POWERS
— AND —
THRONES

DAN JONES is an internationally bestselling historian. His books, including *The Plantagenets*, *Magna Carta*, *The Templars* and *The Colour of Time* (with Marina Amaral), have sold more than one million copies. He has written and hosted dozens of TV shows including the acclaimed Netflix/Channel 5 series, *Secrets of Great British Castles*.

ALSO BY DAN JONES

Summer of Blood:
The Peasants' Revolt of 1381

The Plantagenets:
The Kings Who Made England

The Hollow Crown:
The Wars of the Roses and the Rise of the Tudors

Magna Carta:
The Making and Legacy of the Great Charter

Realm Divided:
A Year in the Life of Plantagenet England

The Templars:
The Rise and Fall of God's Holy Warriors

Crusaders:
An Epic History of the Wars for the Holy Lands

WITH MARINA AMARAL

The Colour of Time: A New History of the World, 1850–1960

The World Aflame: The Long War, 1914–1945

POWERS
AND
THRONES

A New History of the Middle Ages

DAN JONES

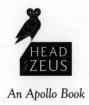

HEAD
ZEUS

An Apollo Book

An Apollo book
First published in the UK in 2021 by Head of Zeus Ltd

9 7 5 3 1 2 4 6 8

A catalogue record for this book is available from
the British Library.

ISBN (HB): 9781789543537
ISBN (E): 9781789543551

Typeset by Ben Cracknell Studios
Maps by Jamie Whyte

Printed and bound in Great Britain by
CPI Group (UK) Ltd, Croydon CR0 4YY

Head of Zeus Ltd
5–8 Hardwick Street
London EC1R 4RG
www.headofzeus.com

For Anthony,
who thinks of everything

What has been is what will be,
and what has been done is what will be done,
and there is nothing new under the sun.
Is there a thing of which it is said,
'See, this is new'?
It has been already
in the ages before us.

ECCLESIASTES 1:9–10

CONTENTS

PART IV: REVOLUTION
(C. AD 1348 – AD 1527)

LIST OF MAPS

AUTHOR'S NOTE

THIS BOOK COVERS MORE THAN A thousand years and its geographical scope encompasses every continent save Australasia and Antarctica. You are about to encounter lots of different languages, currencies and cultures. Some will be familiar. Others will not. In the interests of clarity and enjoyment, I have not tried to apply any rigid system of monetary conversion or spelling convention. I have opted instead for familiarity over strict propriety, and common sense above everything else. I hope you understand.

INTRODUCTION

In the sixteenth century the English historian John Foxe looked over his shoulder at the great sweep of the near, and distant, past. History, thought Foxe (or ecclesiastical history, which was the stuff that really mattered to him), could be sliced into three great chunks.

It began with 'the primitive time', by which he meant those ancient days when Christians hid in catacombs to dodge persecution by wicked, faithless Romans, and tried to avoid being crucified or worse. It culminated in what Foxe called 'our latter days' – the era of the Reformation, when the grip of the Catholic Church on life in Europe was challenged, and when western navigators began to explore the New World.

Sandwiched between these two periods was an awkward slab consisting of about one thousand years. Foxe called this 'the middle age'. It was, by definition, neither fish nor fowl.

Today we still use Foxe's label, although we have added a plural. For us, the years between the fall of the western Roman Empire in the fifth century AD and the Protestant Reformation are 'the Middle Ages'. Anything relating to the time is 'medieval' – a nineteenth-century adjective, which literally means the same thing.[1] But if we have added an extra letter, our periodization is largely the same. The Middle Ages were (it is usually supposed) the time when the classical world had vanished, but the modern world was yet to get going; when people built castles and men fought in armour on horseback; when the world was flat and everything very far away. Although some twenty-first century global historians have tried to update the terminology, speaking not of Middle Ages but of a Middle Millennium, that has not yet caught on.[2]

Words are heavily loaded. The Middle Ages are often the butt of a big historical joke. *Medieval* is frequently deployed as a dirty term, particularly by newspaper editors, who use it as shorthand when they want to suggest stupidity, barbarity and wanton violence. (An alternative popular name for this period is the Dark Ages, which does much the same job: caricaturing the medieval past as a time of permanent intellectual night.) For obvious reasons, this can make today's historians quite tetchy. If you should happen to meet one, it is best not to deploy 'medieval' as an insult – unless you want a lecture or a punch on the nose.

The book you are about to read tells the story of the Middle Ages. It is a big book, because that is a big task. We are going to sweep across continents and centuries, often at breakneck pace. We are going to meet hundreds of men and women, from Attila the Hun to Joan of Arc. And we are going to dive headlong into at least a dozen fields of history – from war and law to art and literature. I am going to ask – and I hope, answer – some big questions. What happened in the Middle Ages? Who ruled? What did power look like? What were the big forces that shaped people's lives? And how (if at all) did the Middle Ages shape the world we know today?

There will be times when it may feel a little bit overwhelming.

But I promise you, it is going to be fun.

I have divided this book into four broadly chronological sections. Part I looks at what one brilliant modern historian has labelled the 'inheritance of Rome'.[3] It opens with the Roman Empire in the west in a state of retreat and collapse, rocked by a changing climate and several generations of mass migration, among other things. It then looks at the secondary superpowers that emerged in Rome's wake: the so-called 'barbarian' realms that laid the foundations for the European kingdoms; the remodelled eastern Roman superstate of Byzantium; and the first Islamic empires. It takes the story from the beginning of the fifth century AD to the middle of the eighth.

Part II opens in the age of the Franks, who revived a Christian, pseudo-Roman empire in the west. The story here is partly but not exclusively political: besides tracing the rise of the dynasties who carved Europe into Christian royal realms, we will also look at the new forms of cultural 'soft' power that emerged around the turn of the first millennium. This part of the book asks how monks and knights came to play such an important role in western society during the Middle Ages – and how the fusion of their two mindsets gave birth to the crusades.

Part III begins with the stunning appearance of a new global superpower. The rise of the Mongols in the twelfth century AD was a sharp and hideously brutal episode, in which an eastern empire – with its capital in what is now Beijing – achieved fleeting domination over half the world, at the cost of millions of lives. Against the background of this dramatic shift in global geopolitics, part III also looks at other emerging powers in what is sometimes called the 'high' Middle Ages. We will meet merchants who invented extraordinary new financial techniques to make themselves and the world richer; scholars who revived the wisdom of the ancients and founded some of today's greatest universities; and the architects and engineers who built the cities, cathedrals and castles that still stand 500 years on, as portals back to the medieval world.

Part IV of this book brings the Middle Ages to a close. The section begins with a global pandemic that ripped through the world, from east to west, devastating populations, reshaping economies and changing the way that people thought about the world around them. It then looks at how the world was rebuilt. We will meet the geniuses of the Renaissance, and travel alongside the great navigators who struck out in search of new worlds – and found them. Last of all, we will see how shifting religious dogma, allied to new communication technology, brought about the Protestant Reformation – an upheaval which (as Foxe recognized) brought the curtain down on 'the middle age'.

That, then, is the basic shape of this book. I should also say a few words about its preoccupations. As the title suggests, this is a book about power. By that I do not simply mean political power, or even human power. We will come across many mighty men and women (although since this is the Middle Ages, there are inevitably more of the former than the latter). But I am also interested in mapping great forces beyond human control. Climate change, mass migration, pandemic disease, technological change and global networks: these sound like very modern, or even post-modern, concerns. But they shaped the medieval world too. And since we are all, in a sense, children of the Middle Ages, it is important that we recognize how similar we are to medieval people – as well as acknowledging our real and profound differences.

This book focuses mostly on the west, and sees the history of other parts of the world through a western lens. I make no apology for that. I am fascinated by the histories of Asia and Africa, and I have tried to show throughout this story how deeply intertwined the medieval west was with the global east and south. But the very notion of the Middle Ages is one that is specific to western history. I am also writing in the west, where I have lived and studied for most of my career. One day I – or most likely someone else – will write a complementary history of the Middle Ages that turns this perspective on its head, and sees the period from 'the outside', as it were.[4] But today is not that day.

This, then, is the shape of things to come. As I have already said, this is a big book. Yet it is also a hopelessly short one. I have covered more than one thousand years of history here, in less than one thousand pages. Every chapter of this book has an entire scholarly field dedicated to it. (The endnotes and select bibliography will help readers to dip further into the fields they find interesting.) So while there is plenty to see here, there is also much that has been left on the cutting-room floor. All I can say is that my aim with all my books is to entertain as well as inform. If this one does a little bit of both, I shall consider it a blessing.

Dan Jones
Staines-upon-Thames
Spring, 2021.

Part I

Imperium

C. AD 410 – AD 750

1

ROMANS

'Everywhere... the name of the Roman people
is an object of reverence and awe.'

AMMIANUS MARCELLINUS,
ROMAN HISTORIAN AND SOLDIER

They left the safety of the road and tramped out into the wilderness, lugging the heavy wooden chest between them. How their limbs must have ached as they carried it some two miles across the uneven landscape – for the box, while only a metre in length, was well built, densely filled and sealed with a large silver spring-lock. To move it any distance required at least two people, or a small cart, for crate and contents together weighed half as much as a person.[1] But the value of the goods inside far exceeded the cost of a human being. A slave imported from Gaul, brought across the British Sea (*Oceanus Britannicus* – today the English Channel) and converted into cash on the markets of London (*Londinium*) might in those days cost 600 *denarii* – assuming he or she were fit, young and either hard-working or good-looking. This was no small price: around twice an ordinary soldier's annual wages.[2] But if it was a lot, it was also nothing at all for an elite citizen of the Roman Empire in the fifth century AD. Inside the oak box that creaked as they hiked across the gently sloping countryside was a fortune sufficient to pay for a whole houseful of slaves.

The precious load inside the oaken case included nearly 600 gold coins known as *solidi*. These jangled against 15,000 silver *siliquae* and a couple of handfuls of random bronze pieces. The coins were stamped variously with the faces of emperors from three dynasties, the most recent of them the ill-fated usurper Constantine III (r. 407/9 – AD 411). Nestled among the coins were even greater treasures: an assortment of gorgeous gold necklaces, rings and fashionable body chains designed to cling to the curves of a slender young woman's body; bangles etched with geometric patterns and lifelike hunting scenes; tableware including silver spoons, and pepper-pots in the shape of wild beasts, ancient heroes and empresses; elegant toilet utensils including silver earwax-scrapers and toothpicks made to look like long-necked ibises; bowls, beakers and jugs; and a tiny elephant-ivory pyxis – the sort of trinket that rich men like Aurelius Ursicinus, whose name was etched into many of the items, liked to buy for refined women like the lady Juliane (*Iuliane*). A bespoke bracelet was personalized with a loving message spelled in tiny strips of beaten gold: VTERE FELIX DOMINA IVLIANE (*Use this happily, Lady Juliane.*) And ten silver spoons advertised the family's devotion to the young but pervasive religion of the day: each was stamped with the symbol known as the Chi-Rho – a monogram made up of the first two Greek letters in the word 'Christ'. This would have been instantly familiar to fellow believers – Christians – who were part of a community of the faithful which stretched from Britain and Ireland (*Hibernia*) to north Africa and the Middle East.[3]

This hoard of coins, jewellery and home furnishings was by no means the sum total of the family's valuables, for Aurelius and Juliane were members of the small, fabulously wealthy Christian elite of Britain – a villa set who lived in similar comfort and splendour to other elites right across Europe and the Mediterranean. But it was a significant nest-egg all the same – and the family had taken some trouble in selecting what to include in it. That was only right, because this rich cache was effectively an insurance policy. The family had instructed that it be buried somewhere discreet for safekeeping, while they waited to see whether Britain's increasingly turbulent politics would tip over into governmental collapse, civil unrest or something worse. Only time would tell what fate held for the province. In the meantime, the best place for an affluent clan's riches was underground.

The bustle of the busy road – the route that joined the eastern town of Caister-by-Norwich (*Venta Icenorum*) with the London-to-Colchester (*Camulodunum*) thoroughfare – had long receded into the distance, and the small group carrying the box found themselves alone and out of sight. They had walked far enough that the nearest town – Scole – was more than two miles away; satisfied that they had found a good spot, they set the box down. They may have rested awhile, perhaps even until nightfall. But soon enough, shovels hit the earth, the soil – a mixture of clay and sandy gravel – heaped up, and a shallow hole emerged.⁴ They did not need to dig far – there was no need to waste effort, for they would be only making work for themselves in the future. So when the hole was just a few feet deep, they carefully lowered the box into it and backfilled the soil. As they did so, the stout oak case containing Aurelius' spoons and silverware, Juliane's delicately wrought jewellery and many handfuls of coin disappeared: buried like grave goods, those prized possessions of the deceased which had been laid to rest with their owners in half-remembered days of generations past. The diggers took note of the spot, then set off, relieved and unburdened, back towards the road. They would, they may have said to themselves, be back. When? It was hard to say. But surely, once the political storms battering Britain eased, and the barbarous invaders who attacked the eastern seaboard with wearying regularity were finally driven away, and the loyal soldiers returned from their wars in Gaul, Master Aurelius would send them back to dig up his valuable cargo. In AD 409, they did not know – and could not have begun to imagine – that Aurelius Ursicinus' treasure trove would in fact remain under the ground for nearly 1,600 years.*

At the dawn of the fifth century AD, Britain was the furthest-flung part of the Roman Empire, a superpower with a glorious history stretching back more than a millennium. Rome began as

---

* The box of treasure is today known as the Hoxne (pron. 'Hoxon') Hoard. It was found by metal detectorists looking for a lost hammer in 1992, and is now is displayed in the British Museum.

an Iron Age monarchy – tradition dated its origins to 753 BC – but following the reigns of seven kings (who, according to Roman lore, became increasingly tyrannical) in 509 BC it became a republic. Later still, in the first century BC, the Republic too was overthrown and Rome was ruled by emperors: at first a single emperor ruled in Rome, but later as many as four emperors ruled simultaneously from capitals including Milan, Ravenna and Constantinople. The fourth Roman Emperor, Claudius (r. AD 41–54), began the conquest of Britain in AD 43, assaulting the native peoples of the islands with an army of 20,000 fierce Roman legionaries and a war machine including armoured elephants. By the end of the first century a large part of southern Britannia had been conquered, up to a militarized zone in the north which was eventually marked by Hadrian's Wall. Britain was henceforth no longer a mysterious zone at the limits of the known world, but a territory that had in large part been pacified and incorporated into a Mediterranean superstate. For the three and a half centuries that followed, Britain was joined to the Roman Empire: a political behemoth only rivalled for size, sophistication, military muscle and longevity by the Persian mega-states of the Parthians and Sassanids, and the empire of the Chinese Han dynasty. Ammianus Marcellinus, a Greek-born historian who lived and wrote in the fourth century AD, called Rome 'a city destined to endure as long as the human race survives'. The Roman Empire, meanwhile, had 'set its foot on the proud necks of savage peoples and given them laws to serve as the eternal foundation and guarantee of liberty'.[5]

There was hyperbole here – but only a pinch. Ammianus Marcellinus was by no means the only serious Roman writer to look upon Rome and its empire and see a series of triumphs stretching back to the dimness of prehistory and forward to infinity.[6] Poets and historians such as Virgil, Horace, Ovid and Livy gave voice to the superior nature of the Roman citizen and the epic character of the city's imperial history. Virgil's *Aeneid*, which wove Romans a magical origin myth, told of an 'empire that will know no end' under 'the people of Rome, the rulers of the world, the race that wears the toga'.[7] 'It is our Roman way to do and suffer bravely', wrote Livy.[8] Four centuries later, and even after an exceptionally troublesome age in which the empire had been wracked by civil war, usurpation, assassination, invasion, political schism, epidemic disease and near bankruptcy, Marcellinus could still maintain that 'Rome is accepted in every region of the world as mistress and queen... Everywhere the authority of its senators is paid the respect due to their grey hairs, and the name of the Roman people is an object of reverence and awe.'[9]

Yet a generation after Marcellinus wrote these paeans, the western half of the empire was in a state of final collapse: Roman garrisons and political rulers were everywhere abandoning lands they and their forebears had occupied and ruled since the dawn of the millennium. Imperial rule dissolved in Britain in AD 409–410, never to be restored; the shock of Britain's abrupt exit from this pan-European union was precisely what led elite families like that of Aurelius Ursicinus and Juliane to pack up their riches and put them in the ground, a financial hedge that became, quite unintentionally, a glittering time capsule preserving the end of an era. By the end of the fifth century the Roman Empire in the west no longer existed. It was, wrote the great eighteenth-century historian Edward Gibbon, 'a revolution which will ever be remembered, and is still felt by the nations of the earth'.[10]

The decline and fall of the western Roman Empire is a historical phenomenon that has exercised modern historians for centuries, for the legacy of Rome remains with us even to this day, stamped into language, landscape, law and culture. And if Rome still speaks to us in the twenty-first century, its voice rang even louder during the Middle Ages – the period which this book aims to chronicle and explore. We will examine in detail the end of the Roman Empire in the next chapter. But for now we must turn our thoughts to its *rise* (or rather, its mutation out of the Republic) around the turn of the first millennium, and sketch the land as it lay immediately before the Middle Ages. For to see the medieval west properly we must first ask how and why Eternal Rome (*Roma aeterna*) managed to command an empire connecting three continents, an innumerable number of peoples with their various religions and traditions, and a similarly vast babble of languages; an empire of tribal wanderers, peasant farmers and metropolitan elites; an empire stretching out from the creative hubs of antique culture to the ends of the known world.

Climate and Conquest

ROMANS LIKED TO TELL EACH OTHER they were favoured by the gods. In fact, for much of their history they were blessed with good weather. Between roughly the years 200 BC and AD 150 – when Rome flourished as republic and empire – a set of pleasant and profitable climate conditions settled upon the west. For nearly four centuries there were no massive volcanic eruptions of the sort that from time to time depress temperatures across the globe; during the same age solar activity was high and stable.[11] As a result, western Europe and the broader Mediterranean fringe enjoyed a cycle of unusually warm and hospitable decades, which also happened to be very wet.[12] Plants and animals flourished: elephants roamed forests in the Atlas Mountains, while grapevines and olive groves could be grown further north than at any time in living memory. Tracts of land that in other eras were barren and hostile to the plough could be cultivated, and crop yields on traditionally 'good' land boomed. These boon years, during which nature seemed to offer her greatest prizes to any civilization capable of recognizing its opportunity, are now sometimes called the Roman Climate Optimum (RCO) or Roman Warm Period.

Rome officially became an Empire on 16 January 27 BC, when the Senate awarded Octavian – an adopted son of Julius Caesar – the title of *Augustus*. Prior to this the Republic had been tortured by two decades of bloody civil wars; in the course of these, in 49 BC, Caesar had seized power and ruled as a military dictator. Yet Caesar was an autocrat both of his time and ahead of it, and on 15 March 44 BC – the Ides of March – he was murdered – direct reward, said the scholar and bureaucrat Suetonius (c. AD 70–130), for his vaunting ambition, in which many Romans perceived a desire to revive the monarchy. 'Constant exercise of power gave Caesar a love for it,' wrote Suetonius, who also repeated a rumour that as a young man Caesar dreamed of raping his own mother, a vision soothsayers interpreted as a clear sign 'he was destined to conquer the earth.'[13]

Fame was Caesar's destiny, but true greatness was Octavian's. Imperium was almost written on Octavian's face: his bright eyes and magnetically handsome features were somehow accentuated by a tousled, slightly dishevelled appearance, which would have suggested an utter lack of vanity were it not for the fact that he wore stack-heeled shoes to raise him above his natural height of 5'7".[14] Octavian succeeded where Caesar had not, avenging his father's death and defeating his enemies in battle, eventually emerging as Rome's sole, uncontested ruler. As Augustus he accrued to himself all the carefully separated political powers of the Republic, effectively playing senator, consul and tribune, *pontifex maximus* (high priest) and supreme military commander all at once. Augustus' character divided Roman opinion – was he a high-minded visionary and peerless soldier-politician, or a corrupt, bloodthirsty, treacherous tyrant, wondered the historian Tacitus (c. AD 58–116), without committing to either judgement.[15] But his achievements as emperor – or as he preferred it, First Citizen (*Princeps civitatis*)* – were impossible to gainsay. On taking power he stamped out the embers of the late Republic's debilitating civil war. He transformed the city of Rome with grandiose building projects – some of them already begun under Caesar and others of his own design. The 500-acre Field of Mars (*Campus Martius*), littered with temples and monuments, was radically rebuilt. New theatres, aqueducts and roads were commissioned. Only the finest building materials passed muster: on his deathbed Augustus bragged that he had found Rome a city of brick, but left it a city of marble.[16] He carried out sweeping reforms to government, concentrating power in his own hands at the expense of the Senate,

---

* The first 300-odd years of the Roman Empire are often known as the Principate, after Augustus' preferred title.

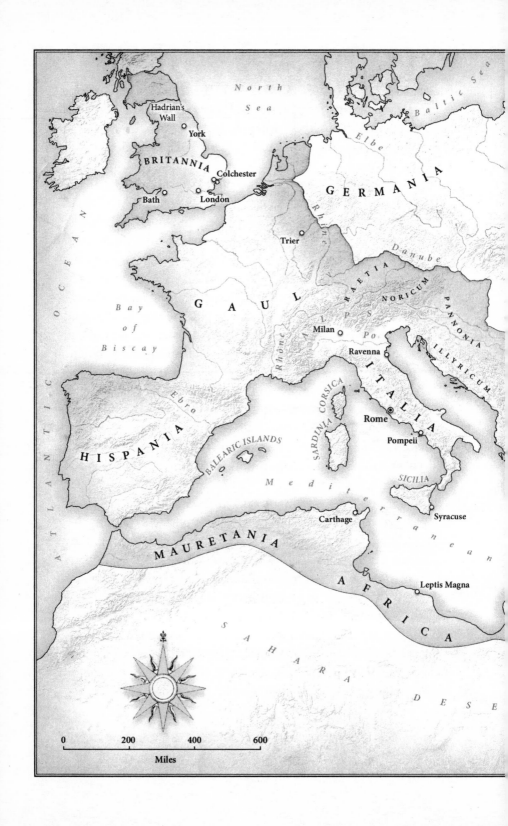

THE ROMAN EMPIRE
AT ITS GREATEST EXTENT

DACIA

Danube

MOESIA

THRACE

MACEDON

Byzantion

Black Sea

Caspian Sea

BITHYNIA

PONTUS

GALATIA

ARMENIA

Corinth

ASIA

CAPPADOCIA

PARTHIA

CILICIA

Delos

(PERSIA)

SYRIA

MESOPOTAMIA

Tigris

Beirut

JUDEA

Sea

Euphrates

Cyrene

Jerusalem

Alexandria

EGYPT

ARABIA

R T

Nile

Red Sea

and encouraging a personal cult of imperial magnificence, which evolved under his successors until some emperors were venerated as demi-gods.

BY THE TIME AUGUSTUS DIED ON 19 August AD 14, at the grand old age of seventy-five, the Roman Empire had been vastly and dramatically expanded, pacified and extensively reformed. Although Britain was still an untapped wilderness (Caesar had blanched at the prospect of a full invasion when he visited in 55– 54 BC, and his son left the Britons alone too), the early Roman Empire included the entire Italian and Iberian peninsulas, Gaul (modern France), transalpine Europe as far as the Danube, most of the Balkans and Asia Minor, a thick slice of the Levantine coast from Antioch in the north to Gaza in the south, the vastly wealthy province of Egypt (*Aegyptus*), won by Augustus in a famous war against the last Ptolemaic pharaoh, Cleopatra, and her lover Mark Antony, and a continuous stretch of north Africa as far west as Numidia (modern Algeria). And the stage was set for even greater expansion during the century that followed.

Rome was the only power in history to rule every shore of the Mediterranean basin, and it added to this an exceptionally deep fringe of territory reaching many miles inland. At its peak under Trajan (r. AD 98–117), who conquered Dacia (modern Romania) the empire covered some 5 million square kilometres, from Hadrian's Wall to the banks of the river Tigris. A quarter of earth's human population lived under Roman rule. This huge conglomerate of imperial territory was not just seized, but reorganized and imprinted with the defining features of Roman civilization. Colossal, centrally commanded, fiercely defended at the fringes and closely governed (if not exactly free or tolerant) within its borders, technologically advanced and efficiently connected to itself and the world beyond, Rome's imperial apogee had arrived.

'They make a solitude and call it peace'

SO WHAT WERE THE DEFINING FEATURES of the Roman Empire? First and most striking to outsiders was Rome's extraordinary and enduring military strength. Warrior culture infused politics. Election to office during the Republic was more or less contingent on having completed a term of military service and military command in turn depended on election to political office. Unsurprisingly, therefore, many of Rome's greatest historical achievements were won on the battlefield. The machinery of state relied upon (and to a large degree existed to serve) a professional standing army which numbered around a quarter of a million men at the end of Augustus' reign, and at its peak in the early third century AD could field 450,000 troops across the empire. Legions, each containing 5,000 heavy infantry recruited from the Roman citizenry, were augmented by auxiliary units (*auxilia*) drawn from the empire's vast non-citizen population and mercenaries (*numeri*) recruited from barbarian forces outside the empire's borders. (As we shall see, the barbarian contingent of the Roman army came to dominate in the later years of empire.) Naval fleets employed another 50,000 men. The cost of maintaining this force, dispersed across millions of square miles from the North Sea to the Caspian Sea, gobbled between 2 per cent and 4 per cent of the empire's entire GDP every year; well over half the state budget was spent on defence.* There were times – during the last days of the Republic in the first century BC, and under the many inglorious emperors who ruled during the so-called Crisis of the Third Century – when Roman military might worked against the cause of imperial

---

* By way of comparison: at the time of writing the USA has by some distance the world's biggest defence and security budget, and as a share of GDP, American military spending is well in line with the Roman Empire's: around 3.1 per cent. However, while this is a *lot* of dollars spent on drones, tanks and troops, 3.1 per cent of American GDP amounts to roughly 15 per cent of the annual federal budget. In other words, Rome's emperors spent three or four times as much of their available income on the military as recent American presidents. In terms of relative deployment capability and escalation potential – the ability, if you like, to bring a rocket launcher to a fist-fight – the modern USA occupies a similar position in the world as the first century AD Roman Empire. It's usually best not to mess with them.

harmony. Yet without the Roman army there could have been no empire at all.

'YOUR TASK, ROMAN,' WROTE VIRGIL (70–19 BC), 'will be to govern the peoples of the world in your empire. These will be your arts – to impose a settled pattern upon peace, to pardon the defeated and to battle down the proud.'[17] The Roman imperial army's size, speed of movement, technological proficiency, tactical nous and terrible discipline was matched by no other power of its time, and made Virgil's lofty aim possible.

The typical Roman soldier signed on to serve for at least ten years; prior to the third century AD the prize for serving in the auxiliaries for twenty-five years was full Roman citizenship. Regular pay was reasonable, while the roles available were many and varied. Besides infantry, trained to fight with a short sword, long, curved shield and javelin, the Roman army employed horsemen, artillerymen, medics, musicians, clerks and engineers. There was a strong culture of reward and honour for distinguished service, but by the same token, discipline was brutally strict, proceeding by starvation, flogging and on occasion summary execution. According to the Greek writer Polybius, who composed a detailed history of Rome in the second century BC, soldiers who failed to stand their ground in battle could be punished by *fustuarium supplicum*, in which their colleagues jointly cudgeled or stoned them to death.[18] In the case of mass failure or disobedience, a legion might be decimated (*decimatio*): one soldier in ten would be selected by lot and beaten to death by his colleagues.

In Republican times the legions had established Rome's hegemony in the Mediterranean with a series of wars for the ages – defeating the Macedonians, the Seleucids and (perhaps most famously) the Carthaginians, whose great general Hannibal marched elephants over the Alps in 218 BC but failed to finish off the Republic, despite crushing the largest army which had ever been assembled by Rome, at the battle of Cannae in 216 BC. Later generations would rue Hannibal's failure: the Carthaginians' punishment for daring to defy Rome was the annihilation of their ancient capital, Carthage, following the Third Punic War in 146 BC. (In the same year, in a separate theatre of conflict, the ancient Greek town of Corinth was also plundered and razed to the ground.) Collectively these wars demonstrated the long-term superiority of Rome's military, which continued into the imperial era. The experience of facing a Roman army in the field was bracing to say the least – as can be shown by way of a single example, from the first century AD, when the imperial army bared its teeth during the invasion and subjugation of Britain.

JULIUS CAESAR MADE THE FIRST EXPLORATORY military expeditions to Britain in 55 and 54 BC. Britain was an attractive target for Rome, promising fertile agricultural land in the south-east and mines across the islands rich in tin, copper, lead, silver and gold deposits. It was also a place where rebels from Gaul tended to flee to avoid Roman authority; besides which there was prestige simply in the prospect of conquering an archipelago reckoned to mark the limit of the navigable world. Caesar's invasions were defeated by native British belligerence and foul weather, but a century later, in AD 43, in Claudius' reign, four legions led an amphibious invasion, sparking a war of occupation that lasted, on and off, for nearly half a century. Tribes like the Iceni, who rebelled under the warrior queen Boudicca in AD 60–61, were wiped out with extreme prejudice. Others cut deals. Britain, and the British, were never the same again. The ruthlessness with which the imperial army conquered and pacified Britain was a matter of considerable pride to Romans, as was summed up wryly by Tacitus in the famous speech he put in the mouth of a doomed tribal chieftain, Galgacus, preparing to give battle against a Roman army under Gnaeus Julius Agricola (who happened to be Tacitus' father-in-law):

> Robbers of the world, having by their universal plunder exhausted the land, they rifle the deep. If the enemy be rich,

they are rapacious; if he be poor, they lust for dominion; neither the east nor the west has been able to satisfy them. Alone among men they covet with equal eagerness poverty and riches. To robbery, slaughter, plunder, they give the lying name of empire; they make a solitude and call it peace.[19]

Shortly after listening to this speech, Galgacus' men were fleeing helter-skelter from Agricola's army of legionaries, auxiliaries and cavalry – 'an awful and hideous spectacle', wrote Tacitus. The tribal warriors 'fled in whole battalions... everywhere there lay scattered arms, corpses and mangled limbs, and the earth reeked with blood.' That night the Roman army partied, but 'the Britons, wandering amidst the mingled wailings of men and women, were dragging off their wounded, calling to the unhurt, deserting their homes... the silence of desolation reigned everywhere: the hills were forsaken, houses were smoking in the distance...'[20] Galgacus had predicted his comrades' fate with absolute accuracy, and in doing so he relived the experience of countless other tribal leaders on the edge of the Roman Empire through the centuries. Even when legions suffered ambush or defeat – as they did from time to time, in Britain, Gaul, Germany (Germania), Dacia, Palestine and elsewhere – the loss was seldom sufficient to vanquish the Roman presence; the underpinning fact of Roman military hegemony was the empire's ability to absorb defeat, escalate conflict and exact pitiless revenge; Rome lost many battles but precious few wars.

For all this, however, the Roman army also won many fine victories in which no swords were drawn, no javelins readied and no blood spilled. The advantage of unapproachable battlefield scale was then – as it has regularly been throughout history – the luxury of winning without fighting. The Roman army's might was not simply an active force, it also acted as a *de facto* deterrent to potential rivals; since no other power in the western world could match the resources of the imperial forces, emperors could use the mere fact of their military capability as a political tool to bludgeon rivals into submission.[21] This is a lesson that most superpowers in world history have come to appreciate.

The golden age of Roman military might came during the 200 years that followed Augustus' accession in 27 BC. This age was known as the *Pax Romana* – a time where (by the standards of the day) Rome could offer exceptional stability, peace and opportunities for prosperity to those who lived under its aegis. It was able to do so because it paid collectively to be protected by the most dangerous army on earth. The *Pax Romana* frayed and began to unravel after the death of the philosopher-emperor Marcus Aurelius in AD 180. For several decades during the third century crisis engulfed the empire, with periods during which it split into three blocs, entertained dozens of emperors, and nearly collapsed altogether – a fate that tested almost to destruction the resolve and capability of the Roman military. Yet by the time of the fourth and early fifth centuries AD, Romans still prided themselves on their armed forces, now increasingly professionalized and posted around the frontiers of the empire (the 'limes'), protecting the fringes of civilization from the incursions of barbarian peoples; ensuring that by and large, despite its divisions and fractures, its power-struggles and its internal feuds, the empire held firm.

So during its heyday Rome was a war state *nonpareil* which could crush any other actor in its sphere; even after the third-century crisis, when it was challenged hard by the Sassanid Persians in the east and barbarians in the west, it remained a formidable force. Yet overwhelming military power and reach alone did not distinguish Rome from other broadly contemporaneous superpowers of the classical world. In the fourth century BC Alexander the Great's Macedonian empire had extended from the Ionian islands of the central Mediterranean to the Himalayas. The various Persian empires of antiquity covered similar territory. Around AD 100 the Chinese Eastern Han ruled over 2.5 million square miles and 60 million people. What made Rome so dominant in the Mediterranean world and beyond was the fact that overwhelming armed force developed in tune with a sophisticated civic machinery: a mesh of state-of-the-art social, cultural and legal systems that Romans considered to be virtuous in and of themselves. Whether or not they were right – and today we may well entertain our doubts about a society that heavily circumscribed the rights of millions of women and the poor, viciously persecuted dissenters from its norms, fetishized blood-sports and other forms of civic violence and depended for survival on mass slavery – the Roman way of life was highly exportable and left deep, often permanent marks everywhere it arrived.

Citizens and Strangers

A FEW YEARS AFTER THE EMPEROR Claudius took his elephants to Britain to subjugate the tribes at the end of the world, he found himself before the Senate, addressing a rowdy group of Rome's leading dignitaries on the intertwined matters of citizenship and political power. The year was AD 48 and the cause at hand was a particular one: whether or not the wealthiest and most respectable citizens of the Roman provinces of Gaul should be allowed to be elected as senators. Claudius – a scholarly if weak-limbed and short-sighted grandson of Augustus, who happened to have been born in Gaul, at Lyon (*Lugdunum*) – believed they should. To emphasize his point, he referred his audience to the ancient history of Rome, stretching right back to the days when their founder and first king, Romulus, was succeeded by a ruler from outside the city: Numa the Sabine. Rome, argued Claudius, had always been a place in which the worthiest outsiders were absorbed. 'I think that provincials should not be rejected, as long as they will be a credit to the Senate,' he said.

Not every senator agreed. Some argued vehemently that it was disgraceful for Rome willingly to have 'a mob of foreigners... forced upon us', particularly since the foreigners in question – Gauls – had once fought bitterly and bloodily against Roman conquest.[22] At the heart of this argument lay two age-old debates which have animated rulers of powerful realms from the beginning of time to the present day: how does a state rehabilitate its former enemies; and does opening up membership of a state or society to non-natives strengthen or dilute its blood and character? It was an argument that rumbled throughout Rome's centuries of imperial dominance, and one that left a legacy to the Middle Ages and beyond.

Before the Senate in AD 48, Claudius was well prepared. To the suspicions levelled against the Gauls' loyalty he said: 'if anyone concentrates on the fact that the Gauls resisted the divine Julius [Caesar] in war for ten years, he should consider that they have also been loyal and trustworthy for a hundred years, and had this loyalty tried to the utmost when we were in danger.' To the more general objections about non-Italians being classed as Roman, he directed his listeners to the examples of the Ancient Greeks. 'What was the ruin of Sparta and Athens but this, that mighty as they were in war, they spurned from them as aliens those whom they had conquered?' Either convinced or browbeaten by their impassioned emperor, the senators eventually agreed. From that point on Gauls could not only attain Roman citizenship but also aspire to the highest political office in the empire.

One of the most important social distinctions of Rome – in the city itself, the Italian peninsula and (eventually) the vast territories the Roman army conquered – was between citizens and the rest. Roman society was obsessed with rank and order, and the small distinctions between the upper-class divisions of senators (*senatores*) and equestrians (*equites*), the middling ranks of the plebians, and the landless poor known as *proletarii* were taken very seriously. But citizenship mattered most. To be a citizen of Rome meant, in the deepest sense, freedom. For men it conferred an enviable package of rights and responsibilities: citizens could vote, hold political office, use the law courts to defend themselves and their property, wear the toga on ceremonial occasions, do military service in the legions rather than the auxiliaries, claim immunity from certain taxes and avoid most forms of corporal and capital punishment, including flogging, torture and crucifixion. Citizenship was not limited to men: although many of its rights were denied to women, female citizens could pass the status on to their children, and their lives were more likely to feature comfort and plenty if they were citizens than if they were not. Citizenship was therefore a prized status, which was why the Roman state dangled it as reward for auxiliaries who served a quarter-century in the Roman army, and for slaves who served uncomplainingly in the knowledge that if their master freed them, they too could claim the right to limited citizenship as freedmen. To lose one's citizenship – the punishment imposed for very serious crimes such as homicide or forgery – was a form of legal dismemberment and social death.

Rome was not by any means unique in fostering this concept of legal and social privilege – there were citizens in ancient Greece, Carthage and numerous other Mediterranean states of the era. But Rome *was* unique in the way that it developed and extended the concept of citizenship over its long history to help sustain its own imperial dominion. The root purpose of the empire was to funnel wealth to be spent in Rome: in that sense it was a racket based on rampant exploitation. Yet through the promise of citizenship – a share in the plunder – conquered aristocrats could usually be brought onside. Accordingly, during the first two centuries of empire, as the imperial provinces expanded, citizenship was gradually awarded to high-status groups far outside Italy. Noblemen and magistrates, auxiliaries who had completed their service in the army, retired officials and their freed slaves could all acquire citizenship – either full-status or one of numerous qualified forms which came with a limited but still desirable slew of rights.[23] Finally, in AD 212, the emperor Caracalla finished what Claudius started and decreed that all free people across the provinces could claim citizenship of some form. The entire populace, announced Caracalla, 'should share in the victory. This edict will enhance the majesty of the Roman people.'[24]

Many historians have seen the edict of Caracalla (sometimes called the Antonine Constitution) as a turning point in the history of the empire, since it was a decision that weakened the imperial system to its core, diluting the appeal to non-Romans of joining the army and denuding citizenship of prestige. Perhaps this is so. But it is also true that an open attitude to assimilation within

24

the empire had been one of Rome's key historic advantages,* for it prioritized the values of the Roman system above everything else, and admitted freely and without hang-ups the possibility that people were capable of entertaining more than one cultural identity. A Roman did not need to have been born within sight of the seven hills of the Eternal City: he or she could be north African or Greek, a Gaul, German or Briton, a Spaniard or a Slav. Even emperors did not have to be ethnically 'Roman'. Trajan and Hadrian were Spaniards. Septimius Severus, who seized power in AD 193 and clung to it until AD 211, was born in Libya (*Leptis Magna*) to a north African father and a Syrian Arab mother; his successors (known as the Severan dynasty) therefore shared this African–Arab heritage. The second emperor of this dynasty was none other than Caracalla. So while Caracalla had good political reasons for issuing his edict of AD 212 – not least widening the tax-base during a parlous time for the public finances – it is perhaps not too anachronistic to suspect the experience of being an emperor with African heritage must have affected his thinking.

Souls for Sale

IF CARACALLA BROUGHT HIS AFRICAN EXPERIENCE to imperial rule, he was not alone. More than a century before he was born, Rome was ruled for ten years by Vespasian, founder of the Flavian dynasty. Vespasian came to power in AD 69 as the victor of a brief, nasty civil war, during which four men ruled in a single year;† but before he was an emperor, he had enjoyed a short career in north Africa during which he was known as a 'mule driver', a euphemism for a slave trader. In this role, Vespasian was known for cutting off the testicles of young boys, so they could be sold at a premium as eunuchs.[25] This habit earned Vespasian a degree of notoriety, but

---

* In this open-armed approach to assimilation the Roman Empire outstripped even the United States during its peak period of immigration at the turn of the twentieth century. Historically, perhaps only the Mongol empire of the twelfth and thirteenth centuries (see chapter 9) demonstrated such an unfussy attitude towards integrating a multitude of peoples.
† The Year of the Four Emperors: they were Galba, Otho, Vitellius and Vespasian.

not nearly so much as it might have done in another historical era. In Rome, slavery, and casual brutality towards enslaved people, was not just rife. It was all-pervasive.

Slavery was a fact of life throughout the ancient world. Slaves – people defined as property, forced to work, stripped of their rights, and socially 'dead' – could be found in virtually every significant realm of the age. In China, the Qin, Han and Xin dynasties enforced various forms of slavery; so too did ancient rulers of Egypt, Assyria, Babylonia and India.[26] 'Your male and female slaves are to come from the nations around you; from them you may buy slaves,' God told the Israelites, asking them only to refrain from enslaving one another.[27] Yet Rome was different. There have been a bare few handful of examples in recorded history of true 'slave-states', in which slavery permeated every facet of society, and on which an entire economy and culture was built. Rome was one.*

Historians cannot agree, because there are no reliable records, how many slaves there were in Rome. One rough guess is that around the time of Augustus there were 2 million slaves on the Italian peninsula, representing perhaps a quarter of the human population there – with many more slaves in the provinces beyond.[28] Slaves could be found performing every imaginable role in society, except for ruling. They worked on large, mass-producing farms known as *latifundia* and on smallholdings where a peasant family might own one or more slaves. The houses of wealthy Romans would be staffed by dozens or even hundreds of slaves, who served as cleaners, cooks, bakers, waiters, doormen, valets, wet-nurses, governesses, gardeners, guards, gatekeepers, teachers, clerks, musicians, poetry-reciters, dancers, concubines or simple sex-objects.

For some slaves, if they were put to work by the wealthy, with the possibility of buying their freedom in middle or old age, life might be comfortable, even luxurious. When Pompeii was buried by volcanic ash in AD 79 one slave's beautiful gold arm-ring was preserved: shaped in the form of a snake, traditionally a

---

* Historians usually name the others as ancient Greece, Brazil and the Caribbean during the colonial era, and the antebellum American South.

guardian-animal, it was inscribed with the words 'From a master to his slave-girl'. (*DOM[I]NUS ANCILLAE SUAE*). But the prospect of gifts to soften chattel status was far from guaranteed. Another contrasting slave accessory is the so-called Zoninus collar, dating to the fourth or fifth century AD, and today displayed at the Baths of Diocletian in Rome. Roughly wrought from iron, it dangled a large – presumably irritating and painful – pendant, of the sort of that people today use to identify lost dogs. The inscription informed any stranger who encountered the wearer on his or her own that this person was a runaway. It promised a reward of one gold coin (*solidus*) for the slave's return.[29]

Slaves, whether sold or born into slavery, were by definition degraded to the level of beasts of burden. We do not and cannot know what it was really like to be a Roman slave, since most left no trace at all of their interior lives. But everything we *do* know about slavery at other points in human history tells us this was a condition which generally consisted of years of unhappiness, with abuse ranging from the upsetting to the downright hellish. In African grain-mills or Spanish mines, slaves toiled in hideous, often fatal misery. The second-century AD writer Apuleius included several grotesque images of maltreated slaves in his novel *The Golden Ass* (*Asinus aureus*, sometimes known as the *Metamorphoses* of Apuleius). Although his vignettes of slaves' lives were fictional, and his story was by turns fantastical, bawdy and satirical, Apuleius still hinted at the squalid truth of slavery. Although his main character spends the early part of the story engaged in a mutually enjoyable *menage à deux* with a friend's pretty house-slave, he later encounters a band of poor indigents labouring in a mill: 'their whole bodies picked out with livid weals... their whip-scarred backs shaded rather than covered by their tattered rags, some with only a scanty loin-cloth by way of covering. There were branded foreheads, half-shaven heads, and fettered ankles; their faces were sallow, their eyes so bleared by the smoky heat of the furnaces that they were half blind...'[30]

***

By the time Apuleius was writing, Rome had been a slave society for half a millennium. Slavery became a vital pillar of Roman life from the second century BC, when the Republic began its period of rapid expansion around the Mediterranean. With dazzling military victories – in the Balkans, the Greek islands, north Africa and elsewhere – came the opportunity to take vast plunder, including human bounty. A year like 146 BC, when both Carthage and Corinth were ground into the dust, brought an influx of tens of thousands of captives. Transported across the sea, with escape to their homelands impossible, slaves became freely, easily available, and a driver of rapid Roman economic development: free labour for the Republic (and later the emperors) to put to work building temples, aqueducts, roads and civic buildings, or to send off to the mines; and a commodity for better-off Romans to buy for their own leisure and convenience, to staff their sprawling urban villas or rural super-farms. The attraction of forced labour was obvious. Slaves could be worked as hard as the owner saw fit, beaten as hard as he or she liked, kept like pigs, bred like cattle, then either set free or simply abandoned when they became too old or sick to serve. Thousands of miles from their home, traumatized and probably unable at first to speak the local language, their presence in Rome transformed the city, the Republic and, latterly, the empire.

As Rome's relentless expansion continued into the imperial age, so Gauls, Britons, Germanic tribespeople and others were sucked into the slave system. Slave piracy was a bane across Europe and the wider Mediterranean. The first-century BC Greek historian and philosopher Strabo described slaver brigands terrorizing the lands around Armenia and Syria, rounding up civilians and shipping them off for sale. '[This] proved most profitable,' he wrote, 'for not only were they easily captured, but the market, which was large and rich in property, was not extremely far away.' The market in question was the slave-hub at Delos, in the Cyclades islands, where Strabo claimed 10,000 slaves were traded every day: all sent away to live, toil and die in foreign lands.[31] Roman slavery was not per se racist (and here is an important point of contrast with slavery in the Caribbean or American South) but it was taken for granted that 'barbarians' from outside the empire were infinitely more suitable for enslavement than Romans themselves. Therefore, as the empire grew, so millions of human beings suffered the fundamental indignity of slavery, an outrage summed up succinctly by the fourth-century AD writer Libanius: 'The slave is one who will at some point belong to someone else, whose body can be sold. And what could be more humiliating… For indeed, has not this body been mutilated, and the soul utterly destroyed?'[32]

Yet despite occasional slave rebellions – most famously the Spartacus War of 73 BC – there was no movement to abolish Roman slaveholding, seemingly on the part of anyone. Only occasionally were efforts made to protect slaves from the grossest abuses: Hadrian (r. AD 117–138) unsuccessfully tried to stop slave-traders from castrating African boys, while Constantine I (AD 306–337) forbade the practice of facial tattooing – an edict very likely made with overzealous slave-owners in mind. But to go very much further – still less to contemplate a world without slaves – would have been nonsensical. Philosophically, slavery was assumed to be essential to a free society – a natural phenomenon without which liberty for the true and noble Roman could not exist. Economically, the entire edifice of Rome and its empire relied upon mass bondage, facilitated by the same long and complex trading networks that supplied the empire with essential commodities and luxury goods. Ultimately, Rome was a patriarchal society in which slaves occupied a position of inferiority that was simply their lot. John Chrysostom, a Christian preacher of the late third century AD, sketched out this hierarchy for his audience. Even in a poor man's house, he said: 'the man rules his wife, the wife rules the slaves, the slaves rule their own wives, and again the men and women rule the children.'[33] During the Middle Ages that followed, slavery declined in scale, yet it remained almost ubiquitous across the west. And even in places where slavery seemed to die out, its place as a pillar of economy and culture was often replaced by serfdom – a system of human bondage to the land. This was not quite the same as chattel slavery, although the difference would have felt slight to the people involved. And a large part of the western attachment to slaving sprang from the fact that slavery had been indivisible from Rome's swaggering glory.

Romanization

IF ROME EXTENDED BOTH CITIZENSHIP AND slavery to the provinces, this was far from the only mark of its influence in the world, which would endure into the medieval era. Beyond the simple fact of its legions and its institutions, Rome possessed a potent cultural brand. Seemingly everywhere the Romans went, law, language and landscape took on flavours of 'Roman-ness'. So too, from the fourth century AD did religion, as the empire became a powerful vehicle for spreading the first of two great monotheistic faiths that emerged in the first millennium AD: Christianity.

This was not an even process, and the differing products of mixing Roman customs with the native practices of the Iberian peninsula, north Africa, Gaul, Britain, the Balkans, Greece and the Levant – among others – produced a wide range of distinctive subcultures, all existing together under the banner of empire. More importantly still, Romanization touched the ruling classes in the provinces vastly more than it affected the ordinary masses, and was concentrated in towns and cities, not the countryside. Despite those caveats, however, the export of Roman institutions, values, technologies and worldviews was absolutely fundamental in the centuries that followed the empire's collapse. For Rome was a highly networked superstate, whose disparate peoples were linked by super-engineered roads, efficiently policed seaways, and trade routes that extended to the ends of the earth. And the connective fibres of empire were not just physical pathways. They were cultural constants that made Roman-ness possible and recognizable across dozens of generations and several million square miles of imperial territory. They ensured that there was a sense of connectedness across the old Roman territories long after the empire itself was defunct.

***

A WELL-TO-DO TRAVELLER ARRIVING IN A strange city within the empire some time in the fourth century AD would, despite the foreignness of his or her surroundings, have known pretty well what to expect. The streets would be laid out in grid fashion. In the smarter sections of town torches might be burning in the courtyards of the sprawling villas occupied by the wealthiest inhabitants: fine homes built in brick or stone and kitted out with underfloor heating, a clean water supply and floors and walls decorated in a distinctive Mediterranean style with nods to classical Greece and ancient Rome. Towards the centre of the city, an open space known as a forum would hold a marketplace and a clutch of official buildings – government offices, shops and temples to various gods. Shopkeepers and stallholders in the market would trade goods that had been sourced and shipped from all over the empire and beyond: wine, oil, pepper and other spices, salt, grain, furs, ceramics, glass and precious metals. These could be paid for in a common imperial coin of gold, silver or bronze, usually bearing the image of a Roman emperor. Advanced water-systems could be seen – and smelled. Aqueducts might bring fresh water into the city while public lavatories would connect to a municipal sewer. For cleanliness, hygiene and relaxation it would not be too much to expect a public bathhouse; those in cities like Bath (*Aquae Sulis*), Trier (*Augusta Treverorum*) and Beirut (*Berytus*) were magnificent complexes featuring sets of bathing chambers heated to varying degrees and offering an enviable range of pampering treatments to those who enjoyed (and could afford) scent, oil and ritual as a part of their ablutions.

A large city might have a theatre and perhaps an arena for chariot racing or gladiatorial blood-sports. This would not be on the astounding scale of the mighty Colosseum in Rome, which was opened by Emperor Titus in AD 80 and could seat somewhere between 50,000 and 85,000 spectators, just as the bathhouses in a provincial town would not be able to rival the massive Baths of Diocletian, which were opened to the public around AD 306. Each imperial town or city's architecture, even where it included tell-tale Roman traits of elegant columns and colourful mosaics, would also reflect local tastes and styles. It is also important to note that outside the cities, Rome's influence on the shape of daily life was sharply reduced. Rome was predominantly an urban empire, and rural areas saw far less of its innovation and interference. Be that as it may: it remains the case that, across the empire, public buildings still deliberately evoked civic life in Rome, and the men and women who worked, worshipped and socialized there would be reaffirming their place in the Roman Empire whenever they walked through the doors.

As we shall see, Rome's distinctive influence on the urban landscape of the west went into abeyance after its political collapse. Yet it mattered greatly in the longer term, for it was rediscovered and lionized during the Renaissance of the fourteenth and fifteenth centuries as the high-water mark of civilization, to be resurrected if possible. But another area in which Rome left an indelible mark throughout the entire Middle Ages was in language. Indeed, one of Rome's most lasting legacies, not only to the Middle Ages, but to schoolchildren even today, was its common tongue.

The official language used across the Roman Empire was Latin. This did not mean that every person from Antioch to St Albans spoke to one another in the epigrams of Martial: the classical Latin of the great Roman poets, philosophers and historians was of no more use to ordinary day-to-day speakers than the syntax and vocabulary of Shakespeare's sonnets would have been to an innkeeper or goatherd in Elizabethan England. In the east of the empire, Latin competed with Greek for the position of the most prevalent, admirable and useful language, particularly after the empire was formally partitioned in the early fourth century. In the west, Latin was adopted, adapted and interbred with local tongues across the empire – a process that produced what would eventually become the great Romance languages of the second millennium AD. But if it was not exactly a universal tongue, Latin certainly was the first language of official imperial business, which allowed educated Romans everywhere to communicate with one another and to advertise their status as sophisticated beings.

Learning Latin – and the skills of grammar and rhetoric – formed an elemental part of elite education. It was not possible to contemplate a political or bureaucratic career without a working knowledge of the language. And to the priests, abbots, chancellors, scholars, lawyers, sheriffs, schoolteachers, nobles and kings of the Middle Ages, Latin would also become an indispensable tool.* Yet even for someone without a full literary education, a little Latin picked up here and there could go a long way. Graffiti recovered in Herculaneum – one of the southern Italian cites destroyed when Vesuvius erupted in AD 79 – gives us a snapshot of the mundane and profane feelings that Romans sometimes scratched onto the walls, using Latin to do so. At an inn beside the public baths, a pair of siblings wrote: 'Apelles Mus and his brother Dexter each pleasurably had sex with two girls twice.' In Pompeii, at a column near the gladiators' barracks, one of the inhabitants left a boast: 'Celadus the Thracian gladiator is the delight of all the girls.'

Aside from bragging about sexual prowess and conquests, one of the most practical applications of the Latin language as a *lingua franca* – one that would endure well into the Middle Ages – was its connection to Roman law. Romans were proud of the ancient history of their lawmaking, which supposedly dated back to the fifth century BC, when the so-called Twelve Tables were inscribed. These drew together Rome's traditions and customs regarding legal procedure, debt, inheritance, families, landholding, religious practice and serious crimes ranging from homicide and treason to theft and perjury; collectively the Twelve Tables provided the bedrock of Roman law for nearly a thousand years.

Of course, during those thousand years, Roman law also developed considerably. The Twelve Tables were supplemented by statutes and the pronouncements of officials ranging from magistrates to emperors. Generations of legal scholars known as jurists devoted their lives to studying these different parts of the law and giving their professional opinion on cases. The result over time was a huge and sophisticated body of law, chiefly concerned with the interests of the powerful: property, wealth, ownership,

---

* Medieval Latin would differ wildly from classical Latin – so much so that medieval Latin is more or less a language in its own right. Nevertheless, the debt to the Roman world was obvious and direct.

contracts and trade. In Rome itself, only citizens were permitted to bring prosecutions, but the spectacle of a Roman trial could be electrifying, as magistrates presided over public courts in which dozens of 'judges' (what we would now think of as a jury) heard the arguments of skilled rhetoricians dressed formally in their togas, then determined their verdict by casting voting tablets inscribed with a C (*condemno*, for guilty) or A (*absolvo*, for acquittal). Romans whose names are still famous to us today, such as Cicero and Pliny the Younger, served as advocates and magistrates in legal cases; Cicero gave one very famous prosecuting speech in 70 BC (and later published several others) in which he condemned a rich and corrupt magistrate, Gaius Verres, for cruel and tyrannical misdeeds while serving as governor of Sicily. Later, during the first and early second centuries AD, Pliny rose to hold very senior judicial posts around the empire under a succession of emperors; his writings still give us a window into the workings of the law in the golden age of the Roman Empire.

The 'purest' form of Roman law existed, of course, in Rome itself, but during the imperial age, the legal system was exported in various forms to the provinces. Provincial governors toured the cities of their jurisdiction on an assize, hearing legal cases and determining them according to the most appropriate law-code to the case. Disputes between Roman citizens – veteran soldiers who had settled in the province, for example – would be subject to Roman law. Cases between non-citizens might be left to the pre-existing laws of the land, allowing the community to keep hold of an important measure of self-determination.[34] In this respect, one of the most famous pronouncements on the reach of Roman law was made by Cicero during the dying days of the Republic in the first century BC. 'There will not be one such law in Rome and another in Athens, one now and another in the future, but all peoples at all times will be embraced by a single and eternal unchangeable law,' he wrote.[35] His point was philosophical as much as pragmatic, and we must remember that Cicero, as one of the most famous Romans of his day, spoke to the concerns of other rich and powerful men, rather than the experience of many millions of ordinary people who lived throughout the empire, whose only interaction with the law might occur if they broke it and faced violent punishment for doing so. Yet at the same time, the influence of Roman law was rich and long-lasting. It thrived not only in the Republic during which Cicero lived, but the empire too, and its influence would be felt very powerfully throughout the Middle Ages and well into the modern era. In this, Roman law was much like Roman language. It was also similar, in its historical robustness, to Roman religion – or at least, the religion that was adopted throughout the empire from the fourth century AD onwards. That religion was Christianity.

From Gods to God

FOR THE FIRST 250 YEARS FOLLOWING the birth, ministry and death of Christ, the Roman Empire was not an especially nice place to be a Christian. Romans had traditionally been enthusiastic collectors of gods, including the Olympian pantheon and various mystery cults from the east. So to begin with, there was little enthusiasm for this odd Jewish sect, whose members sought to keep alive the memory of the carpenter's son who had caused a brief stir in Jerusalem during the governorship of Pontius Pilate. The first generations of Christians were scattered among the cities of the Mediterranean, in sporadic communication with one another but in no position to grow their numbers. Ardent believers like the apostle Paul (St Paul) travelled far and wide, preaching and writing famous letters to all who would listen (and some who would not) describing the miracle of Christ's sacrifice. But in an empire that made gods of everything from the sun and planets to its own emperors, and liberally borrowed from the religious practices of those whom it conquered, men like Paul were nothing new; there was little indication during his lifetime in the first century AD that his enthusiastic wanderings and writings would eventually plant Christ's name in the hearts of literally billions of people during the next 2,000 years of world history. In AD 112,

Pliny the Younger wrote to the emperor Trajan to describe a legal investigation he had undertaken in Bithynia (modern Turkey) following complaints against local Christians. Having tortured a number of them, including young girls, Pliny wrote, he had only really been able to establish that they followed a 'bad... and extravagant superstition' which 'is spread like a contagion.'[36]

In these early years Christians were from time to time mistreated in this fashion, although this did not make them special. Abuse also occasionally rained down on the adherents of other odd new faiths, including 'Manicheans', who followed the teachings of the third-century AD Persian prophet Mani. Yet between around AD 200 and AD 350 Christianity was transformed. First, Christians were taken seriously as a group. Then, in the mid-third century they were persecuted en masse. The really programmatic pursuit of Christians began under emperor Decius (r. AD 249–251), who took umbrage at general Christian refusal to take part in a series of pagan sacrifices that he had ordered for the good of the empire, during the Crisis of the Third Century. Under Decius – and later, under Valerian (r. AD 253–260) and Diocletian (r. AD 284–305), Christians were flogged, flayed, thrown to wild beasts and martyred in many inventive ways. Diocletian was remembered as a sadist and his cruelty provided lurid material for later Christian writers like Eusebius of Caesarea, who collected and chronicled the agonies visited on early Christian martyrs. One passage typical of Eusebius' writings runs as follows:

> Women were tied by one foot and hoisted high in the air, head downwards, their bodies completely naked without a morsel of clothing, presenting thus the most shameful, brutal, and inhuman of all spectacles to everyone watching. Others again were tied to trees and stumps and died horribly; for with the aid of machinery they drew together the very stoutest boughs, fastened one of the martyr's legs to each, and then let the boughs fly back to their normal position; thus they managed to tear apart the limbs of their victims in a moment.[37]

Racking, scraping, branding and barbecuing – all these horrors and more were visited on Christ's unfortunate partisans during the later third century. Yet at the beginning of the fourth century Christians' troubles abruptly eased. First they were tolerated, then they were embraced and finally their beliefs and presence were championed. By the time the Roman Empire in the west suffered its fatal collapse in the early fifth century Christianity was the official imperial religion, and its future as one of the world's biggest faiths was assured. Much of this was down to the emperor Constantine I.

Constantine – born in Niš (*Naissus*) – became emperor in AD 306. A campaigning general of some talent, he was at York (*Eboracum*) when his father, Constantius, died – so it was in that northern British city that his troops proclaimed him emperor. Unfortunately – or perhaps not – this was a time of enormous discord in the Roman Empire, during which the post of emperor had been split into four – the so-called tetrarchy, established by Diocletian, which envisaged two pairs of rulers harmoniously governing the eastern and western parts of the empire in the spirit of compromise and co-operation. Naturally, the actual result of the tetrarchy was protracted civil war; but out of this came Christianity's big break. In the autumn of AD 312, as Constantine was preparing to fight his rival emperor Maxentius at the Milvian Bridge over the river Tiber, he looked to the heavens and saw a blazing cross above the sun, accompanied by the Greek words, 'in this sign, conquer' (Εν Τούτω Νίκα). He took this to be a message from the god of the Christians: clearly a god who at that moment appeared to be more interested in battles and politics than in his son Jesus Christ's programme of charity, forgiveness and reconciliation. In any case, Constantine routed his enemies: Maxentius drowned in the Tiber and was posthumously decapitated. Constantine was now on his way to abolishing the tetrarchy and establishing himself as a single emperor to rule over all. From that moment onwards he heaped all the fruits of imperial patronage on Christian bishops and believers. His soldiers went into battle with the Chi-Rho daubed on their shields. Officials from across the empire were told to enforce a new imperial edict issued in Milan in AD 313, which promised non-discrimination against Christians. In Rome, building works began on what would become St John Lateran and St Peter's. In Jerusalem, the first Church of the Holy Sepulchre was commissioned, to mark the spot where Christ had been crucified and entombed. (Later rumour, which assumed enormous significance during the Middle Ages, had it that Constantine's mother Helena had found the timber of Christ's cross during a visit in AD 327.) And in AD 330, Constantine formally founded Constantinople: a new imperial capital in the east at Byzantium (*Byzantion*, now Istanbul), and filled it with monumental Christian churches.

Now, the Christian God was promoted across the empire, and although to begin with he was not afforded exclusivity over other traditional Roman deities, he soon became a first among equals. Constantine was baptized on his deathbed, and after him only one Roman emperor (Julian 'the Apostate', r. AD 361–63) was not a Christian. By the fifth century Christianity was the official imperial religion and emperors had begun to take seriously its theological minutiae – especially when it came to persecuting heretics and schismatics. In turn, Christianity underwent its first wave of Romanization, developing a distinct military tone, a preference for Latin as the language of exegesis, a network of 'dioceses' (the name was borrowed, ironically, from Diocletian, once the arch-persecutor, who had in his day divided the empire into secular diocese for ease of administration), a taste for monumental architecture and spectacular ritual and – perhaps most enduringly – a nascent divide between its eastern and western branches, mirroring the rupture that defined the Roman Empire from Constantine's day onwards.[38]

Constantine – a hard-headed general whose attempts at preaching to his courtiers were at best stilted and most likely totally inept – was a rather unlikely figure to have launched Christianity on its path, and his reasons for having suddenly cleaved so closely to the faith are still a matter of debate. For generations ordinary Romans continued to balance Christian beliefs with their old fondness for traditional gods and pagan rituals. Yet the power of Constantine's decision in the early fourth century AD is undeniable. Before him, Christians were hounded, hated, and regarded as fodder for the wild beasts of the arena. After him, Christianity was propelled from an unpopular fringe cult to the central worship system in the empire. It was – perhaps appropriately – miraculous.

Legacy

'SOME THINGS ARE HURRYING INTO EXISTENCE, and others are hurrying out of it,' wrote the Stoic philosopher and Roman emperor Marcus Aurelius (r. AD 161–180).[39] If we are to seek 'turning points' in the history of the empire over which he ruled, there are plenty of options. One landmark was the edict of Caracalla of AD 212, when citizenship was radically redistributed in the provinces. Another was the Crisis of the Third Century, when Rome juddered, split, almost collapsed and then reformed. A third was Constantine's reign, when Rome adopted Christianity and the new capital, Constantinople, ensured that the hub and the future of the empire would subsequently be found in the eastern Mediterranean rather than the west. And a fourth (as we shall see in the next chapter) came with the arrival of nomadic steppe tribes in Europe in AD 370, an event that placed enormous and eventually intolerable pressure on Roman institutions, boundaries and power structures.

How we attribute responsibility for the collapse of the Roman Empire between these – and other – factors is not of immediate importance in the context of our story here. What *is* important is that by the turn of the fifth century AD, even as it broke apart, the Roman Empire had been a political, cultural, religious and military force in the west for nearly a millennium. The owners of the Hoxne Hoard, who buried their treasure at that time, had enjoyed access to all the fruits of Roman-ness: Christianity, citizenship, urban comfort, a common language, the rule of law and the freedom to pursue these benefits because of enslaved labour. So too had many others like them, from Britain in the west to the lands that bordered the Sassanid Persian empire in the east.

What was not clear at the start of the fifth century was how much of this Roman-ness would survive. In that regard, only time would tell. In some regions – most notably the old Greek world of the eastern Mediterranean – Rome was destined to live on, updated but not radically altered, for many more centuries. In other places – such as Britain, where we began this chapter – the most obvious signs of Roman influence waned sharply once the legions left; much of Rome's legacy was buried, sometimes literally, as new waves of settlers arrived. For some people the collapse of the western Roman Empire was a seismic event, which demanded that they pack up their possessions, and either bury them in the ground or haul them away to a new life elsewhere. Yet for others it would have registered barely, if at all. Just as there was no single defining experience of life under the Roman Empire, so there was no one typical experience of life without it. It would be naïve to imagine otherwise.

But none of this equivocation is to say that the fall of Rome in the west did not matter, or that it should not still be taken seriously as a pivotal phase in western history. The longevity of Roman rule, its sophistication, its particular geographical extent, its capacity for nobility and abject cruelty – all of these things had been embedded to differing degrees in the western cultural and political landscape. All would continue to matter as the classical world evolved into the medieval. Even when Rome was gone, it was not forgotten. It was the historical foundation on which everything in the Middle Ages was built.

2

BARBARIANS

'Who would believe that Rome, built up by the
conquest of the whole world, had collapsed? That the
mother of nations had also become their tomb?'

ST JEROME, COMMENTARY ON EZEKIEL

For those alert to signs hidden in the fabric of the world, the Roman Empire's collapse in the west was announced by a series of omens. In Antioch, dogs howled like wolves, night-birds let out hideous shrieks and people muttered that the emperor should be burned alive.[1] In Thrace, a dead man lay in the road and fixed passers-by with an unnerving, lifelike glare, until after a few days the corpse suddenly disappeared.[2] And in the city of Rome itself, citizens persisted in going to the theatre: an egregious and insanely sinful pastime, which, according to one Christian writer, practically invited the wrath of the Almighty.[3] Human beings have been superstitious in all ages and we are especially good at adducing portents when we have the benefit of hindsight. Hence the opinion of the historian Ammianus Marcellinus, who looked back on the end of the fourth century into which he was born and reflected that this was a time when fortune's wheel, 'which is perpetually alternating prosperity and adversity', was turning fast.[4]

In the 370s, when Rome's fatal malady set in, the Roman state – monarchy, republic and empire – had existed for more than a millennium. Yet within little more than one hundred years, by the end of the fifth century AD, every province west of the Balkans had slipped from Roman control. In the ancient heartlands of empire, Roman institutions, tax systems and trade networks were falling apart. The physical signs of Roman elite culture – palatial villas, cheap imported consumer goods, hot running water – were fading from everyday life. The Eternal City had been sacked several times, the western crown had passed between a succession of dimwits, usurpers, tyrants and children, until eventually it had been abolished; and territory that formerly comprised the core of a powerful mega-state had been parcelled among peoples whom the proud-hearted citizens of Rome's imperial heyday had previously scorned as savages and subhumans. These were the 'barbarians': a derogatory word which encompassed a huge range of people, from itinerant nomadic tribes quite new to the west and ignorant or dismissive of Roman mores, through to longstanding near-neighbours, whose lives were heavily influenced by Roman-ness, but who had not been able to share in the fruits of citizenship.

The rise of the barbarians was a complex process, involving long- and short-distance migration, a collision of political systems and cultures, and a general collapse in imperial institutions. Although Rome would live on largely untouched in the east, where it thrived in mutant form as Greek-speaking Byzantium, the future of the Roman west now lay in the hands of the newcomers. The age of the barbarian had dawned.

'The most terrible of all warriors'

THE ANTIQUE WORLD CAN BE SAID to have crumbled – and the Middle Ages begun – on the banks of the river Volga in the year AD 370. In that year there appeared at the riverside crowds of people known collectively as the Huns, who had left their homelands thousands of miles away on the grasslands – or 'steppe' – north of China. The origins of the Huns will forever be sketchy, but their effect on the history of the west was profound. When they first appeared, the Huns were what we would today call climate migrants, or even refugees. But in the fourth century they did not come to the west to solicit sympathy. Rather, they arrived on horseback, carrying composite reflex bows which were unusually large and powerful and could shoot arrows accurately to an exceptional range of 150m, piercing armour at 100m. Such weapons were beyond the craftsmanship of any contemporary nomadic people, and the Huns' expertise in mounted archery earned them a reputation for brutality and slaughter, to which they enthusiastically played up. They were a nomadic civilization led by a warrior caste, with access to revolutionary military technology; a people who had been toughened by countless generations of life on the unforgiving Eurasian steppe, for whom migration was the only way of life and violence a basic fact of survival. They would shake the Roman world to its core.

The Huns were related in some way to a nomadic group who populated and dominated the Asian steppe as rulers of a tribal empire from the third century BC.[5] These nomads fought against the Chinese Qin and Han dynasties, and Chinese scribes dubbed them 'Xiongnu', or 'howling slaves'.[6] The name stuck, and was transliterated as Xwn or Hun. Although the Xiongnu empire collapsed in the second century AD, many tribes survived and the scattered descendants of the imperial Xiongnu still retained the name two hundred years later. Xiongnu, Xwn or Hun: who called them what, when and where is only vaguely knowable given the patchy sources of the time. But whichever way the word was rendered it carried a sense of implied horror: the fear and loathing traditionally borne by sedentary civilizations towards alien nomads.

By the late AD 300s the Huns no longer commanded an empire, but they were still a political force. And it was not only Chinese observers who sharpened their pens against them. Around AD 313 a merchant from Central Asia called Nanaivande wrote about the appalling damage a band of Huns had done to towns in northern China, including Luoyang, where the imperial 'palace was burnt and the city destroyed'.[7] A generation later – after a splinter group of Hunnic tribes moved out into new parts of the world, heading towards Europe – western writers also composed screeds elaborating on Hunnic misdeeds. Ammianus Marcellinus called the Huns 'quite abnormally savage'. Certainly they were physically distinctive, often binding their children's skulls so that their heads grew long and conical. Squat-bodied, hairy, coarse and inured to life in the saddle and under canvas, wrote Ammianus Marcellinus, the Huns 'are not subject to the authority of any king, but break through any obstacle in their path under the improvised command of their chief men.'[8]

What caused the Huns to move east in the fourth century has long perplexed historians. Unfortunately, like most tribal nomads of their time, the Huns were illiterate – a people with no record-keeping or chronicle culture. They can no longer speak to us in their language, we will never know their side of the story, and most of our information about them comes from people who hated them. Literary types like Ammianus Marcellinus considered the Huns a scourge of the gods; their appearance in the west was, in his telling, simply a manifestation of 'the wrath of Mars'. What human factors prompted their rise did not detain him very long; insofar as the Huns had any choice in the matter, Ammianus Marcellinus said only that they were 'consumed by a savage passion to pillage the property of others'.[9] Neither he nor any other writers at the time thought to investigate *why* the Huns appeared on the Volga in 370. The fact was, they did.

Yet there is one source that *can* give us a clue about what drove the Huns from their home on the Asian steppe and turned them towards the west. It is not a chronicler or an itinerant Silk Road merchant, but the rugged, spiny Chinese mountain-tree known as the Qilian juniper, or Przewalski's juniper (*Juniperus przewalskii*). This hardy plant, which thrives in the mountains, grows slowly but steadily to around twenty metres in height. Individual trees often live for more than one thousand years, and as they grow they preserve in the rings of their trunks precious information about the history of their world. In this case, the Qilian juniper tells us about the amount of rain that fell in the east during the fourth century AD.[10]

According to tree-ring data provided by Qilian juniper samples from Qinghai province on the Tibetan plateau, it seems that between

AD 350 and AD 370, eastern Asia suffered a 'megadrought' – which remains the worst drought recorded in the last two thousand years. The skies simply dried up. Northern China endured conditions at least as severe as those of the American 'Dust Bowl' of the 1930s, or the Chinese drought of the 1870s – when between 9 and 13 million people starved to death. During that nineteenth-century drought, a missionary named Timothy Richards wrote a harrowing account of conditions among ordinary folk: 'People pull down their houses, sell their wives and daughters, eat roots and carrion, clay and leaves… If this were not enough to move one's pity, the sight of men and women lying helpless on the roadside, or if dead, torn by hungry dogs and magpies should do, and the news… of children being boiled and eaten up, is so fearful as to make one shudder at the thought.'[11] Things were probably similar among the Huns in the 300s. The grass and scrub of the steppe would have turned to mean, biting dust. For the Huns, who depended on grazing animals for their meat, drink, clothing and transport, this was an existential disaster. And it would have presented a stark choice: move, or die. They chose to move.

IN 370 VARIOUS BANDS OF HUNS began to cross the Volga, which empties into the Caspian Sea on the border between modern Russia and Kazakhstan. This in itself was not an immediate threat to Rome. When Julius Caesar had crossed the Rubicon in 49 BC he was about 350km away from the imperial capital; the Huns crossing the Volga were approximately ten times further away from central Italy, and more than 2,000km from the eastern capital in Constantinople. It would be decades before they asserted themselves directly as a first-rank power in the Roman world. Yet in the 370s it was not the Huns who were the problem. It was the people they displaced.

Once across the Volga (in lands roughly equivalent to modern Ukraine, Moldova and Romania) the Huns came into contact with other tribal civilizations: first the Iranian-speaking Alans, then the Germanic tribes known collectively as the Goths. Exactly what took place between these two groups on their first encounters was not reliably recorded. But the Greek writer Zosimus gave the picture in broad strokes. After defeating the Alans, the Huns invaded the Goths' lands, he said, 'with their wives, children, horses, and carriages'. Although as Zosimus understood it, the Huns were so crude and uncivilized that they did not even walk like humans, 'by wheeling, charging, retreating in good time and shooting from their horses, they wrought great slaughter' among the Goths, who were compelled to leave their homes and head towards the Roman Empire, where they 'begged to be received by the emperor'.[12] In other words, a climate emergency in eastern-central Asia fed a secondary migrant crisis in eastern Europe. Drought moved the Huns, and the Huns moved the Goths, so that in 376, huge bands of terrorized Gothic tribespeople showed up on the banks of another major Roman boundary-river: the Danube. There may have been 90,000 or 100,000 refugees in total, although estimating numbers with any real accuracy is impossible. Some were armed, many were desperate. And all were looking for respite within the Roman Empire – which represented, if not paradise, then at least a Hunless zone where stability was the norm and the military offered citizens and subject peoples protection in a time of crisis.

Humanitarian crises are never pretty, and 376 was no exception. The task of dealing with an influx of Goths – deciding who should enter the empire, on what terms and where they should be settled – fell to the eastern emperor, Valens (AD 364–378). A nervous individual, who owed his position as ruler in Constantinople to his late brother (and erstwhile co-emperor) Valentinian I, Valens had spent much of his reign trying to reconcile his apparently boundless military obligations with his limited resources. He was constantly preoccupied with either internal rebellion or conflict with the Sassanid Persians on his borders in Armenia and elsewhere. The Persians had hitherto been by far the most serious menace to Rome's eastern security, and the rivalry between the two empires dominated Middle Eastern politics. Even so, Valens could not ignore the arrival of a large band of indigent outsiders from the realm of the barbarians. It presented him with a practical as well as a moral dilemma. Was it better to admit the bedraggled Goths or turn them back and leave them to be butchered or enslaved by the Huns? To allow them to cross the Danube would bring major challenges: it would be no easy task to maintain public order and a regular food supply while controlling the spread of disease. On the other hand, desperate migrants have throughout history been a reliable source of cheap labour, and the Roman army was always in need of new recruits. If Valens allowed the Goths to enter the empire, he might be able to press their menfolk into military service against Persia, and levy taxes on the rest. The situation was delicate – but not without promise.

In 376 Gothic envoys found Valens in Antioch and formally requested admission for their people. The emperor pondered for a while, then said he would allow some of the Goths to cross the Danube, after which they could settle their families in Thrace (modern Bulgaria and eastern Greece), so long as they sent their menfolk to join the military. Orders went to the frontier granting passage across the water to the Gothic tribe known as the Thervingi; but a rival tribe, the Greuthungi, were to be kept out.* This evidently struck Valens as a reasonable fudge, and according to sources including Ammianus Marcellinus, he was delighted with the outcome: 'The affair seemed a matter for rejoicing rather than dread.'[13] It seemed he had turned a profit from a tragedy. On the Danube, the Roman fleet began a major relief effort, which brought perhaps 15–20,000 of the Goths across the river 'on boats and rafts and canoes made from hollowed tree trunks'.[14] But it did not take long for the Gothic migrant crisis to turn sour. It is easy, with hindsight, to argue that Valens made a catastrophic historical blunder in his approach. Yet this was a situation that might have defeated even an Augustus or a Constantine I. And one thing was

---

* There is some scholarly debate about whether these tribal names meant much to the Goths themselves, or are merely unsatisfactory labels given by Roman outsiders. Think about the difficulties white settlers of the nineteenth-century American interior encountered in describing the tribal structures of Native American people.

certain: once the policy of admitting vast numbers of refugees into the empire had been set, it proved impossible to reverse.

First Blood

THERE WAS RECENT HISTORY BETWEEN ROMANS and Goths. Between 367 and 369 Valens had fought a series of wars against Gothic tribes. These had been settled by negotiation, but the damage done by Roman troops in Gothic lands, combined with economic sanctions, had left bad feeling on both sides. (It is indeed quite likely that war against Rome had played a significant part in weakening the Goths prior to the arrival of the Huns.)[15] And so it did not take much for a state-led refugee settlement programme to turn into an episode of foul exploitation in which 'crimes [were] committed for the worst motives... against hitherto innocent newcomers.'[16]

According to Ammianus Marcellinus, the Roman officials in charge of the Danube crossings – named Lupicinus and Maximus – took advantage of starving migrant Thervingian families by forcing them to give up their children as slaves in return for parcels of dog-flesh. Along with cruelty came ineptitude. Besides abusing the Tervingian Goths, Lupicinus and Maximus also failed to ensure that other refugees, the barbarians *non grata*, stayed out. Guerilla crossings, which dodged Roman river patrols, meant that between 376 and 377 Thrace slowly became home to thousands of disaffected and mistreated Gothic migrants. Some were legal, many were illegal. Most were alienated from their homelands but with no love for their host country. The infrastructure to contain, resettle and feed tens of thousands of new arrivals did not exist. The chief focus of imperial attention remained the Persian borderlands, and Valens had delegated the Gothic issue to men patently not up to the job. The Balkans were becoming a tinderbox.

In 377 Goths inside the Roman Empire began a series of running rebellions. Their plundering of wealthy Thracian villages and estates soon spiralled into all-out warfare, in which the Goths fought Roman military detachments with 'a combination of despair and wild fury'.[17] In one clash, at Ad Salices, not far from the coast of the Black Sea, the Goths attacked Roman troops with 'huge clubs hardened in the fire' and 'plunged their daggers in the breasts of those who put up a stout resistance... The whole field was strewn with corpses... a number had fallen by sling-shot or had been transfixed by shafts tipped with metal. In some cases the head had been split in two by a sword-stroke through crown and forehead, and hung down on both shoulders, a most gruesome sight.'[18]

The first great reckoning with the Goths came in the high summer of 378. By now the Gothic tribes inside the empire had combined their forces. They were joined in the field by groups of Alans and even some freelance Huns, who had also crossed the inadequately policed river-border, and were looking for trouble. Together they had turned much of the large corridor between the Danube and the Haemus Mountains into a scorched and smouldering plain. At one point a war band had ridden within sight of the walls of Constantinople itself. This was no longer a marginal migrant problem on the fringes of empire, but a full-blown crisis that threatened both the integrity and the honour of the imperial state.

Valens had no choice but to act. During a period of brief respite on the Persian front he marched in person to the Balkans at the head of an army. He also sent word to the emperor in the west, his nineteen-year old nephew Gratian, asking for his support. In itself this was prudent, for despite his youth, Gratian had already recorded a series of impressive military victories against Germanic tribes further up the Danube. But Valens was conflicted about asking for the help of his much younger and more successful co-emperor. Both his pride and his advisors urged him to get the job done unaided. So in the end Valens did not wait for Gratian to arrive. Having kept his army in camp throughout much of the summer, in early August he received word that large numbers of Goths were assembling near Adrianople (now Edirne, in Turkey), under a commander called Fritigern. Scouts estimated that they had around ten thousand troops. Valens decided to attack them on his own.

At dawn on 9 August 'the army was put in rapid motion.'[19] Valens marched his men out of their fortified camp at Adrianople, eight miles over rough country under a broiling mid-day sun. When they caught up with the Goths, they found them setting fire to the dry countryside. 'Our men, who were already exhausted by the summer heat, [were now] parched with thirst,' wrote Ammianus Marcellinus. 'Bellona [the Roman goddess of war], raging with more than her usual fury, was sounding the death-knell of the Roman cause.'[20]

When Valens appeared, envoys came to him from the Goths. They claimed they wanted to parlay a truce. In fact, they were playing for time, as the Goths' leaders laid a trap. Following inconclusive negotiations, in the early afternoon Valens lost control of his tired and thirsty troops, who charged unbidden at the Goths. Battle was joined. 'The opposing lines came into collision like ships of war and pushed each other to and fro, heaving under the reciprocal motion like the waves of the sea,' wrote Ammianus Marcellinus. 'Dust rose in such clouds as to hide the sky, which rang with frightful shouts... it was impossible to see the enemy's missiles in flight and dodge them; all found their mark and dealt death on every side.'[21] But the damage was loaded heavily on the Romans' ranks.

The Roman intelligence which had suggested the Goths were only ten thousand strong was wrong. There were many more: easily enough to take on a Roman army of perhaps thirty thousand troops.[22] 'The barbarians poured on in huge columns,' continued Ammianus Marcellinus, 'trampling down horse and man and crushing our ranks so as to make an orderly retreat impossible. Our men were too close-packed to have any hope of escape.'[23] Meanwhile, the Goths had prudently hidden a large detachment of cavalry out of sight of Roman scouts. At a crucial moment during the fighting these horsemen appeared, to devastating effect. Valens had been out-thought and his men were overwhelmed. 'The whole field was one dark pool of blood and [the survivors] could see nothing but heaps of slain wherever they turned their eyes,' wrote

Ammianus Marcellinus. 'At last a moonless night brought an end to these irreparable losses, which cost Rome so dear.'[24]

The costliest casualty was Valens himself. The emperor's exact fate is something of a mystery: one report said he was shot with an arrow and died instantly. Others said he was thrown by his horse into a bog, where he drowned. Others still maintained that Valens was pursued from the battlefield with a few guards and some of his eunuchs, and took cover in a farmhouse. Since those hunting him could not batter down the doors they 'piled up bundles of straw and faggots, set fire to them and burned the house with all who were in it.'[25] Whatever happened, Valens' body was never found. At Adrianople the barbarians killed between ten and twenty thousand Romans, including the eastern emperor. Rome was badly mauled – and over time, her wounds began to fester.

The Storm Returns

ALTHOUGH THE CRISIS OF 376–8 DID severe damage to Roman prestige and to the manpower of the imperial army in the east, it did not plunge the empire immediately into disaster. Plenty of the credit for this must go to a leader who stabilized both halves of the empire in final decades of the fourth century. The emperor Theodosius I took power in Constantinople after Valens' death, and in 392, following an unedifying power struggle in the west, he also took power in Milan (*Mediolanum*) – capital of the western empire since the late third century. Theodosius came to a pragmatic arrangement with the Goths, settling them formally in Thrace, employing their warriors to fill the gaps they themselves had punched in the Roman war machine. He made moves across the empire to suppress traditional Roman paganism and weighed decisively into a tortuous schism within the evolving Christian Church. Most importantly, he made sure that the traditional borders of the empire in Europe – effectively the rivers Rhine and Danube – were not again seriously breached. Theodosius' reign was not entirely untroubled, yet in hindsight it would represent a short golden age – not least because he was destined to be the last emperor to rule over both halves of the Roman state as one.

On a bleak and rainy January day in 395, however, Theodosius died, leaving the Roman state to be ruled jointly by his sons.[26] In Constantinople, a seventeen-year-old youth called Arcadius succeeded. In Milan, the nine-year-old Honorius was named *augustus*. Neither was judged mature enough to exercise power by himself, so rule was subcontracted to a pair of strongmen. The power behind the eastern throne was an energetic brute from Gaul named Rufinus. In the west the position was claimed by a charismatic general called Stilicho. Although Stilicho's contemporaries made much of the fact that he was half-barbarian – his father was a member of the Germanic tribal group known as the Vandals – he would prove himself a stout defender of Rome, even as the empire frayed and fell apart at its seams. It that sense, Stilicho was walking proof of the porous boundaries between Romans and barbarians, whose worlds intersected as much as they stood opposed.

'Since man inhabited this globe never has [any other] mortal been granted all earth's blessings without alloy,' wrote the poet Claudian, who served as Stilicho's personal propagandist.[27] But Stilicho's assumption of power in the west (which included marrying his daughter Maria to young Emperor Honorius) threw him into conflict with a wide range of enemies from within and beyond the empire – and a resurgent swell of mass migration that was about to test the Roman west lead to destruction.

At the time of Stilicho's rise to power in 395, the Gothic crisis of the 370s was a receding memory, now a generation old. Yet the underlying facts that had caused the great Gothic invasion of that year had barely changed. Indeed, they were about to be revived in almost identical form, for in the 390s the Huns were once again on the move.

Although the evidence is unclear and open to multiple interpretations, it is clear that for some reason, between the mid-380s and the mid-420s, the Huns recommenced their westward march.[28] Their journey, which had begun on the drought-stricken steppe north of China, now took them around 1,700km from the Caucasus to the Great Hungarian Plain. They moved in great numbers and, as before, sent other tribal groups scattering before them.*

When the Huns arrived north of the Black Sea in the 370s, they had displaced the Goths. Now, as they swept into the Hungarian Plain, they disrupted other barbarian groups: Alans, Vandals, a Germanic people known as the Suevi and another called the Burgundians, whom Roman writers particularly despised for their chubbiness and rank habit of greasing their hair with sour butter. There had been contact between some or all of these groups and individual Huns during the late fourth century, as enterprising Hunnic warriors struck out west to seek work as mercenaries. (Some Huns also began to tout their military expertise within the Roman empire: both Rufinus in Constantinople and Stilicho in Milan counted Huns among their personal retinues of bodyguards, known as *bucellarii*.) But localized, small-scale encounters with military contractors did nothing to prepare the west for the effects of a second great Hunnic surge. Once again, as the Huns pushed towards the fringes of the Roman Empire, they sparked a secondary panic and waves of uncontrolled migration before them. This culminated between 405 and 410 in a series of devastating assaults on the Roman borders.

Trouble erupted first in the foothills of the eastern Alps, when in the second half of AD 405 a Gothic king called Radagaisus appeared with a vast horde of perhaps one hundred thousand people (around twenty thousand of whom were fighting men) and forced his way into Italy. According to Zosimus (who took his information from a writer called Olympiodorus of Thebes) the news of Radagaisus' impending arrival 'confounded everyone. The cities despaired and even Rome panicked in the face of this extreme danger.'[29] There was good reason for concern. Stilicho, who was charged with repelling these invaders, had more than

---

* Already by the 390s merely the name of the Hun was enough to strike fear into the hearts of Romans far and wide; when a band of runaway slaves and army deserters formed a robber gang in the Balkans in the 390s, they called themselves 'the Huns' despite almost certainly not being Huns. Imitation was a lethally sincere form of flattery: these brigands were taking advantage of what we might call an emerging fourth-century terror brand.

enough manpower to do the job, but not straight away. He needed to draw down troops from the Rhineland, call up mercenary reinforcements from among the Alans and Huns who touted for business as hired swords, and corral the whole armed forces of Italy for a vast military operation. By the time he was ready to take on Radagaisus, it was the middle of AD 406. The Goths had enjoyed six months or so of unopposed plunder, and Radagaisus had cut a swathe as far south as Florence, which he had besieged and reduced to the brink of starvation.

The Goths and their king were roundly punished for their impertinence. Stilicho 'completely destroyed their whole forces,' wrote Zosimus, 'none of them escaping, except a few which he added to the Roman auxiliaries.' Radagaisus was captured and beheaded outside the walls of Florence on 23 August. Stilicho, naturally, 'was very proud of this victory, and returned with his army, universally honoured for freeing Italy miraculously from such inevitable danger.'[30] The battle was won decisively and in relatively short order. But in drawing down so many troops from around Europe, Stilicho had left large regions of the imperial west poorly defended and vulnerable. He had also come nowhere near addressing the source of Rome's problems. The war – which was not so much against a single king or a single people as against demography and human movement itself – had only just begun.

THE EFFECTS OF STILICHO'S THINNING-OUT OF Roman defences on the Rhine were seen within the year. On 31 December 406, a huge, mixed band of Vandals, Alans and Suevi crossed the river into Gaul.[31] Whether the river was frozen in midwinter or simply poorly defended is now lost to us – but the crossing threw Gaul and provinces beyond, including Britain, into turmoil. According to a letter by the Biblical scholar and Church Father St Jerome, violent outsiders plundered the city of Mainz, massacring thousands of churchgoers in the process. They besieged and reduced Worms, and ran riot in Reims, Amiens, Arras, Thérouanne, Tournai, Speyer, Strasbourg, Lyon and Narbonne. 'Those which the sword spares without, famine ravages within,' wrote St Jerome. 'Who will hereafter credit the fact… that Rome has to fight within her own borders not for glory but for bare life?'[32] The Christian poet Orientius adopted much the same tone: 'All Gaul burned as a single funeral pyre.'[33] As many as 30,000 warriors and 100,000 other migrants were now at large in the province. The Rhine border had burst, and would never properly recover.

From this point, things degenerated fast. The crises in Italy and Gaul had spread deep uncertainty to the most westerly fringes of empire, and in Britain, the Roman army – having not been paid for many months – entered a state of semi-permanent mutiny. During 406, two leading officers, first Marcus and then Gratian, declared themselves emperor. Each 'reigned' for a matter of months before being murdered by his men. In early 407 a third usurper-emperor tried his luck. Constantine III seized control of the British legions, announced that he was now the leader of the western empire, and began a fateful withdrawal of all military units from Britain. During the months that followed, Constantine shipped thousands of soldiers out of Britain into Gaul, to try to save the Rhine frontier. The British were left to fend for themselves – nominally still part of the Roman Empire, but effectively abandoned and horribly vulnerable to raids from Germanic tribes bold enough to cross the North Sea. The time was fast arriving when Britain would be Roman no more.

But still the raids kept coming. In 408 the Huns made their first direct attack on the empire, when a warrior known as Uld (or Uldin), once a mercenary ally of Stilicho's, crossed the lower Danube near Castra Martis (today on the border of Serbia and Bulgaria) and announced that he was ready to conquer every place on earth that was touched by the sun's rays. In fact, Uld was sold out by his own men, defeated and disappeared – either sold into slavery or more likely killed outright. Be that as it may; the Roman Empire was now under siege.

***

ONE OF THE MOST DANGEROUS BARBARIAN leaders – a petty king who would prove a regular torment to Stilicho – was a military officer known as Alaric. Early in his career Alaric was something of a poster-boy for Gothic integration into the Roman way of life. He was a Christian. He led a war-band of Goths and other non-Roman troops who served within the Roman army. Indeed, throughout his career he seemed to covet nothing so much as a legitimate place within the Roman political and military world. Nevertheless, in around 395 he broke off friendly relations with Rome's leaders and had himself elected king of a Gothic coalition now known as the Visigoths. This gave him a military following numbering in the tens of thousands. Twice, in 401–2 and 403, Alaric used it to invade Italy. On both occasions he was bested by Stilicho, who triumphed over the Visigoths in battles at Pollenza (*Pollentia*) and Verona. 'Learn, presumptuous peoples, not to despise Rome,' crowed Claudian, when he wrote of Alaric's defeat at the former.[34] But Alaric would have the last laugh.

Although supposedly reconciled with the western empire after his battlefield reverses, in 406 Alaric refused to come to the Romans' aid when his countryman Radagaisus led his own massive Gothic invasion of Italy. Then, in 408, when Gaul fell into chaos, and Britain into the hands of usurper-emperors, Alaric gleefully joined the fray. Still with tens of thousands of troops at his disposal, he sent word to the western emperor Honorius's court – which had now moved from Milan to Ravenna, where it was closer to the east – that he would once more invade Italy, unless he was immediately paid 3,000 pounds of silver. The Senate bridled, but Stilicho – conscious that the imperial military was now impossibly stretched and in no position to open any more fronts – persuaded them to submit to Alaric's demands. There was widespread unease at this decision, with one senator, Lampadius, muttering that 'this is slavery rather than peace'.[35]

This unease soon curdled into political revolt. In the summer of 408, with fires raging across the empire and Visigoths waiting to pounce, Stilicho's enemies in the Senate moved against him. A whispering campaign, playing on Stilicho's Vandal heritage, maintained that the general was in secret alliance with Alaric, and suggested that his ultimate goal was to place his son on the imperial throne in the east, where Arcadius had recently died. With his personal authority rapidly draining away, Stilicho was unable to save his skin. In May 408 several of his loyal officers were murdered in a coup. Honorius summarily cancelled payments to Alaric's Visigoths. And three months later, Stilicho was arrested in Ravenna and imprisoned. On 22 August he was executed for treachery, going to his death without complaint. According to Zosimus, Stilicho calmly 'submitted his neck to the sword. He was the most moderate of almost all those in power at that time.'[36] Without lifting a finger, Alaric had rid himself of his most dangerous foe. He made the most of the opportunity.

Within weeks of Stilicho's execution, Alaric and the Visigoths were on the march through Italy, intent on helping themselves to the richest spoils of the imperial heartlands. Their numbers swelled as they marched, for the wider reprisals that followed Stilicho's death had included waves of xenophobic assaults on migrants. Thousands of barbarian soldiers in the Roman army had been hideously mistreated, and their families abused or killed. Now, for many who joined Alaric, the campaign was not just about plunder. It was personal. So they headed straight for the prize guaranteed to wound the empire most grievously: the symbolic heart of the Roman Empire, the city of Rome itself.

In November Alaric put the Eternal City under siege, stopping all food deliveries and demanding as his ransom all the gold the citizens possessed. With around three-quarters of a million mouths to feed, Rome could not go hungry very long. After two months Alaric received from the court at Ravenna a promise of 5,000 pounds of gold and another 30,000 of silver, along with supplies to feed and clothe his army – if he withdrew. This was a steep price, but the emperor Honorius – now twenty-four years old – realized he had no other option but to resurrect Stilicho's old strategy and pay the bribe. In Gaul, the usurper-emperor Constantine was gathering support daily. The Roman countryside was in tatters – economically crippled for years to come. Crises were piling up everywhere.

Having retreated from Rome, however, Alaric proposed new terms for a settlement that would see him leave Italy altogether. These went back to the issue that had seen the Goths cross the Danube in the first place: their lack of a homeland, now that eastern Europe was overrun with Huns. Alaric asked the emperor to allow his Visigoths to settle in territory roughly comprising modern Austria, Slovenia and Croatia. He also asked for high Roman military office – as a successor to Stilicho himself. He proposed 'friendship and alliance between him and the Romans, against everyone who took up arms and was roused to war against the emperor.'[37] It was not an unreasonable offer. But Honorius blanched, refused to negotiate and dared Alaric to take what he could not achieve through talking.

In 409 Alaric took his army back to Rome and laid siege to the city for a second time. Now he tried to threaten Honorius with deposition, by browbeating the Roman Senate into nominating an alternative emperor, Attalus, as a sort of Gothic sock-puppet. Alaric briefly left Rome, and took his army on a tour of several other Italian cities, where they advised the citizens to accept Attalus' imperium, or taste the sharp edges of Gothic swords. Yet still Honorius sat in Ravenna and declined to compromise, waiting for reinforcement troops to reach him from Constantinople and hoping to bore Alaric into submission. This was a catastrophic misjudgement. In August 410, Alaric cancelled Attalus' pseudo-reign. He returned to Rome, and his original plan. On the second anniversary of Stilicho's beheading, the barbarians were outside the gates. Two days later, on 24 August 410, the gates swung open. By either trickery or simple intimidation, Alaric had persuaded the citizens to let his men in.

The sack of Rome had begun.

EIGHT HUNDRED YEARS HAD PASSED SINCE Rome had last been sacked – on that occasion by Celts from Gaul known as the Senones, who plundered the city after defeating the Roman army in battle a few miles outside the city walls. The awful memory of that day in July 387 BC was lodged in Roman folklore and romantic history, having been described by Livy, in a passage fairly bubbling with melodrama. 'No mercy was shown; houses were ransacked, and the empty shells set on fire.'[38] In fact, archaeological study has shown no evidence of a major inferno that year; rather, it seems that in 387 BC the Senones came, took what they could carry, and were, after some time, chased away by a relieving army.[39] Nevertheless, it mattered deeply to Romans that their city had once – but only once – been sacked. Now, at long last, history was about to repeat itself.

The Visigoths' sack of AD 410 was no annihilation; the attachment of Alaric and many of his followers to the Christian faith ensured that. But it was definitely an enthusiastic looting spree. Having entered Rome through the Salarian Gate, the Goths toured Rome's shrines, monuments, public buildings and private houses, stripping them of valuables but leaving most structures standing and most people unmolested. Ordinary civilians were allowed to take refuge in the large basilicas of St Peter and St Paul, which were designated places of Christian sanctuary. Visigoths ran riot in the Forum, burned the Senate house and ruined several large mansions, but otherwise the majority of Rome's famous landmarks were left intact. Some high-value items, including a 2,000-pound silver tabernacle, were stolen, and wealthy citizens were held up with menaces.

It was a frightening few days, and the stories that circulated of barbarians on the rampage grew more apocalyptic with each telling, crystallizing in accounts like that by St Jerome, writing in Antioch, who cast the fate of Rome in terms borrowed from the Old Testament, where Psalm 79 lamented the destruction of Jerusalem by the Babylonians: 'Oh God, the heathen have come into your inheritance. Your holy temple they have defiled... the dead bodies of your servants are meat for the fowls of the heavens, the flesh of your saints is taken by the beasts of the earth... A sovereign city of ancient date has fallen and lifeless in its streets and houses lie numberless bodies of its citizens.'[40] In north Africa St Augustine took Alaric's sack as the inspiration for a number of sermons, which formed the basis for his monumental *City of God*, a work that poured scorn on Rome's ancient pretensions to eternal empire and argued instead that the only true everlasting kingdom was to be found in heaven.

This was theology, not reportage. In fact, in grand strategic terms, the sack of Rome changed little: after three days of sacking, Alaric called off his Visigoths, and they left the city, heading south, in the direction of Sicily. By the autumn, Alaric was dead, possibly of malaria, leaving command of the Visigoths to his brother-in-law Athaulf. After this, a general called Flavius Constantius slowly but steadily brought back a semblance of calm in the west, persuading Athaulf to bring the Visigoths permanently into the Roman fold, and settling them with a homeland in Aquitaine, in south-west Gaul. Constantius also captured and killed the would-be emperor Constantine III. Although by AD 418 about half the population of the city of Rome had left, never to return, the situation in the wider western empire was much improved.

All the same, the thunderous responses of writers like Jerome and Augustine still communicate the deep shock caused by Alaric's sack of Rome. Like the fall of the Berlin Wall, or the 9/11 terrorist attacks on the United States of America, the terrible symbolism of an assault on a world superpower far outweighed the immediate physical damage done. Alaric's Goths struck at the heart of the Roman Empire, leaving scars that only hardened and deepened as the years went by.

Coming of the Tyrants

ALTHOUGH ALARIC HAD STRUCK AT THE centre, the western empire began to fall apart from the periphery. So in surveying the barbarian realms that emerged in its stead, we must begin at the fringes. And nowhere did the collapse occur so swiftly as Britain: the last of the major Roman provinces to have been conquered and the first to be lost.

During the crisis years of 406–11, Roman defences in Britain vanished. The army there had produced three would-be usurpers,

Marcus, Gratian and Constantine III. But as it did so, the province's military defences were being systematically stripped. When the fifth century dawned, troops in Britain were in serious arrears with their wages and presumably very disgruntled. But before long there were none left to grumble about their lot. By 407 all had been withdrawn to defend Gaul and the Rhine frontier from barbarian incursions and to bolster Constantine's pretensions to the purple. Soon after, Roman civilian administrators were also on their way out.

There is some – contested – evidence to suggest that in 410 the emperor Honorius, besieged by Alaric in Ravenna, wrote to the major Roman cities in Britain and told them that they would be entirely responsible for defending themselves. If he did indeed send such a letter, it was no more than a statement of reality. With no army and no financial or bureaucratic links back to the imperial centre, Britain's ties to the Roman state withered almost immediately. By the 440s most of the obvious social signs of Roman-ness – plush villas, sophisticated urban living, a sense of elite attachment to international culture – were in sharp decline in Britain. Estates were abandoned. Trade networks shrivelled and dissolved. Towns shrank. Political units – tax regions, and spheres of government – shrank alarmingly as the province shattered. The silver spoons, delicate pieces of gold jewellery and mountains of Roman coin that were buried in the Hoxne Hoard* attest to the chaotic retreat of the Roman ruling class from Britain. All over the islands, rich families evacuated the failing state with all that they could carry, abandoning or burying that which they could not.

The process of Britain's departure from the Roman Empire was hastened not only by the turbulence across the sea in Gaul and Italy, but by the arrival in Britain of significant numbers of warriors and their families from another part of Europe, well outside the empire. The eastern seaboard of Britain had long been a tempting entry point for raiding parties of Picts, Scots and Germanic tribes known collectively (if imprecisely)

* See chapter 1.

as Anglo-Saxons. There had been a serious invasion crisis in 367–8, known as the Great Conspiracy, in which a troop mutiny on Hadrian's Wall preceded a massive series of coastal raids by non-Roman aligned northern British tribes, apparently in league with Saxons and others from outside the province. Now the same route lay open once again.

From the early fifth century Britain was steadily settled by warbands and migrant groups from the North Sea fringe. There was no single, co-ordinated military invasion such as the Romans had landed in the time of Claudius, or the Normans would stage in 1066; the invasions were piecemeal and staggered over many years. Some of the names later applied to the peoples who arrived included the Saxons, Angles and Jutes. But ethnic terminology would have mattered much less to fifth-century Britons than observed reality: Roman functionaries and soldiers had disappeared across the sea in one direction, while Germanic settlers bringing new languages, cultures and beliefs arrived from another.

At some time around 450, during the reign of the emperor Valentinian III, the beleaguered chieftains trying to resist Saxon raids sent a begging letter known as the Groan of the Britons to the Roman *generalissimo* in the west, Aëtius. Aëtius was an old-fashioned war hero, who specialized in fighting barbarians in a rearguard struggle for imperial honour. Clearly, he was regarded as the last hope. 'The barbarians drive us to the sea, the sea drives us to the barbarians,' wailed the British. 'Between these two modes of death we are either killed or drowned.'[41] But Aëtius declined to rescue them. Britain was already too far gone.

The writer who preserved the Groan of the Britons was a sixth-century monk called Gildas, whose account of this turbulent period, *On the Ruin and Conquest of Britain*, described an epic struggle for mastery between invading Saxons and native Britons, culminating in a semi-legendary clash of arms known as the battle of Badon, perhaps at some time late in the fifth century. It is often suggested that a decisive part in the battle of Badon was played by 'King Arthur', sometimes identified as the nephew of a soldier called Ambrosius Aurelianus – 'a gentleman who perhaps alone of all the Romans had survived the shock of this notable storm,' wrote Gildas.[42]

The futile debate over whether Ambrosius Aurelianus was the 'real' Arthur need not trouble us here. What is important is that after Badon – or at least, by the time Gildas was writing – Britain was roughly partitioned along a diagonal north-east to south-west line. The Saxon kingdoms that coalesced on the eastern side of that line were tightly bound into trade and cultural networks across the North Sea, towards Scandinavia. Those on the other side looked to the Channel, the Irish Sea and themselves. 'Neither to this day are the cities of our country inhabited as before, but being forsaken and overthrown, still lie desolate,' Gildas wrote, 'our foreign wars having ceased, but our civil troubles still remaining.'[43]

Ultimately, Gildas viewed the agonies of the British after the Romans left as just punishment from God. Britain's rulers, he wrote, deserved everything they got, for 'they plunder and terrorise the innocent, they defend and protect the guilty and thieving, they have many wives, whores and adulteresses, swear false oaths, tell lies, reward thieves, sit with murderous men [and] despise the humble'.[44] The Saxons, he thought, were devils. Of course, Gildas was a churchman, inclined to see the wrath of God and man's evil everywhere. (His most famous aphorism is 'Britain has kings, but they are tyrants: she has judges, but they are unrighteous men'.[45]) And his hysterical account can distract us from the fact that the Saxon barbarians were capable of dazzlingly high culture; take, for example, the famous helmet unearthed at the ship-burial site at Sutton Hoo in Suffolk: a piece of Roman-style head armour complete with eerie face-mask, wrought from iron and bronze and decorated with dragon heads, which may once belonged to King Raedwald of East Anglia. It is a priceless piece of art of which any Roman soldier would have been proud. Nevertheless, it is easy to understand the horror Gildas felt as he surveyed an age of such disorienting demographic change and political reshaping.* Mass

---

* Modern polemicists and politicians are scarcely immune from the same sort of rhetoric, and it is not hard to think of those in our own times who have characterized migrants who disrupt perceived social and cultural orders as cockroaches, vermin, rapists or diseased perverts.

migration, rightly or wrongly, stirs fear and loathing, for as the history of the western Roman Empire makes abundantly clear, it has the power to turn worlds upside down.

WHILE BRITAIN WAS SECEDING FROM THE Roman west, elsewhere in the empire an even more serious rupture was opening up. In this case the lords of misrule were the Vandals. Unsettled by the Huns, many Vandals had joined in the great barbarian crossings of the river Rhine in 406–8. But this was only the beginning of their journey. From the Rhineland, the Vandals pushed south through the convulsing provinces of Roman Gaul, traversed the Pyrenees and headed into Iberia. As they travelled they fought against other barbarian tribes, including the Visigoths and the Suevi, whom they battled to a standstill at the rich and powerful city of Mérida in 428. Then they moved on towards the southern tip of the peninsula.

By this point the Vandals numbered around fifty thousand migrants in total, of whom perhaps ten thousand were seasoned fighting men. They were led by an extraordinarily resourceful and ambitious general called Geiseric. Intelligent and spare in his habits, Geiseric walked with a limp, having fallen from a horse in his youth. Critically for the Vandals, he had a deep affection for and knowledge of sailing and naval warfare.

In May 429, Geiseric loaded his followers and their possessions onto a fleet of ships and took them across the Strait of Gibraltar. His reasons for doing so have been debated at length, but it is likely that he was permitted to enter Roman north Africa by the governor there, Bonifacius – a close ally of Galla Placidia, mother of the emperor Valentinian III and the power behind the throne in Ravenna. If this was so, it was a colossal error by Bonifacius. Having arrived on the southern shore of the Mediterranean, the Vandals turned sharply left, and set off on a plunderous cakewalk through Roman territory, looting every significant city in their path.

According to the Greek scholar Procopius, who took a keen interest in Vandal history, Bonifacius realized his error and tried to make amends: 'he besought [the Vandals] incessantly, promising them everything, to remove from Libya… [However,] they did not receive his words with favour, but considered that they were being insulted,' he wrote.[46] In June 430 they arrived at the port city of Hippo Regius (now Annaba in Algeria), and laid it under siege.

St Augustine, a citizen of Hippo, was lying in his sickbed as the Vandals arrived. He was doubly despondent at their presence, for not only were they barbarians, they were Christians of the Arian sect, rather than the Nicene rite to which Augustine belonged.* He wrote to one fellow churchman arguing that the best course of action for those in the Vandals' path was to flee until the menace had passed.[47] But Augustine never took his own advice: he died in the summer of 430 with the barbarians still camped outside Hippo's walls. In August 431 the city fell, and Geiseric made it the capital of the new barbarian kingdom he was building out of the Roman colonies along the coastal littoral of modern Algeria, Tunisia and Libya.[48]

Hippo was the Vandal capital for only a few years, for in 439 the Vandals took Carthage, the greatest city on the north African coast. The conquest was all too easy. In theory, the Vandals and Romans were at peace that year. But on 19 October, while most of Carthage's population watched entertainments at the hippodrome, Geiseric marched an army into the city. The attack was unannounced, unanticipated and unopposed. It was brazen almost beyond belief. Yet it worked. In a single day, the mighty city for which the Roman Republic had fought the Punic Wars between 264 BC and 146 BC was severed from the empire.

This was more than just a matter of wounded pride. The entire Roman economy depended on Carthaginian grain exports: now these were cut off. In wresting Carthage and so much more of north Africa away from Roman control, the Vandals had sliced

* Most Germanic barbarians were Arian Christians. Arianism rejected a Trinitarian approach to the nature of Jesus Christ – asserting that God the Son was a distinct entity created at a single point in time. Nicene Christians thought otherwise. The Nicene Creed states: 'I believe in one God, the Father Almighty, Creator of heaven and earth, of all things visible and invisible; and in one Lord Jesus Christ, Son of God, the only-begotten, born of the Father before all ages.' This doctrine was formulated at the Council of Nicaea in 325 – hence the name.

through the life-root of the western empire. And in the years that followed, they were able to consolidate their hold over their southern Mediterranean kingdom. Geiseric built and strengthened his fleet, and through his command of the southern Mediterranean coastline was able to construct what amounted to a pirate polity, preying on local shipping and playing havoc with the busy trading networks that were essential to the economic health of western Europe. He raided Sicily, and took control of Malta, Corsica, Sardinia and the Balearic Islands. In AD 455 he even led an army all the way to Rome, emulating Alaric by putting the Eternal City to its second sack of the century. He came back from this adventure with his pockets full. According to Procopius, Geiseric placed 'an exceedingly great amount of gold and other imperial treasure in his ships sailed to Carthage, having spared neither bronze nor anything else whatsoever in the palace... He plundered also the temple of Jupiter Capitolinus, and tore off half of the roof.'[49] Perhaps most scandalously of all, his booty included the western empress Licinia Eudoxia and her two daughters. They would remain honourable prisoners in Carthage for seven years, during which time one of the girls married Geiseric's son and heir, Huneric.

For Rome, this was nothing short of a disaster. For the Vandals it was a triumph to trump their wildest dreams. Geiseric had established a kingdom which, after his death in 477, he passed on to Huneric, and thereafter a dynasty of Vandal kings. The eastern emperors tried to help, sending several naval fleets of their own, in 460 and 468, to try and recapture Carthage and cut off the snake's head. But they failed. The Roman west was left battered and critically diminished.

Unsurprisingly, those on the wrong side of the Vandal conquest left scathing accounts of their times. One especially vehement critic was a churchman known as Quodvultdeus, bishop of Carthage and a correspondent of St Augustine. Having made his distaste for Arianism publicly known, Quodvultdeus was taken captive, put into a rickety boat with no sails or oars and shoved out to sea, eventually washing up in Naples, where he would live his life in exile. In his letters Quodvultdeus described the Vandals as heretics, devils and wolves.[50]

Was Quodvultdeus being fair? Certainly the Vandals were fierce and violent occupiers who shed much blood during their conquest of north Africa. Then again, violent bloodshed is the business of occupying forces. In 146 BC the Roman army under Scipio Aemilianus had hardly treated Carthage civilly: they had burned it to cinders, roasted citizens in their homes, seized all the surrounding land and taken as many as fifty thousand slaves. Likewise, before the Roman emperors converted to Christianity, they had sponsored vigorous bouts of anti-Christian persecution in the province, with victims including the so-called Scillitan martyrs of AD 180 who were executed for their faith and their failure to swear obedience to the then-emperor Marcus Aurelius. The Vandals were unflinchingly severe in persecuting Nicene Christians, but even so, there was nothing intrinsically barbaric in the violence that engulfed north Africa under the Vandals; this was simply the way of the world.

Indeed, we might go further, for there is some evidence to suggest that the Vandal kingdom in north Africa was far from a land of pirates and demons, but actually a fairly stable polity whose rulers were by no means seen by everyone as tyrants. Although the Vandals cut off the vital grain supply chain between Carthage and Rome, there was not a total economic blockade: shipments of popular 'redware' pottery continued across the Mediterranean. The Vandals minted their own, imperial-style coins and evidently got along well enough with the local population (who vastly outnumbered them) to stave off popular revolt.[51] They do not seem to have disrupted the internal mechanisms of Roman government, and surviving Vandal-era mosaics hint at a fine and luxurious material culture. One piece, today on display in the British Museum, but originally unearthed at Bord-Djedid, depicts a north African horseman riding away from a large walled city. Even Procopius, who wrote in detail about the Vandals and their relations with Rome, admitted that these barbarians knew how to live. His account is worth quoting at length:

For of all the nations which we know that of the Vandals is the most luxurious... For the Vandals, since the time when they gained possession of Libya, used to indulge in baths, all of them, every day, and enjoyed a table abounding in all things, the sweetest and best that the earth and sea produce. And they wore gold very generally, and clothed themselves in [silks] and passed their time, thus dressed, in theatres and hippodromes and in other pleasurable pursuits, and above all else in hunting. And they had dancers and mimes and all other things to hear and see which are of a musical nature or otherwise merit attention among men. And the most of them dwelt in parks, which were well supplied with water and trees; and they had great numbers of banquets, and all manner of sexual pleasures were in great vogue among them.[52]

The Vandals did not have very long to live in this state of heightened sensuality and sexual freedom – as we shall discover.* But while they did, it seems that they affected to be more Roman than the Romans whose empire they had – to use the modern idiom – vandalized.

From Attila to Odoacer

AT ANY TIME SINCE THE END of the Punic Wars, losing Carthage and suffering the emergence of a new and destabilizing kingdom in north Africa would have been a grave problem for the Roman west. In the middle of the fifth century it was all the more so, because at exactly the same time, the emperors in Ravenna were forced to deal with the emergence of another rival state on a vulnerable frontier. This was the short-lived but disruptive kingdom of Attila the Hun. A genuinely larger-than-life character whose name remains notorious today, Attila took command of the Huns in the mid-430s, shortly before Carthage fell to the Vandals. And in the

---

* See chapter 3.

two decades of his reign he dragged the western Roman Empire yet further along its path to ruin.

According to the Greek diplomat and historian Priscus, Attila was a short man, with a flat nose and thin eyes, set within a large, swarthy face. His thin beard was speckled grey and he carried himself proudly among his courtiers, 'rolling his eyes here and there, so the power of his proud spirit appeared in his body's movement'. He was a considered, self-possessed leader, but if provoked, could be fierce. 'He was a man born to shake the nations, the scourge of the world,' thought Priscus, remarking that Attila's reputation alone was enough to terrify most men.[53] The western emperor Valentinian III went further. To him, Attila was a 'universal despot who wishes to enslave the whole earth… [he] requires no reason for battle, but thinks whatever he does is justified… He deserves everyone's hatred.'[54]

Attila was born in the first decade of the fifth century, the son of a Hunnic leader called Rua, who died in 435, supposedly when he was struck by lightning. By then the Huns had already been active from the Caucasus to the Hungarian Plain for two generations, but once Attila reached adulthood, they were no longer entirely itinerant nomads. Their tribes had become established across an area that sprawled from the Rhineland to the Black Sea. They had started to follow the rule of a single dynasty, whose royal court was semi-sedentary, and located in a suite of buildings, rather than around the saddle of the king, wherever he might happen to be. The heart of the Hunnic realm was the Great Hungarian Plain – the only grassland in Europe large enough to feed the enormous numbers of horses on which the Hunnic war machine relied.[55] But – as Valentinian observed – the plain alone was not enough for the Huns. Their political system was rooted in forcing other groups to submit to their mastery, rather than acquiring fixed parcels of territory. So as they sought to expand, to dominate and to exact tribute from their neighbours, a large number of Germanic peoples had to accept Hunnic authority, including Goths, Alans, Sarmatians, Suevi and Gepids, as well as tribes like the Sciri, Heruli and Rugi. By the middle of the fifth century the Huns were becoming a serious nuisance to the Romans.

The Huns' original rise in the east had been predicated on excellent horsemanship and superior military technology, in the form of the composite bow. These gave huge tactical field advantage over the nomadic peoples they drove before them, but was of less use against imperial powers whose people occupied walled cities and whose troops commanded timber or stone-built fortresses. However, at around the time of Attila's accession, the Huns added to their armoury a critical new technological skill – siege engineering. Although they could not match the resources of the great powers whose lands they neighboured – principally the Sassanid Persians and Romans – they posed a very serious danger. They could stage campaigns far more devastating than mere horseback raids, for when they captured cities, the Huns could take hundreds or thousands of captives at a time, to be driven back into Hunnic territory and either enslaved or ransomed at high cost.

In the early fifth century there were long periods when the Huns entered partnerships with the Roman army, selling their military prowess as mercenaries. But during the 440s Attila began to send missions against eastern Roman cities. His riders – and siege engineers – left towns like Belgrade (*Singidunum*), Niš (*Naissus*) and Sofia (*Serdica*) smouldering, with dead bodies heaped in the streets and live ones led away in prisoner-columns. Huge areas were depopulated, particularly in the Balkans, where it is possible that Attila took between 100,000 and 200,000 prisoners in total.[56] His price for peace was gold – and a lot of it. In particularly lucrative years, Attila and his troops earned as much as 9,000lbs of Roman gold in private ransoms and official settlements for peace – comfortably more than the tax revenue of many Roman provinces during peacetime.[57] He also managed to extract from the eastern emperors an honorary generalship in the Roman army, with an annual pay-packet to boot.[58]

Not long after he became sole ruler of the Huns, Attila switched his focus of attack from the eastern Roman Empire to the west. In AD 450 he broke off cordial relations with Valentinian III's court in Ravenna, crossed the Rhine and embarked on a rampage around Gaul so shocking that it would live, infamous in popular memory, for more than fifteen hundred years.* The pretext for this invasion was said later to have been a direct appeal sent to Attila from Valentinian's sister Honoria, who asked Attila to rescue her from dishonourable imprisonment, to which she had been sentenced for a tryst with one of her servants. This may or may not be true. Regardless, in early 451 Attila thundered into northern France with a large multi-ethnic army including Goths, Alans and Burgundians. They crossed the Rhine and rampaged all the way to the river Loire. A later chronicle recorded the Huns 'slaying the people with the edge of the sword and killing the very priests of the Lord before the holy altars.' When they arrived at Orléans 'they strove to take it by the mighty hammering of battering rams.'[59]

The insult to Roman honour was almost incalculable, and it was only through a monumental effort that Attila was stopped, when an allied Roman and Visigoth army, led by the mighty general Aëtius, ground out a rare and bloody battlefield victory over the Huns on 20 June 451, an engagement known as the battle of the Catalaunian Plains. 'The slaughter of all those who died there was incalculable – for neither side gave way,' wrote Prosper.[60] But the Roman and Gothic army narrowly prevailed, breaking the momentum of Attila's campaign and sending him back east across the Rhine. Unused to such humiliation, the Hun leader called an end to the campaigning seasons, supposedly having first considered suicide to assuage his shame. However, he was not finished with the west. In 452 he launched a new attack, this time into the Italian peninsula.

Weakened by a severe famine, Italy was in no shape to resist Attila. The cities of Friuli, Padua, Pavia and Milan all fell before his siege engines and swords. Aquileia, one of Italy's richest and most prestigious cities, which stood at the head of the Adriatic, was taken by storm and razed – a sack that had deep and lasting

---

* Not for nothing were the Germans, who ransacked France during the First World War, and whose emperor Wilhelm II publicly praised Attila, nicknamed 'the Hun'.

implications for the locality, providing, in the long term, for the rise of the new city of Venice. It seemed as though all of Italy lay before the Huns, until – as later legend had it – the bishop of Rome, Pope Leo I the Great, mustered all his holy majesty and persuaded Attila to leave. One account of this miraculous meeting claimed that when Leo met Attila, the Hun inspected the pope's splendid vestments silently, 'as if thinking deeply. And lo, suddenly there were seen the apostles Peter and Paul, clad like bishops, standing by Leo, the one on the right hand, the other on the left. They held swords stretched out over his head, and threatened Attila with death if he did not obey the pope's command.'[61] This was a great yarn. But, more likely, the dwindling resources of a ravaged Italy, disease among Attila's followers and the prospect of losses to the eastern Roman army back in the Hunnic heartlands persuaded him it was time to go home.

In 453, Attila died, apparently choking to death on his own blood thanks to the combination of a massive drinking binge and an equally massive nosebleed, on the night of his wedding to a beautiful woman called Ildico. Whatever the truth, the Hunnic empire over which Attila had stretched his hand self-combusted astonishingly quickly. Yet this was not wholly good news for Rome. True, a tyrant and tormentor who had scourged the western empire was dead. Yet the Huns' collapse as a unified state had severe repercussions, for it sent scattering across Europe more huge groups of unsettled Germanic tribespeople, now freed from Hunnic dominion. History was repeating itself. For twenty years after Attila, groups of restless, wandering migrants were again on the move. The Huns were dispersed, no longer operating as a distinct political and military unit. But their legacy lived on.

DEALING WITH THE CONSEQUENCES OF ATTILA's death was a daunting prospect. And the task was made all the harder by the fact that it coincided with a new political crisis in Ravenna. In September 454 Aëtius, victor at the Catalunian Plains, was murdered: his killer was none other than the emperor Valentinian, who had been encouraged by factions at court to regard his finest general, a veteran of thirty years' service, as a rival for the throne. During a finance meeting, Valentinian cut Aëtius to ribbons with his sword. Later, fishing for praise among his courtiers, Valentinian asked whether they thought it was a deed well done. One replied, 'Whether well or not I do not know. But know that you cut off your right hand with your left.'[62]

Revenge indeed followed quickly. In March 455 Valentinian was murdered by two of Aëtius' grieving bodyguards, who ambushed him during an archery contest. (Priscus heard that a swarm of bees sucked up the blood that oozed from the emperor's death-wounds.[63]) And so began a cycle of coup and counter-coup which saw nine emperors occupy the western throne in twenty years. Few of them died in their beds, and politics at the court in Ravenna were dominated by the struggles of strongmen – notably the Germanic-born Flavius Ricimer – to cling to power while dealing with barbarian incursions throughout the collapsing empire. With Vandals in Africa, Visigoths and Suevi carving up Aquitaine, Iberia and southern Gaul, and new powers including the Franks* and Burgundians also on the march, there was plenty for generals like Ricimer to do. But it was also the very definition of a losing game. In the west, Rome now controlled less territory than it had for more than one thousand years: little more than the Italian peninsula between the Alps and Sicily, along with patches of Gaul and Dalmatia. Tax and provisioning networks were in disarray. The army was shrunken, underfunded and institutionally mutinous. The strongest bonds of political loyalty across the west had ceased to be between disparate peoples and their emperors or the abstract imperial system. They were now to the tribe, the general and the momentarily ascendant warlord. Landowners across the provinces had paid tribute to (and held office in) the Roman Empire on the understanding that it offered military might to defend their lives, laws to protect their property and an aristocratic culture to bind them to their neighbours. Now all of

* See chapter 5.

73

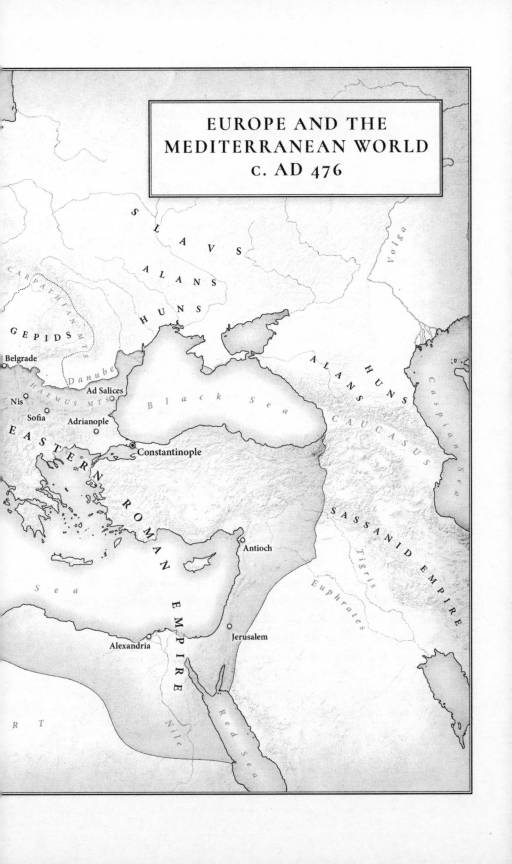

EUROPE AND THE
MEDITERRANEAN WORLD
c. AD 476

S L A V S

A L A N S

H U N S

CARPATHIAN MTS

GEPIDS

Belgrade

Danube

HAEMUS MTS

Nis

Sofia

Ad Salices

Adrianople

Black Sea

Constantinople

ALANS

HUNS

CAUCASUS

Volga

Caspian Sea

E A S T E R N   R O M A N   E M P I R E

SASSANID EMPIRE

Antioch

Tigris

Euphrates

Sea

Alexandria

Jerusalem

R T

Nile

Red Sea

this was broken. Rome's consensus – its collective identity – had been shattered. An end was in sight.

THE LAST OF THE WESTERN ROMAN emperors is traditionally reckoned to be Romulus Augustus – nicknamed Augustulus, or 'little emperor'. A puppet ruler, he was aged around fifteen when, in October 475, he was raised to the throne as an avatar for his father, the general Orestes – who had at one time served as a secretary to none other than Attila. Amid the convulsions of his times, a young emperor like Romulus was a sitting duck. Moreover, he had a rival for the title in the form of a former governor of Dalmatia, Julius Nepos, who had the blessing of the eastern emperor, Zeno. The hapless teenager held on to his position for just eleven months before a barbarian crisis brought him down.

This time the instigators were a coalition of Gothic tribespeople – the Heruli, Rugi and Scirii – who had been set loose from the collapsing Hunnic empire and absorbed into in the Roman army. Deciding that they deserved better reward for their service, in 476 they rebelled under a leader called Odoacer, a canny and resourceful officer distinguished by his physical height, his bushy moustache and his belief – gathered from a youthful meeting with the Catholic holy man Severinus of Noricum – that he was destined for great things.[64]

In 476 Odoacer marched a sizeable body of troops against Ravenna. On 2 September they defeated Romulus Augustulus' father, Orestes, in battle at Pavia and executed him. Two days later, the sixteen-year-old emperor was forced to abdicate and sent off to live out his retirement with relatives. Now in his place Odoacer ruled Italy – not as an emperor but a king (*rex*). He explicitly acknowledged supreme Roman authority as stemming from Constantinople – though the eastern emperor Zeno was unimpressed and refused to acknowledge the new arrangement. Odoacer proved to be a tenacious leader of Italy and its surroundings, limiting his horizons to defending what was left of the Roman west, and successfully conniving at the murder of Julius Nepos, the one remaining serious claimant to the throne. After Julius Nepos' death, Odoacer sent the imperial regalia – the crown and cloak – to Constantinople, marking the physical impossibility of making another western emperor. With that, the title slipped into oblivion. It was a historic landmark, but only the logical result of the steady ruin of Roman networks, power structures and political units which had taken place over the previous seventy years.

Endgame

BY 493 KING ODOACER HAD RULED Italy for more than a decade and a half – longer by far than any of the petty western emperors had managed in the years that preceded his reign. But holding on to power had not been easy, and his relationship with Constantinople vacillated between uneasy and fraught. He did exceptionally well to survive amid a time of relentless change and the intertwined pressures of mass migration and collapsing political certainties. But eventually he fell victim to the forces that had created him.

The blow was struck, perhaps inevitably, by yet another Gothic leader. By the end of the fifth century, Goths of various flavours could be found all over Europe. The Visigoths – the branch who had originally stormed Rome in 410 under the command of Alaric – had energetically established a kingdom with its capital at Toulouse. At its maximum extent their rule ran from the river Loire in central France all the way to the southern tip of Iberia. Far to the east of them in the Balkans roamed the other significant branch of the Goths: a loose federation of many Germanic tribes known as the Ostrogoths. At the end of the fifth century their leader was Theodoric Amal.

Theodoric had received a very conventional classical upbringing. He was born to a leading Gothic family within the Hunnic empire at around the time of Attila's death, in 454. However, when the Huns imploded, Theodoric, aged around seven, was sent to Constantinople. He was officially a hostage: a human guarantor of peace terms between the Eastern emperor and the Ostrogoths. But during his time in the capital Theodoric received an elite education, which moulded him into a literate, cultured young aristocrat – barbarian born but otherwise roundly Romanized.

When he was about sixteen, Theodoric's time in Constantinople drew to a close. He returned to his Ostrogothic people and by the early 470s he had risen to become their king. At first this brought him into conflict with a rival from another Gothic tribal group – Theodoric Strabo, 'the Squinter' – whom he defeated and killed. Then, in the 480s, he led his people into a running conflict with the eastern emperor Zeno, which culminated in 487 when Theodoric led an army to lay siege to Constantinople, the city that had given him so much. By now Zeno was thoroughly weary with Theodoric – but he also saw an opportunity. From Italy, King Odoacer had been making aggressive advances on eastern Roman territory. Zeno decided to solve both his problems in a single stroke: he made peace with Theodoric and sent him west with a simple bargain dangling before him. If Theodoric could depose Odoacer, he could have Italy for himself. Barbarian was now turned against barbarian.

In the summer of 489 a vicious war broke out between Theodoric and Odoacer. In one early battle, fought at the end of August that year on the Isonzo river (the location of a dozen terrible clashes nearly fifteen centuries later, during the First World War), Odoacer's army lay in wait for Theodoric's men, but were beaten and sent scattering backwards into Italy. In 490 Odoacer besieged Theodoric in Pavia. Subsequently the two leaders' armies clashed repeatedly. And slowly but surely the war turned in Theodoric's favour. In 493 he had driven Odoacer back to Ravenna, where he set his final siege. After several months of heavy blockade, winter had set in, and with it a stalemate. Unable to fight on, Odoacer sued for peace, and the two leaders agreed upon a pact by which they would split the kingdom between them.

On 15 March 493 a grand banquet was assembled to celebrate this happy end to a gruelling war. It would be the last banquet Odoacer ever tasted. As Odoacer sat at the feast, he was seized by Theodoric's men. Ambushed and outnumbered, he could not defend himself, but only watch in horror as Theodoric advanced on him with his sword drawn. 'Theodoric leaped forward and struck [Odoacer] on the collarbone with his sword, while Odoacer cried out, "Where is God?"', recorded a later Greek historian called John of Antioch. 'The blow was mortal, for it pierced Odoacer's body through to the lower part of the back.' Theodoric sneered at his fallen rival: 'This scoundrel does not even have a bone in his body.'[65] Then he and his henchman headed out into Ravenna to hunt and kill Odoacer's family and associates. In a matter of hours the coup was complete. It had taken him three and half years, but Theodoric was now king of Italy.

After 493 the Ostrogoths settled around Ravenna and several other northern Italian cities, and over the following three decades Theodoric undertook an audacious new programme of state-building, following in the grandest Roman traditions. His campaigns in Italy had been relentless and his final seizure of the throne bloody and ruthless, but Theodoric had no intention of a further bloodletting among an already beleaguered Italian elite. He resisted purging the aristocrats and bureaucracy of his new kingdom, and sent embassies to Constantinople to confirm his legitimacy in the eyes of the emperor there, playing up his Roman education and calling his own royal rule 'a copy of the one empire'.[66] Around 497 his energetic sycophancy bore fruit, as Zeno's successor Anastasius I cautiously recognized his kingship.

Although many squabbles with Constantinople lay ahead, Theodoric was momentarily assured of his acceptability to the Roman establishment. He therefore set about imitating Roman-ness to the full. Although an Arian Christian, he made strenuous efforts to accommodate and respect the Nicene bishops and Church of Rome. He emphasized obedience to Roman law codes, rather than issuing his own, as was the practice in many of the nascent barbarian states of the west, not least the kingdoms of the Franks and Burgundians. Through military campaigns and marriage alliances he secured peace with the Vandals of north Africa and established close political ties with the sprawling kingdom of the Visigoths, where in 511 he imposed his own king (his grandson Amalric), assembling a huge pan-Gothic kingdom which extended from the Atlantic Ocean to the Adriatic Sea.

Theodoric was destined for the sobriquet 'the Great', and he lived his life like he knew it. In showpiece cities such as his capital, Ravenna, he spent prodigiously on defensive walls, grand palaces, basilicas, mausoleums and public works, decorated by master craftsmen. A visit even today to Ravenna reveals the stunning artistic vision of the Ostrogothic king: the mosaic decorations in the Basilica of Sant'Apollinare Nuovo – much of which was created under Theodoric's commission – are breathtaking. These and other monuments in the city, including Theodoric's mausoleum, stand testament to the surprising glory of the new barbarian era. Theodoric self-consciously styled his kingship on the model of the late Roman emperors. But his was not a Roman empire. Across the west, things had changed forever.

No matter how magnificently and conventionally Theodoric comported himself, and notwithstanding the fact that he reigned for more than thirty years, by the time the Ostrogoth king died in AD 526 the world had shifted radically. Not only had the ethnic identities of rulers and landowners changed, so had their political horizons and the systems of government. The empire lived on in Constantinople, where many new challenges – new religions, new technologies, new networks and new diseases – would re-mould it during the centuries to come. But in the west, kings and kingdoms were rapidly supplanting emperors and empires, ushering in an age that will, when we turn to it again, look more recognizably 'medieval' than the world of wandering barbarians and child emperors has thus far.

WHAT A STRANGE, LURCHING TIME IT had been, in the century-and-a-bit since the Huns had crossed the Volga in 370. Everything had been turned upside down, heaved into motion through the irresistible power of climatic fluctuation and human migration, allied to the usual random historical movers of chance, ambition and individual agency. For those at the time, life could seem bewildering, and it is perhaps not surprising that writers of the fourth, fifth and sixth centuries turned to a metaphor that would prove wildly popular throughout the medieval west: that of fortune's wheel. Ammianus Marcellinus had seen events in the fourth century in this way, and so too did another notable author at the other end of the period, who lived and worked under Theodoric in Ravenna. Anicius Manlius Severinus Boëthius – usually just Boëthius – was born to a well-bred Roman family in Italy the year before the last western emperor, young Romulus Augustulus, was turfed out of office by Odoacer. Boëthius had a brilliant mind and impeccably aristocratic credentials, and by the age of twenty-five he had become a senator in Theodoric's mock-Roman kingdom. A quarter-century later, in 522, Boëthius, now middle aged, had risen to the highest rank in the government bureaucracy, that of *magister officiorum*. But from such a height it was a long way to fall.

In 523 Theodoric was nearing the end of his life and trouble was afoot in his kingdom. Tension had arisen with the eastern emperor Justin I, and rumours dogged the Senate of traitors there who were in contact with Constantinople. During a heated debate on the matter, Boëthius found himself accused of shielding enemies of the state. As a result he was arrested, imprisoned, tried and sentenced to death.

Throughout his life Boëthius had written on a wide range of subjects: his interests included mathematics, music, philosophy and theology. But he composed his most famous work in jail while awaiting execution for his crimes. *The Consolation of Philosophy* attempted to place earthly troubles in a divine context. Written in the form of a dialogue between Boëthius and Lady Philosophy, it asked its readers to accept that there were higher powers at work behind the vicissitudes of man's fleeting life. In the course of his musings, he turned to the notion of fortune's wheel. 'So now you have committed yourself to the rule of Fortune, you must acquiesce in her ways,' he wrote. 'If you are trying to stop her wheel from turning, you are of all men the most obtuse.'[67]

Shortly after he finished his work, the great philosopher was horribly tortured and clubbed to death. Within two years, the great Ostrogothic king Theodoric had also breathed his last.

Ahead of them, a strange new world was opening up.

3

BYZANTINES

'Vanity of vanities, all is vanity!'

GELIMER, KING OF THE VANDALS

J ohn of Ephesus was sent off by the emperor to baptize pagans in Asia Minor. But he found himself travelling through a death zone. In town after town, the sick and suffering staggered through the streets, their bellies swollen and eyes bloodshot, pus leaking from their mouths. Grand houses in which entire families and their servants had died stood silent, every room occupied by corpses. Contorted bodies lay unburied, their midriffs rotting and bursting in the heat of the day, the flesh half-eaten by hungry dogs. The roads and highways were empty, the usual thrum of trade and traffic interrupted. In desolate villages no one was left to harvest crops and fruit trees; animals were left unshepherded to roam the countryside as they pleased.

The living went about in fear. It felt like the end of the world. On his journey, John met travellers who had tied home-made dog-tags to their arms: 'I am such a one, son of such a one, and of such a neighbourhood; if I die, for God's sake, and to show his mercy and goodness, let them know at my house, and let my people come to bury me.'[1] He heard stories of thousands – even tens of thousands – dying in the largest cities every day, their bodies stacked in heaps until such time as they could be hurled into mass graves. John kept a record of the horrors he witnessed, modelled on the Old Testament prophet Jeremiah's Book of Lamentations. 'Death has come up into our windows, it has entered our gates, and made our palaces desolate,' he wrote.[2] 'Now all of them have perished since they did not remember the name of the Lord.'[3]

The apocalyptic scenes John conjured in his writings formed a memoir from the front line of the first global pandemic in recorded history. A form of bubonic plague, caused by the bacterium *Yersinia pestis*, spread by fleas which hopped between small mammals, black rats and human beings, the disease slashed its way across all three continents of the known world in the middle of the sixth century AD, ravaging sub-Saharan Africa, Persia and the Middle East, China and Central Asia, the Mediterranean coastal bowl and north-western Europe. According to the writer Procopius of Caesarea, the sickness 'left neither island nor cave nor mountain ridge which had human inhabitants; and if it passed by any land, either not affecting the men there or touching them in indifferent fashion, still at a later time it came back.'[4] Modern archaeological studies have confirmed the presence of *Y. pestis* as far west as Britain, Gaul, Spain and southern Germany.[5] Wherever it spread, symptoms included large, black bubonic swellings of the lymph nodes in the armpits and groin, delirium, coma, vomiting of blood, and, in the case of pregnant women, miscarriage.

Although exact numbers will never be known, this awful disease – named the Plague of Justinian after the eastern emperor in whose reign it occurred* – probably killed millions, or even tens of millions of people, a large proportion of them between the years 541 and 543. Recently, some historians have argued that writers like John of Ephesus overhyped the spread, mortality and importance of the pandemic. Scholars have argued for greater scepticism about the overall death toll.[6] They may have a point. Nevertheless, there still were many in the sixth century AD who felt they were living through an era of juddering historical importance.

---

* Some modern historians, preferring strict fairness to poetry and believing that the disease is best understood without reference to a single ruler, refer to the Plague of Justinian as the early medieval pandemic (EMP). See, for example, Horden, Peregrine, 'Mediterranean Plague in the Age of Justinian' in Maas, Michael (ed.), *The Cambridge Companion to the Age of Justinian* (Cambridge: 2005), p. 134.

They were right. The Plague of Justinian did not on its own transform the world. But it was a significant part of a larger story of transformation, reform, realignment and a struggle for pre-eminence which took place between the 520s, where our last chapter ended, and the 620s, where our next will begin. This was a formative hundred years for the rump of the Roman Empire; for relations between the Mediterranean east and west; for the cultural balance between the 'Greek' and 'Latin' spheres; for regional relations between the Roman and Persian empires; for lawmaking; for great religions; for urban planners; for great artists. During an age that was buffeted not only by the first world pandemic, but also by a global climate shock, political realities and patterns of thought were set that would affect the Mediterranean world for nearly one thousand years.

To understand all this, we must focus on the birth – or rebirth – of the eastern Roman Empire during the sixth century. This is the time when historians generally stop speaking of Rome and the Roman Empire and refer instead to Byzantium: the Greek-speaking inheritor state that served as a buffer between east and west, surviving for centuries until it was ravaged by crusaders and later consumed by the Ottomans – an event that heralded the end of the Middle Ages. There is no better character to launch us on that journey than Justinian himself.

Often described as the last true Roman, Justinian had many detractors – for he did not care whom he trampled over as he attempted to rebuild his empire in the aftermath of the barbarian conquests. The writer Procopius called him a demon in disguise, who had the blood of one thousand billion* men on his hands; who 'cheerfully banished wealth from Roman soil and became the architect of poverty for all.'[7] Many would have agreed. Yet for others, particularly those who did not have to deal with him at first hand, Justinian was a totemic emperor who deserved

---

* Literally 'ten thousand times ten thousand times ten thousand'. Needless to say, this is not meant to be taken as a serious census of mortality. Procopius' talent for inflating big numbers from the implausible to the impossible was unsurpassed, even in the Middle Ages, when chroniclers made poetic exaggeration an art form.

mention in the same breath as Augustus and Constantine. To them, he was a titan whose terrible magnificence shone far beyond the confines of his own times – so fiercely that many centuries later Dante Alighieri placed him in Paradise as the archetypal Roman: peerless lawgiver and a radiant, supremely gifted caesar, who appeared in the afterlife surrounded by a light as bright and blinding as the sun.[8]

Justinian and Theodora

ON 1 AUGUST 527 THE ELDERLY Roman emperor Justin died from an infected ulcer on his foot, and after nine years in office left the throne of Constantinople to his nephew and adopted son Justinian. The transfer of power was smooth, for Justin had already appointed Justinian as his co-emperor, and the younger man had begun to make his mark about the eastern provinces, sending out judicial orders (*rescripts*) to calm riots in unsettled cities, founding churches in Jerusalem and paying for repairs and humanitarian relief in the Syrian city of Antioch, which had been razed by a gigantic earthquake in the spring of 526. Prior to this, Justinian had served in high office as consul, sponsoring extravagant civic games to mark his tenure. Even before his official elevation to the purple, many had supposed Justinian was the real power in the empire. After 527, he was.

On becoming sole emperor Justinian was in his mid-forties. In a famous gold-flecked mosaic above the high altar in the Basilica di San Vitale in Ravenna, Justinian is a round-faced, slightly ruddy man with heavy-lidded brown eyes, naturally pursed lips and pearls woven into strands of his hair, which is cropped above the ears. This chimes with a description by the Greek chronicler John Malalas of Antioch, who said Justinian was born at Bederiana (today in North Macedonia) and was handsome, if slightly short with a receding hairline. He was a Latin-speaker of the same Balkan peasant origin as his uncle, and he favoured the Chalcedonian form of Christianity, at a time where the empire was riven with religious schism between Chalcedonians and Miaphysites (or Monophysites),* and emperors were encouraged to line up aggressively with one or other of these rival camps. Malalas thought Justinian 'magnanimous and Christian'.[9] But there would be plenty during his reign of nearly four decades who thought otherwise.

One of the emperor's most syrupy sycophants – and fiercest detractors – was the chronicler Procopius of Caesarea. For many years a trusted member of the imperial administration, Procopius wrote several fulsome accounts of Justinian's achievements in war and civil administration, which blended narrative history with unapologetic propaganda. But over the years he came to loathe his master, and in a coruscating pamphlet entitled the *Secret History*, written in the 550s, Procopius demonstrated that there is no enemy so vicious as a former friend. He sneered that while there was a certain natural geniality in Justinian's plump cheeks, he actually resembled a famous statue of Domitian, which had been made after that notorious tyrant of the first century AD was assassinated. This comparison was intended to be politically damaging as well as just plain mean: Procopius went on to call Justinian 'dissembling, crafty, hypocritical, secretive by temperament, two-faced... a treacherous friend and an inexorable enemy... passionately devoted to murder and plunder; quarrelsome and above all an innovator... quick to devise vile schemes and to carry them out and with an instinctive aversion to the mere mention of anything good.' It seemed, concluded Procopius, 'as if nature had removed every tendency to evil from the rest of mankind and deposited in the soul of this man.'[10]

This was a bracing pen portrait. But it was as nothing compared to the calumnies Procopius heaped on Justinian's wife and empress Theodora.

---

* This schism, like many others during Church history, focused on the nature of Christ. To simplify a tortuously complex story: Chalcedonians agreed with the conclusion of the AD 451 Council of Chalcedon (a town that is today a district in Istanbul), which stated that Christ had two natures, human and divine, combined in one being. Miaphysites thought that Christ had only one nature: the divine.

Like Justinian, Theodora rose a long way through society to reach the imperial palace. Her father was a bear-trainer in the circus and her mother an actress. Theodora spent her youth and teens as a theatre performer and – if her detractors were to be believed – far worse. Opposite her husband in the San Vitale mosaic, she appears elegant and slender, with a porcelain complexion, small mouth and dark eyes that gaze serenely from beneath an opulent jewelled headdress. Malalas characterized her as charitable and pious.[11] But Procopius gleefully repeated rumours that Theodora had once been a child prostitute who specialized in anal sex, a sharp-tongued teenage streetwalker who cracked dirty jokes and sold her body to large groups of men, a burlesque dancer who trained geese to peck barley grains from her knickers and finally a courtesan to depraved imperial officials, in which capacity Justinian picked her up.[12]

Much of this sprang from misogyny, some of it from distaste for Theodora's adherence to the sect of Miaphysitism, and the rest from personal spite. Certainly Justinian had been obliged to change imperial law to marry Theodora, on account of her lowly social origins. However, Procopius' wicked character-assassination ignored the fact that throughout her life Theodora played a vital part in imperial governance, particularly by helping Justinian to juggle the theological factions that did spiritual and sometimes physical battle throughout his empire. Yet like any talented tabloid journalist today, Procopius knew that sex, slander and sneering always found a willing audience for whom truth came second to prurience. Justinian and Theodora were a couple whose achievements and celebrity were simply too delicious to ignore.

Law Codes and Heretics

WHEN JUSTINIAN AND THEODORA CAME TO power in the summer of 527 there were plenty of issues facing the empire. Although Constantinople had survived the barbarian crisis that had engulfed the west, resisting attacks by Huns and Goths, and although the imperial finances were still fairly robust, during the first decade of Justinian's reign he would be forced to fight major wars on two fronts, put down a domestic rebellion that threatened to topple him altogether and rebuild major parts of his capital city. However, on his accession Justinian thought the most pressing matter facing him was legal reform. He was a passionate legislator, whose attitude to rule was summed up by a maxim from one of his legal texts: 'The imperial majesty should be armed with laws as well as glorified with arms, that there may be good government in times both of war and of peace.'[13] In his mind, legal tidiness was intimately linked with godliness, and divine sanction for his rule. So, within six months of his reign beginning Justinian ordered the reform and recodification of the entire body of Roman law.[14]

The commission Justinian appointed to carry out this gargantuan task was assembled under the leadership of a young, energetic Greek lawyer called Tribonian. With him worked some of the most acute legal minds in Constantinople, and together they reviewed millions of lines of imperial constitutions – statements of the law made by emperors all the way back to Augustus. Just twenty months into Justinian's reign, these lawyers had digested, edited and compiled these statements into a single, definitive account of Roman law known as the Justinianic Code (*codex iustinianus*). The Codex was issued on 7 April 529 and sent to every province in the empire, where it automatically superseded every other legal code. It was not perfect: in December AD 534 a second edition was required to clean up inconsistencies. Nor did it set in stone a single Roman law, perfectly formed and unchangeable for eternity; law by its nature is constantly evolving and Justinian by *his* nature was addicted to issuing new legal commands, which were collected by scholars as the Novels (*novellae constitutiones*). But the Code was a phenomenal achievement nonetheless. It ran to twelve books, covering civil, ecclesiastical, criminal and public law. It was an exercise in clarification and bureaucratic streamlining that set a gold standard for constitutional reform in the Middle Ages. 'Finding the laws obscure because they had become far more numerous than they should be, and in obvious confusion because they disagreed with each other, he preserved them by cleansing them of the mass of their verbal trickery,' wrote Procopius.[15] From a chronicler whose stock-in-trade was verbal trickery, this was high praise indeed.

The Code was, however, just one of the legal reforms of Justinian's early reign. The year after it was issued, Tribonian was given another mammoth task. Having dealt with the minutiae of specific Roman laws, he now empanelled experts to make sense of jurisprudence, as it was contained in the collective writings of the great classical jurists. Most of the great jurists of the imperial era – men such as Gaius, Papinian, Ulpian and Paulus – had lived and written during pre-Christian times. So their pronouncements were not only frequently contradictory, they also flirted with irreligion. As they were pagans, their opinions were naturally devoid of Christian sentiment. And impieties did not please Justinian. So Tribonian was tasked with creating a single statement of Roman jurisprudence, in which the great works of the ancients were rationalized and improved by references to Almighty God. This project appeared in two stages: the so-called Fifty Questions (*quinquaginta decisiones*), then the Digest or Pandects of December 533. And here again Tribonian came good, providing the emperor with an elegant solution to a bureaucratic mess. For generations, Romans had complained of the archaic complexity, slowness and corruption of the law. Now it had all been whipped into shape.

The last of Justinian's legal reforms, which followed directly after the publication of the Digest, was the creation of the Institutes (*Institutiones Iustiniani*), which was effectively an index to the Digest, designed for the use of trainee lawyers in the official imperial law schools at Beirut and Constantinople. This text served as a practical primer to the new law, and made sure budding young lawyers would be taught to think exactly as Justinian wished. One of Justinian's constitutions stated that 'our subjects are our constant care, whether they are alive or dead.' It was the preamble to a law regulating funerals, but the words could easily be read as a general statement of the emperor's ambition: to leave his mark on every aspect of Roman life, past, present and future – and to do so by the word as well as the sword.

Of course, the reforms to Roman law that occured during the sixth century did not take place in a vacuum. In the barbarian kingdoms of the west – the realms of the Franks, Burgundians and Visigoths – other rulers were busy commissioning their own law-codes. But theirs were small beer indeed compared to the successful and lasting overhaul of the entire Roman system. In Constantinople and the eastern empire Justinian's legal reforms marked the start of a new era in lawmaking and a particularly 'Greek' era in legal history. And in the west, Roman law as laid down in the age of Justinian would come to have foundational status. In the twelfth century it was esteemed to the point of fetishism in the medieval universities that sprang up in Bologna, Paris, Oxford and elsewhere.* As late as the nineteenth century the Napoleonic Code (*Code Napoléon*) – the great French civil law reform of 1804 – was modelled explicitly on Justinian's example.[16] Indeed, it is possible to argue that any nation in the world today which has a codified law (as opposed to, say, the common law that dominates the legal system in the United Kingdom) owes a debt to Justinian and Tribonian. Even if this was not the original intention, it was an incredible accomplishment. In little more than five years of intensive administrative activity Justinian had rewoven the legal fabric of the empire and refashioned legal thought in ways that would still be palpable fifteen centuries later. And he was just getting started.

WHILE TRIBONIAN OVERSAW JUSTINIAN'S PROGRAMME OF legal reforms, the new emperor was also turning his mind to the intertwined issues of heresy, unorthodoxy, disbelief and sexual malpractice.

Here, too, there was much to do. One of his toughest tasks was trying to negotiate a path through the difficult issue of schism and

---

* See chapter 11.

heresy within the imperial Church. By the time of his accession, wranglings between Arian and Nicene Christians, which had tormented the western empire during the barbarian invasions of the fifth century, had been complicated by another dispute, between Chalcedonians and Miaphysites, who disagreed over the exact nature of Christ, and the balance between His human and divine qualities.[17] Today the issues at stake between these two groups can seem arcane to all but specialist Church historians. But in the sixth century they were enough to cause popular riots and international diplomatic crises. Bishops had been murdered by mobs for professing views at odds with their congregations'; a formal schism between the churches of Rome and Constantinople had endured between 484 and 518 over the matter.* And while the imperial capital was staunchly Chalcedonian, large areas outside it were just as steadfastly Miaphysite. These included Egypt, the breadbasket of the empire itself. The prospect of losing the province over a matter of faith was not an enticing one. But it was real.

In light of this Justinian was forced to walk a tightrope between Chalcedonians and Miaphysites for his entire reign. He was helped somewhat by the fact that his wife Theodora was herself strongly Miaphysite, and went out of her way to shelter members of the sect, thereby giving the impression of imperial even-handedness. But Justinian never really grasped the problem with the firmness that he had shown in reforming Roman law. The best that could be said was that he avoided escalating the dispute into another official schism in the Christian world.

Elsewhere, however, Justinian's suppressing instinct and pursuit of orthodoxy would be felt rather more deeply. He was an especially keen persecutor of sexual deviance. Moral turpitude bothered Justinian's neat mind – and there seemed to be plenty of it to worry about. The emperor's special bugbears included sodomy and paedophilia, and he did not hesitate to punish their practitioners. John Malalas recorded details of one ferocious campaign to drive up standards among the Roman clergy. In AD 528, he

---

* The 'Acacian' Schism, named for Patriarch Acacius of Constantinople.

wrote, 'some of the bishops from various provinces were accused of... homosexual practices. Among them was Isaiah, bishop of Rhodes... and likewise [a Thracian bishop] named Alexander.' These two clerics, and others, were brought to Constantinople for questioning by the city prefect. Sadly, they did not have good excuses. So the prefect 'tortured Isaiah severely and exiled him and he amputated Alexander's genitals and paraded him around on a litter.' Other suspects had sharp straws inserted into their penises and were publicly humiliated in the forum. This was not merely cruel Roman sport, but imperial policy. Justinian subsequently decreed that everywhere homosexuals and 'those detected in pederasty' should be gelded. Many died in agony. 'From then on there was fear among those afflicted with homosexual lust,' wrote Malalas.[18] It was a cruel demonstration of a prejudice that would endure throughout the Middle Ages.

Finally, alongside sexual deviancy was the troubling matter of spiritual degeneracy, and specifically the fact that in an empire that was ostentatiously Christian (doctrinal disputes notwithstanding), there remained some stubborn outposts of old-fashioned paganism. It was by now a long time since Constantine's Edict of Milan of 313 had preached religious tolerance, and love for the old gods was becoming ever-harder to square with life as a Roman. No emperor had embraced paganism since Julian, who had died in 363. Olympic Games had been banned since the time of Theodosius II in the 390s. Non-Christians were banned from serving in the army or the imperial administration. As we have seen, part of Tribonian's goal in revising the law was to apply an explicitly Christian flavor to the pagan jurists' writings collected in the Digest. This was not mere window-dressing. The time was fast approaching where pagan beliefs would not only be marginal, but illegal.[19]

Among the rash of laws passed in the first decade of Justinian's reign was a decree that pagans were not allowed to teach students. In itself this did not stand out from the other collections of anti-pagan legislation collected in Justinian's law codes. But its effect on one important institution was soon made clear. John Malalas spelled out what it meant. In an entry covering the year 529, he wrote, 'the emperor issued a decree and sent it to Athens ordering that no-one should teach philosophy nor interpret the laws.'[20]

Another chronicler, Agathius, reported that the last headmaster of the Athens school was forced to leave not only the school and the city, but the empire itself. (In 531 he and several of his fellow teachers fled to Persia.) And this was more than mere relocation. In effect, Justinian's diktat had spelled the end for the famous school in the ancient Greek capital – the city of Plato and Aristotle – where students had absorbed the insights of classical philosophy and natural science for generations.

The closure of the Athens school was important. It did not kill at a stroke all non-Christian learning in the eastern empire.[21] Nor did it immediately throw up an intellectual wall between the classical age and the dawning era of Christian hegemony in Europe and the west. But it was both significant and symbolic. For while scholarship in Persia and other eastern parts flourished, with libraries in Baghdad and other Middle Eastern capitals preserving and transmitting copies of the works of Aristotle and other non-Christian greats, Justinian's reign, and the sixth century in general, was marked by a self-blinkering in the Christian world. Doctrinal minutiae assumed ever bigger and bloodier importance, while anything non-Christian was regarded with gathering suspicion. The Roman Empire had once been a super-spreader of classical learning across its vast territories. But as it fell to pieces in the west and became ever more doctrinally obsessed in the east, it became an active blocker to knowledge chains across the ages, and the transmission of ancient learning throughout the empire began to fail.

One reason that the label 'the Dark Ages' has proven so hard to untie from the neck of the Middle Ages is that for hundreds of years – between the sixth century and the first beginnings of the Renaissance in the late thirteenth – the scientific and rational insights of the ancient world were forgotten or suppressed in the west. This was not simply an unfortunate symptom of creeping cultural dementia. It sprang from the deliberate policies of eastern emperors like Justinian, who made it their business to hound out of their world the self-appointed but unfortunately unchristian guardians of priceless knowledge.

Rioting and Renewal

GIVEN THE SCALE OF REFORM IN the empire, and the pace with which Justinian pursued change during the first years of his reign, it is perhaps not surprising that there was a serious outbreak of popular rebellion against his rule within five years of his accession. This took place in the first, wintry days of AD 532, on the streets of Constantinople, and although the causes of it were peculiar to the politics of the city, its material consequences were very long-lasting, and can still be seen in Istanbul today. Before we move on from the first period of Justinian's epoch-shaping reign in Byzantium, we must therefore look at the so-called Nika riots: an eruption of violence which took Byzantium to the brink of anarchy.

By the start of the sixth century one of the most keenly attended forms of public entertainment in Constantinople and other large cities of the eastern empire was chariot racing. In the capital, races took place in the Hippodrome, a huge, U-shaped racetrack in a stadium complex that backed onto the imperial Great Palace. Here, four massive bronze horse-statues stood on top of one of the spectator stands, indicating the entertainment that took place below, in which equestrian teams thundered around the track, at literally breakneck speeds.* The races were exciting, dangerous contests, which made stars of the fastest and most skilful charioteers and frothing partisans of the fans.

Over time the most ardent racing supporters had come to organize themselves into factions, and in Constantinople there were four: the Greens, Blues, Reds and Whites. By far the largest and most powerful were the Greens and Blues, whose rabid members

---

* These horses are now on display at St Mark's Basilica in Venice, where they were taken after Constantinople was sacked in the Fourth Crusade. See chapter 8.

sat in blocs in the Hippodrome, and took 'team' positions on religious and political matters, expecting their collective voices to carry weight among the imperial administration. The Hippodrome factions shared with modern European football ultras a pompous self-regard, a taste for violence, and a collective fixation on clothes and haircuts.* Very thin-skinned, they could easily be stirred to violence when they felt they had been slighted or ignored.

As a young man rising through his uncle's palace service, Justinian had been a prominent supporter of the Blues. But by the time he was crowned emperor he was trying to shift his position, treating all the factions with disdain.[22] Both approaches were problematic: emperors who over-indulged one faction fuelled ill-feeling between the rival groups; but those who withheld their support entirely often pushed the factions into each others' arms. This was what Justinian achieved in the winter of AD 531–2. It nearly cost him his throne.

Trouble flared in January, when Constantinople's city prefect botched the hangings of a group of Green and Blue supporters who had rioted following a race and caused a number of deaths. One Green and one Blue had been found guilty of homicide and sentenced to death, but cheated justice when the gallows snapped during their execution. The men escaped and briefly took sanctuary in a nearby church, but before long were back under royal guard, imprisoned at the house of the city prefect, known as the praetorium. In other circumstances this might have been mere execution-day drama. But it morphed into a full-blown collapse of public order.

According to John Malalas, the prisoners were kept under guard by the city authorities for three days. All the while, the Greens and Blues agitated for their release and pardon. On Tuesday 13 January

---

* The fashionable look for Hippodrome faction members in the 630s was a long moustache and beard, a 'mullet' haircut cropped close on top and left long at the back, and expensive 'designer' clothes apparently too costly and gaudy for their social station, with tunics cut tight at the wrists and absurdly wide at the shoulders. This was known as the 'Hunnish' look. In spirit we are looking at the mentality of the travelling English football hooligan of the 1990s–2010s, who would typically be seen on the terraces wearing an £800 Stone Island jacket, with his hair cut into a tight skinhead or, latterly, an alt-right fade.

Justinian appeared in the imperial box at the Hippodrome for a series of races. Throughout the day Blue and Green supporters chanted together, asking the emperor to show mercy. Justinian – as usual, a stickler for law and order – paid no attention. And so – on the basis that the only thing worse than being denied is being ignored – as the races drew to a close, the *factionistas* turned on Justinian himself. 'The devil prompted evil counsels in them and they chanted to one another, "Long live the merciful Blues and Greens!"', wrote Malalas. Then they poured out into the streets around the Hippodrome, yelling the Greek word '*nika*' ('conquer') – a popular chant during chariot-racing – and setting fire to buildings. As night drew in, flames licked the praetorium. The two prisoners were freed and disappeared into the crowd, never to be heard from again. The 'Nika' rioters had now achieved their objective. But by now, many other, more general complaints had been added to their original grievances. Most were the perennial grousings of urban populations throughout history: high taxes, corruption and religious sectarianism.[23] (According to Procopius, they had a particular dislike for John of Cappadocia, a city prefect who spent his days swindling and his lunch-hours feasting until he threw up.[24]) But if the rioters were not original, they were certainly dangerous. And their blood was up.

For Justinian, the Nika riots could not have come at a worse time. Besides his massive reforms to the law and campaigns against pagans and heretics, he was also in the midst of highly sensitive negotiations with a new Persian king of kings, Khosrow I, for an end to a bloody war that had erupted between the two empires in their Middle Eastern borderlands. Foreign policy was thus at a critical juncture, and it was not a convenient moment for Rome's capital city to be set ablaze by ordinary people chafing at his heavy-handed rule. Yet that was what was happening. On the morning of Wednesday 14 January Justinian announced another day of chariot races, hoping to distract the rioters back to good behaviour. But all this did was breathe further life into the disruptions. Rather than settling down to enjoy the games, the rioters set fire to the Hippodrome, and began to shout for the dismissal of various imperial officials, including the master of laws, Tribonian. Justinian reluctantly agreed. But it did no good. By now the riot had taken on a life of its own, and the only route out was a messy one.

During the next five days, Justinian lost control of his capital city. On Wednesday he lurched from acquiescence to vengeance, sending in the rising star of his army – a tough-minded general named Belisarius, who had been prominent in the recent Persian campaigns – to crack skulls with a band of Goth mercenaries at his back. 'There was fighting and many of the faction members were cut down,' wrote John Malalas. '[But] the mob was incensed and started fires in other places and began killing indiscriminately.'[25] For seventy-two hours flames engulfed a large part of central Constantinople. Two nephews of a former emperor – Hypatius and Pompeius – were separately proclaimed as Justinian's replacement. Despite a surge of troops from Thrace who arrived in the capital to reinforce Belisarius, by nightfall on Saturday 17 January the city was still in uproar.

Matters came to a head the following day. Not long after dawn, Justinian appeared at the charred Hippodrome, holding the Gospels. When he was jeered back inside the palace, he considered fleeing the city with a fleet of ships. According to Procopius, Theodora came to the rescue. She scolded him, arguing that 'for one who had been an emperor it is unendurable to be a fugitive,' and added that she would not wish to 'live that day on which those who meet me shall not address me as mistress.'[26] Justinian listened. And he realized there was effectively one option left. Only extreme action would now bring his people to heel. Thousands of rioters were assembled inside the Hippodrome, where they were cheering Hypatius' name. The field was set for battle. Belisarius was ready to lead the charge.

When imperial troops rushed the Hippodrome that Sunday, they found tens of thousands of protestors penned in. The troops had orders to massacre them. And it was easy. Soldiers funnelled in from two sides of the stadium, 'some with arrows, others with swords.'[27] According to Procopius, 2,000 prisoners were taken, and 30,000 civilians killed. If these numbers were true, then around

7 per cent of Constantinople's population was slain in a single day. And even if it was an exaggeration, this was still a phenomenally bloody occasion, and a terrible warning of the power of the emperor, and his capacity for cruelty. The rioters' candidate Hypatius was captured and killed the next day, and his body hurled into the sea. For nearly a week afterwards Constantinople was placed in lockdown, with all shops except essential food outlets closed. Meanwhile Justinian, saved from ignominy, sent word out to the nearby cities of the empire announcing his victory and promising to rebuild Constantinople on an even grander scale than before. He had not won any friends. But he had survived.

To DISTRACT FROM THE HORRIFYING VIOLENCE of the Nika riots, Justinian did what many other autocrats throughout history have also done: he decided to build his way back towards glory.

Among the most distressing architectural casualties of the Nika riots was the city's Great Church, dedicated to Hagia Sophia (Holy Wisdom): a vital landmark in the imperial and civic centre of Constantinople that was arranged around the avenue known as the Mese (Middle Street). This area, which included the Hippodrome, was the worst affected by the rioters' arson, and Justinian decided rebuilding it was of paramount importance. The basilica had been a fine, large, wooden-roofed building with an oblong footprint of about 5,000msq. But now the wooden roof was destroyed completely, and according to Procopius the whole church 'lay a charred mass of ruins'. Yet in the ashes lay a great opportunity. 'The Emperor,' wrote Procopius, 'disregarding all questions of expense, eagerly pressed on to begin the work of construction, and began to gather all the artisans from the whole world.'[28] He planned to build the greatest church on earth.

The men Justinian hired to lead this project were among the finest minds on the planet. One was Isidore of Miletus, a professor of geometry and mechanics who had worked on editions of Archimedes' texts, was quoted as an authority alongside ancient geniuses like Euclid, and had invented a special compass for drawing parabolas. The other was Anthemius of Tralles, who was an expert on lenses, prisms and mechanical tools, as well as one of a brood of amazing siblings who included a professor of literature, a famous lawyer and a great physicist. Together, Isidore and Anthemius have been compared by modern historians to Christopher Wren and Leonardo da Vinci.[29] Whether that is fair or not, their engagement on the new Hagia Sophia was certainly a masterstroke. Procopius wrote that 'one might with good reason marvel at the discernment of the Emperor himself, in that out of the whole world he was able to select the men who were most suitable for the most important of his enterprises.'[30] The Hagia Sophia, which Isidore and Anthemius produced in five years between 532 and 537, stands comparison with the most magnificent buildings ever constructed.

The new church soared above the Constantinopolitan skyline. It occupied roughly the same area as the original basilica, but whereas that one was long and narrow, its replacement was built on a central plan, closer to a square shape, topped with a stunning, almost unfathomably vast dome, bigger even than that on the Pantheon in Rome. Procopius thought the great dome of the Hagia Sophia so graceful that it seemed to be 'suspended from Heaven', and its beauty was magnified by its relationship with other, smaller domes which interlocked with it and created a wonderful array of interior shapes, all bathed in natural light, which entered through carefully positioned openings. 'All these details, fitted together with incredible skill in mid-air and floating off from each other and resting only on the parts next to them, produce a single and most extraordinary harmony in the work, and yet do not permit the spectator to linger much over the study of any one of them, but each detail attracts the eye and draws it on irresistibly to itself,' he wrote.

Although Procopius' writings on architecture were heavily laced with flattery for Justinian (for unlike his excoriating tell-all, the *Secret History*, this was official propaganda), in this case the hyperbole was justified. Inside the church, natural patterns in the white Proconnesian marble cut in the quarries of Marmara Island vied for attention with swathes of mosaic decoration. The interior of the dome was densely covered in gold mosaic – glass tesserae threaded with beaten gold leaf – which gave the impression of the entire surface having been lacquered in precious metal.[31] 'Who could recount the beauty of the columns and the stones with which the church is adorned? One might imagine that he had come upon a meadow with its flowers in full bloom,' wrote Procopius. 'Whenever anyone enters this church to pray... his mind is lifted up toward God and exalted, feeling that He cannot be far away.'

Of course, transcendence did not come cheap. The inner sanctuary of the Hagia Sophia alone was endowed with 40,000 pounds' worth of silver ornaments and artworks. But the effect was sensational. The Hagia Sophia was the centerpiece of a singular campaign of urban renewal driven through with the same energy and speed that had characterized the emperor's changes to Roman law. And the renovation of Constantinople was in turn only one part of an empire-wide monumental building programme, which included marvels such as four giant pillars at Ephesus topped with statues of the evangelists, and a city founded in what is now Serbia to commemorate the place of the emperor's birth and provide a palatial home for a new archbishopric of 'Justiniana Prima'.

The wonder of these works sang down through the ages. Some four centuries after the Hagia Sophia was completed (during which time the dome had been damaged by an earthquake and rebuilt at even more magnificent height), a pair of diplomats from Kiev visited Constantinople on business. They were granted a tour of the church, which now homed a splendid collection of the world's best Christian relics.[32] And they could hardly believe their eyes. The ambassadors wrote home in astonishment, praising the Greeks as far superior in religion to the Bulgars or Germans. In the Hagia Sophia, they said, 'we knew not whether we were in heaven or earth... we cannot forget that beauty.[33]

Destroying the Vandals

REBUILDING THE HAGIA SOPHIA WAS THE most direct and obvious way Justinian found to recover from the ignominy of the Nika riots. But it was not his only response. Much further from home in the early 530s the emperor secured what he came to regard as the signal achievement of his long reign. This was the conquest – or, rather, reconquest – of north Africa from the Vandals. The province and its prestigious capital, Carthage, had been wrenched from Roman hands during the tumult of the barbarian migrations. So its recapture would be both a lucrative enterprise, given the continuing prosperity of the region under Vandal rule, and a fillip for Roman pride.

Justinian's Carthaginian project was made possible in strategic and practical terms because in September 532 the emperor agreed a treaty with the Persian king of kings, Khosrow I. This new monarch had come to power in autumn 531, aged around eighteen. He needed time to secure his shaky domestic position, so agreed to end a bitter war that had been raging between Rome and Persia around Armenia for four years. The deal Justinian's ambassadors struck with Khosrow was known as the Eternal Peace. This title was bombastic, inaccurate, and its terms obliged Justinian to pay Khosrow 11,000 pounds of gold in return for a ceasefire. Nevertheless, it left the emperor free to focus on campaigns in the west. And he wasted no time. Just nine months after hostilities in Persia ceased, in the summer of 533 a huge invasion fleet mustered in the waters off Constantinople. It carried 15,000 mixed infantry and cavalry in hundreds of transporter ships, accompanied by ninety-two oared warships known as dromonds. At the head stood Belisarius, the general who had cut his teeth in Persia, then sunk them into the Nika rioters in the Hippodrome. This was a fearsome armada.

In summer 533 Belisarius sailed this fleet out of Constantinople and headed towards Vandal territory, some 1,500km away. After a couple of weeks at sea he made port in Sicily and Belisarius took stock of the latest intelligence from Carthage. The news was promising. The Vandal king of the day was called Gelimer. Three years previously he had seized the Vandal throne by deposing his cousin Hilderic. At the time of Gelimer's usurpation Justinian had written to lecture him on his impertinence; what came by return of post was a letter laced with irony, informing him that Gelimer was well within his rights, and advising Justinian to quit his meddling. 'It is well for one to administer the kingly office which belongs to him and not to make the concerns of others his own,' wrote Gelimer. '[If you] should come against us, we shall oppose you with all our power.'[34] But in 533, Gelimer's powers of opposition were vanishingly slight.

The Vandal king was caught off-guard by Belisarius' arrival: he was absent from Carthage, and a large number of his best troops were on campaign in Sardinia. Apprised of these facts on Sicily, Belisarius headed straight across the Mediterranean, landed in Tunisia and, in early September, marched on Carthage. He crushed a Vandal army in the field at Ad Decimum, killing their commander, Gelimer's brother Ammata. On 14 September he rode into the Vandal capital. The general entered Gelimer's palace on top of the Byrsa Hill, sat on his throne and helped himself to a lunch prepared the previous day by Gelimer's own chefs.[35] 'It fell to the lot of Belisarius on that day to win such fame as no one of the men of his time ever won nor indeed any of the men of olden times,' wrote Procopius, who was there when lunch was served.[36]

Even if we allow for Procopius' addiction to hyperbole, Belisarius had achieved a major coup. Justinian was so thrilled when news of Carthage's fall arrived back in Constantinople that he awarded himself the names *Vandalicus* and *Africanus*. And even greater victories followed. For a short time Gelimer led an insurgent campaign against the occupying imperial army, offering payment in gold for each Roman head that the farmers and peasants of the north African countryside brought before him. But the guerilla war was soon over. In December the Vandals were defeated in a second battle, at Tricamarum. Gelimer fled to a mountain hideout near the ancient city of Medeus. Here he was surrounded by Belisarius' troops and, after a few months of a winter siege, starved into submission. By the time he was taken prisoner, the Vandal king had drifted into a state of remarkable zen. During final negotiations to lift the mountain siege he said his only desires were a loaf of bread, a sponge to help him wash his eyes, and a lyre on which to compose a lament. Later, when it was clear he could no longer avoid capture, he wrote: 'I cannot resist fortune further nor rebel against fate, but I shall follow straightway wherever it seems to her best to lead.'[37] Fortune, through the agency of Belisarius, saw fit to lead him to Constantinople, where he was presented to Justinian as an prisoner of war.

In the summer of 534 a formal triumph took place at the Hippodrome to mark the completion of the African campaign, which Procopius called the greatest since the days of Titus and Trajan. The crowning moment came when Gelimer was paraded in front of the citizens, along with 2,000 other Vandal prisoners, all tall and fair. Brought before the feet of the emperor, Gelimer was stripped of his royal robes, and made to lie prone. Yet even at this humiliating moment the Vandal ruler kept his cool. 'When Gelimer reached the Hippodrome and saw the emperor sitting upon a lofty seat and the people standing on either side and realized as he looked about in what an evil plight he was, he neither wept nor cried out,' wrote Procopius.[38] He recited again and again the words of the Preacher at the start of the Old Testament book of *Ecclesiastes*:

'Vanity of vanities, all is vanity.'[39]

This enigmatic display was enough to convince Justinian to show mercy. Gelimer had gamely served his purpose in entertaining the public, so he was pensioned off with his family to live out a long retirement in Asia Minor. Meanwhile, his fellow warriors were co-opted into the Byzantine army, and sent east on the Persian frontier, where the Eternal Peace with Persia was soon to prove rather less eternal than advertised. And the image of the humbled barbarian became a mainstay of Justinianic propaganda – elaborated in brilliant mosaic murals on the ceiling of the main entrance to the imperial palace, and many years later literally stitched into the fabric of his funeral decorations.

There was good reason for this. Reconquering Roman north Africa was a substantial achievement. It threw up considerable policy complexities for the occupying Byzantine government, no doubt, for Arianism had to be stamped out in the province, and a continuing balance struck between Chalcedonians and Miaphysites. Incursions by Moorish tribes in the south also required constant military vigilance. Balanced against this, though, was the fact that defeating the Vandals had reactivated trading networks between north Africa and the eastern Mediterranean, the effect of which lasted a long time: there would be a Byzantine presence in Carthage until the end of the eighth century. And most immediately, the Vandal campaign provided a roadmap to further conquests in the central Mediterranean. Justinian's next target was Ostrogoth Italy, where Rome's 'other' capital was, like Carthage, in barbarian hands.

However, rebuilding the old Roman Empire would not prove so easy as a regime change in one of its former provinces. And this was not only because the costs were vast. Justinian's vision of Roman reconquest was complicated by the appearance of an enemy far more obdurate and deadly than any number of barbarian armies.

It was *Yersinia pestis*: the bacterium that caused bubonic plague.

'God's Education'

IN THE FIRST DECADE OF HIS reign Justinian had reformed and rebuilt the eastern Roman Empire in ways that would outlive him by many centuries, forming the basis for a distinctive new 'Byzantine' era of imperial history. And he was showing no signs of letting up. Following Gelimer's defeat, and the occupation of Vandal north Africa, the emperor sent Belisarius back to the west. This time he was to take on the Ostrogoths of Ravenna, who, as kings of Italy, now ruled the lands of Romulus, Julius Caesar and

Augustus. As usual, Belisarius performed brilliantly, sweeping through Sicily before setting his sights on the Italian mainland. But he did so amid ominous portents, which seemed to suggest that the very universe, and not only the Roman Empire, was twisting into a strange new shape.

The first sign came in 536, when out of nowhere the whole atmosphere seemed to change. Across the world the sun dimmed, the sky darkened to a murky gloom, and temperatures dropped appreciably, much as happens during a solar eclipse. Unlike an eclipse, however, these odd sights did not pass in the space of a few minutes, but lasted eighteen months. It was, wrote Procopius, 'a most dread portent', for 'the sun gave forth its light without brightness, like the moon, during this whole year.'[40] The deathly gloom was probably the result of a massive volcanic eruption, perhaps in North America, perhaps in Iceland, perhaps in the mid-Pacific, which released gargantuan clouds of ash and dust. And it was followed in 539/40 by another vast volcanic eruption, probably at Ilopango in modern El Salvador.[41] Together these natural explosions spewed out several dozen cubic miles of rock and pumped more than 1 million tons of sulphur and ash into the earth's skies, ushering in one of the sharpest global environmental crises in human history. As a result the world's climate changed for as much as a decade. Temperatures fell by at least 2°C globally and summers effectively disappeared. From Ireland to China, crops withered and harvests failed. Agricultural production collapsed. Tree growth slowed – in some cases trees died where they stood. Procopius was sure it marked a major and historic shift in imperial fortunes. 'From the time when this thing happened,' he mused, 'men were free neither from war nor pestilence nor any other thing leading to death.'[42]

The first round of deaths was man-made. Beneath leaden skies, Belisarius led Byzantine forces on a rampage north through Italy, taking Reggio and Naples before riding bloodlessly into Rome, whose citizens chose not to resist him. By May 540 he had fought his way to the royal capital at Ravenna, and a truce was eventually drawn up by which Italy was partitioned between the Ostrogoths north of the river Po, and the Byzantines to the south. Although the Ostrogoths' king, Vitiges, was deposed and taken back to Constantinople, his people were subjected to a surprisingly gentle peace. But clemency was a matter of necessity, for in June of the same year a Persian army under Khosrow I invaded Byzantine Syria and sacked the great city of Antioch, burning and plundering it with terrible loss of life. Another cycle of war between Rome and Persia loomed. Although this was only clear in hindsight, the eastern empire was about to enter a debilitating phase of conflict on both fronts: with fighting in Italy dragging on until the 560s, and the Persian conflict for two generations more.

Then, amid all this, came the plague. Although its origins cannot be precisely placed, the disease may first have originated in the Tian Shan mountains (which today separate China from Kyrgyzstan and Kazakhstan), and followed the Silk Road trading superhighway west. So it was by no means an unknown ailment by the sixth century AD – outbreaks had occurred in the Roman world as recently as the 520s. Yet plague had seldom been anything more than an intense, local phenomenon, until, somehow, between the 520s and 540s, possibly in south-east Africa, around the ivory markets of what is now Zanzibar, the disease mutated into a super-lethal strain. It then met with environmental conditions ripe for easy infection – the climate crisis of 536 contributed to this by weakening human and rat populations and forcing them into closer-than-usual cohabitation.[43] And it spread rapidly along the long-established and booming trade networks around the Mediterranean.

In July 541 the population of the small Egyptian delta town of Pelusium (now Tell el-Farama) started dying in droves, their armpits and groins swollen and black, nightmarish fever-visions dancing before their agonized eyes. From this incubator town, the disease raced off in two directions: north-east with the merchant ships and caravan trains that worked the Palestinian coast towards Syria and Asia Minor; and west through the busy ports of north Africa. For nearly two years it spread, and spread and spread, in a manner that terrified contemporaries and has puzzled historians for many years.*

The hideous scenes that greeted writers like Procopius, John of Ephesus and the Syrian scholar Evagrius Scholasticus – empty streets and corpse-piles from which bodily fluids leaked like juice from grapes, shuttered shops and hungry children, the raving sick driven demented by the sight of ghosts, the brokenhearted bereaved who tried suicidally to infect themselves, the miscarrying mothers and the hundreds upon thousands of lost souls – wracked the world, flaring up at different places and different times.

In Constantinople, where the pandemic was said by Procopius to have killed 10,000 people a day during a four-month peak, Justinian himself was infected, suffering dangerous swelling around a flea-bite on his thigh. After a fashion he recovered, and his capital city eventually returned to some semblance of normality; on 23 March 543 the emperor declared 'God's Education' over. But this was the same wishful thinking that has traditionally accompanied any political statement about pandemic disease delivered with certain authority. Bubonic plague in fact continued to sweep and swirl around the Mediterranean world for the rest of the decade, resurfacing time and again all over the world until AD 749. How many people it killed in total during these pestilent years is today a matter of live historical debate – most of it largely speculative, with a range of opinions running from hardly anyone to 100 million people. But the economic disruption was real: wildly fluctuating wheat prices, rapid wage inflation as ready labourers vanished, an overwhelmed inheritance system, and a near-total crash in construction. It compounded the strains on Justinian's fiscal system, which was already stretched by the emperor's military adventures. Tax rates soared, and remained high for many years.[44] And this was all quite beside the horrors that pulsed through

---

* There are many unanswered questions about just how a bubonic plague which relied on rat-flea-human transmission chains (and did not seem to spread effectively from human to human) could have raced around the world at such devastating speed, particularly in an age before motorized mass transport. They are well summed up for the general reader in Horden, Peregrine, 'Mediterranean Plague in the Age of Justinian', Maas, Michael (ed.), *The Cambridge Companion to the Age of Justinian* (Cambridge: 2005), pp.134–160.

the accounts of eyewitnesses like John of Antioch. The aghast testimony of these survivors tell us all too bleakly of the scars the pandemic left on the popular psyche.

Things Fall Apart

IN 547 THE BASILICA DI SAN Vitale in Ravenna was officially consecrated. A thickset, imposing church built in terracotta and marble to an octagonal plan, it was the product of more than twenty years' work, the foundations having been laid early in the reign of Theodoric's daughter, the Ostrogothic queen regent Amalasuntha. Yet by the time that the archbishop of Ravenna, Maximian, came to consecrate San Vitale, the Ostrogoths had been driven from Ravenna and momentarily seemed to be in retreat throughout Italy.

Pride of place among the stunning mosaics that decorated the glorious new basilica therefore went to portraits of the Byzantine emperor and empress, Justinian and Theodora. Justinian glared out menacingly from the wall, flanked by barbarian mercenaries and a number of stern-faced clerics, some tonsured and others uncropped and unshaven. Theodora, meanwhile, commanded her own posse – two male clerics were pictured assisting her as she offered an exquisite gold vessel to a gushing font, while around her demure women looked on, all finely clothed, with their hair covered. Even today, visitors to the basilica can still find themselves entranced by the sheer majesty of Justinian and Theodora's portraits, swayed, even if they think they know better, by the force of the political narrative.

Simply to have these images on display in Ravenna in 547 was quite an achievement. It had been more than fifty years since the Roman capital had been lost to the Ostrogoths, but the emperor refused to accept it was never coming back. The great warrior Belisarius – himself represented in the basilica's mosaics, on Justinian's side – had led the charge, fighting his way from Sicily all the way up to Ravenna, which had fallen in 540. True, the war for

Italy was far from over – for even as the Basilica of San Vitale was consecrated, Belisarius was busy on the other side of Italy, fighting over the city of Rome with a tenacious and powerful Ostrogoth king called Totila. All the same, here was a moment to celebrate a rehabilitation of Byzantine fortunes in Europe, and perhaps even the first step towards restoring something of the Roman Empire in the west.

Yet if the consecration of the Basilica of San Vitale was a boon – and the Byzantine mosaics inside it are still one of the most astonishing sights in all of Italy – it was not long before tragedy followed. The following year, in June, Theodora died, probably of cancer. She was around fifty years old and her death grieved Justinian – now over sixty-five – very bitterly. The two had been true political partners, and it was Theodora who had saved them from oblivion during the Nika riots. She had forged a quite amazing path from her wild days on the seedy fringe of the Hippodrome to her position as *augusta*, whose toes petitioners at the imperial court had to kiss before submitting their requests.[45] Justinian wept at her funeral and it is not hard to imagine that his tears were of genuine sorrow, and not merely for public display.

And this was more than mere personal tragedy. For in retrospect Theodora's death marked, or at least coincided with, a turning point in Justinian's fortunes. The hard-won victories of the first half of his reign – the sweeping legal reforms, survival in the face of the Nika riots, the building of the Hagia Sophia, reconquests in Africa and Italy – were in the past. More trouble than triumph now lay ahead.

SOME OF THE DEEPEST AND MOST intractable problems Justinian faced concerned religion. Try as he might, he never found a satisfactory route through the violent theological arguments that tortured the empire and the Church throughout the sixth century. Divisions between Chalcedonians and Miaphysites were harder than ever to reconcile after Theodora's death, for her strong support for the latter had offered balance within the imperial palace, allowing Justinian a degree of insurance in his religious policy. Without her he was dangerously weakened. Additionally, many of his policies actively created religious problems. His attempts to recapture old Roman territories were a case in point. Almost wherever Byzantine troops set foot, sectarianism loomed. And by laying claim to barbarian lands – such as Carthage – Justinian was increasingly exposed to the nasty divisions that raged between Arians and Nicene Christians.

Justinian was by no means blind to these troubles. But he singularly lacked a way to fix them. And his great attempt at religious healing – a gathering of the Church known as the Fifth Ecumenical Council, held in Constantinople in the early summer of 553 – was an expensive, public failure. Hardly any western bishops attended, and in the end the council served best to highlight the dismal fractures in the Church and the seeming impossibilities of agreeing a common position on the precise nature of Christ – as well as hinting at a future in which the churches of Constantinople and Rome, much like the Roman empires that had nurtured them, would strike out in separate directions. A generation later, the great scholar Isidore of Seville dismissed the validity of the Fifth Ecumenical Council altogether. Isidore thought the Justinian was a tyrant and a heretic. In sixth-century theology there were no merits awarded for effort.

Nor were things any easier in foreign policy. In Italy, the consecration of San Vitale in Ravenna was not followed by a pacification and full re-annexation of the peninsula. Instead, violence and Ostrogothic resistance peaked. The Ostrogoth king Totila – whom Procopius saw in person, and described as devastatingly skilled on horseback, typically riding into battle with a gold-cheeked helmet on his head, tossing a javelin expertly from hand to hand and swivelling on his mount 'like one who has been instructed with precision in the art of dancing from childhood' – proved a very tough nut to crack.[46] In January 550 he scored a resounding victory when his men swept through Rome itself, killing everyone they could lay their hands on. 'There was a great slaughter,' recalled Procopius, who went on to describe the roadblocks Totila set up on all the major routes away from Rome, which helped them catch and kill Byzantine soldiers trying to escape the rout. Time and again, the Ostrogoth had the better of Justinian's generals, and it took repeated surges of tens of thousands of troops into Italy to stop it from being overrun.

Only in 552 was Totila finally defeated. In 554 Justinian issued a decree known as the Pragmatic Sanction, which declared Italy a province of the empire with its capital at Ravenna. (Separate government systems were established for the island states of Sardinia, Sicily and Corsica.) But even then, Italy remained unstable. For while the Ostrogoths had been destroyed, so had much of the Italian countryside. Thousands had died during the fighting. Cities were ruined by siege. Aristocratic estates lay ravaged. Slaves had run away. Italy was considerably poorer than it had been at the outset of the war, because the Byzantine army had pursued victory so doggedly they ended up slashing the value of their prize. So although Italy was theoretically theirs, Byzantine control of the territory was patchy at best. What emerged therefore was a government trying to project power from Constantinople, nearly two thousand kilometres away. Meanwhile, across the Alps, a barbarian group known as the Lombards – some of whom had served as mercenaries in the Byzantine army – were now beginning to plot an Italian invasion of their own. Within three decades of the Pragmatic Sanction's promulgation, many of Justinian's hard-won gains in Italy had been lost, the colony too feeble to defend itself when another power threatened. Although the Byzantine empire would retain an interest in Italy and its islands until the tenth century, after Justinian's day the prospect of reconnecting the two old halves of the Roman Empire seemed to diminish with every passing generation.

ONE OF THE REASONS THAT JUSTINIAN had such difficulty crushing the Ostrogoths in Italy was that he was also troubled sporadically throughout his reign by the Persians in the east. His main tormentor in those parts was Khosrow I. The Persian king was a highly intelligent and judicious ruler with an omnivorous curiosity, an especially keen interest in philosophy and a rigorous approach to legal reform. Although the dominant religion in Persia was Zoroastrianism, he understood the value of making his empire safe for renegades – like the pagan scholars of the Athens philosophy school – as well as the burgeoning Christian populations in his major cities. Like Justinian, Khosrow was also an avid builder, famed for erecting huge fortifying walls around his kingdom. His own masterwork, every bit as glorious as the Hagia Sophia, was the Taq Kasra, a palace whose signature architectural flourish was its astonishing brick-built vault, the lonely ruins of which are the only visible remains of the once-mighty city of Ctesiphon, in modern-day Iraq. Khosrow's building projects mattered, because they were an extension of his sense of self: he fancied he was a new Cyrus the Great.*

The detailed history of Justinian's wars with Khosrow lies beyond the scope of this chapter. Suffice it to say, however, that besides the longstanding historical tendency of two neighbouring empires to jostle for position and pre-eminence, Byzantium and Persia both nursed an economic interest in the lucrative Silk Road mercantile trails which ran through their borderlands. The economic and geographical reality of this was the chief reason why their 'Eternal Peace' of the 530s lasted less than ten years. In 540 Khosrow invaded Syria, capturing and deporting tens of thousands of prisoners and slaves. Thereafter came a cycle of seemingly ceaseless wars and peaces: a truce in 545, broken by 548; a truce in 551, broken in 554. A 'Fifty-Year' Peace in 562, which proved to be anything but. And so on. The empires sponsored proxies in a war between rival Arab tribes on their borders, and they clashed directly over sensitive border spots like a triangle of territory known as Lazica, which lay on the eastern coast of the Black Sea. There was precious little respite, and seemingly no end to the financial and military demands that the war place on Constantinople.

---

* Empire-builder and founder of the Achaemenid dynasty, Cyrus II assembled what was at the time the largest empire the world had ever seen, stretching from northern India to Asia Minor. When he died in 530 BC he was known as King of the Four Corners of the World.

In the 540s Justinian had unveiled a massive monumental column to himself in the centre of his capital, in the square known as the Augustaeum,* which lay between the Hagia Sophia and the Great Palace. On top of a steepling, brick-and-bronze pillar, the emperor was depicted on horseback in bronze sculpture. He carried an orb in his left hand – the world surmounted by a cross – and raised his right in salute to the east, the direction of Persia. ('Spreading out his fingers, he orders the barbarians in that place to remain at home', wrote Procopius.[47]) A headdress, lavishly plumed, was an unsubtle attempt to suggest ancient Achilles. But for all the bluster of this sort of visual propaganda, Justinian ultimately found the Persian problem as intractable as his wranglings over the Church. Byzantium and Persia seemed destined for an endless war – at least until some other great power arose in the region. One would – as we shall see in the next chapter – but Justinian was not around to bear witness to it.

UNSURPRISINGLY, ALL OF THIS TOOK ITS toll on Justinian himself, who shared the misfortune of many great rulers in living to see his achievements creak and fall. In 557–8, a series of earthquakes and tremors brought down the dome of the Hagia Sophia. A year later a coalition of barbarian Slavs from beyond the Danube – a tribe called the Kutrigurs – overran imperial defences and menaced the walls of Constantinople itself. Although they were repelled, the terror in the capital was palpable, and Justinian was forced to call an ageing Belisarius out of retirement in order to chase the Kutrigur horsemen away. It was the old general's swansong: two years after saving the city, Belisarius was implicated in a plot against the emperor and forced to undergo the humiliations of a public trial. Although pardoned of his supposed crimes, Belisarius died in the spring of 565 with his reputation in shreds.

The emperor died soon after Belisarius, on 14 November 565. He lay in stately splendour in his palace, having nominated as

---

* Now the Hagia Sophia square (Ayasofya Meydani) in Istanbul.

successor his nephew Justin II. His funerary bier was decorated with images of his pomp: grinding Gelimer beneath his heels as barbarians looked on in fear. Here was the emperor of the 530s, hell-bent on restoring the glory of Rome, driving back the tides of history even as he did so. Yet as Gelimer had warned, for earthly kings, all was vanity. And once Justinian was dead, many of his achievements were in danger of melting away. Amid the uncertainty of the 560s, Justinian's heyday must have felt like a very long time ago.

After Justinian

IN ANY AGE JUSTINIAN'S REIGN WOULD have been a hard act to follow, and his immediate successors struggled to deal with the legacy he bequeathed. His nephew Justin II reigned for thirteen years, during which time he shored up the parlous imperial finances, but acquired a reputation as a tyrant and a miser, who was troubled by the Lombards in Italy, tribal raids across the Danube and perpetual difficulties on the Persian border. Eventually, and perhaps understandably, Justin went mad, his descent coming after a disastrous reverse on the Persian front, during which Khosrow took the critical Byzantine border-fortress of Dara. From 574 until his death in 578 Justin was intermittently incoherent, and power was shared uneasily in Constantinople between his wife, Sophia, and the commander of the palace, Justin's adopted son Tiberius.

Tiberius eventually became emperor in his own right, although without very much more success than Justin. His greatest historical legacy, perhaps, was that he was a native Greek-speaker, for whom Latin was a comprehensible but nonetheless foreign language. After him, Greek would become the tongue of the palace and the empire, as Constantinople sloughed off ever more of its cultural ties to the 'old' Rome and the world of the western Mediterranean. His other notable achievement was the bizarre nature of his demise: he died, or so the story went, when he ate a dish of poisoned mulberries, in August 582.

Tiberius' successor was his son-in-law, Maurice, a general cut from much the same distinguished cloth as the late Belisarius. Maurice was the author of a seminal military text known as the *Strategikon*, which became staple reading for aspiring officers across the west for nearly one thousand years. It was just as well that Maurice knew how to plan a battle, because his twenty-year reign threw up a lot of them. In Persia, Maurice achieved a significant coup when he interfered in a Persian succession dispute to depose Hormizd IV and replace him with his son Khosrow II. Maurice formally adopted Khosrow, and agreed a new 'perpetual' peace with Persia. But things did not go so well in Italy, where Byzantine territory was now designated the Exarchate of Ravenna.* There, the Lombards remained an immovable presence. Maurice fell out frequently with Pope Gregory I the Great, who resented the patriarch of Constantinople's claim to be the 'ecumenical' leader of the entire Church. And in the Balkans, Maurice spent his entire reign struggling to hold the Avars at bay. In 602 he appeared to have pushed them back beyond the Danube for good. Yet even this was not the boon it seemed. Maurice's insistence that his troops overwinter north of the Danube, combined with his longstanding drive to hold down military pay, sent the army into mutiny under an officer called Phocas. In November, rebel soldiers marched on Constantinople, the people rioted, and Maurice fled. He was later caught and killed, along with his sons. His corpse was abused and displayed in public. This was a frightening new insertion of violence into imperial politics, and this would become something of a Byzantine speciality: hereditary monarchy attenuated by murder. After eight years of fairly incompetent rule, Phocas was himself deposed and slaughtered in 610.

PHOCAS' KILLER, HERACLIUS, WAS IN A sense, the real heir to Justinian. This was not only because he contracted a somewhat

---

* Byzantine possessions around Carthage were likewise organized as the Exarchate of Africa.

scandalous marriage: his second wife was his niece Martina, an incestuous match which should have been illegal. He reigned for more than three decades and brought to conclusion many of the tiresome struggles that had begun nearly a century earlier. Under his rule, Byzantine ambitions in Italy were quietly downgraded from dreams of conquest to maintenance of what was held. The Balkan front was shored up. North Africa was secured, but a small Byzantine presence in Visigothic Spain was abandoned, finally ending Roman interests in old Hispania. And the Persian question was spectacularly settled in the favour of the empire – although the effort came at near-fatal cost to both sides. In other words, after Heraclius' reign, the empire's territorial transformation from Rome to Byzantium was complete. It was now a Greek-speaking state, focused on dominating the eastern Mediterranean, with power concentrated in Constantinople and its most important geopolitical rivals lying to the south and east. That was how it would remain, more or less, for eight and a half centuries.

But there was one last twist in the story. The defining struggle of Heraclius' reign was the war with Persia. Shortly after his usurpation, Byzantium was on the verge of annihilation. During the 610s, Khosrow II – having conveniently forgotten that it was Byzantium who had put him on his throne – sent armies slicing through Roman territory. They took Mesopotamia, Syria, Palestine, Egypt and much of Asia Minor. When the city of Jerusalem fell in 614, the Persians seized Christianity's most precious relic: a fragment of the True Cross on which Jesus had died. To make matters worse, the chaos they sowed in the east had enabled tribes like the Avars to sweep into the Balkans. The next year, Persians could be seen on military manouevres in the Bosphorus, and Heraclius was making desperate plans to remove the capital of his empire to Carthage and leave Constantinople to its fate. Never had Rome come so close to destruction. Had Heraclius not sued for a costly and desperate peace, 615 may well have been the end of the story.

Yet it was not. Having saved his city, Heraclius spent the next seven years rebuilding his military, preparing to take the fight back to Khosrow. In the 620s that is what he did – with spectacular results. His policy of marching his armies behind banners showing icons of Christ, giving an explicitly holy aspect to his war of reconquest, would echo loudly several centuries later during the crusades. And just as would happen during the crusades, Christ seemed to grant his people dazzling success.

In four campaigning seasons Byzantine soldiers destroyed their Persian opponents in Armenia and Mesopotamia. After a thunderous victory at the battle of Nineveh in 628, Heraclius came close to capturing Ctesiphon itself. He regained the True Cross, which was sent back to Jerusalem in triumph. The same year Khosrow II was overthrown in a palace coup and murdered. His son, Kavad II, who led the plot, straightaway sued for peace and returned all the territories his father had seized. Here, at last, was a form of eternal peace. Six centuries of intermittent war between the Roman and Persian empires died with Khosrow II. Heraclius adopted a new style of title: he would no longer be *augustus*, but *basileus* (βασιλεύς) – a Greek term implying an equivalent majesty to the Persians' king of kings. Every Byzantine emperor would follow the tradition.

However, if victory over the Persians was resounding and total, this did not mean that the Byzantine empire was free to return to regional supremacy. Because for all that he had achieved, Heraclius found in the end that he was every bit as vulnerable as Justinian to fortune's ever-turning wheel. Vanity, Gelimer had warned. All was vanity. No sooner had Persia been defeated, than a new power reared its head.

The Arabs were coming.

4

ARABS

'Allahu Akbar!'

TRADITIONAL ISLAMIC EXCLAMATION
AND BATTLE CRY

In high summer, some time between 634 and 636 AD,* the Sword of God (*Sayf Allah*) arrived outside the east gate of Damascus.¹ The Sword's name was Khalid ibn al-Walid, and he was a tough general: a veteran of many battles, highly motivated by desert warfare and booty. He was among the most senior officers in an army which had recently burst out of the Arabian peninsula, equipped with nothing more than sharp blades and strong, new faith. Khalid was a Muslim – a member of the Quraysh tribe, and one of the first followers of Islam. Indeed, he had been given his nickname by the Prophet Muhammad himself, the man to whom the word of God (*Allah*) had been revealed.

Muhammad had died on 8 June 632, and Khalid now owed his high military command to Muhammad's earthly successor (*khalifa*, or caliph) and leader of the Believers (*amir al-mu'minin*),

---

* Dating the events of the early Arab Conquests with precision is difficult almost to the point of futility. The sources on which any account – including this one – must rely are by turns contradictory, inadequate and indifferent to the sort of neat sequencing of events that the modern historian expects. It should be taken as read that virtually every sentence in the narrative that follows in this chapter could be contested, and that in many cases different conjectures of dates and events have deep theological implications, which still animate scholars and believers today. Do not be disheartened by this public service announcement. The long-running and rancorous beefs over the origins of political Islam and the Arab Conquests are, in many ways, what makes this passage of medieval history so intriguing – and so important today.

a slight, elderly former merchant with sunken cheeks and a thin, dyed beard, named Abu Bakr.[2] In promoting Khalid, the caliph had acknowledged the general's loyal service during the previous decade. Though Khalid had opposed Muhammad during the earliest days of Islam's growth as a political force and spiritual movement in western Arabia – and had even inflicted a stinging military defeat on the Prophet – he had converted in the 620s and since served with distinction. In Arabia he had fought rival tribes and other would-be caliphs. Outside it, he had stormed Iraq and bested Persian troops. To get to Damascus he had dragged his brigade on a hellish six-day march through the arid Syrian desert. Their only means of transporting enough water for this march had been to force around twenty fat old she-camels to drink massive volumes of water, binding the beasts' mouths to prevent them chewing their cud, and then killing several of them daily to retrieve the water from their stomachs.[3] Now, as Khalid stood outside Damascus, he was setting his arm against his most dangerous foe so far.

Damascus was one of the leading cities in Byzantine Syria: a prestigious imperial redoubt on the desert's edge, a city as ancient as some of the oldest Biblical tales, criss-crossed by streets and fine canals, run through by a broad thoroughfare known as the Street Called Straight, dotted everywhere with churches and home to the magnificent Christian relic of John the Baptist's head. Damascus' stout stone walls – originally built in rectangular form by successive Roman emperors of the second and third centuries AD – stretched 1,500m on their longest sides and half that on their shortest. The seven gates punctuating them were stiffly guarded, and a fortress in the north-east corner contained a Greek–Armenian garrison who were duty-bound to hold it in the emperor Heraclius' name. The city also sheltered the remnants of a Byzantine field army the Arabs had recently routed in the Jordan Valley, and who had fled there to regroup. To take Damascus, Khalid would need to be smart, as well as tough.

Initially, the prospect of taking the city did not look good. The Arabs had put some of their finest generals and most seasoned troops in the field – including Amr ibn al-As, who was every bit as battle-hardened as Khalid, and who had taken up position to the west of Damascus, outside St Thomas' Gate. They had set up roadblocks on the route north of the city at a little village called Barza. Yet the Arab generals did not have large siege engines or advanced weaponry – they had even been forced to raid nearby monasteries to obtain ladders. In these circumstances, the only plausible means of taking a city were by scaring, starving or boring the inhabitants into submission. This usually meant enforcing a blockade: barricading every gate to the city, and allowing no one other than envoys in or out. Most critically it meant finding a way to get inside the minds of the besieged – convincing them that their chances of escaping with their lives would be improved by letting their attackers in, rather than holding out.

Exactly how long Khalid, Amr and their comrades spent outside Damascus is a matter of some conjecture: accounts range from four months to more than a year. Certainly it was long enough to convince the citizens that they could not expect any relief from emperor Heraclius. After a number of reverses to the Arabs – including the loss of the magnificent southern Syrian city of Bostra – Heraclius was wary of expending too much energy on enemies who were momentarily ascendant, but whose resources, dedication and unity could soon be expected to collapse. The Arabs were not the Persians. After all, it was not as though they were about to take over the world.

Except – they were.

LIKE SO MUCH ABOUT THE ARAB Conquests of the seventh and eighth centuries, contemporary (and near-contemporary) accounts of the siege of Damascus are tangled and hard to reconcile. But what we can say with some confidence is that after a long wait, Khalid ibn al-Walid and the Arab army had whittled away at the defiance of the Damascenes until there was nothing left. In one telling, Khalid established a network of spies who let him know when the Byzantine governor of the city was organizing a large party to celebrate the birth of a son; when the party was in full flow, Khalid's men threw up ropes and grappling hooks, scaled the battlements around the eastern gate, cheered *Allahu Akbar* (God is great*), hacked down a skeleton guard and let themselves in. In another version, the siege-weary citizens pre-empted such an invasion by opening negotiations on Amr's gate, and agreeing to surrender. It may be that both these stories are true.[4] Whatever happened, in 635 (or possibly 636) the city was formally handed over to the Muslims, under financial terms thrashed out in a peace conference at a covered market in the city centre. 'Damascus was conquered and its inhabitants paid the *jizyah*', wrote the chronicler al-Tabari, who composed a monumental history of Islam during the early tenth century.[5] (By *jizyah*, he meant a 'head tax': the financial levy imposed on Jews, Christians and other monotheists, in return for which they could live and worship in peace.) The boost to Arab morale was huge. The insult to Byzantine pride was palpable. And there was much more to come.

When Heraclius realized he could not simply ignore the Arab threat and hope it would go away, he sent an army into Syria which later accounts numbered at 150,000 troops.[6] (Around 20,000 is more likely.) It was a medley of Greeks, Armenians and Christian Arabs, many of whom could or would not speak to one another, either because of differences in language, religious sect or political opinion. The Arabs rushed a similar number of men to the region, and the two large armies clashed near the valley of the river Yarmuk, which today lies on the sensitive border between Syria, Jordan and the Golan Heights. A long-running battle took place over the course of a number of weeks, perhaps in August 636, and at one vital moment during the fighting Khalid – who was again one of the chief officers in the field, although he was now out of favour with a new caliph, Umar – gave a stirring speech to inspire the troops. He told them this was 'one of God's battles' and asked them to 'strive sincerely, seeking God in your work,' and accepting that they may be giving their lives in the name of Allah.[7]

---

* Or perhaps more accurately, 'God is greatest'.

This appeal to the Muslims' inherent zeal, along with Khalid's canny cavalry tactics, chronic Byzantine internal dissensions, a plague outbreak and a massive dust-storm combined to grant victory to the Arab upstarts. Writing around four thousand kilometres away and a couple of decades later, one Frankish chronicler, well informed about eastern affairs, lamented that at the battle of Yarmuk, 'the army of Heraclius was smitten by the sword of the Lord.'[8] God had picked sides, and it seemed his favour belonged to the armies of Islam.

The siege of Damascus and the battle of Yarmuk laid the foundations for an astonishingly rapid Arab conquest of Byzantine Syria, Palestine and Egypt. In 638 Jerusalem was surrendered by the patriarch Sophronius, who handed over control of the city in peaceable fashion but later bewailed its fate in sermons, telling the faithful that the arrival of the 'vengeful and God-hating Saracens' was more clear evidence of God's irritation with Christian sinfulness.[9] Yet it was apparently too late for Christ's flock to mollify their lord. In 641, following a series of sieges, Muslim armies took the strategically vital port city of Caesarea. Many of the 7,000 defenders were not able to evacuate by ship to Constantinople and were executed after the city fell.[10] Heraclius died in the same year. Around the time of the fateful battle of Yarmuk he had uttered words which turned out to be utterly prophetic: *Sosou Syria* ('Rest In Peace, Syria'), he said.[11]

THE ARAB CONQUEST OF SYRIA IN 632–642 was one of the most astonishing accomplishments of its age. In the first place it finally and permanently cut off an eastern wing of the Byzantine empire, which had been Roman territory for nearly seven hundred years; the border of Byzantium was now pushed back to the Amanus mountains on the eastern edge of Asia Minor, beyond which it would seldom reach for the rest of the Middle Ages. Much more significantly, though, Syria was one of the first major triumphs of a new power that was about to sweep across the world, branching out to the borders of China and the Atlantic seaboard of Europe, establishing an Islamic state that covered more than 12 million square kilometres. Between Muhammad's death and the collapse of the Umayyad Caliphate in AD 750, Arab armies appeared everywhere from Central Asia, through the Middle East and north Africa, throughout the Visigothic Iberian peninsula and even in southern France. They imposed Islamic governments and introduced new ways of living, trading, learning, thinking, building and praying. The capital of the vast caliphate they established would be Damascus itself, crowned with its Great Mosque – one of the masterpieces of medieval architecture anywhere in the world. In Jerusalem, the Dome of the Rock was built on top of the site of the old Jewish Second Temple – and its gleaming dome became an iconic landmark on that city's famous skyline. Elsewhere, great new cities like Cairo (Egypt), Kairouan (Tunisia) and Baghdad (Iraq) grew out of Arab military garrison towns, while other settlements like Merv (Turkmenistan), Samarkand (Uzbekistan), Lisbon (Portugal) and Córdoba (Spain) were renewed as major mercantile and trading cities.

The caliphate established by the Arab Conquests was more than just a new political federation. It was specifically and explicitly a faith empire – more so than the Roman Empire had ever been, even after Constantine's conversion and Justinian's reforms; even after a promulgation late in Heraclius' reign that all Jews in Byzantium were to be forcibly converted to Christianity. Within this caliphate, an old language – Arabic – and a new religion – Islam – were central to the identity of the conquerors and, as time went on, became ever more central to the lives of the conquered.

The creation of a global *dar al-Islam* (abode, or house of Islam) in the seventh and eighth centuries AD would have profound consequences for the rest of the Middle Ages, and indeed for the world today. With the exception of Spain and Portugal (and, later, Sicily), almost every major territory that was captured by early medieval Islamic armies retained, and still retains today, an Islamic identity and culture. The spirit of scientific invention and intellectual enquiry that thrived in some of the larger and more cosmopolitan Islamic cities would come to play a key role in the Renaissance of the later Middle Ages.

The schisms that arose during medieval Islam's formative years dogged the medieval near and Middle East, and have also continued to inform foreign affairs in the modern world. The roots of the Sunni–Shia divide can be traced back to the days of the very first caliphs, while the Arab–Persian division that emerged in the eighth century lives on in the modern Middle East in geopolitical rivalry between Saudi Arabia and Iran. The complex legacy of conflict and co-existence between Muslims, Jews and Christians springs partially from the early medieval Arab Conquests. Battles refracted through the lens of faith continue to rage, often on the self-same sites they did 1,500 years ago: Palestine, Jerusalem, Syria, Egypt, Iraq, Iran and Libya. To take just one example, the city of Damascus was not just besieged in the 630s; it was assaulted by the armies of the Second Crusade in the 1120s, besieged by Muslim Mongols and Turks in 1400, suffered religious massacres in the 1840s and 1860s, was bombed by the French in the 1920s and has been fought over bitterly by the various factions of the present-day Syrian Civil War. During the last of these conflicts, a notorious battle took place in a district of Damascus known as Yarmuk Camp.

This is an incredible legacy. But it is not all. For more than anything else the Arab Conquests laid the foundations for Islam's rise as a major world religion. In 2015 it was reported that there were 1.8 billion Muslims in the world – around 80–85 per cent of them Sunni, and 15–20 per cent Shia. In the Middle East Islam is by far the dominant religion; but it is also the largest faith in northern and eastern Africa, the second largest in Britain and continental Europe, and the third-largest in the USA. In all, one quarter of the world's population follow some version of the faith professed by Khalid ibn al-Walid, Amr al-As and their companions as they stood before the walls of Damascus in the 630s.

Birth of a Faith

THE CITY OF MECCA SITS IN a hot valley, roughly halfway down the western Arabian peninsula, in the region known as the Hijaz. It is around eighty kilometres from the coast, sheltered from the vast sands of the Arabian interior by the Sirat mountains (*jibal al-sirat or al-sirawat*).[12] Mecca is temperate in the winter months, but savagely hot during its long summers, when daytime temperatures often creep beyond 45°C. Yet despite the sweltering climate, which in the early Middle Ages rendered serious agriculture impossible, geography and spirituality have long made the city important. In the seventh century AD Mecca enjoyed a thriving economy, since it was a stopping point on a major caravan trail, along which swaying camels and their drivers plodded, carrying goods between the Red Sea's busy ports and the bustling marketplaces further north. Perfumes, spices, slaves and animal skins all passed through on their way to larger Arabian oasis cities like Yathrib, and, beyond them, the wealthy markets of Persia and Byzantium. The most successful Meccans of the seventh century were more than just traders: they were a class of busy merchants and investors – proto-capitalists who knew how to exploit the opportunities geography and access to ready finance afforded them. But below them sat a disgruntled underclass, cut off from the profits of business and investment, who were increasingly conscious of a deepening gulf between rich and poor.[13]

Passing trade, however, was not Mecca's only advantage. It was also a site for pilgrimage to the Ka'ba: a cubic temple of black volcanic rock first built, or so tradition had it, by the Old Testament patriarch Abraham.[14] Pilgrims came many miles to pay obeisance to the gods whose idols were housed in and around the Ka'ba, and to see, in its eastern corner, the long-revered Black Stone. This sacred rock – which some traditions suppose was a meteorite, hurled to earth from the heavens – was even more ancient than the Ka'ba itself. Of all the gods and goddesses worshipped at the Ka'ba the most important was Allah, but in the early seventh century other names were also revered there: Hubal loomed large among them, as did the three goddesses, Manat, Allat and al-Uzza.[15] There was even a picture inside the Ka'ba of the Virgin Mary and Jesus. Traditional history suggests there were fully 360 idols in and around the site.

It is impossible to know whether this number should be taken literally. What we can say is that early medieval Arabia was a rich melting-pot for cults and deities. In some cities and regions (notably the region we now call Yemen) there were thriving communities of Arab Jews and Christians. But in many more places pagan polytheism was the norm. Then there were what we might describe as pagan monotheists – believers in a single God who was not the same as the God of Christian or Jewish scripture. Desert prophets, mystics, monks and hermits abounded, some following in the traditions of the early Christian 'desert fathers' who had sought proximity to God through ascetic living in the sunbeaten sands.* In short, Arabian religion was diverse, shifting and heavily localized, and this was only natural. Arabian society was essentially tribal, and despite the nearness of several regional superpowers – Byzantium and Zoroastrian Persia, as well as Christian Ethiopia – none had ever been able to bring the Arabs under their command for long enough sponsor or enforce the spread of a settled 'state' faith. The best the Byzantines and Persians had been able to do was to enlist two northern Arabian tribal groups, the Lakhmids and Ghassanids, into their proxy wars. This was clientelism, not colonialism. In Arabia, change was destined to come from within.

From the middle of the fifth century AD, the chief tribe in Mecca was the Quraysh – and it was this tribe into which Muhammad was born in around 570. Although he was born to a reasonably affluent family of the Banu Hashim clan, his childhood was punctuated by personal loss. By the time he was eight he had lost both his father, Abd Allah, and his mother, Aminah. From late childhood he was raised by his grandfather, and later an uncle, Abu Talib, the leader

---

* It has often been noted that the three great Abrahamic faiths – Judaism, Christianity and Islam – all have deep connections to the desert, to the extent that they could be described collectively as 'the desert religions'. The notion of a single God can be traced back to the sands of ancient Egypt in the age of Akhenaten (c. 1351–1335 BC).

of the Banu Hashim. When Muhammad was around two years old he spent time as a foster-child with Bedouins in the desert.* One day his foster-brother saw angels dressed all in white appear, remove Muhammad's heart, clean it with snow and return it, now purified, to his body.[16] After this, throughout his youth, mystics and monks would predict that he was destined for greatness – or at least, these were the stories they later told, once greatness had descended upon him.

Yet greatness did not arrive until relatively late in Muhammad's life. He was working as a merchant when, at around the age of forty (in c. AD 609/10), he began to experience dreams, visions and visitations from celestial beings. The turning point came while he was in a cave in Mount Hira, on the outskirts of Mecca, a place he liked to go now and then to meditate and reflect. One day he was visited there by the angel Gabriel, who addressed him directly and commanded him to recite. Muhammad came to understand he had been chosen as Allah's Prophet and messenger – the last such in a long line that stretched back through Jesus, Solomon, David, Abraham, Noah and Moses all the way to the first man, Adam. This was big news, but he overcame his initial terror and confusion. His next visitation took three years to arrive, but when it did, Muhammad began to receive the word of God regularly, sometimes in spoken form and sometimes as a ringing sound which had to be deciphered. The angel showed him ritual ablutions and the best way to pray to Allah. These were the basic rites of a new religion: Islam. Muhammad's revelations, as he recited them in Arabic, were eventually collected as the Qur'an. Later on, fragments of the Prophet's speech, along with oral memories of his opinions and actions, known as *Hadith*, were compiled as the *Sunnah* – which contributed to the formation of an Islamic legal code and moral framework.

***

---

* This was traditional practice at the time among the Quraysh: young children were temporarily fostered by nomadic people in order to improve their health and imbue them with the spirit of the desert. See Lings, *Muhammad*, pp. 23–4.

OF COURSE, A NEW RELIGION WAS nothing without a following. Muhammad was by no means the only prophet in early medieval Arabia, and the monotheistic, ritual-based faith he now devoted his life to promoting was still just one of hundreds of belief systems and cults alive among the tribes. His struggle, therefore, was to convince others to follow him in worshipping Allah correctly. Shrewd and intelligent, with a reputation for trustworthiness, prudence and self-control, Muhammad had little difficulty persuading his family and friends of his cause; the first of his companions included his wife Khadijah, his nephew Ali, his dear friend Abu Bakr, and his adopted son Zayd. But other Arabs – including those of the Quraysh – took a little more persuasion. Muhammad's message – that all other gods and idols were to be rejected in favour of Allah alone – was hardly a promising commercial proposition in a city whose economy depended in large part on polytheistic pilgrim tourists. Several years earlier, Muhammad had been instrumental in setting the sacred Black Stone into a new position in the Ka'ba, which had been rebuilt in handsome fashion. Now he was preaching a new religion which threatened to undermine everything the Ka'ba stood for.

Muhammad's public preaching career began in earnest in 613, to a mixed response. Although his advocacy for charity, prayer and monotheism found a willing audience and ready converts among ordinary Meccans, particularly, although not exclusively, the indigent and struggling poor, as well as with Arabs scattered throughout the wider Hijaz, the most powerful and influential groups in Mecca regarded the Prophet as bothersome at best and perhaps downright dangerous to public order. As that other great prophet and preacher Jesus of Nazareth had demonstrated 600 years before, any charismatic and pious individual who sought to build a religious creed around the themes of poverty and social inequality very quickly amassed rich and powerful enemies. Muhammad soon found himself an outcast in his own tribe. The first crisis arrived in 619 – the 'Year of Sorrow' – when both Khadija and Abu Talib died. This double loss severely weakened Muhammad's standing within the Banu Hashim clan and Quraysh tribe at large. During the next three years the danger became existential. At first Muhammad and the Muslims were goaded and teased, then they were actively persecuted. Several were tortured to death, and a number fled the Hijaz altogether, emigrating across the Red Sea seeking refuge in Ethiopia.

In 622 – the foundational year in Islamic history, and the date from which the Muslim calendar begins – Muhammad also left Mecca. He had been approached by tribal elders from Yathrib, who asked him to bring the community of Muslims en masse to their city, where they would be granted an honoured place, and Muhammad would be tasked with settling long-running feuding among the pagan tribes and sizeable Jewish population of the city. In June, he and his followers therefore left Mecca, narrowly escaping an assassination plot. After an eight-day journey of about 320km – known as the *hijrah* – they reached Yathrib, which was later renamed Medina.* He drafted a deal known as the Constitution of Medina that united the bickering factions there in a community or *umma*, bonded by faith – faith above blood, faith above tribal loyalties, faith above everything. Before long he was the leader of the city, and had begun to construct a spiritual and legal polity that was far more than a simple federation of tribal allies. It was, even in its emerging form, the first Islamic state. Within this state, political solidarity, monotheism and religious obedience were one and the same. Islam informed everything – it was a complete way of life. This absolutism, which became increasingly pronounced during Islam's early medieval history, would come to be its attraction, its strength and its inherent menace to those who had not yet submitted to its teaching.

When the Muslims arrived in Medina, they were in the habit of praying towards Jerusalem, but soon afterwards Muhammad adjusted their sights, and his followers began the practice of praying in the direction of Mecca. They also took aim at Meccan trade, making a living by robbing caravan trains. This was a precarious way to get by, and in March 624 one large caravan raid

---

* Short for Medinat an-Nabi (City of the Prophet) or Medinah al-Manuwarra (Enlightened City)

turned into a full-scale battle – the battle of Badr – a handsome, against-the-odds victory in the face of vastly superior force. More battles followed. Not all went the Muslims' way: they were defeated by the Meccans at the battle of Uhud in 625, and Medina was almost lost at the battle of the Trench in 627. But as the decade neared its end Muhammad had sufficient followers, warriors and momentum that he could contemplate returning to Mecca and avenging the insults that had been heaped on him there at the start of his ministry. In 630, with 10,000 men at his back, he marched on his former hometown, swept into the city, smashed the idols in the Ka'ba and took political control. Having spent long enough resisting Muhammad, the Quraysh and the rest of the Meccans now converted to Islam. Only a few obstinate unbelievers held out, and they were executed. In short order Muhammad proceeded to bring tribes all over the Hijaz and beyond into the faith. The momentum and tactical acumen of his campaigning, the purity and clarity of his religious message and the practical realization that the Muslims now controlled trade routes and essential marketplaces all over western Arabia: these were the chief factors that underpinned his success. When the Prophet died in 632, he appeared to have achieved the impossible: the Arabs were becoming united, spiritually and politically, in the *umma*.

Their unity was destined to last longer than anyone might have predicted.

The 'Rightly Guided' Caliphs

WHEN THE ARABIC SPEAKERS OF THE desert told one another stories of their origins, they traced their lineage back to Abraham. They were the Hagarites: the descendants of Abraham's union with his wife Sarah's slave-girl Hagar, which had produced a son called Ishmael. At the time Ishmael's very existence had been a mixed blessing, for it aroused Sarah's extreme and lasting enmity. But it had also – so the stories went – produced the Arab people, a race quite distinct from the sons of Abraham's second son, Isaac, who was revered as patriarch of the twelve tribes of Israel. In one sense all this was ancient history – but in another it mattered deeply. The Old Testament prophesied Ishmael's life in memorable terms: 'He shall be a wild ass of a man: his hand shall be against every man, and every man's hand against him...'[17] This description might well have been applied to his descendants, the seventh-century Muslims of Arabia, as they banded together under the banner of Islam, then set out to subjugate their neighbours.*

After Muhammad died in 632 and was buried in Medina, the unity of the *umma* he left behind was severely tested. The Prophet's old friend Abu Bakr claimed to be his successor, but there were a large number of Arab tribes who took the view that their loyalty had been to Muhammad as God's messenger, and was not to be transferred as a matter of course to his replacement. Other prophets, encouraged by Muhammad's example, laid their own claims to have a special relationship with God, which naturally privileged their own tribal groups. As a result, a short but bloody conflict known as the Ridda Wars broke out, in which Abu Bakr was compelled – somewhat reluctantly – to send the armies of Islam against Arab apostates, to bring them forcibly back into the faith and fold.

The Ridda Wars lasted for around nine months, and during the campaigns across the peninsula commanders including Khalid bin al-Walid and Amr ibn al-As showed their true mettle. Within less than a year the Muslim generals had defeated the rebellious tribes and brought insurgent Arabian cities back under obedience. Victory ensured the unity of the *umma* would last beyond the leadership and lifespan of the Prophet. It also set in motion an Islamic military machine with extraordinary momentum and self-belief, primed to spill out into the lands of the decadent empires to the north.†

---

* A similar sentiment also underpins the notorious Millwall FC terrace chant familiar to followers of English football since the 1970s: 'No one likes us/We don't care.'
† The Ridda Wars had another important consequence for the history of Islam. In one battle, fought at Yamama, in central Arabia, the slaughter included several dozen *huffaz* – scholars who had memorized every word of the Qur'an's 114 surah, comprising 6,000+ verses. As a matter of necessity, Abu Bakr authorized the compilation of a definitive edition of Muhammad's revelation, known as the *mushaf*. In the years that followed, under the rule of the caliphs Umar and Uthman, this text produced was copied and its Arabic standardized.

Geography laid a clear path for conquest outside Arabia. The natural places for the Muslims to turn as they expanded were the regions that lay at the fringes of the great Syrian desert: southern Syria and Iraq. In 633, Muslim armies headed out into both. They met with initial resistance from the representatives of the Byzantines and Persians. But the two empires were structurally and materially exhausted from long decades of war against one another. Emperors in Constantinople were so short of their own troops that they were forced to recruit the majority of their armies from among the Turks – a new nomadic steppe power that had appeared in the region around the Caspian Sea from the sixth century.[18] The Muslims, by contrast, were battle-hardened but not yet battle-weary. In swift order their armies ripped through both sets of imperial defences. In Syria, Damascus was in Muslim hands by AD 635/6; by 648 almost the whole Levantine coast as well as the desert interior was conquered. And that was not all. Having conquered southern Syria, in 639 Amr ibn al-As took an army swarming across the Sinai Peninsula into Egypt, towards the Nile Delta. Within three years all the major cities in Egypt, including the coastal capital Alexandria, were in Muslim hands. In 641 Amr established a new garrison town called al-Fustat (loosely, 'Tent City'), and built the first mosque in Egypt there. This became the Muslim capital of the newly conquered province; today it is a suburb of Cairo. Egypt, the breadbasket of the Mediterranean, now no longer fed the Byzantine empire: it answered to the caliphs in Medina.

Meanwhile in Iraq, invasion proceeded simultaneously and at roughly the same pace. In 636 (or possibly later – the chronology is contested) a Muslim army shattered a large Persian force equipped with war elephants, at the three-day battle of al-Qadisiyya. Early the following year they marched on the great Persian capital of Ctesiphon. During their approach to the city they were briefly detained by a Persian detachment whose mascot was a trained lion called al-Muqarrat; sadly for the beast, its teeth and claws were no match for a Muslim warrior called Hashim ibn Utbah, who killed it with his sword. (The blade was subsequently given the honourable name 'Strong One'.)[19]

After the lion fell, so did the city. Following a short catapult bombardment, a pitched battle with the city's defenders and a daring amphibious raid across the river Tigris, Ctesiphon's two centres were taken by the Muslims in the spring of 637. The treasure they discovered in the great White Palace of the Sassanid kings of kings was almost too much to comprehend: huge baskets full of gold and silver, jewels, crowns and royal vestments, and armour that had once belonged to the Byzantine emperor Heraclius, seized during the Byzantine–Persian war earlier in the century. Bounty thus became bounty again. The best was sent back to the caliph Umar in Medina 'for the Muslims to see and the nomadic tribesmen to hear about'.²⁰ Ctesiphon's magnificent Taq Kasra became a mosque. And the Arab war machine rolled onwards. At the battle of Jalula, which took place shortly after the fall of Ctesiphon, the lion-killer Hashim ibn Utbah once again put a Persian army to flight.

The Sassanid dynasty was now on the ropes. The death-blow came in 642. The new king of kings, Yazdegerd III, had painstakingly rebuilt his military forces after the terrible losses of the 630s. But his new army went the same way as the old: at the battle of Nahavand tens of thousands of Persians fell beneath Muslim swords, and in the aftermath Yazdegerd's state collapsed. News of the victory at Nahavand was reported in a letter that began 'Rejoice, Commander of the Faithful, in a victory with which God has honoured Islam and His subjects and with which He has disgraced unbelief and its advocates.'²¹ On reading it, and learning of the many Muslims who had fallen as martyrs, Umar burst into tears.

UMAR HAD BECOME THE SECOND OF the 'Rightly Guided' (*Rashidun*)* caliphs in 634, when Abu Bakr died. Around fifty-three years old, he was famous for his physical strength, stubbornness

---

* The label 'Rashidun', although the standard name for the first, pre-Umayyad caliphs, is not used by many Shia Muslims, who consider Abu Bakr, Umar and Uthman to have been illegitimate.

and literacy. Although he did not lead Muslim armies in person, he was an outstandingly competent commander-in-chief, able to dictate military strategy hundreds of miles from Medina, trusting his generals to find the most effective means to achieve the wider goals of the expanding Islamic state. As caliph he carefully curated his public image: on entering Jerusalem to take possession of the city from the patriarch Sophronius, he appeared in ragged clothes, dirty from his long journey, so that his humble appearance would contrast pointedly with the churchman's finery.

Yet Umar was not successful simply because he was charismatic and capable. He was also the chief executive officer and spiritual leader of a machine built for and fed by conquest, and perfectly attuned to its day. When the Muslims were expanding and consolidating their rule in Arabia under Muhammad and Abu Bakr, conversion to Islam was a prerequisite of conquest. But once they ventured outside the Arabic-speaking world, the Muslims did not attempt simply to repeat this model. Whether they swept through regions populated by desert nomads or drew up their horsemen and siege catapults outside the great cities of Byzantine and Persia, they made it clear that they did not come as a dogmatic army hell-bent on converting or killing every man, woman and child before them. Their only demand was that communities surrendered quickly and submitted to government by a Muslim ruling elite. Christians, Jews and other monotheists were not expected to become Muslims – and in some cases actively discouraged from doing so on the grounds that they would contribute higher tax yields as infidels than they would as believers. They were exempted from military service and obliged only to pay the *jizyah* poll tax and rule their own communities in an orderly and civilized fashion. Meanwhile, the Muslim soldiers who formed the conquering armies were largely kept separate from the populace, garrisoned in military towns and paid a stipend known as the *ata*, funded by taxation. They were not, however, rewarded with tracts of land nor confiscated estates: a policy that helped reduce civil tension in the short term, and in the long run meant that the Muslim armies did not blend over a couple of generations into the local population, in the Roman fashion.

The roots of this tolerance for conquered people who submitted without resistance was of course not original: it had been in, essence, the package offered by the generals of the Roman Republic and early empire.²² Pragmatic acceptance of local practices – at least in the short term – has always been an effective way of pursuing military expansion without provoking long insurgencies. Yet in the seventh century the offer of religious tolerance may have had particular appeal. Given the poisonous sectarian violence that had swirled around the Christian world in Byzantium, the arrival of a new ruling power that cared little for the tortuous debates over reconciling Christ's spiritual and human natures – one which taxed unbelievers, rather than persecuting them – may have come as blessed relief.

This is not to say, however, that the Arab Conquests were wholly heartfelt and peaceful. Cities and tribes that resisted the Muslim armies forfeited their right to be welcomed into the fold in an orderly fashion. During the wars in Arabia, Muhammad had approved the beheading of hundreds of male members of the Jewish Banu Qurayza tribe, and the enslavement of all their women and children.²³ The many battles fought between the Muslims and their various imperial opponents were also bloody affairs, and the accounts of these, too, overspill with tales of thousands, tens of thousands – even (improbably) hundreds of thousands of warriors slain at a time. After one battle in Persia, reported al-Tabari, 'the youngsters of the [Muslim] army went to inspect the dead... they gave water to the Muslims in whom there was a breath of life and killed the polytheists in whom there was a breath of life... [Meanwhile, others] went in pursuit of the Persians who had fled... they killed them in every village, in every thicket, and on every river bank, then returned in time for the noon prayers.'²⁴ This was the way of war, and in part the way of Islam. Although there were many examples of Muhammad preaching tolerance and peace, the *Hadith* compiled during Umar's caliphate also contained striking pronouncements advocating for war and violence. In one,

Muhammad was reported to have said: 'Allah guarantees that He will admit the Mujahid [holy warrior] in His Cause into Paradise if he is killed, otherwise He will return him to his home safely with rewards and war booty.'[25] The concept of *jihad* (meaning struggle) demanded that all Muslims make strenuous effort for the cause of Islam. Very often during the Middle Ages this meant taking up arms and killing other human beings in the expectation of reward in the afterlife.

The Fitnas

THE VIOLENT AND TURBULENT SIDE TO the Arab Conquests was laid bare in 644 when the second caliph, Umar, was murdered by an enslaved Persian soldier called Piruz Nahavandi (also known as Abu Lu'lu'ah). The man went on a rampage during morning prayers at the Mosque of the Prophet (*al-masjid an-nabawi*) in Medina, slashing out with a double-edged knife and fatally wounding seven people, including the caliph himself, whom he stabbed as many as half a dozen times in the midriff. According to one account preserved in the *Hadith*, when the blade slipped in Umar groaned 'the dog has killed or eaten me'.[26] He survived four days before dying of his wounds.

During those four days, Umar convened an emergency deathbed council of six of the most senior Muslims, all of whom were Companions of the Prophet – the select and slowly dwindling group of people who had met and followed Muhammad during his lifetime. He charged them with picking one from among their number as his successor. The man they chose was Uthman, a merchant of the prestigious Umayya clan of the Quraysh.* Uthman was of medium height, thickset and hairy, with bandy legs but a handsome face pockmarked by smallpox scars.[27] He had been one of the early converts to Islam and he was of good standing among

---

* The Banu Umayya were a sub-clan of the Banu Abd-Shams, a larger group within the Quraysh.

the faithful, in his mid-sixties and very wealthy, albeit without the same military reputation as Umar. He was a serious and credible candidate. But in electing Uthman the council passed over the claims of Muhammad's cousin Ali, and this decision would eventually have enormous consequences for the history of Islam and the wider world.

During Uthman's twelve-year caliphate, Muslim armies continued to press out ever further east and west and to develop their fighting capability in the west. In the late 640s they campaigned in Armenia and eastern Asia Minor. In the east, they rolled ever further through the disintegrating Persian empire, so that by 651 almost all of it was under Muslim control, with the frontier at the borders of what is now Afghanistan. Meanwhile, in the west, an army of 40,000 men began to chew through north Africa, stripping away Byzantine territory in the Exarchate of Africa, working their way at one point to within a few days' march of Carthage.

Battles were fought on the high seas as well as on land. One of the outstanding generals who had emerged during the wars against Byzantium and Persia was Muawiya ibn Abi Sufyan, a tall, bald and distinguished military officer who was a leading light in the conquest of Syria and then its governor for two decades. Having a free hand over Syria's long coastline gave Muawiya access to many of the finest naval ports of the eastern Mediterranean, from Beirut (modern Lebanon) all the way through Palestine to Alexandria, in Egypt. Like the caliph, Muawiya was a member of the Umayya clan, and with Uthman's backing, he now fast-tracked the development of a Muslim navy to rival the powerful Byzantine sea-fleet. During the late 640s and 650s Muslim ships conquered Cyprus, and raided Crete and Rhodes. In (or around) 654 they sailed towards Constantinople itself. Off the coast of Lycia, in Asia Minor, they won a ferocious and very bloody naval battle against a Byzantine fleet commanded by the emperor Constans II, a clash that is known now as the battle of the Masts. Only dreadful storms in the aftermath of the victory (and severe losses sustained in the heavy fighting) prevented the Muslims from making a full attempt on the beating heart of the Byzantine empire.

All of this amounted – superficially at least – to a steady period of growth. Yet one had barely to scratch the surface to see that under Uthman's rule all was not well. Although the caliph oversaw several important spiritual and domestic reforms, including the compilation of an 'authorized' edition of the Qur'an, the caliphate assembled at lightning speed had begun to breed serious tensions and factional rivalries. In the summer of 656 they exploded.

Opposition to Uthman's rule was in equal parts personal and political. As the Islamic state grew, it began to echo with grumblings, heard loudest in Egypt and Iraq, that influence and reward were being concentrated unduly in the hands of the Quraysh. Of course, this was a delicate matter: the Quraysh were both Muhammad's tribe and the people who had opposed him most bitterly in the beginning. They had provided caliphs and generals of the standard of Khalid ibn al-Walid and Syria's governor and naval admiral Muawiya. They were, insofar as there was such a thing, Muslim aristocracy. Yet other Arabian tribes who had participated wholeheartedly in the decades of constant military conquest felt – rightly or wrongly – that they had been denied just return on their investment, and resented the arrogance with which, under Uthman, high-ranking Quraysh seemed to be allowed to help themselves to whatever they desired throughout the conquered lands. The most bitter complaints in this regard were raised by a tribe known as the Qurra. But they were not alone.

Whether through ignorance or inability, during the 650s Uthman failed to heed the signs that a major revolt was looming within the empire. When he began to take action to answer grievances and settle disputes, around 655, it was all too late. In the spring of 656 protestors began to travel from Egypt to Medina and demonstrate outside Uthman's house. By June a large mob had effectively cut off the residence and placed it under siege, pelting the walls with stones and calling for Uthman's head.[28]

On 17 June they got it.[29] A small band of rebels managed to break into Uthman's compound, evade the heavy guard and confront the caliph in his rooms. After a struggle, they overpowered Uthman, beating and stabbing him to death, and seriously assaulting one of his wives, who lost two of her fingers in the fight and had her buttocks groped as she fled.[30] The rebels then pillaged Uthman's house, attacking his servants and other of his wives. Several days later, when Uthman's body was taken for burial, Medina was still in uproar, and a mob threatened to stone the mourners. Rifts had opened that could not be healed.

UTHMAN'S SUCCESSOR AS CALIPH WAS MUHAMMAD'S exceptionally pious and upstanding cousin Ali, a proven warrior and intimate member of the Prophet's family, who had grown up with Muhammad and was married to his daughter Fatimah. Ali was a widely respected figure, and an impeccably holy character, who had the distinction of having been born inside the Ka'ba itself, and who had built his reputation as the most Muslim of the Muslims – a paragon of old-fashioned virtue whose partisans, known as the *shia*, were entranced by his ability to expound and espouse the values given to them by the Prophet.

Ali had been passed over at the time of Uthman's election. Yet now his time had finally come, he seemed wholly unable to turn the Islamic world back towards the purity of its first, golden years in the 630s and 640s. Although he had not connived at Uthman's death, Ali quickly became a polarizing figure, rather than a soothing one. The *umma's* unity now quickly fractured, and a civil war known as the First Fitna blazed into life. In the short four and a half years Ali's caliphate lasted he was sucked into a ceaseless struggle against disaffected Uthmanites whose leaders included such venerable Muslims as Muhammad's widow Aisha (who on one occasion personally led troops into battle while she was mounted on a camel*) and the worldly, hard-bitten governor of Syria, Muawiya. Many of the battlegrounds in this war were in Iraq, and Ali was forced to uproot the caliphal headquarters from Medina and move to Kufa, a garrison town on the banks of

---

* The 'battle of the Camel', so named for Aisha's mount, was fought near Basra, Iraq, in November 656.

the Euphrates (in modern Iraq). In the Great Mosque of this city, during the last days of January 661, Ali himself was murdered, when a member of a radical, fundamentalist sect known as the Kharijites, who thought he had compromised too much, burst in and stabbed him with a poison-tipped sword.

Tales later circulated that Ali had predicted his own death, or else had been told of such a prophecy by a close companion. But it is hard to imagine he or anyone else could have predicted the legacy of his murder to more than a millennium of world history. In the chaotic months that followed Ali's murder, Muawiya fought the late Ali's forces to a standstill, and browbeat Ali's elder son Hasan – a grandson of the Prophet Muhammad – until he accepted a large sum of gold to abdicate his claim to be caliph. Hasan was thus forced from power and in the summer of 661 Muawiya demanded oaths of loyalty from the leading regional commanders in the Islamic world, receiving them at holy sites in Jerusalem. He was now the caliph – the first ruler of a dynasty history has come to call the Umayyads, after his (and before him, Uthman's) clan, the Banu Umayya. With Muawiyah's rise from leader of Islamic Syria to become commander of all the Muslim faithful, the age of the Rightly Guided caliphs came to an end, and the Umayyad period began.

Although the Umayyads were in power for less than a century, it was an exciting and transformational time. The capital of the Islamic world swung away from Medina to Damascus, while the boundaries of the abode of Islam stretched as far into the barbarian west as the south of France. And within this ever-expanding abode, a cultural revolution took place. Arabic and Islam permeated the societies to which the Muslims had staked their claim, while the caliphate became more worldly and less theocratic. The Umayyads were responsible for making the Arab Conquests permanent, and for building a true empire out of a series of conquered states. Yet at the same time they opened divisions that would wrench the Islamic world apart.

At the root of this lay the fact that the Umayyads' rise to power and subsequent consolidation of their hold on it scored deep lines in the fabric of the *umma*. Ali's partisans could not and would not forget his murder, and during the reign of Muawiya these 'Alids' fomented against what they saw as an illegitimate regime. At the end of Muawiya's rule in 680 a second *fitna* erupted. This time power was contested between Muawiya's son and designated heir Yazid, and Ali's surviving, younger son Husayn. When Muawiya announced his intention to hand the caliphate on to his son, Husayn refused to take an oath of allegiance. He set out on a long march of protest, from Arabia towards Iraq, and on his way was killed in a desert skirmish; he was decapitated and his head sent as a trophy to Damascus. Once more, the Umayyads had triumphed.

While this bloody piece of theatre ensured the Umayyads' survival, it also cemented a schism within Islam that has survived for more than thirteen hundred years. The sects and factions that formed during the first and second *fitnas* gave birth to what we now know as the Sunni–Shia divide.* Shia Muslims refused to accept the legitimacy of the Umayyad caliphate, or indeed the legitimacy of Abu Bakr, Umar and Uthman's regimes. Instead, they insisted that Ali was Muhammad's rightful successor: the first *Imam*. This in turn implied an alternative succession, through Hasan and Husayn, then a bloodline of further imams descended from Muhammad. Now this was not solely a dynastic dispute. The Shia framework of Islamic history proposed a significantly different model of organizing the *umma*, and a different set of leadership values.

The Sunni–Shia divide came to be tremendously important during the later Middle Ages, particularly (as we shall see) during the crusading era. But it has lasted far longer than that. During the twentieth century, a revived, poisonous sectarianism established in part along Sunni–Shia lines began to inform world geopolitics

---

* Sunni Muslims regard Ali as the fourth and last of the Rightly Guided caliphs. But to Shia Muslims, he is a man whose importance in the history of the faith is even greater than that – second only to Muhammad's. In this reading of early Islamic history, Ali ought to have been the Prophet's direct successor; the reigns of Abu Bakr, Umar and Uthman are regarded as illegitimate. Ali is the first successor from within Muhammad's immediate family, known as the first Imam. (In addition, almost all members of the mystic Sufi orders regard Ali as a founding father.)

– playing a role in the interconnected Iran–Iraq War, US-led Gulf Wars, and long-running 'Islamic cold war', which has pitted Saudi Arabia and Iran against one another for regional hegemony in the Middle East since 1979; as well as other, painful and deadly conflicts that have been fought in Pakistan, Iraq and Syria.* That all this can still be traced back to the machinations of powerful men in the seventh century AD may seem astonishing – but, as so often proves the case, the Middle Ages remain with us today.

The Umayyads

IN 691 AN EXTRAORDINARY BUILDING WAS erected on top of the huge stone platform in Jerusalem which, centuries before, had been the site of Jewish Second Temple. That famous and sacred complex had been reduced to rubble after a siege in AD 70, when the Roman general (and future emperor) Titus came to Jerusalem to put down a Jewish rebellion and instigated a clash of arms and arson that entirely razed the city. The loss of the Temple was a near-apocalyptic disaster for the Jewish people: its destruction had broken the back of the rebellion, scattered the Jewish people far and wide across the Middle East and left a permanent black mark on Jewish cultural memory. And it had never been rebuilt. At the dawn of the Middle Ages, all that remained was the vast platform, with the old city on one side and Mount of Olives on the other. Jewish prophecy held that one day, when a new Messiah came to earth and the ends of days approached, a Third Temple would finally be erected. But in the seventh century the end of days seemed to be some way off. Jerusalem was under Umayyad rule, and the ruling dynasty was about to leave its own spectacular

---

* Some prominent journalists have in recent years read the United States' Middle Eastern policy from around 2008 to have been explicitly anti-Shia, as an extension of its government's deep-seated suspicion of Iran. See for example, Hersh, Seymour, 'The Redirection', *The New Yorker* (February 2007); Nasr, Vali, 'The War for Islam', *Foreign Policy* (January 2016); Erasmus, 'Why Trump's pro-Sunni tilt worries human-rights campaigners', *The Economist* (May 2017).

mark on the Temple Mount. The structure they placed there was the Dome of the Rock.

The Dome of the Rock was – and is today – a beautiful, elegant, eight-sided shrine, which shares the Temple Mount (known to Muslims as the Noble Sanctuary or *Haram al-Sharif*) with two other Umayyad structures: the great, oblong al-Aqsa Mosque (*Masjid al-Aqsa*) and a smaller prayer house known as the Dome of the Chain. The Dome of the Rock is the most dazzling of these three structures, and in modern times it has gained iconic status – a symbol of supra-national Arab fraternity which appears on knick-knacks, trinkets, postcards and cheap wall-prints all over the Muslim world and beyond. It is as instantly recognizable as the Statue of Liberty or the Eiffel Tower. The Dome that tops it is a round, gilded half-sphere, 25m at its highest point, which gleams when it catches the sun, and can be seen from miles outside Jerusalem as a traveller approaches along the roads that cut through the Judean hills.[31] The yellow limestone rock within, which the shrine was built to contain and honour, has come to be revered as the spot from which Muhammad ascended to heaven in AD 621, for a tour of paradise in the company of the angel Gabriel. Pious mosaic inscriptions and Qur'anic quotations, written in the 'Kufic'* style of Arabic script current in the seventh century AD, run for 240m around its inside. Yet there is more than a hint of Byzantine artistic influence in the mosaic-work and decorative motifs that adorn the Dome, as well as a reference in the inscription of 'Jesus son of Mary', who is mentioned respectfully, albeit alongside a reminder that he should not be regarded as the son of God. The Dome is often mistaken for a mosque. It is not one. But it is certainly a strange and mysterious building which abounds with evidence of the swirling and competing cultural currents of Jerusalem in the seventh century.

Although almost everything we see when we look at the Dome of the Rock today is a combination of sixteenth-century Ottoman decoration and restoration work carried out in the second half

---

* Named for Kufa, the prominent garrison city in Iraq already mentioned in this chapter.

of the twentieth century, the substantive structure is still that which was commissioned by an Umayyad caliph, Abd al-Malik, in the 690s.[32] The cost of building the shrine was said to be seven times the annual revenue of the province of Egypt. But this was not mere heedless profligacy. The vast expense lavished on such a monumental construction project, the care and craftsmanship that went into its decoration and the very impulse to build it at all are tangible hallmarks of the Umayyad caliphate, which tell a story of ninety critical years in history, during which the *dar al-Islam* was transformed from a military machine into a fully fledged early medieval empire, infused with elements of the cultures it encountered, yet highly distinctive in its own right.

AFTER THE FIRST *FITNA* ENDED WITH Muawiya's triumph, the hub of the caliphate shifted from the holy cities of Medina and Mecca to Damascus, the capital of Muslim-ruled Syria. This physical move also represented an important shift in mentality. Under the Rightly Guided caliphs, the supreme leader of the *umma* was by definition a spiritual guide entrenched in Islam's historical heartlands, as well as a political and military commander-in-chief. But once the Umayyad caliphs left Arabia, these two roles were not quite so easily combined. The caliph was not suddenly stripped of his religious dignity – but he looked very much more like an emperor than before.

. In part, the adoption of imperium was a matter of osmosis. In Syria, the Umayyads abutted directly against Byzantium. Once the Umayyad caliphs set themselves up next door to the old Roman state their rule came to absorb a distinct flavor of Roman religious imperium. But this was not a peaceful process. The Umayyads were so intent on emulating Byzantium that between the 660s and 710s they repeatedly tried to take over the old Roman state wholesale. The result was a wide-ranging war across the near east and southern Mediterranean, which lasted for more than a century. The two great powers clashed frequently in north Africa, as Arab-led armies pushed towards the Maghreb (modern Algeria and Morocco). And they fought a series of battles on the high seas around Asia Minor, culminating in two spectacular sieges of Constantinople. These battles were nothing short of a war for the world, as the Umayyads strove to claim for Islam the most magnificent city in the western hemisphere, and the beating heart of Byzantium. The outcomes of these clashes would shape geopolitics across eastern Europe and the Balkans for centuries.

Muawiya launched the first direct tilt at Constantinople in the early 670s. Twenty years on from the battle of the Masts, the general-turned-caliph was as determined as ever to prove that Arab ships could match the notoriously agile and dangerous Greek vessels. So year after year, he sent ships, often crewed by Christian sailors fighting under Muslim commanders, to attack islands and ports in the Aegean Sea, menacing the sea-routes around the Byzantine capital and setting up a command centre at Cyzicus, which lay directly across the Sea of Marmara from Constantinople. According to the Greek chronicler Theophanes, they used this base to launch 'military engagement[s] every day from morning until evening', nibbling constantly at Byzantine defences.[33]

Then, in the autumn of 677, a full assault commenced.

It was an epic, furious encounter. The Byzantine empire may only have been a shadow of the once-unassailable Roman state, but in the 670s they had a secret weapon. Military technicians working for the emperor Constantine IV (r. 654–85), led by a scientist from southern Syria known as Kallinikos, had perfected a deadly, oil-based jelly, known variously as Roman Fire, marine fire, artificial fire or (most famously) Greek Fire.[34] When this incendiary liquid was sprayed under pressure, flame-thrower style, from jets mounted on the prows of specially equipped Byzantine fireships, it turned everything it clung to into an oily fireball. Greek Fire burned in the air, it burned on water, it could only be put out by smothering it with sand or diluting it with vinegar, and it could obliterate whole fleets during the course of a single engagement. Greek Fire was a game-changing weapons system, and a military secret the Byzantine state would guard closely for nearly five hundred years, so closely indeed that the knowledge of how to manufacture and deploy it was ultimately forgotten. In the meantime, however, it became notorious as one of foulest horrors of medieval battle, the equivalent of First World War poison gas, the napalm used in Vietnam, or the white phosphorous deployed against civilians in the recent Syrian Civil War. Its testing ground was the war against the Umayyads. In 678 the emperor turned Greek Fire on Muslim ships, and sent them away from the sea-defences of Constantinople with their masts smoking and sails blazing. As they scattered, they were smashed by powerful storms off the coast of Asia Minor. Up to thirty thousand men drowned. The fleet was 'dashed to pieces and perished entirely,' wrote Theophanes.[35] It was a triumph for Byzantium, a pivotal point in the history of warfare, and a round humiliation for the Muslims.

The second *fitna* of 680–692 interrupted the Umayyads' arm-wrestle with Byzantium, but not for good. A generation later, in 717, the caliph Sulayman tried once more to claim Constantinople as a grand prize for the Muslims. Encouraged by political unrest and plotting within the Byzantine empire, Sulayman sent a land army swarming towards the city's legendarily massive landward walls, while a rebuilt Muslim fleet tested its luck and skill in the waters one more. Accounts of the second siege of Constantinople describe a scene even more dramatic than the first. On land, famine and disease ripped through the Arab armies. Theophanes claimed 'they ate all of their dead animals, namely horses, asses and camels. It is said that they even cooked in ovens and ate dead men and their own dung which they leavened.'[36] This is likely poetic slander rather than factual reportage. Still, conditions were plainly awful. And while starvation ruled on land, Greek Fire once again lit up the seas. 'Fiery hail fell upon [the Arab ships] and brought the sea-water to a boil, and as the pitch of their keels dissolved, their ships sank in the deep, crews and all,' wrote Theophanes.[37] The Byzantine capital was saved – again.

Once more, the Umayyads had come agonizingly close to wiping out Byzantium; once more they had fallen at the gates of Constantinople. Rather than installing the caliph there, the siege of 717–8 only succeeded in helping a scheming Byzantine general,

Leo the Isaurian, to depose the reigning emperor Theodosius III and claim the throne for himself. The experience put paid forever to Umayyad ambitions in Asia Minor, and in retrospect, many historians have seen the failure of the second siege as a turning point in western history: the moment when the spread of the first Islamic armies towards the Balkans was halted. Afterwards, Constantinople remained in Christian hands until the end of the Middle Ages, and Islam only burst through the old Roman territories into eastern Europe with the Ottoman conquests of the fifteenth and sixteenth centuries.* The counterfactual game that asks 'what if' the Umayyads had taken Byzantium drives towards an alternative reality in which minarets and not church spires dotted the skyline of medieval Europe. The real events of 717–718 are often supposed to have turned the world away from such a fate. Whether they did or not is unknowable – but what is incontestable is that the shape of the Umayyad caliphate, and of the Muslim near east, was determined by the failure of the two sieges of Constantinople in 677–8 and 717–718.

INSTEAD OF EXPANDING THROUGH ASIA MINOR and the Balkans, then, under the Umayyad caliphs of the late seventh and early eighth centuries, Islam branched out east and west. Having seized Persia, Muslim armies eventually made their way into what is now Pakistan, Afghanistan and 'Transoxania' (the Central Asian 'stans' of Uzbekistan, Tajikistan, Turkmenistan and Kyrgyzstan). They also marched through north Africa, eventually overrunning Byzantine Carthage in 698, which struck a death-knell for Byzantine control in the region. Then they pressed on through Algeria towards what is now Morocco – the western coast of the continent. In 711 they crossed the Strait of Gibraltar and began to ride through the Iberian Peninsula. The arrival of Islam in modern Spain and Portugal created the territory known for centuries as al-Andalus.

---

* See chapter 15.

According to al-Tabari, the doomed caliph Uthman had once claimed the only way to take Constantinople was by first taking control of Spain.[38] But it is not very likely that such grand strategic thinking underpinned the Umayyad invasion in 711. It was much more probable that, having torn a path through north Africa, temperate and fertile southern Europe seemed a better prospect for further expansion than the merciless expanse of the Sahara. And no doubt the task seemed straightforward. The old Roman province of Hispania lay in the hands of the Visigoths. And for all their success during the age of barbarian migrations, the Visigoths had not made the leap to become a major regional power. The people of Morocco had been sailing across the straits to pillage Visigoth territory for generations; and now there was every reason to think that the Umayyad war machine, bolstered with Moroccan troops, might follow the same path.

In the event, they did not so much follow the path as race along it at full pelt. Under the energetic leadership of the general Musa ibn Nusayr, the Umayyads' forces ran the Visigoths out of Spain inside three years. One traumatized account preserved by the author of the so-called Mozarabic* Chronicler recalls that Musa 'cast down fine cities with the burning fire, and condemned to crucifixion the senior and powerful of the generations, while butchering the young and infants with daggers.'[39] At the battle of Guadalete in 711, the Visigothic king Roderic was slain and his kingdom lay open to the invaders. 'Even if all limbs were turned into tongue, human nature will never at all be able to tell of the ruins of Spania and indeed such great evils that befell all of it,' the Mozarabic Chronicler wailed.[40]

In 714 the last Visigothic king, Ardo, took power in a pathetic kingdom reduced to a strip of land between Béziers (today in France) and Barcelona. He clung on there for around seven years, and when he died in around 720/1, the Visigoths were done.

---

* The Mozarabs were the Christian people of southern Spain, who adopted many Arabic customs, including speaking Arabic, but did not convert to Islam, choosing instead to pay the *jizyah* and continue to worship God through Christ, albeit with a distinctively Hispanic liturgy, which sometimes drew the disapproval of medieval Roman popes.

Whether this rapid fall of a ruling power that was 300 years old stemmed more from the fragility of their rule or from the sheer irresistibility of the Muslims on the charge is a moot point, and not an easy one to answer given the sketchiness of eighth-century chronicle sources. But they were hardly the only regime to have melted away before Arab swords, and their retreat marked a sea-change in the history of the Iberian peninsula.

By the 720s, then, the Ummayads were in control of the largest conglomeration of territory since the collapse of the greater Roman Empire in the fifth century. They had also set about transforming it. The great levers of change in this respect were language and architecture. And the two most influential figures were the fifth and sixth Umayyad caliphs, Abd al-Malik (685–705) and his son, al-Walid (705–715).

The elder of these, Abd al-Malik, became caliph in the midst of the second *fitna*, when provinces across the Muslim world were in open revolt. His first priority was to restore the unity and stability of Umayyad power across the still-expanding Islamic world. He did so by centralizing and 'imperializing' authority, appointing powerful provincial governors who were closely accountable to his court in Damascus, including the supremely capable al-Hajjaj ibn Yusuf, who was critical to maintaining Umayyad authority in Iraq, and al-Malik's brother Abd al-Aziz, who kept a steady hand on Egyptian affairs from Fustat. But as well as making good personal appointments, al-Malik also took revolutionary measures to press the image and reality of Umayyad power into the daily lives of ordinary people everywhere: not only of the Muslim faithful, but non-Muslims as well.

One of al-Malik's more important reforms was his introduction of an Islamic coinage. When the first Muslims rode out of Arabia, they had taken care not to disrupt the valuable commercial and monetary systems of the lands they came to conquer.[41] But by the 690s things had changed. Al-Malik ordered the mints across his former Byzantine and Persian provinces to strike a series of coins, the design of which trumpeted the nature of the new Umayyad empire. In place of the gold Byzantine *solidus* – which had been familiar currency around the Mediterranean since the age of Constantine the Great – Umayyad-controlled mints now began producing a coin known as a *dinar*. The first of these to be designed bore the image of the caliph standing in quasi-imperial splendour – a sign that al-Malik was trying to out-emperor the emperor in Constantinople. By 697, however, this iconography – which sat ill with Muhammad's pronouncements against graven images – had been abandoned and *dinars* emerged from the mints emblazoned with verses from the Qur'an and other godly phrases stamped in Kufic script, praising the name Allah and celebrating his mercy and compassion.[42]

Coin production has always been a tool of political propaganda as well as commerce, and the Umayyad coin reform was no different. Across the Muslim world, old gold was now recalled to Damascus with menaces, to be turned into *dinars*. These were pure, pious and consistent with the Qur'an's apparent position on numismatics: 'And give full measure when you measure, and weigh with an even balance.'[43] At the same time, although with a little less urgency, silver and copper coins (*dirhams*) were also redesigned, reminted and recirculated. Silver coins were struck all over the Muslim world, while gold was tightly controlled from Damascus. *Dirhams* therefore often matched the weights and shapes of coins current in the regions where they were circulated. But everywhere the fundamental shift in decoration remained the same. Gone were images of old, infidel kings. In their place, pithy Arabic pieties advertising Muhammad's revelation were soon passing every day through the hands of merchants and market-goers from the banks of the river Tagus, in Spain, to the river Indus, in Asia.

This change did not take place in a vacuum. When caliph al-Malik first remade the Islamic coinage, the language that decorated his coins was unfamiliar to most of even the educated people who used them. As we have already seen, the early caliphs left in place the monetary systems of the conquered territories; they also declined to force Islam upon the masses. The Muslims had preferred to tax infidels and to keep their colonists segregated in newly founded garrison towns. The result was that the *umma* was spread widely across the world, but not very deeply. Al-Malik set out to change this. He worked – in time-honoured fashion – through the middle classes.

Around the year 700 al-Malik ordered that public servants across the Umayyad world should use one language only: Arabic. The commonest tongues used by the non-Arabs who made up the vast majority of the caliphate's population were Greek and Persian. Al-Malik made no provision against people speaking them as they pleased – but he decreed that they could no longer do so while working for him. At a stroke, the Christians, Jews and Zoroastrians who had found gainful employment as scribes, middle managers and government bureaucrats were faced with a stark choice. Unless they knew or very quickly learned Arabic, they were out of a job.

This simple administrative change was in fact a moment of juddering cultural importance in the history of the Islamic world – for it ensured that there *would be* an Islamic world in perpetuity, rather than a short-lived federation of former Roman and Persian territories ruled over by a thin monotheistic elite. As we saw in chapter 1, the Roman Empire in its pomp had been bound together over millions of square miles in part because Latin was a common language of cultural discourse as well as base communication. Al-Malik now set Arabic on a similar path. By enforcing its use of a universal tongue across the caliphate he transformed it into a global language of record and enquiry. Arabic became a *lingua franca* every bit as potent as Latin and Greek. As a result it was as useful to scholars as it was to civil servants. During the Middle Ages Arab scholars compiled, translated and preserved hundreds of thousands of texts from across the classical world, and the Arab-speaking Islamic world inherited the Greek and Latin world's position as the west's most advanced intellectual and scientific society. This would not have been possible without al-Malik's decision in the 690s to impose the Arabic language on the Umayyad caliphate's bureaucrats.

Yet that was not all. Arabic was more than a tool of bureaucracy and study. Unlike Latin, for example, Arabic was the language in which God himself had spoken. The Qur'an had been revealed to Muhammad in Arabic; it was preserved in Arabic; the first Muslims were Arabs who were by definition Arabic-speakers; the call to prayer (*adhan*) that had rung out from mosques ever since it was sung from the Ka'ba when Muhammad captured Mecca in 630 was made in lilting, musical Arabic. It was impossible to imagine Islam without the language of its first people, and once that language became mandatory for all who wished to interact with the state, the faith did not follow too far behind. From the early eighth century, Arabization was gradually followed by conversion across the Muslim-held territories – a shift that can still be seen, felt and heard in almost every part of the old medieval caliphate in the twenty-first century.*

IN 705 AL-MALIK DIED AND WAS succeeded by his son al-Walid, who found himself in charge of a treasury filled with new gold *dinars*. His father's centralizing efforts had created a highly efficient financial system to funnel tax revenues and the booty taken during new conquests back to Damascus. True, much of this revenue was required to maintain the large standing armies and navies that pushed the frontiers of the *dar al-Islam* east and west, and to fight Byzantine fire-ships in the stormy waters of the Mediterranean. Yet even after these huge expenses, al-Walid enjoyed a healthy budgetary surplus, and he used it to develop his father's policy of rooting Islam in the fabric of the early medieval world. Al-Malik pointed the way his son would follow when he commissioned the Dome of the Rock in Jerusalem in the 690s, pioneering pseudo-imperial monumental building with a distinctive Islamic flavour. Al-Walid took this idea and ran with it. In doing so, he created some of the most extraordinary buildings conceived in the last two

---

* The notable exception to this is Iran, where Persian proved far harder to eradicate than al-Malik and his Umayyad successors had hoped. Although Iran went through a long process of conversion to Islam during the early Middle Ages, the Iranians stuck steadfastly to the Persian language and to Persian culture, producing a distinctive new form of non-Arab Islam, which heavily influenced the development of Islam in the wider region, including modern Afghanistan, Pakistan, India and Turkey.

thousand years – many of which stand today, not just as historical relics but as living, breathing buildings for Muslim worshippers to commune with God, one another, and their medieval past.

At the heart of this epic project was a triptych of mosques at the three most important cities in the Umayyad world outside Mecca. These were the Great Mosque of Damascus, al-Aqsa Mosque in Jerusalem, and the Prophet's Mosque (*masjid an-nabawi*) in Medina, which was extensively renovated, enlarged and modified to house the graves of Muhammad, and the caliphs Abu Bakr and Umar. These three vast, congregational houses of worship spoke in different ways to critical stages in the Muslims' expansive history, while showcasing the wealth and imperial self-confidence of the Umayyad caliphs. The Great Mosque of Damascus, built in 706, is today the least-altered of the three, and in it visitors can still see how the plan, purpose and unique decorative styles of the Islamic world were developing in the first years of the eighth century. The mosque was placed on a site that had originally been a pagan temple to Hadad and Jupiter, then a Christian church to John the Baptist, which the Umayyads bought and demolished. The mosque that arose on this hallowed spot included the first known concave *mihrab* – a feature in the mosque wall indicating the direction of Mecca, which is a unique and essential part of every mosque in the world today – yet this is set within a building that is decorated with mosaics far more reminiscent of the great churches of Byzantium than later monumental mosques would be. There are no representations of people, but there are many intricate images of houses, palaces, places of worship, trees, rivers and foliage, which suggest earth and paradise all at once, and hint at a style of Islamic art that borrowed heavily from the Christian tradition of the time.[44]

Yet if the Great Mosque of Damascus seems exotic and strange in this respect, it is also the first of many great mosques which have, over the centuries, absorbed local styles and fused them with uniquely Islamic elements: the elaborate mosques of the late-medieval Ottoman empire, which fairly bubble with elaborate domes evoking the basilicas of the Eastern Orthodox Christian

Church; structures like the magnificent Mughal-era Badshahi Mosque in Lahore, Pakistan, fashioned from red sandstone in a seamless blend of Indian and Persian styles; the ultra-modern Istiqlal Mosque in Jakarta (Indonesia), erected in 1987 at the height of the New Formalism movement that produced notable American municipal buildings such as the World Trade Center in New York City, the John F. Kennedy Center for the Performing Arts in Washington D.C. and The Forum in Los Angeles. The architectural confidence to create mosques that spoke to Islam's unique and deliberately exclusionary character while also borrowing liberally from the world around them can be traced directly back to the age of the Umayyads, and particularly to the caliphate of al-Walid.

By the time al-Walid died in 715 the Umayyads stood at the peak of their powers. The conquest of Visigothic Spain was well underway. Great houses of worship had been built. A massive scheme of public works was underway throughout the Islamic state, as the caliph invested in new roads and canals, street-lighting in cities and irrigation ditches in the countryside. Arabic had been instituted as the language of commerce and administration, as well as prayer, and the ground was laid for Islam's extension into the lives of millions of people across the medieval world. The irksome defeat in the first siege of Constantinople lay in the rapidly receding past, while the second siege of 717–718 lay in the unrealized future. This was a mighty set of accomplishments, whose consequences would endure for centuries. But they would not endure long under the Umayyads themselves. For within thirty-five years the dynasty would be destroyed and the limits of expansion reached. It is to the end of the Umayyads that we must now turn, as we bring our story of the Arab Conquests to a close.

The Black Flag Rises

IN 732, EXACTLY 100 YEARS AFTER the Muhammad's death, Umayyad warriors swept over the Pyrenees and raided the lands of the Franks. They destroyed palaces and robbed churches in the duchy of Aquitaine. They crushed a Frankish army in battle by the banks of the river Garonne. They plundered mightily, taking 'male and female slaves, and seven hundred of the best girls, besides eunuchs, horses, medicine, gold, silver and vases.'[45]

The Muslims who charged over the mountains had steeled themselves for a long campaign. Their leader, Abd al-Rahman, had in his sights a grand basilica just outside the city of Tours, some 750km deep into territory ruled over by a Frankish dynasty known as the Merovingians. The basilica was named after the long-dead Christian hero St Martin, whose tomb lay within. During his life in the fourth century St Martin had quit the Roman army to become a 'soldier of Christ', and subsequently performed miracles such as exorcising demons from angry cows and setting fire to the emperor Valentinian's buttocks.[46] Now his cloak was venerated as a holy relic, his shrine was a site of Christian reverence and the basilica was the repository of much moveable plunder.[47]

Yet before Abd al-Rahman reached the doors of the basilica he ran into trouble. It arrived in the form of Charles Martel.

Not quite a king, Martel was nonetheless one of the dominant aristocrats in the Frankish realm. As we shall soon see, he would one day be recognized as the founder of the Carolingian dynasty that produced illustrious rulers including Pippin the Short and Charlemagne. But in 732, when the Umayyads approached, Charles Martel held the prime ministerial title of Mayor of the Palace of Austrasia.* His nickname (*Martellus*) meant 'the hammer'. He was, in the words of one near-contemporary, 'a mighty man of war' who took 'boldness as his counsellor'.[48] On this occasion – a Sunday in October – he had rallied an army to defend Tours and protect the southern lands of the Franks from conquest.

Having learned about the depredations of the Arabs from the duke of Aquitaine, Martel sought out Abd al-Rahman on the road between Tours and Poitiers. After a seven-day period of phoney

---

* Merovingian Francia (the territory that corresponded roughly to Roman Gaul) was divided into three principal territories: Neustria, Austrasia and Burgundy; various other lands were linked to the kingdom, including the duchy of Aquitaine. For more on this see chapter 5.

war he brought the Muslims to battle. When the fighting broke out Martel lined up his men, ordered them on foot in a shield-wall as immobile and rugged as a glacier and marshalled them so that 'with great blows of their swords they hewed down the Arabs. Drawn up in a band around their chief, the people of the Austrasians carried all before them.'[49] Chroniclers looking back on Charles Martel's victory (exhibiting the usual combination of wishful thinking, poetic exaggeration and bravado that characterized medieval estimations of armies and massacres) credited the mayor with slaying between 300,000 and 375,000 Muslim warriors, among them Abd al-Rahman himself. Frankish losses were calculated at just 1,500 men.

The battle of Tours (also known as the battle of Poitiers) was well known to contemporaries and has been celebrated by western writers for more than one thousand years. Its salient details and exemplary moral lesson were fixed within no more than three years of its conclusion by writers including the Venerable Bede, who wrote in his *Ecclesiastical History of the English People* (completed at some time before Bede's death at Jarrow in England in May 735) that 'a dreadful plague of Saracens ravaged France with miserable slaughter, but they not long after in that country received the punishment due to their wickedness'.[50] Many others followed Bede's example, both in the Middle Ages and the present day. To the chronicler of St-Denis – writing more than six hundred years later during the apogee of French sacral kingship in the thirteenth century – Charles Martel saved 'the Church of St Martin, the city and the whole country' from 'the enemies of Christian faith'. To Edward Gibbon, writing his *Decline and Fall of the Roman Empire* between 1776 and 1789, the defeat of Abd al-Rahman saved all of Europe from Islamification and prevented an alternative history from unfolding: one in which Arab conquests reached Poland and the Highlands of Scotland; where 'the interpretation of the Koran would now be taught in the schools of Oxford, and her pulpits might demonstrate to a circumcised people the sanctity and truth of the revelation of Mahomet [sic]'.[51] Two hundred years later, during the 1970s, the

Charles Martel Group formed in France as a right-wing terrorist organization devoted to opposing Algerian migration to France through a series of bombings. In twenty-first century America an organization called the Charles Martel Society organizes white nationalists and publishes an overtly racist journal giving a platform for pseudo-scholarly articles on subjects including eugenics and racial segregation.[52] So even today, Martel's victory is regarded as a historical turning point: a battle that changed the world; the moment at which the seemingly unstoppable sweep of Arab conquests in the century following Muhammad's death was checked.

Yet of course, as we have already seen, this is far too simple a reading of history. For one thing, it is not totally clear that Abd al-Rahman wished to conquer the kingdom of the Franks at all: the most useful Mediterranean ports between the Pyrenees and the Rhône were already in Muslim hands by the 730s, and had been pacified with a judicious use of exemplary violence (bishops were occasionally burned alive in their churches, while rumours had spread up from Visigothic Spain telling of Berber troops boiling and eating obstinate Christians) alongside the routine application of the *jizyah*. Tours and the surrounding areas were interesting fields of plunder, but it is no certain thing that in the 730s they were being lined up for full Muslim conquest.

Moreover, the battle of Tours alone was nothing when placed alongside two earlier defeats which stand as much more convincing examples of historical turning points for the caliphate's expansion. The first was the failed 717–718 siege of Constantinople, described above. The second is the battle of Aksu, also in 717, in which an Arab-led army, bolstered by troops of Turkic and Tibetan origin, was wiped out by the Tang Chinese in the Xinjiang region of modern China. This defeat heralded a gradual winding-down of the Muslim charge eastwards; by the 750s the borders of the Islamic world and Tang China had been settled in Central Asia, where the two powers shared control of the Silk Road trading routes. The middle decades of the eighth century marked the point when the Islamic conquests hit their geopolitical limits, not only in Europe but across the world. Charles Martel's victory in 732 was only one small part of that much larger process.

IN FACT, THE MOST SIGNIFICANT INCIDENT which fixed western Europe's medieval future, and the place of Islam within it, occurred between June 747 and August 750, when the Umayyad dynasty was overthrown in Damascus. The causes and course of this revolution were complex, but in short, various dissident groups within the caliphate – including Shiites, and non-Arab Muslim converts (known as *mawali*) who were excluded from many of the legal privileges of the *umma* – banded together under the leadership of a mysterious and secretive character from eastern Persia known as Abu Muslim al-Khorasani. Beginning with a local rebellion in the eastern city of Merv, they spread the spirit of full revolution throughout the caliphate, igniting a third *fitna* which ended with military defeat for the caliph Marwan II at the battle of Zab (Iraq) in January 750. Three months later Damascus fell, and after this the surviving members of the dynasty were hunted and assassinated, one by one. Marwan was murdered after he fled to Egypt, and replaced by a Jordanian Arab called Abu al-Abbas al-Saffah – whose sobriquet translates to English as 'blood-spiller'. Al-Saffah was thus the founder of a new dynasty named the Abbasids, who claimed descent from Muhammad's uncle al-Abbas and identified themselves with a plain black flag.*

The Abbasids made sweeping changes to the Islamic empire they had wrested from the Ummayads. They moved the capital 800km east from Damascus to a new city in Iraq called Baghdad, and devolved sweeping political and legal powers to local rulers throughout the caliphate known as 'emirs'. The Abbasids also worked hard to integrate non-Arab Muslims into the *umma* on roughly equal terms. As a result theirs was a time of political

---

* This plain black flag has sinister overtones today, for it was imitated by the short-lived 'caliphate' of Abu Bakr al-Baghdadi, the leader of the Islamic State (ISIS, ISIL or Daesh), the fundamentalist Islamist group which emerged from al-Qaeda and brutally controlled large parts of Syria and Iraq between 2013 and 2019.

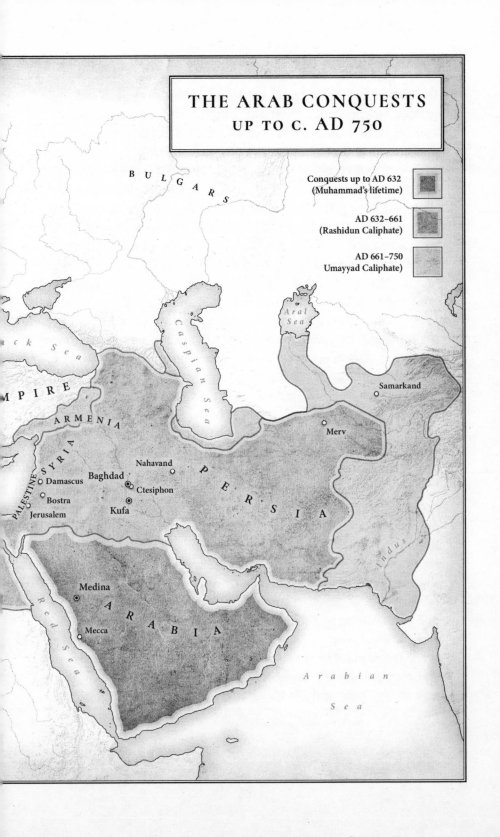

THE ARAB CONQUESTS
UP TO C. AD 750

Conquests up to AD 632
(Muhammad's lifetime)

AD 632–661
(Rashidun Caliphate)

AD 661–750
Umayyad Caliphate)

BULGARS

Aral
Sea

Caspian Sea

ck Sea

MPIRE

ARMENIA

SYRIA

Samarkand

Merv

Nahavand

Damascus

Baghdad

Ctesiphon

PERSIA

PALESTINE

Bostra

Jerusalem

Kufa

Indus

Medina

ARABIA

Red Sea

Mecca

Arabian

Sea

fracture within the Islamic world, when emirs gained steadily greater independence from the caliphs, and schismatic Sunni and Shia blocs emerged, as well as rival dynasties such as the Fatimids in Egypt and Almoravids and Almohads in modern Morocco. Never again would caliphs wield as much political and spiritual power over such a massive swathe of territory as they had during the heyday of the Rightly Guided caliphs and the Umayyads. Nevertheless, the Abbasid age (which lasted until 1258, when the caliphate was destroyed by the Mongols*) would come to be known as the Golden Age of Islam, during which art, architecture, poetry, philosophy, medicine and scientific enquiry flourished. In the eighth century the Abbasids stole the secrets of paper-manufacturing technology from the Tang Chinese, and in the thirteenth they learned the secrets of making gunpowder from the Song. They assembled massive libraries such as the House of Wisdom in Baghdad, where millions of pages of books were translated, copied and studied for the benefit of society at large. Many of the late-medieval advances of the European Renaissance would have been quite impossible without the preservation of classical knowledge and technology from across the world in Islamic institutions like the House of Wisdom.

Yet the Abbasid age was also one in which the Muslim world's centre of gravity shifted, like its capital, to the east. The caliphs now sat geographically and culturally removed from the old Roman territories that – along with Arabia – had formed the core of the first two caliphates. Developments in the *dar al-Islam* therefore affected the western world at one or more steps of remove. One of the great and lasting stories of the Middle Ages is one of increasing ignorance and hostility between the Islamic east and Christian west – a distinction that would have made very little sense at this point in our story, when the Umayyads were invested and engaged directly in affairs of the western Mediterranean as well as the near and Middle East. This supposed civilizational divide is today a favourite trope of the far right and extremists of

* See chapter 9.

various persuasions throughout the world – it owes at least part of its genesis to events that were rooted in the eighth century AD.

Having said all this, however, we should also remember that although the Umayyad caliphate was overthrown in 750, the Umayyads themselves lived on, and their legacy can be felt powerfully in one particular region of the west today: in the southern halves of Spain and Portugal, which had been conquered so efficiently during al-Walid's reign in 711–714. Amid the tumult of the Abbasid revolution, one of the old caliph al-Malik's grandchildren ran away from Damascus, hotly pursued by would-be assassins intent on adding him to the list of slaughtered Umayyads. Having evaded them he wandered in exile for six years, making a long clandestine journey through north Africa until he arrived in southern Spain, where he proclaimed himself as caliph in his own right, and established an independent capital in the sweltering city of Cordoba – in the hottest part of Spain, where temperatures rival the roiling heat of Arabia. Over the following two decades he steadily brought the Muslim territories in Iberia in what became known as the Emirate of Cordoba.

Like Baghdad, and the city of Kairouan in the province of Ifriqiya (modern Tunisia), which remained part of the Abbasid caliphate until the early tenth century, Cordoba gained immense renown in the Middle Ages as a city of learning and extraordinarily rich culture. Its population bloomed to around four hundred thousand inhabitants – a scale that put Cordoba comfortably in the league of Constantinople or even ancient Rome. The religious life of the city pulsed around the Great Mosque of Cordoba.* Built on a scale to rival the jewel of the Ummayad empire in Damascus, it absorbed Roman stonework and Moorish decorative influences, and was paid for with the rich plunder taken from the vanquishing of the Visigoths and raids into neighbouring Frankish lands.

For a century between around AD 900 and AD 1000, the city of Cordoba and the rump Umayyad emirate it controlled had a

---

* Now a Catholic cathedral, although in the twenty-first century Spanish Muslims have lobbied unsuccessfully for the right to pray there.

strong claim to be the most advanced and sophisticated state in western Europe, and the fabulous legacy of that time is still tangibly embedded in southern Spanish and Portuguese culture. The very names of the region still bear clear Arab influence: Lisbon (*al-Usbuna*), Gibraltar (*Jabal Tariq*), Malaga (*Malaqa*), Ibiza (*Yabisa*), Alicante (*al-Laqant*) all carry a heavy flavour of Arabic in their names, as do many other well-known Iberian towns, cities and tourist destinations. The glorious palace of Alhambra in Granada is the best known, but the Alcazar in Seville – still a working Spanish royal palace – was built on the foundations of a late medieval Muslim ruler's fortress. The Arab Baths in Jaén, meanwhile, hint at a fragrant and sophisticated civic culture in Islamic Spain which would have comfortably stood comparison with old Roman Hispania.

There was a Muslim presence in Spain throughout the Middle Ages, and although Islamic rule was steadily denuded from the eleventh century onwards by the western crusades known as the *Reconquista*, it was not until January 1492 that the last Muslim emir was forced off the mainland, to live out a life of exile in Morocco.* This amounted to more than seven centuries in which the Iberian peninsula was at least in part connected formally to the *dar al-Islam*, and that long association has been a live and sometimes deadly part of Spain's national and cultural history in the modern age. It is not universally a cause for celebration: in what is today a strongly Catholic country, there are plenty who are uncomfortable with Spain's Islamic heritage.

By no means were all of medieval Spain's Muslim rulers enlightened intellectuals devoted to the twin causes of building libraries and public baths: the Berber dynasties known as the Almoravids and Almohads, who controlled al-Andalus from the eleventh to the thirteenth centuries, were austere zealots responsible for much violent oppression and persecution of non-Muslims. A degree of popular prejudice and suspicion of the *moro* – the Moor, or Spanish Muslim, whose true loyalties supposedly

* See chapter 15.

lie in north Africa – is a continuing feature of Spain's political discourse. Half-memories of the medieval past have often been blended with less faraway recollections of the course of the twentieth-century Spanish Civil War, which began in Morocco and involved tens of thousands of Muslim troops from north Africa, fighting on the side of the Nationalists under General Francisco Franco. This all amounts to a complicated, delicate situation. History continues to swirl around us, shaping attitudes, belief, prejudices and worldviews. So it is that the word of God revealed in a cave in the Hijaz in the seventh century still affects the everyday lives of men and women living in the era of the smartphone and self-driving car.

Part II

Dominion

C. AD 750 – AD 1215

5

FRANKS

'Oh the iron! Woe for the iron!'

CRY OF DESPAIR AMONG THE LOMBARDS,
AT THE APPEARANCE OF THE FRANKISH ARMY

In the second half of the year 751* Childeric III had an expensive haircut. For eleven years he had been king of the Franks, the people who ruled the old Roman provinces of Gaul after the barbarian migrations brought down the western empire. Although Childeric had never wielded practical power – one dismissive chronicler thought his sole function was 'to sit back on his throne… satisfied with the name of king and the appearance of ruling' – he had nevertheless been the man in possession of majesty, which he symbolized by growing his hair and beard as long as he could, in the time-honoured fashion of his royal dynasty, the Merovingians.[1] This preference for tousled locks had earned the Merovingians the name *reges criniti* ('long-haired kings'), which was more than just a trademark or an idle nickname. Hair was an essential symbol of their power. Like Samson in the Old Testament, if a Merovingian was given a crew-cut he was deemed to be shorn of all power. So in 751 Childeric was not merely being restyled. He was being ceremonially deposed. His kingdom was in the throes of a revolution, and this was its symbolic climax. The old king was tonsured and packed off to live out his life under house arrest in

---

* Or perhaps the early spring of 752. For a succinct explanation of the problem with dating this event, see Costambys, Marios, Innes, Matthew and MacLean, Simon, *The Carolingian World* (Cambridge: 2011), pp. 31–4.

a monastery at Saint-Omer, not far from the sea in the far north of the Frankish kingdom. He was replaced by the man who had ordered his disgrace: a warrior politician named Pippin the Short.

According to one chronicler, Pippin was 'chosen king by all the Franks, consecrated by the bishops and received the homage of the great men.'[2] This writer recorded his judgement in the Royal Frankish annals, which were sponsored by Pippin and his descendants and therefore painted them in the softest and most flattering light. Be that as it may, the year 751 still marked a formative time in European history, as Francia entered the Carolingian age. The Carolingians were named in honour of their patriarch, Pippin's father Charles Martel (*Carolus Martellus*): the man who had smashed the Umayyads at the battle of Tours. They produced more than one famous Charles, including Charles the Bald, Charles the Fat and Charles the Simple. But the most illustrious of all was Charlemagne (*Carolus Magnus*). During a reign that spanned forty years Charlemagne united the lands we now know as France, Germany, northern Italy, Belgium, Luxembourg and the Netherlands into a European superstate under his own command. In AD 800 this European union was granted empire status by the pope, and its Francified, sanctified, militant nature was personified by Charlemagne himself, who would be remembered as a figure as heroic and grand as the legendary British king, Arthur.[3] Charlemagne was one of the most powerful and influential rulers in the whole of the Middle Ages. And he left a legacy to Europe that has been strongly felt – and heard – ever since.[4] His Latin name – *Carolus* – has passed into many modern European languages such as Polish (*król*), Bulgarian (*kral*), Czech (*král*) and Hungarian (*király*) as the literal meaning for 'king'.[5] And his political achievement has been just as long-lasting. Uniting the lands on either side of the Rhine into a superstate centred on modern France and Germany took monumental effort. Keeping them together proved beyond the capabilities of most of Charlemagne's successors. It has remained beyond the talent of most statesmen ever since.*

---

* With the possible exception, at the time of writing at least, of the European Union.

Yet mighty as Charlemagne was, and as far as his imperium extended, the Carolingian Franks were not the only great power to come to prominence in this period. From the eighth century onwards, vigorous bands of pagan explorers, traders and killers from Scandinavia were also on the march. Today we know these people collectively as the Vikings. Inevitably, the Franks and Vikings clashed as much as they co-operated while they jockeyed for resources and power within the same regions of northern and western Europe. And in the end, in a process resembling nuclear fusion, the white heat of their collisions produced a third people, who would have their own important part to play in medieval history. They were the Normans, who will loom large as the second part of this book unfolds.

Merovingians and Carolingians

WHEN WE FIRST MET THE FRANKS, in chapter 2, they were a coalition of at least half a dozen Germanic war-bands, who had charged across the Rhine in the age of the great migrations, blazed their way around Roman Gaul and then coalesced into a single group who settled and gradually wrested for themselves what little remained of the Roman state. Roman writers of the third century AD therefore viewed the Franks as common-or-garden peripatetic barbarians. However, in the intervening centuries the Franks had come up in the world, and as they did so, their bards and scribes concocted a grand origin myth. The way the Franks told it, they had settled in Europe during the bronze age; their ancestors were a band of warriors who had left the Trojan War and wandered west.[6] Whatever the case, from 460 they were a force to be reckoned with. Having settled west of the Rhine, they steadily imposed themselves on their neighbours – most notably the Visigoths and Burgundians – until by the seventh century they occupied all the territory of modern France, save the Breton peninsula and the coastal littoral between Arles and Perpignan (today a balmy seaside strip of Languedoc-Roussillon.) The Franks also took tribute from Germanic tribes east of the Rhine as far as

Bavaria, Thuringia and parts of Saxony. Much of this expansion took place in the two and a half centuries during which the Franks were ruled by the long-haired Merovingian dynasty.*

The first Merovingian king about whom we know very much at all was another Childeric – the first. This Childeric used his military talents to gather a large following in the lands north of the Loire during the mid-400s. He fought against Visigoths and Saxons, and died in 481, when he was buried in Tournai along with his fabulous collection of jewellery. When Childeric's tomb was opened in the seventeenth century† it was found to contain a cache of gold and silver coins, a gloriously decorated sword with a gold hilt, scores of gold trinkets, hundreds of beautiful ornamental gold bees, a ceremonial signet ring inscribed with the legend CHILIRICI REGIS, a spear, throwing axe, the remnants of a shield and at least two human skeletons. It lay at the centre of a large Frankish cemetery full of warriors, women and expensive war-horses, possibly sacrificed in elite burial ceremonies.[7] Together all these resting places had once formed a literally monumental graveyard, built around a royal tumulus (burial mound) visible for miles around. Childeric I's grave tells us the Franks were more than wandering warlords. As early as the late fifth century their rulers had all the appurtenances of kingship, and saw themselves as commanders of lands stretching many days' ride in all directions.

The Merovingians were at the peak of their powers in the fifth and sixth centuries. After Childeric I came a mighty king called Clovis. Clovis brought together the Frankish tribes into a coherent political and cultural unit. His wife, a Burgundian princess called Clothilde‡, converted him from paganism to Catholicism. In 486

---

* The Merovingians had a fanciful origin story of their own: they claimed to have descended from a queen who was raped by a 'Quinotaur' – a fantastical monster which resembled a giant walrus. The chronicler Fredegar described it as a 'beast of Neptune'.

† Childeric I's tomb was uncovered when it was stumbled upon by a deaf-mute stonemason working on a building site near a medieval church. Sadly, his glorious grave-goods are now mostly lost – during the nineteenth century the hoard was stolen in Paris and the bulk of the gold was melted down.

‡ Now St Clothilde, patron saint of brides and adopted children. Clothilde was the subject of a tenth-century hagiography by the Benedictine Abbot Adso of Montier-en-Der, an author better known for his authoritative work on the nature of the Antichrist.

he ended lingering Roman interests in the old province at the battle of Soissons. In 507 he crushed the Visigoths of Iberia in the battle of Vouillé, ending their influence in the region of south-western Gaul known as Aquitaine. As a result, Clovis bequeathed to all subsequent Frankish rulers a sense of their own entitlement to rule everywhere between the Low Countries and the Pyrenees. He also authorized the Salic Law (or Laws of the Salian Franks) – a legal text issued between 507 and 511. Salic Law would be a core component of Frankish law throughout the early Middle Ages, and was still cited in royal succession disputes 800 years later, in the fourteenth century.[8] Clovis' reign marked the true beginning of Frankish collective identity – which later became the sense of French nationhood. He is often described as the first real Frenchman.

Yet after Clovis, the story of the Merovingian Franks was one of grandeur increasing in inverse proportion to political power. When Clovis died in 511, he divided royal rule in Francia between four of his sons. This division, while intended to provide strong leadership in each of the major constituent parts of the Frankish realm, more often contributed to its disunity. As a result, while the Merovingian dynasty wore the crown – or more accurately, the crowns – of the Franks for two and half centuries, few of Clovis' descendants matched his extraordinary achievements. Indeed, from the later seventh century they came to be defined by their political impotence. The feeble later Merovingians were known derisively as *rois fainéants* (do-nothing kings). In each of the main royal divisions of Frankish lands (Austrasia, Neustria, Aquitaine, Provence and Burgundy), power was gradually devolved to officials known as mayors of the palace (*maior palatii*). These mayors led armies and controlled military policy and strategy; they resolved disputes and conducted foreign diplomacy. They were a cross between magnates and prime ministers, in whose hands lay all the sweeping political authority that had leeched to them over the generations from their kings. Meanwhile, the kings wore hollow crowns. According to the chronicler Einhard, a typical *roi fainéant* 'listened to ambassadors, wherever they came from, and when they departed he gave replies which he had been taught or ordered to say. Apart from the empty name of king and a small stipend... he owned nothing else of his own but one estate, and that with a small income... When he needed to travel he went in a cart pulled by yoked oxen and was led by a cowherd in the country manner.'[9]

In the first half of the eighth century Charles Martel took the office of a Frankish mayor and upgraded it into fully fledged and publicly acknowledged kingship. During Martel's long life he gained political control in both Neustria and Austrasia, then brought all the other regions of Francia under his sole control as 'Duke and Prince of the Franks'. The chronicler Einhard wrote admiringly of Martel's achievements: he 'brilliantly discharged [his] civil office... overthrew the tyrants who claimed rule over all of Francia and... completely defeated the Saracens [i.e. the Umayyads]'.[10] By contrast, the Merovingian from whom Martel theoretically derived his power, Theuderic IV, was the very definition of a *roi fainéant*. Martel ensured he spent his entire sixteen-year reign under house arrest in monasteries. In 737 this lame-duck monarch died. Martel did not bother to replace him, preferring to exercise quasi-royal power in his own right. So for several years the Franks were technically kingless. This was not quite the end of the Merovingians, but it was a major acceleration of their decline. In 743, when Charles Martel was dead and his sons and relatives were squabbling over his legacy and their inheritances, the unfortunate Childeric III was installed as Theuderic's successor. But as we have seen, Childeric III turned out to be the last of the Merovingians. In 751 his hair was cut off on the orders of Martel's son Pippin the Short.

And with that, the dynasty fell.

MAKING THE STEP UP FROM BEING a mayor of the palace to a king was not totally easy for Pippin the Short. His problems were twofold. In the first place, his father had instructed him to share power over the Frankish lands with his younger brother Carloman. This issue was largely resolved in 747 when Carloman retired from politics and went to live in the famous Benedictine monastery at Monte Cassino, halfway between Rome and Naples. However, it still left another problem. In removing Childeric, Pippin had meddled with the fabric of the universe. Useless as the Merovingians had been, their kingship had lasted for centuries and carried with it the implied approval of the divine. It was a little unseemly to simply shove them aside. Pippin needed to find a way to justify his own regime in the eyes of man – and God.

For a solution he looked to the popes in Rome. Before Pippin moved against Childeric, he wrote to Pope Zachary (r. 741–752), asking him to back his coup. Pippin asked Zachary 'whether it was good that at that time there were kings in Francia who had no royal power.' It was rather a leading question, and Pippin had a strong idea of what the pope would say. Zachary was worried about the power of the Lombards, whose territorial ambitions in Italy were a threat to the papacy and their usual secular defenders: the Byzantine Exarchs of Ravenna. Zachary needed friends he could call upon if the Lombards moved against him. Pippin was well placed to be such a friend. So Zachary was inclined to give helpful answers to innocent questions about the Frankish crown. He wrote to Pippin to say it would be far better to have an active than an inactive ruler. And 'by means of his apostolic authority, so that order might not be cast into confusion, he decreed that Pippin should be made king.'[11]

The ball was now set rolling. With the theoretical backing of the pope, Pippin decided his coronation as Childeric's replacement should not be a matter of mere political acclamation, but should have an explicitly theological flavor. As a child Pippin had been educated by monks at the abbey of St-Denis in Paris, where he had been imbued with an acute sense of Biblical history. So in 751, when Pippin was crowned as the new king of the Franks by the papal legate Boniface, archbishop of Metz, he drew on the examples of Old Testament kings. Boniface anointed him with holy oil – slathered on his head, shoulders and arms – before he was raised to his throne.

This was no ordinary coronation. Part baptism, part priestly ordination, it was a piece of sublime public theatre. It advertised the support of the Church, and not merely the Frankish aristocracy, for Pippin's elevation. And it would have long-lasting consequences. From this point onwards Frankish kings would only be considered 'made' once they had been anointed by a bishop or archbishop's hands. Like Roman emperors in the Christian age and the first Islamic caliphs, Frankish kings now claimed there was a sacral character to their rule. The stage was set for kings to begin to regard themselves as in direct contact with God: approved and protected by the Almighty and entitled to think of themselves as His deputies on earth. And at the same time, the Church had been granted the right to judge the performance of French kings. The implications of this new pact would be felt long into – and indeed after – the Middle Ages.[12]

A single sacred anointing might have been enough for many rulers. But Pippin had a taste for theatre and a nose for holy oil. So three years after the ceremony at Soissons, he went even further. By this time Pope Zachary was dead, but his replacement, Stephen II, was similarly pliable. Over the winter of 753–4 the new pope traversed the Alps, and at Epiphany (6 January) he appeared in solemn splendour at the Frankish palace at Ponthion, to ask for military assistance: 'so that he might thereby be freed from [Lombard] oppressions and their double-dealing', as one chronicler put it.[13] In keeping with papal dignity, Stephen arrived trailing priests by the dozen, all chanting and singing hymns. Pippin met them solemnly. 'The bountiful man [i.e. the pope] with all his companions rendered in a loud voice glory and unceasing praise to Almighty God,' wrote a papal chronicler. 'And with hymns and spiritual chants they all set out with the king towards the palace together.'[14]

After this melodramatic meeting, a series of equally tightly choreographed ceremonies followed. In each, pope and king took turns in throwing themselves on the ground before one another and groveling in the dust. In the background their ambassadors horse-traded. And after a fashion another broad-ranging pact between Roman popes and Frankish kings was thrashed out. The pope would turn to the Franks as his secular defenders and throw his legitimizing influence behind the new Carolingian monarchy – if in return Pippin would incur vast costs and take considerable military risk by riding south over the Alps to deliver the papacy from its enemies. It was a high-stakes deal on both sides. But in retrospect it has come to represent a moment of seminal importance in western history: the moment at which the bishops of Rome no longer looked east to Constantinople for support, but to the barbarian-descended peoples of the west.[15]

It was also the first time that Pippin's son Charles – the future Charlemagne – met a pope. Young Charles was only around six years old in 754, but he was placed at the heart of the papal and royal pageantry. First he was sent out into the freezing winter at the head of a diplomatic escort to accompany Pope Stephen on the last 100 miles of his journey to the royal palace in early January. Then, a little over six months later, on 28 July 754, he joined his father as the pope capped his visit with yet another anointing and coronation, at Saint-Denis. A third ceremony might have felt a little like overkill, except that this time it was not only Pippin who was anointed and blessed by the pope, but also Charlemagne, his brother Carloman* and their mother Bertrada. This was more than the coronation of a king. It was the sacred affirmation of the whole Carolingian dynasty. Between them, these first two generations of Carolingians would redraw the map of western Europe.

'Father of Europe'

PIPPIN RULED FOR SEVENTEEN YEARS AFTER his second coronation by the pope. During that time, he steadily expanded the Carolingian territories, and he executed his pact with the pope diligently. Twice in the years immediately following Pope Stephen's visit the Frankish king charged into Italy, and on both occasions he chastised the Lombards and their king, Aistulf, very severely.

---

* Not to be confused with Pippin's brother Carloman, aforementioned.

'Far and wide in all directions he ravaged and burnt the lands of Italy until he had devastated all that region, pulled down all the Lombard strongholds and captured and taken in charge a great treasure of gold and silver as well as a mass of equipment and all their tents,' wrote the chronicler Fredegar.[16]

Faced with these onslaughts, the Lombards backed down. Aistulf was forced to give up lands he had conquered, and pay a heavy annual subsidy to the Carolingian king. Pippin revelled in his triumph, and he granted lands he seized from the Lombards to the papacy, for popes to rule as earthly lords. This became known as the so-called 'Donation of Pippin', the basis for the existence of the 'Papal States', a region of Italy that survived until the nineteenth century. (Today the pope only rules the tiny sovereign state of Vatican City, in Rome.) Aistulf, humiliated, did not live very long afterwards. In 756 he went out hunting, crashed his horse into a tree and was killed. Pippin, meanwhile, turned his attention back to Francia.

Outside Lombardy, the two areas that Pippin had deemed ripest targets for his ambitions were Aquitaine and Saxony. In the case of the former, Pippin was troubled by a truculent duke by the name of Waifer, against whom he fought for nearly fifteen years. Aquitaine was not subject to the Frankish kings' oversight, but Pippin felt it should be, and in pursuit of that goal he launched a series of campaigns against Waifer, consisting chiefly of arson, siege, punitive robbery, and pitched combat. This was warfare by attrition, and Pippin only triumphed in 766 when the waves of brutality he had sent crashing over Aquitaine had ensured that virtually no peasant was willing to risk his or her life working for Waifar. In addition to this, most of the duke's family had been captured and killed. In 768 Waifar himself was murdered, by assassins who may well have been on Pippin's payroll.[17] The last duke of Aquitaine who could credibly claim to be independent of any royal ruler was dead.

In Saxony, things were different. Saxony presented specific military challenges to invading armies: marshy, roadless terrain made systematic conquest difficult to contemplate, while a scattered tribal society meant that there was no controlling duke like Waifar who could simply be killed and replaced. So Pippin took another approach. He did not try to conquer Saxony, but treated it as a source of handy plunder for his followers. Warfare in the early Carolingian age was still rooted in warlord ways. It revolved around annual campaigning in frontier zones, and relied on a ready stream of supporters willing to bear arms in the hope of winning gold, silver, goods and slaves. Pippin embraced this, and season after season sent Frankish troops to plunder Saxony. This did not push the frontiers of his Carolingian kingdom very deep into the Saxon wilds, but Pippin certainly used their inhabitants and their wealth for his own ends. And when he died in 768, after a short illness that killed him in his mid-fifties, he left a war machine well tuned for deployment across all terrains, as well as political borders and alliances that extended hundreds and even thousands of miles in every direction. His son Charlemagne took this legacy and ran with it.

Charlemagne was described by the chronicler Einhard as being large and strong; when his grave was exhumed in the nineteenth century he was measured at a little over 6'3" – a prodigious height for his times. 'The top of his head was round, his eyes large and lively, his nose was a little larger than average, he had fine white hair and a cheerful and attractive face,' Einhard wrote. He was a strong swimmer and liked keeping clean, doing much of his business while in the bath. When clothed he tended to wear 'a linen shirt and linen underwear, a tunic fringed with silk and stockings… and he covered his shoulders and chest in winter with a jacket made of otter-skin or ermine and a blue cloak, and he was always armed with his sword, which had a gold or silver hilt and belt.' Only on feast days or visits to see the pope in Rome would he wear gold robes or jewels; 'on other days his costume was little different from that of the common people.' He was ostentatiously pious, a keen reader who could also write to a basic standard, a light sleeper and a healthy eater, although never a drunk. He was, then, in Einhard's sympathetic eyes at least, the very image of a mighty king.[18] And on his accession in 768 he could not have been given a more promising inheritance – with one exception.

That exception was his brother, Carloman. In keeping with the old Merovingian customs, Pippin had declined to choose a single king from between his sons. Instead he insisted that Charlemagne and Carloman succeed him as joint rulers. This arrangement, predictably, did not survive long. Nor did Carloman. In 771 he died, from a suspiciously convenient nosebleed. Charlemagne was free to govern alone and as he pleased. He was inconvenienced by the survival of his brother's sons, but for only a few years. Perhaps fearing nosebleeds of their own, they took refuge from their uncle in Lombardy, with a new Lombard king, Desiderius, who planned to obtain papal support to install them as alternative Frankish rulers whom he might be able to control, or at least defy. This was very naïve. Far from worrying, Charlemagne went out and finished the job his father had begun. In 773 and 774 he entered Italy and crushed the Lombards out of existence. The memorably named chronicler Notker the Stammerer composed a vignette describing Charlemagne at the head of his army:

> Then could be seen the iron Charles, helmeted with an iron helmet, his hands clad in iron gauntlets, his iron breast and Platonic shoulders protected with an iron breastplate: an iron spear was raised on high in his left hand; his right always rested on his unconquered sword... All who went before him, all who marched on his side, all who followed after him and the whole equipment of the army imitated him as closely as possible. The fields and open places were filled with iron; the rays of the sun were thrown back by the gleam of iron... the horror of the dungeon seemed less than the bright gleam of iron. 'Oh the iron! Woe for the iron!' was the confused cry that rose from the citizens...[19]

By 776 Desiderius had been captured and imprisoned, and Carloman's sons had disappeared: woe for the iron indeed. To make his victory absolute, Charlemagne declared himself the new ruler of Lombardy. He replaced the Lombard dukes, to whom day-to-day governance was devolved, with Frankish counts.[20] This was an extraordinary power grab. In two centuries no western king had seized another king's throne by force.[21] But Charlemagne's desire for predominance over as much of the west as possible was never a secret, and he liked a good coronation just as much as his father Pippin had. At the end of his Lombard wars he had himself crowned with the Lombards' famous Iron Crown. This stunning piece of regalia, layered with gold and studded with garnets, sapphires and amethysts, was even then at least 250 years old. Its name referred to the fact that it was also set with a thin ferrous band supposedly hammered out of one of the nails used to crucify Jesus.* The crown's provenance allegedly went back to the days of Constantine the Great, whose mother, Helena, was said to have commissioned it. So all in all, it was a wonderful prize – a piece of booty that bolstered Charlemagne's wealth, his pious reputation and the extent of his power. And it was not the end of his ambition.

Over the course of the next two decades Charlemagne took aim at the pagan tribes of Saxony, whom he set out not simply to rob, as his father had done, but to conquer and convert. Between 772 and 804 he fought a long series of wars against them, which cost a lot and shed much blood. But the wars ended with the near-total subjection of the pagan Saxon tribes, who found their lands invaded and colonized, bishoprics established and abbeys founded where the word of Christ had hitherto gone unheard.

This was a massive military undertaking, not least because during the same period Charlemagne also tussled with independent-minded lords in Bavaria, with the Muslim-ruled Basque people of north-east Spain, and with Avars, Slavs and Croats in eastern Europe. Year after year he marshalled Frankish armies and drove them to the ever-expanding frontiers. Year after year they returned home rich with the spoils of battle. And he seldom had trouble recruiting followers. Charlemagne was personally charismatic and a superb strategist. He picked his targets carefully. The Saxons were

---

* The Iron Crown is today kept in the Basilica of Saint John the Baptist in Monza. It was restored many times during the Middle Ages, including by Charlemagne's own craftsmen. When it was scientifically examined in the 1990s, its 'iron' band that was supposedly a relic of the Crucifixion was found in fact to be a thin layer of sliver.

attacked because they were pagans. The Avars, steppe nomads not dissimilar to the Huns, were attacked because they were rich. And when Charlemagne took on the Muslim rulers of Hispania, from 795, he posed as the builder of a bulwark against Islam's supposed designs north of al-Andalus, by creating a 'Spanish March' across the Pyrenees.*

This is not to say that Charlemagne won every battle that he fought. Yet even his defeats somehow turned out to be strange victories. In 778, Charlemagne was leading his army back into Francia after a sojourn in Iberia, where they had swept through Barcelona and Girona and conducted a long siege of Zaragoza. As they traversed the Roncesvaux (Roncesvalles) pass in the Pyrenees, Charlemagne's host was ambushed by enemies who had been silently stalking them. The Franks were surprised and outflanked. Their baggage train was captured. Their rearguard was surrounded, cut off and – after a long fight – slaughtered. Einhard wrote that 'the dead could not be avenged' because the attackers fled so fast into the night.[22] This should have been remembered as a humiliation. Yet it was not. For among the dead of Charlemagne's army was an officer known as Roland.

Although Roland scarcely merited a mention in the chronicle accounts of the battle, during the Middle Ages he would gain a form of meme status. His name became the byword for and archetype of the courageous Christian knight who died heroically for his lord and faith, fighting in a losing cause but emerging with the greater glory for it. In the eleventh century, one version of the many minstrel songs composed about Roland was written down in verse as The *Song of Roland* (*La Chanson de Roland*). Today this is revered as the oldest surviving work of French literature, and although the world it describes bears little actual resemblance to Carolingian Francia (it is much closer to France during the

---

* It is worth noting here that Charlemagne was not anti-Islamic per se. In fact, he cultivated cordial relations with the Abbasid caliph in Baghdad, who at the start of the ninth century sent him the marvellous gift of an Asian elephant called Abul-Abbas, which was transported hundreds of miles by sea and land to the Carolingian court by a diplomat known as Isaac the Jew.

No Roman emperor left so vast a legacy to the Middle Ages as Constantine the Great (r. 306–337) (*above*). His decision to convert to Christianity, along with his refounding of Constantinople gave the medieval west its dominant religion and one of its most important cities.

The Hoxne Hoard, on display in the British Museum, is a glorious trove of jewellery, ornaments and coin, buried for safekeeping when Roman rule in Britain collapsed at the start of the fifth century AD. This gold body-chain (*above*) is just one of its treasures.

(*below*) The Sack of Rome, AD 410, depicted by nineteenth-century artist Thomas Cole. Although Rome was not the capital of its own empire in 410, its pillaging by Alaric and the Goths symbolised a superpower at the end of its life.

The stunning mosaics at the Basilica of Sant'Apollinare Nuovo in Ravenna date from the time of Theodoric the Great, Ostrogoth king of Italy in the early sixth century AD. He may have been a barbarian, but Theodoric was a sophisticated and magnificent ruler with a truly Roman taste for fine art and architecture.

Attila the Hun (d. AD 453) is one of the most famous figures in western history, who rose to power as the western Roman Empire collapsed. His name would become a byword for ferocious cruelty and conquest, but he was far from a mere bloodthirsty warlord. This woodcut portrait was made in Germany more than one thousand years after he died.

The sixth-century Byzantine emperor Justinian completely overhauled Roman law. This manuscript page is from a copy of his Digest, and dates from the late thirteenth century. The legal text in the centre of the page is surrounded by dense commentary, showing how deeply generations of medieval lawyers thought about Roman law.

Hagia Sophia, recently reconverted into a mosque, was originally built as the greatest church in Byzantine Constantinople. Its vast dome was commissioned

by Justinian in the aftermath of the Nika riots of AD 532, which nearly toppled him from his throne, and destroyed much of the city centre.

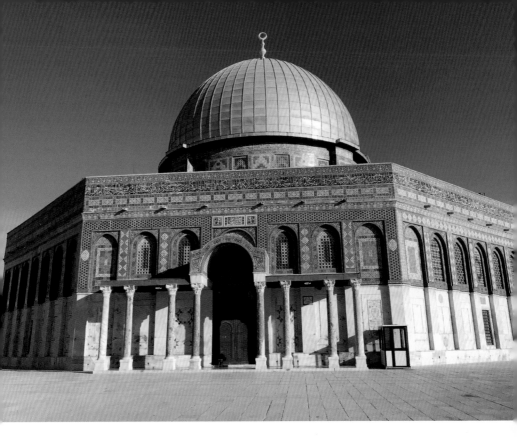

The Dome of the Rock in Jerusalem was built by the Umayyad caliph Abd al-Malik in the seventh century, and later extensively renovated by the Ottomans. It is one of the oldest and most instantly recognizable buildings in the world, and a symbol of the swaggering might and sophistication of Islamic powers in the Middle Ages.

A burlesque dancer who became Empress of Byzantium, Theodora was one of the most fascinating figures at the dawn of medieval history. Her marriage to Justinian was a meeting of minds, and she saved him from defeat during the Nika riots. This mosaic image of her is in the Basilica di San Vitale, Ravenna.

This late medieval Persian manuscript illustration shows the Battle of the Camel, AD 656. It was fought at Basra, Iraq, between the Prophet Muhammad's cousin Ali, and his widow, Aisha, who is sitting on camelback in the top left of the scene. Its outcome still reverberates today in Islam's Sunni–Shia divide.

Charlemagne (*right*), as imagined long after his death by Albrecht Dürer, is rightly known as the 'father of Europe'. His conquests, which united modern France, Germany, Belgium, Luxembourg and northern Italy, have shaped the dreams of European politicians from Napoleon to the architects of the European Union.

The Iron Crown of Lombardy (*below*), which Charlemagne confiscated in 774, was thought to incorporate a flat-beaten nail from Christ's crucifixion. Sadly, modern analysis has shown this to be a myth.

The Great Viking Horde that invaded England in the ninth century murdered
King Edmund of East Anglia, who was later considered a Christian saint.
The legend that the Vikings tied him to a tree and shot him to death
with arrows spoke to the fear that generations of medieval people
had of these fierce Scandinavian warriors.

crusades), the story was no less popular for it. Describing the climactic moments at Roncesvaux, the *Song* told of Roland blowing a mighty horn to alert Charlemagne to his desperate plight. The warrior puffed so hard into the instrument that his temples literally burst and blood spurted from his mouth.[23] Later in the *Song*, once all his companions were dead and he himself was dying, Roland summoned his last ounce of strength to defeat a Saracen who was trying to steal his sword, beating his eyes out of his skull and laying him dead on the ground. Eventually, Roland himself died, but before repenting his sins and joining hands with the archangels Gabriel and Michael his last thoughts were for 'the fair land of France, the men of his lineage [and] Charlemagne, his lord, who raised him.'[24]

Needless to say, this was all fantasy. Neither Charlemagne nor the unfortunate, real-life Roland could have imagined that a dismal defeat at the Pass of Roncesvaux would eventually inspire such a dramatic scene – let alone a foundational text in European literature. Yet somehow, for Charlemagne, even abject failure often contained the seeds of triumph.

AS THE EIGHTH CENTURY DREW TO a close, Charlemagne's relentless, annual assaults on his neighbours had succeeded in extending the borders of the Frankish realm and the power of the Frankish crown to unprecedented scale. He was unquestionably the most potent ruler in western Europe, and besides corresponding and exchanging gifts with the Abbasid caliph in Baghdad,* he was also on familiar (if not always friendly) terms with the imperial court in Constantinople. At one point he even betrothed his daughter Rotrud to the Byzantine emperor Constantine VI, although, sadly for all, the marriage never took place. (Constantinopolitan politics remained as unsentimental as

---

* Besides the elephant, Notker the Stammerer reports that Charlemagne received from the Abbasids monkeys, a lion and a bear. In return he sent Spanish horses and mules, along with hunting dogs to scare off tigers.

ever, and in 797 the emperor's mother Irene deposed and blinded her son, rendering him useless for marriage to anyone.)

Difficult relations with Byzantium notwithstanding, Charlemagne was now ascendant at home. He had crushed the independent-minded lords of autonomous regions like Aquitaine, and forced everyone within the Frankish world to accept a new reality in which the old, decentralized Merovingian system of rule was replaced by a structure focused directly on a single king at the centre of the political world. Those who rejected this new reality of a centralized, Europe-wide union, or who plotted against the king, were liable to be savagely punished, with mutilation and summary execution the order of the day. Meanwhile, Charlemagne also commanded the Low Countries, most of modern Germany, the mountain passes into Muslim Spain and much of Italy. True, this was not a state that could rival in size the first Islamic caliphates, or Rome at its height. All the same, though, the inhabitants of around 1 million square miles of territory theoretically obeyed Charlemagne's decree. Given the reach of his power and his personal dedication to an explicitly Christian kingship, Charlemagne began to see himself as a new Constantine the Great. And as his power neared its peak he set out to build monuments to it. His most lasting work was a magnificent new royal palace which he had built at Aachen, the remnants of which survive today, bearing vivid testament to Charlemagne's royal vision.

The Palatine Chapel in Aachen, on which work began in the 790s, was built on an octagonal plan. It had a domed roof designed by the architect Odo of Metz. And it was the centrepiece of a palace complex that outshone any of the dozens of fine Carolingian royal compounds, cathedrals and monasteries that were built throughout the Frankish lands in the eighth and ninth centuries. (Some of these foundations visible today include the ruins of the imperial palace at Ingelheim and the remains of Lorsch Abbey – both in modern Germany.) In his designs for Aachen, Odo consciously mimicked features of famous late Roman buildings. The eight-sided walls of the chapel chimed with the Basilica di San Vitale in Ravenna; a 125-metre-long audience hall evoked Constantine the Great's audience hall in Trier. A long covered walkway echoed the Byzantine royal palace in Constantinople. Although the interior decoration visible at Aachen today is twentieth-century reconstruction, the chronicler Einhard recorded how it looked at the turn of the ninth century: it was, he said, 'a church of great beauty... adorned with gold and silver and lamps and with railings and portals made of solid bronze.' Much of this splendour had been imported from many miles away. 'Since [Charlemagne] could not procure columns and marble from anywhere else he took the trouble to have them brought from Rome and Ravenna.'[25] One of Aachen's great attractions was its famous natural hot springs, whose waters had long ago been associated with the pagan deity Granus – from which Aachen, in Latin *Aquis Granum* – derived its name. But when Charlemagne was not relaxing in these, he was often to be seen in his fine church, seated high up in a royal box, from which he could gaze down to the altar or up towards a fine mosaic image of Christ on the inside of the great dome.[26]

Aachen was not, however, simply a place for bathing, praying, and impersonating Constantine the Great. Under Charlemagne's literate patronage it became the hub for a royal court in which aristocrats needed to show their faces. In the years 786–7 Charlemagne had personally travelled more than 3,500km in the effort to ensure his empire was governed and defended as he saw fit. This was a record-breaking itinerary, which may never have been matched by any other ruler in the Middle Ages. But it was not sustainable. Soon afterwards Charlemagne decided, as it were, that the mountain should come to Muhammad.[27] He had a large number of children (at least nine of them by his second wife, Hildegard), and by the 790s his elder sons were men. So Charlemagne delegated to them much of the military responsibility of leading campaigns, while he received visitors at his principal palaces, including Aachen. From this more settled position he could concentrate on the voluminous other business of kingship: making laws, sponsoring a large campaign of church-building and admonishing his subjects to live more Christian lives, as he often did in letters to the faithful Franks, urging them to 'love

God the Almighty with all your head and with all your prayers, and whatever pleases him, do that always.'[28]

These letters were not startlingly original in their content, but the fact that Charlemagne wrote them mattered. For as he governed by decree out of palaces like Aachen, Charlemagne was assuming responsibility for both secular policy and for reform of the Church in the Frankish lands. This was quite an expansion of the duties of kingship. But it followed logically from the relationship that had been established between the Carolingians and the Roman Church during his father's reign. The Frankish kings had been touched by God through the popes. In Charlemagne's eyes this gave him the right to speak with a special authority on matters that touched every one of his subjects' souls.

SINCE CHARLEMAGNE WAS A WILDLY ENTHUSIASTIC issuer of charters, letters and directives to all corners of his territories and beyond (often contained in documents known to historians as 'capitularies'), his palace base at Aachen also became a centre for both intellectual enquiry and manuscript production. One of the most famous of the king's associates was an English churchman, poet and scholar known as Alcuin of York, who could turn his hand to everything from philosophical dialectic to poems about the stench of latrines,* and was reckoned by one chronicler to be one of the cleverest men in the world.[29] Under Alcuin's supervision Aachen became an elite school for rhetoric, religion and the liberal arts, in which the master encouraged all his pupils to copy him in nicknaming Charlemagne 'King David'.

Making manuscripts was as important in Aachen as reading them, and during the early ninth century the school's scribes began a massive programme of knowledge preservation, creating a super-archive of information passed down from the classical

---

* Alcuin's sign composed for a lavatory is worth quoting, since it triangulates vulgar humour with Christian instruction: 'O reader, understand the rankness of your devouring belly, for it is that which you now smell in your putrid shit. Therefore, leave off feeding the gluttony of your belly, And in good time let the sober life return to you.'

world. During the ninth century perhaps one hundred thousand manuscripts were produced there, preserving what today represent the earliest surviving copies of texts by writers and thinkers ranging from Cicero and Julius Caesar to Boethius. In order to perform this epic feat of storing and organizing medieval 'big data', the scribes at Aachen developed a new style of writing, known as Carolingian minuscule. This script – exceptionally plain and well-spaced, with a then-unusually generous use of lower- and upper-case letters and punctuation marks – was designed to make manuscripts readable to literate people anywhere across the broad sweep of the Carolingian territories – much as today certain fonts and coding languages are designed to be universally readable to all mainstream computers and smartphones.

But the manuscript copyists at Aachen were not solely in the business of churning out useful texts in plain font. They also worked on masterpieces such as the Coronation Gospels – a vellum book illuminated with full-page portraits of the evangelists dressed in Roman-style togas, with leather sandals on their feet. The illustrations in the Coronation Gospels were heavily influenced by Byzantine art, and were very possibly the work of a Greek master called Demetrius who had travelled west to work on commission for Charlemagne. The book was so brilliantly produced that it became one of Charlemagne's most prized possessions – when he died he was entombed sitting up, holding it in his lap.* Plainly, Charlemagne valued fine consumer goods and the word of God. But beyond the simple fine craftsmanship, Charlemagne had another reason to think of this particular book as his most prized treasure. For it was on it that he swore a sacred oath on Christmas Day, AD 800: a day that would mark the zenith of Carolingian rule and shape the course of European history for a millennium thereafter. This was the third major coronation of his lifetime, a

---

* Today the Coronation Gospels are part of the Imperial Treasury held at the Hofburg palace in Vienna, Austria. The book was removed from Charlemagne's tomb in around the year AD 1000 and in the early sixteenth century it was bound in with stunning gold cover produced by the great German goldsmith Hans von Reutlingen.

ritual which raised Charlemagne from the status of a mighty king into a fully fledged emperor.

From Kings to Emperors

IN THE SPRING OF 799 POPE Leo III encountered some misfortune. Leo had become pontiff four years earlier, after the demise of the independent-minded Hadrian I. To welcome Leo to his office, Charlemagne had sent him a huge gift of gold and silver, confiscated from the Avars. But wealth brought trouble. For while this precious metal had enabled Leo to sponsor charitable works and luxurious building projects in Rome, it had also aroused the jealousy of those who had been close to his predecessor Hadrian. This faction disliked the idea of strong Frankish influence in Rome. They determined to do something about it.

On 25 April 799 Leo was leading a procession through the city streets when several hoodlums jumped him. They wrestled him prone, stripped him of his vestments and attempted to gouge out his eyes and sever his tongue. Next, they dragged the unfortunate Leo to a nearby monastery where, as one account had it, 'for the second time they cruelly gouged his eyes and his tongue yet further. They beat him with clubs and mangled him with various injuries and left him half dead and drenched in blood.'[30] They announced that Leo was deposed, and imprisoned him in agony for more than twenty-four hours, until some of his supporters, led by Frankish ambassadors present in Rome, found and rescued him.

The experience left Leo badly hurt and very scared, but by good fortune (or, as some had it, God's miraculous intervention), he was not killed or permanently blinded. And as soon as he was well enough to travel he fled north across the Alps to seek out Charlemagne, then in Paderborn, a week or so east of Aachen, in a region he had conquered from the Saxons.[31] Leo's choice of defender was sensible. Not only was Charlemagne well known for his piety and interest in Church reform, he was also the most powerful ruler in the west, nicknamed – according to the author of the contemporary poem known as the *Paderborn Epic* (or *Karolus magnus et Leo papa*) – as 'the lighthouse' and 'father of Europe'.[32] Just as his papal predecessors had sought out Pippin to save them from the Lombards, so Leo now implored Pippin's son to restore him to his dignity – and his office.

When Leo arrived at Paderborn there was great celebration, of the sort that must have reminded Charlemagne of his childhood, and the arrival of Pope Stephen to meet his father in 754. Charlemagne hosted Leo 'in great honour for some time,' wrote one annalist.[33] The author of the *Paderborn Epic* painted a more vivid picture: 'Charles invites Leo to his great palace. His gorgeous court-hall shines inside with colorful tapestries and its chairs are covered in purple and gold... In the middle of the high hall they celebrate a great banquet. Golden bowls overflow with Falernian wine.* King Charles and Leo, the highest prelate in the world, dine together and quaff sparkling wine from their bowls...'[34] It almost sounded like fun. And Charlemagne could afford to be merry. He had the pope at his disposal.

Beyond good wine and pleasantries, what high politicking took place between Charlemagne and Leo at Paderborn in 799 is not reliably recorded. Nevertheless, a deal was thrashed out – and it extended the Carolingian–papal compact considerably. It recognized the fact that since the 750s, the Carolingians had become not only masters of Francia, but of a huge swathe of central and western Europe. It acknowledged that the Franks and not the Byzantines were now the secular defenders of the papacy. And it rewarded Charlemagne for using the spoils of his wars against unbelievers – the Muslims of al-Andalus, the Avars and the Saxons – to sponsor his programme of building churches and monasteries. It was, in short, a deal that conferred on Charlemagne a status he had long hankered after – a title to set him alongside his hero Constantine the Great. Charlemagne agreed to send Leo back to Rome with Frankish troops at his back and vanquish his enemies.

---

* The most famous wine in ancient Rome. Probably used here allegorically to foreshadow the imperial status Pope Leo was to bestow on Charlemagne – although it is possible that Leo really did bring some of Rome's finest vintage to impress the Frankish king.

In return, Charlemagne was to receive yet another coronation. This time he would rise not as a king, but as an 'Emperor and Augustus'.[35]

So it was that in late November 800 Charlemagne was received into Rome with the highest papal pageantry. When he arrived, Leo rode a full twelve miles outside the city limits to greet him and later welcomed him formally on the steps of St Peter's Basilica. For several weeks Charlemagne busied himself purging the city of papal opponents. Finally, on Christmas Day at St Peter's, he attended a Mass dressed in full Roman costume, including a toga and sandals.[36] Leo publicly crowned him emperor, then bowed down at his feet.

The chronicler Einhard later claimed – unconvincingly – that Charlemagne had been unaware of Leo's plans and was surprised to be offered such high honour.[37] This was nonsense: Einhard's dissembling was aimed at Byzantine readers who disapproved of Charlemagne usurping the title of emperor. In fact, far from being an embarrassing accident, Charlemagne's elevation was deliberate, meticulously planned, and revolutionary. It restored to western and central Europe the fact of imperium, which had gone missing on the ground several hundred years earlier, and which seemed to be wobbling even in Constantinople, where – horror of horrors – a woman, the empress Irene (797–802) occupied the Byzantine throne. What took place in St Peter's that Christmas was supposed to be the resurrection of the western Roman Empire.

Or at least, that was how Charlemagne saw it. In February 806, when he formally announced his plans to hand over his empire to his three sons, Charles, Pippin and Louis, he announced himself 'In the name of the Father and Son and Holy Ghost, Charles, the most serene augustus, the great and pacific emperor crowned by God, governing the Roman Empire, and also by the mercy of God king of the Franks and Lombards.'[38] Four centuries later, during the reign of Frederick I Barbarossa, a tradition arose where those emperors formally crowned by a pope could call themselves 'Holy Roman Emperors'. And in that form, the office endured until the Napoleonic Wars at the turn of the nineteenth century.

The Empire Fractures

As CHARLEMAGNE GREW OLDER, HIS HEALTH failed and his associates began to observe portents of his death. 'For three successive years... there were frequent eclipses of the sun and moon, and a dark spot was seen on the sun for seven days,' recalled Einhard. The timbers in the palace at Aachen seemed to creak eerily, as though they knew their founder was ailing and felt his pain too; the church, in which he intended to be buried, was struck by lightning. Although Charlemagne breezily waved the omens away, acting 'as if none of them were related to his affairs in any way,' to others the emperor's demise seemed imminent.[39] It was. At the end of January 814, in the forty-seventh year of his reign, Charlemagne came down with a fever, accompanied by a pain in his side. He tried to cure himself with extreme fasting, but this made things worse. At nine o'clock in the morning on 28 January the emperor died, and was buried with great solemnity at Aachen. 'The Franks, the Romans, all Christians are stung with worry and great mourning,' wrote an anonymous monk from Bobbio, in northern Italy. 'The young and old, glorious nobles and matrons, all lament the loss of their Caesar.'[40]

During his long life Charlemagne had produced a large number of offspring. Between four wives and at least six concubines he had eighteen or more children, including his three legitimate sons Charles, Pippin and Louis. It had been expected that the Carolingian territories would be divided among them at the time of his death, with one son taking the Iron Crown of Lombardy, another the large central and northern kingdoms of Austrasia and Neustria, and a third Aquitaine and the Spanish March. The old-fashioned Merovingian fantasy Charlemagne entertained as he made these arrangements was that his sons would rule his Christian empire in a spirit of Christian peace and harmony: dealing strictly with the various enemies on their collective borders but peacefully with one another, tied together by the bonds of blood and mutual

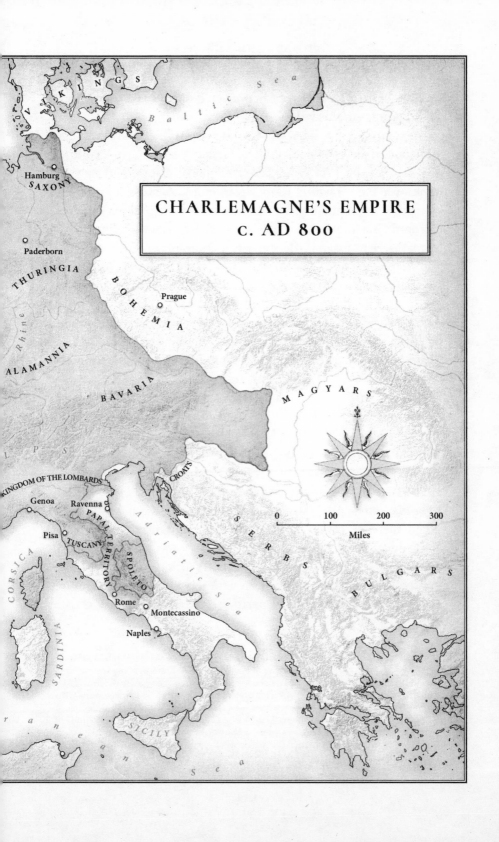

CHARLEMAGNE'S EMPIRE
c. AD 800

VIKINGS

Baltic Sea

Hamburg
SAXONY

Paderborn

THURINGIA

BOHEMIA

Prague

ALAMANNIA

BAVARIA

MAGYARS

L P S

KINGDOM OF THE LOMBARDS

CROATS

Genoa

Ravenna

PAPAL TERRITORY

Pisa

TUSCANY

Adriatic Sea

SERBS

BULGARS

CORSICA

SPOLETO

Rome

Montecassino

SARDINIA

Naples

SICILY

...ranean Sea

0   100   200   300

Miles

respect for their great European project. It did not take long for the shortcomings in this vision to appear.*

As it turned out, by 814 Louis (known as 'the Pious') was the only one of the brothers left alive. He had been crowned co-king the previous year, in anticipation of his accession, and now he took over the sprawling Carolingian empire wholesale, with the exception of Lombardy, which was settled on a nephew called Bernard. But inevitably, Louis struggled to hold together what his father had assembled. Some of his problems stemmed from the simple magnitude of the task: governing such vast territories and defending a million square miles from attack. But many more came from within the family. From the early years of his reign Louis struggled to find a way to satisfy the ambitions of his male relatives, including his own four sons. All now set their sights on a share in the empire, and they were not prepared to wait patiently to receive it.

Within three years of Louis' accession, Bernard, king of Lombardy, the son of one of Charlemagne's illegitimate children, known as Pippin the Hunchback, began the rot. The flashpoint was the publication of constitutional document known as the *Ordinatio Imperii* in 817. In it, Louis tried to clarify the hierarchy of the Carolingian empire and make provisional plans for its rule after his own death. Louis implied (although he did not state) that when the time came, Bernard ought to recognize the supreme lordship of Louis' eldest son Lothar. This was not particularly unreasonable. But it needled Bernard's pride.[41] Aggrieved, he started to think of his association with the pan-European empire not as a mutually beneficial partnership, but as a binary choice

---

* Although the analogy is far from exact, the map of Europe on the eve of the First World War comes to mind here: a large number of kingdoms whose kings were mostly related to one another (and indeed, almost all descended from Charlemagne), mutually deluded by the sense that their blood relations might override their rivalries and antagonisms. This was most famously, and calamitously, expressed in the so-called Willy–Nicky Telegrams of September 1914, in which the cousins Tsar Nicholas II of Russia and Kaiser Wilhelm II of Germany tried to talk one another down from war with reference to their personal links. ('I beg you in the name of our old friendship to do what you can to stop your allies from going too far. Nicky.')

between independence and subservience.* Very soon, Bernard was rumoured to be plotting to break off his Italian kingdom and enjoy all the supposed fruits of full sovereignty. When these whispers reached Louis' ears he had Bernard arrested, tried and sentenced to death. Although Louis showed what he claimed was mercy, by commuting death to blinding, the punishment was sufficiently brutal that Bernard died from his tortures – a combination, perhaps, of blood loss, infection and shock.

Besides illustrating the fragility of a European empire that was bound only by assumed common values and what the *Ordinatio Imperii* called 'mutual brotherly love... common welfare and everlasting peace', Bernard's plot and death brought down on Louis a torrent of criticism.[42] In the high summer of 822 Louis publicly confessed his sins and did penance at a great Carolingian family meeting, attended by Pope Paschal I. The pro-royal Frankish annals that described the penance were tight-lipped about the details of what took place, but emphasized that Louis apologized for more than simply killing Bernard. 'He took the trouble to correct with the greatest care whatever things... he and his father had done,' wrote the annalist.[43] Yet apologies and ritual contrition did not solve the basic problem: Louis had been left an empire too big for him to hold together.

Between 830 and 840 a series of three major rebellions broke out in which Louis' sons banded together in various combinations to try and improve their portions of the imperial inheritance. In keeping with Carolingian custom, many cruel, murderous and disgraceful deeds were perpetrated, including further blindings, drownings, exilings, accusations of witchcraft and adultery levelled against Louis' wife and empress Judith, and a general commitment to naked self-advancement. In June 833, at a meeting in Rothfeld, in Alsace, Louis was confronted by his eldest son, Lothar, who had proven himself an attentive student of Carolingian family history, and persuaded Pope Gregory IV to back him as supreme ruler. Lothar's play for power spooked Louis' supporters, and almost to

---

* See also: Brexit.

a man they abandoned him for his eldest son: an act of collective spinelessness which earned the meeting the nickname 'The Field of Lies'. Louis was now a prisoner. Lothar wore the imperial crown. And the son dragged his father around Europe with him as he tried his own hand at rule.

This farcical state of affairs collapsed, perhaps inevitably, under the weight of its own iniquity. Louis was restored to the crown in another family coup a year later. But the writing was on the wall for Charlemagne's empire. Like Alexander the Great before him, Charlemagne had built an empire which quickly proved itself possible only as an extension of one man's political self. Louis died in 840, at which time three of his sons were still alive. After yet another round of civil war, they decided in 843 to abandon the European dream. The Carolingian empire was formally partitioned under the Treaty of Verdun, creating the three kingdoms of West Francia, the Middle Kingdom and East Francia. (These approximated, respectively and very roughly, to modern France, northern Italy and Burgundy, and western Germany.)

Further carve-ups of western Europe would take place during the remainder of the ninth century, along with intermittent war between the realms whose Carolingian rulers, as descendants of Charlemagne, generally fancied themselves as significantly mightier than nature had allowed. For a brief moment towards the end of the century, Charlemagne's hapless, idle and unfortunately epileptic great-grandson, Charles III the Fat, staked a claim to all the lands of the Franks. But when he died in 888 the empire fell apart, splintering into component pieces of East and West Francia, Germany, Burgundy, Provence and Italy. Many would dream during the Middle Ages of piecing all these fragments back together, but it would take nearly a thousand years for one ruler to once again hold the whole Carolingian inheritance in his hands. He was Napoleon Bonaparte – another irresistible warrior and accumulator, but one whose career only served to emphasize what Charlemagne's had done: it has only been possible to unite Europe once or twice in every millennium, and even then, not for very long.

Coming of the Northmen

IN THE SPRING OF 845, WHEN Louis the Pious' youngest son Charles the Bald was ruling West Francia, a Danish warlord called Ragnar brought a fleet of 120 ships up the river Seine. It has sometimes been said that this Ragnar was the model for the legendary Ragnar Lodbrok ('Hairy Britches'), star of Danish chronicles, Icelandic sagas and a highly successful twenty-first century television series: a physically vast, sexually potent, highly skilful sailor who had sailed the high seas and snaking rivers as far afield as England and the Baltic lands of the Kievan Rus'.[44] It is hard to know for sure whether or not this is so. But either way, the Ragnar who attacked the Franks in 845 was still very dangerous.

After travelling about seventy-five miles up the river, Ragnar and his followers disembarked their sleek ships, to raid and plunder. 'Ships past counting voyage up the Seine, and throughout the entire region evil grows strong,' wrote one despairing chronicler. 'Rouen is laid waste, looted and burnt...'[45] Far from exhausted – indeed, now pumped for more excitement – Ragnar's men carried on up the river until they arrived in Paris, around Easter. A city of probably just a few thousand souls, Paris was not yet the powerhouse it would become in the later Middle Ages. But it was rich. The treasures of the royal abbey of St-Denis were especially alluring. And if there was one thing Ragnar knew how to do it was robbing houses of God.

As king of the western Franks, Charles the Bald could not stand aside and allow this Danish hooligan to fill his boots. The Danes, along with other 'Northmen' – or Vikings, meaning either pirates or 'bay-dwellers' – had already been threatening the Carolingians for decades. But in recent years the scope and scale of their raids into Frankish territory had escalated. Charles the Bald therefore assembled an army, divided it into two – one for each bank of the Seine – and went out to drive Ragnar away.

It did not go to plan. Whereas long ago the Lombards had cried 'woe' at the sight of the Franks, Ragnar and the Northmen bared their teeth. They isolated one group of Frankish warriors, took them prisoner and rowed them to an island in the middle of the Seine, where Charles the Bald and the rest of his cohort could see, but not help them. Once they had beached on the island, Ragnar summarily hanged 111 of the prisoners. Helpless to evict the Northmen and terrified that if they stayed there might be very little left of Paris to remember them by, Charles the Bald now agreed to pay Ragnar 7,000 pounds of silver and gold to retire. This was an astronomically large sum, and its size alone was a miserable humiliation for the Frankish king. Charles' only consolation was that he was not the only ruler to suffer the indignity of such an attack. That same year Scandinavian fleets attacked Hamburg (in Louis the German's East Francia), Frisia (in Lothar's Middle Kingdom) and Saintes, in Aquitaine. Once upon a time the Franks had been the most feared military force in the west. Now it was the Northmen's turn.

The Northmen – or Vikings – are often said to have burst out of their coastal settlements in what is now Sweden, Norway and Denmark at the end of the eighth century. The most famous account of their arrival into the Christian realms of the west comes from Britain. In 793 warriors appeared off the coast of Northumbria, leapt from their ships and robbed the island of Lindisfarne, desecrating the monastery and murdering its brothers. This ferocious raid sent shock-waves rippling out from Britain. When the news reached Charlemagne's court in Aachen, Alcuin of York wrote to the king of Northumbria, deploring the fact that 'the church of St Cuthbert is spattered with the blood of the priests of God, stripped of all its furnishing, exposed to the plundering of pagans.'[46] He suggested to the king that he and his noblemen might mend their ways, starting by adopting more Christian haircuts and clothing styles.

But it was too late for any of that. The Northmen had announced themselves as a major power in the western world. The next year, 794, raiders appeared on the other side of the British Isles, in the

Hebrides. In 799 Vikings raided the monastery of Saint-Philibert at Noirmoutier, just to the south of the river Loire. Sixty years later Viking raids would be a painful feature of life not only in the North and Irish Seas but as far away as Lisbon, Seville and north Africa, as Northmen tangled with Anglo-Saxons, Irish, Umayyads and Franks. In 860 a band of Viking-descended warriors from what is now north-west Russia even sailed to Constantinople via the river Dnieper and the Black Sea, and laid the city under siege. Although exposed only to a tiny part of this, the chronicler of Noirmoutier wrote what could have been an epigram for the entire age: 'The number of ships grows, the endless stream of Vikings never ceases to increase... the Vikings conquer everything in their path and nothing resists them.'[47]

THE PEOPLE OF SCANDINAVIA WERE NOT somehow conjured into existence in the late eighth century. More than a millennium earlier, around 325 BC, the Greek explorer Pytheas made a famous journey to the freezing north-west of the then-known world and came into contact with a partly populated place called 'Thule', which may (or may not) have been Norway or Iceland.[48] Around the same time, people living around Denmark were capable of constructing clinker-built* boats: the so-called Hjortspring boat, retrieved in a bog on the Danish island of Als in the 1920s, shows that these ancient Scandinavians went to sea in vessels that held crews of twenty.

Over the centuries that followed, the northerners remained an acknowledged presence on the edge of the known world. In the days of Augustus the Roman military scouted Jutland. In AD 515, a Danish ruler called Chochilaicus raided Frankish territory in the Low Countries. (Chochilaicus may have been the model for King Hygelac, king of the Geats and uncle of the eponymous hero in the great medieval epic poem *Beowulf*.) Yet until the eighth

---

* Vessels in which overlapping planks are arranged to form a hull – a considerable improvement on earlier techniques of canoe-building, which relied on hollowing out a single trunk.

century, glimpses of the Northmen had been just that: few, far between and fleeting. Although the northern world was linked to trade routes that connected ultimately with the Silk Roads, the links were relatively weak and had been severely disrupted by the barbarian migrations of the fifth and sixth centuries AD. And geography itself was isolating. It is telling that in the early Middle Ages neither Christianity nor Islam touched the northern world, which remained resolutely cut off from the desert monotheisms and their worship of the book and the word until the turn of the first millennium. Left to develop on its own course, Viking culture was highly idiosyncratic, infused with the unique landscape and conditions of the lands on the Arctic fringe.

The Vikings' worldview was informed particularly by climate. Possibly thanks to the shock of the great volcanic eruptions that caused global temperatures to plummet and harvests to fail during the 530s and 540s, the Vikings' stories of genesis and apocalypse revolved around the lives of trees and the impending arrival of the *Fimbulwinter*, when the earth would freeze and all life would end. The Northmen celebrated a colourful pantheon of gods such as Odin, Ull, Baldr, Thor and Loki. They knew their lives were affected by other supernatural beings, too, including the female beings known as Valkyries and *fylgjur*, as well as elves, dwarves and trolls. They detected the magical and mystical everywhere in a varied and often extreme natural world that was vividly and deeply interconnected with the 'other'.[49] And they interacted with this invisible realm in ways far removed from the liturgical, institutionalized forms followed by the Christians, Muslims and Jews of Europe and the Middle East, ranging from leaving offerings of food to practising ritual human sacrifice.

Historians have puzzled for generations over why the Vikings suddenly, in the course of two generations, broke their relative isolation and surged out to terrorize – and colonize – the west. Political turmoil, cultural revolution, climate change and demographic pressure have all been proposed as causes.[50] Like all huge questions, it has no straightforward answer. But for our purposes here, it seems to be that at exactly the moment that economic conditions and popular technologies were changing within the Scandinavian world, the Frankish world and its established order fell to pieces.

From around the fifth century Scandinavian boat technology had been improving, perhaps driven by the opportunities for trade around the North Sea, including the long, fjord-pocked thousand-mile west coast of Norway.[51] Boats became larger and faster, equipped with strong keels, powerful sails, deep, flat hulls more than twenty metres in length and crews large enough to work in rotation for twenty-four hours at a time.[52] At the same time there was rising cultural pressure on young Viking men to travel and enrich themselves. In a society that still allowed men to marry more than one woman (and possibly to kill female babies), men had to pay a 'bride-fee' for a prestigious marriage and to advertise their social credit. The best ways to raise this were trade and piracy – or a bit of both.

Against this background, then, came the sweeping changes in Europe wrought by the Carolingians. Under Charlemagne the Franks became increasingly interesting to the Northmen. For one thing, Charlemagne's campaigns against the Saxons drove the Frankish frontier north, until it was nudging up against the lands of the Vikings. (From AD 810/11 there was a 'Danish March' in the north of the empire, which served as a militarized buffer zone against the northern pagans.) And for another, the Carolingians founded and enriched monasteries and other Christian holy sites. Large amounts of moveable wealth were placed in the hands of monks: physically the weakest men in society. Moreover, many monasteries – such as the Saint-Philibert at Noirmoutier, nestled on a spit of land at the mouth of the Loire – were on the coast or beside rivers, or in locations far from secular society, where the brothers were deliberately isolated from social violence – or so they thought.

These fruits could not have hung lower, nor seemed riper, to a society of highly mobile warrior bands equipped with the finest ships outside the Mediterranean, whose viciousness Alcuin of York compared with that of the ancient Goths and Huns.[53] When the 830s and 840s saw the Frankish rulers falling into a mutually destructive civil war, and eventually into three-way partition of the once impervious empire, it was time for the fruit to be plucked.

From Vikings to Normans

FROM THE MIDDLE OF THE NINTH century onwards, the Franks had to contend with the fact that they were near-neighbours to an outwardly mobile society with ambitions that stretched across the western world. There were few places anywhere that were off-limits to the Vikings, and as they travelled ever further afield, the nature of their attacks began to change. In place of small, smash-and-grab hits on coastal targets which had characterized their forays at the end of the eighth century, by the ninth century came huge missions equipped for siege, subjugation and settlement.

Almost everywhere, established powers struggled to contain the Viking threat. In England a 'Great Heathen Army' of Vikings invaded in 865, possibly led by four of Ragnar Lodbrok's sons, including Ivar the Boneless, who may have earned his name because of a disability which affected his legs. In previous generations Vikings had preyed on monasteries and thriving cities such as London, Canterbury and Winchester. But the Great Heathen Army was a fully formed army of conquest, bent on breaking the power of the Saxon kings who now ruled the petty kingdoms of Northumbria, Mercia, Wessex and East Anglia. With the army travelled a settler community including many women; they had come to live, not just raid. And they succeeded. In 869 Edmund, king of East Anglia, was put to death by the Vikings.* By the 880s around half of England was under Scandinavian control or direct rule; the Viking advance was halted only after a long struggle led heroically on the Saxon side by Alfred, king of Wessex.

---

* Later hagiographical legend, enthusiastically encouraged by the monks who controlled access to the royal shrine at Bury St Edmund's, held that the king refused to give up his kingdom unless the Northmen converted to Christianity, so was tied to a tree and riddled with arrows before having his head removed.

A treaty agreed at some time between 878 and 890 formalized the partition of England, with the large portion of 'Viking' territory, in the north and east of the country, known as the Danelaw. Within the Danelaw, a different legal system operated, Anglo-Scandinavian coinage circulated (including pieces emblazoned with Thor's hammer), new languages came into use and place-names changed.* Old gods and new commingled, as the settlers simultaneously imported the Norse pantheon and adopted the rites of Christianity. Scandinavians would retain an interest in some or all of England until 1042, when Harthacnut, joint king of Denmark and England, died.

But England was only part of the picture. The Vikings traded, fought and settled on the island kingdoms of Scotland and the Irish Sea: Orkney, the western isles of Scotland, Man and Anglesey. In Ireland Viking colonists established a major kingdom around Dublin, which survived until the early eleventh century. (This kingdom of Dublin was built on a flourishing slave market: slaves known as 'thralls' taken inland in Ireland might be sold into servitude in lands as distant as Iceland, rubbing shoulders in slave markets with other unfortunate people captured across the western world, from as far away as north Africa or the Baltic.)

Meanwhile, thousands of miles away in eastern Europe, Scandinavians (known as the Rus') began to travel in ever-larger numbers towards Constantinople. By the middle of the tenth century, Byzantine emperors had come to envy the martial abilities of the Northmen so much they maintained a personal bodyguard known as the 'Varangian Guard', recruited from Viking stock. (Norse rune graffiti can still be found at the Hagia Sophia, possibly etched there by guardsmen called Halfdan and Ari.) From Byzantium, a few intrepid Northmen even reached Abbasid Persia; according to the Arab scholar and geographer Ibn Khurradadhbih, the Viking Rus' traded in Baghdad in the 840s, bringing goods overland on camel-back and posing as Christians

---

* Today a city like York, once a major centre of Viking settlement in England, still carries a legacy of Scandinavian occupation in its road names: Coppergate, Stonegate and Micklegate all descend etymologically from the Old Norse word 'gata'.

to take advantage of a tax regime that offered preferential rates to people of the book over pagans.[54] Soon, silk and slaves were being exchanged between the Viking world and the Abbasid caliphate at a record rate, and silver Abbasid *dirhams* were flooding into the Scandinavian west.* The Vikings seemed to be eternally expanding their global networks and the frontiers of their societies. By around the year 1000 the Scandinavian west would include settlements in Iceland, Greenland and even 'Vinland' – Newfoundland in modern Canada, where an abandoned Viking settlement has been excavated at L'Anse aux Meadows.†

LET US RETURN NOW, THOUGH, TO those Northmen who invaded the world of the Franks. Although Ragnar had been paid to leave Paris alone in 845, this had by no means put an end to Viking ambitions in the Frankish kingdoms. Indeed, it seemed to many among the Franks that the Northmen would soon be the greatest power in the land: in 857 Pippin II of Aquitaine, who was disputing the kingship of that region with his uncle Charles the Bald, made a pact with the Vikings to employ their military muscle in his wars for control of the Loire valley; Pippin was even said to have abandoned Christianity for paganism before he was killed in 864. By and large, however, Frankish rulers preferred to resist the Vikings rather than attempting to join with them. In the same year Pippin died, the Frankish emperor Charles the Bald issued the Edict of Pîtres. Amid a raft of legal pronouncements on matters such as coin production, labour laws and the plight of refugees, the edict also ordered Frankish subjects to contribute to measures against the Vikings, including a royal bridge-building programme, by which vulnerable waterways such as the Seine would have regular militarized crossings along their course,

---

* As were accounts of the Vikings' strange and often sadistic cultural ways. Ibn Khurradadbih's near-contemporary, the Abbasid ambassador Ibn Fadlan, recorded in terrifyingly vivid prose a different side to the Viking Rus' whom he witnessed carrying out the ritual funeral of one of their great men – a ceremony that included the drugging, violent rape and murder of a slave girl, who was buried with her dead master.
† See chapter 15.

guarded with forts and theoretically able to block the Northmen's boats.[55] This worked for a time, although it did not so much send the Northmen home as divert their attentions to other parts of the region, both in Frankish lands and in England.

Many parts of the Frankish world that were unprotected by bridge-barriers must have felt as though they were permanently under assault. One monastic chronicler writing around that time wailed: 'the Northmen ceased not to take Christian people captive and to kill them, and to destroy churches and houses and burn villages. Through all the streets lay bodies of the clergy, of laymen, nobles, and others, of women, children, and suckling babes. There was no road nor place where the dead did not lie; and all who saw Christian people slaughtered were filled with sorrow and despair.'[56] Naturally, monks wondered why God was so angry that he had sent the Vikings. Another chronicler reflected that it must have been their sins: '[The] Frankish nation... was overflowing with foul indecencies... Traitors and perjurers deserve to be condemned, and unbelievers and infidels are justly punished.'[57]

By the 880s Charles the Bald was dead, his bridge defences had failed, and Viking raiders were back with a vengeance. And this time they struck at the symbolic heart of the Carolingian state. In 882 a Viking army that had spent the previous winter despoiling Frisia entered the river Rhine and advanced towards Charlemagne's palace-city of Aachen. They took over the palace and used Charlemagne's once-beloved imperial chapel as a stable for their horses.[58] Throughout the Rhineland, the invaders 'brought to their death servants of [Christ] by famine or sword, or sold them beyond the sea.'[59] To the chroniclers (almost all of whom were based in monasteries, and thus directly in the sights of the raiders), it seemed as if the devastation would never end. But for the Scandinavian adventurers, business was booming. One modern historian has estimated that during the ninth century Vikings active in the Frankish lands stole or extorted in ransom and protection payments around 7 million silver pennies; approximately 14 per cent of the total that were minted. The Carolingians had grown rich and powerful, and sponsored well-endowed abbeys, by plundering unbelievers on their borders. Now that process was being ironically and very uncomfortably reversed. The hunters had become the hunted.

In 885, a Viking army returned to Paris, where Ragnar had found such easy pickings four decades previously. This time the city was better defended, but the Northmen put it under siege and tormented the inhabitants for nearly a year. A famous account known as the *Wars of the City of Paris*, by a monk called Abbo of St Germain, recounted the chaos as 'fear seized the city – people screamed, battle horns resounded... Christians fought and ran about, trying to resist the assault.'[60]

For eleven months the citizens of Paris held out, often at great cost to their lives, liberty and wellbeing. Eventually, in October 886, the Carolingian king of the time, Charles the Fat, appeared at the city with a relieving army. Yet to the intense dismay and disgust of the Parisians, Charles did not use his troops to grind the Vikings into the dirt. Instead he followed the example of his predecessor Charles the Bald, and paid them to leave Paris alone. Over the course of the following decade, Viking attacks on the Frankish kingdoms slowed down. But the events of the 880s left an important legacy in the history of all parties concerned.

FOR THE CAROLINGIANS, A HALF-CENTURY OF Viking attacks eventually proved fatal. Charles the Fat was seriously damaged by his craven response to the siege of Paris. By contrast, the city's leader, Odo, count of Paris, was lauded as a hero for his willingness to stand and fight. And as a result, when Charles the Fat died in 888, Odo was elected as king of Western Francia. Odo thus became the first non-Carolingian to rule over a Frankish kingdom since the lifetime of Charles Martel. And he is remembered today as the first of the Robertian kings – the dynastic name a reference to his father, Robert the Strong. Although there would be another Carolingian king after him – and the further branches of the Carolingian family would produce claimants to the western and eastern Frankish thrones until the middle of the tenth century – no ruler was ever again able to do as Charles the Fat had briefly done, and rule the full empire assembled by Pippin and Charlemagne.

Undone by their own family rivalries, the challenges of holding together such a vast and culturally diverse collection of territories and peoples, and the depredations of the Northmen (as well as other enemies on their eastern frontiers, including the Magyar tribal groups who had started to launch massive raids into imperial territory from what is now Hungary), the Carolingians drifted, generation by generation, from pre-eminence to irrelevance. Behind them they left to the Middle Ages several distinct polities. Western Francia became the kingdom of France. Eastern Francia became an empire centred on Germany and northern Italy that would in time become known as the German, or Holy Roman, Empire. (Middle Francia, sometimes known as Lotharingia, was gradually squeezed out of existence.) For long stretches of the later Middle Ages, and well into the early modern period, France and the German empire would be the dominant powers on the European continent. Their successor states, France and Germany, occupy the same status in the early twenty-first century.

Yet there was another political entity that emerged from the age of Carolingians and Vikings. Over time, the Northmen evolved from Scandinavian raiders to become the rulers of more conventional, mainstream, Christian states of the west. Most obviously these included the kingdoms of Sweden, Norway and Denmark. There were also notable Viking-ruled kingdoms around the North Sea and Irish Sea (ranging from the small island kingdom of Orkney and the Irish kingdom of Dublin to the massive Danelaw, which consisted of much of modern England) as well as the Kievan Rus', a vast patchwork of territories in modern Russia, Belarus and Ukraine, which was ruled over by the Viking Rurik dynasty, whose roots lay in eastern Sweden. Yet none was so influential on the subsequent course of medieval history as that which they carved out from the Frankish state: the realm of the Northmen, or Nordmannia – known as Normandy.

The creation of Normandy was directly linked to the dramatic siege of Paris in 885–6. Among the Viking leaders of that expedition was a man called Rollo (or *Hrolfr*), who was probably born in Denmark, and whose career was described by a later biographer, Dudo of St Quentin, in idealized but undeniably thrilling terms. Dudo described Rollo as a preternaturally tough and dogged soldier, 'trained in the art of war and utterly ruthless,' who could typically be seen 'in a helmet wonderfully ornamented with gold and a mail coat'.[61] Rollo was one of the most violent men of his exceptionally bloody times: on one occasion he prevailed in battle by ordering his men to kill all their animals, chop their carcasses in half and build a makeshift barricade out of freshly butchered meat. But he was a canny negotiator. During the second half of the ninth century, Rollo made a tidy living among the Franks, doing as all thrusting young Northmen did: burning, laying towns and villages to waste, plundering and killing. By the early years of the tenth century he and his Viking comrades had driven the rulers of the Franks to distraction and their people to a state of abject war-weariness. According to Dudo's account, in 911, following a spate of Viking raiding, the subjects of the then-king of West Francia, Charles the Simple,* petitioned their ruler, complaining that the land in the Frankish realm was 'no better than a desert, for its population is either dead through famine or sword, or is perhaps in captivity.' They urged him to protect the realm, 'if not by arms, then by counsel.'[62]

Fatefully, Charles agreed. By a treaty probably sealed at Saint-Clair-sur-Epte, halfway between Rouen and Paris, Rollo came in from the cold, agreeing a 'a pact of love and inextricable friendship' with the Franks. Under its terms he undertook to give up raiding, marry the king's daughter Gisla and convert to Christianity. Whether the marriage to Gisla took place is uncertain – not least because Rollo had previously seized and taken into either concubinage or wedlock another young woman by the name of Poppa of Bayeux. But Rollo certainly did accept baptism. He was 'imbued with the catholic faith of the sacrosanct Trinity,' wrote

---

* Charles the Simple was the last Carolingian king of West Francia. His reign was sandwiched between that of the first Robertian king, Odo (888–898) and the second, Robert I (922–3).

Dudo, '[and] caused his own counts and warriors and his entire armed band to be baptized and instructed through preaching in the faith of the Christian religion.' He also changed his name to that of his new godfather, Robert, the future Robert I, king of the Franks.

This was quite a U-turn for a man who had made his name robbing churches. But it was worth it. For in return, Charles the Simple granted Rollo all the lands spreading out from the Seine valley, which would come to be known as Normandy. The newly Christian Viking now controlled the riverine approach to Paris, along with a swathe of famously fertile landscape and a coastline studded with strategically useful ports, from which passing sea-traffic as well as vessels bound for nearby England could be monitored.

It was clear – to Dudo at least – who had got the better deal, as the chronicler illustrated by way of an anecdote. When the time came to make formal submission to Charles the Simple to seal their deal, Rollo declared: 'I will never kneel before the knees of another, nor will I kiss anyone's foot.' Instead, he asked one of his henchmen to do the job on his behalf. The warrior, wrote Dudo, 'immediately grasped the king's foot and raised it to his mouth and planted a kiss on it while he remained standing, [which] laid the king flat on his back. So there rose a great laugh, and a great outcry among the people.'[63]

So, WITH THE FARCICAL SIGHT OF the hapless Frankish king Charles the Simple upended on his backside, the Viking duchy of Normandy came into being. Rollo – or Robert, as he was now known – ruled between 911 and his death in 928, when he handed over to his son William 'Longsword', who expanded Normandy's borders through military campaigns against his neighbours before being assassinated in 942. At this point, two generations after Rollo's conversion, it might be assumed that the new Norman leaders' essential 'Vikingness' would have been diminished. But it was not quite so. Under them, Scandinavian settlers flooded into Normandy, and although over time they mixed, married and integrated with the Frankish inhabitants of Normandy, the Normans retained a sense of themselves as a people apart long into the Middle Ages.

Rivalry between dukes of Normandy and kings of France would be a pronounced and important feature of the eleventh- and twelfth-century political landscape in the west, especially after the year 1066, when Rollo's great-great-great grandson, William 'the Bastard' of Normandy, launched his invasion of England, sending a flotilla of ships across the Channel to kill his rival Harold Godwinson and seize the English crown.* (In the famous Bayeux Tapestry, which tells the story of the Norman Conquest in embroidered comic-strip format, William's ships are distinctly Viking in appearance, with ornate, carved prows and large square sails.) Norman dukes would rule England until 1204, and with the wealth and military resources of the English crown behind them, were able to cause enormous trouble for the French kings, many of whom would rue the day that Charles the Simple had innocently handed over a large corner of his kingdom to a gang of hard-nosed men of the north.

ALL THIS SAID, HOWEVER, IF THERE was one area where the Norman dukes did depart wholesale from their Viking roots, it was in their Christianity. The Franks had converted to Christianity centuries earlier, and as we have seen, their intimate political and ritual connection to the Church had been a source of enormous prestige and 'soft' power. By contrast, in the Scandinavian world Christianity was a long time coming. Even at the dawn of the 1100s, pagan beliefs still commingled freely with advancing Christian rites among more conservative tribal people in Sweden.[64] But the Vikings who colonized Normandy were distinct and different. They converted early and decisively and never looked back.

---

* William of Normandy was one of two 'Viking' claimants to the crown of England in 1066. The other was Harald Hardrada, king of Norway – a one-time member of the Byzantine emperor's Varangian Guard.

Perhaps no more intriguing example may be found than that of Duke Richard II of Normandy, who ruled between 996 and 1026. Richard's grandmother was a Breton woman called Sprota, whom Richard's grandfather, William Longsword, took captive during a raid on Brittany and forcibly married in what was euphemistically termed 'the Danish fashion'. Richard grew up in regular contact with his distant cousins in the Scandinavian world, and was never shy of employing Viking mercenaries in his military campaigns. Yet he was a duke who looked in both directions. On the one hand he lived in the same century as Rollo: Norse blood flowed in his veins. But Richard II was also, unquestionably, a man of the Frankish world: a Christian, the first Norman ruler to use the title duke (*dux*), and the man who commissioned Dudo of St Quentin to write the history of his family, from which we learn about Rollo's conversion and his assumption of power within the Frankish world.

So, far from robbing monks, Richard II actively sponsored and patronized them – and not only in Normandy. This child of Viking heritage and Frankish temperament was so well known for his pious generosity that every year Christian monks from the Sinai desert in Egypt travelled the better part of 5,000km to Normandy to beg alms from Richard for their upkeep.[65] The poachers had become world-famous gamekeepers.

The Normans would climb further still on their journey from scourges of the Church to its fiercest defenders – as we shall see when we turn to the crusades in chapter 8. But before that it is time for us to look at some of the other powers that rose to shape the west between the tenth and twelfth centuries. Unlike those we have surveyed so far, these were not empires or dynasties, but supranational movements centered on religious and military expertise. The groups we will examine in the next two chapters produced perhaps the Middle Ages' most enduring archetypes, whose images spring immediately to mind whenever we think of this period – and whose costumes are a mainstay of all good fancy-dress outfitters.

They are monks and knights.

6

MONKS

'The world is full of monks.'

BERNARD OF CLAIRVAUX, c. 1130

At some time in 909 or 910 Duke William of Aquitaine was forced to find a new home for his hunting dogs. The duke had decided to found a new monastery, and had turned for advice in this enterprise to one of the most respected monks of his day, a fellow called Berno. Berno had once been a nobleman himself, but had given up the fineries of the world to devote himself to God's praise and service.[1] He had built an abbey of his own (at Gigny, in eastern France) and was subsequently headhunted to take over another at nearby Baume-les-Messieurs. Under Berno, both houses were renowned for the quality of their management and their ordered way of life – as well as for the harshness of their discipline. Monks under Berno's care were frequently whipped, imprisoned in their cells and starved for minor infractions. But these were not necessarily thought to be bad things; in fact they enhanced Berno's reputation as a hard-nosed spiritual CEO with an excellent track record. In turning to Berno for advice, William was approaching one of the leading authorities on monasticism in all of the Frankish lands.

But, as the story was later told, once engaged on this new project, Berno immediately presented the duke with a problem. The prime site he had identified for a new monastery was a hunting lodge at Cluny, on one of William's extensive estates in Burgundy. The duke was fond of this part of the world, and the grounds that spread out around his lodge; he kept large packs of hounds there to allow him to enjoy the exhilarations of the chase. Now Berno told him Cluny was the only place that would do for the abbey – and the dogs would have to be re-kennelled elsewhere.

'Impossible,' said William, according to a later chronicle that described their exchange. 'I cannot have my dogs removed.'

'Drive out the dogs,' replied the abbot, 'and put monks in their place. You know full well what reward God will give you for dogs, and what for monks.'[2]

Reluctantly William agreed. For the sake of a pious foundation that might well save his immortal soul, he consented to hand over his hunting lodge. With the agreement of his wife Engelberga, he drew up charters entrusting it to the protection of Saints Peter and Paul, and in their absence from earth, the pope in Rome. Berno would oversee its practical conversion into a dwelling for a community of monks. The brothers who came to live there would be sustained by its woodland and pastures, vineyards and fishponds, villages and serfs – unfree peasants who were legally obliged to work the land. In return they would be expected to engage in rounds of constant prayer and devotion, offering their hospitality to passing travellers and living in respectable chastity, obedient to the Rule of St Benedict – a code of monastic conduct drawn up hundreds of years previously in southern Italy by the sixth-century monk Benedict of Nursia. Popes would be their guardians. Berno would be their abbot. Their financial benefactors and physical protectors would be Duke William and his descendants.

Thus was an abbey born, in a process that was not, on the surface of things, very unusual. During the Carolingian years many rich Franks founded monasteries and there were plenty of would-be monks and nuns to fill them.[3] But compared to many contemporary institutions, what was odd about Cluny was how little control Duke William demanded for himself and his heirs. William might have asserted his family's right to appoint Cluny's future abbots and have a hands-on role in running the house. Yet he did not. Instead he promised Berno and all future monks of Cluny would be allowed to govern themselves, free of interference from secular powers and even local bishops. Anyone who tried to meddle with Cluny Abbey's affairs would, according to the charter of foundation, be damned to suffer the eternal inferno and the gnawing worms of hell. More immediately, they would also face a fine of one hundred pounds.[4] Insofar as it was ever possible for medieval monks to be fully inured from harm and left to their own devices, the brothers of Cluny would be.

Construction began around 910. It was a big, costly project. Berno and the monks he invited to populate Cluny needed a church, communal living quarters, a dormitory, refectory and library, individual cells and spaces for study, along with kitchens and animal-sheds for their lay servants. This took many years, and the job was nowhere near complete when William died in 918 or even when Berno followed him to the grave in 927.

Yet if Cluny's foundation was slow, shrouded not in glory but in clouds of builders' dust, it would still turn out to be a hugely significant event in the history of the medieval west. During the next 200 years monasticism boomed. Many variant types of monasticism were spawned: besides the Benedictines there were orders known as the Cistercians, Carthusians, Premonstratensians, Trinitarians, Gilbertines, Augustines, Paulines, Celestines, Dominicans and Franciscans, as well as military orders which included the Templars, Hospitallers and Teutonic Knights. But it was Cluny, located in Burgundy but with influence extending throughout France into England, Italy, the Iberian peninsula and western Germany, which would grow to become the pre-eminent monastery in Europe. From the mid-tenth century it was the headquarters of an international organization which at its peak included many hundreds of subsidiary or 'daughter' houses. All of these were answerable to the abbot of Cluny, who controlled astonishing wealth and economic resources. By the late eleventh century abbots of Cluny were on even terms with kings and popes, and participated in the highest conversations and conflicts of their age. Like branches of a spiritual McDonald's, Cluniac houses could be found almost everywhere west of the Rhine, and particularly along the international road-routes walked by pilgrims visiting holy sites such as Santiago de Compostela, in north-western Spain. True, Cluny's reach did not extend to much of Germany, nor was it pre-eminent in the Christian parts of eastern and central Europe, let alone Byzantium, where a distinctive 'eastern' form of monasticism developed. All the same, for several generations Cluny was armed with a rare degree of 'soft' power that crossed jurisdictions and borders.* And the Cluniac system spearheaded a more general monastic explosion, which altered the relations between Church and state, and recharged and reshaped cultural life in the Christian world, transforming not only religious observance but also literacy, architecture, fine art and music.

All this was exemplified at Cluny itself. Although a visitor there today will find depressingly little to see, save a small set of buildings which escaped dynamiting by anticlerical philistines during the French Revolution of the eighteenth century, in its day Cluny was the site of arguably the grandest church in the world, fit to rival St Peter's in Rome and the Hagia Sophia in Constantinople. From a hunting lodge and dog-pound Cluny's abbey church, at 517 feet long, grew to become the biggest building of any sort in Europe: the location of a world-class library and artistic centre, the home to a prestigious and elite community of religious men and the nerve centre of a golden age of monasticism. Its story takes us into a wider period of intense monastic activity, invention and growth. Its influence, and the broader influence of monks of various orders and lifestyles, would be felt across the Latin world until the end of the Middle Ages.†

From the Desert to the Hilltop

NOTHING BETTER SUMMED UP THE BUSINESS of being a monk than Christ's words in the parable of the rich young man, as

---

* A very loose comparison today would be to think of the wealth and power controlled by non-state, corporate titans and social media entrepreneurs such as Amazon's Jeff Bezos or Facebook's Mark Zuckerberg.
† By the Latin world, we mean that part of the world where Latin was the dominant common language – as opposed to Greek, Arabic or any other commonly spoken medieval tongue.

reported in the Gospel of St Matthew. 'If you would be perfect,' Jesus said, 'go, sell what you possess and give to the poor, and you will have treasure in heaven. Then come, follow me.'[5]

The young man to whom Christ addressed these words was not willing to listen. He departed lamenting that it would be quite impossible for him to give up his money. (Christ responded with his famous line about camels and needles.*) But several hundred years later minds had changed. From the third century AD, pious men (and some women) throughout the Christian world of the Roman Near East had come to the conclusion that in order to save their souls they needed to strip their lives of all luxuries, fripperies and temptations. They began to give up their possessions and abandon the secular world and take off into the wilderness, to live in physical squalor but moral purity: praying, contemplating the world and surviving on donations and scraps.

Like so many of the key developments in western monotheism during the first millennium AD, this trend for what historians now call 'asceticism' emerged in the deserts of the Near East, and especially in Egypt. Among the most famous of the Egyptian Christian ascetics was St Anthony the Great. Anthony was himself quite literally a rich young man – the son and heir of a wealthy family who at the age of twenty went to church and heard Christ's exhortation to poverty, and promptly 'sold all he had, gave the proceeds to the poor and from then on lived the life of a hermit.'[6] His devotion to self-denial was a legendary model for generations of monks who came after him. Anthony's contemporary Athanasius, bishop of Alexandria, recorded the hermit's struggles and deeds in an entertaining (and enduringly popular) hagiography. According to this, Anthony was regularly bothered in his cave by demons disguised as small children, vicious wild beasts, piles of treasure or gigantic monsters.† Thanks to the strength of his forbearance

---

* 'Again I tell you, it is easier for a camel to go through the eye of a needle than for someone who is rich to enter the kingdom of God.' *Matthew* 19:24.
† The grotesque and bizarre torments of St Anthony fired the imaginations of many later artists, ranging from late medieval masters like Hieronymus Bosch and Michelangelo to modern figures including Dorothea Tanning and Salvador Dalí.

and faith he defied them all. Meanwhile, he set a fine example to the other hermits and disciples who gravitated to him, inspired by his life of hard manual labour and rigorous, searching prayer. Despite the harshness of his existence Anthony lived – or so it was said – to the age of 105 and after his death he became known as the Father of All Monks.⁷ However, he was by no means the only prominent ascetic of his day. The formative age of Christianity produced a whole host of 'desert fathers' and 'desert mothers'. They included Anthony's leading disciple, Macarius; a Roman soldier called Pachomius, who pioneered 'cenobitism', or the custom of ascetics living together in what became known as monasteries; a reformed bandit called Moses the Black; an anchorite or female hermit called Syncletica of Alexandria; and one Theodora, also of Alexandria, who joined a community of male ascetics, living undetected as a man until her death.

Together these early ascetics were an eclectic and varied bunch of pious pioneers – experimental, often (to our eyes) eccentric, but connected by a remarkable desire to experience extreme physical deprivation, usually in remote and inhospitable places. Together they alighted on the essence of what became medieval monasticism, and generations of monks and other ascetics would return to their example throughout the ensuing eleven centuries.

AFTER ITS BEGINNINGS IN THE DESERT, the monastic movement grew steadily between the third and sixth centuries AD, creeping out of Egypt to all parts of the Christian east and west, with notable early centres in Caesarea-in-Cappadocia (modern Kayseri, Turkey), Aquileia (Italy) and Marmoutier (France) – the last being the base of operations for a particularly saintly character called Martin, a Roman cavalry officer who saw Christ's light and abandoned the life of saddle and slaughter to become the hermit-bishop of Tours.⁸

There were, broadly speaking, two types of monk. Hermits operated singly. Some removed themselves to the middle of nowhere – extreme practitioners of eremitism might choose to become 'stylites', meaning they lived on top of pillars, while other hermits wandered the towns and countryside, preaching, begging for their upkeep and offering spiritual guidance to ordinary laypeople. Then there were cenobites, who formed single-sex communities, living together, usually in a fixed abode with common areas and individual cells, praying, studying and labouring their days away. Both types of monasticism (the word stems from the Greek μονος, suggesting a oneness with God) co-existed throughout the Middle Ages, and indeed can still be found today. And both types caused some consternation for the established Church. Ascetics disrupted traditional social hierarchies. They were in most cases pious laypeople, not ordained priests. They did not fall under the jurisdiction of bishops, and could often drain authority and charitable funds from 'official' representatives of the Church. At the Council of Chalcedon, held in Byzantium in 451, there was an attempt to force monks to live in monasteries and quit wandering, but this had little long-lasting effect.[9] For one thing, it was practically very difficult to police individual piety. And for another, global cultural networks in the early Middle Ages were already wide and strong enough to mean that men and women were living monastic lives far beyond the discipline of Constantinople: by the fifth century Christian hermits could already be found as far afield as Ireland and Persia. Wherever there was Christianity, there were monks and hermits, and for a long time there seemed to be very little way to impose any sort of order or discipline on their spontaneous, vigorous and localized subcultures.

Unquestionably the most important figure in applying form and consistency to monasticism – in the west at least – was an Italian called Benedict of Nursia. The details of Benedict's life are by no means certain,* for, like St Anthony, he was the subject of a tremendously popular hagiography, in this case written by Pope Gregory I 'the Great', which was not written to satisfy modern

---

* Some historians think that Benedict may not even have been a single figure, but rather may represent a composite 'ideal' abbot, created by Gregory the Great for his own didactic purpose.

tests of historical veracity. But from what we can tell, Benedict appears to have been born around the year 480. He had a twin sister called Scholastica and the siblings came from a well-to-do family. Benedict lived for a time in Rome but left the city as a young man, 'giving over his book, and forsaking his father's house and wealth, with a resolute mind only to serve God.' In Gregory the Great's telling, Benedict was looking 'for some place where he might attain to the desire of his holy purpose'. He found it in a cave near Subiaco, in the Lazio.[10] There a more experienced ascetic, Romanus of Subiaco, instructed Benedict in the ways of being a hermit. But the student soon excelled his master in holy reputation and was headhunted to come and run a nearby monastery.

Although initially reluctant to embrace the communal life over the rigours of the cave, Benedict soon thrived. According to Gregory the Great's hagiography, he performed scores of miracles. He escaped numerous attempts at poisoning by disgruntled monks who resented the strictness of his regimen. He revived a little boy who had been crushed by a collapsing wall. He outwitted a Goth called Riggo who was pretending to be the barbarian king Totila, and he disconcerted the real Totila by predicting the date of his death. (Accurately, as it turned out.) He seemed to have a sixth sense for knowing if the monks in his charge had stashed illicit flagons of wine, accepted gifts (monks were forbidden personal property) or even entertained proud thoughts. He exorcised demons, raised the dead and cured a woman of insanity. Once a year he saw his sister Scholastica, who lived in a nunnery;* she was also able to perform miracles, which included persuading God to conjure up thunderstorms on demand.

But most important of all, Benedict of Nursia founded twelve monasteries in southern Italy, including one in a magnificent hilltop location on Monte Cassino, halfway between Rome and Naples, the site of an abandoned pagan temple to the Roman god Jupiter. To ensure that his own standards were kept at Monte

---

* i.e. a community for women living the cenobitic life – these had roots just as ancient as male-only monasteries. Tradition holds that Scholastica's nunnery was at modern-day Piumarola, but archaeological evidence does not definitively agree.

Cassino and other similar foundations, Benedict 'wrote a rule for his monks, both excellent for discretion and also eloquent in style.'[11] It laid out the principles by which, in Benedict's words, monks could renounce 'your own will, once and for all, and armed with the strong and noble weapons of obedience... do battle for the true King, Christ the Lord.'[12]

The Rule of St Benedict (*Regula Sancti Benedicti*) was by no means unique. It was not the first monastic rule to have been written: St Augustine of Hippo had composed one in north Africa around the year 400, while Caesarius of Arles had written a rule specifically for women (the *regula virginum*) in 512. Nor was it even especially original, owing much to the writings of a fifth-century ascetic called John Cassian and an anonymous sixth-century text called the Rule of the Master. Nevertheless, Benedict's Rule was simple, elegant and influential. It would become the template for western monasticism for generations afterwards. Monks who lived under its provisions would be known as Benedictines, or, in reference to the mandatory colour of their robes, Black Monks.

The Rule of St Benedict, comprising of seventy-three chapters, set out the basis of life for a monk living in a community under the guidance of an abbot. Its essential principles were prayer, study and manual work, supplemented by frugal living, personal poverty, chastity and a restricted diet. The Rule provided for the hierarchy within the monastery. It specified what food could be eaten (or not) and when. And it laid down rules for sleeping arrangements, clothing, the terms on which monks could sell their produce, the manner in which monks should travel and even how much they ought to smile. Punishments for infractions against the Rule ranged from a scolding to excommunication, although there were exemptions for those who fell sick. The Rule was detailed enough to be adopted by abbots who were looking for some guidance and certainty in running their own houses, but flexible enough to allow a degree of individuality between monasteries. It was, in short, an elegant and thoughtful piece of work, which was why Gregory the Great praised and publicized it in his account of Benedict's life. Those who followed the Rule, wrote Gregory, might 'understand all [Benedict's] manner of life and discipline.'[13] They too could aspire to perfection by obeying the commands of what we might now describe as a holy algorithm. Just as St Anthony in the desert had established an example for early ascetics in the Roman Empire to follow, so Benedict on his hilltop at Monte Cassino had now assembled a step-by-step recipe for the monastic lifestyle. Over subsequent generations this would be exported all over the Christian west.

Towards the Golden Age

IN THE SECOND HALF OF THE seventh century, around one hundred years after Benedict of Nursia died, his bones, along with those of his twin Scholastica, were dug up from their resting place at Monte Cassino and stolen. At that time, the monastery lay in ruins, having been ransacked by the Lombards in 580; it would not be rebuilt and re-inhabited until 718. So the graverobbers, according to a later account, thought they were doing a good deed. They were themselves monks, from central France, hundreds of miles away to the north, and they were guided to the exact location of the tomb by a combination of holy visions brought on by fasting and the local knowledge of a swineherd. After some effort – they had to cut through two thick marble slabs – they found Benedict and Scholastica's remains, scooped them up, washed them, and 'laid them upon fine clean linen... to be carried home to their own country.'[14] Specifically, this meant their monastery at Fleury (subsequently known as St Benoît-sur-Loire, about 150km due south of Paris). There the abbot, Mommolus, recognized a good thing when he saw one. The linen in which they were wrapped now seemed to be soaked in miraculous holy blood: Mommolus declared this a sure sign of their authenticity. So the remains were reinterred with honour in a shrine that catapulted Fleury Abbey to new fame.*

---

* A shrine is still maintained by the community of Benedictine monks at Fleury today. But it should be said that the monks at Monte Cassino today disagree with virtually everything written here. They dispute the whole story of the removal of Benedict and Scholastica's relics

St Benedict's posthumous removal from Italy to the lands of the Franks was not only an exciting caper. The burglary would have long-lasting repercussions, for it gave rise over the century that followed to a newfound enthusiasm north of the Alps for Benedict and his Rule. During the early Middle Ages, a wide range of monastic practices was to be found in Merovingian Gaul. The influence of Irish monasticism – which emphasized extreme personal hardship and missionary wandering, as exemplified by the missionary saints Columba and Columbanus* – was particularly strong.[15] But there were many different opinions current as to how to run a monastery, with no overall consensus as to which was the best way. Accordingly, monks and nuns who lived together in communities obeyed a whole hotchpotch of 'mixed' rules, composed or compiled ad hoc by their abbots. It was often rather hard to tell the difference between a house of monks and a group of canons – priests and clergy who lived together under an agreed rule of their own, but were allowed to keep personal property and interacted as a matter of course with the world and people around them. Benedict's arrival was destined to change all that.[16]

The agents of change, as with so much in early medieval Francia, were the Carolingians. As we saw in chapter 5, Charlemagne rapidly expanded and centralized Frankish authority, reviving the notion of a Christian imperial power in the west, while taking a keen interest in study, literacy and pious building works. Unsurprisingly he also liked the idea of imposing uniformity on the monks in his territories. Both Charlemagne and his son Louis the Pious saw the Rule of Benedict as a useful way to bring order to Christian practice and exercise meaningful imperial power over

---

and maintain their own shrine, marked with a black marble stone. This bears an inscription stating that the twins lie under the high altar of their cathedral, which was rebuilt in the twentieth century after being flattened by heavy Allied bombing during the Second World War.
* St Columba took Christ's word out of Ireland and into Scotland, where among his other impressive deeds he was said to have banished a fierce creature that had been terrorizing the River Ness to the depths of Loch Ness – a story that seems to mark the beginning of the legend of the Loch Ness Monster. Columba was buried in 597 on the island of Iona, but his remains were removed during the Viking invasions and were taken to various places on either side of the Irish Sea. His contemporary St Columbanus went much further afield, travelling around the lands of the Merovingian Franks and across the Alps into Lombardy.

the ordinary lives of their subjects. This was an especially pressing matter in the case of monks, who occupied an awkward position outside direct ecclesiastical control, as unanswerable to bishops as they were to secular lords. Meanwhile, founding Benedictine monasteries in newly conquered pagan territories was also a reliable way to promote good Christian practice on the fringes of empire – a form of colonization and missionary activity rolled into one. Finally, the Carolingians recognized that monasteries were the only real way to provide serious education, where clever young men (and women) could learn to parse Christian scripture while also studying Latin and pagan writings preserved from the ancient world.[17] Charlemagne and Louis therefore swung the weight of their governments behind the rule of Benedict. It was a decisive moment in the history of the western Church.

The man charged with the practical responsibility for this religious policy was another Benedict – of Aniane. He was given sweeping powers to impose reform across the Frankish lands, a task he undertook with great energy, culminating towards the end of his life in a series of Church councils held in the glorious palace at Aachen between 816 and 819. At these gatherings, Louis and Benedict of Aniane ordered that all Frankish monasteries should henceforth observe standardized practices. There ought to be fixed processes of initiation, an emphasis on obedience to the abbot, lifestyles focused on prayer, work and study, and above all, adherence to the Rule of St Benedict, which could be augmented only by additional regulations that were in keeping with its spirit. Any monk who felt that he might not be up to the rigours of the life was to seek ordination as a cleric – joining the ranks of the institutional Church and coming under the jurisdiction of their local bishop.

There were, therefore, two ways to go within the Frankish empire: you were either in the Church proper, or under the imperially approved Benedictine Rule. This did not instantly tidy up every aspect of Christian religious life across the vast Carolingian lands. But it ensured Benedictine practice became the norm across large swathes of Europe. Every mainstream monastic movement from this point on would build on the Benedictine standard – including the Cluniacs of the tenth century, to whom we can now return.

WHEN DUKE WILLIAM OF AQUITAINE HANDED over his hunting lodge at Cluny for Abbot Berno to transform into a monastery, he knew what sort of place he imagined it becoming: a well-run Benedictine establishment, strictly governed by a rigorous abbot, but shielded from earthly influence by anyone except the pope. All the same, William cannot possibly have realized just how successfully Cluny would grow – and how powerful it would become.

When Berno died in 927 he passed command of Cluny to a new abbot called Odo, who had trained from boyhood as a warrior in Duke William's household, but experienced a crisis of faith in his late teens and ran off to live as a cave hermit. Later Odo became a monk under Berno's strict regime at Baume, where he was known for his impeccable humility. When he eventually succeeded as Berno's successor at Cluny, Odo brought the monastery's first phase of building works to completion. He obtained royal and papal confirmation for the terms of Duke William's foundation charter, successfully solicited land and money from other supportive nobles, and maintained Berno's tradition of close enforcement of the Benedictine Rule. He was not always especially nice about it: the brothers at Cluny were harshly punished for such tiny errors as failing to gather up and eat the crumbs from their plates at mealtimes.

Most importantly, however, Odo began to export Cluny's high standards to other monasteries. He visited Benedictine houses in central France as a sort of freelance standards inspector, advising them on improving their communal life. This almost always meant reverting to the first principles of hard physical labour and constant prayer. Odo was a stickler for silence unless absolutely necessary, and insisted on a rigorously policed diet, free from all meat. He was punctilious about dress code. His chief interests, in the words of his biographer, John of Salerno, were 'contempt for the world, and after that, zeal for souls, the reform of monasteries, and of the clothes and food of monks.'[18]

If Odo's measures now sound harsh, however, the need for such reform seemed strong. Despite repeated demands from Carolingian rulers – and others besides – that monasteries should be run well, and the Benedictine Rule observed, surviving sources from the time abound with lurid examples of monastic standards slipping as brothers and sisters decided to relax a little and enjoy their isolation from the world. The eighth-century northern English monk and historian known as 'the Venerable' Bede left one typically unflattering account of a double monastery (a house established under a single abbot or abbess with communities of both monks and nuns) at Coldingham (today in Berwickshire in Scotland). There, Bede claimed, the monks and nuns spent half their time in bed, sometimes with each other. Their cells were 'converted into places for eating, drinking and gossip', and the nuns spent 'all their time weaving fine clothes... either to adorn themselves like brides or to attract attention from strange men.'[19] Even allowing for the stiff-necked Bede's natural hostility to women and the high probability of confirmation bias ensuring that anyone who went looking for examples of imperfection in monasteries would find them, his anecdote paints a colourful picture of moral laxity among so-called ascetics.* Odo never made it to the British Isles – reform there was led, a generation later, from within the established English church by Dunstan, archbishop of Canterbury, Aethelwold, bishop of Winchester and Oswald, archbishop of

---

* Of course, we must always take care with literary depictions of monastic vice, for the 'bad monk' was a staple trope of complaint and humour writing throughout the later Middle Ages. Writing much later than Bede, in the fourteenth century, Geoffrey Chaucer and Giovanni Boccaccio would have enormous, bawdy fun with the stereotype of the greedy, lazy, sexually incontinent 'ascetic'. Boccaccio's *Decameron* includes one very entertaining story about a layman who pretends to be a deaf-mute to cadge a stay at a nunnery, but ends up becoming the sexual servant of all nine of the sisters, including the abbess. The plot of this story (and the caricatures it promotes) is not very far removed from that of a typical 1970s sex-farce movie, such as *Confessions of a Window Cleaner*. For Boccaccio, see Steckel, Sita, 'Satirical Depictions of Monastic Life', Beach, Alison I. and Cochelin, Isabelle (eds.), *The Cambridge History of Medieval Monasticism in the Latin West* II (Cambridge: 2020), pp. 1154–1170.

York. But it was precisely the sort of misbehaviour that had been characterized by Bede that he was determined to stamp out.

The example of Coldingham might have served as a dire warning in itself for wayward monks and nuns, for according to Bede, God allowed the abbey to catch fire and burn down 'because of the wickedness of its members'.[20] But as Odo travelled ever further across Europe rolling out Cluny's monastic template, he found there was plenty of work to do. Naturally, not all the monks he visited were overjoyed to receive him. When Odo came to reform Fleury – the resting place of Benedict and Scholastica's relics – the monks threatened him with spears and swords. They later claimed they had been traumatized by Viking raids and were therefore leery of all outsiders; either way, Odo calmed them down, took them to task, improved their obedience and then moved on. Over the course of the next decade he brought Cluniac reform to houses as far afield as Normandy and southern Italy, where his projects included reforming Monte Cassino itself. One of Odo's specialities was returning monks to monasteries which had been desolated by attacks from non-Christians – especially Vikings, Muslims in northern Spain or Slavs raiding from central and eastern Europe. When he visited a monastery to reform it, he usually left behind one of his trusted, experienced fellow monks to ensure that his standards were maintained.[21] In many cases these men would serve not as abbots, but as priors, answerable directly to Odo himself at Cluny. This practice soon became a system, and with every reformation he undertook, the abbot of Cluny expanded his authority. He was becoming more than just the head of a single house and an itinerant trouble-shooter for others: he was actively folding newly reformed houses into the spiritual community of Cluny itself. By the time he died in 942 Odo had carried the name and the brand of Cluniac reform far and wide across western Europe.

BY THE MIDDLE OF THE TENTH century, Cluny was becoming famous. Better still, it was becoming famous at exactly the right moment, for money and property were flooding into the monastic world, particularly in the west, and communal spirituality was a booming business. Benedictine monasteries such as the glorious foundation at Gorze, near Metz in north-east France, had independently begun to reform themselves along similar lines as Cluny, operating as hubs for monastic renewal in their own regions. Germany's royal rulers were taking a leading hand in establishing and patronizing Benedictine houses in their realms. At the same time, Christianity was marching afresh into new parts of Europe, and bringing the life ascetic with it. The rulers of Bohemia (in the modern Czech Republic), Hungary, Poland and Denmark all converted in the tenth and eleventh centuries and often established monasteries in their realms to mark the occasion. (Some of the earliest Polish monks arrived as settler-missionaries from near Ravenna and set up a monastery under the protection of the Polish duke Bolesław the Brave. Unfortunately they were all murdered by bandits.)[22] A little later, during the crusades, western Benedictine convents would be built in Palestine and Syria, on holy sites in Jerusalem and at the coastal city of Antioch.[23] Yet it was Cluny – the nimble start-up with designs on becoming an international brand – which best exploited the wealth flooding into the market.

The reasons for this explosion in monasticism around the turn of the first millennium have been hotly debated by historians. Many factors played a part. One elemental cause may have been climate change. Between around 950 and 1250 global temperatures in the northern hemisphere rose, and although this rise was by no means evenly felt across the globe, it provided the longest sustained period of benign climate conditions in the west since the Roman Climate Optimum.[24] Although as we shall see, the so-called Medieval Warm Period would not last throughout the Middle Ages, it made conditions in Europe relatively favourable to agriculture. This natural advantage coincided with the development of new horse-harnesses and large iron ploughs ('heavy' ploughs) which allowed massively more efficient large-scale agriculture.[25] And as this technology combined with the effects of a fluctuating climate, landholding became ever more profitable and landowners had ever more disposable income to spend.

But what to spend it on? One very good answer was: salvation. As we have seen, the rise of the Carolingians changed the way western Europe was politically constituted. The drawing-together of numerous fractured, post-Roman 'barbarian' polities into a revived Christian empire provided a firmer central government, and directed major spheres of warfare to the fringes of the organized Christian west – pagan central Europe, Muslim Spain and (eventually) Scandinavia. But it also set the conditions for more small-scale fighting within the west itself. Frankish elites were increasingly tied to their rulers and rewarded for their loyalty with grants of land. They defended their territories by fighting one another. We will explore in more detail later how this changed aristocratic warrior culture. But in simple terms, the consequence was a sharp rise in lethal violence between Christian warriors, and a concomitant desire among those warriors to make sure that they did not go to hell for their sins.

Monasteries provided a neat solution. To atone for sins, the Church recommended penance and prayer. This was time-consuming, uncomfortable and impractical for people who had jobs to do fighting and killing one another. Fortunately the Church was very open-minded about how penance was to be done, and Church authorities had no problem with the rich paying others to do their penance for them. By founding monasteries – as Duke William did at Cluny – the landowning, warrior classes of Europe could effectively offset their sins by paying for monks to beg forgiveness on their behalf in the form of masses.* The result was that from the ninth century onwards, founding, endowing or donating to monasteries became a popular pastime for rich men and women. And like all rich-people pastimes throughout history it quickly became the object of fashion, competition and one-upmanship. Monasteries that could demonstrate the finest

---

* Think about carbon offsetting among modern companies and individuals who are interested in making up for the damage they have done to the environment through long-distance travel, freighting, excessive use of the central heating, etc.

standards of observance, grandest churches and libraries, largest and most devout communities and best international reputations were highly prized. The super-wealthy founded them. The wealthy donated to them. And in turn the affluent and just-getting-by followed suit.[26] Monasteries sprang up in their hundreds. Looking back on this explosive time of growth, the tenth to twelfth centuries have often been labelled a 'golden age' of monasticism.

Pathways to Heaven

WHEN ODILO, THE FIFTH ABBOT OF Cluny, was a young boy, he suffered a crippling condition that deprived him of the use of his legs. His family were affluent and his parents well known in their corner of the Auvergne, in southern France. When they travelled, servants carried little Odilo on a stretcher. This was a comparative luxury, which most children in his position would never have been able to enjoy. But Odilo still suffered, and seemed destined never to be able to walk.

One day, however, the strangest thing happened. The family was out on an expedition, and as they passed by a church, Odilo's attendants stopped to rest. They put his stretcher down near the door and left him on his own for a moment. When they returned they were stunned to find that the boy had rolled off his litter, crawled into the church, pulled himself up on the altar-side and was now prancing around. It was a miracle, and one that would shape the course of Odilo's long life. His parents were overwhelmed, and as a sign of their gratitude they gave the boy to a local house of canons in the Auvergne, to be raised for a career in the service of God. Gifting children to religious houses in this fashion – as 'oblates', literally meaning 'offerings' – was common aristocratic practice, since it ensured the child would receive an education, while reducing the number of potential heirs among a large family. And if to us today this seems cruel, it suited some oblates very well. Odilo thrived among the clerics, and in his late twenties moved on to Cluny to become a monk. He impressed his fellow brothers there so much that in 994, upon the death of the fourth abbot, Maiolus, he was elected to lead them.[27] He steered the house through the unsettling turn of the first millennium, when many worried the world might end. And he went on to govern Cluny with great distinction for the next fifty years, during which time the prestige, presence and resources of the Cluniac movement grew enormously.

Odilo was described by one chronicler as an 'archangel of monks'. He counted as his confidantes not only a succession of popes, but several Frankish kings and emperors, who hosted him as a palace-guest at Christmastime and on other high ceremonial occasions. When Henry II, king of the eastern Franks (or as we can now call them, the Germans) was crowned emperor in 1004, he presented his papal coronation gift – a golden apple topped with a cross – to Abbot Odilo. It was sent back to Cluny to join an increasingly well-stocked vault of precious trinkets and jewels. But Odilo was not merely a gold-digger or princely ligger. He persuaded his powerful friends to protect Cluny and its daughter-houses from attempts by unscrupulous neighbours to deprive them of lands or infringe on their independence. And he used the wealth that accrued from their fabulous gifts to develop Cluny's buildings. Their abbey church had been remodelled during his first years as a monk there (modern archaeologists refer to this second church as 'Cluny II'). Odilo now set about reconstructing the monks' communal spaces at great expense – ordering the works done in marble and decorating the buildings with extraordinary sculptures. He likened himself to Augustus in Rome's heyday, saying that he had found Cluny built of wood and left it built of marble.[28]

It was not merely the fabric of Cluny's buildings that took grandeur from Odilo's time. Inside them, increasingly spectacular daily rounds of praise took place, in the form of communal prayers, psalms, readings and hymns, which were known collectively as the offices (or canonical hours). Offices were performed eight times in each day, beginning before dawn with matins and lauds, proceeding to *prime* around daybreak, *terce* in the mid-morning, *sext* at midday, *nones* in the mid-afternoon, with *vespers* and *compline* towards the day's end. (The length of the canonical hours varied by the season, according to the amount of daylight.) There was also a daily Mass to be heard. Performing these services was known as *opus Dei* (God's work), and it was the essential point of monasticism: this was the monks' contribution to society and an economy which placed great value on providing for souls as well as bodies. As a result, performing the offices was what most Benedictine monks spent most of their time doing. It behoved them to perform their duty to the best of their ability.

That meant a lot of singing. The Benedictine Rule was extremely enthusiastic about music, which, said St Benedict, ensured that 'our mind may be in harmony with our voice.'[29] It required the monks to organize themselves into a choir, ensuring only the best singers were allowed to have a prominent part in the performance.[30] Benedict recommended they learn the melodic style of plainchant which had been popular during his day in the basilicas of Rome: this was commonly called Gregorian chant, after Benedict's friend and cheerleader Pope Gregory I the Great, who was often (probably wrongly) said to have invented it. But beyond this he did not lay down too many specifics. There was, therefore, plenty of room for musical creativity during the monastic boom of the tenth and eleventh centuries.

Naturally, at Cluny, music was a central part of life. Although the destruction of the mother abbey and its archives means that it is now impossible to recreate the sound of Cluny's brethren in full voice, the importance of music was literally scored into the fabric of the buildings. Surviving columns contain etchings of musicians and verses about the importance of music to the praise of God.[31] From at least Odilo's day there seems to have been considerable experimentation there with different styles of psalm-chant, in which a delicate and harmonious balance could be struck between the performance of a single soloist and the whole choir singing together.[32] And of course, under such strict rule, there was plenty of chance for practice. On an ordinary day a typical Benedictine monk in one of the hundreds of monasteries across Europe might be awake for nineteen hours, of which fourteen were spent in some form of liturgical duty. But Cluny went even further. Almost every second could be accounted for by some form of procession to, from or within a service, by offices dedicated to specific feast days or the souls of the departed, or by humble ceremonies such as the ritual washing of paupers' feet. By the eleventh century, when the famous monk, reformer and cardinal Peter Damian paid a visit to Cluny, he was surprised to find that there was so much of God's work to be done there that the brothers had less than half an hour's respite from the choir each day.[33]

Later generations of monastic reformers grumbled that St Benedict would not have approved of marble pillars in the monks' dining hall, and singing all day taking precedence over hard manual labour. But at Cluny, opulent surroundings were understood to magnify the power of the divine praise that took place there.

Compostela and Cluny III

BY THE HIGH MIDDLE AGES* MONASTERIES had taken on most of what we now think of as the basic functions of the liberal welfare state. They were centres of literacy, education, hospitality, medical treatment, tourist information, elderly social care and spiritual counselling – in addition to their main role as a retreat for the godly. As a result they had wandered a long way from their origins as places of impoverished retreat, and now had close and lucrative links with the outside world.

One of the most visible ways that Cluny and its daughter houses became integrated in secular society was in their monopolization of the pilgrim routes which led to the holiest sites in western Europe. The most famous of these spiritual superhighways converged at the north-western tip of the Iberian peninsula, at the shrine of Santiago de Compostela in Galicia. Here, in AD 814, a hermit called Pelagius saw lights dancing in the sky, which led him

---

* Broadly speaking, the period from the eleventh to mid-thirteenth centuries.

miraculously to discover the remains of St James the Apostle.* And once St James had been discovered, his presence was marketed assiduously around the western world. A church was built to mark the site of his grave; it is still the site of one of the most spectacular cathedrals anywhere in the world, blending successive Romanesque, Gothic and baroque features into a monumental and magnificent whole. For Christian pilgrims fit enough to travel long distances, Compostela was (and is) an irresistible attraction. Outside the Holy Land only St Peter's Basilica in Rome could also boast the remains of one of the apostles. The obligation to pray at such a venerable shrine in one's lifetime was not incumbent on Christ's faithful in quite the same way as performing *hajj* was to Muslims. But it was still important.

To trace on a map the major medieval roads that led to Compostela is to draw an arterial system, with pathways that begin in Italy, Burgundy, the Rhineland, northern France and Flanders slowly but steadily converging on a few mountain passes through the Pyrenees, before a religious superhighway drives east-to-west parallel with the northern coast of the Iberian peninsula, until it hits Santiago itself. A medieval handbook for pilgrims planning to travel this road was written in the twelfth century. It gave much practical advice to the intrepid traveller, noting spots along the way where the wine was good and the local people honourable. But it also warned of the perils of the trip: giant wasps and horseflies around Bordeaux, the greed and drunkenness of Gascons, the risks of being swindled or even deliberately drowned by rogue ferrymen at river crossings, and the absolute barbarousness of the Navarrese, who spoke like barking dogs and copulated with mules and mares during the night.[34]

The dangers and discomforts of travelling long distances like this were, of course, part of the penitential purpose. Earning God's forgiveness was not supposed to be easy. But they also presented a

---

* According to various Christian traditions, following Christ's death and resurrection, James had preached the gospel all the way into Hispania. Having returned to the east he was murdered on the orders of the king of Judea, Herod Agrippa, then brought back to the Spanish peninsula for burial.

golden business opportunity. Many centuries earlier, when Rome had been at the peak of its imperial power, the Roman roads that criss-crossed the empire were lined with purpose-built *mansiones* – effectively service stations for imperial officials, kitted out with stabling, overnight facilities and hospitality. Now, along the pilgrim routes, there sprang a similar need.[35] The Cluniacs recognized it and exploited it. Monasteries became the new *mansiones*, catering to the faithful as they struck out to seek salvation in northern Spain.

The genius in this phase of Cluny's development was Abbot Hugh 'the Great', who succeeded Odilo when he died at the advanced age of eighty-seven, on the first day of January 1049. Much like Odilo, Hugh was a saintly character – he became a monk at fourteen, was ordained to priesthood at twenty and was elected abbot at twenty-four. According to one of his contemporaries, Arnulf of Soissons (the patron saint of Belgian beer), Hugh was 'most pure in thought and deed... the promoter and perfect guardian of monastic discipline and the regular life... [and] the vigorous champion and defender of the Holy Church.'[36] Like Odilo, Hugh would also prove an astonishingly durable abbot, remaining in office for sixty years. In that time he continued where Odilo had left off: reinforcing the sense that the abbot of Cluny was a natural peer to kings and popes, exerting his political power across Europe and seeing to it that Cluny stayed institutionally rich. He was a brilliant administrator with a sharp eye for business. Under Hugh's leadership the Cluniac network grew towards its peak of around 1,500 houses.

Under Hugh, monastic houses either controlled directly by Cluny or influenced by its observances sprang up along the roads to Santiago. An eleventh-century pilgrim starting his or her journey to visit St James hundreds of miles away in the gently rolling heartlands of southern England might conceivably set out from the Priory of St Pancras, near Lewes in Sussex, the first Cluniac establishment in England. Lewes was founded by the earl of Surrey, William de Warenne and his wife Gundrada, and grew to become one of the largest and most lavishly appointed monasteries in the realm. Had our pilgrim then crossed the Channel and picked up the pilgrim road south from Paris, he or she would have encountered dozens more Cluniac houses along the way, whether at major urban stopping points like Tours, Poitiers, or Bordeaux or at smaller spots in between. Then, after the mountain passes, the pilgrim would have found the Spanish road dotted with further Cluny-affiliated monasteries – at Pamplona, Burgos, Sahagún (a sublime house richly endowed and known as the 'Spanish Cluny') and León.

The grandest of these were designed to evoke Cluny itself, both architecturally and through the atmosphere and routine of monastic life. Many were repositories for saintly relics. The great abbey at Vézelay claimed, amazingly, to possess the body of Mary Magdalen. In Poitiers nuns guarded a fragment of the True Cross, sent long ago as a gift to the Merovingian queen Radegund by the Byzantine emperor Justinian; Sahagún boasted the remains of the local martyrs Facundus and Primitivus, who were beheaded for their faith in around AD 300, and died spouting milk as well as blood from the arteries in their necks.[37] The corporeal remains of all these could be venerated by pilgrims, as part of the warm-up act for the shrine of St James himself in Compostela.

STRANGE TO SAY, THE MOTHER-HOUSE OF Cluny itself was not endowed with relics of comparable magnificence. However, for the time that it sat on top of such a vast pyramid of reformed monasteries, during the tenth and eleventh centuries, Cluny became vastly wealthy. Besides ample donations from direct benefactors, and the money it generated from its large estates, vast riches were funnelled its way thanks to its investment in the Compostela pilgrim ways. Some of this came from contributions of a few pounds of silver sent back 'home' every year by every daughter house. But even more came in from direct payments made to Cluny by the Christian kings of the northern Iberian peninsula, whom Abbot Hugh assiduously groomed for their generous donations. In 1062 King Ferdinand of León and Castile promised to give Hugh 1,000 pounds in gold every year for the good of the Cluniac movement. In 1077 his son, Alfonso VI, bumped up the contribution to 2,000 pounds.

These were enormous sums, bigger by far than the entire revenue Cluny Abbey generated from its landed estates.[38] But they were also a testament to how well the Spanish kings thought of Hugh – and how much they valued what he could offer them in return. Cluniac houses not only lubricated the valuable tourist trade through the Spanish kingdoms, but also were able to offer what Ferdinand and Alfonso saw as the most elite soul-laundering service on earth. The eleventh century marked the beginnings of the *Reconquista* – the wars between Christian powers in the northern Iberian peninsula and Muslim powers in the south (al-Andalus). The kings of Leon and Castile, tightly bound up in these wars, were compelled to spill a lot of blood. But they earned a great deal of gold, in either plunder or tribute, taken after the conquest of Muslim cities, whose rulers sometimes agreed to pay annual tribute in return for peace.

These rich pickings allowed the Christian kings to make amends for the grave sins incurred in military campaigning. They did so by ploughing funds into Cluny. In return for their generous donations, Hugh agreed that Cluniac houses would sing literally non-stop for the Spanish kings' souls, those of their ancestors and – most impressively – those of their as-yet unborn descendants. At Cluny itself a special altar was set up, at which Masses sung would only be deemed to assist the salvation of Alfonso himself.* This was angel investment, to be sure, and Hugh of Cluny used it to endow his mother-house and the Cluniac movement at large with a church that would be for several centuries a true wonder of the western world.

***

---

* One feature of late capitalist angst is to fret about a digital economy in which money is lavished on services and products which have absolutely no tangible existence outside the realm of computer servers, vastly enriching a small group of companies and their executives. It is perhaps comforting to think that in the Middle Ages a comparable economy certainly existed.

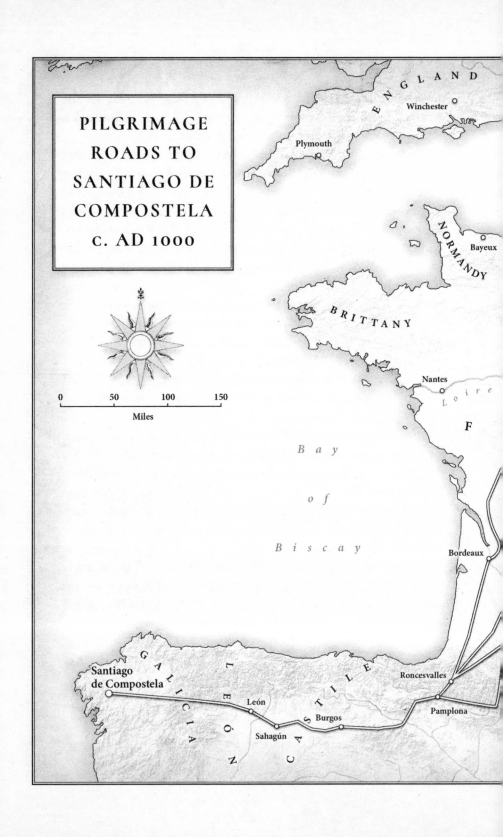

PILGRIMAGE
ROADS TO
SANTIAGO DE
COMPOSTELA
c. AD 1000

0   50   100   150
Miles

ENGLAND

Winchester

Plymouth

NORMANDY

Bayeux

BRITTANY

Nantes

Loire

F

Bay

of

Biscay

Bordeaux

GALICIA

Santiago
de Compostela

LEÓN

León

Sahagún

Burgos

CASTILE

Roncesvalles

Pamplona

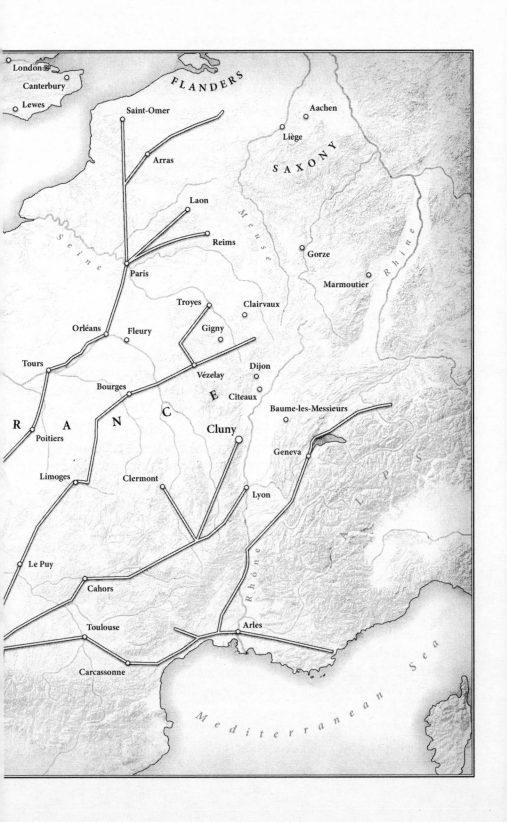

CLUNY III, TO GIVE HUGH'S NEW abbey church the unromantic name favoured by modern historians, was begun in the early 1080s. According to later tradition, the plans were allegedly drawn up by none other than the saints Peter, Paul and Stephen, who appeared together one night in the dreams of a crippled monk named Gunzo, formerly the abbot of Baume. In Gunzo's dream, saints laid out their plans for the new church, including precise architectural dimensions. They told Gunzo to pass the details on to Abbot Hugh and said if he relayed the message he would regain use of his legs. (They also threatened to paralyse Hugh if he failed to do their bidding).[39] Neither Gunzo nor Hugh needed further prompting. Hugh entrusted the job of realizing the saints' plans to a brilliant mathematician from Liège, not far from the old imperial court at Aachen. His name was Hezelo, and he seems to have been well versed in mathematical proportions described by the great Roman engineer Vitruvius – whose work intrigued many other medieval geniuses, including Leonardo da Vinci.[40] Hezelo's designs were for a church nearly 200m in length, theoretically large enough to accommodate not just the 300 monks who inhabited Cluny, but, so it was said, every single monk and nun within the Cluniac world. Cluny III was more than twice the size of Justinian's Hagia Sophia and substantially bigger than the Umayyads' glorious Great Mosque of Damascus. No religious building of any sort in the medieval west even began to rival it for size – not even Santiago de Compostela or 'Old' St Peter's in Rome.*

The church was built on a long, cross-shaped plan, with an extraordinarily long nave, divided into two aisles, with eleven bays along its length. It rose to three storeys in height.[41] Outside, a thicket of square and octagonal towers rose above the apse and transept, and over the centuries other buildings and towers would be added to the central works. On the church's southern side, cloisters, courtyards, dormitories, an infirmary and other outbuildings stretched over at least the same area again. The church's elongated

* 'Old' St Peter's, which was demolished in the early sixteenth century, was around 110m long. The current basilica, which replaced it, and is today the largest Christian basilica in the world, is 186m long – almost identical to Cluny III.

cruciform design, with thick walls and masses of columns and rounded arches, set it well apart from earlier monumental buildings like Charlemagne's palace cathedral at Aachen or the squat, early medieval basilicas of Ravenna and elsewhere. Cluny III was a masterpiece of an architectural style that would come to be known as Romanesque, so named because it drew on elements of ancient Roman architecture, and the engineering theories that had made them possible. It was a swaggering expression of the capital wealth that was circulating in the west around the turn of the first millennium – and the willingness of men like Abbot Hugh and his patrons to invest it in long-term building projects. Put up in stages, partly because it was hamstrung by a collapse in funding that was brought about by a turn in fortunes in the wars of the *Reconquista*, Cluny III was not consecrated until 1130 – nearly half a century after ground was broken. By this stage, everyone who had conceived of the project was dead, and fashions in monasticism were beginning to change. But Hugh's vision had not been abandoned.

Although only a tiny portion of Cluny III remains standing today – a small section of the transept – there are still clues suggesting the wonder this behemoth of a building once inspired. Ten kilometres south of Cluny lies the chapel of Berzé-la-Ville, where the walls are literally plastered from floor to ceiling with dazzling, brightly coloured frescoes illustrating scenes from the Gospels and the lives of the saints. These jaw-dropping images were almost certainly commissioned by Abbot Hugh, and a similar aesthetic would have been visible on a much grander scale in Cluny III.* Meanwhile, records from the early twelfth century also hint at the opulence of the abbey's fixtures and furnishings: the family of Henry I of England gave silver candelabras and beautiful bells. Cluny III was a fabulous achievement, and its imprint in archaeology can still be seen in surviving Romanesque buildings all the way from England to Poland and Hungary.

However, while Cluny was a wonder of the new monastic world, it was also a far cry from the original ideal of reformed,

* See plate section.

stripped-back Benedictine practice. The monks who had been paid handsomely by high-net-worth clients to sing perpetual masses for their souls wore fine linen and ate well. Their liturgy was complex, highly structured and beautifully performed. The ordinary brothers' throats may have ached from perpetual chanting, but their hands were not calloused from manual labour, which was given over to serfs. Inside the abbey buildings could be found finely stocked libraries, wine cellars and huge collections of religious relics housed in jewelled reliquaries and fine painting and sculpture.

Cluny's monks were scholars. Its abbots were saints. But people were starting to grumble. History was coming full circle.

New Puritans

THERE WERE MOMENTS DURING THE PEAK of Hugh of Cluny's power when much of Europe seemed to dance to the abbot's tune. Cluny's – and Hugh's – influence was everywhere. In 1050, the German king and emperor Henry III asked Hugh to stand as godfather to his son, and took his advice on what to name the child. (Hugh obliged, although he didn't exercise much imagination: the child grew up to be the emperor Henry IV.) When William the bastard, duke of Normandy, invaded and conquered England in 1066 he struck up a correspondence with Hugh, and asked him to send monks from Cluny to set up priories in his new realm. When the French king Philip I – a man whose lifestyle choices left him in dire need of spiritual help – was getting old he contacted Hugh to sound him out about the possibility of retirement into monastic life.[42] At one point Hugh even travelled in person to visit King Andrew I of Hungary. And the abbot nurtured especially close links with Rome, where the reforming instinct that had underpinned Cluny's success and been rolled out far and wide in the monastic world was being adopted, adapted and extended by a series of 'reforming popes'.

Foremost among these was a monk named Hildebrand, who grew up in Tuscany and the Rhineland, found his way into a career in papal administration and – largely through his insatiable capacity for hard work and battering-ram personality – rose to be acclaimed Pope Gregory VII in 1073. Although very different in temperament, Gregory and Hugh struck up a close friendship, which cut across their occasional political differences. It rested on their shared, deep-seated belief in improving and ordering the institutions of Christian faith, and negotiating a place for the Church that sat squarely at the heart of everyday life across the realms of the west.

Gregory's fierce desire to clean up the Church and impose papal authority in every Christian realm caused serious political disquiet in Europe. And when Gregory went to war with Hugh's godson, the emperor Henry IV, in a conflict known as the Investiture Controversy – since it concerned the rights of secular rulers to appoint or 'invest' bishops – Hugh was caught somewhat in the middle. He felt much sympathy for Gregory. Yet he was friendly, both personally and politically, with key players on both sides. He tried his level best to remain impartial, and offered his services in mediation on several occasions. But for the most part all he could do was to stay removed from the ugly squabbling between his peers and hope that in time, a change of personalities might ease the troubles.[43] Which, in the end, they did. In 1088 a Cluniac monk called Odo of Châtillon – formerly Hugh's deputy at Cluny – was elected as Pope Urban II. His papacy redirected the violent energy of the Investiture Controversy towards a new experiment that would loom large over the next two centuries of monasticism in particular and western history in general: the crusades. But this is a story we shall pick up again in chapter 8. In the meantime, Hugh and Cluny faced challenges closer to home.

IN 1098, TOWARDS THE END OF the fourth decade of Hugh's abbacy, a small group of disaffected monks and hermits from Molesme in Burgundy decided that they wished to return to the first principles of asceticism, and find somewhere to live communally, according to a stripped-back version of the Benedictine Rule. The place they chose was Cîteaux, a highly unpromising patch of marshy land about 130km due north from Cluny, near Dijon. Here they founded a new monastery, intended to be as uncomfortable – and therefore as godly – as possible. Under their first abbot Robert of Molesme, and an English reformer known as Stephen Harding, the monks of Cîteaux went back to basics: hard labour, inadequate diet, austere surroundings, social isolation, lots of prayer and no fun.

With hindsight it feels only natural that this small band of spiritual warriors who assembled at Cîteaux – and thus became known as Cistercians – would come to steal Cluny's thunder. Such is the timeless story of radical movements. But the Cistercians, much like the Cluniacs, might never have turned austerity into popularity without the influence of their own charismatic leader. In this case, their guiding light was an affluent young Burgundian called Bernard. Born around 1090, Bernard entered the order as a teenager along with a couple of dozen of his well-off friends, and rose to become a new superstar of religious life and thought. In 1115 Bernard established his own Cistercian abbey at Clairvaux, and from there he corresponded energetically with all the sorts of people whom Hugh of Cluny had once petitioned, and many more beside. Popes, emperors, kings, queens and dukes were all in his contacts book; but so too were wayward young clerics and runaway nuns.

As we shall see, Bernard was a leading voice in the Second Crusade, which he preached in the 1140s. He was also a driving force in establishing the military Order of the Temple – the Templars. And just as Hugh of Cluny had seen a close ally elected Pope Urban II, so Bernard would celebrate one of his own protégés becoming pope: Eugenius III. But where Hugh of Cluny had worn the customary black habit of the Benedictines, Bernard of Clairvaux girded himself in Cistercian white, the colour chosen to symbolize purity. And whereas Hugh presided over a palatial, sensory, aristocratic form of Benedictine monasticism, Bernard insisted on an utter lack of adornment and dedication to the simplest possible existence, stripped bare of art, philosophy, complex rites and expensive architectural projects. These were incompatible approaches and ultimately only one could triumph.

For many years Bernard exchanged letters with Hugh's successor at Cluny, a famous and formidably gifted scholar-abbot known as Peter the Venerable. They argued constantly, and it was a contest of ascetic versus aesthete: of angry radical against reasoned traditionalist. The two men took opposite positions on many of the greatest issues and scandals of their days – not least the notorious case of a love affair between a brilliant Parisian scholar called Peter Abelard and his young female student, Heloïse.* Bernard of Clairvaux excoriated Abelard for his immorality – and for what he also saw as heretical scholarship. Peter the Venerable, by contrast, extended his sympathy to Abelard, taking him to Cluny when he was old and weak, and nursing him through the last months of his life in several comfortable Cluniac properties, until he died in 1142.[44]

In taking Abelard in and protecting him from trial for his scholarly opinions, Peter the Venerable was explicitly thwarting Bernard of Clairvaux. But in a sense, none of it was personal. Bernard and Peter butted heads as rivals but not as enemies. They could be by turns cutting, patronizing, dismissive, pedantic, snide and outright rude on parchment. But they always respected one another, and even spent Christmas together in 1150 – in the comfort of Cluny, of course, and not amid the frigid austerity of Clairvaux. What connected them – monasticism, contemplation, rules, order, earthly sin, heavenly redemption and high politics – was stronger than what drove them apart.

All the same, theirs was a correspondence that seemed to illustrate the turning of the wheel. Cluny's fortunes peaked under Hugh the Great. But they began to wane as the middle of the twelfth century approached. Abbots Odilo and Hugh had ruled between them for a century, a time during which there were twenty popes (and several rival 'antipopes'). But in the fifty years that followed Peter the Venerable's death in 1156, nine abbots came and went.[45] Secular rulers and popes began to release Cluniac priories

* See chapter 11.

from obedience to the mother-house. There was no flood of new foundations to replace them. The world had moved on.

By contrast, the power of the Cistercian order, inspired through Bernard of Clairvaux's impassioned leadership, grew and grew, and long outlasted Bernard's death in 1153. By this time more than three hundred Cistercian houses had been founded or reformed along Cistercian lines. They included Melrose Abbey in Scotland and the stunning Fountains Abbey in Yorkshire, England. There was a slew of new foundations in Ireland, where Benedictine monasticism had previously been pitifully under-represented. In France the movement earned the backing of the crown, when Louis VI 'the Fat' sent his son Henry to train for a career in the Church under Bernard at Clairvaux. Cistercians were drawn, just as Cluniacs had been, into the wars of the *Reconquista*, putting down roots in the expanding Christian kingdoms of Iberia. And the order pushed into central Europe too, with foundations in Germany, Bohemia, Poland, Hungary, Italy, Sicily and the western Balkans. By 1215, the Cistercians were culturally ascendant: the Fourth Lateran Council recognized them as the exemplar of the life ascetic, and instructed that the Cistercians should take the lead in organizing monastic councils, to gather every three years in each province subject to the religious authority of Rome.[46]

And so was a new age in western monasticism confirmed. At their peak, the Cistercians could boast more than seven hundred houses across Europe. Yet if the Cistercians were now clearly the west's leading monastic order, they did not enjoy that position unchallenged, as Cluny once had. For in their wake there emerged a whole myriad of other monastic 'orders' – groups who followed different rules, ways of life and dress codes – who felt they were better suited to a changing economy and religious climate. These included international military orders such as the Templars, Hospitallers and Teutonic Knights, whom we will meet again in chapter 8, along with smaller, localized military orders in Spain and Portugal, such as the orders of Calatrava and Santiago.

Meanwhile, more traditional, peaceful monastic orders for men and women also abounded. The Premonstratensians (or

Norbertines) were founded in the early twelfth century as a reformed, austere order of canons, who obeyed the rule of St Augustine rather than that of St Benedict, but who modelled their lives on the ascetic model espoused by the Cistercians. Around the same time the Carthusians – an order originally founded in the 1080s by St Bruno of Cologne – began to expand. Carthusian men and women pursued a simple, lonely life in which they dwelt, ate and prayed communally but spent most of their time in contemplation in their cells. Then, the dawn of the thirteenth century saw the rise of the mendicant* orders – the Franciscans and Dominicans, whose members (often called friars) stepped out from the cloister and, like the first generations of ascetics, took to wandering in towns and countryside, ministering and preaching and begging for alms to sustain themselves. Monasticism was in a sense returning to its roots – with a welter of different approaches, suited to local tastes and the whim of devout and sometimes eccentric individuals who sought their own idiosyncratic relationship with God, and did not feel the need to sign up to a giant multinational spiritual corporation such as Cluny had been in its heyday.

THE EXPLOSION OF WESTERN MONASTICISM BETWEEN the eleventh and the thirteenth centuries is a story that should feel as familiar to us as it does strange. Few people in the western Christian world now seek permanent retreat into a monastic order. A life of such intense voluntary hardship, chastity, poverty and repetitive liturgical worship holds scant appeal for rich young men and women in the twenty-first century. But what we can certainly recognize today is the rise of vastly rich and powerful international institutions and corporations who exercise enormous 'soft' power, and whose leaders have the ear of the world's political grandees. We are at ease with the idea of voluntarily adapted 'orders' for life, designed to improve our individual and collective virtue: veganism

---

* The name mendicant comes from the Latin *mendico* – to beg.

is one of the most popular in the west today. Finally, we take for granted that there will be institutions in our lives which provide education, pastoral care, medicine and respite for the retired elderly, whether run by the state or the community. We are in that sense perhaps not so far removed from a world run by monks as we may think.

We will come back to monasticism throughout this book, not least in the final chapter, when we discuss the religious upheavals of the Reformation in the late fifteenth and sixteenth centuries. We will also see monks again when we look at the crusades. But for the moment it is time to leave the safety of the cloister, and look at the other cultural movement that swept through the western world in tandem with monasticism. We will now turn our gaze on that group in society whom Bernard of Clairvaux scorned, in his trademark acid prose, as those who 'fight with such pomp and pains... to no purpose save death and sin.'[47] These were knights: people whom the monasteries had grown in part to save from damnation, but who represented the opposite way of life to monasticism, in which their power was executed not in word and song but at the end of a lance or sword.

7

KNIGHTS

'Are you God?'

PERCEVAL, CHRÉTIEN DE TROYES

In the middle of August 955, a time of year when specks of stardust always seemed to sparkle in the night sky, Otto I, king of the Germans, assembled an army a little way west of the city of Augsburg.[1] Otto was an experienced king and a veteran of many skirmishes and battles. He had ruled Germany for nearly twenty years, working hard to bring the disparate territories of what had once been Carolingian Eastern Francia under his direct control, strengthening the crown's authority and stamping down rebellious nobles who tried to resist him. Experience had made him tough. As a chronicler named Widukind of Corvey put it, Otto had learned to play 'the dual roles of the most powerful warrior and the highest commander.'[2] And at Augsburg he would need to draw on every ounce of his talent, for the city was in grave peril from a dangerous enemy known as the Magyars.

The Magyars had a long history of encroaching on the German sphere of interest. They were a pagan, tribal people who had migrated towards central Europe from the east, to settle the vast plains which spread out from the foothills of the Carpathian Mountains. Magyar fighting men were skilled riders who fought with bows and arrows from the saddle. They were dexterous, lightning fast and deadly. Christian writers in the German realm spread tall stories of their unique ferocity. They claimed the Magyars 'destroyed fortifications, set fire to churches and killed the people, alleged that 'to spread fear they drank the blood of their victims' and swore the first thing Magyar mothers did on giving birth was to 'take a sharp knife and mutilate their [babies'] faces, so that they will be able to tolerate wounds.'[3] Needless to say, this was little more than hearsay and libel. But it spoke to a fear of the Magyars deep-rooted among the ordinary folk of Germany; a fear that was every bit the equal of the western Franks' terror of the Vikings. So in the midsummer of 955, when Otto of Germany heard a Magyar army had set its sights on Augsburg, it was his duty as king to drive them away.

It ought to have been possible, if not easy, to defend Augsburg. Nestled between the duchies of Swabia and Bavaria, the city was the fortified seat of a senior bishop. Its walls were low and without defensive towers, but it occupied a reasonably safe geographical spot at the junction of two waterways, which impeded the approach to the city on three sides. Just north of the city walls, the river Wertach merged with the Lech, which then flowed on a few dozen miles until it emptied into the Danube. Plenty more tributary rivers cut through the plains to the east, feeding large areas of swamp almost unnavigable to conventional troops.

The problem, however, was that the Magyars were no conventional troops. Like the 'barbarian' tribespeople who had swept into Europe in the twilight years of the western Roman Empire, they excelled at fighting in open, grassy terrain, for their ancestors had learned the ways of war on the Eurasian steppe. They knew their way around plainlands, and the efficacy of their battle tactics had been proven in past generations. In 910 the sixteen-year-old Carolingian king Louis the Child had fought a Magyar force at Augsburg and been humiliated as Magyar horsemen feigned retreat, lured his troops forward, then cut them down without mercy. This had been the undoing of Louis the Child, who died a year or so later, tormented by melancholy stemming from his military failure. Otto could not afford a similar defeat. So he approached Augsburg with care.

Otto arrived on 10 August to find the city totally surrounded. One monastic annalist estimated, very improbably, that there were

100,000 Magyars outside it. Whatever their real numbers, these Magyar warriors, under leaders called Bulcsu, Lehel and Taksony, were unquestionably battle-hardened, having already plundered their way through Bavaria, 'which they devastated and occupied from the Danube to the dark forests on the rim of the mountains.'[4] Moreover, they were equipped with siege towers and catapults, with which they had been pelting the city for several days. The citizens of Augsburg had manned the walls, where they were bravely commanded by their bishop, Ulrich, who sat on horseback in his episcopal robes, 'protected by neither shield nor chain mail, nor helmet, as missiles and stones whizzed around him.'[5] But it was clear they would not be able to hold out for very long. Bishop Ulrich was committed to his cause, but he had little to work with. Besides his efforts to organize the citizens, he could do no more than pray, perform the Mass and instruct a group of nuns to parade around the city streets carrying a cross.

Otto had better weapons at hand. He travelled to Augsburg from Saxony, where earlier that summer he had been fighting Slavs. Although his forces were smaller, numerically, than the Magyars, they were disciplined, led by capable nobles including Conrad the Red, duke of Lorraine, and trained to fight in a quite different way to the Magyars. Rather than sitting light in their saddles, loosing off arrows and relying on agility and speed, the German troops were organized around a core of heavy cavalry. These were mounted warriors who wore thick armour, including helmets, and fought with sword and lance, running their enemies down and hacking them to pieces. Riding in good order and given the chance to fight at close quarters, heavy cavalry could usually be expected to defeat light mounted archers. The only question was whether the Magyars would give Otto's men the sort of battle they wanted.

As it turned out, they did. After arriving on 10 August Otto ordered his men to confront the Magyars. Unwilling to abandon the city, the Magyars stood and fought. Initially the battle was evenly contested, particularly when the Magyars took aim at Otto's baggage train, and tried to exploit difficulties in communication along the German lines. But eventually Otto's forces' organization told. Realizing they could not break their opponents' ranks, the Magyars reverted to their favourite tactic: the feigned retreat. They turned tail and fled east, across the river Lech, hoping Otto's men would follow, just as Louis the Child's had done in 910. But Otto was a grizzled warrior and cannier than Louis had been. Instead of sending his men galloping into a trap, he ordered them to advance only cautiously, crossing the Lech but going no further, stopping instead to capture the Magyar's camp on the riverbank and release the German prisoners who had been taken during the fighting. Meanwhile, he sent messengers to outride the retreating Magyars, asking Bavarian Christians further east to impede the enemy's flight by blocking bridges.

With this done, over the course of the following two or three days Otto was able to lead out detachments of his mounted troops to round up the now-fractured Magyar forces. The chronicler Widukind left a gory account of what happened: 'Some of [the Magyars], whose horses were worn out, sought refuge in nearby villages, where they were surrounded by armed men, and were burned along with their buildings,' he wrote. 'Others swam across the nearby river but... were swept away by the torrent and perished... Three leaders of the Hungarian people [i.e. the Magyars] were captured... and were hanged, suffering a shameful death which they richly deserved.'[6]

Victory was total. Otto's army had defeated the Magyars, saved Augsburg and, in the eyes of the monastic writers, at least, given living proof of God's ability to award victory to the righteous. Otto himself was lauded as a great king and formally crowned as emperor in Rome in 962, just as Charlemagne had been in 800. His dynasty – the Ottonians – ruled Germany for another sixty years. And the clash, which came to be known as the battle of Lechfeld, gained semi-legendary status. Its casualties – like Duke Conrad the Red, who was killed in the fighting when he loosened his armour to cool off and was hit in the throat by an arrow – were hailed as heroes and even martyrs. And the outcome of the battle came to be seen as a pivotal moment in the history of the

Germans and Magyars. After Lechfeld, the waves of attacks from the dreaded, baby-defacing Hungarians seemed to come abruptly to an end. A curtain fell on the waves of so-called 'barbarian' migrations that had been a feature of western European life for nearly five centuries. Within a generation a Magyar leader called Vajk would convert to Christianity, change his name to Stephen and rule (from 1001 to 1038) as a king within the orbit of the Roman Church.

All of this could be traced – or so the theory went – to the turning point of Lechfeld. Yet Lechfeld was notable also for another, less immediately obvious reason. Although today it is a battle scarcely known outside central Europe, Lechfeld can be seen as a symbolic moment in the grand march of medieval history. For the triumph of heavy cavalry over light mounted archers coincided with the dawn of an age in which the sort of armoured, lance-wielding horsemen whom Otto commanded began to take centre stage in western warfare. For the next two centuries, powerful, mounted warriors dominated battlefields, while also beginning to burnish their status in society at large. The battle of Lechfeld did not cause that shift. But it did show which way the wind was blowing.[7] The European knight was coming of age.

From the tenth century, the status and importance of knights rocketed across the medieval west. Within a couple of generations Frankish-style heavy cavalry evolved to become pre-eminent on battlefields from the British Isles to Egypt and the Middle East. As they did so, the social cachet of being able to fight in the saddle also soared. By the twelfth century, the knight was a man whose importance in wartime was rewarded with landed wealth and high rank during peacetime. And around him was emerging a distinctive cult of knightliness known as chivalry, which would inform art, literature and high culture long beyond the end of the Middle Ages. Indeed, the tropes and rituals of knighthood and chivalry persist in many western countries right down to the present day. In terms of popular perception, the knight is arguably the most distinctive legacy the Middle Ages have left to us. How knighthood came to be, and what occurred during the high

Middle Ages to make it such a powerful, enduring, international institution is the question we will try to unravel in the remainder of this chapter.

Spears and Stirrups

HUMANS AND HORSES HAVE CO-OPERATED IN battle since at least the Bronze Age. The Standard of Ur, a magnificently decorated box created in the mid-third century BC (today a treasure of the British Museum in London) depicts a detailed procession of men in war array.* In fine mosaics of bright shell and coloured stone, the Standard shows some soldiers marching on foot while others ride in horse-drawn carts. Man and beast work together here in bloody synchronicity: the cart-riders brandish spears and battle-axes; the horses, wide-eyed, proud and decked out in fine ceremonial harness, trample over enemy troops' prone bodies. It is a frightening scene, and far from the only source that emphasizes just how important a role horses have played in war for the last 4,500 years.

The ancients knew all about using horses in battle. In Athens in the fourth century BC, the historian Xenophon wrote extensively about military horsemanship, advising his readers on the best ways to pick, break and train a war-horse, and recommending body-armour to protect one's midriff 'when the [rider] intends to fling his javelin or strike a blow.'[8] Several hundred years later, Republican Rome institutionalized the concept of military horsemanship: equestrians were the second-highest rank of society below the senators. And although for most of the Roman imperial age equestrians were not fighting men, but soft-handed financiers and bureaucrats, there was nevertheless a place for real cavalry

---

* The Standard of Ur is slightly misleadingly named. Ur is accurate: the box was lifted in pieces from the ground by archaeologists investigating a royal tomb at that ancient Sumerian city, now in southern Iraq, in the 1920s, and subsequently restored. Whether it is a 'standard' – a sort of battle flag – is less certain. It can be viewed at the British Museum (location G56/dc17) or online at www.britishmuseum.org/collection/object/W_1928-1010-3

within the infantry-dominated Roman army. During the fourth century AD Vegetius – the late Roman Empire's foremost author of military manuals – wrote in detail about the best horses for use in battle. (These were those bred and used by the Huns, Burgundians and Frisians.)[9] Later, in Byzantium, when Justinian's great general Belisarius campaigned against the Persians and Goths, he deployed cataphracts (*kataphraktoi*): men and horses who were both protected by full-length metal armour. These cataphracts rode against their enemies in shock formation, charging headlong while waving spears and maces. And they were not alone. Persians and Parthians, Arabs and barbarians, the ancient warrior classes of China, Japan and India: in one way or another all of these developed the use of horses in battle.*

Yet if it was not original, medieval knighthood was still revolutionary. Once the western Roman Empire collapsed, the only settled powers in Europe who used horses to a significant degree on the battlefield were the Arabs and Visigoths. The Franks knew how to trade, breed and deploy war-horses. But for a long time, when it came to the biggest clashes between their armies and those of foreign powers, the Franks fell back on foot-soldiers. When Charles Martel defeated the great Arab army at the battle of Poitiers of AD 732, the Frankish army stood as an immoveable wall to repel the Arab cavalry. Yet just two generations later, Frankish methods on the battlefield had moved on.

Here, and not for the first time, the Carolingians shook things up. Squabbling and skirmishing were embedded into the Carolingian world, but much of the toughest fighting took place on the frontiers against Saxons, Slavs, Danes and Spanish Muslims. As a result, Carolingian foreign policy demanded very large, highly mobile armies that could move long distances at pace. To serve this need, Charlemagne demanded all significant

---

* Only in the Americas and Australasia were horses not generally part of medieval war culture. Horses were extinct in the Americas from around the sixth century BC until their reintroduction in the fifteenth century AD, after which they certainly did become part of warrior culture, not least in clashes between Native Americans and European settlers. Horses arrived in Australia in the eighteenth century AD.

landowners make themselves or a representative available for his army. He also developed corps of horsemen who could ride both to and into battle. In 792–3 Charlemagne issued a law ordering all cavalrymen to carry a spear, to be thrust and stabbed towards the enemy, rather than thrown, javelin-style. This proved so effective that over the following two centuries spear-wielding horsemen became an increasingly important part of western medieval armies. The Latin term for such men was *miles* (plural: *milites*); the Old German term *kneht*. By the eleventh century the word had entered Old English as *cnihtas*, from which today we have the word knight.

Until the turn of the millennium, however, western horse-warriors still did not quite resemble knights, for one of the crucial pieces of military technology – or rather, combinations of military technologies – was not yet in place. The knight of the high Middle Ages was defined not only by his horse, but also by the specific weapons he wielded. These included slashing and stabbing sidearms, like swords and daggers. But most important was the couched lance: a long, strong, metal-tipped mutation of the spear, three or more metres in length, with a handle at its blunt end for the rider to hold. The lance was designed to be tucked under the right arm and aimed directly at the enemy as one's horse thundered forward. This was a difficult skill, but once mastered it offered a quite different proposition to what had gone before. In the Bayeux Tapestry, embroidered in southern England to chronicle and commemorate the Norman Conquest of 1066, we can still see the old-style cavalry ways in use: most of William of Normandy's horsemen rumble towards Harold's Anglo-Saxons holding spears javelin-style in their raised right hands, ready to jab or throw, but not to pile-drive like a boring engine. The difference between this approach and the couched-lance attack was profound. With a spear, a horseman could be dangerous, agile, shocking and scary. But he was not doing much different to the footman with the same weaponry who ran beside him. With a couched lance at his disposal, however, the knight was no longer an infantryman on horseback. He had become the medieval equivalent of a guided missile.* Riding in tandem with half a dozen or more other guided missiles, he was almost unstoppable. As the Byzantine princess Anna Komnene wrote in the twelfth century, a Frank fighting on foot was easy prey, but a Frank on horseback could put a hole in the walls of Babylon.[10]

Yet the lance did not develop on its own. It required other technological advances to make it effective: the stirrup and the cantled saddle. Both served the same purpose. They counteracted the laws of physics, protecting the rider from his own momentum and allowing him to transfer all the acceleration and force of his charge through the shaft and tip of his lance. The cantled saddle was designed with a high back, to keep the rider in place on impact. Stirrups allowed him to deploy his legs for balance and further resistance. The lance made him a killing machine. Without these pieces of technology, there could have been no knight.[11]

Quite when the lance-stirrup-saddle technological combination became widespread in the west, and what its consequences were, has been a matter of intense historical scrutiny and argument. (It is sometimes known as the Great Stirrup Controversy.) What seems reasonably certain is this: perhaps in the fourth century AD and certainly by the fifth stirrups were invented in the far east, by nomads in Siberia and what is now Mongolia.[12] They were enthusiastically embraced by the Chinese, Japanese, Koreans and Indians, but took rather a long time to spread to the west. Eventually, however, the knowledge was transmitted via Persia and the Arab realms to the post-Roman Christian empires of the near east and the west, so that by the eighth century stirrups had arrived in Europe. By the 780s, stirrups were considered sufficiently commonplace that the author of a lavishly illustrated Spanish Biblical commentary known as the *Beatus* could picture the Four Horsemen of the Apocalypse wearing them around their diabolical feet.[13]

---

* The force of a direct hit from the tip of a lance delivered by a knight on horseback charging at full tilt has been estimated at roughly 5KJ. This is comparable to the muzzle energy of a round fired by a standard twentieth-century military service rifle.

Although it took some time for stirrups to catch on everywhere – not until the late eleventh century were they ubiquitous – eventually they transformed the way people rode and fought.[14] True, the stirrup's rising popularity in the west coincided with a more general age of military invention: siege engines were improving, and castle-building was following suit; from the twelfth century it became increasingly common across Europe to build fortresses out of stone rather than timber and earthworks.[15] But stirrups were no less important for being part of a general improvement in military hardware. They allowed individual riders to stay in the saddle at greater speed and to fight with greater ferocity, and the result was that knights became dominant on the battlefield, and highly valued by emperors, kings and other aristocrats. Finally, as the demand for knights rose, their social position, rank and presence began to alter as well.

The most contentious part of the story of the knight's origin, however, is not how stirrup technology spread. It concerns the degree to which the rising preference for heavily armed, mounted warriors directly caused a social revolution in Europe, and ushered in 'the age of feudalism': an all-pervasive, notionally pyramid-shaped system of social organization, in which lords granted land to their vassals in exchange for formal promises of military service, and the vassals then subcontracted it to poorer men in return for further service, either in the form of military assistance or agricultural labour or both.[16] Most historians would now hesitate at drawing a direct link between these two phenomena, and some argue that 'feudalism' as a concept is far too simplistic a model to explain how medieval society really worked. Yet it is still just about uncontroversial to note that at the same time as horse-mounted warriors were becoming more firmly seated in the saddle, the structure of landholding across Europe was also changing.

From the knight's point of view, at least, the root cause of change was the cost of doing business. Fighting in the saddle was beastly expensive. At the turn of the first millennium a single, fully equipped mounted warrior would need at least three horses, mail armour, a helmet, weapons including lances, a sword, an axe or mace, dagger, underclothing, several tents and flags and one or more assistants who needed to be supplied with grooming tools, cooking utensils, food and drink. This was no small outlay. To supply and sustain a single knight for one year cost approximately as much as sustaining ten peasant families for the same period.[17] It was an astronomically expensive career, and one that could only be contemplated by those who were born rich or else could be made so.

One way for a knight to sustain himself was to chance his arm: battle offered the opportunity to seize plunder, equipment and prisoners for ransom. But this was a precarious way to fund a career. A more reliable route was to find a patron and eventually become a landowner. Thus, from around the ninth century onwards, across the west, men who fought on horseback were awarded hundreds of acres of farmable land, which they held in exchange for making themselves available to fight for the person – a higher lord or king – who had granted it to them. In the Frankish realms, some of this land was obtained by the blunt method of confiscation; under the Carolingians, many Church estates were simply seized, parcelled up and handed out to military retainers. Given these to manage and farm, fighting men could afford to sustain themselves, and could also be bound into a system of obligation to the king or lord who allowed them to hold the land in the first place. The bond was deepened by the need for aspirant knights to learn their trade: this generally happened when parents placed their sons from mid-childhood in the household of wealthy lords, who would take on responsibility for their education and physical training, in expectation that the boys would grow up to join their military retinue.

Here, in outline, was the basis of a complex but effective way to organize political society. And it was not limited to the lands of the Carolingian Franks. Outside the Frankish realms, feudal structures (or, if we are avoid the word feudal, the land-for-arms social compact) developed. They could be found, adapted to local custom and tradition, in Normandy, England, Scotland, Italy, the Christian kingdoms of the northern Iberian peninsula, the crusader states that were established in Palestine and Syria in the twelfth century* and eventually in the newly Christianized states of Hungary and Scandinavia.[18] And by the same token, even when the western half of the Carolingian empire experienced a dearth in strong kingship following the deaths of Charlemagne and his immediate successors, the social mechanisms of lordship and military service continued. Indeed, they became all the more important as French kingship declined from its Carolingian high-water mark, and dukes, counts and other lords – including high-ranking churchmen – began to tussle with one another for the security of their individual patches.

The long-term results of all this were threefold. In the first place, an ever more complex set of laws and procedures emerged to define the relations between land-givers and land-holders: semi-sacred rituals of homage bound people to serve and protect one another (in theory at least) and a whole raft of legally enforceable rights, obligations, payments and taxes developed around the bonds of land-grants. (If 'feudalism' existed, then this is what it comprised: a complex nexus of interlocking personal relationships which, when taken as a whole, presented a haphazard but distinctive system of government.) In the second, the success of a system by which large numbers of warriors could be sustained contributed to a sense, part-real and part-imagined, that society in the west was becoming more violent and dangerous. And in the third, the fact that warriors were now endowed as a matter of course with estates that could support an aristocratic lifestyle helped create an upper-class consciousness that lauded – indeed, fetishized – supposedly knightly virtues. The code of conduct and honour, which eventually came to be known as chivalry, would by the end of the Middle Ages become something akin to a secular religion.

That, at least, is the theory. But theory is hard for us to visualize. In order to better understand what the 'new' warrior of the early second millennium looked like, how he worked within the turbulent medieval world, what he might hope to achieve in life

---

* See chapter 8.

through sheer force of arms, and how he might come to be lionized by later generations, it is better that we move from generalities to particulars, and look at the career of one of the most famous characters of this early age of knighthood. The knight in question was called Rodrigo Díaz de Vivar. He was not a Frank, but a man of the Iberian peninsula, where war was endemic, authority was fragmented and opportunities for advancement by the strength of one's arm abounded. Those who knew him in life called him the Champion (*el campeador*). But he is better remembered by a bastardized, Arab–Spanish colloquial nickname that was given him by bards who sang of him after his death. They knew him as *al-Sayyid*, or El Cid.

'El Cid'

IN THE EARLY 1040S, RODRIGO DÍAZ was born to a noble warrior family in the town of Vivar, in the kingdom of Castile in what is now northern Spain. His father was a faithful follower of the Castilian king Fernando I, and in return for taking part in battles against Christian folk in the neighbouring kingdom of Navarre, the old man was permitted to hold large landed estates and a castle called Luna.[19] He also introduced his boy Rodrigo to the next generation of Castilian royalty. Rodrigo was sent to be raised, educated and trained in the ways of war at the Castilian royal court. There he was taken under the wing of Fernando's son and successor, Sancho II of Castile, who, as Rodrigo grew and flourished in the arts of fighting, groomed him as a leading officer in the royal army. When he was a young man, and deemed ready to play his part in the wars of the Castilian crown, Sancho 'girded him with the belt of knighthood'.[20] This ceremony, by which a sword was publicly and ritually fixed to a young warrior's side with a belt, was by the mid-eleventh century an important public recognition of a fighter's competence and high status. Aristocrats of the eleventh century were, almost by definition, members of a military caste, and girding with a sword was therefore a major life moment for male members: they were passing out of adolescence, inexperience and the civilian life into an existence in which commanding troops and fighting would be the norm.[21]

For Rodrigo the girding ceremony was the first step on an illustrious early career. Before long he had risen to high command. 'King Sancho valued Rodrigo Díaz so highly, with great esteem and affection, that he made him commander of his whole military following,' related one near-contemporary biography. 'So Rodrigo throve and became a most mighty man of war.'[22] Besides being maintained financially by his patron the king, Rodrigo was given the duty of carrying Sancho's royal standard into battle. And the accounts of his military prowess give a sense for just how dangerous a single, properly trained and well-armed knight could be on the battlefield. At one siege in Zamora (today a picturesque town halfway between León and Madrid, with a domed Byzantine-era cathedral), Rodrigo was reckoned to have fought fifteen enemy soldiers, seven of whom were protected by mail armour. 'One of these he killed, two he wounded and unhorsed, and the remainder he put to flight by his spirited courage,' wrote his biographer.[23] These were impressive numbers; to repeat an old but appropriate cliché, the knight was in many ways the tank of the medieval battlefield. But just as intriguing is the reverence in this account for Rodrigo's personal valour, which cannot easily be unpicked from his military achievements.

By the time Rodrigo was in his mid-thirties he was famous. He was also moving on in the world. King Sancho was murdered, and the new power in northern Spain was his son (and very possibly his murderer), Alfonso VI, who became king of Castile, León and Galicia. Rodrigo joined the new king's entourage in the early 1070s. In return for his loyalty he was granted marriage to one of Alfonso's relatives, a young woman called Jimena. For employment he was sent to a new theatre of political intrigue and martial combat: Alfonso commissioned him as an ambassador to the Islamic court of al-Mu'tamid, the louche but charismatic poet-emir of Seville and Córdoba. This was in theory a friendly posting: al-Mu'tamid was a vassal king, who owed annual tribute payments to the Castilian crown as a result of previous military defeats.* And while posted to Seville, Rodrigo helped al-Mu'tamid to fend off attacks by a rival Islamic ruler – a victory that resulted in 'great carnage and casualties', but which earned him much booty, which he sent back to swell Alfonso's coffers. Unfortunately, Rodrigo's success made him unpopular, as did his growing penchant for independent campaigning. (On one unauthorized raid into Muslim-held land around Toledo he and his friends took thousands of captives and vast booty.) Soon he had attracted the jealousy of a faction of nobles at Alfonso's court, and in the middle of the year 1080, Rodrigo fell from Alfonso's favour. He was exiled from the kingdom. Thus was one of the major flaws in the whole system of knighthood illustrated. When an able, highly trained killer was bound by obligation and reward to the service of a ruler, he could be contained and controlled. But cut loose, the warrior could be unpredictable, disruptive and dangerous.

AT THE START OF THE 1080s Rodrigo Díaz was free to sell his military talents to the highest bidder. After offering his service to the count of Barcelona, and being rebuffed, the clients he settled upon were the Islamic rulers of the *taifa* kingdom† of Zaragoza, members of a clan known as the Banu Hud. On their behalf he threw himself into a campaign of raiding against the Christian kingdom of Aragon, which he 'ravaged', and 'stripped of its riches, and led off many of its inhabitants captive'.[24] When the king of Aragon allied with a dissident member of the Banu Hud to try to attack Rodrigo directly, Rodrigo met them in battle and bested them, capturing a large number of high-value prisoners and taking 'unreckonable booty', an event which was the cause of riotous partying in the streets of Zaragoza.[25] Rodrigo continued in this vein for more than five years, building up a substantial personal

---

* As we saw in chapter 6, Alfonso VI sent much of this tribute north to the abbey of Cluny, where it paid for perpetual prayers for his soul.
† The *taifa* kingdoms were the independent Muslim-ruled polities into which Islamic Spain – al-Andalus – fractured after the collapse of the Umayyad caliphate in 1031.

military retinue said to be 7,000 strong, and a reputation as one of the most talented, if unpredictable, warriors in the Iberian peninsula. It was probably around this time that he earned his nickname, *El Cid*.

Soon, however, events on the peninsula underwent a radical change. Earlier in the century a Berber dynasty of austere, conservative Muslims known as the Almoravids had conquered Morocco in north-west Africa, and in 1085 they set their sights on al-Andalus. They invaded and began what amounted to a full-blooded takeover of all the petty Islamic *taifa* kingdoms, whose rulers they scorned as decadent, weak-willed and ripe for removal. Neither did the Almoravids hold the Christian kings of the northern kingdoms in very high regard. In 1086 they took aim at Alfonso of Castile: in October an Almoravid army crushed a Castilian one at the battle of Sagrajas. Shell-shocked, Alfonso realized he needed to swallow his pride. He recalled Rodrigo to his service. Being in no position to bargain, Alfonso fairly begged him to come, promising 'that all the lands or castles which he might acquire from the Saracens [i.e. the Almoravids], should be absolutely his in full ownership, not only his but also his sons' and his daughters' and all his descendants.'[26] This was the measure of the power that a skilled and resourceful knight could wield. He could write his own cheques.

Yet as Alfonso quickly found, Rodrigo was not contented simply to write cheques. Although he helped drive the Almoravids back out of Alfonso's Castilian territory, the king suspected – quite rightly – that Rodrigo had designs on setting himself up as a great lord. So it did not take very long for old grievances to resurface. By 1090 Rodrigo had fallen out with the king again, and found himself accused at the royal court as 'an evil man and a traitor' who was plotting to have Alfonso set up and murdered by the Almoravids. Irate, Rodrigo protested his innocence, appealing to the king with explicit reference to the knightly code: he was a 'most faithful vassal', he told Alfonso, offering to fight a royal champion in single combat to prove his innocence.[27] But the king would hear none of it. So Rodrigo was an exile again. He headed back out into the world – now not as a lance for hire but as a would-be conqueror. He had set his sights on taking the Muslim-ruled city of Valencia, roughly halfway down the east coast of modern Spain, between Barcelona and Dénia. The final act of his career was about to begin.

The full conquest of Valencia and the surrounding area took Rodrigo Díaz the better part of four years. It brought him into conflict with Muslim and Christian enemies in equal measure. In the course of his campaign he fought a memorable battle against Ramon Berenguer, count of Barcelona, in which the count was captured and imprisoned for a vast ransom and his camp roundly sacked. Rodrigo also raided Alfonso's lands, burning villages with 'relentless, destructive, irreligious fire'.[28] When the leader of the Almoravids, Yusuf ibn Tashfin, 'sent letters to [Rodrigo] strictly forbidding him to dare to enter the land of Valencia,' Rodrigo 'spoke of Yusuf in terms of the strongest contempt,' and sent his own letters all over the region, advertising his willingness to meet an Almoravid army of any size in battle, and settle things one way or the other.[29] He stuck stubbornly and unwaveringly to his principles of violent aggression in the field and meticulous attachment to a code of honour off it. And eventually his efforts were rewarded. On 15 June 1094 Valencia fell. Rodrigo's men robbed the city enthusiastically, helping themselves to vast amounts of gold and silver from the citizens, so that 'he and his followers were rendered wealthier than it is possible to say'.[30] Rodrigo was at last the undisputed master of his own land. It was not a kingdom, but it was still a rich and strategically critical lordship, and Rodrigo would have to fight tooth and nail to defend it. In 1094 Yusuf ibn Tashfin sent a massive army to evict him. The Almoravid force was said by chroniclers to number 150,000 men. This was an exaggeration, by at least 600 per cent.[31] But the scale of the crisis was plain.

What happened next was one of the most extraordinary encounters of the *Reconquista*, and the stories of what took place would understandably be heavily romanticized in later years. Rather than waiting for Yusuf to lay Valencia to siege, Rodrigo put his city into a state of emergency, sequestering every available iron item for melting down to make weapons. Then he rallied as large a force as he could, and rode them out of the city intent on outflanking the Almoravid force and driving them away.

One of the more understated chronicles of the time gave a terse account of the battle that followed, which took place on the plain of Cuarte. Rodrigo and his men approached Yusuf's army, 'shouted at the enemy and terrified them with threatening words. They fell upon them and a major encounter ensued. By God's clemency Rodrigo defeated all the Moabites [i.e. the Almoravids]. Thus he had victory and triumph over them, granted to him by God.'[32] A slightly later Old Spanish epic poem, known as *The Song of the Cid* (*El Cantar de mio Cid*), originally sung by bards intent on memorializing Rodrigo's heroic deeds, gave the battle a full blood-and-thunder treatment:

> My Cid used his lance, took his sword in hand,
> he kills so many Moors that they were not counted,
> from the elbow down the blood dripping.
> He had struck three blows against King Yúsuf,
> he got out from under his sword, for his horse ran fast...[33]

In truth, what seems to have happened is that Rodrigo relied on a timeless military trick: he sent a small party towards the Almoravid army as a distraction, before leading his main force directly against the army's unguarded battle camp, routing it, taking many prisoners and sending panic through the ranks. Whether the victory was down to personal heroism or low cunning, the outcome was the same. Rodrigo had struck a blow against the Almoravids which showed that this Islamic invading army was far from invincible. There were echoes of Charles Martel's victory against the Umayyads at Poitiers in 732. There was plenty more campaigning to be done, but in retrospect the clash at Cuarte could be identified as a turning point in the *Reconquista*: a point from which momentum eventually shifted in favour of the Christian states of the Spanish north.[34]

***

RODRIGO DÍAZ, THE KNIGHT WHO HAD become a lord, lived and ruled in Valencia for five years after he took it and died there in 1099. Writing his obituary, even his detractors had to grant that he was 'the scourge of his time' who 'by his appetite for glory, by the prudent steadfastness of his character, and by his heroic bravery, was one of the miracles of God.'[35] The author of this surprisingly generous eulogy was an Arab poet from Santarem (now in Portugal) named Ibn Bassam. As a Muslim and an admirer of the Almoravids, Ibn Bassam was culturally a long way removed from the Frankish realms that had incubated the culture of knighthood, a culture to which Rodrigo Díaz had wholeheartedly subscribed. Yet it is striking that he identified in El Cid all the paradigmatic qualities of the eleventh-century knight: proud, constant, courageous and dangerous. And Ibn Bassam was not alone. As other writers wrote, rewrote, romanticized and embellished El Cid's life and career, as his deeds were set to song and mythologized, they became a vehicle for not only exciting tales of derring-do, but also for exploring the whole ethos of knightliness. Relics associated with him were treasured with reverence: a beautiful sword known as Tizón (or Tizona), said to be one seized from the Almoravid leader Yusuf when El Cid defeated him at Valencia, can today be seen at the municipal museum of Burgos in northern Spain. Since the fourteenth century it has been a prized treasure connecting its various owners to a figure who has become a national hero in Spanish culture, co-opted (somewhat dubiously) as a Christian soldier and even claimed by Hollywood.

So, very soon after his death, El Cid was on his way to join a new pantheon of immortals. Just as the Church had its saints to give lesser mortals a lesson in good moral conduct, so the secular world was developing its own demi-gods, both real and mythical. Alongside El Cid we can count Roland, King Arthur, Perceval and Lancelot; these heroes exemplified a way of living and a warrior-code that coalesced as chivalry. In the later Middle Ages, chivalric knightliness, like Christian saintliness, became a powerful psychological institution, which was disseminated through literary culture and informed the real-life behaviour of men and women across the western world.

Roland and Arthur

THE WISH, PERHAPS EVEN THE NEED, to glamourize violence and romanticize warriors has been a part of human psychology since the dawn of civilization. One of the oldest cave paintings in the world is an ancient mural discovered on the island of Sulawesi, Indonesia, in 2017. Daubed in red pigment on limestone walls, a cartoon-like scene shows human-like figures attacking wild boar and buffalo with spears. It is at least 44,000 years old: at the time it was painted, *homo sapiens* still shared the earth with Neanderthals and the end of the most recent Ice Age lay two dozen millennia in the future. Yet one glance at the image shows us that a straight thematic line runs from the prehistoric humans who decorated the cave in Sulawesi to the themes of war stories from the *Iliad* to *Saving Private Ryan*. The compulsion to process brutality is the oldest theme in art.

This being so, it is hardly surprising that when the Middle Ages forged a new way of fighting, people came up with a new genre of art to match. The reality of going to war on horseback in the Middle Ages was objectively terrible. It was not only expensive, tiring and frightening, it also hurt. A skeleton found in the 1990s in southern England, recently radiocarbon-dated to the time of the battle of Hastings, shows the dreadful physical degradation knighthood entailed. The bones of the wrists, shoulders and spine bear the scars of painful, lifelong wear-and-tear: joints and vertebrae worn ragged by arduous days and months spent training, riding and fighting in the saddle. The side and back of the skull bear six separate, severe wounds, administered with swords when the person was around the age of forty-five. These lethal blows were the reward for a life of toil.[36] And they were entirely normal. The reality for medieval warriors was a hard life concluding in a nasty death, followed by the distinct possibility of hell as punishment for all the slaughtering and maiming they had done. Yet the impulse among medieval fighting men and the poets who wrote for them was not to report this godforsaken reality in plain prose, but to overwrite it with a heroic new literature that painted knights as lovers and questers whose ethical code perfumed the dubious reality of their deeds. As T. S. Eliot wrote in the twentieth century, humankind cannot bear very much reality.

The first great surviving written work that sought to elevate and sanctify the deeds of knights is one that we have met before, in chapter 5. The *Song of Roland*, which dates in its earliest known manuscript to about 1098, tells of the warrior who fought for Charlemagne in the Spanish march and died, surrounded by 'Saracens' and blowing a horn until his head popped, at the Pyrenean mountain pass of Roncesvalles in 778. The *Song of Roland* is in a loose sense historical, yet its concerns are not for sober recollection of long-ago deeds or meticulous scrutiny of evidence. Rather, the *Song* uses the setting of Charlemagne's wars against the Umayyads to expound on the natures of bravery, love, friendship, wisdom, faith, and justice. It is part of a broad genre of epic, historical, narrative poems that are collectively called *chansons de geste* ('songs of deeds').

The *Song of Roland* today occupies a foundational place in French literature, as much as *Beowulf* does in English and the *Song of the Cid* in Spanish. And no wonder. It is dazzlingly entertaining, melodramatic and at times ultraviolent. The main characters – Roland himself, his level-headed friend Oliver, his weak-willed and duplicitous stepfather Ganelon, the Muslim king Marsile – are vivid and memorable. The battle scenes are steeped in blood. There is extraordinary dramatic tension at the height of the great showdown at Roncesvalles, as Roland holds off blowing the horn that will summon help, arguing that to do so would be to betray the highest ideals of knightly courage. Accordingly, there is haunting pathos to Roland's last moments, when he puts his lips to the horn, summoning both his king and his own death. And, finally, there is rough justice. Few listeners who heard the *Song* sung in the eleventh century, late at night before some great lord's hearth, would have forgotten the grisly scene at the poem's end, where, in the aftermath of Roland's demise, the knights Thierry and Pinabel engage in mortal combat to determine the guilt or innocence of Ganelon. When Pinabel strikes Thierry's helm, his sword sends out a constellation of sparks that sets fire to the grass around the dueling men; Thierry responds to this near-fatal blow by slamming his own blade so into Pinabel's head that his skull is cleft in two, all the way down the nose. His brains ooze out.

'With this blow the combat is won,' says the poet. '"God," say the Franks, "has performed a miracle!"'[37] But this is not quite the end of the matter, for Pinabel has been fighting to clear the traitor Ganelon's name. Since he fails, thirty hostages who have also stood as character witnesses for Ganelon are taken away and hanged, and Ganelon himself is sentenced to be bound limb by limb to four stallions and torn apart. 'A fearful ending for Ganelon,' muses the poet, in a rare moment of understatement.[38]

What are we to make of all this? At its heart, the *Song* is a timeless war epic, in which heroes and villains struggle, battle, live and die. But what sets the *Song of Roland* apart is its wholehearted advocacy for the values of knighthood. Its story is designed to reflect back to its audience the most flattering image possible of their own martial world: one in which the best life is defined by faithful sworn obligations between vassals and lords and the knight's near-pathological devotion to keeping his word and taking up the offer of a fight, no matter how insane the odds. And of course, at the end of it all, the ultimate reward for the soldier – as for the saint – is a good death.

THE *SONG OF ROLAND* IS GREAT. But it is not unique. Hundreds, perhaps thousands of other *chansons de geste* were written from the early twelfth century onwards. Those few dozen that survive in manuscripts today can only represent a fraction of the songs that are lost, and an even smaller fraction of the songs that were sung but never committed to parchment. Another famous *chanson* is the *Song of William*, which narrates the deeds of the southern French count William of Orange as he fought against Muslims in the late eighth century. A third is *Gormond and Isembart,* an interesting subversion of the Roland story, in which the hero, a knight from France called Isembart, is mistreated by his king, so renounces both his monarch and his Christian faith and goes over to the infidel, led by King Gormond. Unlike the *Songs* of Roland and William, *Gormond and Isembart* wrestles with the dilemma of the knight who must rebel against an unjust lord. It has obvious links with the story of El Cid, and it paints in bright and vivid colours a sympathetic picture of knighthood, whose values of honour and personal courage are by definition virtuous. The knight, even as he renounces his oath to a perjured lord, proves once again to be too good for the world. Knightliness, like cleanliness, lives next door to godliness. Taken together the tales of Roland, William and Isembart are not just evidence for a literary genre that boomed in the twelfth century. They are a guide to the complex self-image of the knightly and aristocratic classes in the medieval west – particularly those lands that spoke dialects of French and Italian.

Like modern superhero movie franchises, the *chansons de geste* spawned sequels, prequels, 'remakes' and character-led spin-offs, as successive poets and scribes refashioned the stories for their times. And as with superhero franchises there were a number of dominant 'worlds', with their own casts of characters. Those like the *Songs* of Roland and William, which were set in the times of Charlemagne, were described from the fourteenth century onwards as being concerned with the Matter of France. Others, which took as their setting the long-ago events of the Trojan War, the foundation of Rome and other classical topics, were said to deal with the Matter of Rome: they treated heroes like Theseus, Achilles or Alexander the Great as off-the-shelf medieval knights.*

---

* Interest in the classical world and its heroes was a theme that ran throughout many genres of literature during this period of the Middle Ages, including more straightforward monastic histories. Often there was a self-conscious attempt to backdate the institutions and values of knighthood to the half-imagined, ancient past. The thirteenth-century Saxon World Chronicle (*Sachsische Weltkronik*) – the oldest surviving piece of High German prose writing – tells a story of Romulus founding ancient Rome and selecting 100 councilors to be known as senators, and 1,000 warriors to be called knights. Famously, in the fourteenth century, Geoffrey Chaucer chose Athens in the era of Theseus as the setting for the Knight's Tale, the first story proper in his *Canterbury Tales.*

The third great 'world', which is today arguably the most famous and enduring of all, was the world of the romances, set in the court of the legendary King Arthur and concerned with the Matter of Britain.

Tales of King Arthur are still fertile material for storytellers in the age of Netflix. And for good reason.[39] Even in their earliest known forms, concocted between the pseudoscholarly *History of the Kings of Britain* by Geoffrey of Monmouth and the out-and-out fantastical romances of the French writer Chrétien de Troyes, they are wonderfully entertaining yarns, throwing together memorable characters such as Arthur himself, the wizard Merlin, the ambiguous Queen Guinevere and the knights Perceval, Gawain and Lancelot in a sprawling universe full of adventure and surprise. The themes of love, lust, loyalty, infidelity, betrayal, questing, belief and brotherhood pulse beneath the surface of stories that feature mystical kings and beautiful maidens, holy grails and giants. Extended, reimagined and rewritten over the course of the Middle Ages and beyond, the Arthurian romances have long been vehicles for exploring aristocratic and courtly values, which have shifted and evolved over time. Always common to the tales, however, is the sense that humanity can be explored through the deeds of knights. Some of these knights exemplify their code. Many more of them show how difficult true knightliness – or chivalry – is to achieve. But to be a knight is always by definition a man's highest calling. Early in Chrétien de Troyes' story *Perceval*, the title character is presented as a young boy throwing spears in the forest, teaching himself war and enjoying the simple pleasures of nature. He hears, and then sees, 'five armed knights, in armour head to toe, coming through the woods... the glittering hauberks and the bright, shining helmets, the lances and the shields... the green and vermilion glistening in the sunshine...'

Convinced he must be seeing angels, he asks their leader: 'Are you God?'

'No, by my faith,' replies the man. 'I am a knight.'[40]

Stranger than Fiction

CHANSONS DE GESTE, ROMANCES AND SIMILAR stories have left us a rich impression of the grandiose self-image of the medieval knight. Yet they were only one part of a broader literature exploring knightly culture, which we can refer to by the broad but slippery term 'chivalry'. Writers in the thirteenth century produced texts that were effectively handbooks for chivalric conduct: the earliest an allegorical poem of around 1220, known as the *Ordene de chevalerie*, the most famous the Mallorcan philosopher Ramon Llull's *Book of the Order of Chivalry* (*Libre del Ordre de Cavalleria*). Later, in the fourteenth century, the French nobleman Geoffrey de Charny wrote another *Book of Chivalry*. Through allegorical stories and straightforward agony-uncle-style prescription, all these books (and many others besides) laid out their vision for the knightly life, which as time went on became about far more than fighting in the saddle. As knights developed a courtly status and good standing in society as landlords and members of the noble elite, so writing about knightliness came to focus on its spiritual and emotional aspects. Knights were exhorted to demonstrate courage, honesty, charity, piety, concern for the poor and downtrodden, gracious deportment in the halls of great lords, purity of heart and unblemished devotion to one's lady – who might not be one's lady at all, but rather the unattainable wife of a social better.

Several of these chivalric manuals described the dubbing ceremony by which one became a knight. Whereas in the age of El Cid an aspiring warrior was girded with sword and belt and sent out to kill, by the thirteenth and fourteenth centuries an elaborate ritual of purification, bathing, oath-swearing and dubbing had become the ideal preparation for passage into knighthood: a process not far removed from ordination into priesthood, or anointing as a king. Once inducted into this life, a knight of the thirteenth and fourteenth centuries had far more to think about than simply where his next meal and kill were coming from. How many knights lived up – or even tried to live up – to the meticulous standards of treatises on chivalry is hard to say. The answer is probably: not many. But there were those who tried, and perhaps none lived a more extraordinary life than William Marshal, a knight whose long life bridged the twelfth and thirteenth centuries, and who strove to turn the ideal of chivalric knighthood into reality. He is often described as 'the greatest knight' who ever lived – an accolade that would have pleased him immensely.[41] His career is worth considering for a moment as an example of what could happen when the literary ideals of chivalry collided with the reality of medieval life, war and politics.

ACCORDING TO THE LONG, OLD FRENCH verse biography of William Marshal, which was commissioned by his family soon after his death, Marshal's first encounter with the business of war came when he was around five years old and King Stephen of England put him in the sling of a siege catapult. The king's plan was to hurl the boy at the ramparts of a castle held by his father, John Marshal.[42] But William, demonstrating a childish naiveté which would foreshadow his instinctive bravery in adult life, charmed his way out of certain death by hopping gladly into the catapult's business end and rocking back and forth on it as though it were a playground swing.* The sight of young William enjoying himself so gaily plucked the king's heart-strings. Although the boy was a hostage, and his father was defying Stephen by refusing to surrender his castle, which gave the king every right to catapult him to his death, Stephen relented and saved his life. For the next few months he kept William as a personal companion, allowing him to play all manner of pranks and games and generally cause mischief.

Thus was the pattern of William Marshal's life set. The civil war in which he was caught up as a child was the Anarchy – a struggle

---

* The style of catapult described here is a long-armed trebuchet with a counterweight at one end of the throwing arm and a sling for projectiles at the other. When 'fired', the arm arced through around seventy degrees, whipping the sling from behind it. This gave added momentum to the projectile: usually a heavy stone but from time to time something else, such as a beehive, dead cow, unlucky messenger or, in this case, a helpless child.

for the English crown between King Stephen and his cousin, Matilda, the widowed former empress of Germany. This war had been raging for a decade when William was born in 1146–7, but it was settled in 1154, when Stephen died and Matilda's son Henry II became the first Plantagenet king of England. The Plantagenet dynasty's arrival was the making of William. Besides England, the new king Henry also controlled Normandy and the central French counties of Anjou, Maine and Touraine. He claimed lordship over Ireland and harboured military ambitions in Wales. His wife Eleanor, meanwhile, was duchess of Aquitaine, which constituted the south-west quarter of modern France. The couple produced a large family, with four sons and three daughters surviving to adulthood. And most importantly of all, they did a lot of fighting, against rebellious vassals, neighbouring rulers and each other. All this meant that there were plenty of Plantagenet patrons for a hungry young knight to latch onto, and few years that did not offer some opportunity for war.

From the time that he was returned to his family from the royal court, around the age of eight, William began to train for knighthood. His father sent him to Normandy to be educated for eight years in the household of a cousin who was selected for his chivalric reputation: a man who 'had never brought shame on his family line at any time.'[43] Although William did not immediately impress the other squires of the household, his cousin had faith in him. According to his biography, the man would respond to any complaints about the boy with a quiet admonition: 'you'll see, he'll set the world alight yet...'[44]

This was easier said than done. William was his parents' fourth son. He was knighted around the age of twenty, but inherited nothing when his father died in 1166. He therefore had to make his way in the world by the force of his arms alone. There were some hard lessons to learn. In his first battle, fought in Normandy in the late 1160s, William fought bravely (smiting his enemies 'like a blacksmith [hammering] on iron') but too boldly, and he ultimately lost his horses, the best of which was killed under him.[45] This was a disaster for a knight, whose fortunes rose and fell according to how many prisoners, horses, saddles and weapons he was able to seize while fighting, and later exchange for ransom. At the victory banquet, William was ribbed for having fought recklessly instead of with an eye to profit. Having failed to line his pockets, he had to sell his clothes to buy a new riding-horse, and beg his cousin for a charger. He had more to learn than he knew.[46]

Fortunately, William had a quick brain, and he absorbed many of his lessons about warfare on the tournament field. In the twelfth century tournaments bore no resemblance to the choreographed jousts in front of soccer-style spectator stands that were popular between the fourteenth and sixteenth centuries and which have become a mainstay of today's Hollywood portrayal of the Middle Ages.* A tournament in William's day was a mock battle, contested by dozens or even hundreds of riders who ranged across miles of open countryside, fighting in teams or in single combat, aiming to capture rather than to maim or kill, but not always managing to stay the right side of the line.

Tournaments took place from about the 1090s and were advertised in advance so that would-be participants could travel – sometimes from hundreds of miles away – to join the action. Along too came crowds of spectators, entertainers, pedlars, stallholders, blacksmiths, horse-trainers, fortune-tellers, musicians, spivs, thieves and ne'er-do-wells. The crucibles of the tournament were the Flanders and the Netherlands, and the lands between the kingdom of France and its Carolingian cousin, the German empire.[47] But as tournaments became more popular, they spread to other regions too; borderlands between lordships were always popular locations, since they gave a chance for knights to play out local rivalries within a semi-safe context. During William's lifetime, tournaments became immensely popular. And no wonder. Tourneying was a glamorous, perilous rich man's sport, played by kings, great noblemen and their hangers-on, in which the going was tough and the stakes were

---

* See, for example, Brian Helgeland's excellent, if not entirely historically accurate, film *A Knight's Tale* (2001).

high.* On the tournament circuit a knight could hone his skill for war and impress potential patrons (or lovers) with his ability in the saddle. When he rode into the melee, he staked his fortune, his reputation and his life. The Church attempted on numerous occasions to ban tournaments, and from time to time individual rulers would outlaw them as a menace to public order. But for the most part these attempts were futile. Like twenty-first century raves, tournaments were part of an irrepressible culture that celebrated and indulged the excitable impulses of youth. As the author of a twelfth-century German romance called *Lanzelet* wrote, the tournament was a chance to win 'fame and honour: there one can thrust and slash at will; all the celebrities will participate; and there one can meet distinguished knights and ladies. To stay away would be a disgrace.'[48]

During William Marshal's early years as a knight, one of the wealthiest and starriest figures on the tournament scene was Henry the Young King, the eldest son and heir apparent of Henry II and Eleanor of Aquitaine.† Young Henry was rich, good-looking and open-handed. He was seven or eight years William's junior; the two met because Henry's mother recruited Marshal in 1170 as a sort of personal tutor to teach her fifteen-year-old son how to fight and ride. William quickly became a cornerstone of Young Henry's household. He introduced him to the tournament field, rode with him and looked out for him. And in 1173–4, when Young Henry rebelled against the older Henry, in a Plantagenet family conflict dubbed the War Without Love, William sided with his lord against the old order and – according to his biography – knighted the eighteen-year-old Young King at

---

* For a modern comparison, imagine a sport with the high-society cachet of polo, the thrill of high-stakes gambling, the roughness of professional rugby, and the technical demands of cage fighting.

† Henry the Young King was crowned king of England in 1170, and thereby established as a 'junior' king to rule alongside his father, 'the Old King'. This arrangement proved unsatisfactory for all parties, and the younger king's frustrated ambitions for full rule in his father's lifetime were one factor in the Plantagenet civil war of 1173–4. Since Henry the Young King predeceased his father, he is ignored by the system of regnal numbers in use for English kings – although since he was anointed and crowned he really ought to be known as Henry III. (This would make the famous Tudor king with six wives Henry IX.)

the outset of the rebellion, to mark his formal suitability to be the leader of a war.

The way Marshal's biographer told it, the two enjoyed an impeccably chivalrous bromance: Young Henry 'so worthy and courtly, more generous than any other Christian... who surpassed all the princes on earth in his sheer handsomeness, honourable conduct and loyalty'; and William, 'the best instructor in arms that there ever was in his time or since... who devoted himself utterly to the King and never once failed him.'[49] This description of king and knight as inseparable comrades could have come straight from the pages of one of the *chansons de geste* or Arthurian romances. And indeed, these were the stories that reflected and reinforced the cultural milieu in which Marshal and the Young King moved. King and Marshal rode together, travelled Europe together and fought side by side – they were lord and master, student and master, and brothers in arms.

Yet life imitated art in more ways than one. In Chrétien de Troyes' Arthurian romance 'The Knight of the Cart', the tragic-heroic knight Lancelot betrayed Arthur by allowing his chivalric adoration of Queen Guinevere* to spill over into a fully consummated love affair.[50] A recurring theme of the romances was precisely this difficulty in policing the line between chaste courtly love and actual fornication and adultery. Around the year 1182 William Marshal fell foul of exactly this problem. Having forged a close bond with the Young King, William also came to know his young queen, Margaret of France.† This acquaintance became a matter of scurrilous gossip in the Young King's circle, and it was folded into resentments about William's prowess on the

---

* This occurs in the course of a deliciously convoluted story, in which Lancelot takes on the task of rescuing Guinevere from imprisonment by the villainous Meleagent. Having ridden two horses to death in pursuit of the queen, he accepts a ride in a cart driven by a taciturn dwarf. This is considered a most undignified form of transport for a knight; the story that unfolds is a dual narrative of Lancelot struggling to overcome the shame of having been carried on the cart, while also attempting to realize his helpless love for Guinevere, which at times drives both of them to the brink of suicide.

† Born in 1158, Margaret was the elder daughter of Louis VII of France (to whom the Young King's mother, Eleanor of Aquitaine, had once been married). After the Young King's death, Margaret was married to Bela III, king of Hungary. She died in the Holy Land in 1197.

tournament field, where he seemed to be taking the lion's share of bounty and ransoms for himself. Rumours of a 'wild affair' were reported to the Young King, who was furious, 'and ill-disposed to the Marshal so much that he would not speak to him'.[51]

The rancour this alleged infidelity caused was very real. William was forced away from court to take a few months' knightly sabbatical: he visited pilgrimage sites in Germany and spent some time at the count of Flanders' court. He was eventually reconciled with the Young King, but only just. In early 1183 the Young King fell ill and died. William saw him at his bedside and as they made their peace, he promised to fulfil by proxy a vow Henry had made to visit Christ's tomb in Jerusalem. This was no small undertaking. But to a knight like Marshal, whose life-goal was to personify the chivalric ideal, word was bond. He spent two years in the crusader kingdom of Jerusalem before coming back, now aged around forty, to begin the second half of his career in Plantagenet service. It would be every bit as lively as the first.

HAVING SERVED THE YOUNGER KING HENRY, Marshal now went to work for the elder. Henry II was coming towards the end of his life and reign, and beset on all sides by enemies, a new Capetian king of France, Philip II Augustus, chief among them. In 1189 Philip tempted Henry's two surviving sons, Richard and John, into allying with him in a war against their father, now sick and weak. It would have been understandable if William had chosen to transfer his allegiance to the incoming generation of Plantagenet princes, for it was clear that before long Richard would be king of the English realm and John his most powerful baron. But William put great store in his reputation for loyalty above all other virtues. He stuck with Henry II to the bitter end, and was thus at the deathbed of another king when Henry died at Chinon on 6 July. During the course of the fighting against Henry's sons which preceded this, William came face to face in combat with Richard – a soldier-prince already renowned across Europe for his martial expertise, who would come to be known as 'Lionheart' (*coeur de lion*). Lionheart or not, Marshal bested Richard, killing his horse from under him but sparing the young man's life. 'Let the Devil kill you,' he famously told Richard. 'I won't be the one to do it.'[52]

This combination of chivalrous propriety with bloody lethality earned William a high place in the Lionheart's esteem, and when Richard was crowned king, Marshal slid from one Plantagenet's service to another's. This time, however, it was more than just knightly service he rendered. Richard promoted William handsomely, giving him extensive aristocratic estates in England, Wales and Normandy, and awarding him marriage to the wealthy teenage heiress Isabel de Clare, a match which lasted until William's death. Isabel bore him a large number of children and brought landed interests in Ireland. In return for this generosity, Richard set him to work. Between 1190 and 1194 Richard left his lands to lead the Third Crusade, a long absence made longer still by the fact that he was kidnapped and imprisoned by the German emperor Henry VI on his way home. During this time William was one of the lords tasked with supervising the English justiciars who led day-to-day government. He had also to act to restrain Richard's brother, John, who agitated (decidedly unchivalrously) to take control of the realm himself.

Like El Cid before him, William had now stepped up from the world of knightly adventure to the front rank of regional and international politics. But he would still throw himself headlong into battle when the situation called for it. At one encounter between English and French troops at Milly castle in northern France, Marshal climbed from the bed of the empty moat and up a ladder to the top of the ramparts, while wearing full armour and carrying his sword. At the top of the ramparts he singled out the constable of Milly and 'dealt such a blow at him that he cut through his helmet [so that the constable]... fell down unconscious, battered and stunned...' Marshal, 'now weary', sat on the defeated constable to stop him from waking up and escaping.[53]

For once, William Marshal was not present at the death of the king in 1199, when Richard I succumbed to gangrene after being hit with a lucky shot from a crossbow bolt while besieging a castle in Châlus-Chabrol. He was, however, involved in the politicking that placed Richard's brother John on the Plantagenet throne at the expense of his young nephew Arthur of Brittany – a decision that would ultimately prove fatal for Arthur, whom John captured, imprisoned and killed. For supporting John, William was rewarded with yet more valuable prizes, including the earldom of Pembroke in west Wales, which linked together his now extensive English and Welsh estates with those in Ireland. Once more, his chivalric values – chief among them loyalty – seemed to have served him right.

Yet William could not get on with John. The new king's character was neatly summed up by a chronicler known as the Anonymous of Béthune. Although John was capable of lavish hospitality and generosity, noted the writer, adding that he gave out handsome cloaks to his household knights, John was otherwise 'a very bad man, more cruel than all others, he lusted after beautiful women and because of this he shamed the high men of the land, for which reason he was greatly hated. Whenever he could, he told lies rather than the truth… He hated and was jealous of all honourable men; it greatly displeased him when he saw someone acting well. He was brim-full with evil qualities.'[54]

This was far from the only damning judgement passed of King John, who between 1199 and 1216 enjoyed one of the least successful reigns in English history. Even a summary list of his failures runs quite long: John lost most of the Plantagenets' lands in France (including the duchy of Normandy); he murdered Arthur of Brittany; he irritated Pope Innocent III to such a degree that he was excommunicated; he extorted so much money from his barons in taxes and semi-legal fines that he pushed many of them to the verge of either bankruptcy or rebellion; he wasted all the money he had plundered from his people on a hopeless war to regain his French lands; he drove his realm into a civil war, during which he was forced to grant a peace treaty circumscribing his royal powers, later known as Magna Carta; he reignited the civil war by renouncing Magna Carta and consequently suffered a full invasion of his realm by the heir to the French crown, Prince

Louis; and in the end, he died, abandoned by most of his allies, having lost many of his crown jewels in the marshlands in eastern England known as the Wash.

To what degree precisely all of this was John's fault is not our concern here.* What is significant, though, is that the Anonymous of Béthune, who was probably in the service of a Flemish lord from that town, near Calais, saw John's failings through an unmistakably chivalric prism. John was not merely incompetent, an unskilled leader, unlucky or undiplomatic. He was also untruthful, dishonourable, lustful, untrustworthy and spiteful. Forasmuch as William Marshal's biographer would portray his rise through life as the reward for his dedication to knightly virtues, so too would chroniclers like the Anonymous of Béthune ascribe John's freefall through kingship as just deserts for his unchivalrous approach to life. Knightliness – or the perception of knightliness – could make or break a man in the twelfth and thirteenth centuries. It made William Marshal. It unmade King John.

William fell out with John early in his reign, and spent the middle seven years of it in self-imposed exile in Ireland. John summoned him back to England in 1213, as the wheels began to fall off his regime – Marshal used this as yet another opportunity to demonstrate his unwavering fidelity, by riding to the service of a lord who hardly deserved it on any other grounds save the oath Marshal had sworn to support him on becoming earl of Pembroke. He stuck ostentatiously by the king's side during the rebellion that produced Magna Carta – just as he had done during the last year of Henry II's life, when men (including John) had abandoned the old king and looked to a new regime. Even as England collapsed into civil war, he refused to abandon his monarch – although he allowed his sons to join the rebel side, in order to hedge the family's bets and ensure that someone ended up having backed the winning party. When John finally died, in October 1216, Marshal was as usual not far away. He took personal responsibility for

* Interested readers may want to see my previous books *The Plantagenets* (London: 2009), *Magna Carta* (London: 2015) and *In the Reign of King John* (London: 2020).

John's nine-year-old son Henry: knighting him, attending him on his coronation as Henry III in Gloucester Abbey, and going on to lead the war effort that removed French troops from English soil and reunited the realm under the new young king's rule. His final charge into battle took place at Lincoln in 1216, by which time he was about seventy years old and had to be reminded to put his helmet on before he spurred his horse towards the enemy.

Lincoln was a dramatic victory, which turned the course of the war. What was more, it cemented William Marshal's reputation as the greatest knight who had ever lived. When he died a few years later in 1219, he summoned the young king Henry to his deathbed and gave him a solemn lecture. 'I beg the Lord our God that... he grant you grow up to be a worthy man,' croaked William. 'And if it were the case that you followed in the footsteps of some wicked ancestor, and that your wish was to be like him, then I pray to God, the son of Mary, that He does not give you long to live.'

'Amen,' replied the king, and left Marshal to die in peace.[55]

WILLIAM MARSHAL'S EXAMPLE MATTERS. HE LIVED through the zenith of medieval knighthood, when the potency of heavy 'Frankish' cavalry on the battlefield was at its peak, and when the values of chivalry were highly developed in both the literary and political worlds. The biography that his son William and friend John of Earley commissioned to commemorate his extraordinary life is one of the greatest documents extant from all of western medieval history, for it represents the perfect fusion of chivalric literature with political reportage. Frequently, of course, it is self-serving propaganda masquerading as lyric history: we seldom see William behaving badly, moaning about his bad luck or having an off-day on the tournament field. But the account is no worse for its hagiographical tendencies, for it shows us better than any other work how the idealized knight's life could play out in practice. Although we cannot always take its assertions and its slant on events as objective truth, Marshal's biography is unbeatable as an applied demonstration of just how deeply the culture of chivalry informed and underpinned political events. It crystallizes what it meant to be a knight, and it shows how one man whose shoulders were broad enough to bear the burden of an exacting moral code could materially shape his times. Just as anyone interested in the events and spirit of the years 1939–45 must at some point turn to Winston Churchill's self-serving but majestic *The Second World War*, so too must all people with even a passing interest in the early Plantagenet dynasty, the wars of Henry II, Richard I and John with the kings of France, and the mindworld of chivalric Europe at some point read the history of William Marshal.

Knighthood's Legacy

IN 1184, AROUND THE TIME THAT William Marshal was travelling home to England from a pilgrimage to Jerusalem, the Benedictine abbey at Glastonbury, in south-west England, caught fire and burned to the ground. This was a disaster – but also a once-in-a-lifetime opportunity, which the then-abbot of Glastonbury, Henry de Sully, spied and leapt upon. In the 1180s, the cult of Arthur and associated romantic, fantastical ideas of knighthood were flourishing. There was a seemingly limitless appetite among the well-to-do of England and western Europe for Arthuriana. Accordingly, Abbot Henry commissioned a dig among the charred ruins of the abbey. And his excavators 'found' exactly what they went looking for: a double tomb in which lay the skeletons of a royal couple. They were identified (on the basis of a lead cross supposedly bearing their names) as the remains of King Arthur and Queen Guinevere. The waspish Welsh scribe Gerald of Wales, and a number of other learned scholars who curried favour among the rich and powerful – these were the medieval equivalent of what we would now call 'influencers' – were invited to inspect the remains. They agreed the find was genuine. Thus were Arthur and Guinevere located. Glastonbury was on the map. And the Arthuriana which was peddled there by monk-guardians of the tomb would have important consequences for future generations.

284

As time went by, the Arthurian romances continued to exert a firm grip on the medieval upper-class imagination. When Richard the Lionheart left England in the 1190s for his crusade to the Holy Land he carried with him a sword that he identified as Arthur's 'Excalibur'. In the 1230s, Henry III of England's younger brother, Richard earl of Cornwall, took over Tintagel Island, a peninsula on the north Cornish coast, and built a castle which he actively promoted as marking the spot where King Arthur had been conceived.[56] And perhaps most significant of all, at Easter in 1278, when Henry III's son Edward I 'Longshanks' (r. 1272–1307) was king of England, he decamped his whole court to Glastonbury itself to pay a personal visit to Arthur's supposed tomb. There, accompanied by his twelve-year-old queen, Eleanor of Castile, he ordered that the royal tombs be opened. He inspected Arthur and Guinevere's remains: the couple were reported to be strappingly tall and winsomely beautiful, respectively. Edward and Eleanor personally wrapped the bones in fine cloth before placing them in the tomb: a black marble casket with a lion at either end. (This no longer survives, having been destroyed when the abbey was dissolved during the Tudor years.)[57]

On one level, this was just so much courtly hokum: a secular pilgrimage enlivened with ritualistic theatre. Yet in the context of Edward's reign, it was more than that. For the chivalric Arthurian romances also had a political context: the Matter of Britain. Arthur's lasting accomplishment was supposedly the fact that he had fought to unite the fractured polities of the British Isles under his own rule. At the end of the thirteenth century this was no longer some obsolete matter lost in the mists of the half-remembered past. It was live public policy. The central goal of Edward I's reign was the king's drive to stamp English royal power over Scotland and Wales, so that he alone could claim to be the master of the British – pre-eminent over the kings of Scots and native princes of Wales. In theory it was the Welsh who had the strongest historical claim to kinship with Arthur, as descendants of the Romano-Britons who had been forced west and corralled beyond the river Severn during the Saxon invasions of the fifth and sixth centuries

AD. But by co-opting Arthur, Edward was stripping the Welsh of their claim to kinship and the legitimacy of their independence. He, Edward, a renowned warrior and conscientiously chivalric king, was laying the Arthurian claim to be lord of all the Britons. Once more knightly literature collided with politics, with real, lasting effect.

In 1277, the year before he visited Glastonbury Abbey, Edward had launched a major amphibious invasion of Gwynedd, the heartland of native Welsh power in the north of the country. His huge army contained hundreds of heavily armed knights, who were far better armed and equipped than the Welsh resistance. The sheer scale of the attack was terrifying. And in 1282–4 the king followed it up with another huge military campaign. This one culminated in the death of the last independent prince of Wales, Llywelyn ap Gruffudd (also known, aptly, as Llywelyn the Last). Edward and his successors would now rule Wales as well as England. To make this state of affairs permanent the English king's engineers erected a chain of huge stone castles in north Wales, designed to house knights, settler lords and colonists. The grandest of these – at Caernarfon, Beaumaris, Flint, Rhuddlan and Conwy – still loom out of the steep north Welsh landscape today.* Driving along the coast road between Chester and Bangor, you can still appreciate (or rue) the scale of Edward's fierce assault on the free Welsh: a merciless war of conquest that took as its theme a real-life manifestation of Arthuriana.

BY THE TIME THAT EDWARD I was living out his own personal romantic fantasy, however, the role of the knight was beginning to change. For one, their role on the battlefield had to adapt to innovations in tactics and developments in armour. In the British Isles, one of the most catastrophic days in the history of knightly combat occurred on 24 June 1314, the second day of the battle of Bannockburn, at which hundreds of English knights under

* See chapter 12.

the command of Edward I's hapless son Edward II (r. 1307–27) were skewered by pike-wielding Scottish infantry marshalled by the heroic king Robert the Bruce. In the century that followed, English knights began radically to change their fighting methods, abandoning their traditional reliance on the couched-lance charge and often riding into battle but fighting on foot as what military historians call 'dismounted men-at-arms'. They were protected by ever-heavier armour, which was evolving from chain-link mail to 'plate' style armour, in which interlocking sheets of hammered steel provided better protection from sword, lance and axe-blows. No longer was the missile-barrage of the old 'Frankish' cavalry charge the chief weapon in the medieval general's armoury. Besides knights fighting on foot, English kings deployed longbowmen (often recruited from Wales), while their continental counterparts used crossbowmen – of whom the Genoese were renowned for producing the most skilled.

Furthermore, by the thirteenth and fourteenth centuries, the way armies were raised was also shifting. Kings no longer depended so heavily on the 'feudal' system of land grants in exchange for military service when they went to war. Instead, taxes levied across society were used to pay for contracted soldiers and mercenaries, who agreed to turn up and fight on fixed-term deals, typically of forty days. Knights were still an important part of any army for many years to come – indeed, we may remember that as late as the First World War, horse-mounted cavalry were being sent charging across the battlefields of western Europe, even as howitzers boomed and machine-gun fire raked barbed-wire-brambled no man's land. But by the fourteenth century the knight's moment of military supremacy had passed.

Strangely, however, this did not dim the allure of knighthood. Far from it. For as knights became relatively less critical on the battlefield, their standing in society was rising. From the mid-thirteenth century English knights began to be summoned to parliaments, where they sat in what became the commons – the second (but today the most important) of the two English parliamentary cameras. This development was mirrored in the Spanish kingdoms (where *caballeros* had a right to be summoned to the parliamentary bodies known as Cortes), and in France (where Louis IX summoned nineteen knights to his first *parlement*). And as knightliness took on new social functions outside wartime, so knighthood became the badge of a much broader-based social class – known as the gentry.[58] Noblemen would still be knighted as a matter of course – for knighthood was still linked to the martial spirit of the baronial caste and its tropes of masculinity. But it also extended down to the families who were wealthy but not rich, who controlled estates but not regions, who fought in wars but did not command divisions, and whose jobs in peacetime included serving as members of parliament, judges, sheriffs, coroners and tax collectors. By and by, these tasks overtook military duties of knights, to the point where gentlemen became somewhat loath to seek knighthood at all. (In England they were sometimes compelled, for tax purposes, to do so, in a process known as distraint of knighthood.)

There is more – far more – we could say on this topic. For now, though, it is worth considering briefly the astonishing longevity of knighthood, which outlasted the existence of actual knights by around five hundred years. In the sixteenth century, long after guns and cannon and professional armies had arrived and any vestiges of feudal government had disappeared, the allure of armoured cavalry, knightliness and chivalry still remained irresistible to the European upper classes. It was still just possible for knights to earn the sort of international renown that El Cid and William Marshal had enjoyed: one such was the German freelance mercenary and poet Gottfried von Berlichingen – better known as 'Götz of the Iron Hand'. In an episode that rather summed up the impending redundancy of knightly combat skills, von Berlichingen lost his sword hand to cannon fire in 1504, when he was helping to besiege a city in Bavaria. But he continued his military career thanks to a prosthetic lower right arm, and spent his life sniffing out trouble across the German empire, where he specialized in engaging in blood feuds. (He also, in the 1520s, led a rebel militia in the German Peasants' War.) By some miracle von Berlichingen lived until the 1560s, when he was in his eighties, and died at home in his bed.

And von Berlichingen was hardly the only advertisement for the physical dangers of the chivalric life in the twilight of the Middle Ages. In 1524 Götz's contemporary, King Henry VIII of England, was badly injured while jousting at a tournament. Undaunted, Henry continued to joust until it happened again. In 1536 an even more serious fall in the lists damaged his health permanently and nearly cost him his life, much to the terror of his court and then-queen, Anne Boleyn. And even this did not dampen his enthusiasm for the trappings of knighthood, which was an essential part of his self-image. A visitor to the Tower of London or Windsor Castle today can see the gargantuan suits of armour Henry commissioned around the time of his last military campaigns in France in the 1540s – armour that would have been quite useless had the king ever been hit with a cannonball, but which advertised his self-image as a chivalrous soldier in the romantic tradition stretching back centuries before his birth.

Nor was Henry the last English king to indulge in medieval cosplay. The Tower of London also displays fine, ornately decorated suits of armour made for Charles I (1625–49) and James II (1685–88), neither of whom, despite the troubles of their reigns, had much real use for medieval armour beyond ceremonial showboating. Yet the appurtenances of knighthood were by their times tightly woven into the fabric of monarchy and aristocracy. Indeed, they still are. Today one of the highest and exclusive public honours in the United Kingdom is the award of knighthood; more exclusive still is membership of the Order of the Garter – an Arthurian-style club originally founded for two-dozen jousting partners of Edward III in 1348. Current members of the Order of the Garter include senior members of the royal family, former prime ministers, high-ranking civil servants, spies, bankers, generals and courtiers; members known as 'Stranger Knights', selected from overseas royalty, include the monarchs of Denmark, Spain, Japan, Sweden and the Netherlands.

Yet the United Kingdom has no monopoly on modern chivalry. Institutions of knighthood still exist across the world, including in Austria, Denmark, Germany, Italy, Poland, Scotland, Spain and Sweden.[59] Even in the United States one can find knights and knightly institutions. While writing this book I attended an investiture ceremony of a modern-day American chivalric order, held at a church in Nashville, Tennessee. The new knights and dames were formally dubbed with a sword, in a ceremony constructed on the basis of the multi-volume, heavily romanticized twentieth-century history of the Plantagenet dynasty by the Canadian-born author Thomas Costain. They thereby became members of a private chivalric networking club that boasted among its members two-star and three-star military generals, members of the US security services, judges, lawyers and Wall Street financiers.[60] It struck me then that knighthood is today as it always was: an avowedly elite and international affair; partly fantastical and sometimes outright silly; less a way of fighting and far more a set of shared assumptions; but an institution that once comprised the philosophy of the most powerful people in the west and allowed them to shape the world around them.

8

CRUSADERS

'Pagans are wrong and Christians are right'

THE SONG OF ROLAND

In the last week of August 1071 the Byzantine emperor Romanus IV Diogenes contemplated the Seljuk sultan Alp Arslan from a position of some discomfort and total disadvantage, his neck being held under Alp Arslan's boot. Romanus' hand hurt where he had been injured the previous day. He was muddy and bloody. It had taken some effort for him to convince the sultan that he was in fact the leader of anything at all, let alone the inheritor state of Rome. And once he had persuaded Alp Arslan of that fact, the Seljuk leader had insisted on performing ritual humiliation by standing on his neck. Romanus was not having a wonderful day.

The events that had brought him to such a woeful position were these: earlier that summer Romanus had summoned a huge army, consisting of perhaps forty thousand men, drawn from a wide area. Besides Greek-speaking warriors from the imperial interior, he had gathered together Franks and Viking Rus', Pechenegs and Oghuz from Central Asia and Georgians from the Caucasus. He had marched them to the east of the Byzantine empire, where Alp Arslan had been raiding imperial territory from the direction of Armenia and northern Syria. Romanus' aim was to send the sultan and his own large army of light cavalry (mounted archers) packing, and prevent them making further inroads into his provinces in Asia Minor. But events had not gone his way. On 26 August he had tried to bring the Seljuks to battle at Manzikert, near Lake

Van (today in eastern Turkey). But Alp Arslan had outsmarted him. The light cavalry had refused to come to blows, retreating and forcing the Byzantine army to follow them. Then, as dusk was falling, the Seljuks had suddenly turned and charged, creating confusion, panic and even defection among Romanus' ranks. With embarrassing ease, the Byzantine troops had been put to flight, and although Romanus had fought hard, he had lost his horse from under him, had his sword-hand slashed to ribbons – among other injuries – and was eventually surrounded and captured.[1] After a grim night spent bleeding, he had been dragged before Alp Arslan. And now, beneath the sultan's heel, he lay.

Fortunately for Romanus, this awkward state of affairs did not last long. Having made his point, Alp Arslan released the emperor, pulled him to his feet and told him not to worry. Although a captive, he would from now on be treated decently, fed well, given medical care and kept honourably in the sultan's company. After a week or so he would be allowed to go back to Constantinople, where he could recover his strength and go about his business as he pleased. This was a show of calculated magnanimity that emphasized the sultan's nobility. And it saved Romanus Diogenes' life – for a time.

The Seljuks, whom Alp Arslan led, were Turks. They were Sunni Muslims descended originally from nomadic tribes who lived around the Aral Sea (which today lies between Kazakhstan and Uzbekistan). But since the late tenth century they had risen to become the dominant power in the Islamic world, conquering their way out of Central Asia into Persia, taking control of Baghdad in 1055 with the approval of the Abbasid caliph, and subsequently branching out towards Syria, Armenia, Georgia and the eastern fringes of Byzantium. By the time Emperor Romanus stood up to them, the Seljuks were ascendant across a huge stretch of the Middle East, perhaps three thousand kilometres wide. And they had ambitions to push further still: into Egypt, ruled from AD 909 by Shia caliphs of the Fatimid dynasty; northwards through the Caucasus towards the lands of the Rus'; and all the way across Asia Minor as far as the Bosphorus strait on which sat Constantinople. That was why Romanus had been compelled to stand up to them.

That was why his failure, ensured by defeat and embarrassment at Manzikert, mattered.

WHEN ROMANUS SET OUT FOR CONSTANTINOPLE, things did not go well. For as Alp Arslan knew, the one thing guaranteed to sow even more discord in Byzantium than killing an emperor was sending one back who had been beaten. Besides the reverse on the battlefield, Romanus had lost the northern Syrian cities of Antioch and Edessa, as well as Manzikert itself. He had agreed to pay Alp Arslan an onerous yearly tribute, and had promised to marry one of his daughters to one of the sultan's sons. He manifestly could not now be depended on to defend Asia Minor from future attacks – and there were obvious questions about whether he would be able to keep European rivals at the other end of the empire from stripping away imperial territories in the Balkans too. He was a lame duck emperor. And Byzantium did not tolerate those.

The rebellion began as soon as news of Romanus' defeat reached his capital. A rival emperor, Michael VII Doukas, was proclaimed; Michael had been one of the senior officers at Manzikert, but escaped the battlefield unscathed. Michael sent his son Andronikos Doukas to intercept Romanus before he could reach Constantinople, and the old emperor was captured. To render him politically dead, Andronicus had Romanus blinded and transported to the island of Proti, just off the coast of the Peloponnese. Unfortunately, the blinding also rendered Romanus literally dead. According to one chronicler, Romanus' wounds became infected, so that 'his face and head [were] alive with worms.' Not surprisingly, he perished very soon after, in the summer of 1072. It was now up to the Doukas clan to save Byzantium from dismemberment by the Seljuk Turks.

In this, the Doukases failed. Sniffing weakness and dissent at the heart of Byzantium, the Seljuks rushed into Asia Minor, sweeping through Byzantine territory. Michael VII proved wholly overmatched, and suffered a series of revolts against his rule before he resigned the throne in 1078. When the 1080s dawned, a major reordering of the Near and Middle East was underway, and it threatened to squeeze Byzantium until the pips squeaked. The Byzantines were not only frozen out of Asia Minor: their reputation as the regional bulwark for Christianity in the eastern Mediterranean had also been dealt a severe blow. In 1009 they had proven powerless when a Fatimid caliph in Egypt, al-Hakim, had ordered the destruction of the Church of the Holy Sepulchre, which protected Christ's tomb. Now they were in an even weaker position. In their place, the ascendant powers in the east were the Seljuks, and to a lesser extent the Fatimids of Egypt.

The Fatimids and the Seljuks were themselves at odds, of course: divided by religious schism and economic rivalry in Syria and Palestine. Yet between them they were picking away at the spiritual and territorial potency of Byzantium – without an emperor able to take urgent action, there might soon be very little of the old Roman Empire left. It was hard to see where salvation would come from.

Then, however, in 1081 a new emperor, Alexios I Komnenos, came to the throne. A brilliant military officer and a veteran of the battle of Manzikert, Alexios had a vision of how the fortunes of Byzantium might be restored. Salvation, he thought, lay in a part of the Roman Empire that had detached from Constantinople some seven hundred years previously. In the second decade of his reign, Alexios sent an SOS call that would change history. Byzantine ambassadors were packed off to the realms of the west, to ask for military and moral support from the 'other' half of Christendom: western Europe and the lands of the Franks. They had set in chain events that would coalesce as one of the most astonishing events in medieval history – the First Crusade.

Urban II

ON 12 MARCH 1088 A MIDDLE-AGED French bishop called Odo of Châtillon was consecrated as Pope Urban II. Already Odo had enjoyed a distinguished career in the Church. As a young man he had taken vows as a Benedictine monk, and proved himself a star in the Cluniac system, becoming its second-most senior official when he was prior of Cluny Abbey during the tenure of the great Abbot Hugh. As we saw in chapter 6, Cluny's dignitaries during its golden era tended to be at ease in high company, and Odo was no different. Like Abbot Hugh, he ingratiated himself with leaders across Europe, and became particularly close to the great reforming pope Gregory VII. Around 1080 Gregory plucked Odo out of Cluny to appoint him cardinal-bishop of Ostia. This was his springboard to the papacy itself.

The political circumstances under which Odo became Pope Urban were highly unpromising. For a start, the Church was in a double schism. The first schism was doctrinal and dated back just over three decades to 1054. In that year, disagreements between the churches of Constantinople and Rome (concerning matters such as the appropriate duration of fasts and what kind of bread to use for the Eucharist) had flared up in an exchange of mutually contemptuous letters, followed by tit-for-tat excommunications. Relations between the eastern and western halves of Christendom were delicate, and Urban had to seek ways to smooth them where he could.

The second schism had its origins across the Alps. In 1076 the so-called Investiture Controversy had erupted between Gregory VII and the German king Henry IV. Although this was ostensibly a disagreement over whether secular rulers could appoint (or 'invest') bishops without papal approval, the contest really drove to the heart of a much bigger question, the roots of which lay in Charlemagne's reign, when the rulers of Frankish Germany had been allowed to develop notions of imperium. This posed deep constitutional questions. Were popes the single highest authority in the west, as Gregory had asserted in 1075 in a document known as the *dictatus papae*? Or were kings supreme in their realms, under God alone? That was Henry's position.[2] With so much at stake, affairs became rancorous, then violent. When Urban was elected, a German-sponsored antipope, Clement III, was at large, and Rome had recently been attacked by the Normans of southern Italy.

Added to all this were other pressing matters of governance. Urban was a Gregorian reformer, who shared his late mentor's ambition to enforce high standards of clerical behaviour and extend papal control across the Christian west. This was not only about paying attention to morality inside monasteries. There was a secular dimension too.

Since the late tenth century European churchmen had been fretting over what they could do to rein in the violence perpetrated by knights engaged in local feuds. The popes had direct experience of this through the Normans of southern Italy. But trouble was – or seemed to be – endemic. Two early attempts to impose Church discipline over unruly knights were known as the 'peace movements': the Peace of God (*Pax Dei*) and the Truce of God (*Treuga Dei*). These were mass advocacy programmes, through which clergy tried to impress on fighting men the need to refrain from plundering churches, killing, raping, maiming or robbing civilians. Bishops tried to enforce the Peace by putting towns and regions under the Church's explicit protection, and threatening God's curse against trespassers who did their inhabitants harm. The Truce, meanwhile, named days and times of the year when fighting was forbidden.[3] Both the Peace and the Truce of God proved widely popular among the common people, but they were not enormously effective. So among the many things that vexed Urban at the outset of his papacy was how to support moral censure with positive action.

Then, in 1095 an intriguing solution presented itself. In the first week of March, ambassadors from Alexios I Komnenos' court in Constantinople appeared in the west.[4] They tracked down Urban in the city of Piacenza, where he was holding an ecclesiastical council known as a synod. And they made him a proposal. According to the German chronicler Bernold of St Blaisen, they 'humbly implored the lord pope and all Christ's faithful people to give [the Byzantines] some help against the pagans in defence of the holy Church, which the pagans had almost destroyed in that region, having seized that territory up to the walls of the City of Constantinople.'[5] It was a big ask. Yet their pleas fell on willing ears. This was not the first time that such a request had arrived from Byzantium: after the catastrophe at Manzikert, an anonymous letter addressed to the count of Flanders had begged western military aid against the Turks; Pope Gregory had separately lobbied secular princes to 'bring aid to the Christians who are grievously afflicted by the most frequent ravagings of the Saracens.'6 Until now there had been little serious interest. But in the 1090s it was a different story.

From the spring of 1095 onwards Pope Urban threw himself into an extraordinary rallying tour, concentrated on southern France and Burgundy. He glad-handed powerful noblemen and bishops – influential men such as Raymond count of Toulouse, Odo duke of Burgundy and Adhémar, bishop of Le Puy – and he excited preachers both official and unofficial to take his message far and wide. That message was truly explosive. Urban called upon the fighting men of the Roman Church to take up arms and march east, where they would help the Byzantine emperor drive out the perfidious Turks from his lands. And this would be just the first step. The end goal was not Constantinople, but Christ's Sepulchre in Muslim-ruled Jerusalem. If Byzantine emperors could not protect Christian interests there, Urban reasoned, popes would step in. They would not just save Byzantium. They would usurp the role of Roman emperors as guardians of the holiest places in the Christian world.

One reason Urban could conceive of such a grand plan lay in his years spent in Cluny's cloisters. As we have seen, under the leadership of Abbot Hugh, Cluny had been knitted into the economy of warfare against non-Christian powers through its relationship with kings like Alfonso VI of Castile, an enthusiastic *Reconquista* warrior. Cluny's financial strength and regional spread had been aided in no small part by the profits of the *Reconquista*, and the Roman Church's mission on the Iberian peninsula had also been boosted by the triumphs ground out in the 1080s and 1090s by men like El Cid. Might it be that what had worked in the west could transfer at scale to the east? It would not be easy. Urban's vision of conquering Jerusalem was a medieval moonshot. But the pope was confident. In October 1095 he visited Cluny, where the world's biggest church was under construction. He blessed Cluny's high altar and stayed a week among his former colleagues and friends. Then, in November, he convened another Church council, ninety miles away at Clermont. And on 27 November, he gave a sermon as destined to be spoken of for a thousand years. The exact text is lost, but according to a chronicler known as Fulcher of Chartres, Urban implored his audience to:

> ...hasten to carry aid to your brethren dwelling in the East, who need your help for which they have often entreated.
> For the Turks, a Persian people [sic], have attacked them... and have advanced as far into Roman territory as [Constantinople]. They have seized more and more lands of the Christians, have already defeated them in seven times as many battles, killed or captured many people, have destroyed churches, and have devastated the kingdom of God.
> Wherefore with earnest prayer... God exhorts you as heralds of Christ to repeatedly urge men of all ranks whatsoever, knights as well as footsoldiers, rich and poor, to hasten to exterminate this vile race from our lands and to aid the Christian inhabitants in time...[7]

To this stirring – and, we may note, bracingly violent – entreaty Urban added an incentive. All who went on his campaign of extermination and died along the way would be rewarded with 'remission of sins'. Their earthly misdeeds would be forgiven; their passage to heaven smoothed. In an age where offsetting sin had become a serious moral and financial concern for the people of the west, this was a highly alluring offer. Urban had produced a new and enduring spiritual calculus. Those who committed to leaving home and slaughtering other human beings thousands of miles away would earn the wages of heaven. It went down a storm. So did the pope's plan to send his armies from Byzantium to the Holy Land. In a report of Urban's sermon recorded by a chronicler known as Robert the Monk, when the pope mentioned his plan to liberate

Jerusalem – the 'royal city at the centre of the world [that] begs and craves to be free' – his audience threw back their heads and roared.[8]

'Deus vult!' they cried. 'Deus vult!' God wills it – God wills it.*

Like a modern-day politician at an election rally, Urban had established a call-and-response catchphrase which would motivate his supporters long after he had moved on. He also invented a neat piece of theatre. At the climax of the Clermont rally, the pope's most committed supporters, starting with Bishop Adhémar, threw themselves on their knees, begging to join the glorious expedition. Urban commanded all who wished to participate to mark themselves out from their neighbours by fixing a sign of the cross to their shoulders or chests, before going out into the world to spread the word and prepare for departure. Although the term 'crusade' was not yet coined, Urban had created the first crusaders.[†] A phenomenon known first as the 'great stirring' and later as 'the First Crusade' had begun.

The First Crusade

THE FIRST PEOPLE TO FEEL THE wrath of Urban II's crusaders were not Turks at the gates of Constantinople, nor Seljuks in Syria, nor Fatimids in Jerusalem. Rather, they were ordinary Jewish men, women and children in the cities of the Rhineland, who in the late spring of 1096 fell victim to the murderous instincts of Christian mobs worked up into a frenzy by preachers promising a quick path to heaven. In cities such as Worms, Mainz, Speyer and Cologne, roving bands stalked the streets, burning synagogues, beating and killing Jewish families and forcing individual Jews to convert to Christianity or commit suicide. Accounts of the atrocities at that time are a depressing reminder of the long and stubborn history

---

* Today Deus Vult has been adopted as a watchword and a meme, notably by the alt-right, white supremacists and anti-Islamic terrorists. Be careful before shouting it in polite company.

† As I have written elsewhere, the word for a crusader (*crucesignati*), denoting an individual who had committed to going to fight for the Church, long predates the term 'crusade'. See the introduction to my book *Crusaders* (London: 2019).

of European anti-Semitism, which came to a head in the twentieth century. In 1096, Jews were dragged around the streets with their necks in nooses, herded into houses and burned or beheaded in the streets before cheering crowds.[9] 'From this cruel slaughter of the Jews [only] a few escaped,' wrote the chronicler Albert of Aachen. Then 'that intolerable company of men and women [i.e. the crusaders] continued on their way towards Jerusalem.'[10]

This was not quite as Urban II had intended. His vision for the first crusade was one in which powerful nobles would lead large military divisions towards the Holy Land, in a reasonably organized fashion. Yet the first wave of crusaders to depart Europe for the east consisted of poorly trained and barely controllable zealots egged on by populist demagogues, including a shabby but charismatic ascetic called Peter the Hermit and a rich but disreputable German count called Emicho of Flonheim. The 'People's Crusade', as this amateur vanguard was later known, swept eastwards through Europe during the summer of 1096, followed the Danube through Hungary into the Balkans, and pitched up at the gates of Constantinople in early August. The emperor Alexios Komnenos was not delighted to see them. They had announced their arrival by rioting and skirmishing in Byzantine towns along their route, and their lack of military expertise and discipline made them worthless for the task at hand: driving Turkish armies commanded by a warlord and self-appointed 'sultan of Rum'* Qilij Arslan I out of Asia Minor for good.

Alexios' erudite and literate daughter, Anna Komnene, recalled consternation in Constantinople as word whipped around of the crusaders' approach. She thought Peter the Hermit was mad as a cuckoo. And she was dismissive of his followers: a mere handful of warriors, surrounded by 'a host of civilians, outnumbering the sand of the seashore or the stars of heaven, carrying palms and bearing crosses on their shoulders.'[11] This hotchpotch band camped across the Bosphorus from the Byzantine capital while they waited for more crusaders to turn up. They camped, made

---

* i.e. Rome. The allure of the Roman Empire remained irresistible.

merry, and attempted a few half-cocked raids inland against Qilij
Arslan's Seljuks. In the course of the skirmishing, many of them
were killed. It was not an auspicious start.

BY 1097, HOWEVER, THINGS WERE LOOKING more promising for
the crusaders, as better-organized armies commanded by lords and
staffed by knights began to appear in Byzantine territory. These, at
least, were serious warriors. Among the leaders of this so-called
'Princes' Crusade' were Raymond, count of Toulouse; the French
king's brother Hugh of Vermandois; William the Conqueror's son
Robert 'Curthose', duke of Normandy; Robert, count of Flanders;
and a pair of ambitious brothers called Godfrey of Bouillon and
Baldwin of Boulogne.

Bishop Adhémar of Le Puy travelled as Urban's representative
and papal legate. The Normans of Italy were represented by
Bohemond of Taranto: one of the most controversial – and
charismatic – men of his age. Bohemond's father, Robert Guiscard,
had been a thorn in Alexios Komnenos' side for many years, using
his base in southern Italy as a raiding-station for attacks on western
Byzantium. So Bohemond was already known in Constantinople:
Anna Komnene described him as spiteful, malevolent and utterly
untrustworthy, a villain who wished to destroy Byzantium under
the guise of rescuing it. (Anna did, however, grudgingly admire
Bohemond's macho charm, describing him as tall, thick-chested
and handsome, short-haired and clean-shaven with sparkling blue
eyes.)[12] Bohemond was a divisive presence among the armies who
arrived to save Constantinople. Nevertheless, he and his colleagues
including as many as eighty thousand armed pilgrims, were about
to effect a radical reordering of the near east.

Having arrived in Constantinople during the early months
of 1097, and enjoyed Emperor Alexios' sumptuous hospitality
for a few weeks over Easter, Bohemond and the other 'princes'
eventually got down to business at the end of the spring. Their
task was a huge one: driving Qilij Arslan and any other Turkish
warlords back through Asia Minor, and restoring captured cities

to the control of the Byzantine emperor, before making their way through Syria towards Jerusalem. It would be very difficult, even for an army with a core of 7,500 knights trained in lethal, Frankish couched-lance warfare. They would have to fight in unfamiliar country, relying on military advisors provided by Constantinople, such as Tatikios, an Arab–Greek eunuch who had been deprived of not only the usual parts, but also his nose, in place of which he wore a gold prosthesis. To survive, the crusaders would have to march hundreds of miles, cope with fiercely hot summers and steep, uneven terrain, repel constant harrying by Turkish horsemen and even see off the threat of hostile wildlife. (This was no joke: during the summer of 1097 Godfrey of Bouillon was attacked by a gigantic bear, which nearly mauled him to death.[13]) Most of all, they would have to fight against an enemy that all the might of Byzantium had thus far been unable to hold at bay.

What transpired during 1097 and early 1098, therefore, was little short of a miracle. A sensible betting person would have backed the crusaders to be starved, parched or hacked to death within a few weeks of their departure from Constantinople; Alexios surely packed them off on their mission suspecting that he would never hear from most of them again. Instead, the westerners undertook one of the greatest marches of the Middle Ages, all the way across Asia Minor and down through the Amanus (Nur) mountains into Syria. They survived almost indescribably terrible privations, trudging onwards no matter what hardships they endured. And when they stopped from time to time to fight, they recorded battlefield victories that left them – and future generations – in no doubt that God himself was on their side, protecting them as they marched in Christ's name.

Their first stop was at the city of Nicaea where, in late May and early June, the crusading army conducted a successful siege of several weeks, during which severed heads were used as ammunition for catapults, and from which many Frankish knights came away gleefully wielding Turkish scimitars they had prised from the dead hands of Qilij Arslan's light cavalrymen. Next, on 1 July, the crusaders bested 'an innumerable, terrible and almost overwhelming mass of Turks' in battle at Dorylaeum. As the Turks charged they gave a terrific battle cry, yelling what the author of a chronicle known as the *Gesta Francorum* called 'some devilish word I do not understand'; this was almost certainly *Allahu Akbar!* In response the crusaders passed their own motto up and down the lines. 'Stand fast altogether, trusting in Christ and in the victory of the Holy Cross,' they shouted. 'Today, please God, you will all gain much booty!'[14] It was not exactly pithy. But it summed up exactly the reasons why people in the Middle Ages would go off so regularly to fight in the name of the Lord: the terrifying hardship of the mission offered the prospect of spiritual and earthly riches in roughly equal measure.

By the autumn of 1097 the crusading army had marched the entire length of Asia Minor and come down through the mountain passes into Syria. They were now depleted and tired, and their leaders were prone to squabbling among themselves. But their collective spirit was unbroken. On the contrary, they were ready for greater struggles. And this was just as well, for many more hardships lay before them. In October the crusaders laid siege to the ancient Roman city of Antioch, held by a white-bearded governor called Yaghi-Siyan. Yaghi-Siyan was an effective leader and Antioch was blessed with extraordinary natural and man-made defences. But it was no match for the crusaders. They camped outside the walls for nine months, during one of the bitterest winters many of them had ever experienced, and finally forced their way into a starving Antioch by trickery in June 1098. By that time they were ill, tired and fractious, so when they got inside the city, they relieved their miseries by carrying out a dreadful massacre: an orgy of mass murder so hideous that, as one chronicler put it, 'the earth was covered with blood and the corpses of the slaughtered... the bodies of Christians, Gauls as well as Greeks, Syrians and Armenians mixed together.'[15] Once the city fell, Bohemond of Taranto installed himself as its new ruler – assuming the title prince of Antioch and, incidentally, extending the reach of the Normans all the way from Hadrian's Wall in northern England to the banks of the river Orontes. At the same time, another of the crusade leaders, Baldwin of Boulogne, had led a small breakaway mission which captured the northern Syrian city of Edessa. He set himself up there as count of Edessa. The first two of what would eventually become four 'crusader states' of the near east had been established.* And the end goal of the First Crusade – Jerusalem – was slowly coming into view.

That endgame began almost a year after Antioch fell. Having spent many more difficult months fighting their way south down the Levantine coast, the crusade armies were spotted sending up dust clouds in Judean hills in June 1099, their rank and file singing hymns and weeping with joy as they marched through hallowed country. The job of preventing the crusaders from entering the holy city belonged to a Shia governor called Iftikhar al-Dawla, who was answerable to the Fatimid caliph and his vizier (a prime ministerial figure) in Cairo. His ought to have been a straightforward job: as anyone who visits Jerusalem today sees immediately, the city is located a long way from any major natural water-source, protected on one side by the deep Valley of Jehoshaphat (Kidron Valley) and surrounded by walls that connect to the plunging stone-works of the huge Temple platform.† Yet al-Dawla did not take advantage of Jerusalem's natural or man-made defensive structures. He was also cut off from reinforcements in Egypt. The crusaders, meanwhile, were aided by the timely arrival of reinforcements and siege equipment aboard a small fleet of Genoese galleys in early summer. This, combined with the now irresistible zeal of the besiegers, was enough to tip the balance.

After besieging Jerusalem for around a month, the crusader army breached the city's walls at two points on Friday 15 July. As had happened in Antioch a year previously, they rushed in and put the city to the sword. Even pro-Christian chroniclers could not gloss the horror; they described scenes which seemed to foreshadow the apocalypse. The governor al-Dawla cut a deal and

---

* The four crusader states – all of them fairly short-lived – were the principality of Antioch, county of Edessa, county of Tripoli and kingdom of Jerusalem.
† Note, however, that the walls surrounding Jerusalem's Old City today mostly date to Ottoman times, as does the citadel (Tower of David) that stands guard over the Jaffa Gate, through which most western tourists enter and leave.

ran away. Behind him, the warrior pilgrims who had endured so much in their four years of campaigning tore through Jerusalem, looting and killing with bestial abandon. 'Some of the pagans were mercifully beheaded, others, pierced by arrows, plunged from towers, and yet others, tortured for a long time, were burned to death in searing flames,' wrote Raymond of Aguilers. 'Piles of heads, hands and feet lay in the houses and streets, and indeed there was a running to and fro of men and knights over the corpses.'[16] Echoing one of the lurid prophecies from the Revelation of St John, chroniclers wrote of horses riding in blood up to their bridles. They exaggerated, but not by much. Hundreds of Jewish people were incinerated in a synagogue. Thousands of Muslims were trapped on the Temple precinct (*Haram al-Sharif*) near al-Aqsa Mosque. Some were murdered; others took their own lives by leaping from the platform's steep sides. When news of the atrocities reached the Abbasid caliph in Baghdad, it 'brought tears to the eye and pained the heart.'[17] Many at the caliph's court cursed the world, and at least one blamed Islam's Sunni–Shia sectarian divide for having weakened the unity of the *umma* to such an extent that the Franks (*ifranj*, as westerners were generically known to educated Muslims of this time) had been able to conquer their sacred lands. But they could do little more than gnash their teeth and rail. Against all the odds, Urban II's audacious plan to strike at Byzantium and Jerusalem had worked. The 'Franks' had come to the east. They would remain there for nearly two hundred years.*

Kingdom of Heaven

WRITING WITH THE BENEFIT OF LONG hindsight, the Iraqi chronicler Ibn al-Athir† identified an intriguing – and to him somewhat

---

* Unfortunately for Urban II, he never heard of Jerusalem's fall. He died on 29 July 1099, before word had travelled back to Italy.
† Ibn al-Athir's life straddled the turn of the twelfth to thirteenth centuries. His mammoth, multi-volume history of the world, which is an essential source for all crusades historians, is known as *al-Kamil fi'l Ta'rikh*: The Perfect Work of History.

depressing – pattern of events across the Mediterranean world at the end of the eleventh century. On the Iberian peninsula kings like Alfonso VI had made territorial gains at the expense of the Muslim powers who had ruled al-Andalus since the days of the Umayyads. In Sicily between the 1060s and 1080s the Normans had conquered the island and driven out the Arab governors; in the early twelfth century Sicily became a Christian monarchy under the Norman King Roger II (r. 1130–54). At the same time, ports in the north African Muslim province of Ifriqiya (what was once Carthage) suffered sporadic raiding by Christian pirates. And of course, in Palestine and Syria, the warriors of Urban II's First Crusade had won their own sensational battles against Turks and Arabs alike. At that precise moment in world history, thought Ibn al-Athir, Christians were on the march, and Muslims were in retreat.

Ibn al-Athir had a point. Yet we must be cautious about following too closely. For generations, historians have been trying to fight the idea that the medieval crusades were at root a 'clash of civilizations' between the Christian and Islamic worlds. For one thing, such a stark and binary reading of medieval history plays uncomfortably into the narratives of extremist factions today, ranging from white supremacists and neo-fascists in America and Europe to Islamist fanatics and followers of al-Qaeda and ISIS.* For another, to characterize the crusades as a simple faith war between Islam and Christianity is to ignore the complex regional and local politics that informed successive waves of crusading from the late eleventh century onwards. Crusading was about more than a tussle of ascendant monotheisms. It was about the changing shape of the western world at large. From the time of the first crusade until the end of the Middle Ages, popes ordered or sanctioned military campaigns on three continents, against enemies who included Turkish warlords, Arab sultans, Kurdish generals and Spanish–Arab emirs, as well as Baltic pagans, French

---

* Characterizing all westerners as either Jews or Crusaders has been a staple trope of Islamist propaganda in the early twenty-first century. Likewise, it is rare to find the manifesto of any modern-day white supremacist mass murderer that does not make mention of crusading battles, the Knights Templar, Deus Vult, etc., etc.

heretics, Mongol chieftains, disobedient western Christian kings and even Holy Roman Emperors.

In other words, Islam held no monopoly on victimhood when it came to holy war; even if we ignore the many differences between the Muslims of Spain, Egypt and Syria, still the so-called 'Saracens' were one enemy among many. And just as importantly, it was never the case that Christians and Muslims of the crusading period were automatic and implacable enemies. There were times when they tore each other to shreds. But there were many other times and places in which crusaders and Muslims rubbed shoulders, traded and interacted without feeling the least need to behead or burn each other to death. This is not to write the crusades out of existence – simply to say that the importance of crusading in medieval history and its legacy to the world today is very often misconstrued as being about relations between Christians and Muslims – and nothing more. As we shall see in the remainder of this chapter, crusading was important precisely because it was such a varied phenomenon and a malleable concept. It did not simply define relations between Christianity and Islam; rather, it set a template for the projection of military power against enemies of the Roman Church wherever they could be perceived.

HOW, THEN, DID THIS CRUSADER WORLD evolve? To begin with, in the Holy Land where the crusaders of 1096–99 had landed with such spectacular force, there was a period of slow but ultimately small-scale colonization by 'Franks' or 'Latins', who arrived from all over the west, but especially from France, Flanders and northern Italy. Some of the first crusaders stayed on in the Holy Land: Godfrey of Bouillon became the first ruler of the kingdom of Jerusalem, and on his death in 1100 was succeeded by his brother, Baldwin of Boulogne, erstwhile count of Edessa.*

---

* Godfrey declined to take the title of king, preferring to be styled 'defender of the Holy Sepulchre'. Baldwin was therefore the first official 'king' of Jerusalem, reigning from 1100 to 1118, when he was succeeded by another first crusade veteran, Baldwin of Bourcq, who became Baldwin II (r. 1118–1131).

Others went home. Others still came to the party late, in piecemeal mini-crusades that supplied vital annual reinforcements of men and materiel. This allowed the Franks of Jerusalem to expand their holdings beyond the towns they had seized in 1098–9. They focused on the coastal cities: Beirut, Tyre, Acre, Antioch, Ascalon and Tripoli. One by one, these were besieged by land and sea and eventually captured.

Participants in the battles for these cities of the place western Christians called 'outremer' ('beyond the sea') arrived from far, wide and occasionally unlikely sources. In 1110 the city of Sidon, partway between Beirut and Tyre, was prised away from its Muslim rulers by an army that included a party of Norwegian Vikings, who had sailed to the Holy Land from Scandinavia led by their intrepid teenage king, Sigurd I 'Jerusalemfarer'.[18] Sigurd helped reduce Sidon, then returned to Scandinavia with a splinter of Christ's True Cross, the holiest relic in Jerusalem, as reward for his service. This created a bond between Norway and the Holy Land which really mattered, at a time when Viking territories were transitioning from paganism to the ways of Christ. And Sigurd had done his business for the crusader states, too. Thanks to conquests like Sidon, by the 1130s the Levantine coast was home to four interconnected, militarized states with the kingdom of Jerusalem at their head. No doubt, these were small and surrounded by hostile powers. Moreover, the countryside was prone to Biblical torments: plagues of locusts, earthquakes and other natural disasters. But the Latin settlers survived, putting down roots in the Holy Land, while remaining linked to the west by ties that were by turns spiritual, emotional, dynastic and economic.

From the very first years of the crusader states' existence, enthusiastic pilgrims flocked to see and worship in them. Christian pilgrimage had not been impossible under Muslim rule, but under Latin occupation, Jerusalem became a distinctly more alluring destination. Pilgrim diaries that survive from the early twelfth century describe a land that was beguiling and deadly in equal measure. A British pilgrim called Saewulf, who visited Jerusalem in around 1103, suffered shipwreck and piracy during his long sea journeys to and from the east, and complained that the roads around Jerusalem, Bethlehem and Nazareth were plagued by brigands who hid out in caves, 'awake day and night, always keeping a lookout for someone to attack.' (By the roadside, he wrote, lay 'countless corpses which have been torn up by wild beasts.')[19] Yet he also spent months touring shrines that connected him to Biblical characters ranging from Adam and Eve to Christ and the Apostles.

Another pilgrim, an abbot called Daniel from near Kiev (in what he called 'the Russian land' – now Ukraine) spent sixteen happy months touring every corner of the Holy Land, and went away with a small chunk of Christ's tombstone, which was gifted him as a souvenir by the monk who held the key to the shrine.[20] Returning home he was able to boast to dozens of his friends, family and local nobles that he had said Masses for their souls at the holiest sites in the Christian world; moreover, he had left the names of particularly eminent Russian princes, their wives and their children with the monks of a desert monastery near Jerusalem, so that they could be prayed for regularly there. These were more than just kind wishes – Abbot Daniel had created a meaningful spiritual link between his own home country and the kingdom of Jerusalem more than three thousand kilometres away.

And it was not just religious ties that bound the new crusader states with the wider world. As the kingdom stabilized under the new monarchy it began to resemble a western 'feudal' state – with barons and knights granted estates and villages in return for sworn military service to the crown. Jerusalem was never a fabulously wealthy realm or an imperial power on the scale of any of the earlier medieval empires that had laid claim to the same territory. But it was a place where young knights could come and seek their fortune. A significant number of noble and even royal families put down roots in the east, creating blood networks from one end of the Mediterranean to the other. For some families – such as the interrelated Montlhéry and Le Puiset clans, from the Champagne region of France – sending menfolk to participate in the military defence of Jerusalem and its surrounding regions, or to take up lordships there and remain in the east, became a badge of honour.[21]

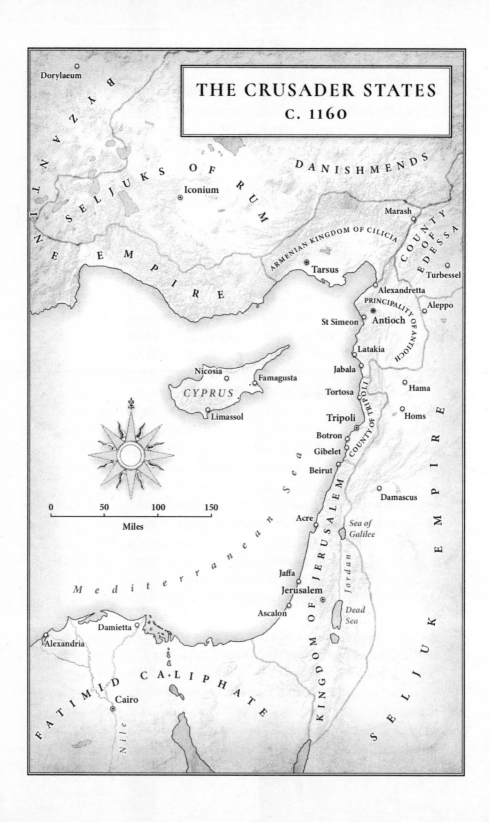

THE CRUSADER STATES
C. 1160

Dorylaeum

BYZANTINE

SELJUKS OF RUM

Iconium

DANISHMENDS

EMPIRE

ARMENIAN KINGDOM OF CILICIA

Marash

COUNTY OF EDESSA

Tarsus

Turbessel

Alexandretta

PRINCIPALITY OF ANTIOCH

Aleppo

St Simeon Antioch

Latakia

Jabala

Hama

Nicosia   Famagusta

CYPRUS

Tortosa

Homs

Limassol

Tripoli

COUNTY OF TRIPOLI

Botron

Gibelet

Beirut

Damascus

Mediterranean Sea

Acre

Sea of Galilee

EMPIRE

Jaffa

KINGDOM OF JERUSALEM

Jordan

Jerusalem

Ascalon

Dead Sea

Damietta

Alexandria

Mediterranean Sea

FATIMID CALIPHATE

Cairo

Nile

SELJUK

0   50   100   150

Miles

For others it was a matter of duty. In the late 1129, Fulk count of Anjou, in central France, was persuaded to hand over his lands to his son Geoffrey and travel to Jerusalem to marry the ageing king Baldwin II's daughter and heir, Melisende. Two years later Baldwin died: Melisende was queen of Jerusalem and Fulk was king. He stayed in the east until his own death in 1143. This in turn meant that, back home in the west, Fulk's descendants remained conscious that they now had family in the Holy Land. Fulk's grandson Henry II of England was petitioned in the 1180s to honour family history by taking over the crown of Jerusalem during a succession crisis there. Henry demurred, but the Plantagenets remained keen supporters of crusading ever after: every Plantagenet king until the early fourteenth century took crusader vows, and two of them (Richard the Lionheart and Edward I) fought in the Holy Land with distinction – as we shall see.*

AS ROYALS AND NOBLES INVOLVED THEMSELVES in crusading and the crusader states, so too did western businessmen. For European merchants, the crusader world offered a tantalizing business opportunity, thanks to its numerous coastal cities, which served as trading *entrepôts* connecting sea traffic from the eastern Mediterranean with the Silk Road caravan routes overland to Central Asia and China. These were buzzing trade hubs: in the thirteenth century the city of Acre was said to produce more annual revenue than the kingdom of England. As a result, every major city conquered by the crusaders quickly became home to a colony or colonies of expatriate merchants trading in goods including fruits, honey and marmalade, cane sugar, cotton, linen, camel-hair cloth and wool, glassware and exotic items traded over long distances such as Indian pepper and Chinese silks.[22] (A sunken crusader ship found wrecked off the coast of Israel in 2019

---

* Richard led one contingent of the Third Crusade. Edward visited the kingdom of Jerusalem before he succeeded to the crown in 1272.

contained four tonnes of lead ingots, useful for construction and weapons-making.[23])

The most enterprising and ruthless of these merchants came from the powerhouse trading cities of northern Italy: Genoa, Pisa and Venice. These merchants had long experience of operating foreign trading posts – there had been Italian colonies in Constantinople, among other places, for many years.* And such was the importance of these outposts that the Genoese, Pisans and Venetians could usually be relied upon to pull their weight financing and defending their economic assets when they were threatened. In 1122–5 the *doge* of Venice personally commanded a fleet of 120 ships to help secure the seas for merchants, and participated in the capture of the city of Tyre (modern Lebanon) for which they were rewarded with a third of the revenues of that city in perpetuity, along with major tax breaks on their business dealings there. And this was no exception. Time and again during the two centuries in which there were Latin states in the east, Pisans, Genoese and Venetians arrived in sleek fighting galleys and troop transporter ships, sometimes to bolster the defences of their commercially valuable cities, and sometimes to fight one another for trading advantages.

Finally, there were the military orders, crusading institutions spawned during the first decades of the twelfth century, which famously included the Knights Hospitaller and the Knights Templar. Both of these organizations emerged in Jerusalem in the immediate aftermath of the First Crusade, when they were conceived as sworn brotherhoods of pious knights, whose members agreed to abandon their possessions, live according to a quasi-monastic rule emphasizing chastity, poverty and obedience, and devote themselves to the medical treatment of injured or ill pilgrims (Hospitallers) or their defence on the highways (Templars). What set the military orders apart from actual monks was that to fulfil their duties in dangerous lands they kept up their weapons training, so that they were able to use sword and lance

* See chapter 10.

to attack Christ's enemies and serve, if required, as special forces units in Jerusalem's royal armies.

The notion of a military order, which seemed to fuse the two hitherto distinct roles of knight and monk, was obviously paradoxical. But it gained acceptance in the Church thanks in large part to the advocacy of Bernard of Clairvaux – the energetic Cistercian abbot whom we met in chapter 6. Bernard and his protégé Pope Eugene III, who became pontiff in 1145, were fascinated by the notion of reforming the decadent institution of knighthood, just as the Cistercians had tried to reform the bloated and indulgent corpus of Benedictine monasticism. Accordingly they patronized the Templars and their first grand master, Hugh de Payns, in particular; in the 1120s and 1130s Eugene granted the Templars their first official Rule, along with a distinctive uniform of white cloaks emblazoned with red crosses, and extensive tax breaks and other liberties within the fold of the Church. Bolstered with papal approval, a promising financial basis on which to solicit donations and income, and no shortage of work to do patrolling the Holy Land, the Templars thrived. Their membership ballooned. They received handsome awards of landed estates, revenue and other patronage from wealthy supporters across Europe and the near east. And they built up a network of monastic-style houses in almost every Christian territory of the west, where non-fighting brothers worked to finance the military wing in the east.

The Templars were closely followed in all this by the Hospitallers, and later imitated by the German Teutonic Knights and a number of smaller, Spanish and Portuguese military orders. Collectively, these military orders became the nucleus of a permanent crusading army in both the Holy Land and the Iberian peninsula. They became particularly expert in building and manning huge castles – such as the mammoth strongholds of Krak des Chevaliers and Château Pèlerin (today in Syria and Israel respectively) or the near-impenetrable fortresses at Monzón (Spain) or Tomar (Portugal). As the years went by, the military orders took on ever more responsibility for the day-to-day business of crusading, until by the fourteenth century it had become almost a private enterprise. Before that, however, they were called repeatedly into action as the crusader states came under grave pressure from hostile neighbours on their borders.

Second Comings

LONG BEFORE IBN AL-ATHIR DIAGNOSED THE success of the crusaders as stemming from disunity in the Islamic world, the Christian cleric Fulcher of Chartres made much the same point. Fulcher took part in the First Crusade, and he was one of those who remained in the east long after it was over, serving as chaplain to King Baldwin I. In his official history of the crusade, known as the *Deeds of the Franks* (*Gesta Francorum*), Fulcher marvelled at the fact that the crusaders had survived at all. 'It was a wonderful miracle that we lived among so many thousands of thousands and, as their conquerors, made some of them our tributaries and ruined others by plundering them and making them captives,' he said.[24] Fulcher made the last revisions to his chronicle in or around 1128, and apparently died soon afterwards. At that point, the crusader states were still young and expanding. Had Fulcher lived very much longer he would have seen the tide begin to turn.

The troubles began in the 1140s, when a Turkish soldier and career politician known as Imad al-Din Zengi attacked the city of Edessa – capital of the smallest and most vulnerable of the crusader states. Edessa was a long way from the coast, halfway between the Latin-held city of Antioch and Aleppo, where Zengi was governor, and that fact of geography alone made it vulnerable. Zengi had a reputation for drunkenness and extreme cruelty to his troops and enemies alike, but he was a brilliant strategist, with ambitions to unite as many Syrian cities as possible under his leadership. Taking Edessa from its crusader rulers was not a matter of religious duty so much as part of a master-plan to assemble from the fractured pieces of Seljuk Syria a realm that he could call his own.

In 1144 Zengi appeared outside Edessa with troops, siege towers and professional diggers. The miners tunnelled beneath the city walls while artillerymen used giant catapults known as mangonels to bombard the citizens from above. It did not take long for the Turks to break Edessa's resistance. When they broke in, civilians panicked and women and children were crushed to death in a stampede to flee. For Zengi this was a useful victory. But for the crusaders it was a disaster. The territorial loss was one thing. Much worse was the sense that nearly half a century on from the victories of 1096–99, God had ceased to smile on them.

When news of Edessa's capitulation filtered back to Europe, it prompted general dismay. Yet it also presented an opportunity. Pope Eugene III was not enjoying a peaceful papacy. He was struggling with continuing schism and attempts to set up antipopes against him. Communards had been rioting on the streets of Rome. Heretic preachers were reported to be stirring up anticlerical feeling in France. This was a worrying set of problems, and, like Urban II before him, Eugene felt he needed a cause around which to build his papacy and rally political support. He found it in the Second Crusade.

The Second Crusade was closely and deliberately modelled on the First. This time, however, the driving intellectual and rhetorical force behind it was Eugene's mentor, Bernard of Clairvaux. Between them, Eugene and Bernard concocted a brilliant mission statement for their project. It was a generation since Jerusalem had fallen, they argued, and in that time Christians everywhere had drifted from the path of righteousness and self-sacrifice which had once brought about wonderful victories. It was time to get back to basics. Now was the moment for noblemen and knights across Europe to prove that 'the bravery of the fathers will not have proved to be diminished in the sons.'[25] The best way they could do that was to repeat their fathers' deeds – as closely as possible. At Easter in 1146 Bernard preached this message at a crusade council in Vézelay designed to emulate Urban's in Clermont. Although by this stage of his life Bernard was thin and painfully frail from relentless fasting, he was still intensely charismatic. As one chronicler described it, Bernard 'poured forth the dew of the divine word [and] with loud outcry on every side, people began to demand crosses.'[26] In a piece of bravura public theatre, Bernard ripped his cloak into strips to make enough to go around. The crowd chanted 'Deus Vult' – of course. And in the following weeks a popular French song averred that going crusading was a sure route to paradise, for 'God has organized a tournament between Heaven and Hell.'[27] Once again a grand announcement ignited crusading fever across the west, and all the usual ingredients were present. Bernard's announcement of the crusade (backed by a papal bull known as *Quantum Praedecessores*) was followed by an intense spate of preaching and negotiation with possible military leaders. Knights and untrained civilians signed up in droves. And popular enthusiasm spilled over as before into zealotry, bigotry and anti-Semitic attacks, in which a new generation of Jews in the Rhineland were beaten, robbed, mutilated, blinded, murdered or hounded until they committed suicide. This was historical re-enactment on a grotesque scale. And it would have further tragic consequences.

One of the few unavoidable points of difference between the First Crusade and the Second lay in the state of its secular leadership. Whereas in 1096 Urban had only been able to persuade counts and bishops to lead his armies, in the 1140s, Bernard of Clairvaux and Eugene III managed to persuade two of Europe's greatest kings to take charge.* When Bernard preached at Vézelay he was accompanied on stage by one of them: Louis VII of France (r. 1137–1180). Not long afterwards the king of the Germans, Conrad III (r. 1138–1152†) also succumbed to Bernard's diplomatic pressure and signed up. The involvement of two such mighty princes was a considerable boon. They would be the first kings to go crusading since Sigurd of Norway – and they had at their

---

* Despite Bernard's prominence in preaching the crusade, and his extensive writings about fighting in the Holy Land, he never left Europe during his lifetime, preferring to regard his Cistercian abbey at Clairvaux as his own personal Jerusalem.
† Conrad was never crowned emperor, although he often styled himself 'King of the Romans'.

disposal the financial and military might of all the old Frankish territories. It was hard to imagine how they could fail.[28]

But fail they did. After its promising beginnings, the Second Crusade was a disaster at virtually every turn. The kings set out in style around Easter 1147: Conrad made a show of crowning his son Henry as king in case he did not return; Louis departed from Paris, after great and solemn celebrations at the abbey of St-Denis, flanked his wife, Eleanor of Aquitaine, a company of Templar knights and tens of thousands of pilgrims. But they soon ran into catastrophic difficulty. They had decided to follow quite literally in the footsteps of the first crusaders: along the Danube, through the Balkans to Constantinople, then overland across Asia Minor into northern Syria. This had a certain poetic appeal and fulfilled Bernard and Eugene's call for a repeat performance of 1096–99. But in reality times had changed. And what had been an unlikely journey in the 1090s was now an impossible one. A new Byzantine emperor in Constantinople, Manuel I Komnenos (r. 1143–80) had not summoned crusaders, did not want them on his doorstep, and did only the bare minimum to help them on their way. A new 'sultan of Rum' – Qilij Arslan's son Mas'ud – had an even firmer grip on Asia Minor than his father had enjoyed. Both Conrad and Louis' armies were savaged by Turkish warriors as they stumbled through Asia Minor: in October 1147 Conrad fought the Turks at Dorylaeum. But this time the crusaders were crushed and Conrad lost much of his baggage train. Several months later, in January 1148, Louis VII only narrowly escaped with his life when his own army was ambushed at Mount Cadmus (Honaz).

By the time they all arrived in Syria, Louis was virtually broke and both armies had lost thousands of men. Moreover, they had to reckon with a new enemy. Zengi was dead, having been stabbed to death by a disgruntled servant while he was passed out drunk in his tent. His place as the driving force behind the unification of Syria had been taken by his brilliant son, Nur al-Din, who had no intention of allowing the crusaders to upset his plans for restoring order to the Muslim Near East. So Edessa was a lost cause, and there was little hope of making gains anywhere else, either.

Conrad and Louis tarried for several months in the Holy Land, trying desperately to come up with a plan that would save some face and make the vast expense and discomfort of their crusade worthwhile. What they came up with was arguably worse than doing nothing at all. In July, they and the king of Jerusalem, Baldwin III (r. 1143–63), attempted to besiege the mighty city of Damascus. It was a fiasco. The crusaders failed even to break through the orchards in Damascus' suburbs before their discipline failed and they were beaten away. The siege was over within a week. With nothing left to do, Conrad quickly took his ship back to Germany. Louis hung around Jerusalem for six months of sightseeing and prayer, and left at Easter 1149. But by this time he was estranged from his wife, Eleanor of Aquitaine, whose experience of the crusade had been one of tedium and misery, enlivened only by the company of her uncle, Raymond prince of Antioch, with whom she was later accused of having an incestuous affair.[29] By the following year she and Louis were divorced, and Eleanor had married the soon-to-be Plantagenet king of England, Henry II, a union that was disastrous for Louis and brought about a state of sporadic warfare between the English and French that was only settled in 1453.[*] It was the final humiliation of a second crusade that was not so much a pale shadow of the first as a terrible parody. And it was still not the end of the story.

UNSURPRISINGLY, AFTER THE FAILURE OF THE Second Crusade, western interest in any more major crusading campaigns to the east waned for several decades. The military orders continued to build their strength, and small individual groups of fighters continued to travel on armed pilgrimages to Syria and Palestine. The kings of Jerusalem, meanwhile, began to eye expansion into Egypt, where the Shia caliphs and their viziers were presiding over

---

[*] By marrying Henry II, Eleanor linked Aquitaine to the English, rather than the French crown. The dispute over who truly 'owned' the duchy (and its later medieval successor, Gascony) was unsettled until the culmination of the Hundred Years War at the battle of Castillon on 17 July 1453.

an increasingly corrupt and fragile government in Cairo. Yet for many in western Europe, there were better opportunities to fight for Christ, much closer to home.

In Spain and Portugal the *Reconquista* continued at pace. In 1147 a band of English and Frisian crusaders travelling by ship to join the French and Germans on the Second Crusade had stopped during their long journey to conquer Lisbon from its Muslim rulers – a major milestone on the conquest of western Iberia and the creation of a kingdom of Portugal. What was more, the Almoravids who had swept through al-Andalus in the eleventh century were now in a state of protracted collapse; they were deposed in a revolution in Morocco and replaced by an even more puritanical Muslim sect known as the Almohads. This instability made the Iberian peninsula a ripe field for warfare, and warriors who travelled there to do battle in the name of Christ were explicitly granted crusader status (and the attendant forgiveness of sins) by Pope Eugene III.

Meanwhile, a third front of crusading had also opened up. When Bernard of Clairvaux preached the Second Crusade in Germany, groups of Saxon nobles had asked his permission to crusade on their own doorstep, ignoring the Holy Land and instead fighting to colonize lands in what is now northern Germany and western Poland, which were at that time home to pagan Slavic peoples known collectively as the Wends. Bernard had given his approval, calling the Wendish unbelievers the enemies of God, and demanding bluntly that they be converted or wiped out. This was of only limited consequence at the time, but its significance to later generations was huge. Although the Wendish crusade was small and sparsely attended when compared to the royal-led mission to Syria, or the battles of the *Reconquista*, its categorization *as* a crusade was a critical event in medieval history, which framed colonialization and conversion in north-east Europe as holy war. After the 1140s, 'Northern Crusades' aiming to bring pagans into the Church, baptize their people and steal their lands would continue until the fifteenth century.[30]

Given all this, the fact that crusading to the east did not simply stutter to a standstill at the second attempt it is perhaps strange.

That it did not owed a great deal to a Kurdish politician and general called Salah al-Din Yusuf ibn Ayyub – better known today as Saladin.

Even today, Saladin remains one of the most famous, notorious and controversial characters in all of medieval history.[31] Born around 1138 to a well-to-do Kurdish family, Saladin rose in the service of Nur al-Din, establishing himself as a reliable civil servant and absorbing many of the older man's insights into the nature of politics in the fractious Levant, where Nur al-Din spent the 1150s and 1160s piecing together a coherent realm out of the self-contained city states within the Seljuk Turkish world. In the 1160s Saladin was sent to Egypt. For several years he fought there to resist the crusader king Amalric I, who had designs on expanding the kingdom of Jerusalem into the Nile Delta. But at the same time Saladin was part of a group within the Egyptian Muslim world that was calmly engineering the destruction of the Fatimid caliphate, the Shia authority that had ruled Egypt since 969. In 1171, Saladin effected a palace coup which deposed the last Fatimid caliph. Egypt's political allegiance was transferred to Nur al-Din in Syria. Religious obedience was switched to the Sunni Abbasid caliph in Baghdad. This on its own was a massive accomplishment (and one that has earned Saladin eternal opprobrium in the Shia world). But Saladin was not finished. Far from it.

When Nur al-Din died in 1174, he left a delicate situation in the near east. During the course of a quarter of a century he had painstakingly assembled something resembling a unified Syria. But without his personal leadership everything risked collapsing back into disorder. So Saladin set his heart on making himself Nur al-Din's effective heir. And through a combination of audacious military manoeuvres and diplomatic cunning, he achieved exactly that – and more. By the late 1180s he had pieced together a realm in which much of Syria and all of Egypt were joined under his personal rule. The Abbasid caliph recognized him as a sultan. His family took plum positions in government. And as he grew in stature, Saladin began to present himself as the saviour of Islam itself: a *jihadi* warrior who was fighting not for personal gain but for the benefit of Muslims everywhere. In large part this was to distract from the fact that Saladin actually spent many years of his life fighting and killing fellow Muslims. Nevertheless, as he came to ever-greater success, the sultan was filled with what one Islamic writer called 'zeal for waging holy war against the enemies of God'.[32] In practice, this meant turning his attention and his military campaigns directly against the leading infidel power in the region: the crusader kingdom of Jerusalem.

Throughout the 1180s, Saladin and the rulers of Jerusalem eyed each other uneasily. During this time the crusader realm was tortured by a series of succession crises and internal disputes, while Saladin was occupied consolidating his hold on Syria.* So for a while, neither side was willing to risk all-out war, and a series of truces kept a delicate peace. But in 1187 Saladin felt confident enough to attack. Seizing on a raid against a Muslim caravan train by a crusader lord called Reynald of Châtillon as a pretext, in the spring of that year Saladin stormed into the kingdom of Jerusalem with 'an army whose numbers could not be counted'.[33]

The reckoning came on 3–4 July, when Saladin lured the hapless and widely disliked king Guy I of Jerusalem, and an army comprising almost the entire military force of Guy's kingdom, out to the twin peaks of an extinct volcano known as the Horns of Hattin, near the Sea of Galilee. Once there Saladin's men cut off Guy's army from any water source, set fire to the brush and scrub of the hot, parched landscape and then rode them down. In the course of a cataclysmic battle the crusader army was annihilated, Guy was captured, and the True Cross – the most precious relic in the Christian world – was confiscated, never to be seen again. After the battle 200 Templar and Hospitaller knights – the crack troops

---

* These stemmed from the accession in 1174 of King Baldwin IV of Jerusalem, who suffered from painful and debilitating leprosy, which eventually killed him. Although Baldwin was physically strong and very brave, his reign saw an inevitable wasting away of royal leadership. In 1185 he died, and was succeeded by a six-year-old child, Baldwin V. The next year the boy-king also died, leaving the crown to his mother, Sibylla, and her roundly scorned husband Guy. This disastrous run of dynastic luck understandably emboldened the crusaders' enemies, including Saladin.

of the army – were captured and ritually beheaded by Saladin's courtiers and clerics.

In the ensuing months, Saladin took almost every crusader city on the Levantine coast, including the most important trading port of Acre. In October, he besieged Jerusalem itself, which was mostly defended by women and youths, since the garrison had been among the army that was wiped out at Hattin. After some token resistance, it surrendered. Saladin ostentatiously refused to allow his troops the pleasure of a massacre. But the shock still reverberated around the western world. And it prompted the last really serious crusade to the Latin kingdom: the Third Crusade. Preached with an urgency that stemmed from abject humiliation verging on existential crisis, it was led by a new generation of warrior kings: Philip II of France and Richard the Lionheart. They prepared their realms for war at pace, with Richard auctioning public offices, levying a 10 per cent income tax known as the Saladin Tithe and stockpiling huge quantities of goods and weapons as he prepared to travel east. Dozens of lords and churchmen set out to assist in the war to save God's kingdom. But this time there was no compulsion to follow slavishly in the footsteps of old crusaders. The German ruler and Holy Roman Emperor, Frederick Barbarossa, who did attempt an overland route, was drowned while bathing in a river in Asia Minor. Richard and Philip, meanwhile, sailed to the east, stopping at Sicily and Cyprus, bickering as they went but in no doubt as to the importance of their mission. For good luck, and to summon the martial valour of King Arthur, Richard took with him a sword named Excalibur.

Philip and Richard reached the Holy Land in 1191. In an expedition that lasted two years they retook Acre, before Richard led a large army down the Levantine coast, massacring prisoners, skirmishing with Saladin's troops and recapturing cities as he went. But even Richard – the greatest general of his age – came up short when he contemplated the city of Jerusalem. Twice he approached it, and twice he turned back, daunted by the scale of the siege it would require. The closest he came to taking Jerusalem was when he tried to negotiate a remarkably progressive two-state solution for Palestine at large, under which the state would be ruled jointly by his sister Joanna and Saladin's brother al-Adil (also known as Saphadin). This stalled when the couple could not agree religious terms on which to marry, and eventually the project – and the crusade – petered out. So Jerusalem stayed in Saladin's hands. And the crusaders, as they always did, either settled down or departed.*

By 1192 the crusader kingdom had been rescued – but reshaped. Thanks to the intervention of the Third Crusaders, it had not been annihilated. But the Holy City was gone, and the polity itself now consisted of a string of ports dominated by merchant factions, and inland castles maintained by the Templars and Hospitallers. The county of Tripoli and principality of Antioch survived, but were also somewhat reduced in size and power. All three would hold out for nearly another hundred years. But the age of mass crusades to Syria and Palestine was over. A significant shift in the crusading movement was underway. As the twelfth century passed into the thirteenth, Christian holy war was about to be turned in extraordinary new directions.

'A detestable business'

POPE INNOCENT III, LONG OF FACE and razor-sharp of mind, was elected as pontiff in 1198 at the exceptionally young age of about thirty-seven. Innocent was an Italian aristocrat, born Lotario dei Conte di Segni (Lothar, of the counts of Segni), and in his short but successful career as a canon lawyer and cardinal he had developed a grand and cosmic worldview, the result of much hard thought about both the fundamental nature of man's existence and the deepest systems of power that underpinned the Christian universe. On the first topic Innocent had produced a philosophical

---

* Philip Augustus, whose relationship with Richard had grown progressively worse during the journey to the east, had left the crusade in high dudgeon immediately after the siege of Acre. After Richard departed the Holy Land late in 1192 he was shipwrecked in Istria (modern Croatia). He tried to make his way home overland but was captured and imprisoned by the German king and Holy Roman Emperor Henry VI.

polemic called 'On the Misery of the Human Condition' (*De Miseria Humanae Conditionis*),* which spelled out the unremitting terribleness and squalor of all humanity. Despite its gloomy title and pessimistic content, *De Miseria* became a medieval bestseller, copied many hundreds of times and circulated for generations throughout the west.[34]

On the second matter, that of the hierarchy of western power, Innocent had become a wholehearted believer in the political theory of the sun and moon: an astronomical allegory which asserted papal supremacy in all Christian realms. In this view, the pope was the sun, emitting light; royal rulers (particularly the Holy Roman Emperor) were like the moon, merely reflecting it. They were not equals. In 1198, right at the start of his papacy, Innocent wrote: 'Just as God, founder of the universe, has constituted two large luminaries in the firmament of Heaven, a major one to dominate the day and a minor one to dominate the night, so he has established in the firmament of the Universal Church, which is signified by the name of Heaven, two great dignities, a major one to preside... over the days of the souls, and a minor one to preside over the nights of the bodies. They are the Pontifical authority and the royal power.'[35] This was not a new idea: by the time of Innocent's elevation to the papacy, popes had been tussling with kings for pre-eminence for almost four hundred years. But Innocent went further than almost any other pope in history towards turning high philosophy into political reality. His papacy, which lasted from 1198 until his death in 1216, was a *tour de force* of legalistic

---

* *De Miseria Humanae Conditionis* was a survey of the general awfulness of humanity, in the long tradition that also informed the turn to monastic or ascetic orders. In a largely derivative but expertly constructed text, Innocent described the pain and decay attendant to humankind's physical existence, the moral repugnance of just about everyone, and the inevitable humiliating torment of man's judgement after death and the tortures of hell. A typical passage from the first part of the book describes the hideousness of ageing: 'if, however, one does reach old age, his heart weakens straightaway and his head shakes, his spirit fails and his breath stinks, his face wrinkles and his back bends, his eyes dim and his joints falter, his nose runs and his hair falls out, his touch trembles and his competence fails, his teeth rot and his ears become dirty... But neither should the old man glory against the young person nor the young be insolent to the old person, for we are what he was, someday will be what he is.' (This translation: Lewis, Robert E., *Lotario dei Segni (Pope Innocent III) / De Miseria Condicionis Humane* (Athens, GA: 1978), pp. 106–9.)

papal statesmanship, in which Innocent tried to impress the power of Rome over everyone and everything, with some extraordinary results.

In crusading terms, the immediate background to Innocent's election was the failure of the Third Crusade to seize Jerusalem. European kings were consequently rather queasy about contemplating another tilt at the holy city, despite Saladin's death in March 1193 – for the Third Crusade had seemed to demonstrate only the extraordinary difficulty of repeating the miracle of 1099. Yet this did not turn Innocent off the idea of crusading per se. In fact, no pope after Urban II would be more important in the history of crusading, for Innocent took the faltering concept of Christian holy war and remade it for a new century. Just as Urban and Eugene III before him had done, Innocent understood how useful the crusade could be as a bolster for the power of the papacy. But whereas his predecessors had largely aimed the weapon against enemies outside the Christian world, Innocent decided to turn it inwards as well. Besides using crusading to hound Muslims and pagans, he would deploy it (or allow it to be deployed) against heretics and dissenters within the Christian world. This was a momentous turn of events. Thanks to Innocent, the thirteenth century would see an explosion in crusade preaching throughout the western world. Yet – partly as a result of Innocent's reimagining of what the crusade was for – it would also see the decline and ultimately the demise of the crusader states of the Near East.

THE FIRST OF INNOCENT'S CRUSADES STARTED out in predictable fashion, although it did not remain predictable for very long. Shortly after his election the pope issued a bull (known as a *Post Miserabile*) which challenged the young knightly men of the west to avenge the loss of Jerusalem and the True Cross: 'the deplorable invasion of that land on which the feet of Christ had stood'.[36] This claim chimed well with rumours that the devil had recently been born in Cairo, which were exciting the ordinary people of Europe, and had convinced many of them the apocalypse was on its way.

And it prompted a small group of western lords (most notably the counts of Flanders, Champagne and Blois) and their associates to start planning for a new invasion of the Holy Land. This Fourth Crusade would be a daring amphibious assault, in which a huge fleet of warships would strike at Alexandria, on the west of Egypt's Nile Delta. There they would disgorge an army which could fight its way up into Palestine and liberate Jerusalem from the south, rather than the north. It was a bold, even visionary plan. However, it required around two hundred war galleys and a fleet of transporter ships with full crews, as well as an army of around thirty thousand men to do the fighting. This logistical obstacle would prove the Fourth Crusade's undoing.[37]

To build their galley fleet the French turned to the citizens of the Republic of Venice, who cherished their own reputation as longtime crusaders with a proud civic record for pious deeds and a keen pecuniary interest in maintaining the crusader states as trading posts. After tough negotiations, the leader of Venice – the blind, ninety-year-old *doge* Enrico Dandolo – took on the shipbuilding contract in early 1201. Within just a year Venice's shipyards had produced the fleet, stocked it with food, wine and horse fodder and were ready to go crusading. Innocent kept track of these developments and declared himself satisfied. Unfortunately, the French counts then let him – and everyone else – down. In the early summer of 1202 they were supposed to have supplied 30,000 men and 85,000 silver marks, to fill and pay for the ships. But when early summer came, it was clear that the French had neither. They had mustered less than one third of the promised army and barely half the funds. This was not just a diplomatic disaster – it threatened to bankrupt the city of Venice.

In response, Enrico Dandolo took a fateful decision. Rather than stepping back, he stepped up – effectively taking command of the crusade himself. In October 1202 he took his crusading vows, having his cloth cross pinned to his hat rather than his shoulder. A few days later the fleet left port, with his personal galley, decked out in vermillion and silver, leading the way. They set out to make good the city's losses. Far from heading to Alexandria, the

Venetians, with those French allies who had turned up to fight, sailed along the Adriatic coast of what is now Croatia. They weighed anchor outside the Christian city of Zara (Zadar), which had offended Venice some years previously by refusing to pay the citizens tribute, instead claiming allegiance to the Christian king of Hungary. Despite howls of protest from the citizens, who hung banners bearing crosses on the city walls to advertise the fact that many of them had taken crusader vows too, the Venetians and French set to work with a catapult barrage that forced them to swing open the gates. The invaders moved in and lived off the citizens for the winter, then departed in the spring of 1203 leaving the city plundered, its walls pulled down and every building except for the churches burned to a shell. The writer Gunther of Pairis called it a 'detestable business'.[38] Innocent III, when he heard the news, agreed, and after threatening to excommunicate everyone involved, relented and let the crusaders off with a warning not to repeat the trick. Alas, a repetition was exactly what was coming – on a scale that was scarcely imaginable. The next city they visited was also a Christian stronghold. Indeed, it was the greatest Christian city in the world: Constantinople.

The crusaders were initially drawn to Constantinople by the pleas of a foolish young man, Prince Alexios, the son of the former Byzantine emperor Isaac II Angelos. Isaac had taken power in Constantinople following a coup in 1185, and had spent the next ten years of his reign cordially frittering it away. He in turn was deposed by his brother (Alexios III Angelos) blinded, imprisoned and left to rot in jail. The brother was now in power and the nineteen-year old Prince Alexios was after revenge. No promise was too outlandish for him to make, and so it was with a straight face that he had approached the leaders of the Fourth Crusade with an offer to pay them 200,000 silver marks, provide a permanent garrison of 500 knights to the kingdom of Jerusalem and bind over the city of Constantinople to the religious authority of the pope in Rome – if they would just place him on the throne from which his father had been toppled. This was an offer manifestly too good to be true, but the crusaders snapped it up. In June 1203 the

Venetian-led fleet sailed into view of the Queen of Cities. It would remain there for nearly a year.

During that time, events moved chaotically – and often fast. In the summer of 1203 Alexios III abandoned Constantinople. Isaac was pulled from his jail cell and placed back on the throne, with his son playing co-emperor, as Alexios IV. With that, the crusaders' mission in Constantinople was theoretically accomplished. But once again, the Venetians had encountered a ruler who could not pay for services rendered. They took their satisfaction the hard way, by plundering churches throughout the city. As a result, riots and street-fighting between Greeks and westerners broke out and in August huge fires were lit. Flames ripped through around four hundred acres of the city's ancient centre, threatening to destroy even the Hagia Sophia and the Hippodrome. Eventually, a delicate peace was made, in which Alexios IV promised to pay his debt in instalments and offered the Venetians further work fighting his enemies in Thrace and the wider empire. But by December 1203 the money had again dried up, and the ancient Venetian *doge* had threatened the young emperor with deposition.

In the end Dandolo did not have to lift a finger. In late January 1204 old Isaac died, and in yet another Byzantine palace coup, Alexios was strangled to death on the orders of a rival called Alexios Doukas 'Mourtzouphlos' – a nickname that referred to his enormously bushy eyebrows. In the early spring, Mourtzouphlos tried to get tough with the Venetians, demanding that they leave or face slaughter. The Venetians just laughed. On 9 April they began to bombard the city from the sea. Three days later they landed men on the ramparts with flying bridges from their ships' masts. With the walls breached, the whole might of the crusading army rushed in and began a dreadful sack. Homes, churches and offices were looted. Rape and murder were commonplace. Nothing was off-limits to the plunderers, including the four ancient bronze sculpted horses adorning the Hippodrome, which were taken down and loaded onto the Venetian ships. (They can still be seen in Venice today, at St Mark's Basilica.) Inside the Hagia Sophia a prostitute from the crusader camp cavorted around the patriarch of Constantinople's holy throne. Mourtzouphlos fled the city, but he was tracked as he ran, and eventually brought back to his capital, where he was tortured, then hurled from the top of the column of Theodosius. As he smashed to pieces on the ground, so the Byzantine empire died a sort of death. No Greek was raised up in his place: instead the crusader Baldwin count of Flanders was hailed as a Latin emperor of Constantinople. Meanwhile, the Venetians, having made back their outlay on the crusade, declined to go to Alexandria or anywhere else besides. They weighed anchor and went home to count their winnings. The Greek chronicler Niketas Choniates called the whole thing 'outrageous'.[39] He was not far wrong. The Fourth Crusade was one of the most disgraceful and notorious escapades in the whole of the Middle Ages, and Innocent III raged and complained about it bitterly. Yet for all its horrors and corruptions, the Venetians had also shown what was possible under the banner of crusading. And for all his bluster in the aftermath of Constantinople's sack and fall, Innocent would make full use of the insight.

DURING THE EIGHTEEN YEARS OF HIS papacy, Innocent preached five other crusades, prepared a sixth and inspired a seventh. Not one of them went to Jerusalem. Yet his crusading gaze reached every point of the compass. In Spain and Portugal Innocent urged the Christian kings of the region to band together and fight against the Almohads. They duly did so, and in 1212, reinforced by members of the Templars and Hospitallers, as well as other crusaders from across the Pyrenees, they crushed the Almohad caliph al-Nasir at the battle of Las Navas de Tolosa – a milestone in the *Reconquista* which began a rapid drive southwards by the Christian powers, who pushed the Almohads steadily back towards the Mediterranean. Meanwhile, far away in northern Europe, Innocent was also wholeheartedly encouraging Danish, German and other Scandinavian lords to attack pagans in the unconverted north-east of Europe – a campaign known as the Livonian Crusade, in which all Christian warriors, including the newly formed Teutonic Knights, could claim forgiveness for their sins in return for colonizing new lands around the Baltic. These military campaigns had dire consequences for both Spanish Muslims and pagan Livs. But more revolutionary still was Innocent's use of crusading in the heartlands of western Europe. During a dispute with King John of England over the appointment of an archbishop of Canterbury called Stephen Langton, Innocent prepared (but did not publish) documents authorizing a crusade against John, whom he had excommunicated for his disobedience and general impertinence. And around the same time, in 1209, he preached crusade against a heretical Christian sect in southern France who were known as the Cathars. This campaign, usually called the Albigensian Crusade, since some of the activity took place around the southern French city of Albi, would last for twenty years.

Enemies Within

CATHARS, WHO WERE THE UNLUCKY TARGETS of Innocent's Albigensian Crusade, had been known in Europe since at least the 1170s, when a grand assembly of Church leaders known as the Third Lateran Council declared their beliefs 'a loathsome heresy'. And it was true that these were unorthodox people, who took the tradition of Christian asceticism far beyond what had been developed even by Bernard of Clairvaux's Cistercians. Their first principles were uncontroversial: Cathars regarded human flesh as by its nature sinful and detestable – a view which, as we have seen, Innocent had once professed wholeheartedly to share. They thought the only route to escape from mortal corruption was by living according to a strict doctrine of self-denial: sexual abstinence, vegetarianism and simplicity of life. In this they were not very different from, say, the orders of mendicant friars who were emerging in Europe at roughly the same time. However, Cathars crossed from Christian asceticism into heresy by rejecting the hierarchy of the western Church in favour of their own private priesthood, and refusing the Eucharist, baptism and other Church rites. This put them quite beyond the pale – especially for a pope like Innocent, so firmly fixated on imposing command-and-control authority on the Church at large.

Catharism was also troublingly close to home, for it had a close following among citizens of towns in southern France and northern Italy. One typical Cathar-friendly settlement was the city of Viterbo, which bore the full brunt of Innocent's wrath in 1205 when the citizens elected several Cathars to the city council. 'You have rotted in your sins like a beast in its dung,' the furious pope told them.[40] But Innocent found he could not stamp out Catharism with poison-pen letters. Catharism was off-beat and extreme, but it inspired great devotion and loyalty in its adherents. Moreover, several lords of the French south – most notably Raymond, count of Toulouse – were content to turn a blind eye to the heresy, which for all its oddness did very little tangible harm to the moral and religious fabric of society. And so the pope decided to act. As he wrote to Philip II Augustus of France in 1205, 'wounds that do not respond to the healing of poultices must be lanced with a blade.'[41]

In 1208 the pope had his *casus belli* when one of his leading diplomats, Peter of Castelnau, was murdered following a fruitless meeting to discuss Catharism with Raymond of Toulouse. Within weeks Peter had been declared a martyr. And at the same time, Innocent sent letters to the great lords and princes of the west, defaming the Cathars as 'more dangerous than the Saracens' and calling for a general effort to wipe them from the face of the earth.[42] He summoned a crusading force to meet at Lyon in the summer of 1209 and deal with the enemies of God once and for all.

Although calling a crusade on Christian soil was a drastic and unprecedented step, it found rapid favour with the king and northern French nobility. The south of France was to them an almost foreign realm. Hot and sensuous, and linguistically different from the north with its Occitan dialect, it had for a long time been distant from the reach of royal government. This was highly displeasing to Philip Augustus, whose goal throughout his reign was to establish his crown's authority over a greater portion of the kingdom than had recently been the case.* Philip had no great wish to go crusading himself – his experience on the Third Crusade as a younger man had been quite enough excitement – but he still lent his tacit support of the crusade against the Cathars within his realm, calculating that it would be useful means of breaking the autonomy of men like the count of Toulouse. Command of the anti-Cathar army was entrusted to an experienced crusader: Simon de Montfort, a veteran of the Fourth Crusade and a tireless, stiff-necked zealot, whose life's driving passion was slaughtering infidels wherever he could find them.† In the Albigensian Crusade he found the perfect outlet for his bloodlust.

From June 1209, for a full two years, Simon de Montfort and his fellow crusaders cut a swathe through the French south, besieging towns suspected of harbouring Cathars and burning, slicing or torturing people to death. De Montfort hunted heretics in places like Béziers and Carcassonne, Minerve and Castelnaudary, and when he found them he showed no mercy. According to one of the authors of a chronicle known as *The Song of the Cathar Wars*, 'there was so great a killing that... it will be talked of till the end of the world.' The crusaders torched and bombarded their way around Cathar country, massacring citizens in their thousands to ensure no heretic would escape their punishment. They sang religious anthems like 'Veni Creator Spiritus' and they threw women down wells. By 1210 their victims numbered in the tens of thousands. And de Montfort was in no mood to quit. Indeed, he was having such success that he had started to assemble a large southern lordship of his own, created out of lands he had confiscated from lords who refused to back his actions against heretics. By late 1212 he was in charge of a considerable portion of southern France,

---

* A goal that had already been achieved spectacularly in Normandy, where in 1203–4 Philip evicted the English duke of Normandy, King John, and took the duchy under French royal control for the first time in many centuries.
† This is Simon IV de Montfort, sometimes known as Simon de Montfort the elder, to distinguish him from his son Simon V de Montfort, earl of Leicester, the leader of a major rebellion in England which in 1264–5 temporarily deposed king Henry III. Simon the elder had left the Fourth Crusade after the debacle at Zara and travelled on his own to fight for a while in Syria – a decision that meant he was untainted by association with the sack of Constantinople of 1204.

which he governed according to a set of strict and divisive laws called the Statutes of Pamiers. He was also completely out of control. In 1213 de Montfort attempted to extend his crusader state into territory belonging to Pedro II, king of Aragon and count of Barcelona, whose dominions stretched north of the Pyrenees. Pedro was a *Reconquista* hero, who had been crowned king by Innocent himself and who in 1212 had taken part in the huge battle against the Almohads at Las Navas de Tolosa. No matter: on 12 September 1213 de Montford drew Pedro into battle at Muret, not far from Toulouse, crushed his army and killed the Aragonese king. Whatever danger Catharism had threatened to the unity of the church, no Cathars had been responsible for slaughtering crusader monarchs. It was de Montfort who now seemed to represent the greatest threat to order in the French south.

Innocent, however, either did not care or could not rein in his man. The pope had now begun to plan a Fifth Crusade, which was to be announced at a Fourth Lateran Council in 1215, with its target the Nile Delta city of Damietta. And while de Montfort was certainly a distracting presence during the preparations for this mission, he was not distracting enough to convince Innocent of the need to call a halt to persecuting Christ's enemies. So the pope allowed the persecutions to continue, and de Montfort was still alive and active in June 1216 when Innocent fell sick and died at Perugia, at around the age of fifty-five. De Montfort continued to enjoy his role as scourge of the Cathars for another two years, before he too died: killed while besieging the city of Toulouse, where he was struck by a rock hurled from a catapult operated by a group of the city's women. It was a lucky hit. But the damage had long ago been done. After de Montfort died, the Cathar wars were taken on by Philip Augustus' son Louis 'the Lion', who in 1223 succeeded his father as Louis VIII of France. Louis continued the war on southern heretics until the end of the 1220s, by which time he had successfully stripped away the county of Toulouse of any last vestiges of independence. Whether this had tackled the root problem of heresy was much less certain. Catharism remained alive in the south until the fourteenth century, no more or less dangerous than it had ever been to the moral fabric of western society. So whatever the Albigensian Crusade had achieved in terms of political reorganization, it had not been able to crush the spirit of the heretics themselves.* But it had normalized the sight of crusaders fighting within the Christian realms of the west. During the thirteenth and fourteenth centuries this would become an increasingly familiar sight.

Crusaders Everywhere

THE FIFTH CRUSADE PLANNED BY INNOCENT and promulgated at the Fourth Lateran Council of 1215 was eventually overseen by his successor, Honorius III, with very limited success. Despite the deployment of large, predominantly French and German armies to assault Damietta, four years of war between 1217 and 1221 produced no lasting gains. Damietta was taken and lost, and an attempt to storm the Egyptian capital Cairo was easily defeated by the sultan, Saladin's nephew al-Kamil, who flooded the Nile valley and sunk the crusader army into fields of sapping mud. This, along with an almost identical crusade to Damietta led by Louis IX of France in 1248–54, were the last, faintly farcical mass assaults on the east, which was thereafter left increasingly to the defence of the military orders, bolstered occasionally by independent expeditions raised privately by great lords.

But this did not mean an end to crusading. For as the age of the great campaigns diminished, many smaller fields of crusader warfare emerged in their stead. In Spain, the victory over the Almohads at Las Navas de Tolosa in 1212 began a new phase of the *Reconquista* in which the Christian powers were increasingly ascendant, working their way steadily southwards until by 1252 only the emirate of Granada in the far south of the peninsula remained under Islamic rule. Meanwhile, in northern Europe,

---

* One of many historical examples of the futility of wars against abstractions. See, in our times, the War on Terror, War on Drugs, etc.

crusading became effectively permanent, as the Teutonic Knights put down roots in frontier country and led annual raids into pagan lands around the Baltic regions known generically as Prussia, to convert unbelievers by force and carve out new estates for Christian secular lords and bishops. This was a slow but ultimately successful process, which for a time created a military crusader state in the Baltic, stretching all the way from what is now northern Poland to Estonia. At the same time, as we shall see in chapter 9, the crusade became a means of defending the borders of Christendom in eastern Europe from a new world superpower – the Mongols.

Yet while these crusaders and others like them were at least fighting non-Christians, from the thirteenth century onwards many others took their vows to fight in Christ's name and ended up making war on their co-religionists. Indeed, one of most notorious crusading leaders and later targets of the age was the Holy Roman Emperor Frederick II Hohenstaufen. One of the most striking men of his age, Frederick was nicknamed 'the wonder of the world' (*stupor mundi*) for his piercing intellect, political genius and perpetual restlessness. Raised on Sicily, where he became king at the age of three in 1198, Frederick was possessed of an easy familiarity with the Arabic language and Islamic culture as well as his own Christian faith. He also had a lifelong obsession with scientific enquiry, natural philosophy, mathematics and zoology, and wrote a highly regarded textbook on the art of hunting with birds of prey. In 1220 Frederick was crowned as Holy Roman Emperor, extending his authority from Syracuse in the south to the German borders with Denmark in the north. Even without accounting for the force of his personality he was the dominant secular ruler in the Christian world. And when he turned his attention to crusading, he achieved spectacular results.

Although he never led a mass crusade to the east, Frederick did travel to the kingdom of Jerusalem in the late 1220s, where he used his rare rapport with his the sultan al-Kamil to achieve what many had given up as impossible: the return of Christian rule to the Holy City. In a negotiated settlement brokered via personal diplomacy between himself and the sultan, Frederick secured recognition for Christian oversight, on the understanding that Muslims would be allowed unmolested access to the Haram al-Sharif so that they could worship at the Dome of the Rock and al-Aqsa Mosque. Frederick claimed the title and crown of king of Jerusalem for himself, but left day-to-day government in the hands of appointed deputies when he returned to Europe. Although this happy balance of powers lasted only sixteen years, it was a miraculously even-handed and bloodless revolution for which Frederick might have expected the thanks and adulation of all of Christendom. Unfortunately, he received no such thing.

During the course of his life, Frederick Hohenstaufen quarrelled with popes constantly and was excommunicated a remarkable four times. Indeed, at the very moment that he was crowned king of Jerusalem at the Church of the Holy Sepulchre in 1229 he was technically barred from communion with the Roman Church. He made a mortal enemy of Pope Gregory IX (r. 1227–41), an imperious and querulous individual cut from much the same cloth as Innocent III, whose driving mission was to stamp out heresy, persecute unbelievers everywhere and make all earthly princes aware that their power was nothing when compared with the papal majesty. Terrified that Frederick's power in Sicily, southern Italy, Germany and Lombardy would enable the Hohenstaufen dynasty to surround and dominate popes in the papal states, Gregory repeatedly accused Frederick of heresy and encouraged other rulers to invade Hohenstaufen lands. This enmity outlived both men: from the 1240s until the 1260s successive popes preached warfare against Frederick and his successors, encouraging belligerents to wear crusader crosses, claim remission of sins and commute vows to make pilgrimages to the Holy Land in favour of staying in the west to fight the Holy Roman Emperor. Eventually the Hohenstaufen were brought low, their luck running out in 1268 when Frederick's sixteen-year-old grandson Conradin, the titular king of Jerusalem, was captured by papal allies during fighting for rule of Sicily, taken to Naples and beheaded. It would be difficult to think of a greater inversion – or even perversion – of the original mission of crusading than a

Latin king of Jerusalem losing his head in a war against the pope. But that was the way the world was moving.

FROM THE MID-THIRTEENTH CENTURY ONWARDS, THE crusader states of the east entered a terminal decline. Geopolitics in Syria and Palestine were changing radically, in part thanks to disruptions caused by the rise of the Mongols. In 1244 the city of Jerusalem was invaded and sacked by the Turks of Khwarazm, who had been displaced and forced out of Central Asia by the Mongol advance. Then from the 1260s, a new ruling dynasty in Egypt – a Turkish slave-soldier caste known as the Mamluks – began to chip away at the remaining coastal redoubts and fortresses of the kingdom of Jerusalem, county of Tripoli and principality of Antioch. Over the course of three decades they ground the vulnerable and increasingly neglected crusader cities into the dust, culminating in a huge siege of Acre in May 1291, which ended in a forced evacuation by sea. Thereafter the Latin kingdom of Jerusalem relocated to Cyprus, where it withered away.

Crusading to the east was dying, and its institutions were following suit. In the early fourteenth century the Knights Templar were destroyed in a cynical and systematic attack led by the French government of Philip IV 'the Fair'*, whose ministers accused Templar leaders of blasphemy, sexual deviance and gross misconduct.[43] Although many writers from the fourteenth century to the sixteenth fantasized about a new age in which the spirit of 1096–9 would once again descend, and all Christendom could reclaim Jerusalem, it would be 1917 before another western general could walk through the gates of the Holy City as conqueror, when Edmund Allenby strolled in to take command on behalf of the Allies, who had driven out the Ottomans in the First World War.

Yet at the same time, crusading continued, and in some cases even in its original form against non-Christian 'infidels'. The Teutonic Knights continued their war on pagans in the Baltic

* See chapter 11.

well into the fifteenth century. The Knights Hospitaller set up an international headquarters on Rhodes where they fought running sea-battles, policing the Mediterranean against Muslim pirates from Asia Minor and north Africa, under the guise of a holy war. And when the Ottoman empire began to sweep towards eastern Europe, Christian knights rallied to the cause with crosses pinned to their plate armour. But just as often, crusading became a badge to wear to give any war fought by a Christian power an added gloss of legitimacy. In 1258, when Pope Alexander IV wished his allies (including the Republic of Venice) to make war on Alberigo of Romano, ruler of Treviso, he sent a papal legate to preach a crusade against Alberigo in St Mark's Square – a parade at which the legate produced a bevy of naked women whom he claimed had been sexually assaulted by the Trevisan. Soon after, in the 1260s, Simon de Montfort the younger, son of the Cathar crusader of the same name, declared his rebellion against King Henry III of England to be a crusade.* A century later, Henry III's great-great-grandson John of Gaunt, duke of Lancaster, claimed to be a crusader when he went to fight on the Iberian peninsula in the hope of seizing the crown of Castile in the name of his wife, daughter of the murdered king Pedro 'the Cruel'. In the 1380s the English bishop of Norwich, Henry Despenser, led a crusade to Flanders, which was supposedly to wipe out supporters of an antipope, Clement VII, but really a side-campaign in the long-running Anglo-French struggle known as the Hundred Years War. The fifteenth century saw five crusades launched against the Hussites – followers of a Bohemian heretic called Jan Hus, an early dissident theologian of what would come to be known as the Reformation.† And in 1493, the Genoese explorer Christopher Columbus sailed back from his first encounter with the Americas announcing in terms strikingly reminiscent of crusader rhetoric his discovery of a land of great

---

* De Montfort's rebellion was indeed prompted by Henry III's foolish promise to lead an anti-Hohenstaufen crusade to Sicily, where he imagined he could oust the Christian ruler and instead install his son, Edmund.
† See chapter 16.

wealth and many pagans, which could be claimed on behalf of all Christendom.

And this was far from the last mention of the C-word. Crusading outlived the Middle Ages, and remains today a favoured trope of the alt-right, neo-Nazis and Islamist terrorists, all of whom cleave to the decidedly shaky idea that it has defined Christian and Muslim relations for a millennium. They are not right, but they are not original in their error, either. Crusading – a bastard hybrid of religion and violence, adopted as a vehicle for papal ambition but eventually allowed to run as it pleased, where it pleased, and against whom it pleased – was one of the Middle Ages' most successful and enduringly poisonous ideas. Its survival is a sign of both its genius and of the readiness of people both then and now to throw themselves into conflict in the name of a higher cause.

Part III

Rebirth

C. AD 1215 – AD 1347

A taste of the opulent decoration that would once have filled Cluny III:
these frescoes, commissioned by Abbot Hugh of Cluny, were uncovered in the
chapel of Berzé-la-Ville in the late nineteenth century. Cluniac monasticism inspired
some of the greatest art and music before the Renaissance.

Only a tiny part of the Burgundian abbey known as Cluny III still stands. Yet in the high Middle Ages this was the biggest building in Europe, and a symbol of the immense wealth and influence of the Cluniac monks.

St Bernard of Clairvaux – imagined here by the sixteenth-century artist El Greco – was the driving force behind the Cistercian Order, and played a crucial role in winning papal approval for the Knights Templar in the twelfth century.

William Marshal, earl of Pembroke, was by his own reckoning the greatest knight of his age. He served five Plantagenet kings of England and was still fighting in the thick of battle in his seventies. His tomb effigy, pictured right, lies in the Temple Church in London.

tout le pays. Et sait Il fist rappareillier leglise de monseign~
saint Jaques et plusieurs autres. Et quant il eut chasse les
sarrazins hors du regne Il se mist au retour vers france

La bataille de ronchenaulx et la mort rolant et oliuier.

This late medieval manuscript shows the battle of Roncevalles, AD 778, and the death
of Roland. Originally based on a military campaign of Charlemagne's reign,
the Song of Roland made a chivalric hero of its title character. It was one of the
most popular tales of the Middle Ages.

Eleanor of Aquitaine
marries the king of
France, Louis VII,
while a ship waits to
transport them east on
the Second Crusade.
Eleanor's visit to the
Holy Land was not
very successful, and
she was divorced from
her husband when they
returned to Europe.

The thirteenth-century Mongolian warlord Temüjin, better known as Genghis Khan, founded the largest world empire of the medieval period. Today he is revered as a national hero: this giant statue of him looms over the landscape outside Ulaanbaatar.

Floor tiles made at Chertsey Abbey in England depict Richard the Lionheart jousting with Saladin during the Third Crusade. No such fight ever took place, but in the late Middle Ages the rivalry between the two rulers was legendary.

The Mongols practised medieval total warfare. When Genghis Khan's descendant Hülagü besieged Baghdad in 1258 his troops killed the Abbasid caliph, and threw so many priceless manuscripts into the Tigris that the river flowed black with ink.

The Polo family are presented with a golden tablet by Kublai Khan, the supreme leader of the Mongol empire. Marco Polo blazed a trail as merchant and diplomat, and his Travels is one of the best-known books of the Middle Ages.

Meticulously reconstructed after being shelled in the First World War, the Cloth Hall in Ypres is a testament to the vast wealth of European merchants in the later Middle Ages – particularly those who dabbled in the English wool trade.

Abelard and Heloïse were two of medieval history's most famous lovers. Peter Abelard was the most brilliant scholar of his day, but his affair with Heloïse led to public disgrace for both, his brutal castration and her confinement to a nunnery.

The original parchment roll detailing the confessions of the Templars
in France in 1307. The confessions were heard by the scholars of the University
of Paris, whose opinion helped convict the Templars of terrible crimes.

The Sainte-Chapelle in Paris is one of the most dazzling achievements of Gothic architecture.
Commissioned by Louis IX as a repository for his relics, including Christ's Crown of Thorns,
the chapel's vast stained-glass windows and soaring ceiling evoke
a sense of stepping from earth into heaven itself.

9

MONGOLS

*'They came, they sapped, they burnt, they slew,
they plundered and they departed...'*

ATA-MALIK JUVAINI ON THE MONGOLS

At the great Nile Delta city of Damietta during the cool early months of 1221 strange news arrived from the east. Damietta was at that time in the hands of an international crusader army. For four years they been conducting a tedious military campaign against the sultan of Egypt, and although they had taken the city they had not managed to do much else. Fighting in Egypt was proving hot, expensive, uncomfortable and unsanitary. The Ayyubid sultan al-Kamil was sitting impervious in Cairo, and further gains at his expense seemed as though they would be difficult and most likely impossible. Much money had been spent and many lives lost for an overall position that amounted to stalemate. But the letters that reached Damietta seemed to change everything.

They were forwarded to the crusader army by Bohemond IV, prince of Antioch, and they reported rumours which had reached the crusader states from spice merchants working the trade routes that ran through Persia to the west coast of India. According to explosive documents provided by these traders, a tremendously powerful ruler called 'David, King of the Indies' was battering his way through the Islamic realms of Central Asia, scattering all before him. King David had, it was said, already defeated the Shah of Persia and captured massive and wealthy cities including

Samarkand, Bukhara (both in modern Uzbekistan) and Ghazna (modern Afghanistan). Yet he was far from satisfied. He was now heading relentlessly west, smashing infidels as he went. 'There is no power on earth that can resist him,' heard one chronicler. 'He is believed to be the executor of divine vengeance, the hammer of Asia.'[1]

The man who received this startling military intelligence in Damietta was Jacques de Vitry, bishop of Acre, an industrious scholar-churchman whose love for letters extended to wearing an episcopal mitre made out of parchment.* De Vitry had every good reason to believe what he read. For at around the same time, a small group of crusaders who had been captured months earlier during fighting outside Damietta had made it back to the city telling similar tales of an incredible adventure. Having been seized in Egypt by the sultan's forces, they were sent as prisoners-of-war to the court of the Abbasid caliph in Baghdad. From there they were given as human gifts to diplomats working for a powerful king from much further east. This same, mighty monarch had in his turn sent them all the way back to Damietta to bear witness to his strength and magnanimity. It was a curious tale, and since these crusaders' adventures had taken them ever further from lands where European languages were spoken, they had not really understood all they had seen nor everyone whom they had met. But given the context, it seemed reasonable to suppose that their saviour was none other than King David.

Archbishop Jacques de Vitry spread the news far and wide across the west, writing personally to such high dignitaries as the pope, the duke of Austria and the chancellor of the University of Paris.[2] The crusade was saved, he announced: King David was on his way to help smite the Egyptian sultan. Conflating various Christian prophecies with the undoubtedly exciting eyewitness reports given by the prisoners-of-war, de Vitry and other churchmen like him decided this King David must be a descendent of a mythical Christian warrior-ruler called Prester John. In their

---

* Today a treasure of the Musée Provincial des Arts Anciens in Namur, Belgium.

forefathers' times men had spoken of this Prester John, ruler of a dimly perceived place called 'the Three Indies', to whom dozens of kings allegedly paid tribute – predicting he would visit Jerusalem 'with a huge army befitting the glory of our Majesty to inflict a humiliating defeat on the enemies of the Cross'.[3] Sadly for them, this had never happened, for the simple reason that Prester John did not exist. But it was now supposed that his son – or possibly his grandson – was on his way to carry out the task. If the combination of intelligence reports and prophecies could be believed, then soon the crusaders could expect to capture Alexandria, then Damascus, before joining up with King David to sweep triumphantly into Jerusalem.

At long last, things were starting to look up.

Except, of course, they weren't. When the crusaders at Damietta, buoyed by news of their impending reinforcement by King David, set out to attack the sultan and begin their sweep to victory, they were easily defeated and drowned in a flooding Nile. And when further groups of crusaders travelled to the Holy Land in the ensuing years, they saw neither hide nor hair of any King David. The prophecies of imminent victory were shown up to be fantasy, and soon King David's name was mentioned no more.

Yet for all this, the rumours of King David were not entirely fictitious. For the Indian spice merchants and the crusader prisoners-of-war had not been lying when they spoke of an all-conquering ruler advancing unstoppably from the east. They had simply not known what they were looking at.[4]

What they had thought was 'King David', grandson of Prester John and saviour of the Christian west, was in fact Genghis Khan (or as many scholars now prefer, *Chinggis Qan*), a down-and-out nomad boy from the steppe of Mongolia who had risen to become the most successful conqueror of his age. In two decades, Genghis had created a merciless and apparently invincible Mongolian war machine, then set it loose on the world around him, from Korea to Mesopotamia. In doing so he had torn up the political structures of Central Asia and the Middle East, bringing about the demise of two of the eastern world's greatest imperial dynasties: the Jin in China and the Khwarazmians in Persia. And there was more to come.

From Genghis' rise in the early 1200s, until 1259, when the superstate he conquered was formally partitioned into four huge quarters, the Mongols controlled the biggest contiguous land empire in the world. And although their period of global pre-eminence lasted only 150 years, their achievements in that time stood comparison with those of the ancient Macedonians, Persians or Romans. Their methods were more brutal than those of any other global empire before the modern age: the Mongols did not hesitate to level entire cities, wipe out whole populations, ruin vast regions and leave once-busy metropolises smouldering and desolate, either to be rebuilt to their own liking or simply wiped from the map.[5] Yet weighed against their appalling legacy of slaughter, waste and genocide was the fact that the Mongols rebooted the whole shape of trade and interaction across Asia and the Middle East. The severely policed order they imposed on their conquered territories created a relative period of peace sometimes known by historians as the *Pax Mongolica*. It permitted epic journeys of overland exploration, and an easier transfer between east and west of technologies, knowledge and people. It may also, as we shall see in chapter 13, have allowed for the transmission of the worst pandemic in world history.

The Mongols pioneered the administrative tools of a global empire: a world-class postal system, universal law code, rationalized and decimalized military reform and an extremely harsh but efficient approach to metropolitan planning. Their imperial systems set a gold-standard that had not been seen on such scale since Rome's demise and arguably would not be seen again until the nineteenth century. More than any empire since the pre-Christian Romans, they were largely relaxed about religious dogma (although Genghis Khan forbade Islamic ritual halal slaughter of animals), relatively flexible about permitting local customs under the umbrella of Mongol rule and respectful of religious leaders without preferring one sect or faith to another.

As a result of these achievements and more besides,

historians have credited the Mongol khans with everything from revolutionizing medieval banking to forging the worldview of the American founding fathers. In their own day they inspired both envious admiration and sheer, slack-jawed terror. It is impossible to tell the story of the Middle Ages and the making of the west without the Mongols. And so it is with their own founding father we must start: Temüjin, the poor boy from the steppe who became Genghis Khan.

Genghis Khan

ACCORDING TO *THE SECRET HISTORY OF THE MONGOLS* – the most contemporary (if not entirely reliable) account of Genghis Khan's life – the great conqueror was descended originally from a 'blue-grey wolf with his destiny ordained by Heaven above', who was married to a fallow doe.[6] His human ancestors also included a cyclops who could see for dozens of miles and an uncountable number of nomadic tribal warriors who inhabited the rolling plains of what is now north Mongolia, living in tents, moving with the seasons, and hunting or raiding for survival. And at some time in or around 1162 near the sacred mountain of Burkhan Khaldun the baby who would become Genghis Khan was born into this world, supposedly 'clutching in his right hand a clot of blood the size of a knucklebone.'[7] He was named Temüjin, because his father, a famous warrior in the Borjigin clan, had been fighting against the Mongols' deadly enemies, the Tatars, and had taken a valuable captive of the same name. But when Temüjin was nine years old, the Tatars poisoned his father. The boy and his six siblings were left to be raised by their mother, Höelün – a hard state of affairs made worse when the family was rejected by their tribe and abandoned to fend for themselves. They did so by foraging for wild fruit and small animals like the ground squirrels called marmots native to the Mongolian steppe. It was not much of a start to a life.

Fortunately, when Temüjin and his family fell on hard times, conditions on the steppe were uncommonly gentle. Studies of ancient trees in the pine forests of central Mongolia have shown that during the exact time that Temüjin was growing up, the area enjoyed fifteen consecutive years of mild weather and abundant rainfall.[8] This was the most hospitable period of weather the region had experienced in eleven hundred years. The grasslands thrived, and the people and animals who lived on them did too. Temüjin and his family survived their hard years in the wild, and by the time the boy was in his mid-teens he had learned to ride, fight, hunt and survive. He and his family were eventually accepted back into the tribal system. Temüjin acquired animals to graze and milk, and he married a girl called Börte, the first of at least a dozen wives and concubines who would frequent his *ger* (the traditional Mongolian yurt or animal-hide tent), often simultaneously, throughout his life. Physically strong and energetic, with darting eyes like a cat's, he was making his way in nomadic society. But rejection shaped him in ways that would inform his leadership ever after. Temüjin grew up to be extraordinarily tough and self-disciplined, and placed a higher value on loyalty than anything else: he would never tolerate even a sniff of betrayal or dishonesty, and reacted ferociously when he was rejected, resisted or thwarted.

Tribal life on the steppe revolved around grazing and raiding animals, and politics was organized according to complex and regularly shifting alliances between tribes. Warfare between these tribes was commonplace, and Temüjin excelled in it. By his mid-twenties his reputation was such that he had been acclaimed as leader (*khan*) of a tribal confederation known as the Khamag Mongol. This was a prominent position, which allowed Temüjin to call upon tens of thousands of mounted warriors when he went to war with neighbouring tribes – including, most dramatically, a rival coalition led by his childhood friend and sworn blood-brother Jamukha, whom he defeated and eventually killed as punishment for his betrayal. As the twelfth century drew to a close Temüjin was proving to be one of the most adept leaders in his region.

The reasons for his success were simple but effective. Besides a personal talent for fighting and marrying, both of which were essential tools of steppe diplomacy, he had also lighted upon some radical reforms to traditional Mongol tribal and military organization. Like Muhammad uniting the bickering tribes of Arabia during the seventh century AD, Temujin saw that bonds of clan and blood repelled as often as they attracted, and that by weakening them in favour of a direct bond to himself he could create a whole that was much more powerful than its constituent parts.

This necessitated some simple but important practical steps. One was to introduce a strong element of meritocracy into his military organization. Mongol society was customarily arranged according to tribal hierarchies based on ancestry and wealth. Temüjin tore this tradition to shreds. He chose his allies and his military officers on the strict basis of talent and loyalty. Then he gave his officers regularized units of men to command. The base unit was a company of ten men called an *Arban*, comprising six light mounted archers and four more heavily armoured lancers. Ten of these companies made a *Zuun*. Ten *Zuuns* made a *Mingghan*. And the largest unit, ten thousand men strong, was a *Tumen*. Critically for the unity of the military as a whole, these units were not constructed from tribal groupings. They cut across family and clan lines.[9] Once troops had been placed in their unit, they could not transfer – on pain of death. But if they rode and won together, they could expect to amass coin, women and horses – the three most eagerly sought-after currencies of the steppe.

Outside his army, Temüjin also focused on ways to bind together the society under his rule. Here he bore some resemblance to the great Byzantine emperor Justinian. A law code known as the *Jasaq* or *Yassa* enjoined everyone under Mongol rule to refrain from stealing from or enslaving one another, to exhibit strict protocols of generosity and hospitality, to obey the authority of the khan above all others and to disdain rape, sodomy, washing clothes in thunderstorms and urinating in sources of water. Harsh and usually mortal punishments were levied without sentiment on anyone who offended Temüjin or his code: ordinary people found guilty of crimes were beheaded with a sword, while distinguished officers or leaders had their backs broken so they died without their blood being spilled.

Severity was a hallmark of Mongol conduct across the board. During the course of his campaigns and conquests, Temüjin and his generals also operated according to strict and hideously bloody rules of engagement. Any people or city that immediately submitted to Mongol rule would be welcomed into the fold. But the faintest hint of resistance or insubordination invited massacre and scorched-earth destruction. Rivals who mistreated Mongol envoys could expect to be hounded personally to death. Communities who lied about how much wealth they possessed were liable to be killed en masse, often in grotesque and exemplary manner. This served two ends. First, it was a form of psychological warfare: Temüjin realized that his enemies were more likely to crumble at his mere approach if they suspected the alternative to immediate surrender was immediate death. Second, annihilating all but totally subservient opponents ensured that Temüjin could win wars with relatively small armies, since he did not need to leave large numbers to police conquered communities.

Yet balanced against rule by terror was a surprising degree of tolerance for those whom the Mongols allowed to survive. Clans and tribes who surrendered to the Mongols were actively integrated into Mongol society. Their men were expected to join the army and the women and children were folded into the rest of the community. Meanwhile, most religious faiths were tolerated – a fact that would become increasingly important once the Mongol world started to expand outwards. (Temüjin was fascinated by religious faiths in general, and usually viewed them as useful additions to Mongol shamanic paganism, rather than competitors.)[10] So from early in his career Temüjin conceived of a Mongol world characterized by overwhelming military force, but also a strong degree of enforced social cohesion. Many a dictator in world history after him would have similar ideas. Few would ever pursue or achieve their goals with such devastating success as Temüjin.

By around 1201 Temüjin's Khamag Mongol was the most powerful coalition on their region of the steppe. Five years later

Temüjin had defeated all the other neighbouring powers, including the Merkits, Naimans, Tatars and Uighurs. Each of them bowed before his name – which in 1206 became Genghis Khan (loosely, 'fierce ruler') when a council of high tribal chiefs known as a *quriltai* awarded him the title in recognition of his extraordinary feats of conquest. As *The Secret History of the Mongols* reported it: 'when the people of the felt-walled tents had been brought to allegiance in the Year of the Tiger [1206], they all gathered at the source of the Onon River.* They hoisted [Temüjin]'s white standard with nine tails and there they gave [him] the title of *qan*.'[11] Genghis had richly earned his sobriquet, for the Mongols he commanded were the terror of the steppe. As one despairing enemy put it: 'If we engage them and fight them to the end, they will not blink their black eyes. Is it advisable for us to fight these tough Mongols, who do not flinch even if their cheeks are pierced, and their black blood gushes forth?'[12] Many millions more would ask themselves the same question in the following century.

March of the Khans

AFTER HIS TRIUMPHS IN 1206 GENGHIS Khan expanded his dominions far and wide beyond the Mongolian plains. In northern China he attacked the Western Xia and Jin dynasties, crushing Chinese armies in battle, and massacring hundreds of thousands of combatants and non-combatants alike. In 1213 he sent troops smashing through the Great Wall of China at three separate points, before descending towards the Jin capital Zhongdu, which was besieged, taken and sacked in 1215. The emperor Xuanzong was forced to submit to the Mongols and abandoned both his capital city and the northern half of his realm, fleeing to Bianjing (modern-day Kaifeng), more than 350 miles away. It was an abject humiliation from which the Jin dynasty would never recover. But

---

* This flows from northern Mongolia north into modern Russia, where it becomes the river Shilka.

for Genghis Khan and the Mongols it was just one more victory. Afterwards they headed west and targeted the Qara Kitai (also known as the western Liao). According to *The Secret History of the Mongols*, Genghis 'slew [the Qara Kitai] until they were like heaps of rotten logs.'[13] By 1218 Mongol armies were heading east in the direction of Korea, while in the other direction they had Central Asia and the lands of the Persians in their sights.

At this time the rulers of Persia and many surrounding territories were the Khwarazmians: Turks who had once been mamluks, but had risen up to become the masters of their own huge empire, which sat across the rich cities and Silk Roads of Central Asia. In 1218 Genghis Khan planned to negotiate a trade deal with their leader, the Khwarazm-Shah, so sent him a diplomatic delegation of 100 Mongol officials. Unfortunately, on their way to the Khwarazm-Shah's court, the envoys were stopped at the Khwarazmian city of Otrar (modern Kazakhstan). All were summarily executed on suspicion of spying. Needless to say, Genghis did not find this amusing. He vowed 'to take revenge to requite the wrong', a policy which he carried out with extreme prejudice.

The campaign Genghis waged against the Khwarazmians was the same one that eventually echoed in the ears of the fifth crusaders, recast as the conquests of 'King David'. In 1219 an army that was numbered in one wild estimate as being 700,000 strong* crossed the Alai mountains (which straddle modern Tajikistan and Kyrgyzstan), beginning a two-year campaign that left Khwarazm broken, its cities destroyed and the Khwarazm-Shah running for his life out of Central Asia towards India, where he took refuge from the Mongols, never to return. Some of the greatest cities in Central Asia were put to the sword, including Merv (today in Turkmenistan), Herat (Afghanistan) the Khwarazmian capital of Samarkand (Uzbekistan) and Nishapur (Iran). 'They came, they sapped, they burnt, they slew, they plundered and they departed,'

---

* This estimate, by the Persian chronicler Rashid al-Din, is obviously a hysterical exaggeration; the entire Mongol military around this time numbered less than 150,000 men. The leanness of the Mongol military was in fact one of its key tactical advantages.

wrote the Persian scholar Ata-Malik Juvayni, quoting one rare and lucky soul who had escaped the Mongol onslaught.[14]

The sack of Merv was particularly heinous. A cosmopolitan metropolis home to perhaps two hundred thousand souls, Merv was a beautiful oasis in an otherwise harsh plateau, located at the crossroads of several major international trade routes, with numerous fine manufacturing industries of its own and a thriving agricultural hinterland fed by a state-of-the-art artificial irrigation system.[15] Genghis sent his son Tolui to demand the city's surrender. Tolui's instructions were as usual: if Merv did not immediately bow down to Mongol authority, it should be devastated. Tolui did not let his father down. When Merv resisted Tolui placed his troops around the city, then invited all citizens to leave in peace with all their possessions, promising that they would be safe. They were not safe: thousands emerged from the city, only to be robbed and murdered. Then the city was sacked, stripped of anything and everything valuable. The irrigation system was studied so that it could be copied, then demolished. So too were Merv's walls. A few citizens who had hidden in basements and sewers were smoked out and slaughtered. And when the Mongols were satisfied that there was no one left to resist them, they moved on.

They repeated the performance with only minor variations across the Khwarazmian lands, wrecking cities while also undertaking methodical sieges of hill fortresses, until at last the whole empire was at their mercy. Mongol governors were installed everywhere, and rebellions against them put down by shocking means. Mass beheadings were commonplace, and many cities were decorated with separate mountains of heads and torsos, left to rot in the open. Hundreds of thousands – perhaps millions – of people, mostly civilians, were killed. Countless others were forcibly drafted into the Mongol army or sent back to Mongolia as slaves, either for work or sexual exploitation. Leaderless and helpless, the Khwarazmian people had been terrorized into submission and their state destroyed. Even accounting for structural weaknesses within the Khwarazmian state, which was riven by factionalism and sectarian divisions between ethnic Iranians and Turks, it was a chastening experience.

By 1221 Genghis had made his point, and was ready to pull his troops back to Mongolia. Yet despite all he had achieved against the Khwarazmians, he was not inclined to go quietly. To predators, everything looks like prey, and there was still plenty for the Mongol generals to feed on. After subjugating Persia, Genghis divided his forces. He himself worked slowly eastwards towards his homelands, raiding and plundering Afghanistan and northern India. Meanwhile, his two finest generals, Jebe and Subedei, headed further west and north, skirting the Caspian Sea and pushing into the Caucasus and the Christian realms of Armenia and Georgia. Here they proceeded in their customary fashion: massacring whole cities and visiting terrible fates on their populations. Jebe and Subedei ordered gang rape, mutilated pregnant women and chopped their unborn children to pieces, and tortured and decapitated with abandon. During the summer of 1222 they twice defeated George IV of Georgia in battle, wounding him so badly that he died of his injuries. Shortly afterwards, George's sister and successor, Queen Rusudan, wrote to Pope Honorius III offering a significant corrective to the garbled 'King David' tales the pope had been fed by the likes of Jacques de Vitry. Far from being a godly people, she told Honorius, the Mongols were pagans who would merely pose as Christians in order to trick their enemies. They were she said, 'a savage people of Tatars, hellish of aspect, as voracious as wolves... [and] brave as lions.'[16] They were virtually impossible to resist. By this time the Mongols had already passed through her kingdom. On this occasion they did not stop to conquer – but they would return to complete the task a generation later.

From Georgia, the generals Jebe and Subedei raced out onto the Russian steppe. As they approached the Crimea, they were met by envoys from the Republic of Venice – who had demonstrated only a few years earlier on the Fourth Crusade to Constantinople that they were almost as capable as the Mongols of ruthlessness in the pursuit of profit. The Venetians struck a deal by which the Mongols agreed to attack their trading rivals, the Genoese, in their lucrative colony at Soldaia, on the Crimean peninsula in the Black Sea. This was the start of a lasting partnership between Venice *doges* and Mongol *khans*, which endured well into the fourteenth century, paving the way for the famous adventures of Marco Polo (see chapter 10) and making the Republic of Venice very rich. Devils, it seemed, could ride together.

Having overwintered in the Crimea, Jebe and Subedei now began a long, circuitous trek back to join Genghis. On the way they fought and crushed various Turkic tribes of the steppes, including the Cumans and Kipchaks. Then they headed north towards Kiev (modern Ukraine). News of their progress along the river Dniester was spread among the Kievan Rus' by distraught Cumans, although there remained great confusion about who exactly the Mongols really were. The well-informed author of the *Novgorod Chronicle* knew only that they had been sent as a divine scourge 'for our sins'. Otherwise, he could only say that they were 'unknown tribes... no one exactly knows who they are, nor whence they came out, nor what their language is, nor of what race they are, nor what their faith is; but they call them Tatars.'[17] Still, it was clear that these mysterious visitors meant trouble. A coalition of Russian princes, including Mstislav the Bold, prince of Novgorod, Mstislav III, grand prince of Kiev and Daniel, prince of Halych, raised an army and tried to chase them off. That this was foolhardy hardly needs to be said. But when the princes executed ten Mongol ambassadors sent to negotiate with them, idiocy became suicide.

At the end of May 1223, the princes of the Rus' caught up with the Mongols near the river Kalka. Although they managed to kill around a thousand warriors from the Mongol rearguard, when they met Jebe and Subedai's main force they were routed. As many as 90 per cent of the Russian troops were killed in the battle and three of the princes were captured. The Mongols had not forgotten the Russians' impertinence in executing their ambassadors, and took ghoulish revenge. Mstislav III of Kiev and two of his sons-in-law were rolled up in carpets and shoved beneath the wooden floor of the Mongol leaders' *ger*. A celebratory dinner was then held on top of them, so that they were crushed and suffocated to death with the sounds of a victory banquet ringing in their ears.[18] On this occasion the Mongols did not remain long enough to add the lands of the Rus' to their now handsomely expanded empire. But they had sighted them, along with the grasslands at the European end of the steppe. As in Georgia, they would be back.

IN THE MEANTIME, IT WAS A long ride home to Mongolia for Genghis Khan, his generals and their armies, made longer by their predilection for fighting almost everyone they encountered, and holding lavish, drunken banquets to advertise their success. But by 1225 they were reunited in their homelands, where they were able to survey the new world they had created. By now Genghis was in his early sixties, and he was the master of a domain that stretched from the Yellow Sea in the east to the Caspian Sea in the west. The sheer size of the thing was almost surreal. The Iraqi chronicler Ibn al-Athir, writing later in the century, declared that 'these Tatars had done something unheard of in ancient or modern times,' and wondered how his readers would ever believe their eyes. 'By God, there is no doubt that anyone who comes after us, when a long time has passed, and sees the record of this event will refuse to accept it.'[19] And along with simple vastness of conquest came the juicy fruits of imperialism. Mongolia was enriched beyond its people's wildest dreams. The conquering armies had driven back before them thousands of stolen horses. Gold and silver, slaves and transported artisans, exotic new foods and powerful alcoholic drinks all flooded in from the subjugated lands many months away. Never especially culturally dogmatic, the Mongols had eagerly harvested technologies and customs from the lands they had visited. Chinese shipbuilders and Persian siege engineers had been co-opted into the military. Uighur scribes had been drafted into the government administration, and a new official script adopted for bureaucracy across the empire. In 1227 Genghis issued a paper currency, copied from the defeated Jin dynasty of China, and backed by silver and silk.

The same year – 1227 – the fierce conqueror died, in the second half of August. The cause of his death is now unknown, but a number of colourful explanations were given during the Middle Ages: it was variously said that Genghis was struck by lightning, poisoned by an arrow or fatally wounded by a captive queen who went to his bed with a razor blade hidden in her vagina.[20] Whatever the case, it was in bed that he died, and his last orders were fitting: he demanded his successors build a new city called Karakorum to serve as the capital of the Mongol empire, then gave instructions for the mass execution of the Tangut emperor Modi and the royal family of the Western Xia, against whom his armies had recently been fighting. They were tied to stakes and hacked to pieces.

Where Genghis' body now lies is as obscure as the cause of his death, for he had his burial place kept deliberately secret: horses trampled the burial spot beyond identification, after which the burial party was supposedly murdered, and their murderers murdered, and the gravediggers murdered. By this stage, the number of lives wasted by Genghis in his charge to rule the world was far beyond reckoning. Looking back several generations later Marco Polo would claim Genghis was a man of 'approved integrity, great wisdom, commanding eloquence and eminent for his valour'.[21] This assessment left out as much as it kept in. But after the lightning territorial expansion and cultural leaps taken in Genghis' reign, the Mongols' future as the only world superpower of the thirteenth century seemed to be assured. All that remained to be seen was who would oversee the next stage of their domination – and how far they could go.

Among the 'Tartars'

SHORTLY AFTER EASTER IN 1241, FOURTEEN years after Genghis' death, Mongol armies were back in the west. They scored two stunning battlefield victories in central and eastern Europe, which, occurring within just seventy-two hours of one another, seemed to set the stage for the Mongolization of the whole continent. On 9 April Mongol generals called Baidar and Kaidan scythed down a combined force of Polish, Czech and Templar soldiers near Legnica (today in southern Poland). They killed Henry II, duke of Lower Silesia, and took his head on a spike to parade before the horrified inhabitants of Legnica itself. After the fighting was concluded, a detachment of Mongol soldiers cut off the right ear of each dead enemy combatant as a trophy to be sent back to Mongolia. (There were enough ears to fill nine large sacks.) Two days later, on 11 April, a separate and much larger Mongol army at large in Hungary dealt an equally severe defeat to King Béla IV at the battle of Mohi (Muhi) in Transylvania. Béla lost the bulk of his army and was forced to flee for his life into Dalmatia. The Polish chronicler Jan Długosz shuddered at the awesome sight of Mongol armies on the rampage. 'They burn, kill and torture as they like, since none dares stand up to them.'[22]

As leaders like Béla fled in panic, the Mongols ran riot across eastern Europe. News soon spread of the terrors they inflicted. Horrified at the 'Latin' world's invasion by the 'Tartars' (the already-inaccurate name Tatars had now been bastardized as a pun on *tartarus*, the Latin name for hell) Pope Gregory IX decided he had to act. Although he had been trying for nearly two years to muster political support for a crusade against the Holy Roman Emperor Frederick Hohenstaufen, he now switched tack.[23] In June he issued a bull asking crusaders who had promised to go to the Holy Land, the Baltic, the Latin kingdom of Constantinople or the lands of the Hohenstaufen to transfer their vows and go to Hungary to take on the Mongols. Unfortunately for Béla and the Hungarians, the sheer number of crusades that were underway in 1241 meant that virtually no one heeded the pope's call. Christmas came and went; by March the Mongols were closing in on Dalmatia, to try and capture Béla himself. Things looked very bad indeed.

Yet then – all of a sudden – the Mongols abruptly halted their pursuit. They wheeled their horses around and rode away, back in the direction of their imperial heartlands. From the brink of apparent annihilation, eastern Europe was suddenly Mongol-free. It was as if God had taken pity, reached down and plucked the tormentors of His people from the earth. According to the Croatian chronicler Thomas the Archdeacon, the reason for this abrupt departure was that the Hungarian steppe, although expansive, did not provide enough grass to feed the huge herds of horses the Mongols required for long campaigning.[24] But Mongol politics had also taken a sharp turn: Ögödei Khan, Genghis' third son and successor as supreme khan, died in late December 1241, and there was a momentary power vacuum in Mongolia. Prudent generals and officials headed home together to witness the transition to a new leader. The Mongols were not giving up on the west – the riches of Italy and Germany remained just as tempting as those of the Khwarazmian empire or the cities of northern China. But for the moment they were forced to pause.

THIS STRANGE HIATUS NOTWITHSTANDING, IN THE 1240s the Mongols still ruled a gigantic area of the world's landmass. During the fourteen years of Ögödei's reign they had added relentlessly to their dominions, deploying new siege technology they had adopted from their Chinese and Muslim subjects.[25] Azerbaijan, northern Iraq, Georgia and Armenia were all under Mongol overlordship, as was Kashmir. Seljuk Asia Minor was being lined up for invasion. The nomadic tribes of the central steppe and princes of the Rus' had all been given hidings of varying degrees of severity. Virtually every city in the Kievan Rus', including Kiev, with its double ring of defensive walls, had been sacked. A chronicle account of the ruin of Riazan' (Ryazan', about 250km south-east of Moscow) described how the Mongols 'burned this holy city with all its beauty and wealth... And churches of God were destroyed... and not one man remained alive in the city. All were dead... And there was not even anyone to mourn the dead.'[26] The Mongol empire was now bigger than ever. And it connected regions of the world that had for a long time been cut off from one another. As a result, from the middle of the thirteenth century, intrepid explorers began to strike out into strange new lands, documenting what they saw and describing the exotic conditions that existed under the command of a superpower of a size unseen in the whole of the Middle Ages.

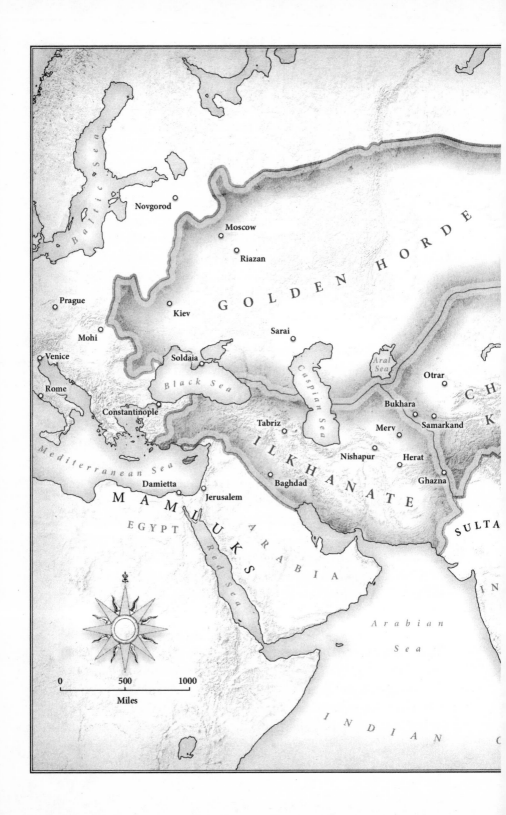

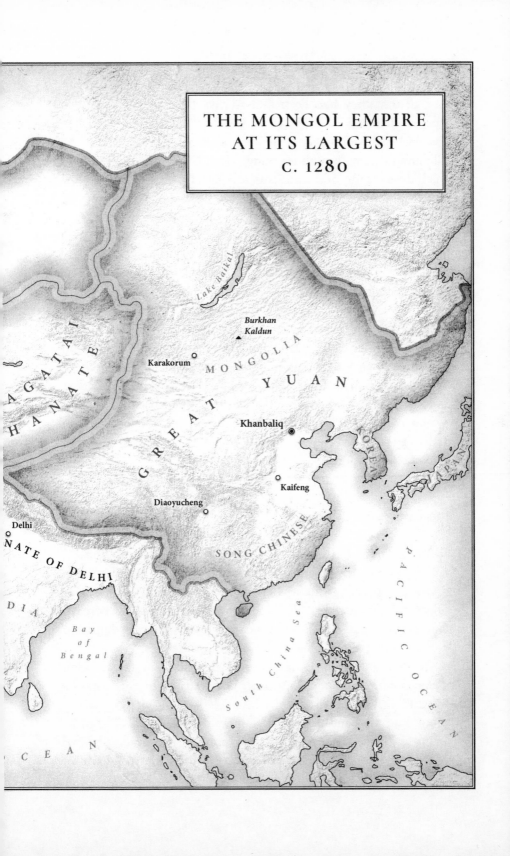

THE MONGOL EMPIRE
AT ITS LARGEST
C. 1280

For all that they had destroyed worlds, the Mongols had also opened them up for exploration. Even during Roman times, the Far East had been beyond the horizon of a single traveller – the silk and other commodities traded from China had arrived only via indirect trade, and India was scarcely any better known. Now under Mongol hegemony, all that would change – at least for a time.

Some of the medieval travellers who struck out into new lands in the thirteenth century kept accounts of their travels. So today we can still glimpse life in the Mongol realms through their eyes. Among them were a Flemish Franciscan called William of Rubruck, who went east from Constantinople in 1253, visited Mongolia and returned to the crusader state of Tripoli in 1255. A generation later came the Venetian merchant Marco Polo, who stayed away far longer wandering far and wide and remaining in the land of the khans for a quarter of a century. But the pioneer among this intrepid group – the globetrotter who wrote the first western account of life on the ground among the Mongols – was an Italian friar turned clergyman who went by the name of Giovanni da Pian del Carpine.

GIOVANNI DA PIAN DEL CARPINE SET out to visit Mongolia in 1245. He departed from the papal court, then temporarily at Lyon in France. And he was carrying letters from Pope Innocent IV, calling on the great khan to desist from attacking Christian lands and consider converting to Christianity, since 'God was seriously angered' by his actions.[27] This was a hopeful mission, and perhaps a futile one. But del Carpine pursued it despite great hardship along the way, and his reward was a tale for the ages.

To get to Mongolia, del Carpine travelled initially through Prague and Poland and on through the lands of the Rus' towards Kiev. Five years previously the Mongols had laid the city waste: around 90 per cent of its inhabitants were killed and most of its important buildings burned to the ground. It was a mere shadow of a place when del Carpine arrived. But there was no doubt of the dominant power in the region. Each prince of the Rus' whose territory del Carpine entered directed him nervously towards the travelling court of the Mongols' supreme western military commander, Batu, a grandson of Genghis Khan, whose blessing he would need to travel any further. Del Carpine was also repeatedly told that the only way to get on in the Mongol world was to appeal to that people's innate love of gifts and consumer goods. He and his attendants carried with them fat sacks of Polish beaver pelts with which they glad-handed all who demanded tribute.

Del Carpine met Batu at Easter-time in 1246. The encounter was a learning experience, to say the least. Before the westerners even entered the camp they had to go through the thirteenth-century's equivalent of airport security: del Carpine and his companions were told to walk between two large fires so that 'if you plan any evil for our lord, or if you bring any poison, the fire will carry it away.'[28] They were warned in dire terms not to step directly on the threshold of Batu's audience tent, since the Mongols considered this such bad luck that they would execute anyone who did it. When presented to Batu, del Carpine found him wise and judicious, but scary. 'This Batu is very good to his people, yet they fear him greatly,' he wrote.[29] This was the essence of the Mongols' rule: tolerance policed by terror.

After a short stay at Batu's camp, del Carpine and his companions were told they should continue further on towards Karakorum, where the new *khan*, Ögödei's son Güyük, was soon to be enthroned. This was an exciting prospect, if a daunting one. The spare Mongol diet of millet and much alcohol given to guests at court did not agree with them – in particular they never developed a taste for the alcoholic fermented mare's milk that is still today a staple social lubricant in Mongolia.* So he and his travelling partners were alternately sick, uncomfortable and very cold. And their journey took many months, even allowing for the

---

* A western traveller who has trekked the Mongolian steppe on horseback in recent years reports of this much-loved delicacy: 'Nomadic families keep a barrel in their *gers* and drink it from bowls. They keep a string of mares with foals at foot tied in a long line, so they can milk them when they need to. The milk is like fizzy cheesy milky yoghurt. Fucking rancid.'

remarkable system of horse relay posts which had been established as part of the imperial postal system built by Ögödei, under which tired horses could be changed as many as seven times every day so that officials could travel as fast as their own bodies would allow all day, every day.

Yet if the journey was long, it was also full of wonders. The Mongols as a people fascinated del Carpine, and their appearance, habits and customs were a matter of awe. 'Tartars have eyes and cheeks wider apart than most men,' del Carpine wrote. 'Their cheeks stick out a good deal from the jaw and they have a flat middle-sized nose and small eyes and eyelids raised to the eyebrows. They are generally narrow in waist... and almost all are of middling height. Few of them have much of a beard, though some have a small amount of hair on the upper lip and in the beard which they seldom trim.'[30] He was intrigued and appalled by Mongol religion, which was monotheistic but shamanistic, idolatrous, astrologically obsessed and full of superstitions enforced with capital punishment: death was the sentence for intentionally putting a knife in a fire, spitting food on the ground, striking bones against one another or pissing in a tent. 'However, to kill men, invade others' lands, acquire others' goods by unjust methods, to fornicate, to do injury to other men, to act against the commands received from God is not a sin among them,' he wrote.[31]

He was perplexed by the many curious and contradictory character traits of the Mongols he met: physically resilient, obedient to their lords, generous, unquarrelsome and peaceable with each other; yet proud and haughty, hostile and false to outsiders, unruffled by dirt and squalor, hopelessly drunken and willing to eat literally anything, be it mouse, louse, dog, fox, wolf, horse or even human. And he found Mongol women especially fascinating: 'Girls and women ride and gallop on horses as skilfully as men. We even saw them carrying quivers and bows, and the women can ride horses for as long as the men; they have shorter stirrups, handle horses very well, and mind all the property. The Tartar women make everything: skin clothes, shoes, leggings and everything made of leather. They drive carts and repair them, they load camels, and are quick and vigorous in all their tasks. They all wear trousers, and some of them shoot just like men.'[32]

Del Carpine and his associates travelled for many long weeks through the lands these people had subjugated, observing as they went 'innumerable destroyed cities, destroyed forts, and many deserted villages.'[33] It was summer when they arrived in Mongolia – and they tracked down the imperial court, as planned, in time to witness Güyük's acclamation as *khan*. They were welcomed into the new khan's camp as honoured guests – given ale, at last, rather than mare's milk – and found their hosts excited but on edge. The place buzzed with visitors from all over the world, including a large contingent of westerners – Russians, Hungarians, French and Latin speakers and more beyond. At the centre of everything was Güyük's tent. It was lined with fine silk and held up with golden pillars, but sneaking a glimpse of it was hard, since anyone who crept too close was liable to be stripped naked and beaten up by the khan's guards. Del Carpine was embarrassed to arrive with little more valuable in his possession than beaver skins; the mountain of precious gifts brought by other guests filled around fifty wooden wagons. He was also nervous for his life, for a Russian prince who had come to pay his respects to the khan was found dead in his tent, stretched out ashen-faced as though he had been poisoned. But after a fraught wait of several days, del Carpine was eventually granted his audience with Güyük.

He found the new khan to be 'forty or forty-five years old, or more... of medium height, very wise and extremely clever and very serious, and strict in his morals, so that no one ever easily sees him laugh or make a joke.'[34] Through interpreters, the khan asked him about del Carpine's master, the pope, wishing to know who he was, and whether he spoke Mongol, Arabic or Ruthenian (a Slavic language common among the Rus'). Latin seemed to strike Güyük as a hopelessly parochial. But del Carpine got the distinct impression that the *khan* had designs on the pope's dominions, if not his lexicon, for Güyük insisted on giving him Mongol companions to travel back to the west in a capacity that del Carpine was sure would be that of spies or military scouts.

There was, however, little that he could do about it. Güyük dictated letters to be sent back to the pope, declining his offer of baptism and curtly instructing the leader of the Roman Church to bow down to him or face unpleasant consequences. After these letters had been translated into Latin as well as Arabic, del Carpine was dismissed. He and his companions were given fox-fur cloaks lined with silk, and then they were packed off back in the direction whence they had come. Another very long ride by postal stages lay ahead of them, and del Carpine endured many more freezing nights sleeping in snow. When he made it back to Kiev, the Russians there were astonished – it was as if, they said, he had returned from the dead. Yet del Carpine was not dead. He had endured – and at times enjoyed – the trip of a lifetime, to a land which was only just opening up to Europeans of his age. And in mid-1247 he was back in Europe to deliver the *khan*'s letters to the pope at Lyon, tell his tale and receive his reward: promotion to the posts of archbishop of Antivari, in Montenegro, papal legate and ambassador to King Louis IX of France, who himself had a keen interest in all matters Mongol. Carpine survived only another five years – his life perhaps truncated by the hardships of his adventure. But before he died he wrote down what he had seen, as an illustration of the new world that was evolving – and the danger that was lurking – in the new empire of the east. His only fear was that people would call him a fantasist and a liar, for what he had written down of his adventures was at times quite literally incredible.

The Empire Splits

A WHOLE SLEW OF ADVENTUROUS DIPLOMATS and missionaries followed hot on del Carpine's heels. At around the same time, one Lawrence of Portugal was commissioned to go east, although little was heard from him afterwards. In 1247 the Dominican friars Simon of Saint-Quentin and Ascelin of Lombardy visited the Mongol regional commander Baiju in Persia. In 1249 the brothers André and Jacques de Longjumeau went to Karakorum bearing gifts and letters from the French king and pope.[35] And in 1253 another Franciscan friar set out for Mongolia, this time with a view to converting pagans, which was one of the foundational duties of a follower of St Francis.*

This latter friar was a Fleming called William of Rubruck, and like del Carpine he kept a vivid diary of what he saw, compiled in the form of a report to Louis IX of France. Friar William took a somewhat different route to del Carpine: he set out from Constantinople and crossed the Black Sea to the merchant port of Soldaia, the former Genoese trading colony which was now under Mongol control, albeit with thriving groups of Italian merchants doing business within it. He too met the western khan Batu, spending five weeks in his company travelling down the river Volga, before heading off towards Mongolia itself.

On his way, William noted of many of the same unfamiliar Mongol customs that had caught del Carpine's eye: the dirt and filth, the strength and industry of Mongol women, the complex superstition, the social violence and easy resort to death sentences, the vileness of mare's milk (which by now many Christians in the Mongol empire refused to drink on religious grounds), the obsession with gifts, the ignorance of, tempered with prurient interest in, the west (one of William's interviewees had heard that the pope was 500 years old), the general fear of thunderstorms, the disgusting omnivorousness which extended to eating mice, and the odd haircuts favoured by both sexes. Like del Carpine, William was tortured at times by the discomforts of long-distance travel and he too spent much of his time sick, cold, thirsty or starving. But like del Carpine, he never quit.

Two days after Christmas in 1253 William arrived at the *khan's* camp, just outside the walls of the city of Karakorum, which he thought rather shabby compared to European wonders like the abbey of St-Denis but nevertheless wildly cosmopolitan and

---

* St Francis had been personally committed to converting infidels to the way of Christ, and had led the way in memorable fashion when he attempted to convert none other than al-Kamil, the Ayyubid sultan of Egypt, during a visit to the front line of the Fifth Crusade in 1219.

multicultural, with twelve temples, two mosques and a church. Güyük was dead, and had been succeeded by his cousin Möngke. Otherwise, the good times were still in full swing. The Mongol capital remained very rich and a hub for merchants and envoys from all corners of the globe; it was not unusual to see an Indian dignitary parading down the street with a train of horses carrying greyhounds or leopards on their backs. It was also a home to a smattering of western and Christian expatriates: a Nestorian Christian who served as Möngke's private secretary, a Parisian called William Buchier who worked as a court goldsmith, an Englishman called Basil who was a widely travelled polyglot but seemed to have no obvious purpose in the depths of Mongolia, and a kindly French girl called Pacha who had been taken prisoner by the Mongols in Hungary and transported to their realm to work as a cook.

Although William was comforted by this homely company, his journey was not an overwhelming success in terms of his remit to convert unbelievers. He stayed many months, and tried his best to preach the word of Christ to the great Möngke in person. But he was fobbed off several times and eventually rewarded with only a lecture from the *khan*, who swigged heavily from a drink while holding forth about the general decadence of westerners, who were too undisciplined to match the standards of the east.* Like all smart Mongol rulers, Möngke was very happy to adopt and adapt the best aspects of cultures his armies subjected. But he would not be bounced into conversion to a half-baked faith that seemed to offer little evidence for its self-proclaimed superiority. 'God has given you the Scriptures, and you do not observe them,' said Möngke, 'whereas to us he has given soothsayers, and we do as they tell us and live in peace.'[36]

Thus thwarted, William eventually left the royal court in July 1254, following a round of hugely drunken feasts. He was packed off with a letter from Möngke to Louis IX, which advised the French king that it would be best if he offered his immediate

---

* A common theme, to this day.

submission to the khan, since at some point the Mongols would inevitably come for him too. Möngke told Louis he would only rest 'when in the power of the everlasting God the entire world, from the sun's rising to its setting, has become one in joy and in peace'. Geography would be no protection against the Mongol war machine, he warned, for 'if, on hearing and understanding the order of the everlasting God, you are unwilling to observe it… and say, "Our country is far away, our mountains are strong, our sea is broad"… how can we know what will happen?'[37]

As it transpired, for all of Möngke's passive-aggressive menace, the Mongols never made it to the kingdom of the Franks. However, William of Rubruck did make the long journey back to the west, and tracked down Louis IX on crusade in the Holy Land in late 1254. He suggested that it would be quite sensible if Louis were to dissuade any other friars from making the same journey as he had, for now its perils were quite plain. But he added that there was still much that they could all learn from his experiences in the east – particularly with regard to crusading. 'I tell you with confidence that if our peasants – to say nothing of kings and knights – were willing to travel in the way the Tartar princes move and to be content with a similar diet, they could conquer the whole world,' he wrote.[38] But that never came to pass, either. For the crusader world of the east was on the verge of collapse. And more important, the Mongol world was about to undergo a radical transformation, too.

IN 1258 A MONGOL ARMY SACKED Baghdad. One of the greatest cities in the Islamic world was wrecked in the usual monstrous fashion. An army led by Möngke's brother Hülagü and a Chinese general called Guo Kan swept past the city's defences and massacred tens – perhaps hundreds – of thousands of civilians. Baghdad's House of Wisdom, which had a fair claim to be the finest library in the entire world, was ransacked. Thousands of treatises and books on philosophy, medicine, astronomy, and much else – which had been translated over centuries from Greek, Syriac, Indian and Persian languages into Arabic – were thrown into the river Tigris.

So many books were lost that the river-water was said to have run black with their ink.

Then, even more shockingly, Hülagü had the Abbasid caliph, al-Musta'sim, put to death. Al-Musta'sim had made the error of refusing to capitulate when the Mongols approached, so there was no helping him. The supreme spiritual leader of the Sunni Muslim world was rolled up in a carpet and trampled by horses. Thus was the light was extinguished on a dynasty whose history stretched back to the revolution against the Umayyads in AD 750.* There was, it seemed, no limit to Mongol ruthlessness – and nothing in the world that was too sacred for them to destroy.

The following year, however, the invincible, insatiable Mongol empire was severely wobbled. Just as Mongol armies seemed to be on the march again – some went invading Syria and Palestine and scaring the wits out of the Christians of the crusader states, while others returned to eastern Europe, sacking Krakow in Poland – disaster struck in the east. In August 1259 Möngke was killed while conducting a siege of the mountaintop fortress of Diaoyucheng in Sichuan, which was a stronghold belonging to the southern Chinese Song dynasty. Whether he died from dysentery, cholera, an arrow or a fall from a siege ladder is disputed by historians. It will likely never be known for sure.[39] But whatever the case, Möngke was dead. The fallout from his death brought about confusion, civil war and eventually the partition of the Mongol empire into four separate regional powers known as khanates, each of which would develop its own distinctive character an political objectives.

This was by no means a short, sharp process. In the immediate aftermath of Möngke's death, conflict broke out in the far east between his would-be successors as supreme khan. For four years, Möngke's brothers Kublai and Ariq Böke fought for the right to rule.† By 1264 Kublai Khan had triumphed. But trouble was far from over. Barely had Kublai settled into his rule than he was challenged by his nephew Kaidu (son of the late Ögödei), which prompted a

---

* See chapter 4.
† This conflict is known as the Toluid Civil War, since it was a contest between two children of Tolui, who was himself Genghis Khan's fourth son by his wife Börte.

conflict that rumbled on for nearly forty years. Meanwhile, amid the power-vacuum, a regional dispute broke out between the butcher of Baghdad, Hülagü Khan, and Berke, younger brother of the western commander Batu, who had featured prominently in the writings of Giovanni da Pian del Carpine and William of Rubruck, but who had died in 1255.

Neither the details of these conflicts nor the scores of Genghis Khan's grandchildren and great-grandchildren who contested them need detain us here. The fact is that the Mongol empire, which had functioned very effectively across such a huge expanse for the first half of the thirteenth century, proved unable to hold together when its guiding principle – unwavering loyalty to the authority of a single, undisputed leader – was challenged. The extraordinary postal communications system established under Ögödei, which allowed commanders to keep in contact with one another while fighting thousands of miles apart, was no use if those commanders decided that they were more interested in their own gain than that of the supreme khan and the good of the empire itself. Moreover, the Mongols were in some sense the victims of their own adaptability. Regional commanders who had been sent into China, Central Asia, Persia and the Russian steppe had, over the course of a couple of generations, started to feel a stronger degree of affinity for their own patch of the empire than they did for the concept of the Mongol dominions as a whole. Some gained a fondness for urban living rather than life under the felt of the *ger*. Some adopted local religions, professing Tibetan Buddhism or Sunni Islam, abandoning the shaman-led paganism of the old country. This was, perhaps, only natural: not even the mighty Roman Empire had managed to prevent its regional commanders from going native sooner or later. But in the thirteenth century it meant that the Mongol empire could not stay Mongol forever.

The four khanates that emerged out of the crisis years around 1260 were nevertheless massive power blocs by any standard. The first, and notionally the senior, was centred on China and known as the Great Yuan (or Yuan dynasty). It was established by Kublai Khan in 1271 and was – or quickly became – explicitly Chinese in character and culture, embracing Confucianism and the native Chinese aptitude for technological invention. Kublai moved his capital from Karakorum to a purpose-built city beside the shell of the old Jin stronghold Zhongdu. This new metropolis was called Khanbaliq or Dadu, and it was from here that Kublai and his descendants of the Yuan dynasty aimed to project their imperial might out of China towards Tibet, Korea, eastern Russia and southeast Asia. Today the city still exists, in drastically altered form but with something of the same political role. We call it Beijing.

West of the Great Yuan lay the other three Mongol successor states. The Chagatai Khanate, so named because its rulers were the descendants of Genghis Khan's second son Chagatai, sat squarely over Central Asia, from the Altai Mountains in the east to the Oxus river in the west. This khanate remained nomadic, tribal and highly unstable, with repeated lurches between rival rulers. (In the fourteenth century it split, contracted and morphed into an entity known as Moghulistan.) And for generations its rulers clashed with those of the Mongol Ilkhanate, established by Hülagü and his line on what had once been the Persian empire of the Khwarazm-Shah.

Having destroyed the Abbasid caliphate, wrecked Baghdad and taken command of Persia, Iraq, Syria, Armenia and the western half of Asia Minor, the Ilkhans were, for a short while at least, the dominant players in the Middle East. This made them particularly interesting to westerners, because they naturally became embroiled in the politics of the crusader world, as a result of which many in the west revived their old King David fantasies, trying to kid themselves that the Mongols could be made into servants of Christ. In 1262, Louis IX of France, having read William of Rubruck's account of his journey to Karakorum, tried to pitch the Ilkhan Hülagü an unlikely vision of Christian–Mongol alliance against the new Islamic rulers of Egypt, the Mamluks. Hülagü indulged the dream a little, boasting to Louis that he had recently rid Syria of the sect of the Assassins – a reclusive Shia sect who lived in the mountains and were known for launching surprise terrorist attacks on political leaders of all faiths in the region. He further described himself the 'avid destroyer of the perfidious Saracen peoples, friend and supporter of the Christian religion, energetic fighter of enemies and faithful friend of friends', and vowed to Louis that he would indeed destroy the Mamluks, whom he defamed as 'Babylonian dog mice'.[40]

But as it turned out, Hülagü and his successors had strictly limited success against the Mamluks. Descended from steppe nomads themselves, highly disciplined and adept at warfare, the Mamluks proved to be the bulwark that set the limits of Mongol expansion in the Levant. They secured Egypt, Palestine and eventually much of Syria, and by the end of the thirteenth century had put paid to any Mongol drive into north Africa or Arabia. What this meant was that the Mongols of the Ilkhanate effectively became the latest rulers of the old Persian empire, and as they settled into this role they gradually started to look and sound like every other recent ruler of that part of the world. In 1295 the Ilkhan Ghazan converted from Buddhism to Sunni Islam – quite a decision for the great-grandson of Hülagü to take, since it was the latter who had literally put the Abbasid caliph to death in 1258. This irony aside, Gazan was a cultured and far-sighted ruler. But after he died, the first half of the fourteenth century saw the authority of the Ilkhans gradually beginning to fracture, and petty regional emirs began to exercise their own power; by the middle of the century it was barely recognizable as a Mongol state at all.

This left one more khanate: the so-called Golden Horde.* As we have seen, when travellers such as Giovanni Pian del Carpini and William of Rubruck traversed the Mongol empire, they had found the western portion, which overlays the Russian steppe, under the control of a regional commander, Batu. As the thirteenth century wore on, this region became an independent khanate under its own khan, who had to be a descendent of Genghis Khan through the line of his eldest son Jochi. As in the Chagatai

---

* This name was retrospectively applied to the khanate of the Russian steppe from the sixteenth century. But whether it is a name derived from the golden tent of the western khan, or a bastardized fusion of the Turkic word *orda* (headquarters) and the Latin word *aurum* (gold) is not totally clear.

khanate, the Mongol ruling caste lived a nomadic lifestyle for long stretches of the year. But they did not entirely neglect urban living.[41] Some of the great Russian cities sacked during the years of conquest were reconstructed, but others were built afresh. Like the Soviet dictators who would dominate this part of the world in the twentieth century, the Mongol leaders of the Golden Horde favoured purpose-built settlements, the most famous of which were Old Sarai and New Sarai.

New Sarai, which sat on the river Akhtuba between the Black and Caspian seas, was a prosperous and elegant capital, seen in the later fourteenth century by the Muslim traveller Ibn Battuta, who described it in some detail: 'one of the finest of towns, of immense extent and crammed with inhabitants, with fine bazaars and wide streets,' he wrote. He estimated that it took half a day to walk the breadth of the city, and noted that it had 'thirteen cathedrals and a large number of other mosques,' befitting a highly cosmopolitan population. 'The inhabitants belong to diverse nations; among them are the Mongols, who are the inhabitants and rulers of the country and are in part Muslims, As [i.e. Ossetians], who are Muslims, and Kipchaks, Circassians, Russians and Greeks, who are all Christians. Each group lives in a separate quarter with its own bazaars. Merchants and strangers from Iraq, Egypt, Syria and elsewhere, live in a quarter surrounded by a wall, in order to protect their property.'[42]

This was a cosmopolitan scene indeed, as befitted a city that controlled one of the major Silk Roads thoroughfares. As we will see in the next chapter, the Mongols were in large part responsible for the boom in global trade along these routes that occurred from the thirteenth century onwards, and the Golden Horde was a vast intermediary market for commercial goods ranging from silk, spices, precious metals and stones, furs, salt, skins and slaves. It was also a melting-pot for religions and cultures. As ibn Battuta noted, the Mongol khans had converted to Islam. But they were highly indulgent of Christianity, exempting the Orthodox Church in their lands from taxation and refraining from demanding that churchmen serve in the Mongol army. Indeed, they solicited prayers for their souls from Russian clerics. Likewise, the khans of the Golden Horde were prepared to deal peaceably with princes of the Rus' who acknowledged their overlordship and paid them tribute.

One such was the Russian hero Alexander Nevsky, grand prince of Kiev and Vladimir (d. 1263) and today a saint of the Orthodox Church. Nevsky cultivated excellent relations with the Golden Horde khan Sartaq, whom he saw as a vital ally in his attempt to prevent Christian armies from Sweden and Germany from invading his territory and dragging him into the orbit of the Roman Church. This friendship put political pragmatism above religious solidarity in a crusading age that did not always make easy bedfellows of Christians and Muslims. And it was not entirely unusual. After the shock of the Mongol invasions had subsided, from the middle of the thirteenth century the Golden Horde and the native princes of the Rus' dealt with one another relatively easily: the Mongols took tribute and military service, and in return they kept the peace among the princes, cut them in on their lucrative trade networks and protected them from enemies in the west. By contrast, the khans of the Golden Horde spent much of the same period feuding and fighting with their Mongol cousins in the Ilkhanate, who presented a serious threat to their territorial ambitions in the Caucasus, and were competitors for merchant traffic along their different sections of the Silk Roads.

This curious state of affairs – in which Mongols fought Mongols and indulged princes of the outside world – was in many ways an exact inversion of everything that Genghis Khan had stood for. And slowly but surely, Mongol-on-Mongol violence would bring down the curtain on the empire that had once been the scourge of the world.

The Last of the Khans

ABOUT ONE HUNDRED YEARS AFTER GENGHIS Khan died, in (or slightly before) 1336, the last of the great Mongol conquerors was born, to a Turkic nomad society in what is now Uzbekistan. He grew up to be dazzlingly intelligent, militarily accomplished and physically tough, despite having been permanently crippled during a youthful escapade in which he was shot with arrows in the right leg and hand. His name was Temür – sometimes given as Timur the Lame (*Temüri lang*) or Tamerlane – and although he was unrelated to Genghis, he was the man who came closer than anyone since the old warrior to bringing the world back under the Mongol yoke.

By the time Temür was a man in the 1360s, what had once been the Mongol empire was a highly fractured set of entities in varying states of decay. As we will see in chapter 13, waves of plague beginning with the Black Death had battered Mongol polities as severely as any in the world. And this was not the only problem afflicting the various khanates. In the far east, the Yuan dynasty had completed its transformation from a lean, snarling steppe nomad culture into a stereotypical Chinese imperial autocracy: tyrannical, paranoid and beset by allegations of hopeless loucheness and endemic buggery within the palace walls. A long-running and very violent insurrection known as the Red Turban uprisings, which took place between 1351 and 1367, finally destroyed the Yuan dynasty as a regional force. In 1368 a new dynasty – the Ming – came to power, and the survivors from among the Yuan fled back to the Mongol steppe, where a small and unremarkable rump state known as the Northern Yuan endured until the seventeenth century. And the rot was not limited to the far east. In Persia the Mongol Ilkhanate had dissolved into a patchwork of petty warlord fiefdoms by the 1330s, with the last undisputed Ilkhan dying in 1335 – more or less at the same time that Temür was born.[43] The Golden Horde was increasingly riven by faction and infighting, and so the Chagatai khanate, where Temür had been born, was effectively partitioned. To Genghis, Ögödei or even Kublai Khan this would have all been unrecognizable. The Mongol successor states no longer remotely resembled the superpower they had once comprised.

But spectacularly, if momentarily, Temür rolled back the years. Between 1360, when he first took to the battlefield, and his death in the early fifteenth century, Temür swept up the jagged shards of the great Mongol empire and pieced them back together under his own charismatic rule. His route to pre-eminence was a familiar one. Having risen in the tribal society of Central Asia thanks to his skill in battle and talent for diplomacy, Temür then set his sights outwards. He gathered and motivated a large, multi-ethnic army that roved far and wide, terrorizing those who refused to bow to its approach. He justified his aggression with direct reference to history: although not descended from Genghis, two of his four dozen wives or concubines were from the old khan's line. Temür insisted that this gave him the right to restore what the old man had once assembled. He labelled himself as a son-in-law (*küregen*) of Genghis, and although he was not a *khan* (claiming merely to act in the name of the puppet *khans* at home in Central Asia) he bore the title of Great Amir and carried himself with the imperious bearing of a Mongol noble.[44]

So Temür was acutely conscious of his place in Mongol history. And what history demanded, historical methods were used to achieve. Under Temür, massacre and torture were once again the watchwords. Cities were razed. Heads were lopped off. Bodies were left to rot in the sun as carrion. Crowds of slaves were herded from their homes and packed off to Temür's homelands, never to return. Many hundreds of thousands, if not millions, of civilians died to satisfy Temür's ambition and affirm his belief that the improbable conglomeration of half the world under the banner of Mongol rule was what political success looked like.

Decades of expansionist campaigning throughout Asia, southern Russia and the Middle East brought Temür lordship over three of the four old khanates – the Chagatai, Ilkhanate and Golden Horde; in the end, only the Ming emperors held out against him. Moreover, he fought his way west, deep into Asia Minor, and for a time seemed to be bearing down towards Europe. There, news of his vast conquests worried and excited Christian kings in roughly equal measure. Still in thrall to updated versions of the Prester John fantasy, many wondered whether it was better to tremble at Temür's name or attempt to convert him to Christianity and enlist him to destroy their mutual enemies – particularly the Ottoman Turks who had risen up to take control of many of the former Byzantine provinces in the eastern Mediterranean. Unsurprisingly, as had happened so often before, their hopes were dashed, for Temür was no more a friend of Christians than he was of anyone but himself. Sometimes he left in peace Christian communities in the provinces he ruled, demanding only that they pay him tax and tribute for the privilege. At other times, however, he liked to pose as a *jihadi* Sunni Muslim (despite his absolute ease with killing other Muslims when it suited him). Certainly he persecuted to virtual extinction the Nestorian Christians of Persia and Central Asia.

When he died in 1405, Temür had followed in Genghis' footsteps to a remarkable, if superficial, degree. He had terrorized more or less the whole Asian continent and Middle East, roped together a vast empire which bowed to his personal command, and effected such a rapid redistribution of treasure and artistic talent that the stage was set for a cultural and intellectual golden age in Central Asia, where his capital city of Samarkand – like Karakorum before it – grew fat and glorious on the spoils of war. The city was rescued from the depleted state in which it had languished after Genghis' attacks in the thirteenth century: replanned, rebuilt and repopulated. Artisans and artists kidnapped from other countries were transported there and tasked with this grand imperial refurbishment, and they filled Samarkand with ostentatious monumental architecture, palaces and public gardens, walls, gates, mosques and statues.[45]

Yet just as had been the case in the thirteenth century, Temür's bloodily assembled empire was not built to last. By the time the Middle Ages were drawing to a close in the late fifteenth century, the whole thing had fallen apart. The Temürids, as Temür's branch of the Mongol people were known, were scarcely able to hold together what he had won. The Ming ruled China. A Sunni Turkic tribal confederation known as the Aq Qoyunlu swept through Persia and Mesopotamia. Uzbek tribes overran Central Asia. The Golden Horde, having been severely disrupted by Temür's invasion in the 1390s, fell finally and comprehensively to pieces in the fifteenth century, leaving behind it a smattering of independent 'Tartar' khanates. Two of these – the Crimean state sometimes called Little Tartary and the Kazakh Khanate, which is roughly congruent with modern Kazakhstan – survived the Middle Ages. In Afghanistan and northern India Temür did leave an important imperial legacy, through his descendant Babur, who founded the Mughal empire at Kabul in the early sixteenth century. However, though the Mughals were destined to be a mighty power in the east in the early modern age, they were only dimly recognizable as inheritors of the Mongols. Like Genghis, Temür's greatest talent was for conquest and expansion. Building a stable, unified superstate that could outlive him by generations was not his forte. But nor, to be fair, was it his chief goal.

So, THEN, WITHIN THE SPACE OF less than two centuries, the Mongols had rampaged from the eastern steppe to supremacy over the whole Eurasian world, before imploding, briefly reuniting, then disintegrating again. Theirs was a strange story indeed, and perhaps the bloodiest one of all the Middle Ages. Mongol methods of conquest, pioneered and perfected by Genghis Khan, and imitated ably by Temür, prefigured the terror-autocracies of the twentieth century, in which millions of civilians could be thoughtlessly murdered to service the demented personal ambitions of charismatic rulers, and the goal of spreading an ideology as far around the globe as it would go. Yet alongside their gross bloodlust and a cruelty that cannot be written off with mere historical relativism, the Mongols also changed the world profoundly – for better and for worse.

In some cases the changes were to basic political geography. The Mongols' tendency to burn cities to the ground and either replace or erase them effectively re-oriented whole regions. In the Far East, their conquests created the enduring idea of a Greater China, with one imperial (or quasi-imperial) power dominant over a massive territorial area, ruled from what is now Beijing, extending out onto the steppe and including a huge number of different ethnic groups. In the Middle East, poor ruined Baghdad declined, to be overtaken in importance by Tabriz in Azerbaijan. In Central Asia, Samarkand was catapulted to powerhouse status by Temür's plunderings. In Russia, a trading backwater called Moscow grew to become a regionally dominant trading hub – initially as somewhere that merchants could operate at a safe distance from the Mongols of the Golden Horde, but subsequently as an ally of the Golden Horde khans and, by the sixteenth century, the dominant state in western Asia, whose ruler claimed lordship over all the Rus' as *tsar*.[46]

Then of course, there was religion. The Mongols' initial *laissez faire* attitude towards religious dogma seems refreshing when set against the bigotry of the crusading age – and one modern scholar has even argued that it set such a fine historical example that the principle of religious freedom enshrined in the west in general and the US constitution in particular had its origins in the philosophy of Genghis Khan.[47] But alongside that, the Mongols also made sweeping changes to the religious composition of Eurasia. By converting to Islam, the Mongol rulers of the Ilkhanate, Chagatai khanate and Golden Horde together created a vast Islamic zone that stretched all the way from the Tian Shan mountains to the Caucasus, where it connected with the Turkish and Arabic realms of the eastern Mediterranean and north Africa. The strong Islamic character of Central Asia and southern Russia today owes a huge amount to the Mongols. And this is not only observable with hindsight. The Christian princes and Franciscan friars of the west who implored successive Mongol khans to become 'King David' and convert to Christianity realized that the religious identity of this vast and domineering imperial power would have a lasting effect on balance of world faiths. Had they succeeded in convincing men like Möngke Khan to accept baptism, there might be many more church spires than minarets in Asia today. And relations between modern states like the USA and Iran, or Russia and Turkey, might look rather different.

But that is speculation. What is certain, and what deserves

closer inspection, is the way in which the Mongols reshaped global trade and travel networks. At root was the fact that the Mongols' rampant territorial ambition and the scale of their conquests made it possible to travel thousands of miles beyond the horizon and come back again to tell the tale. Their rearrangement of Central Asia, Persia and the Kievan Rus' was as cruel as any imperial expansion of the nineteenth century. But like the colonial scramble of the nineteenth century, the Mongols' bloody rampage across the world map nevertheless opened up global trade and information networks that ushered in a new age in western history. Dreadful as were their means, the changes they wrought were astonishing and epoch-shifting. Indeed, this transformation of trade is almost certainly the Mongols' greatest significance to the story we are telling in this book. So it is to that part of their legacy that we will now turn, as we discover how intrepid merchants, scholars and explorers from east and west flourished in the aftermath of the Mongol conquests, exchanging ideas, goods and wealth, and remodelling the western world and western minds as they did so.

10

MERCHANTS

'For God and profit'

PERSONAL MOTTO OF TUSCAN MERCHANT
FRANCESCO DI MARCO DATINI

In early September 1298 two fleets, decked for war, bore down on one another in the Adriatic Sea, in the strait between the mainland of what is now Croatia and the large Dalmatian island then known as Curzola (Korčula). Scores of sleek galleys, all bristling with troops, flew the flags of two of Europe's leading maritime states: the Republic of Venice and Republic of Genoa. Located on opposite sides of the Italian peninsula – Venice in the north-east and Genoa in the north-west – these ambitious, autonomous cities (along with a third rival, the Republic of Pisa) had been at loggerheads for nearly fifty years. They had fought in the Holy Land and in Constantinople. They had fought in the ports of the Black Sea, and around the islands of the Aegean and Adriatic. Their contest was for supremacy on the waves, and they played the game very roughly, for victory could bring more than simple neighbourly bragging rights or plunder. The Venetians, Genoese and Pisans were competing to become the leading mercantile power in the west. At the turn of the fourteenth century, this was no small prize. World trade was booming. Commodities and luxury goods were flying halfway around the globe at a pace seldom seen before in the whole of human history. Commercial dominance in this age was worth fighting – and dying – for.

The clash in the strait of Curzola was a bloody, one-sided

affair. The brilliant Genoese admiral, Lamba Doria, a member of a swaggeringly famous noble family, had significantly fewer ships than his opposite number, Andrea Dandolo – a relative of the old *doge* Enrico Dandolo, who had burned Constantinople during the Fourth Crusade. But Doria had luck and the tides with him. As the galleys clashed oars, his captains drove the Venetian ships into shallow waters where many were run aground. The Genoese boarded the stricken enemy vessels, slaughtering and taking prisoners as they pleased, before scuppering almost the entire Venetian fleet. As many as seven thousand Venetian sailors were killed in the fighting. Admiral Dandolo was captured and committed suicide in prison rather than live with the shame of defeat. When news of his humiliation arrived back in the Venetian lido, the city authorities were forced to sue for peace. The battle of Curzola would not be remembered as Venice's finest hour.

Yet strangely, it would not be remembered as Genoa's triumph either. Instead, this bloody skirmish in the blue waters off the Dalmatian coast would come to be associated most closely with one of the Venetian prisoners of war. He was a veteran adventurer from a family of merchants, who had been further around the world than almost any person alive, seeing many extraordinary things and meeting many astonishing people. A survivor and a charmer, he had mind-boggling stories to tell. And after he was captured at the battle of Curzola, he had the opportunity to tell them. He was incarcerated alongside a sympathetic and talented professional writer called Rustichello of Pisa, who drew memories out of his cellmate and wrote them down for posterity. The result was a great popular travelogue, which still sells thousands of copies every year. Of course, the merchant was Marco Polo – and his story is justly one of the most celebrated of the whole Middle Ages.

BORN IN VENICE IN 1253 TO a family of businessmen, Marco Polo was forty-five when he fought at the battle of Curzola. He had spent most of his adult life away from Europe. His father,

Niccolò Polo, and uncle Maffeo Polo were among the vanguard of European travellers to the Mongol court, having made their first journey to visit Kublai Khan in 1260, after liquidating earlier business ventures in Constantinople to escape the restoration of a Byzantine emperor.* On making their way to the Far East they had found the Mongols receptive to western commerce and interested in exchanging diplomatic letters with kings and popes in Europe. So for a decade thereafter Niccolò and Maffeo shuttled back and forth between east and west. When they set out from Venice on one trip in 1271 they took the now-teenaged Marco with them. It was the start of a wondrous journey. The introduction to Marco Polo's memoirs (today known as the *Travels*, but originally called *A Description of the World*) claimed that 'from the time God formed Adam... down to this day there has been no man, Christian or Pagan, Tartar or Indian, or of any race whatsoever, who has known or explored so many of the various parts of the world and of its great wonders as... Marco Polo.'[1] This was hyperbole – ably injected into the story by Rustichello, whose talent for crafting bestselling stories had been honed while composing Arthurian romances for the English king Edward I. But it was not far from the truth.

As we saw in chapter 9, the Polo family were by no means the first European travellers to make the expedition to the land of the khans in the thirteenth century. From the 1240s onwards a regular procession of envoys and missionaries headed out eastwards. We have already met Giovanni Pian del Carpini and William of Rubruck. There were many others. Giovanni da Montecorvino was sent to Khanbaliq (Beijing) in the 1290s under papal instruction to establish himself as the city's first archbishop; he led a successful mission in Mongol China for nearly twenty years, preaching and converting people at the churches he founded, and translating

---

* In 1261 Manuel Palaiologos, co-ruler of the small Greek empire of Nicaea, based mostly in western Asia Minor, overthrew the last Latin emperor of Constantinople, Baldwin II. Manuel VIII, as he now became, sought to turn the clock in Constantinople back to before the Fourth Crusade, repairing buildings, restoring the Orthodox rite in churches, and taking violent revenge on the Venetians in particular for their disgraceful actions at the beginning of the century. The Polo brothers had anticipated this revolution and sold up their assets ahead of it, thereby avoiding confiscation and ruin.

the New Testament into the Mongol tongue. Around the same time, Thomas of Tolentino toured Armenia, Persia, India and China, preaching relentlessly until he was tried and executed for blasphemy in Thane (today part of the greater metropolitan area of Mumbai) for telling the Muslim authorities he believed Muhammad was burning in hell. Later, between 1318 and 1329, Odoric of Pordenone would embark on a marathon preaching tour of China and western India. Giovanni de' Marignolli was sent as spiritual advisor to the last Yuan dynasty emperor between 1338 and 1353.

Yet Marco Polo differed significantly from these other travellers. Almost without exception they were friars – Dominican or Franciscan holy men whose chief responsibility was to the word of God and the wellbeing of the Latin Church, and for whom the hardship of the journey was part of their spiritual calling. But while the Polos were Christians, they were no churchmen. They did not venture thousands of miles from home to save souls. Rather, they were merchants: traders who sought profit, specifically by selling precious stones to wealthy Mongol princes and freelancing as intermediaries in business and international diplomacy. What was more, they were Venetians – citizens of one of the most ruthless and outward-looking mercantile-states in the west. Marco's adventures in the east represented something rather different to the friars'. He went east in search not of salvation but gold.

The Polos' journey east took them along a broadly familiar route. In 1271 they sailed from Venice to Constantinople, and crossed the Black Sea, disembarking at Trebizond in Armenia. A long overland trek on camel-back across Persia took them into Central Asia, and onwards to the khan's summer palace at Shangdu (sometimes called Xanadu), where they arrived after three and a half years of travel. This opulent residence, built in marble and decorated in gold, was home to many bizarre and exotic hangers-on, including sorcerers who sacrificed live animals, ate the flesh of condemned criminals and played conjuring tricks at mealtimes, along with thousands of bald-headed ascetic monks who worshipped fire and slept on the ground.[2] And it was also, of course, the seasonal home of Kublai Khan himself, grandson of Genghis, 'the mightiest man, whether in respect of subjects or of territory or of treasure, who is in the world today or who ever has been.'³ These were Marco's words, and well might he have sung old Kublai's praises. For it was he, the last of the great khans, who gave Marco the opportunities that changed his life for good.

Young, tenacious, clever, culturally sensitive and confident in strange surroundings, Marco caught Kublai Khan's eye as soon as he was presented at court, and was given a place among the Khan's attendants of honour. This was a huge step into the unknown, but Marco thrived, not least thanks to his facility with learning new tongues: 'He acquired a remarkable knowledge of the customs of the Tartars,' claimed the *Travels*, 'and mastered four languages with their modes of writing.'* While Niccolò and Maffeo busied themselves trading jewels and gold, Marco was employed as an itinerant civil servant, trusted by the Khan 'with all the most interesting and distant missions,' transacting official diplomatic business, while keeping a keen eye out for the oddities and peccadilloes of people in the furthest reaches of the Mongol empire, about whom Kublai Khan would always quiz him when he returned to court.⁴

The colourful tales Marco collected for Kublai provided the bulk of the *Travels*, and just as they entertained the khan, so too they dazzled Europeans, with descriptions of many of the great cities of eastern China, Burma, Malaysia, Sri Lanka, west India and Persia, alongside stories about Russia and the 'Region of Darkness' – a place where pale-faced tribes lived in semi-permanent night, trapping wild animals for their furs. Marco was especially attuned to unusual religious practices and foodstuffs, sexual habits, odd illnesses and weird physical characteristics. He also had a keen eye for flora, fauna and topography. But nothing caught his eye so much as commerce. Although his father and uncle were more

* Western schoolchildren today, pressed by their anxious middle-class parents into taking Mandarin classes in preparation for a Chinese-dominated twenty-first century, may take comfort from the knowledge that they are following in a tradition dating back at least to Marco Polo's age.

directly involved in the Polos' actual business ventures in the Mongol empire than he was, Marco never lost his own Venetian's eye for profit.

Almost everywhere he went, Marco took note of business opportunities. He discovered that Sheberghan, in Afghanistan, exported the best dried melon sweets.[5] The countryside around Balkh (also in Afghanistan) yielded incredible rubies whose production and sale abroad was strictly limited in order to keep prices high.[6] In Kashmir, he said, coral was sold 'at a higher price than in any other part of the world.'[7] Hami, in north-western China, had a booming economy based on pimping and prostitution.[8] A place he knew as 'Su-chau' (in China's modern Gansu province) abounded with a delicious variety of rhubarb, 'and the merchants who procure loadings of it... convey it to all parts of the world.'[9] Gouza produced wonderful gauze and gold cloth.[10] The best camphor was from Java.[11] The finest pearls were fetched by professional oyster divers in the Palk Strait between India and Sri Lanka.[12] Kollam (in the Indian state of Kerala) produced great indigo dyes, which could eventually be sold at premium prices in Europe.[13] Marco was so assiduous in his quest for commercial intelligence that he even recorded the trading advantages of places he had not managed to see: the best elephants' teeth and ambergris, he said, came across the Indian Ocean from Madagascar and Zanzibar, while Aden, in Yemen, was the place to trade horses, spices and drugs at the highest profit.[14]

Marco reserved his highest praise, however, for Kin-sai (modern Hangzhou, near Shanghai in eastern China), which he thought was the handsomest place on earth: a warren of streets, canals, marketplaces, squares and 'innumerable' shops. He loved Kin-sai. He adored the wet markets, where live animals were sold for next-to-nothing and killed on the spot. He savoured the fruit, the fish, the local wine, the 'spices, trinkets, drugs and pearls' sold from shops which occupied the street-level storeys of high buildings. He wowed to the daily buzz of crowds of shoppers and traders he estimated at forty or fifty thousand strong. He admired the efficient municipal governance in which a civic police force monitored crime, fraud and riotous assembly, where gongs sounded to mark the passing of the hours, where the streets were paved not with gold but with a practical surface of brick and stone which allowed couriers, carriages and pedestrians to move efficiently and quickly about the city, facilitating swift and easy business in every daylight hour. Kinsai was a mercantile hub of paper money, perfumed courtesans, busy workshops and frictionless trade: a Venice away from Venice, in which 1.6 million families (or so Marco said) lived in 'grandeur and beauty... which might lead an inhabitant to imagine himself in paradise'.[15] Even as he sat in a Genoese prison dictating his memoirs, Marco seemed able to close his eyes and return there.

THE SHEER COLOUR AND EXOTIC DETAIL of Marco Polo's anecdotes alone made (and makes) the *Travels* worth reading. But at the dawn of the fourteenth century AD his work had a significance that elevated it beyond a mere cabinet of oriental curiosities. The *Travels* was not just the medieval equivalent of gap year blogging. It was a tract full of valuable commercial insight. We have just encountered examples of specific guidance for the enterprising merchant looking to trade jewels or ivory or rhubarb. But Marco also made careful note of the wider conditions under which traders could expect to operate. In Persia, he observed, where there was a busy market for transporting horses for sale in India, people in many districts were 'brutal and bloodthirsty... forever slaughtering one another.' But they left merchants and travelers alone, because they themselves lived in terror of the Mongols, who imposed 'severe penalties upon them.'[16] In China, where paper money was used, the advanced attitude to macroeconomics meant the Great Khan 'has more treasure than anyone else in the world.'[17] Along major roads throughout the empire, he observed, trees were planted along the roadside to increase both the safety and aesthetic appearance of the thoroughfare.[18] All of this mattered, for it showed how a new, commerce-focused and globally connected world was coming to life under the *Pax Mongolica* – the vast trading zone pacified and policed by the khans.

Marco was an evangelist for the Mongol regime, which, for all its severity and illiberality, kept the peace and allowed trade to flourish safely and securely over a hitherto unimaginable span of territory, joining up the Christian west directly with the Chinese and Indian east, and making overland travel through Islamic Persia safe and reliable. This was not a totally benign judgement: for millions of massacred civilians and their families the Mongol advance of the thirteenth century had not been so much an economic miracle as a cataclysmic tragedy. But in the amoral worldview of the profit-hungry salesman, the khans had ushered in a boom. And in Marco's mind, eastern trade was there to be seized by adventurous businessmen in Europe, and particularly by the merchants of the advanced Italian city-republics.

Marco Polo had latched onto an important point. And in a sense he was right about the Mongols. Yet he did not tell the whole story. For it was not only long-distance trade that was taking off in the thirteenth century. Major changes were happening closer to home. During Marco's lifetime and the century after it, the western world underwent sweeping economic changes, with increasingly sophisticated ways of trading and financing business invented, and new markets opened up. The name historians have given to the changes that took place in this age is the Commercial Revolution, and this is a deservedly grand term. What took place in the thirteenth and fourteenth centuries was as economically significant as the Industrial Revolution of the nineteenth century and Digital Revolution through which we are presently living. The Commercial Revolution placed power in the hands of new agents besides emperors, popes and kings. It allowed the merchant to assume a prominent place in medieval society and culture. It gave cities in which merchants dominated newfound political status and independence. Tastes in art and literature were moved by the mores of the merchant class, who could afford to act as both patrons and creators. Political regimes and wars were underwritten by merchant money. It is a cliché much-repeated by historians that the medieval world was made up of three groups of people: those who prayed, those who fought and those who worked. But from the thirteenth century onwards, we must also take into account those who counted, moved, saved and spent. It is to the rise of the merchants, and their contribution to both the Middle Ages and the world today, that the rest of this chapter will now turn.

Bust and Boom

TRADE IS ALMOST AS OLD AS human society itself. Two hundred thousand years ago and more, Stone Age people in east Africa (modern Kenya) were transporting and exchanging obsidian, the tough volcanic glass which could be worked into tools and weapons, over distances in excess of 150km.[19] In the Bronze Age, enterprising merchants in Assyria traded goods like tin, silver, gold, luxury fabrics and wool across hundreds of kilometres between modern Iraq, Syria and Turkey, recording their transactions on clay tablets and negotiating protection and safe passage for their caravans with the rulers whose territory they traversed.[20] In the fifth century BC the Greek historian Herodotus described several successful long-distance trade expeditions: he included in his *Histories* the story of a ship captained by a man called Colaeus, whose crew were the first Greeks to venture all the way from Greece to 'Tartessus' (southern Spain) and back. 'The profits made... on their cargo, once they had returned home, were larger than those of any other Greek trader for whom we have reliable information,' Herodotus wrote.[21]

Half a millennium later, during the zenith of the Roman Empire, the Mediterranean world was alive with trade, joined to an unprecedented degree in a single political and economic market, under imperial supervision. Inside this trading zone, goods and people were transferred 'frictionlessly' and in huge quantities between places as far afield as Syria and the lowlands of Scotland, north Africa and the forests of the Ardennes. Empire offered huge advantages for trade: safe, good quality roads in which the chance of being stuck up and robbed was low, reliable coinage and a legal system that could settle commercial disputes. And it allowed regular people to participate, as farmers produced grain to feed armies, wealthy townsfolk sought expensive pottery and imported spices, and workshops and households demanded slaves to do their dirty work.

Interestingly, despite the sheer amount of trade that took place by land and sea, particularly during the first two centuries of empire, the Romans did not hold merchants in especially high regard. Buying and selling was not a profession considered fit for a patrician, and the economic life of the upper classes was usually focused on managing their country estates.[22] Beyond tax collection and coin-minting, the financial tools of the Roman state remained relatively underdeveloped. Still, as would be starkly clear in retrospect, Roman emperors oversaw a trading bloc that was uniquely powerful and diverse in its own time, and which would be badly missed when the empire fell apart. For Roman trading relied on Roman unity. Once Rome shattered and its authority waned, the basic conditions for long-distance and high-frequency trading worsened steeply.

Of course, Rome's 'barbarian' successor states did not do without trade completely. But when Roman towns and political horizons contracted, the once-busy Mediterranean economy slowed down. Trade shrank to the village-to-village level. Long-distance exchange between the post-Roman west and India and China was complicated by political and religious upheaval in the Middle East and Central Asia – not least the Byzantine–Persian wars, the rise of Islam and depredations of the Magyars in eastern Europe. Luxury goods became more difficult to import. Global trade stalled considerably, and so did regional trade around the Mediterranean and the former Roman provinces. Compared to the rest of the known world, from the sixth century onwards Europe became a commercial backwater, with little to export except for Baltic furs, Frankish swords and slaves.[23] Although it would be misleading to write off the whole of the early Middle Ages as a 'dark' period in which all business receded to nothingness and human progress went into hibernation, in the grand scheme of western history it was a period of stagnated economic development, which lasted several hundred years.

Slowly, however, business recovered. From around the year 1000 Europe's population boomed, in tandem with a surge in agricultural production. The Medieval Climate Optimum was kind to farmers, and huge new tracts of land were brought under the plough through forest clearances and marsh-draining. Territory was seized from itinerant, pagan Slavs and put under Christian ploughs – a process which started with the Carolingians and continued under the crusaders.[24] New farming technologies were developed, with heavy ploughs improving soil quality and the 'three-field' crop rotation system preventing soil exhaustion. Shipbuilding also improved, making long voyages by sea safer and faster – whether those voyages were for Viking-style slave-taking and monastery-plundering or buying and selling goods in foreign markets. And from the time of Charlemagne onwards, western Christian monarchs slowly began to stake their claims to ever-larger kingdoms, subjecting them to deeper mechanisms of royal control and governance which (in theory at least) made longer overland trading journeys safer and more secure.

As trading networks began to extend further afield, so institutions appeared to help make business easier. In the eleventh century, markets began to grow and expand in towns across Europe, at predictable times of the week, month or year. Here, surplus grain could be exchanged for wine, leather, worked metal or livestock, which was distributed by travelling traders. Over the next 200 years, markets and fairs (originally markets associated with a religious festival or holiday) became an increasingly important part of economic life in Europe. With the rise of the market came a surge in coin production, along with the silver and copper mining required to mint coins.[25] Meanwhile, basic financial services came to be offered in the growing towns and cities across the west, especially through Jewish commercial networks. Between the ninth and eleventh centuries Jewish people all over the west became prominent in moneylending, as well as long-distance trade, carrying commodities like salt, cloth, wine and slaves throughout the old Roman world.[26] Of course, Europe's Jews were not thanked for this pioneering contribution to the macroeconomic fabric of their world: rather, they were the object of suspicion, derision and bursts of violent persecution, which accelerated during the crusades, and crescendoed in the late thirteenth century with waves of pogroms and expulsions throughout western Europe.* Nevertheless, the Jewish contribution to the great medieval economic revival was significant.

SLOWLY BUT SURELY, THEN, AROUND THE turn of the millennium, western economies began to spring noticeably back to life. One of the most famous trade hubs to emerge in the reinvigorated medieval world could be found in the county of Champagne, east of Paris. From the twelfth century, this county – which clung fiercely to its independence from French royal oversight – became home to an annual series of trade fairs. There were six main fairs, held in the four towns of Lagny, Bar-sur-Aube, Provins and Troyes, according to a calendar in which each fair lasted six to eight weeks. These were much more than bazaars for the people of Champagne to visit for their weekly shopping. Champagne occupied a convenient geographical location where cloth manufacturers in the Low Countries could mingle with vendors of foreign luxury goods imported via Byzantium and Italy, and fur traders from the Baltic.[27] All who attended were protected by the authority of the counts of Champagne, who, by licensing the fairs, also took responsibility for ensuring they were kept free from swindling or brawling, and seeing that there was a fair process for resolving disputes and pursuing those who welched on their debts. The Champagne fairs soon attracted traders from hundreds of miles away, lured by the promise of a stable, safe, fixed location where business could be done at volume.

Initially attendees brought with them large quantities of stock and samples, which could be stored in purpose-built warehouses in and around these towns. But as time went on, the Champagne

---

* In 1290 King Edward I of England expelled Jews from his realm. In France, several kings passed laws expelling Jews for long periods: Philip II did so in 1182, Louis IX in 1254, Philip IV in 1306 and Charles IV in 1322. Jews were expelled from Aragon and Castile in 1492.

Fairs would evolve into something closer to what we would today call a 'stock exchange', with currency, credit and contracts changing hands and real goods being delivered (or not) at some future moment, with much business being done by specialist agents on behalf of wealthy companies, banks and governments. By the late thirteenth century a visitor to the fairs in Champagne or Flanders could expect to find representatives of Italian business consortia bargaining with agents representing multiple north-west European wool producers and cloth manufacturers, drawing up contracts for payment schedules with debts to be cleared at future fairs months or even years in advance.[28] Champagne's fairs were not the only marketplaces of their sort – nearby Flanders also hosted large-scale exchanges in towns like Ypres, where a bustling cloth-making industry was emerging in the later Middle Ages. But they were the longest-lasting and the best known of their times: a bellwether for a dawning age of international commerce.

Rise of the Republics

MANY OF THE MOST HIGH-PROFILE CUSTOMERS at the fairs of Champagne and Flanders travelled there across the Alps from the Italian city republics, of which the most reliably bullish was Venice. The city nicknamed *La Serenissima* had not even existed during Roman times, but during the sixth century a settlement developed around the lagoon and its islands. Initially it was ruled from Constantinople (via the exarchate of Ravenna), but by the ninth century the *doges* of Venice had shaken off Byzantine oversight and started to build up their independent power along the shores of the Adriatic. In their early days the Venetians manufactured salt and glass, but as the Middle Ages wore on, they found there was better business to be done as professional middlemen, who took advantage of their blessings of geography and the necessity of making a living without any farmlands to fall back on, to link together the markets of Arab north Africa, Greek Byzantium, and the Latin west, importing and exporting commodities and luxury goods.

Hand in hand with trading in this world went coin striking, which was carried out in a Venetian mint called Zecca.* Also critical for a port city was shipbuilding. This took place in the shipyard known as the Arsenal, which fielded orders from the city government, its merchants, and would-be mariners from further away, not least twelfth- and thirteenth-century lords and kings who needed to commission fleets to transport their armies on crusade. And since the high seas of the Mediterranean could be violent as well as rough, the Venetians became adept at fighting, whether to defend their convoys, see off hostile Arab and Greek vessels or simply to indulge in out-and-out piracy. The line between trading and raiding was always tenuous in the Middle Ages; the Venetians usually had a foot on either side of it. The city's patron saint was (and is) St Mark the Evangelist, to whom the famous basilica on the Rialto is dedicated, but even he was, in a sense, stolen goods. In 828 a pair of Venetian merchants thieved Mark's relics from the Egyptian city of Alexandria, smuggling the saint's bones through customs inside a barrel of pork, which they trusted – rightly – the Muslim inspectors would not investigate too closely.

Around the turn of the millennium, Venice and a handful of other Italian cities, mostly on the coasts of the long peninsula, began to experience economic lift-off. The motor for their success was their innate sense of adventure. Rather than simply trading from within their own city walls, colonies of Italian merchants set up shop in every other significant trading city that would have them, usually living together as neighbours in protected quarters, where they were allowed to observe their own religious rites, use their own weights and measures and claim immunity from a raft

---

* The Zecca was the collective name for two separate Venetian mints, probably in adjacent buildings on St Mark's Square. One struck the silver *grosso*, which was the Venetian penny, produced from the time of *doge* Enrico Dandolo in the late twelfth century and known at least at first for its exceptionally high silver content. The second struck the pure gold *ducat*, made from the mid-thirteenth century onwards, which rivalled the Florentine *florin* for the status of Europe's standard gold currency. On the history of the Zecca, see Stahl, Alan M., *Zecca: The Mint of Venice in the Middle Ages* (Baltimore: 2000).

of local taxes and tolls. Their favoured status and insular expatriate lifestyle did not always win them friends, and murderous riots against Italian merchants were a regular event throughout the later Middle Ages. In 1182 Constantinople witnessed the dreadful Massacre of the Latins, when tens of thousands of Italian merchants were murdered or enslaved, in a frenzy of anti-western bloodletting encouraged by the imperial government. On that occasion, the papal legate's head was cut off and dragged through the streets tied to a dog's tail.

So trade was not without risk. But the reward was evidently worth the danger, which was why during the eleventh and twelfth centuries Italian merchants fanned out across the west. In the ports of the eastern Mediterranean they did business with Turks, Arabs and other merchants working the Silk Roads into Central Asia – a state of affairs made considerably more lucrative once the crusader states were established in Syria and Palestine. The Black Sea, where the Genoese had a special interest, gave access to the Balkans, Asia Minor, the Caucasus and the lands of the Rus'. During the eleventh century Pisan merchants took a keen interest in the ports of north Africa, and Pisan ships sent troops to sack both Carthage and Mahdia to attempt to permanently yoke them to Pisa's rule. Meanwhile, traders from a fourth Italian city-republic, Amalfi, could also be found in most major Mediterranean ports, although their prominence sharply waned from the 1130s after they were defeated in a war with Pisa. There was intense competition between the Italian city-states and none of them were ever overburdened by moral compunction. During the thirteenth century Genoese traders in the Black Sea port of Caffa struck a deal to run slaves captured in the Caucasus by the Mongols to the Mamluk rulers of Egypt, shipping them to the Nile Delta via the Black Sea and Mediterranean, whereupon the slaves would be forcibly impressed into the Mamluk army. Effectively this meant that the Christian Genoese were directly responsible for supplying workers to a power that was doing its best to crush the western crusader states of Syria and Palestine. Meanwhile, although Venice had no slaves to trade with the Mamluks, they cultivated exclusive trading arrangements between Alexandria and western ports, ensuring that the Mamluk state took a juicy share of the profits of long-distance trade between the far east and Europe. Both Venice and Genoa thereby profited handsomely from supporting the Egyptian economy and military at a time when the stated goal of Egypt was to wipe the crusader states off the map.

None of this stood up very well to ethical scrutiny. Yet then as now, markets seldom suffered pangs of conscience. And neither did merchants. By the time of the Mongol conquests, when Marco Polo was enjoying his adventures at the court of Kublai Khan, Italy's city-states occupied the box seat in Mediterranean trade, and were naturally placed to benefit from the opening-up of commercial routes to the far east. The Persian historian Ata-Malik Juvaini wrote of the Mongol empire that fear of the khans made the roads so safe that 'a woman with a golden vessel on her head might walk alone [across it] without fear or dread.'[29] The Italians did not carry gold vessels on their heads, but they took full advantage of conditions nonetheless.

Yet at the same time, the travels of Marco Polo and others like him had demonstrated the one major hurdle that faced would-be eastern traders: sheer distance. It had taken the Polo family three full years to make their way from Venice to China; the physical toll this took on a person, no matter how well provisioned they might be, was enough to make anyone think hard about making the journey more than once. The same was true on a smaller but still significant scale of trade everywhere: the merchant stood a far better chance of making profit if he could stay in one place and let others move goods on his behalf. This was where the other side of the medieval Commercial Revolution came in. During the thirteenth and fourteenth centuries new financial tools and institutions emerged which could help businessmen realize the goal of making money without traipsing relentlessly around the world in person. These new moneymaking devices lent merchants enormous power, both in their hometowns and beyond. The best way to understand how this worked is to unpack an example from the height of the Commercial Revolution, when the power of mercantile money forged the political shape of a kingdom. The merchants in question were wool-trading bankers from the city of Florence. The realm was the kingdom of England.

White Gold

AT THE TURN OF THE FOURTEENTH century, English wool was considered the finest in the world. Produced by sheep grazed on the lush pastures of regions like Lincolnshire, Northamptonshire and the Cotswolds, it could be woven into thick, durable, good-quality cloth. And there was plenty of it. Even after north-west Europe was struck by a dreadful famine in the years 1315–17, which included a murrain of sheep and other livestock, English wool was still envied by cloth manufacturers and other secondary industries across the west. Tens of thousands of woolsacks were exported every year from ports on England's southern and eastern coastline, and the revenues from taxing the wool trade were a vital part of England's national finances. Wool exports were the subject of a permanent sales tax by the crown, introduced by the Plantagenet king Edward I to fund his expensive wars of conquest in Scotland and Wales and defensive campaigns against the French king in and around Gascony. The wool tax was one of the most important. It was white gold. And it did not just enrich the crown. Thanks to the demand for English wool, English sheep farmers thrived. Many of the biggest wool-growers were monasteries: to take just one example, the monks of Rievaulx in Yorkshire, which had been England's first Cistercian abbey when it was founded in 1132, became dazzlingly wealthy thanks to the huge herds of sheep which grazed their thousands of acres of land. (Their wool-wealth is still tangible in the grand remains of their abbey, which was dissolved during the English Reformation.) And they were not alone. It was said in 1297 – with only a little exaggeration – that 50 per cent of England's wealth came from wool.[30]

These fabulous riches accrued because England's sheep sat at the production end of a long economic chain. Once woolsacks filled on estates such as Rievaulx left the country, they were typically taken across the English Channel to Flemish workshops. There raw fleece was spun into cloth, which was marketed by wholesalers in places like the Fairs of Champagne (or those of Flanders itself). It was very often bought by Italian merchants, who transported it across the Alps, where it could be dyed and cut, before finally being sold on to consumers for clothing and furnishings. Then as now, high fashion and home décor depended on quality raw materials – and in the case of woollen cloth, England was where everything began.

At each stage of this economic chain there was money to be made. But in the first decades of the fourteenth century, sharp-eyed Italian merchants began to realize there was far *more* money to be made if they could make the process shorter. It would be much simpler, they reckoned, if they could cut out the middlemen: buy wool at source, then take it from England to be spun in Italy, or employ the cloth-workers in Flanders directly. But to do that, the Italians needed boots on the ground in England. They also needed a means of safely and securely conveying large amounts of wool in one direction, and large amounts of cash in the other. The system they arrived at, which flourished through the first four decades of the fourteenth century, represented medieval commercial engineering at its finest.

FLORENCE WAS NOT A MARITIME CITY. But it had nevertheless become home to a thriving mercantile community during the economic explosion of the late twelfth and thirteenth centuries. Florentines did (and still do) many things well, but what they did best of all was merchant banking. The first western bank had been created in Venice in the twelfth century. But by the early fourteenth century the most successful houses were the Florentine-based Bardi, Peruzzi and Frescobaldi. (The most famous banking dynasty the Middle Ages produced was the Medici – who in the fifteenth century rose from Florentine financiers to become a dynasty of oligarchs, popes and queens.)* These family-run 'super-companies' bought and sold stocks, offered deposit banking to clients large and small, and provided a whole raft of secondary financial services including loans and investment in business ventures, long-distance cash and credit transfer, and tax collection as the licensed agents of popes and kings.† To run their businesses smoothly, these Florentine companies (and others like them) followed the example of the Genoese, Venetians and Pisans, placing agents in cities across the west, from France, England and Flanders to Syria, Cyprus and the larger Greek islands, all the way east into Khanbaliq and Kin-sai, Sarai and Delhi.[31]

Unsurprisingly, there was a strong Florentine presence in London, England's capital city and a burgeoning commercial hub in north-west Europe. Indeed, the Florentines had enjoyed conspicuous success in London since the 1270s, when Florentine banking agents including those of the Bardi and Frescobaldi had helped Edward I to fund his wars. Having gained the king's trust they were soon subcontracting other aspects of government business, including collecting customs duties and other taxes on behalf of the crown.[32] This was, admittedly, risky business: in 1311, during a baronial rebellion against Edward's son and successor, Edward II, Amerigo Frescobaldi, the head of that company's English branch, was hounded out of the country as 'an enemy of the king and of the kingdom'.[33] His vast credit account to the crown was left unpaid, a stroke of misfortune which briefly bankrupted the Frescobaldi. Nevertheless, despite the obvious possibility of ruin when political winds ran contrary to bankers' interests, the rewards on offer from providing such services were magnificent.

---

* Between 1475 and 1630 the Medici produced four popes (Leo X, Clement VII, Pius IV and Leo XI) and two queens of France (Catherine de'Medici and Maria de Medici). See chapters 15 and 16.

† Many of these functions had been pioneered by the Knights Templar. The Templars collected the papal tax that funded the Fifth Crusade; they bailed out Louis IX of France when he was taken prisoner during his own crusade to Damietta, using a large cash loan drawn from individual crusaders' deposits; they provided private accountancy services to the crown of France and subcontracted treasury functions including paying public servants. But in 1307–14 the Templars were shut down and their members persecuted in a process driven along by the king of France, Philip IV, and a supine Gascon-born pope, Clement V.

After the upheaval of the baronial rebellion died down, Amerigo Frescobaldi's place was taken by the brilliant Francesco Balducci Pegolotti, a representative of the Bardi, another Florentine 'super-company'. In a guide to finance which Pegolotti wrote towards the end of his life, he made a detailed inventory of the best places in England to obtain wool, and at what prices it could be acquired.[34] Pegolotti knew well what he was talking about. From 1317 until the 1340s the Bardi would be heavily knitted into English affairs.

The interlocking set of English interests that attracted both the Frescobaldi and the Bardi was considerable. Most obviously, English kings borrowed heavily from Italian bankers, first relatively small sums – a few thousand pounds here and there – and later, from 1310 onwards, huge ones, equivalent to multiples of the crown's annual revenue, which was repayable out of revenues from the wool trade, which the Florentines were licensed to collect directly.[35] Italian bankers also dealt extensively with major English magnates and other landowners. Sometimes this was connected to the wool industry: for example, when Cistercian abbots wished to build new abbey churches, they could secure large lump sums from Florentines, repayable in future wool-stocks, or discounts on purchases.[36] At other times it was just business. Edward II's extravagantly corrupt favourite Hugh Despenser the Younger was rewarded fulsomely for his friendship with the king in the form of land grants and other revenues; he used the Bardi and Peruzzi to deposit his ill-gotten profits and to borrow against his assets. By the time Despenser was hanged, drawn and quartered for treason in 1326, shortly before the *coup d'état* that brought Edward's tumultuous reign to an end and forced him from the throne, he owed the Bardi nearly £800,* but was owed nearly £200 by the Peruzzi.[37]

Finally, and separately from all this, the Bardi also agreed with the pope to collect papal taxes in England. This was a complex operation to say the least, but it gave the Florentines one more

---

* For rough comparison, one pound at this time was around three months' wages for a skilled craftsman such as a stonemason or carpenter.

stake in England's economic and political life, which by the 1320s amounted to a virtuous financial circle. Thanks to their relationships with wool producers, the Florentines could secure heavily discounted prices before English wool officially hit the export market. And thanks to their loans to the crown, they profited directly from the customs duties levied on every woolsack that left the country, wherever its destination. When they needed ready cash to spend on wool or loan to clients in England, they had it, either in the form of deposits from men like Despenser or in the proceeds of papal taxes. And when the pope demanded the receipts of his tax collection, the bank's representatives in Rome were able to provide it, drawing on deposits from other customers, and profits they made from selling wool and cloth. One way or another, this meant that both English wool *and* English money were flowing into Italy, while Italian credit flowed into England. It was a situation that suited both parties very well indeed – at least, for a time.

IN THE FOURTEENTH CENTURY, AS NOW, even mildly complex financial business bore risk. These risks ranged from the jeopardy that came from dealing with political actors (as Amerigo Frescobaldi had learned the hard way when he was kicked out of England in 1311) to the practical problems posed by transporting money and stock around the western world. There was not much that bankers could do about the first of these problems: affairs of state were delicate, which was why they were lucrative. But the pragmatic issues of cash and stock transfer certainly could be dealt with. Indeed, much of the medieval Commercial Revolution was founded squarely on improving the systems by which money and goods were transferred.

Moving money was one of the first issues to be solved by medieval financiers, through the invention of a cashless credit transfer system which operated on so-called 'bills of exchange'. These were, to use a crude analogy, medieval travellers' cheques: they promised to pay the bearer a fixed sum of money at a destination far from their place of issue, and often in a different currency. The Templars had pioneered their use in the twelfth and thirteenth centuries, creating chits that allowed pilgrims travelling to the east to borrow against their properties and assets at home and withdraw their funds from Templar houses in the Holy Land. Italian bankers used them extensively, and with good reason. These sorts of financial instruments are small beer indeed to us today – but in the Middle Ages they were truly revolutionary. They were a safe way to move credit over long distances, and could be secured against fraud with seals and code-words. They allowed Christian merchants to get around the Roman Church's strict prohibition on usury – for when money was changed between currencies, exchange rates could be manipulated artificially in the lender's favour, effectively allowing profit to be baked into the trade without officially defining this as interest. Better yet, bills of exchange could also be traded and circulated – sold at a discount to third parties who could go on to cash them themselves. This allowed for flexible, adventurous deals to be struck, across long distances. Groups of merchants could act as truly international entities, with sprawling webs of commercial activity, but scant need for international travel, save to transport stock. The merchant who availed himself of the fourteenth century's financial innovations was free as never before to become 'sedentary' – based in a single city but able to do business in many others. It was a great leap forward.

There were many more devices that facilitated the financial strides of the thirteenth and fourteenth centuries – and which directly affected commercial networks such as the Florentine-English wool trade. It was an unfortunate fact of shipping that ships sometimes sank, usually with the loss of their valuable cargo as well as their crews. So from the 1340s at the latest, merchants in Genoa began to draw up insurance contracts, which would pay out if stocks were lost in transit. At roughly the same time, merchants began to formalize ways in which they could work together to invest capital jointly in commercial ventures, thereby sharing out both the risks and the profits between themselves. This was a vital part in the development of the 'company' itself: the practice of multiple partners and investors sharing in the fortunes of a single abstract commercial entity, with new investors being sought out when the company wished to expand and records kept of how the company was performing, what its assets and liabilities were, and how its success (or failure) could be projected into the future.

The notion of keeping business accounts was not original to the Middle Ages: it dated back at least to the Roman Republic. But double-entry book-keeping – in which assets and liabilities were systematically listed in opposing columns and balanced out to describe numerically the state of the company – became a western business norm only in the fourteenth century, when it was adopted by Italian merchants and applied across their businesses, giving them the competitive advantage of understanding their own trading performance and potential to an exact standard. Book-keeping, the notion of corporate risk and sedentary business were the rocks on which companies like the Bardi, Peruzzi and Frescobaldi were built. They remain core components of capitalism today.

THE TENACIOUS AND MUCH-TRAVELLED MERCHANT FRANCESCO di Marco Datini, who was born in Prato, not far from Florence, during the second half of the fourteenth century, left more than 600 account books and nearly 150,000 pieces of business correspondence when he died in 1410.[38] (He also left 70,000 gold florins as capital for a fund to alleviate poverty in Prato, a fund which still pays out interest today.) Datini was in many ways the poster-boy for the bright and busy new commercial world of the later Middle Ages. He opened his account books with his personal motto, which summed up his approach to life. 'For God and profit,' he wrote. But profit, like God, could be capricious, as traders and financiers sometimes found to their great cost. For while the Middle Ages presented them with a wonderful new toolbox of devices to increase their wealth, there were times when markets and events contrived to shred their endeavours. To illustrate this we may return to the Bardi and Peruzzi companies who profited so handsomely from exploiting the English wool trade and attending to the needs of its spendthrift Plantagenet kings in the first half of the fourteenth century.

In 1327 Edward II was forced to abdicate his crown. He was subsequently murdered in prison in Berkeley Castle, a turn of events that placed his teenage son Edward on the throne. Edward II had been a weak, corruptible, inept and unlucky monarch; few were sorry to see him go. But even fewer could have predicted how quickly his son Edward III would launch England into a new age. Soon after this Edward was old enough to exercise royal power independently, he began to plot, prosecute and spend prodigious sums on war against the kings of Scotland and France in pursuit of his right – as he saw it – not only to rule the old Plantagenet dominions in Normandy and Aquitaine, but to claim the French crown itself. This was the beginning of the Hundred Years War, which historians usually date between 1337 and 1453. It was expensive at the outset and never got much cheaper. From 1340 Edward was bleeding money month after month, chiefly on paying continental noblemen to ally with him against the French, and raising armies of soldiers on fixed-term cash contracts whom he could send out on annual expeditionary campaigns.

As Edward's financial commitments grew, he ran up an ever-larger account with the Florentine bankers, who began to operate in partnership as a joint venture in order to meet his need. He was also borrowing from other sources: like a modern-day shopping addict whose wallet groans with maxed-out store- and credit-cards, Edward had accounts with lenders in Florence, Venice, Asti and Lucca, and many other places besides. He taxed England as hard as he could, and on occasion negotiated with domestic merchants in London for a share in the profit of a whole year's wool-stock, which was forcibly purchased and sold on foreign markets, with proceeds split between the merchants who transacted the deal and the government itself.[39] Italian banks took regular repayments on their loans to England in the form of tax receipts and discounted wool sales, but by the mid-1340s both Edward and his Italian creditors found themselves in deep water.

Then a perfect storm hit. In Florence, political and social unrest led to a series of rapid changes in government, in which the Bardi backed the wrong candidate. Meanwhile, wars in Tuscany which they had part-financed also turned out badly. From 1341 the Bardi and Peruzzi were struggling to keep up with the English king's demand for funds. In 1341 they defaulted on a payment they had agreed to make to Flemish merchants on Edward's behalf; under the terms of a deal the parties had struck, Edward was forced to hand over his aristocratic friends the earls of Derby and Warwick as hostages to the Flemings.[40] It was humiliating for all involved.

Things did not improve from here. Edward kept spending; the merchant bankers kept lending. But on both sides the accounts were looking increasingly unsustainable. In 1343 the Peruzzi went bust, amid a series of rapid changes of chairmen, allegations of political corruption levelled against board members and repeated defaults on debts by the English.[41] Then, in 1346, the Bardi were also forced to declare themselves bankrupt. Although they were not totally ruined – and were indeed still loaning large sums of money to the English crown thirty years later in the 1370s – they were nevertheless badly shaken and very nearly put out of business altogether. The banker and chronicler Giovanni Villani estimated that when the Bardi went down, Edward was in debt to the tune of around 1.5 million gold florins – around a quarter of a million pounds, or roughly five years' annual royal revenue. Even if this was a gross exaggeration – and it may well have been – he was plainly up to his neck.[42] Yet curiously this did not much trouble him. Despite the financial meltdown – exacerbated if not directly caused by Edward's failure to honour his debts – England was enjoying spectacular good fortune in the war that the king was straining to pay for. In August 1346 Edward won the first and perhaps the greatest of his land battles in the Hundred Years War, destroying a French army at the battle of Crécy and ushering in a short golden age for English military supremacy in northern Europe. The great twentieth-century economist John Maynard Keynes is often credited with having popularized the idea that 'if you owe the bank £100, that's your problem. If you owe the bank

£100 million, that's the bank's problem.' This was as true in the 1340s as at any time afterwards.

Money and Power

MEDIEVAL MERCHANTS EXERCISED POWER IN LOTS of ways. Wealth was of course a form of power in its own right. And by their sheer command of resources and reserves of gold and silver, Italian cities like Venice, Genoa and Pisa achieved commercial success, which went a long way towards guaranteeing their political independence from kings and emperors. It allowed them to act as states, despite their tiny geographical footprint: going to war, joining and even leading crusades, invading enemies' territory and colonizing non-Christian spaces. At the same time, diplomats like Marco Polo influenced the ways in which westerners were perceived far from home: they were cultural ambassadors as well as diplomatic envoys. And as we have seen in the case of England, merchants and their companies could exercise tremendous economic sway over central parts of a nation's economy.

And this was not only true in Italy, although without question, the Italian city-states were the boiler-room of the Commercial Revolution. In northern Europe, where the Danish peninsula jutted out into the Baltic in something of a geographical mirror-image of the Italian boot in the Mediterranean, a smaller but similarly busy group of merchant city-states also emerged around northern Germany. The Venice of the north was the city of Lübeck, sheltered in a bay where the river Trave flows into the Baltic Sea. Once a pagan settlement, it was refounded as a Christian city in 1143 by Adolf II, count of Schauenburg and Holstein, and in 1226 granted 'free city' status by the Holy Roman Emperor Frederick II Hohenstaufen.

Geography made Lübeck a bustling port linking the Christian states of northern Europe with territory newly colonized around the Baltic, exploiting the rich commercial possibilities of a region abundant in timber, furs, amber and resin. The ambitions of the merchants who lived and worked there ensured that over the years Lübeck became the most influential of a cluster of similar city-states around the Baltic and beyond, including Danzig, Riga, Bergen, Hamburg, Bremen and even Cologne. By the mid-fourteenth century these had banded together in a loose commercial partnership known as the Hanseatic League. The axis of trade for the League's merchants stretched from London and Bruges in the west as far as Novgorod in the east, and throughout this trading region, Hanseatic agents could be found pushing the interests of their bloc. Their collective mercantile power enabled them to defend their freedom from political influence by outsiders; and like the Italians they were prepared to defend their own commercial interests by raising troops and going to war, as they did against Denmark in the 1360s and 1370s. They were troubled towards the end of the fourteenth century by a violent pirate gang known as the Victual Brothers, who plagued Hanseatic coastal ports with their raids, and identified themselves by their motto 'God's friend and all the world's enemy.' But this challenge was eventually seen off, and during the fifteenth century the Hanseatic League was rich and powerful enough to tangle in the affairs of other states, as they did in the 1460s and 1470s in a tussle with native English merchants that dragged the Hanse into the Wars of the Roses.

As the Hanseatic League grew, and the Italian city-states consolidated their hegemony in the Mediterranean, merchants as a class were becoming more and more visible throughout the west. And whereas in classical times theirs had not been considered a genteel line of business, in the late Middle Ages merchants' wealth and omnipresence started to buy them social and cultural respectability. Business could be an unexpectedly levelling career; in early fourteenth-century Paris the two most successful linen merchants were women: Jeanne Fouacière and Erembourc de Moustereul. Or it could be a route to status. In Italy, as early as the thirteenth century it had become possible for a merchant family to spend their way into high society, marrying their children to the offspring of princes and other magnates, and claiming a space in the aristocratic world. Indeed, merchants were often so successful at colonizing the ranks of nobility that they started to behave rather too much like nobles. In Venice, for example, many merchant families rose to power on the back of the city's open embrace of business before lineage. But in the fourteenth century these wealthy families, who ran Venice's government, passed a series of laws that forbade non-noble dynasties from participating in long-distance galley trading – effectively sewing up the more lucrative sector of the Venetian economy, and clamping down on social mobility in the process.[43]

Meanwhile, in England, where Italian merchants had helped to underwrite the first campaigns of the Hundred Years War, the levers of power continued thereafter to be shared by rich men as well as high-born ones. A succession of London- and York-based merchants would play a conspicuous part in managing the war effort as the century went on, taking on considerable personal risk as they did so. In the 1340s the wool and wine merchant turned moneylender Sir John Pulteney lent money extensively and regularly to the crown for services termed only as 'the king's secret affairs'; at the same time he was entrusted as a civil servant to audit Italian bankers' accounts, sit on judicial commissions, raise troops and oversee the maintenance of London's defences. He served one annual term as mayor of London. Along the way Pulteney amassed a handsome property portfolio, with a superb Thames-side mansion called Coldharbour (later inhabited by Edward's son, the Black Prince) and a magnificent fortified country manor, Penshurst Place in Kent, which today still retains its stunning medieval Great Hall, with the chestnut-beam roof Pulteney himself had installed. Yet all this great fortune and luxury could come at a political cost as well as a financial one. When the king's fortunes in war momentarily dipped early in the 1340s, Pulteney was marked as a fall-guy, arrested and imprisoned in Somerton Castle in Lincolnshire, where he served a two-year sentence.[44]

This was no doubt unpleasant, but compared with later London merchants who dabbled in public affairs, Pulteney got away relatively lightly. In 1376 a trio of London traders who had served as city administrators and advisors to central government – Richard Lyons, Adam Bury and John Pecche – were hauled before the 'Good Parliament', impeached for fraud, corruption and embezzlement, severely censured and stripped of many of their offices. Lyons was later murdered by a mob during the populist rising known as the Peasants' Revolt of 1381. His near-contemporary, the grocer and wool exporter Nicholas Brembre, served three times as London mayor and arranged large loans to King Richard II, both from his own pocket and in the form of corporate credit on behalf of the City. Brembre's reward for a surfeit of loyalty to an incapable and unpopular king was to be hanged, drawn and quartered for treason by rebellious noblemen in 1388.

Such were the risks inherent when merchants involved themselves in politics. And perhaps it is not surprising that then – as now – businessmen who sought or accepted political office laid themselves open to allegations of corruption, malfeasance and hopeless conflicts of interest.* Be that as it may: by the end of the fourteenth century it was impossible to deny that in western Europe merchants had come of age, and were leaving their mark on society and culture at large. Some of that legacy was physical: we can still visit the early fourteenth-century cloth hall of Ypres (reconstructed meticulously after being destroyed by artillery in the First World War) and bear witness to the extraordinary architectural relics of cities that were transformed by the Commercial Revolution of the thirteenth century. Visitors to Venice can view the thirteenth-century Ca' da Mosto palace, best known as the birthplace of the fifteenth-century slaver and explorer Alvise da Cadamosto but actually constructed in earlier generations by his wealthy merchant ancestors. Even visitors passing through the somewhat less glamorous English coastal city of Southampton will see the timber frame of Merchant's House, which dates to the late thirteenth century, and be reminded of what medieval wool traders did to transform the prosperity of their world.

* Cf: Donald J. Trump.

But commercial activity was not only memorialized in stone; it also left its mark on the page. When Geoffrey Chaucer wrote his *Canterbury Tales* in the 1390s he gave one of his bawdiest and strangest stories to 'The Merchant'.* It was no surprise that a merchant should feature in Chaucer's riotous compendium, for the author had lifelong experience of business. His father was a vintner, or wine merchant, and travelled widely in the course of his trades. As a boy Chaucer was raised in Vintry Ward, then London's most cosmopolitan district, home to Germans, French, Italians and Flemings, many of them in London for the sole purpose of doing business, and a riverside ward in which merchant ships loaded down with wares from all over the world docked constantly throughout the year.[45] As an adult Chaucer served as a customs official for the English Crown, and he lived for more than a decade in apartments above the Aldgate, one of the main passages in and out of London's walls and a busy portal for traders approaching the city from the east. In 1372–3 he was sent abroad to Genoa and Florence as a trade envoy, with the task of negotiating a base for Italian merchants in one of the cities on England's south coast.[46] Business, as well as poetry, was in his blood.

But Chaucer was influenced by the booming medieval world of trade and exchange in more than just this direct, literal sense. His *Canterbury Tales* were also heavily influenced by an elite, international artistic culture in which ideas and stories were traded as eagerly – and over as great expanses – as Indian spices and English woolsacks, and could do so specifically because the Commercial Revolution allowed it. Chaucer's stories sprang from an international literary culture that most famously produced the historian and poet Petrarch, and the Florentine writer and *Decameron* author Giovanni Boccaccio. And his

---

* In 'The Merchant's Tale', an old, rich, risible merchant called Januarie marries a much younger woman, May, who then takes up with one of his squires. Januarie goes blind, and is tricked into facilitating a sexual encounter between the squire and his wife, which takes place in the unlikely venue of a pear tree. Through an intervention of the (classical) gods Januarie regains his sight and witnesses his wife in congress with his squire; thanks also to a gift of the gods, May talks her way out of the situation, telling her husband that his eyes are fooling him, a psychological manipulation which we might today call 'gaslighting'.

classical education, fluent understanding of French and Italian and European outlook all served his muse as well as his career in business and bureaucracy. It is no exaggeration to say that the great cultural flourishing that occurred towards the end of the Middle Ages owed much to the mercantile flourishing that preceded it.

We shall examine Renaissance culture and the power of late medieval art and literature more closely in chapter 14. But before we leave behind the world of business, there is one more merchant who merits our attention. He was arguably the most successful English businessman of his age, his life spanning the reigns of five kings at the turn of the fifteenth century. Although he is best known – in England, at any rate – as a pantomime character, who wandered London's streets with a knapsack on his shoulder and a prodigal cat at his heels, the reality is very different. Mayor of London four times and mayor of Calais once, he was a financier and trader par excellence, who negotiated the political world more adeptly than many of his contemporaries, and left a deep impression on the physical and mental landscape of his adopted home city in ways that can be practically felt by people today. His name was Sir Richard Whittington, thought he is best known on the stage today as plain old 'Dick'.

'Dick' Whittington

HAD RICHARD WHITTINGTON BEEN BORN A century earlier than he was, he might have been a churchman. As it was, he arrived into the world around 1350, the third son of a knight from Pauntley in Gloucestershire, who struggled to pay his debts, and whose estate was in any case quite insufficient to provide young Richard with a secure future as a landed aristocrat.[47] The traditional path through life might have been a rigorous education before patient progress up the ranks of the clergy. But Whittington was a child of the fourteenth century. Other opportunities were available to him – and he grasped them with both hands.

When Whittington was growing up, Cotswold wool was renowned as the softest and most desirable in England, and by extension the best in the world. Fabric – or the raw materials for it – was all around him. So it was natural that a Gloucestershire lad would gravitate towards the cloth trade. In adolescence Whittington was apprenticed as a mercer: the catch-all name for traders in England who imported fine silks, linens and similar fabrics, and exported wool and its by-products. He was sent to London, where the busiest and best mercers did business. And slowly but surely it became apparent that he had a knack for the job. By 1379, when he was probably in his late twenties, Whittington was doing well enough to loan money to the city authorities; a decade later he had begun to seek and hold minor political offices: first as a member of his local ward council, then as an alderman.* In 1393 he was asked to serve a year's term as one of the city's two sheriffs. Soon after he was appointed as a warden of the newly incorporated Mercers' Company† – a trade association set up to advance and protect the interests of clothmongers all over the city. Like his contemporary Geoffrey Chaucer, Whittington was making his way as a respectable citizen in a buzzing European capital.

He was also, not coincidentally, doing a roaring trade. The young king Richard II was highly enamoured by the finer trappings of royalty, and surrounded himself with courtiers who shared his expensive tastes. The court was not the source of wise or constant governance. But it was a very good place to be a mercer. Whittington made connections there and milked them. He sold silks and other cloth to the value of thousands of pounds a year to some of the richest and most powerful noblemen in the land:

---

* Medieval London was divided into small districts called wards, each of which had its own administrative council. Each ward also elected aldermen each year to serve on London's city council. The city's official leader was the lord mayor, also elected annually.

† The Worshipful Company of Mercers, which is today one of the richest and most prominent livery companies in the City of London, traces its foundation to 1394. It is one of dozens of such companies that had their medieval origins as boards of trade, but now perform broader charitable service and exist as a forum for likeminded London professionals to meet, dine and network. Other notable companies still extant include the Fishmongers, Grocers, Skinners, Merchant Tailors and Goldsmiths.

the king's uncles John of Gaunt, duke of Lancaster and Thomas of Woodstock, duke of Gloucester; his cousin Henry Bolingbroke, earl of Derby; and his best friend, Robert de Vere, earl of Oxford. Most lucrative of all, by the 1390s Whittington could count the king himself as a customer. Richard was a tall, strong man with delicate, slightly effeminate features: he was handsome, he knew it, and he enjoyed dressing up to enhance his good looks. As well as enjoying traditional kingly hobbies such as hunting with birds, hunting with dogs and hunting with weapons, Richard was very interested in fine dining, expensive clothes and accessories. (He was, it seems, the first English king ever to use a handkerchief.[48]) Whittington sourced and supplied Richard with the most luxurious fabrics on the market: velvet, embroidered velvet, cloth of gold, damask and taffeta.[49] In one year midway through Richard's reign, Whittington sold cloth to the value of almost £3,500 to the court. And he was rewarded for his services with more than just cash.

Other merchants – the unfortunate Nicholas Brembre, for example – had fallen foul of proximity to Richard's court, which was regularly beset by conflict, much of it stemming from the incompetent, partial, spiteful style of the king himself. Yet somehow, Whittington was neither consumed by the court nor hated by its enemies. He maintained a professional closeness to Richard, and was granted high political office. Yet somehow he never found himself tainted by association. In 1397, when the incumbent lord mayor of London, Adam Bamme, died in office, Richard demanded that his favoured mercer, Whittington, step in to complete Bamme's tenure. The following year, 1398, Whittington was legitimately elected to continue for a second, full term. This might have seemed to paint Whittington in Ricardian colours. But it did not. In 1399 Richard's reign spiralled into brittle despotism and the king was deposed and murdered in a revolution led by his cousin Bolingbroke. Whittington did not fall alongside his most famous customer and patron. Indeed, when Bolingbroke – now Henry IV – appointed his first royal council, he chose none other than Whittington to sit as one of its members. Whether through professional ambivalence, force of character, or plain good fortune,

Whittington glided through the ugly transition of monarchs. He would make as much money – and find himself even more pressed into civic duty – under Henry IV's new, Lancastrian regime as he ever had under the old.

In the embroidered, romanticized plays and stories of 'Dick' Whittington, which circulated from the very start of the seventeenth century and are still performed today, Whittington's rise to power and fame was rather different to all this. In fiction, he is traditionally a poor boy who comes to London as an apprentice, acquires a cat, finds himself ill-treated and decides to run away, but changes his mind as he marches north through Highgate,* where he hears the Bow Bells of east London ringing, telling him he is destined for greatness if he stays. He sends his cat on a merchant ship to a foreign land, where it kills the mice and rats that are bothering the local king; he is sent a vast sum of money in thanks, and goes on to be mayor of London three times. There is much to recommend this as an exciting fairy-tale, but little of it is true. By the start of the fifteenth century Whittington was on the cusp of high power; one poet called him 'of merchandy that lodestar, and chief chosen flower'.[50] However, his success and his reputation had nothing to do with cats, mice or bells and everything to do with his remarkable tenacity and his talents as a mercer and a civic administrator.

These, certainly, are what served him well for the next twenty years of his life. As well as importing fine cloth, from the start of Henry IV's reign Whittington became prominent in wool. He collected the wool tax on the crown's behalf. He exported a significant number of sacks himself. And he lent large sums of the private wealth he accumulated to the crown, including a substantial advance of 1,000 marks in the winter of 1400–1, when the Byzantine emperor Manuel II Palaiologos arrived in London for a two-month state visit, and was entertained with a glittering round of pageants, tournaments and parties, at vast expense to the new king.[51] He was elected twice more as London's mayor, in 1406

* Today on Highgate Hill, outside a pub called the Whittington Stone and just down the road from the Whittington NHS Trust hospital, there is a small and slightly overlooked statue of a cat, which is a tribute to this fictional journey.

and 1419. He also served as mayor of Calais, the town in north-western France which was ruled from England, and in which a 'staple' – or compulsory export market – had been established. As he aged and stacked up experience, he was drafted into service beyond his sphere of business expertise: on one occasion he served as a papal tax collector, and on another he sat on a royal commission to investigate the heretics known as Lollards. He was even appointed to the committee that supervised refurbishments to Westminster Abbey, which had begun under Richard II and were continued by the new king.[52]

Perhaps most spectacularly, during the reign of Henry IV's irrepressible son, Henry V, Whittington involved himself heavily in war finance. The Hundred Years War was still in full swing in the first decades of the fifteenth century, and in early 1415 Henry had plans to take a large English army to invade and occupy Normandy: a huge undertaking which would include landing an amphibious army on the other side of the English Channel, besieging castles and cities, defending whatever might be won and potentially meeting the French in battle. Costs were not helped by the fact that Henry planned to bring gunpowder-fired cannons and specialist artillery on campaign – a new, exciting, but very expensive addition to a medieval army. To pay for all this Henry leaned into every possible source of finance he could – and Whittington lent a hand, advancing the crown a joint loan of £1,600 (around 3 per cent of the first three months' war budget) and negotiating with other London merchants to find more lines of credit, secured against royal jewels, art collections and chapel plate.[53] During the siege of Harfleur, Whittington made an emergency loan of nearly £500 to keep the English effort going.[54] This was more than just patriotism: it is fair to say that without the goodwill and financial backing of Whittington and his fellow London merchants the Normandy campaign of 1415 could not have been fought – and Henry V would never have won the most famous battle in the whole of the Hundred Years War: Agincourt.

After the Agincourt campaign, Whittington continued his interest in war finance, as he dabbled in the market for ransoms:

the busy (if morally murky) trade in prisoners of war. Once a knight or soldier had been taken on the battlefield, he was legally considered the property of his captor, who was entitled to ask for a cash payment from the king, lord or family of the man in question. Collecting on the ransom (and paying a cut of the profit to the crown) required more effort than an archer or weary man-at-arms might possess. He could therefore sell the prisoner to a merchant, who would enter into a legal arrangement known as a bond to pay the crown's fee, before beginning the process of recovering the ransom. After Agincourt, records show that Whittington bought a French prisoner called Hugh Coniers, and subsequently sold him to an Italian merchant, who paid the very large sum of £296.[55] Whether the Italian merchant was effectively acting as a bail bondsman or intended to sell the prisoner on again we do not know. But it is a startling insight into the way that merchants like Whittington could profit from wars without going anywhere near a castle or a battlefield.

THROUGH THESE MEANS AND MANY OTHERS, Whittington continued to make money. As a moneylender he was well known for his liquidity and willingness to lend to high-status clients. Unusually for his class and time, he never invested seriously in property outside London. Although he married a woman from Dorset called Alice Fitzwarin, they never had children and she died in 1410, more than a decade before he did. Whittington therefore kept almost all of his fortune in assets: cash, loans extended to the great and good and a fine house in central London, set just back from the Thames in the district known as the Royal. He rebuilt a church there, dedicated to St Michael, and made arrangements for a college of priests and scholars to be attached to it, so they could study and pray for the souls of Whittington's friends and colleagues – including the late king Richard and his queen, Anne of Bohemia. Sadly, the college was dissolved in the 1540s during the English Reformation, while the church burned down during the Great Fire of London in 1666. (The replacement, which stands on the site today, was rebuilt by Christopher Wren.) These were the only major personal marks Whittington left on the city of London in which he made his fortune. But they were not meant as monuments, for Whittington was in many ways the archetype and epitome of the publicity-shy business mogul for whom fame and fortune are antitheses and not bedfellows. Instead, his real legacy to London – and beyond – was made through his impersonal but massive charitable and philanthropic spending.

When Whittington died in late March 1423 he left an estate of £7,000 – a hefty sum, almost all of which was in cash. It was his express wish that every penny be given to charity. In his lifetime Whittington had already spent some of his fortune on good causes: repairing bridges, fitting out public toilets, founding a women's refuge for single mothers and building a library for the Franciscans of London's Greyfriars, which by the sixteenth century was richly stocked with works on history and philosophy and collections of sermons. In death he added to the list of works: he paid for drinking fountains in the streets and repairs to the walls at St Bartholomew's hospital. He established a second new library at the Guildhall – the fine Gothic municipal building which still stands today and which was halfway through massive reconstruction works when Whittington died. He left money for the overhaul of Newgate prison, a cramped, squalid and diseased jail on the western edge of the city in which inmates often died from the sheer foulness of the conditions. He made sure his college at St Michael's church was left on a sound financial footing. And he funded an almshouse – an establishment to take care of London's poor and destitute.

This was a long and impressive and wholly civic-minded set of projects, unusual in its day and exemplary across time. And although the city of London has changed radically since Whittington's death, his hand can still be felt. For nearly six hundred years the Mercers' Company has maintained the almshouse Whittington established. It has now moved out of central London and can be found near East Grinstead in West Sussex, not far from Gatwick Airport. Whittington's College, as it is now known, is an estate of more than fifty homes leased at a subsidized rate to retired people who are either single women or hard-up couples. The residents who pass through these homes are the beneficiaries of the charitable instincts of Sir Richard Whittington, mercer, moneylender, war financier and friend of kings, who made money and exercised power in a variety of subtle ways during the Middle Ages.

But they are far from the only people who enjoy the fruits of that age. The changes wrought to medieval society and economy during the Commercial Revolution laid the foundations for the golden age of western capitalism that followed many centuries later. Everyone today whose life is enhanced by Chinese exports, banking credit, travel insurance and investment in stocks and shares owes something to the Middle Ages. We are standing on the shoulders of giants.

11

SCHOLARS

'Almost every monk seemed a philosopher...'

NORMAN CHRONICLER ORDERIC VITALIS

O n Saturday 14 October 1307 a group of the most senior scholars from the University of Paris bustled through the city's streets towards the cathedral of Notre-Dame, to attend an audience with the French king Philip IV's minister, William de Nogaret. They had been summoned to see him at short notice, for de Nogaret had urgent business to put before them. When they arrived before the cathedral's soaring Gothic edifice, they were shown into the chapter-room. De Nogaret came to address them in person.

The minister was a familiar and controversial figure in French society. He too was a scholar, originally: in the 1280s he had trained in law at the University of Montpellier, rising to the rank of professor before he left the academy to carve out a career as a hard-headed political fixer and solver of problems. His reputation as a brute with a brain ran far beyond France. In 1303 he had, with King Philip's approval, tried to kidnap Pope Boniface VIII from his villa in the central Italian town of Agnani, causing a skirmish in which the pope was slapped in the face.* De Nogaret was a tough

---

* The 'Agnani Slap' was the melodramatic climax of a nasty feud between Philip IV and Boniface VIII. Its origin lay in the French king's desire to tax the Church in his realm, but its roots lay in the age-old issue of papal vs royal pre-eminence. Resistance to papal authority was traditionally the preserve of German kings and emperors (e.g. during the Investiture Controversy of 1075–1122 and the subsequent Guelph–Ghibelline wars, which persisted in Italy from the early twelfth century until the end of the fourteenth). But at the turn of

man who demanded to be taken seriously. Yet now he told the Parisian academics a story so scandalous as to strain all credulity. It was a tale of sex and sin, blasphemy and heresy. It concerned the Knights Templar – the military order which had been at the front line of the crusades for nearly two hundred years.

The Templars, de Nogaret revealed to the scholars, had been the subject of a long, covert investigation carried out by the French government and overseen by himself. He claimed his inquiries had revealed foul and endemic corruption running from the top to the bottom of the Templar order. Under the cover of papal protection, generations of high-ranking Templars had turned their noble organization into a hotbed of homosexuality, idolatry and vice, where members were not only allowed but encouraged to disrespect Christ's name. According to an account of the meeting written by the chronicler Jean of St Victor, de Nogaret alleged that in nightly rituals, Templars spat on the cross, trampled on images of Christ and denied His holiness.[1] They worshipped false idols and engaged one another in lewd sexual acts. In formal allegations drawn up by the government, the brothers' supposed deeds were described as 'a disgrace for humanity, a pernicious example of evil and a universal scandal' and the men themselves 'wolves in sheep's clothing… sons of infidelity'.[2]

In light of these revelations, the scholars learned, the French government had taken swift and decisive action. On the previous day – Friday 13 October – every Templar in France, up to and including the Order's grand master, Jacques de Molay, had been arrested by government agents. The Order's property had been impounded. Templar houses (known as preceptories or com-manderies) had been seized and searched. Hundreds of Templars

---

the fourteenth century Philip IV briefly became chief papal tormentor. When Boniface opposed Philip's attempts to assert royal supremacy, de Nogaret travelled to Italy, contracted a small private army loyal to the powerful Colonna family and laid siege to the papal villa at Agnani, aiming to seize Boniface and remove him to France, where he might be put on trial. In the confusion of the siege, de Nogaret and his leading ally Giacomo 'Sciarra' Colonna confronted Boniface. Sciarra slapped the pope in the face. They then imprisoned and seriously mistreated the pope for three days, before he was rescued by the people of Agnani. Boniface died soon afterwards of a fever, during which it was said (inaccurately) that he went mad and chewed his own hands off.

were now in prison. They could expect condign punishment, because this was a case Philip himself took very seriously. The king had been complaining in private of his suspicions about the Templars since at least the spring of 1305.[3] Whether he *truly* believed the Order was riddled with sexual misconduct and godless corruption was not – and still is not – certain. But he was definitely interested in the Templars' wealth as a possible resource to boost his faltering economy and fund his foreign wars, and it pleased him to pose as the scourge of Church corruption. It was a sure bet that Philip would call for the support of the university men as things moved forward. The university was one of the finest in the west, and its scholars were at the cutting edge of theological research and debate. Their collective judgement helped forge French and international public opinion. This was why de Nogaret took pains to update them on what was going on as soon as he was able. Like it or not, they were destined to pay a role in the Templars' survival – or destruction.[4]

THE FRENCH ATTACK ON THE TEMPLARS which began in 1307 was one of the most shocking events in the history of the late medieval west. As we saw in chapter 8, the Templars were famous across the Christian world and beyond. For nearly two centuries, Templar brothers had played a distinguished part in some of the most dramatic battles and sieges in the near east. They had taken on Saladin at Hattin in 1187, slogged through the flooded Nile Delta during the disastrous Egyptian crusades of 1217–21 and 1249–50, and been the last men standing when the Mamluks overran Acre in 1291. The Templars had also developed an institutional expertise in financial services, as moneylenders, accountants and civil servants; they were employed by the French crown to handle important aspects of public finance. Their non-fighting brothers had houses all over the west, in virtually every kingdom, from England and France to the German states, Sicily and Hungary, where their patrons included kings, queens and the highest nobility. So for the French to set their sights on taking down this institution was no small task. But that, with the connivance of Paris's scholars, is what they did.

About two weeks after their initial meeting with de Nogaret at Notre-Dame, on 25–26 October, the Parisian masters were called to a second conference, held at the Templars' own French headquarters – a great, turreted urban fortress in the region of Paris today known as Le Marais.* This time almost all the scholars in the university were called: the regent masters (those who were qualified to teach students), the non-regent masters (who had passed all their examinations but did not teach) and the bachelors (those who had completed half of their studies). Having previously been presented with the case against the Templars, they were now to hear the government's evidence, in the form of confessions read publicly to them by dozens of Templar brothers, including grand master de Molay himself.

The confessions had been exacted under torture. For a fortnight the Templars had been worked on by King Philip's best interrogators, led by his personal confessor, the Dominican friar William of Paris. They had been deprived of sleep, starved, shackled, isolated and beaten. Some had been burned with fire or stretched with the strappado. They had been physically and psychologically broken down until they agreed they were guilty. And now, in long and tragic sequence, these frightened men were brought out and deposed before the academics. One by one they recited their confessions. Then they were taken back to their cells. When the scholars were packed off back to their studies after two long days of bearing witness to this horror-show, they went with de Molay and his brothers' horrible stories ringing in their ears. Yet still this was not the last the scholars would hear of the Templar affair. Soon they would be called upon to give their official judgement on its merits.

Although it took less than three weeks to carry out the initial arrests, and to intimidate the Templars' leaders into confessing

---

* There is no longer any trace of this magnificent building, which was last used as a prison for Louis XVI and Marie Antoinette in the French Revolution, before being torn down in the nineteenth century. Its site is commemorated only through the name of Baron Haussmann's Square du Temple.

their supposed misdeeds, the case soon spiralled out of any single person's control. The pope of the day, Clement V (r. 1305–14), was a Gascon-born milksop who had been elected under French political pressure in the expectation that he would be directly biddable from Paris; he spent his whole reign in France.* But even Clement could not be seen to simply roll over and allow the Templars to be destroyed by a secular prince. Clement therefore attempted to stall Philip's assault by claiming the investigation into Templar corruption as his own, and extending it to every sovereign territory in western Christendom.[5] Two parallel investigations – one into individual Templar misconduct and another into the order as a whole – were set up, and took several years to report back, from lands as far afield as Ireland and Cyprus. During that time the Templars in France were able to organize a collective legal response.

In the course of this, once again both sides appealed to the University of Paris. In or around early February 1308, three months after the first arrests, an anonymous, open letter known as *A Lament for the Templars* was addressed to the doctors and scholars of the university, protesting that the imprisonments had been sudden, arbitrary and outrageous, alleging that many Templars had died under torture and that their bodies had been secretly buried, and complaining that the allegations against the order were false, illogical and absurd. The letter noted that at the time the French Templars were arrested, around one hundred brothers were languishing in an Egyptian jail, refusing all offers to convert to Islam and be released: hardly the behaviour of an unchristian rabble. The letter was a spirited defence of the order, probably written by a secular clerk, and it was a bitter rebuke to the bullying tactics deployed by the French government.[6] But it preceded – or perhaps prompted – a direct response in kind.

* In 1309 Clement officially moved the headquarters of the papacy from Rome to the city of Avignon, theoretically in the independent kingdom of Arles but in reality strongly influenced by France. Seven popes, all of them French, would reside there in what was known as 'Babylonian Captivity', until Gregory XI returned the papal seat to Rome in 1376. A further two antipopes subsequently attempted to rule the Church from Avignon between 1378 and 1410.

In late February a set of seven technical questions written in the king's name were sent to the university's regent and non-regent masters of theology. In dense legalese these asked the masters for their collective opinion on matters pertaining to the right – or the duty – of the French crown to proceed against heretics and apostates in French territory. The scholars were asked to ponder whether a secular ruler was 'obliged or permitted' to act when he 'hears the name of the Lord blasphemed and the Catholic faith rejected by heretics, schismatics or other unbelievers'. They were asked to judge whether the Templars – 'a unique sect composed of many individuals so horrible, so abominable' – could be judged under secular law as knights, rather than only under canon law as churchmen. They were asked whether the fact that 'five hundred and more' Templars had by that stage confessed to misdeeds meant that the Order itself ought to be considered hopelessly corrupt, and whether it was possible to know just how deeply that corruption ran when (so it was claimed) the abuses carried out in the Order were historic as well as recent.[7] These and other leading questions were dangled in front of Paris's theologians, with the obvious intention of securing their further intellectual backing for what was in reality a foregone conclusion.

On 25 March 1308, the reply came. And it made clear where the scholars' sympathies lay. The masters praised 'the most Serene and Christian prince Philip, by the grace of God illustrious king of the Franks' for being 'inflamed with the zeal of the holy faith'. They then launched into a masterclass of evasion, bet-hedging and 'up-to-a-point'-ism. It was hard to argue, said the masters, that the crown had any business judging the Templars, for that right properly belonged to the Church. However, the masters' subsequent answers included so many caveats that Philip's ministers could drive a cart and horses through them. Describing themselves as the 'humble, devoted chaplains... always ready and willing to manifest grateful and devoted service to his royal majesty', the scholars argued that while the pope had the ultimate right to judge the Templars, the confessions already extracted meant that 'a very strong suspicion has been engendered... that all the members of the Order are heretics or sympathisers… that the said heresy was rampant in the Order… [and] this should be sufficient to cause people to condemn and hate them'. Their possessions ought to be used to further the defence of the Church, said the masters, but 'regarding who should look after them, it seems to us that they ought to be collected in the way that will best serve the end.' In short, they equivocated sufficiently that Philip could claim both that he had taken proper legal advice and that he was justified in doing as he pleased. The masters signed off with the plea that 'these [answers] be acceptable to your royal Majesty'. They hoped, they said, that 'a wound that is so scandalous and horrible in the eyes of the whole of Christianity be quickly avenged in accordance with your holy wish.'[8] It was a whitewash.

Perhaps the masters' craven response was understandable. King Philip was undoubtedly a man to be feared, and in his reign to date he had shown no compunction about persecuting to ruin or death those who displeased him. Many of the masters of theology in Paris were also members of monastic orders which, like the Templars, were subject by papal oversight and therefore also potential targets for royal attacks. They had no wish to see the Templars crushed – but equally had no interest in drawing down further wrath on their own orders. What was more, they were pedantic churchmen who had a natural inclination to see heresy wherever they looked. There were one or two dissenting voices within the university – such as an aged Italian hermit-scholar who signed himself Augustine Triumphus and composed a personal demolition of the government's case against the Templars.[9] But by and large, the scholars left the government to go about its dubious business, hoping that having said their piece, they would be left alone to continue their studies and teaching. They were not the first academics in history to make a quiet life their overriding priority. Nor would they be the last.

AFTER A LONG AND BRUTAL LEGAL and political tussle, Philip IV succeeded in having the Templars wound up. In March 1312, at the council of Vienne, Pope Clement declared the Order beyond repair. In March 1314 Jacques de Molay was burned to death in Paris; he died calling on God to avenge him. His death was the final act in a dreadful saga which reflected badly on all involved. And it is remembered today as a turning point in medieval history, when a secular prince took aim against the power of the papacy and scored a difficult but decisive victory.

In accounts of the Templar affair, the role of the University of Paris is usually mentioned only in passing. Yet the opinion of its masters was considered to be of crucial importance by all sides in the debate. This was by no means inevitable. Although there had been semi-formal gatherings and communities of scholars in Paris since the middle of the twelfth century, the university had only been officially founded in 1231 by Pope Gregory IX. It was therefore less than a century old in 1307, and one of only a handful of universities in the world – its nearest rivals being at Oxford and Bologna. Yet despite its youth, this institution was clearly regarded as an important pillar of the establishment, and the opinions of its brightest and best scholars carried political as well as academic importance. In the great scheme of the Middle Ages, this mattered. The University of Paris had in short order become a forum where great questions of theology, society and government were analysed and answered.* It was also, incidentally, a useful recruiting-ground for the French royal administration, which from time to time poached professors to act as civil servants. Education at a university was not yet a standard part of growing up for middle- and upper-class youths; nor was it yet usual to find a university in every major town. Nevertheless, at the beginning of the fourteenth century medieval universities like the one in Paris were beginning to develop into something like the institutions we recognize in the twenty-first century. And they were starting to wield significant power, becoming hubs of scholarship and intellectual enquiry whose discoveries shaped the world outside

---

* Before Philip engaged the Parisian scholars in the Templar affair, he had also dragged them into his dispute with Boniface VIII in 1303, compelling every member of the university to sign papers aligning themselves with his position over that of the pope. See Crawford, 'The University of Paris and the Trial of the Templars', p. 115.

them, and whose legacy endures to this day.* To understand how this came to pass, we must look at the intellectual and cultural tradition that produced them, beginning in the sixth century AD, when the classical world was collapsing and its traditions of fearless academic enquiry slowly disappearing in the west.

The Word of God

WHEN ISIDORE, FUTURE ARCHBISHOP OF SEVILLE and one of the greatest scholars of first millennium AD, was a young man, he went to school. This was not exactly radical, but it was a privilege. Education in the late sixth century was the preserve of the well-to-do, and it was afforded to Isidore only because his parents were members of the old Roman-Spanish elite. At the beginning of the Middle Ages the Iberian peninsula was under Visigothic rule, but an old-fashioned 'Roman-style' education could still be found for an intelligent child. So young Isidore was lucky. And like most high-achievers throughout history, he had the wit to add hard work to good fortune. He made the most of his schooling, devouring learning and setting no limits on his interests.

Isidore's classroom was in Seville's cathedral, where his elder brother Leander was bishop. However, the curriculum he studied there was not strictly Christian. In fact, the basic syllabus taught in Seville and all other schools like it dated back more than one thousand years, to long before Christ was even born. It was a classical programme of study that would have been just as familiar to Aristotle in the fourth century BC as it would have been to Cicero in the first century BC, Marcus Aurelius in the second century AD

---

* Today France boasts around one hundred public universities and two hundred and fifty *grandes écoles*. The United Kingdom has more than one hundred. Germany has just under four hundred. India has more than one thousand. China has nearly three thousand. In the United States there are more than five thousand universities or colleges. In virtually every country in the world a graduate education, usually consisting of at least three years' study at a university (or equivalent), is considered to be at least a useful personal asset and more often an essential prerequisite to a professional or public career. Universities today are the engines of research in fields ranging from law, literature and business management to medicine, engineering and computing. All of this can be traced directly back to the Middle Ages.

or Boethius in the sixth century AD. Its pillars were the so-called seven liberal arts ('liberal' because they were once considered suitable for free people, rather than slaves). These were subdivided into two groups. First came the *trivium*, the arts of expression and argument: grammar, logic and rhetoric. Then came the *quadrivium*, which consisted of the arts of calculation: arithmetic, geometry, astronomy and music. Although the *trivium* and *quadrivium* did not cover the whole scheme of human knowledge – eager young minds would also be expected to apply themselves to theology, medicine and law – they were nevertheless the bedrock of a formal education. Boethius described the *quadrivium* as the foundation-stone on which all philosophical research into the nature of the world rested, and few serious medieval thinkers ever departed from that assumption.*

Isidore took to his education with relish. He had no problem with the *trivium* and *quadrivium*. He also mastered theology. He studied Latin, Hebrew and Greek. He roamed hungrily around topics ranging from war, law and theology to shipping, geography and home economics. As an adult he would be driven by the belief that he could hold at his fingertips all the knowledge in the world. His sheer aptitude for learning dazzled those who knew him. Isidore's friend Braulio described him as 'a man educated in every kind of expression, so that in the quality of his speech he was suited to both the ignorant audience and the learned. Indeed, he was famous for his incomparable eloquence.'[10]

In its own right, Isidore's natural cleverness made him remarkable. He wrote at least twenty-four books during his lifetime, which included historical chronicles, studies of natural scientific phenomena, mathematical textbooks, potted biographies of Church fathers, collections of epigrams and his *Etymologies*, a giant encyclopedia in which he aimed to describe everything an educated person ought to know, ranging from the feeding habits

---

* Isidore certainly did not. In his most famous book, the *Etymologies*, the seven liberal arts were the very first thing he discussed, even before the letters of the alphabet. See Barney, Stephen A., Lewis, W.J., Beach, J.A, Berghof, Oliver (eds.), *The Etymologies of Isidore of Seville* (Cambridge: 2006), p. 39.

of hedgehogs to the geographical arrangement of the world's continents.[11] (Not for nothing is Isidore today considered the patron saint of the internet.) Any one of these would have been a respectable work on its own. Taken together they represented an incredible body of scholarship. And the *Etymologies* was a true masterpiece, treasured by generations of future readers for the breadth and colour of its insights. It was one of the most widely read and influential books in the medieval west.[12]

The huge, enduring success of the *Etymologies* was no fluke. For despite being taught in the Church, Isidore had a massive working knowledge of both Christian and pagan authorities, and could quote just as freely from Aristotle, Cato, Plato and Pliny as he could St Ambrose and St Augustine. His ability to weave together the greatest writers – jurists, theologians, philosophers, poets and polemicists – from the disappearing classical age and dawning Christian one lay at the heart of Isidore's genius. He realized that other scholars of his time felt queasy about mixing Christian and non-Christian sources. But he did not really care. A poem usually attributed to Isidore addressed such concerns: 'You see meadows filled with thorns and rich with flowers./ If you do not wish to take the thorns, then take the roses.'[13] Isidore understood that to be a polymath, one could not afford to be too much of a dogmatist.

So in pure academic terms, Isidore was a highly influential scholar. But he had a hand in politics too. His brother Leander, who had overseen his schooling, was a statesman as well as a churchman, who had befriended Pope Gregory the Great (another superb scholar) as well as the Visigothic royal family that ruled Spain; under Leander's guidance, King Reccared I converted from Arian Christianity to Roman Catholicism: this would later be recognized as a foundational event in Spanish history. And Isidore kept the family's involvement in politics alive. After Leander died, Reccared appointed Isidore as his successor to the bishopric of Seville, and from that point on, Isidore was close to the royal court, where his learned counsel carried great weight.[14]

In all, Isidore served as bishop of Seville for more than thirty years. Towards the end of his life, in 633–4, he presided over a

Church conference known as the Fourth Council of Toledo, which set policies that would have a lasting impact on the cultural and political spirit of Christian Iberia during the Middle Ages. It tightened discriminatory laws against Spanish Jews, and promised close ties between the Church in Spain and its secular Christian rulers. Perhaps most significantly for Isidore himself, the council also commanded that bishops should establish schools alongside their cathedrals, in imitation of the one which had set him along his path to scholarly and political prominence. In part this was an acknowledgement that all the good things in Isidore's life had begun with education. But it also pointed the way ahead in a much broader sense: to a medieval western world in which the Catholic Church would exercise a monopoly over schooling, would provide the institutional environment in which western intellectuals would exist, and would dictate permissible – and forbidden – avenues of study.

FROM ISIDORE'S DAY IN THE SIXTH century until the end of the Middle Ages (and beyond) the Church had a firm grip on western education and scholarship. As much as anything else this was a matter of practicality. Like Judaism and, as it would soon transpire, Islam, Christianity was a religion rooted in the word of God, and His word was transmitted primarily through being written, read and heard. St Paul, the apostle who did more than anyone else to publicize Christ's teachings, was an educated man with a working knowledge of several languages and a healthy smattering of philosophy. The next 500 years produced many more great thinkers and writers like him. Saintly scholars such as Augustine, Ambrose and St Jerome were load-bearing walls in the intellectual and liturgical architecture of the Church – and by extension in the lives of millions of medieval Christians. In the fifth century St Jerome was asked by a friend for advice in how to bring up a young girl called Paula, whose parents had marked her down for a career as an abbess. He was forthright on the importance of education: 'Have a set of letters made for her of boxwood or of ivory and tell her their names,' he wrote. 'Let her play with them, making play a road to learning... Offer her prizes for spelling, tempting her with such trifling gifts as please young children. Let her have companions too in her lessons, so that she may seek to rival them and be stimulated by any praise they win.'[15] The Church had been built by scholars, and it never lost interest in producing them.

Yet the Church had more to gain from scholarship than simply passing on the Good News. Right from the start of the Middle Ages, religious institutions were major landowners. This meant they had practical needs in worldly fields like land conveyancing and administration. Popes had taxes to collect and kings and emperors with whom to argue by long-distance post. Bishops had dioceses full of priests with whom they needed to communicate the latest matters of doctrinal or behavioural reform. Monasteries had obligations to their benefactors past and present, and needed to keep track of whose soul they were meant to be praying for on any given day. (They also had choirs, which needed young boys who could read or understand music well enough to sing the treble parts in their daily offices and Masses.) Bureaucracy never ended. So the Church always needed literate people among its staff at every level.

Obviously, the surest way to maintain a supply of smart, literate people attuned to the latest approved doctrine was to educate them 'in-house' – which was exactly how Isidore had come to his education in Seville, and why at the Fourth Council of Toledo he advocated rolling out a formal system of cathedral schools. It was also why scholarship remained alive in the west after the Roman Empire had retreated beyond the Balkans. It was why, wherever there was a cathedral or a monastery, there tended to be some form of school, a scriptorium and a library.* And it was why the Rule of St Benedict demanded monks spend several hours every day reading the Bible and other religious writings.[16] Throughout the Middle Ages there were monasteries and cathedrals that

---

* Some monastic libraries were very grand indeed: Cluny Abbey library in its heyday would have nearly six hundred books.

based their whole 'brand identity' around high standards of literacy. In the sixth century the Roman statesman Cassiodorus founded the abbey of Vivarium (near Squillace in southern Italy) as a centre of study and the preservation of both Christian and classical texts; 500 years later the newly founded abbey of Bec in Normandy was considered such a magnet for learning that the chronicler Orderic Vitalis thought 'almost every monk seemed a philosopher'.[17]

But the Church did not just educate philosophers. Although going to school was an indispensable grounding for a career in the Church, monasteries and cathedral schools also came to be training grounds for those who needed to be literate, but had ambitions in the secular world: practicing law, doing business, or working as scribes in the civil bureaucracies that attended kings and other landowners.* One very well-trodden path to power throughout the medieval period was to combine the life of a scholar with that of a minister. The Biblical scholar Augustine, prior of St Andrew's abbey in Rome, was selected by Pope Gregory I to lead the famous English mission of 597 which persuaded king Aethelbert of Kent to embrace Christianity and kickstarted the conversion of Saxon England. The mathematician and astronomer Gerbert of Aurillac, who brought the abacus to Europe in the late tenth century and wrote several well-regarded mathematical textbooks, rose to the papacy itself, as Pope Sylvester II. Then there was Alcuin of York, the Englishman who sat for many years at the right hand of Charlemagne. The chronicler Einhard described Alcuin as the most learned man in the whole world; even if this was hyperbole, Alcuin was undoubtedly the most influential public servant of Charlemagne's reign. The emperor took seriously his views on clerical reform in the 780s and on paganism in the 790s. He consulted him about

---

* The experience of going to school, then as now, could be either pleasurable or wholly disagreeable, often depending on the character of the teachers. One nun who taught at the school for girls at Wimborne Minster in south-west England at the turn of the eighth century was so foul to her students that when she died they jumped up and down on her grave. See Orme, Nicholas, *Medieval Schools: Roman Britain to Renaissance England* (New Haven: 2006), p. 24.

matters of heretical doctrine. Alcuin was encouraged to pursue his programme of manuscript copying, which helped disseminate learned texts around the empire. And, like Isidore, he consciously used his political power to serve education itself: cultivating his own private group of students at the palace school at Aachen, and making reforms to the syllabus there which were later mimicked by monastic and cathedral schools that flourished during the Carolingian age and afterwards. By the turn of the millennium, a golden age of education and scholarship was arriving. It was a good time to be a student.

Yet paradoxically, it was also a bad time to be a scholar. For although scholarship in the west was encouraged, respected, patronized and protected during the Carolingian age, during the early Middle Ages the Latin Christian world was also becoming increasingly inward-looking: suspicious of other faiths, other modes of thinking and other authorities. Since scholars were overwhelmingly to be found in monasteries and cathedrals, scholarship as a whole took on an increasingly concentrated Christian flavour, in which the writings of non- and pre-Christians were viewed with mounting suspicion. Whereas in the sixth century Isidore of Seville had roved voraciously across the writings of Greek and Roman pagans as well as the early Church fathers, by the turn of the millennium, this sort of omnivorous scholarship was firmly out of favour. Between the sixth and eleventh centuries, much of the wisdom of the ancients was gradually lost to the Latin world. Greek, which had been petering out in the west even during the sixth century, was effectively dead to western writers by the eleventh. Foundational philosophers such as Plato* were all but unknown.[18] It took until the twelfth century for the intellectual floodgates to re-open, and pagan knowledge to come washing back in.

---

* Had Boethius not been executed for treason in AD 524 (see above, chapter 2), the story might have been rather different: before his early death, he had been planning to translate the complete works of both Plato and Aristotle into Latin.

Translation and Renaissance

ALTHOUGH WESTERN EUROPE DID NOT CONSIDER itself an intellectual backwater around the end of the first millennium AD, the reality was that by the year 1000 it lagged far behind other parts of the world. The Carolingian manuscript-machine at Aachen, cathedral schools dotted across France, England and Germany, and monastic libraries stocked chiefly with texts by Christian writers were all well and good. But any traveller who struck out east for the great cities of the Arab and Persian world would quickly realize where the real engine of global intellectual enquiry lay: in the lands of the caliphs and the realm of Islam.

Although Islam had begun as a religion of merchants, it was by no means anti-intellectual. From the time of the Abbasid revolution in AD 750, education was highly prized. Scholars were generously patronized. And critically, scholarship was detached from religion, allowing eastern Christians and Jews to contribute heavily to the collective body of knowledge within the Islamic empire. Libraries such as Baghdad's House of Wisdom* compiled collections containing hundreds of thousands of manuscripts, translated into Arabic from almost every language in the literate world. Further hubs of education and study existed in cities like Cordoba and Seville in Andalusia, Ctesiphon and Gundeshapur in Persia, Edessa and Nisibis in Syria, and Palermo in Sicily. As the Abbasid period wore on, Muslim-ruled cities also became home to religious schools known as *madrassas* – the oldest of which was attached to a grand mosque in Fez (modern Morocco), where it was founded by the wealthy merchant's daughter Fatima al-Fihri in the mid-ninth century AD. In terms of scale, breadth and sheer force of curiosity, little on earth could match the academic institutions of the *dar al-Islam*, which between the seventh and thirteenth centuries stretched like a string of pearls between Mesopotamia in the east and Iberia in the west.

---

* Wrecked with such wanton violence in 1258 by the Mongols under Hülagü Khan – see chapter 9.

This rich intellectual environment nurtured some of the greatest thinkers in world history, from the ninth-century Persian mathematician al-Khwarizmi, known as the 'father of algebra',* and his contemporary, the brilliant chemist Jabir ibn-Hayyan, to the eleventh-century medic Ibn Sina ('Avicenna') and twelfth century geniuses such as the Andalusian map-maker Muhammad al-Idrisi and philosopher Ibn Rushd ('Averroës'). This period is today known as the Golden Age of Islam, not least because of its intellectual achievements. Yet despite the fact that the Islamic world directly abutted the Christian realms of the Mediterranean, between the eighth and eleventh centuries very little trickled across. It was not until the turn of the twelfth century – not coincidentally, the dawn of the crusading era, when Islamic cities with scholarly communities like Toledo, Córdoba, Palermo and Antioch came under Christian control, and Damascus, Alexandria and Baghdad were suddenly more accessible than before – that the intellectual boundaries thrown up between the Arab and Christian blocs began to collapse, and scholarship both new and forgotten began flooding from the Arab world to the west.

ONE OF THE EARLY HERALDS OF this new age of information exchange was an eleventh-century Benedictine monk called Hermann the Lame (*Hermannus Contractus*) who lived in a monastery on the island of Reichenau in Lake Constance (today at the border between Germany, Austria and Switzerland, in the northern Alps). Hermann was born around 1013 and he grew up a profoundly disabled child: he had very weak arms and hands, he could never walk and his speech was extremely stunted, and he needed assistance even to change his position in a chair.[19] But in about 1020, when he was seven years old, his parents placed him in the care of Reichenau's monks. And there, despite (or indeed

---

* The etymology of algebra is, obviously, western-bastardized Arabic, deriving from *al-jabr*, loosely meaning 'the reuniting of broken parts'.

because of) his physical afflictions, Hermann devoted himself to his studies and grew into a brilliant scholar. In the words of his biographer and disciple Berthold of Reichenau, Hermann had 'a virtually complete grasp of the difficulties of all the arts and the subtleties of poetic mitre.' Like Isidore before him, he ranged easily across history, mathematics and natural sciences, and he was a superb composer of hymns. What was more, he was an unexpectedly brilliant raconteur: Berthold noted that although Hermann's 'feeble mouth, tongue and lips produced only broken and scarcely intelligible sounds of words... he proved an eloquent and diligent teacher, very lively and humorous'.[20] He was also, wrote Berthold, patient, modest, chaste and vegetarian. He was a model scholar.

Although Hermann the Lame was at home in most fields of study, one of his greatest loves was for astronomy. As we have seen, stargazing was a core subject in the *quadrivium*; calculating the movements of the heavens relative to the earth demanded advanced mathematical skills, but promised to yield deep insights into the fabric of God's universe. And it could also have vital practical applications, for astronomers could predict seasonal changes to the length of days and the shifting ratio of daylight to night-time hours – useful indeed for monks who organized their entire lives around the regular chanting of Masses and offices. Hermann used a combination of careful empirical observations and advanced mathematics to work on practical problems relating to timekeeping: calculating the diameter of the earth and the exact length of a lunar month and drawing up star charts illustrating the shifts in the heavens from month to month.

Throughout human history, many devices have been invented to help people map, model and track the changing patterns of the sky, ranging from sarsen stones to the atomic clock. But in the Middle Ages, the most popular was the astrolabe – a mechanical device usually made from metal or wood, which allowed a trained user to measure the position of the stars and planets and to calculate local time and geographical latitude. The astrolabe had been invented by the Greeks in either the second or third century BC, and many different variations had been produced over the centuries by scholars in Byzantium and the Arab world. It had a particular religious use to Muslims, for it could help ascertain the direction of Mecca from anywhere on earth, allowing the proper conduct of daily prayers. It was effectively a finely tuned medieval GPS system which was studied, refined, updated and written about by countless clever men and women throughout the medieval world.*

Until the turn of the millennium the astrolabe was something of a mystery to western Christian scholars. But during his time at Reichenau, Hermann managed to obtain an incomplete manuscript partially describing its workings. This document somehow made its way to his little island from the caliphate of Cordoba, probably via the monastery of Santa Maria de Ripoll, about a hundred kilometres north of Barcelona. It may have been written by Gerbert of Aurillac, the French scholar who became Pope Sylvester II. Whatever the case, it contained scientific intelligence which was well known in the Islamic world, but had seldom if ever been circulated north of the Alps and Pyrenees. Hermann had a scoop.

And he made the most of it. A keen tinkerer, adept at 'constructing clocks, musical instruments and mechanical devices', Hermann used the partial information in the manuscript to work out how an astrolabe might be built.[21] He then redrafted and completed the text to record his findings for posterity. This was in itself a significant achievement for scholarship in Christian Europe, for in the following centuries the astrolabe would transform timekeeping and navigation, ultimately opening the way for the Portuguese voyages of discovery and the pivot to the New World. And in the immediate context of the eleventh century Hermann's work on the astrolabe was just as significant, for it signalled a coming scientific revolution. In Hermann's day the transmission of Islamic scholarship to the Christian world was still in its infancy, and his work on the astrolabe was highly unusual. Yet within a couple of generations,

---

* Among these was Geoffrey Chaucer, who in the fourteenth century wrote a whole book, his *Treatise on the Astrolabe*, to describe its functions for his son.

work like Hermann's would be all the rage. Driven by new networks of information-sharing, Christian scholarship in Europe was on the cusp of a dramatic transformation.

ALMOST EXACTLY ONE HUNDRED YEARS AFTER Hermann the Lame fiddled with astrolabes on Reichenau, another talented scholar struck out for the intellectual heartlands of the Arab-speaking world. His name was Gerard of Cremona, and he had been born, raised and educated in northern Italy. Like Hermann, Gerard was fascinated by the movements of the celestial bodies, and devoted much of his life to studying astronomy. But unlike Hermann, whose physical condition meant he was confined to his monastery, Gerard sensed that if he wished to grow as a scholar he needed to go in search of new frontiers. Specifically, Gerard yearned for a way to read the great classical scientist Claudius Ptolemy. Ptolemy had been a subject or citizen of the Roman Empire, who lived in second-century AD Alexandria and wrote in Greek. His foundational work on astronomy was known as the *Almagest*, which laid out a mathematically informed model of the solar system in which the earth sat in the middle of the revolving planets, moon and sun. Of course, we now know this system to be wrong, but it dominated scientific thought for more than a thousand years until the end of the Middle Ages. So to Gerard there was no better authority available.

By the 1100s, when Gerard became interested in astronomy, the *Almagest* was known only second-hand in the west, and was not available in Latin translation. It was, however, extant in Arabic. And as luck would have it, a vast new corpus of Arabic literature had just fallen into the hands of a western ruler. In 1085 the *Reconquista* king of Castile and León, Alfonso VI, had conquered the city of Toledo from its Muslim rulers. Once one of the finest cities of Umayyad Andalusia, Toledo was full of libraries, which contained Arabic-language editions of classical texts unavailable anywhere else in Europe. So, in the 1140s, Gerard of Cremona moved from Italy to Castile and headed for Toledo. When he arrived, he got straight down to work: learning Arabic and joining a scholarly community that was busy translating the treasures of the city's libraries into languages that could be read throughout the west.

During his time at Toledo Gerard translated nearly one hundred important scientific studies out of Arabic. He laboured long and hard to produce an authoritative edition of the *Almagest*, which would become the standard translation in circulation for the rest of the Middle Ages. He worked on mathematical treatises by Greek giants such as Archimedes and Euclid, and on original Islamic works by astronomers such as the ninth-century mathematician and civil engineer al-Farghani and the tenth-century philosopher and legal writer al-Farabi. He translated the esteemed medical specialist al-Razi and the physicist and the so-called 'father of optics' ibn al-Haytham. And he stayed in Toledo until he died in 1187, by which time his work had contributed mightily to the burgeoning reputation of that city. According to the English philosopher Daniel of Morley, who met Gerard in his pomp and talked astrology with him, Toledo in the late twelfth century was home to 'the wisest philosophers in all the world'.[22]

Philosophers. The plural was important. For Gerard of Cremona was never working alone. Rather, he was part of a buzzing scholarly community, all eagerly rendering into Latin and Catalan texts that had been lost to western minds for hundreds of years. An Englishman called Robert of Ketton went to Castile to work on mathematics and astronomy but ended up translating Islamic religious texts, including the Qur'an and a chronicle of the deeds of the early caliphs. Another Italian scholar also called Gerard translated the works of Avicenna – including his massive medical encyclopedia, the *Canon of Medicine*. A Scotsman known simply as Michael Scot translated works by writers ranging from Aristotle to Averroës; Michael subsequently earned great patronage and a court position from Frederick II Hohenstaufen, the insatiably inquisitive Holy Roman Emperor who had his own lifelong passion for science, mathematics and philosophy.* Meanwhile, Toledo was a fruitful place for Jewish scholars to work, particularly during the enlightened reign of Alfonso X the Wise of Castile (r. 1252–84), who patronized Toledo's translators, including large numbers of Jews, encouraging them to render as much material as possible into Castilian vernacular rather than Latin. In doing so, he – and they – helped to lay the foundations for the Spanish language, which is today spoken by around half a billion people worldwide. As they worked, the Toledo translators were producing the textual core of a new age in western thought, which burst into life during the high Middle Ages.

THE TRANSLATION MOVEMENT WAS A PIVOTAL event, because it ushered in a period that historians call the 'twelfth century renaissance'.[23] The return of classical works to the western mainstream – which would not have been possible without people like Gerard of Cremona – shook up whole spheres of thought, radically transforming academic disciplines including philosophy, theology and law. But it also had tangible, real-world effects, as technologies developed on the basis of new knowledge, and in the spirit of an exciting new scientific age, found their way into ordinary people's lives.

Within the traditional centres of study – monasteries and cathedral schools – the twelfth century saw an explosion in the sheer number of books produced. Many of these were carefully wrought Latin copies of ancient texts – the Bible, of course, the works of the Church fathers, service books for use in church and the works of the early medieval geniuses, Boethius, Isidore of Seville

* Frederick's interest in scholarly matters was legendary. He swapped maths problems with the Egyptian sultan al-Kamil, wrote his own works on natural science and was said by the Italian chronicler Salimbene di Adam to carry out bizarre and sometimes very cruel empirical experiments at court. In one, he supposedly had a man starved to death in a barrel in the hope that he would be able to detect the moment at which the soul left the body; in another he had two men fed identical meals, then sent to perform different activities before they were killed and the contents of their stomachs examined; in a third he ordered a pair of twin babies be raised without anyone speaking to them or fussing over them, to see whether they would speak the primitive language of Eden. The twins died of neglect.

and the northern English monk-historian the Venerable Bede, who in the early eighth century had written the huge *Ecclesiastical History of the English People*. But alongside these now appeared works by Aristotle and Euclid, Galen and Proclus. Roman poets like Virgil, Ovid, Lucan and Terence, and rhetoricians like Cicero, Cato and Seneca did not require translation, of course – but interest in them was revived, and their works were copied and pored over by medieval grammarians, who devoted themselves to analysing classical Latin and creating technical linguistic handbooks based on their findings.[24]

As old works flooded anew into western libraries, trends in scholarship and creative writing were also transformed. In theology and philosophy, Aristotle's influence was deeply felt with the rise of scholasticism: an approach to Biblical study that emphasized logical deduction, with readers encouraged to interrogate texts deeply and reconcile paradoxes and contradictions by resorting to reasoning and structured argument. In the spirit of knowledge compilation and interrogation, a Paris-based scholar called Peter Lombard (d. 1160) wrote his *Sentences*, a massive collection of Biblical passages and supporting material from other Church authorities, organized on fundamental Christian themes from Creation to the mystery of the Trinity. From its completion in around 1150, the *Sentences* became the foundational textbook for all theology students until the end of the Middle Ages. Future generations of great medieval scholars including Thomas Aquinas (see below), Duns Scotus and William of Ockham would all begin their academic careers by writing commentaries on the *Sentences*, and no theologian could consider himself a master until he had wrestled with it.

But it was not only high academic discourse which was transformed in the twelfth century. This was also a time of vigorous writing in less abstract fields – not least romance and history. As we saw in chapter 7, the twelfth century saw a surge in knightly romances and epic storytelling – and it was no coincidence that many of the tales that were invented and popularized in the high Middle Ages reached back to classical times for their subject matter or plots. Athens and Rome, whose great figures had been rescued from the fog of posterity by the translators, now inspired the tales that were told by the fires in lords' halls, and the songs minstrels composed as they wandered the landscape.

At the same time, there was a new vogue for writing huge chronicles of political events both ancient and modern. Hermann the Lame, our early pioneer of interest in the astrolabe in the eleventh century, composed an epic history that narrated the thousand years that had passed between the birth of Christ and his own times, with a focus in its latter chapters on German affairs and the wrangling between emperors and popes; the chronicle was continued after his death by his friend Berthold of Reichenau. Many more would follow his lead. The twelfth and thirteenth centuries saw the historical tradition blossom, along with genres including biography, travelogue and treatises on good government.

In Britain, the scholar and courtier Gerald of Wales wrote many learned and at times hilarious accounts of his travels around Wales and Ireland, and his experiences at the English royal court. The multi-authored *Grandes Chroniques de France*, compiled from the thirteenth century at the French abbey of St-Denis, was a singular achievement, translating earlier medieval sources from Latin into French, and telling the epic history of France and the French kings from the (supposed) westward migration of the Trojans to the time of Louis IX, who originally commissioned the project. Meanwhile, there may have been no greater individual chronicler in the whole Middle Ages than Matthew Paris, a thirteenth-century monk at the notably learned English monastery in St Albans, whose works of English history started with the Creation and worked their way down to the travails of his king, Henry III. They were illuminated with glorious illustrations and maps in Paris' own hand.

And then there were advances beyond the realms of science and literature. It was not only the astrolabe that came west during the twelfth century. From the 1180s, windmills began to appear across the European landscape – devices which harnessed what we now call 'renewable energy' to grind corn into flour – but which depended on an impressive degree of mathematical engineering to build.[25] New clocks were invented: elaborate devices powered by water or weights, which marked the hours without lengthening or shortening them according to the amount of daylight. From the thirteenth century, scholars like the Englishman Roger Bacon began to record recipes for gunpowder – an invention whose arrival in the west would in time come to be associated symbolically with the end of the Middle Ages. All of these inventions and many more besides emerged from the reinvigorated twelfth century. At the root of them all lay education, scholarship and study – still very much the preserve of churchmen, but more connected than ever before to the secular world outside the cloister.

Rise of the Universities

THE TYPICAL SCHOLAR AT THE BEGINNING of the twelfth century tended to be a brilliant individual, generally working in a monastery or cathedral school, itinerant and in contact with other thinkers and writers, but connected to an institution whose sole purpose was something other than the pure pursuit of knowledge. They included people like the German abbess Hildegard of Bingen, a bright German nun prone to magnificent holy visions, and a prolific composer of liturgical music, morality plays, and tracts on medicine, natural science, health, herbology and theology; Adelard of Bath, who travelled in search of knowledge from his home city in the south-west of England to France, Sicily, Antioch and into Asia Minor; and Leonardo 'Fibonacci', the son of a twelfth-century merchant from Pisa who mastered the Hindi-Arab numeral system* when he saw it in use to good effect on his commercial travels around the Mediterranean.

All of these were great thinkers in their own right. But as the Middle Ages wore on, another sort of scholar came to prominence:

---

* i.e. using the numbers 1–9 and 0 as a place-holder, rather than calculating with unwieldy Roman numerals.

not the freelance monk or nun, or the wandering merchant, but the master – who was part of a community dedicated only to the business of study, debate, research and teaching at one of the great universities that were established across the west between the eleventh and fourteenth centuries.

ACCORDING TO TRADITION, THE FIRST UNIVERSITY to be established in the west was at Bologna in northern Italy. In the late eleventh century Bologna sat sandwiched between two great spheres of influence: to the north lay the Alps, and the territories ruled by German emperors; to the south, the papal states. Since there were few times during the later Middle Ages when popes and emperors were not squabbling, from the tenth century Bologna began to attract communities of lawyers – expert in either canon or civil law – who found the city a convenient base from which to attract business.

The official date of the University of Bologna's foundation is usually given as 1088, and although this may owe as much to tradition as hard institutional fact, it is certainly true that from around this date onwards law students had plenty to pore over there. Besides the practical business of mediating and litigating when emperors and popes were at one another's throats, the great Byzantine emperor Justinian's Digest had been rediscovered in the 1070s, to great academic excitement among the jurists of northern Italy. As we saw in chapter 3, the Digest had been a towering legal achievement when it was compiled, and along with the Codex and Institutes, it provided an authoritative guide to the entire body of Roman law as it had been understood during the sixth century AD. Now, at the close of the eleventh century, this vast trove of legal writing offered a tantalizing new basis for thinking about justice and governance. But to make it applicable and useful in the context of a world which had changed profoundly in the intervening 550 years, it also required analysis, commentary and interpretation. So there was plenty for legal students to work on, and no shortage of willing volunteers.

In the 1080s a Bologna-based jurist by the name of Irnerius began 'glossing' Roman law – literally copying it out and adding his own commentary either between the lines or in the margins – and lecturing on its many and various aspects. In 1084 Irnerius founded a school of jurisprudence, which began to attract students from all around Europe. Within a generation Bologna was known as the best place in the west to train as a lawyer, and Irnerius was applying his scholarship in the political world, in the service of the German emperor Henry V. When Pope Paschal II died in 1118, Henry wished to impose his own candidate as successor, despite stiff opposition from the college of cardinals. During the ensuing political tussle Henry hired Irnerius to prepare legal arguments in defence of his rights as emperor and the legitimacy of his man, the antipope Gregory X. Although this was a fight Henry lost – Gregory was excommunicated by the rival pope, Calixtus II, finally captured and imprisoned in monasteries until his death – the very fact of Irnerius' employment was a sign of the esteem in which Bologna legal scholars were already held. This reputation, and the sheer fact that so many lawyers were gathered in one place, was the basis for what became the university.

The mechanism by which Bologna became a university was essentially a process of unionization. Since many – perhaps most – of Bologna's legal scholars from the eleventh century onwards were non-citizens, they did not enjoy the full rights of citizenship, and were subject to onerous laws levied on foreigners. Natives of each different country living in Bologna were regarded as collective entities and punished en masse if one of their number broke the city's laws or defaulted on debt: a legal concept known as the right of reprisal. To resist this, Bologna's eleventh-century students therefore began to organize themselves into mutual aid societies, known in Latin as *universitas scholarium*, which in turn could act collectively as the *Studium*. Thus banded together, students were able to negotiate their collective rights and liberties with the city's authorities – with the implicit threat that they would all walk away from the city and deprive it of their economic custom if they did not get what they want. Students also found it convenient to negotiate as a bloc with their teachers, deciding what they would be taught and how much lecturers deserved to be paid, and censuring or sacking professors who offended them by dint of substandard teaching or unpopular opinions. It took some time for this informal system of student association to be recognized as a bona fide institution – it was only in 1158 that the Holy Roman Emperor Frederick I Barbarossa granted the law known as *Authentica Habita*, which conferred permanent privileges and rights on law students in Bologna and elsewhere.[26] But the elemental features of the medieval university had long since been created – and would soon be copied around Europe.

AS THE TAPS OF CLASSICAL LEARNING were turned on in the twelfth century, so more towns and cities began to see bodies of students collaborating, organizing and claiming institutional privileges for themselves in similar ways to the scholars of Bologna. From 1096 masters were receiving students in the small English settlement of Oxford. In Paris, from around 1150 a body of students and teachers hived off from the cathedral school at Notre-Dame and established what fifty years later was recognized as a university. The fortunes of these two illustrious institutions (today the University of Oxford and eleven different Parisian universities colloquially called the Sorbonne) were intertwined from the outset. Oxford benefitted hugely from Anglo-French political wrangling during the reigns of the Plantagenet king Henry II and Capetian monarch Louis VII: during a particularly sour patch in relations between the two in 1167 Henry ordered all English scholars to leave their studies in Paris, upon which many of them crossed the English Channel, migrated up the Thames valley and settled in Oxford, supercharging its academic profile and development.

There were plenty more besides. In the 1130s a university emerged in Salamanca, a beautiful cathedral city on the banks of the river Tormes in Castile-León. In the early thirteenth century dissatisfied students and teachers from Bologna migrated 120km north to set up a new institution in Padua. Around the same time, in 1209, riots in Oxford sent groups of nervous academics scuttling east across England to a safer spot on the edge of the East Anglian fens, where they became the first scholars of the University of Cambridge. Experts in anatomy and medicine in southern Italy grouped together at Salerno, which became the foremost medical school in Europe. In 1290 the poet-king Dinis of Portugal gave his blessing to a university at Coimbra. And many others proliferated in Italy, the Iberian peninsula, France and England. In the fourteenth century universities appeared far outside these four realms: Irish students could go to the university of Dublin, Bohemians to Prague, Poles to Kraków, Hungarians to Pécs, Albanians to Durrës and Germans to Heidelberg or Cologne. Typically each of these far-flung and varied institutions was known as a *Studium Generale*, and taught the liberal arts, along with one or more of theology, law and medicine. There was an international ethos from the outset, and students and masters could and would travel between these universities, with a degree or qualification to teach gained at one being considered valid at all the others. Bands of scholars, wearing distinctive clerical dress and subject to their own codes of discipline which sat outside the ordinary laws, became a common sight in dozens of 'university towns' across the west. The scholar's moment had arrived. And there is no better way to see what opportunities the university could afford a clever young man than to briefly examine the career of one of the most famous scholars in the whole of the Middle Ages: Thomas Aquinas.

WHEN AQUINAS – CERTAINLY THE GREATEST Christian scholar of the thirteenth century and often cited as one of the greatest the west ever produced – was roughly five years old, in 1231, his parents sent him for education at the monastery of Monte Cassino. The abbey which St Benedict had once presided over was now under the supervision of young Thomas' uncle Sinibald, and it may well be that the family dreamed of young Thomas growing up and taking it over. But Aquinas had set his heart on other, bigger things. For around ten years he applied himself diligently to his studies in the ultra-traditional monastic surroundings. But aged about fifteen, on the cusp of manhood, he veered off course. He announced to his colleagues at Monte Cassino that he was leaving the abbey. He was going to join the new, Dominican Order of friars that had been established by the Castilian priest Dominic de Guzman in 1216.*

To become a Dominican was to devote oneself to a life of preaching and teaching in the wider community, backed up with intensive private study and prayer. To thrive as a Dominican, a man needed a state-of-the-art higher education. So Aquinas also revealed he would be decamping to the new university at Naples, recently established by Frederick as a rival to Bologna, which the emperor considered to be hopelessly anti-imperial. Aquinas' family was not pleased, for the life of a student seemed to them to be synonymous with intellectual navel-gazing, and the life of a friar even more so: an existence predicated on the two great student pleasures of idling around and sounding off. So although they let him go, they subsequently tried everything to dissuade and distract him – at one point kidnapping him from Naples and imprisoning him for a year in their castle at Roccasecca where Aquinas' brothers attempted to test his Dominican credentials by hiring prostitutes to try and tempt him into sin.[27] But for Aquinas, the scent of books was infinitely more alluring than the perfume of hookers' knickers. He stuck stubbornly to his decision, and after a while his family relented. They let him return to the Dominicans and his studies. In 1245 his fellow friars asked him to leave Italy and go north, to the University of Paris, where he was to bring glory to God by embarking on a career as an academic.[28]

It did not start perfectly. Aquinas' early students and colleagues nicknamed him 'the dumb ox', on account of his quiet demeanour. But if he was outwardly a shy man, Aquinas was also a brilliant one, and he had the trust of the leading light of the faculty, the Bavarian theology professor and fellow Dominican Albertus

---

* The Dominicans were known as the 'Blackfriars', in reference to their dark robes, which marked them out from the Franciscan 'Greyfriars' and Carmelite 'Whitefriars'.

Magnus. After a short time in Paris, Albertus took Aquinas to the university in his own hometown of Cologne, where Aquinas worked as a junior professor for four years, lecturing students on the Bible while continuing his own private study. In 1252 he went back in Paris to read for the degree of master of theology, and when he completed this, in 1256, he was recognized as a regent master, with responsibility for teaching. He was now a made man, both in the Parisian theology faculty and the western university system at large. His mature career stretched before him.

Aquinas' time as a senior scholar was actually relatively short – less than twenty years – yet in it he produced a truly formidable body of writing. His crowning study was the massive *Summa Theologiae* – designed as an introduction to, and defence of, the whole of Christian belief, written for what we would now call undergraduates, but accessible to lay readers too.[29] The *Summa Theologiae* dealt with everything from the nature of the world to morality, virtue, sin and the mysteries of the sacraments; is still a set text for divinity students and priesthood candidates today. Aquinas also composed tracts long and short on the whole panoply of issues touched by late medieval theology: natural science, philosophy, economics, ethics and magic. He wrote Biblical commentaries and notes on the works of other theologians and philosophers, from Boethius to Peter Lombard's *Sentences* – the first book on every university student's reading list. He travelled as he worked – spending years away from Paris back in Naples as well as at Orvieto and Rome. And he did not neglect his duties as a Dominican, preaching and delivering sermons, in order to pass on aspects of his learning to the wider public.

Aquinas was an academic devoted to what is known as the 'scholastic' method – resolving intellectual problems through highly structured debate or 'dialectical reasoning'. But more importantly, he was the greatest scholar since Isidore of Seville to see how the wisdom of the ancient pagans could complement Christian theology. Aquinas read and absorbed Aristotle (writing a commentary on the *Metaphysics* and other Aristotelian works), and his understanding of Aristotelian philosophy fed his analysis and exposition of scripture. This was not always straightforward: in 1210 the University of Paris had attempted to ban the use of Aristotle's works in its theology faculty, and repeated proscriptions were made against pagan writers in subsequent years. Aquinas negotiated the prohibitions adeptly. He also embraced the work of later non-Christian scholars such as the Muslim polymath Averroës and the twelfth-century, Cordoba-born Jewish philosopher Maimonides. And for good measure, in his final years, Aquinas experienced holy visions. These convinced him to give up his work on the *Summa Theologiae*, which was why that masterpiece was left incomplete when he died, aged just forty-four, in 1274. But as a medieval Christian intellectual they made him more or less the perfect package. He had depth of understanding of Christian scripture and commentary, a breadth of learning that could triangulate between the works of pagans and believers, and a personal connection to the divine. Not for nothing was Aquinas recognized in the sixteenth century as a Doctor of the Church – the first to be so honoured since the sainted Pope Gregory I 'the Great'.*

Besides the fact that Aquinas produced timeless, seminal theological works, his career was important because it epitomized the intellectual vigour at play in Europe's universities during the thirteenth century. He harvested the fruits of the great revival of learning that characterized the high Middle Ages. Yet at the same time Aquinas was what we might call a 'pure' academic. He spent his life reading, writing, teaching and preaching, mostly in universities. As a Dominican he was not exactly a man in an ivory tower. But neither did he get his hands dirty in politics. It was left to others of his time to connect the intellectual world to the political, and to show how power developed or exercised within the academy might shape the world on the outside.

***

* The original four Doctors of the Church were Gregory, St Ambrose, St Augustine and St Jerome. Thomas Aquinas was recognized as a Doctor in 1567. At the time of writing there are thirty-six Doctors, including Isidore of Seville, the Venerable Bede, Hildebrand of Bingen and Aquinas' mentor Albert Magnus. The most recent Doctor to be recognized was St Gregory of Narek, a tenth-century Armenian mystic poet and monk on whom the status was bestowed by Pope Francis I in 2015.

Unsurprisingly, since universities tended to develop in cities that were close to political capitals, they became recruiting-stations for public servants and ministers. Indeed, it would have been strange if they had not, for at the turn of the fourteenth century a university like Oxford had about 1,600 members at any given time – Cambridge about half as many, Paris substantially more.[30] Among all these clever people, there were naturally some efficient and worldly ones, prime for poaching by secular society.

At the beginning of this chapter we met the diabolical William de Nogaret, a French jurist who became Philip IV's political hitman and the architect of the Templar trials of 1307–12. De Nogaret was no outlier. A few years after his death in 1313 the Italian medic Marsilius of Padua, a graduate of his hometown university and rector of the University of Paris, also became embroiled in a dispute between a secular ruler and the papacy when he was recruited to become an intellectual advocate at the court of Ludwig of Bavaria, the Holy Roman Emperor-elect who was at loggerheads with Pope John XXII. Marsilius was joined at Ludwig's court by the noted Oxford scholar and philosopher William of Ockham (today best known for the philosophical principle of Ockham's Razor); these two serious scholars were weapons every bit as important as those wielded by armies, as emperors and popes continued their interminable struggles.

In the twelfth century Peter of Blois, a Breton who studied law at Bologna and theology at Paris, had a most lively political career: appointed as the tutor-guardian to the boy-king William II of Sicily, he was chased off that island during a populist revolt; Peter went to England and served as a diplomat to the Plantagenet king of England Henry II, shuttling between the English, French and papal courts at a particularly febrile time in relations between all three. At one point Peter even took on the delicate task job of writing a letter admonishing the queen of England, Eleanor of Aquitaine, who was leading a rebellion against Henry, telling her that 'unless you return to your husband, you will be the cause of widespread disaster. While you alone are now the delinquent one, your actions will result in ruin for everyone in the kingdom.'[31]

And Peter of Blois was by no means the only scholar to be mixed up in the topsy-turvy world of Plantagenet politics. Thomas Becket, who served as a chief minister to Henry II in the 1160s, had studied the *trivium* and *quadrivium* at Merton Priory in Surrey and probably at the grammar school attached to St Paul's Cathedral in London. But thanks to his father's untimely bankruptcy in the late 1130s he could not study for his higher degree in theology at the University of Paris, and was forced to take a job as a clerk. This left Becket with a suppurating intellectual wound and an enormous chip on his shoulder. These had tragic consequences when in the 1160s Henry II promoted him – very controversially – as archbishop of Canterbury. Suddenly feeling his intellectual inferiority far more acutely than he felt his duty to the king, Becket overcompensated by becoming an objectionable and obstructive primate who blocked Henry's attempts to control the English Church at every turn, with the eventual result that he was murdered, on Henry's indirect orders, on the floor of Canterbury Cathedral at Christmas 1170. Had he managed to pursue his studies and scratch his intellectual itch this might never have happened. Then again, perhaps it would, as the experience of another Plantagenet archbishop showed: the English-born cardinal and academic Stephen Langton was one of the stars of the University of Paris' theology department, where he had organized the Bible into the chapters that we still use to navigate its text today. But when Langton was appointed archbishop of Canterbury by Pope Innocent III, during the reign of Henry II's son King John, he too caused enormous political problems: John vehemently opposed his candidacy and was drawn into a spectacular arm-wrestle with Rome, during the course of which England was placed under interdict for six years and John was personally excommunicated.

Of course, not all medieval academics were dragged out of the academy simply to be thrust into dogfights. The great crusades chronicler William archbishop of Tyre studied at Paris and Bologna in the twelfth century, before heading back to his birthplace in the Holy Land, where his secular duties included serving as tutor and later chancellor to the unfortunate leper-king Baldwin IV. The thirteenth-century Italian medic Lanfranc of Milan was forced to leave his studies in Italy during political turmoil in the 1290s and sought refuge in the University of Paris, where he wrote his *Chirurgia Magna*, destined to become one of the most important medical textbooks of the Middle Ages.* Nevertheless, one of the most significant – if unintended – consequences of the rise of the universities was that institutions which had been created to facilitate serious study for its own sake developed into finishing schools for politicians.† By the time the sixteenth century dawned a university career was becoming almost as necessary a qualification for public office as it is today.

And at the same time, universities had become the focus of another phenomenon that remains strikingly familiar today, as they became a forum for defining and deciding heresies: avenues of thought which were not only wrong but illegal, and punishable by humiliation, ostracization and even death.

Medieval 'Woke'

LIKE THEIR MODERN SUCCESSORS, MEDIEVAL UNIVERSITIES could be progressive and viciously censorious, often at the same time. Bologna University, for example, was the first to employ a woman as a lecturer: Bettisia Gozzadini taught law, albeit with her face hidden behind a veil, from the late 1230s, and blazed a path for other women to follow – such as the sisters Novella and Bettina d'Andrea, who taught law at Bologna and Padua respectively in the fourteenth century. In the University of Paris, students walked out on strike in 1229 to defend their right to be free from oversight by the city's authorities.‡ And as we shall see in chapter 16, it

---

* Another great medical writer of the age was Trota of Salerno, a southern Italian surgical specialist, whose writing on women's medicine, collected in a multi-authored volume known as the *Trotula*, circulated widely throughout Europe during the later Middle Ages.
† A lament still sung today.
‡ Not that this was a particularly edifying episode for anyone involved: a drunken fight between students and Parisian citizens at the start of Lent 1229 led to demands that the students be punished by the secular courts rather than Church courts; several students were

was at the University of Erfurt that the fifteenth-century student Martin Luther began to ask questions of the established order that sparked the monumental religious and cultural upheavals of the Reformation. All of these, in different ways, spoke to a spirit of intellectual independence that remains a governing ideal in western higher education to this day. Yet if medieval universities could – and did – serve as clusters for radical thought and re-examination of long-held orthodoxies, they were just as often places where debate was stifled and forcibly shut down, in an attempt to preserve prevailing pieties.

RIGHT FROM THE START OF THE twelfth-century renaissance there were powerful figures both inside and outside the universities who found the new spirit of intellectual inquiry to be as much a menace as a force for good. Not least among them was Bernard of Clairvaux. His monastic order, the Cistercians, were almost by definition hostile to book-learning. And Bernard in particular – a mystic, rather than a scholar – was more or less allergic to any system of study that deviated from unquestioning adoration of scripture. Never was his scorn for new-fangled learning more evident than in the late 1130s when he led the charge to prosecute the Breton theologian Peter Abelard for heresy.

Abelard was the greatest scholar of his day. In philosophy he applied himself to the vexing problem of universals, which was the vigorously disputed issue concerning the relationship between language and objects. As a theologian he brilliantly spliced Aristotelian logical reasoning with scriptural study. He helped develop the Catholic doctrine of Limbo as a realm of the afterlife where unfortunate souls such as unbaptized babies might be found. He was a gifted musician and poet. But he was also a controversial, and by the end of his life a notorious, figure. Abelard had been disgraced as a young man when he was master of the cathedral

---

killed by city guards seeking retribution, and the whole student body walked out of lectures for two years until their rights were guaranteed by papal bull.

school of Notre-Dame in Paris: in 1115–16 he took a part-time job as tutor to a girl called Heloïse, the niece of one of the cathedral canons. Unfortunately, in the course of teaching Heloïse, Abelard seduced her, got her pregnant (with a son whom she would name 'Astrolabe'*), married her, then sent her to live in a nunnery. In return for this, Heloïse's irate uncle accosted Abelard and brutally castrated him. Fortunate to survive the ordeal, Abelard retired to live as a monk at the abbey of St-Denis, although he was later forced to leave, having wound up his fellow monks one too many times with his deliberately provocative behaviour and opinions. He lived for a time as a wandering hermit, and gave public lectures on theology in the streets of Paris. All the while, Abelard was writing brilliant but challenging books and treatises, which drew on Aristotelian methods of reasoning, and often came to conclusions which could be construed as heretical. By the late 1130s, he had already been publicly convicted of heresy once (in 1121), on which occasion he was forced to burn a collection of his lectures known today as the *Theologia 'Summi Boni'*.

Bernard found Abelard's methods and theological conclusions utterly unacceptable, and in 1140 he pressed to have Abelard prosecuted once more. He hounded Abelard out of Paris, had his views condemned by an ecclesiastical council and petitioned the pope to add Rome's censure to the verdicts. It is hard to know how much further Bernard would have gone had Abelard not been given sanctuary by Peter the Venerable, abbot of Cluny (see chapter 6); as it was he still managed to break Abelard's spirit and drive him to what was probably an early grave in 1142. Thus was one of the most original thinkers and charismatic teachers of his age 'cancelled': his reputation trashed not only in his own lifetime but for generations afterwards. And so, too, was a playbook written for future heretic-hunters to follow. There would be plenty of them within the late medieval intellectual world.

***

* The tradition of creative geniuses giving their children weird scientific names is not unique to the Middle Ages. Consider Moon Unit Zappa, or the child born to Elon Musk and Grimes during the writing of this book: X Æ A-12 Musk.

In 1277, Etienne Tempier, bishop of Paris, issued an official decree threatening to excommunicate anyone at the city's university who held or taught one of 219 erroneous points of view. Quite why Tempier chose this particular moment to issue his condemnation, and which scholars at the university he felt were particularly guilty of corrupting their own minds and those of the students and masters around them, is no longer very clear.[32] He was, however, following a tradition of scholarly censorship that stretched back more than half a century. In 1210, an earlier group of scholars within the arts faculty at the university had been officially condemned for reading too much Aristotle. A number of that great Greek philosopher's works had been officially forbidden, along with works by other scholars, both ancient and modern, which offered secondary commentary on him.

In 1270 Tempier had repeated this proscription, and specified a number of Aristotelian positions which were henceforth to be considered unutterable. So in 1277 the bishop was repeating what was both well-established thought-policing, and a self-evidently unsuccessful censorship; had the scholars at Paris been diligently ignoring Aristotle as requested, he would surely not have had to need to issue his order. The 1277 condemnations at Paris did not seem to clamp down very hard on the study of Aristotle; in fact, it has been argued that they pushed western scholars to think even harder about the basis for knowledge and belief. Certainly there were no bonfires in the streets, either of books or academics. But the condemnations did demonstrate that what was being said and thought within the universities was seen to have wider significance for the moral order of society. From this point onwards, both in Paris and in the wider world, academics would frequently find themselves embroiled in the politics of correct – or incorrect – belief.

As we have already seen, it was only thirty years after the 1277 condemnations that the masters of the University of Paris were dragged into a far less abstract scandal, when the French crown demanded their judgement in the matter of the Knights Templar. During the Great Schism of the late fourteenth century, when rival popes sat in Rome and Avignon, universities across Europe were constantly under political pressure to declare for one side or the other, while during the Hundred Years War between England and France, French academies were endlessly embroiled in the arguments about legitimate kingship that fuelled that interminable conflict.[33] But nowhere was the entanglement of academy in the secular world played out more dramatically than at Oxford, where in the later fourteenth century a very different sort of heresy emerged, not only splitting that university, but causing ructions throughout political society. The heresy was known as Lollardy, and its guiding figure was the theologian and philosopher John Wycliffe.

A SHARP-TONGUED YORKSHIREMAN WITH A BITING wit and no great optimism about mankind's innate goodness, Wycliffe was active at the University of Oxford from the 1340s, where he was lucky to survive the Black Death. He enjoyed a successful career as an academic, serving at one point as the master of Balliol College; but by the 1370s he had gravitated towards politics, serving as a royal envoy to Flanders, in the Netherlands, before falling into the orbit of John of Gaunt, a dominant figure in English politics during the dying years of his father Edward III and the minority of Richard II. He had also begun to advocate a number of radical ideas and positions, and had translated large portions of the Bible for the first time into English.

Among a number of the controversial ideas that Wycliffe had been formulating during his academic career was the notion that there was no scriptural basis for the papacy, that transubstantiation (i.e. the literal transformation of bread into the body of Christ during the Eucharist) was nonsense, and that secular powers were within their rights to demand back lands that had been granted to the Church. None of these were in any sense uncontroversial stances, but the last of them appealed to Gaunt on political grounds, and the duke therefore gleefully promoted and patronized Wycliffe for many years to come, personally protecting him from public censure by the bishop of London in 1377.

By the end of that decade, Wycliffe had become a minor celebrity, whose views on matters ranging from theology and philosophy to the plight of the poor and the state of international relations were the subject of scrutiny both inside and outside the academic world. After London and several cities across England erupted in populist rioting during the so-called Peasants' Revolt of 1381,* Wycliffe's ideas and preaching were blamed for having incited the trouble. And perhaps inevitably, since the archbishop of Canterbury of the day was murdered during those riots, less than twelve months later an official church council was convened at Blackfriars, where a list of heretical doctrines attributed to Wycliffe were condemned.

This was effectively the end of Wycliffe's career: he was forced into retirement and died two and half years later, on the last day of 1384. But he was not forgotten, either by his enemies or his friends. In the fifteenth century his grave was exhumed and his bones burned, and on papal authority his views were condemned almost in their entirety. But it was too late. Wycliffe's arguments had already gone viral. In England they underpinned a radical clerical reform movement, known as Lollardy, which was considered not only heretical but actively seditious, after several of its followers were associated with an attempt on the life of King Henry V in 1414. Meanwhile across Europe he had inspired other anticlerical writers and activists, chief among them the Bohemian reformer Jan Hus, who was condemned and burned at the stake in 1415, after which a series of five crusades was preached against his followers, who were hunted down with extreme prejudice in a campaign that lasted more than twenty years. Wycliffe the theologian had done far more than ruffle feathers within the academy: he had sparked revolutionary fervour across Europe, the effects of which would feed directly into the Protestant reformations that marked the end of the Middle Ages.

Yet there was more to Wycliffe's story than just this. For while he stamped his mark on the world at large, Wycliffe also left an

* See chapter 13.

important legacy to academic culture inside England's universities. In 1409, in direct response to Wycliffism and Lollardy, the English archbishop of Canterbury (and Oxford alumnus) Thomas Arundel issued a series of thirteen 'Constitutions': clerical rulings directed specifically at Oxford University, which strictly limited the freedom of speech and research among academics, forbade unlicensed preaching and English translation of scripture, demanded monthly inspections by senior University officials to ensure that no untoward opinions were being expressed and forbade teachers to say anything to their students that was not approved Church doctrine. The penalties for contravening these onerous restrictions on free thought included being removed from office, imprisoned and publicly flogged. The Constitutions were granted royal approval, giving them the full weight of law, and they would have a lasting and deleterious effect on Oxford's ability to operate as a leading western university. In the short term the University of Cambridge, hitherto a second-rate power in English academic life, would benefit enormously from Oxford's struggles with censorship and the persecution of heretics, as it attracted thinkers who preferred a less censorious environment.[34] In the long term, however, a template for intellectual life within western universities was set: a template in which two conflicting ambitions are at play. On the one hand universities were to be institutions where the more intellectually vigorous and fearless people in society could go to learn, investigate and challenge the world as they found it. Yet they were also under pressure from both within and without to serve as bulwarks for politically acceptable pieties. It is perfectly possible to look at universities across the western world today and think that by and large, not much has really changed.

12

BUILDERS

'There he saw a great city, and a great fortress within
with many tall towers of different colours'

THE MABINOGION

Dafydd ap Gruffudd, prince of Wales, was condemned to die by an English parliament convened in the Anglo-Welsh border town of Shrewsbury in September 1283. His death was to be cruel and unusual. Dafydd considered himself a freedom fighter, defending the rights of the native Welsh to live as they wished, according to their own laws and customs, and not under the rule of their hated neighbours to the east. The English saw things otherwise. For many years Norman and Plantagenet kings had invested time, money and blood into conquering Wales, and stubborn resistance led by men like Dafydd had begun to test their patience. Letters summoning English magnates to attend the Shrewsbury parliament complained that 'the tongue of man can scarcely recount the evil deeds committed by the Welsh... from time within memory', and described Dafydd as 'the last survivor of [a] family of traitors'.[1] It was time to make an example of him.

Parliament did not take long to decide Dafydd's fate. On the basis that he had plotted to kill king Edward I, Dafydd was found guilty of treason. He was sentenced to be the first person in British history to be hanged, drawn and quartered. This was a horrible way to die, as Dafydd found out at first hand. Having been taken from his prison cell at Rhuddlan Castle in north Wales, he was dragged behind a horse to the scaffold in Shrewsbury, where he was strung up by his neck and left to struggle and choke for a while. Then he was cut down by the executioner, a townsman called Geoffrey, who proceeded to slice out his intestines with a butcher's blade. Only then was Dafydd put out of his misery: beheaded and hacked into four pieces, each of which was sent to a different English city as an advertisement of his fate. Exactly where the pieces ended up was not recorded by the chroniclers. But his head went south. It was set up on a spike at the Tower of London – the brooding fortress that overlooked England's capital city.[2]

Dafydd's death was a grisly piece of political theatre, which introduced a dread new punishment to England. It extinguished a great line of Welsh princes, and it struck a severe blow to Welsh hopes of ever wriggling free of English dominion. Both of these were important political and cultural landmarks in Britain's medieval history. Yet as a demonstration of royal majesty and English hegemony in Wales Dafydd's death was far from the most spectacular or lasting of Edward I's punishments. For at the same time as Dafydd was being publicly tortured to death by an executioner, the northern Welsh landscape that he had called home was being recast forever by architects and masons. To secure his legacy in Wales, Edward I had commissioned a string of massive stone castles, built at staggering cost across the beautiful, mountainous landscape of Powys and Gwynedd. These castles were state-of-the-art military installations and totems to the might of English monarchy. They cost vast sums and employed thousands of people during several decades. And they were hate objects for the subjugated Welsh, whose sense of self was deeply rooted in a liberty they saw as stretching back to Roman times and beyond.

Yet in addition to all this, Edward I's Welsh castles were a potent demonstration of the burgeoning skill and vision of builders in the later Middle Ages. The thirteenth and fourteenth centuries were a golden age of monumental architecture in the west, in which some of the most iconic buildings in world history were erected. They were designed by civic and military architects and executed by master masons who explored new ways to defy gravity, sending spires and towers soaring towards the heavens, telling interwoven stories of wealth, power, piety and dominion. Many of the castles, Gothic cathedrals and pleasure palaces which appeared at this time still stand, serving as popular tourist attractions (and in some cases, working buildings) whose silhouettes have become virtually synonymous with the Middle Ages. No study of medieval power would be complete without reference to this glorious age of stone.

The Conquest of Wales

IF EDWARD I'S WELSH CASTLE-BUILDING PROGRAMME can be said to have begun anywhere, it was in the little French village of Saint-Georges-d'Espéranche, 50km south-east of Lyon, in the year 1273. At that time, Edward was travelling home from the Holy Land, where he had been on crusade, attempting to rally Christian forces in their fight against the Mamluks of Egypt.

During his time in the east, Edward had seen and heard about many extraordinary castles, not least the Knights Hospitallers' gargantuan concentric hilltop fortress of Krak des Chevaliers, a twelfth-century military installation which guarded the dangerous road between the cities of Tripoli and Homs, and the Templars' equally vast coastal castle, Château Pelèrin, a naval base and knightly garrison south of Haifa at Atlit, which could accommodate 4,000 troops, and had stairways broad enough to ride horses up and down. These were among the stand-out achievements of the crusader states' builders, but the Holy Land was dotted from top to bottom with defensive towers and fortresses of all shapes and sizes. The chief mode of warfare was siegecraft: an army tried to capture a castle or fortified town by bombardment, starvation or storm, while the defenders did their best to stand firm until their tormentors lost patience and went away. The basic contest in military technology was therefore between castle engineers and the designers of siege-towers, battering rams and catapults. This was true throughout the western world, but especially so in the crusader states, where war and violence were more or less endemic

– it was only natural, therefore, that some of the world's finest castles were to be found in and around the kingdom of Jerusalem.

Now, when Edward stopped at Saint-Georges-d'Espéranche, he found another fine castle under construction. This one had been commissioned by the local lord, Count Philip of Savoy, who was an old family friend. Works were being overseen by a brilliant young architect-engineer called Master James, who was also engaged on similar projects elsewhere in Philip's lands. Whatever Edward saw in Master James, it impressed him. Four years later, with England's wars against the Welsh in full flow, he summoned him across the Channel and entrusted him with the project of a lifetime.[3] Master James of St George, as he was henceforth known, took on the creative direction and oversight of works on castles in north Wales at sites including Flint, Rhuddlan, Conwy, Builth, Harlech, Aberystwyth, Ruthin, Beaumaris and elsewhere. (He would also work for Edward in Gascony and Scotland.) From the summer of 1277 until his death in 1309 he was Britain's premier military engineer, entrusted with budgets unheard of for fortifications since William the Conqueror had been subduing Saxon England in the 1060s and 1070s. Master James changed the landscape of Wales and set a new standard for military architecture which was scarcely bettered before the close of the Middle Ages. Nowhere were his talents better exemplified than in his masterpiece – a castle that sat on the north-west extreme of mainland Wales, between the Menai Strait and the mountains of Snowdonia, in the town that is today known as Caernarfon.

Once upon a time, Caernarfon had been a Roman legionary outpost called Segontium, and although by the 1280s not much remained of that far-flung imperial outpost, the memory of a Welsh connection with Roman Britannia lived on.[4] Caernarfon was associated (albeit dubiously) with Constantine the Great, as well as the western usurper-emperor Magnus Maximus, both of whom had been declared emperor while in various parts of Britannia.* (See chapter 2.) Maximus – or Maxen Wledig, in Welsh

---

* Received wisdom of the day held – incorrectly – that Maximus was Constantine the Great's father.

– loomed especially large in local folklore. The great national romance known as the *Mabinogion* told in vaunting terms of a dream-vision Maximus experienced:

> He saw himself travelling… and though his journey was long he finally reached the mouth of the greatest river anyone had seen. There he saw a great city, and a great fortress within with many tall towers of different colours… Inside Maxen saw a fine hall: its roof seemed all of gold, its sides of luminous stones all equally precious, its doors all of gold. There were golden couches and silver tables… By the base of a pillar Maxen saw a white-haired man sitting in a chair of elephant ivory, on which was an image of two eagles in red gold…[5]

This was model for the castle that Edward charged Master James of St George with building. The king yearned for a fortress that gleamed with imperial insignia; one which co-opted Welsh dreams of ancient dignity, and brought them under his own command. He also wanted something transcendent – not only of time, but of place. Master James delivered all of this and more. In the summer of 1283, around the same time that Dafydd ap Grufudd was being tried and butchered in Shrewsbury, workmen broke ground on the new fortress. They laid the foundations for polygonal towers, and for walls that were to be decorated with stripes of coloured stone running through them in horizontal bands. One of the towers was to be adorned with three turrets bearing carved eagles, and the whole southern side of the castle would jut out into the mouth of the river Seiont, which emptied into the sea at Caernarfon.[6]

This was a strange and wonderful castle. In part it was the realization of a fairytale. But it was also a deliberate echo of something real: its banded walls recalled the Theodosian defences of Constantinople itself. Of course, Caernarfon was very much Constantinople in miniature: its walled town and garrison never accommodated more than a few hundred royal inhabitants – a far cry from the hundreds of thousands who swarmed the streets of the Byzantine capital at its peak. Nevertheless, the likeness was intentional and meaningful. And Edward made sure to underscore his point. During initial excavations in 1283 the supposed mortal remains of Maximus/Maxen Wledig were found, dug up and reinterred with honours in a local church. And in 1284, when the castle was still no more than a building site with a shanty village of temporary wooden shacks to accommodate craftsmen and labourers, Edward sent his heavily pregnant queen, Eleanor of Castile, to Caernarfon to give birth to the last of their many children, a duty she performed on 25 April, when she bore the future Edward II. This Edward grew up as the first English Prince of Wales, his claim to that name justified by his origins in the quasi-imperial fortress of Caernarfon.* Thus did propaganda, politics and military strategy collide in north-west Wales, under the watchful gaze of Master James of St George.

CASTLE-BUILDING WAS NOT INVENTED IN THE high Middle Ages. The castle's lineal ancestor was the iron-age hill-fort – a military position established on high ground, protected by earthworks and some degree of timber defences. Roman forts (*castra*), often with stone foundations and timber palisades and outbuildings, represented a big step forward in military architecture – a tradition that was maintained and developed in the Islamic world during the Umayyad period, when desert castles (*qusur*) proliferated in the Middle East, blending military functions with more luxurious, palatial features such as farm-buildings, bath-houses and mosques. In the west, by contrast, fortifications remained relatively primitive throughout the first millennium. Huge sums and millions of man-hours were expended on Church buildings, but military architecture lagged a long way behind.

Around the year AD 1000, however, western Europe experienced a revolution in castle building. What prompted this revolution has vexed historians for generations: the answer probably lies in

---

* Caernarfon Castle has kept up this tradition into the modern era: in 1969 Elizabeth II's eldest son Charles was invested there as Prince of Wales.

European instability after the break-up of the Carolingian empire, the external threats to Christian kingdoms posed by Vikings, Magyars and Iberian Muslims, and the increasing prominence of Frankish-style knights, who needed bases from which to operate. Many of the improvements in western castle-building were driven by the Normans – not only in Normandy, but also England, Sicily and the crusader states. The Normans were early adopters of motte and bailey castle design, in which a large mound (the motte) was surmounted with a fortified keep or tower, at first typically made of timber, while outbuildings in the area surrounding the motte (the bailey) were defended with a fence or ditch. From the late tenth century until the late eleventh, this was the cutting edge of castle design.

By the early twelfth century, however, engineers had thrown out the timber-heavy motte and bailey model. Instead, they began to build larger and more elaborate castles in stone – a difficult, expensive and labour-intensive material to work with, to be sure, but one that produced infinitely stronger fortifications, from which military and political power might be projected for miles in every direction. At first these stone castles imitated motte and bailey structures, but by the twelfth century the 'concentric' castle had arrived: sprawling stone-built structures based on complex footprints with inner and outer baileys, two or more sets of walls studded with defensive towers, multiple gatehouses and drawbridges, single or double sets of moats and often palatial living quarters in the most secure parts of the fortress.

These vastly improved castles were only possible to conceive – let alone build – because of the leaps forward in economic activity and mathematics that occurred in the twelfth and thirteenth centuries. But the boom was also down to the basic willingness of later medieval patrons – royalty, nobility and churchmen alike – to throw money and ambition at castle engineers. They did so with the abandon of modern-day oil billionaires commissioning Gulf-state hotels. And some truly awesome castles were realized. In the 1190s, Edward I's great-uncle Richard the Lionheart spent £12,000 – equivalent to roughly 50 per cent of his annual revenue from the kingdom of England – on a single stone castle in Normandy, Château Gaillard, which towered over the Seine at Les Andelys in the fraught Franco-Norman border zone known as the Vexin.[7] (Château Gaillard was supposed to be impregnable, although Richard's feckless brother and successor John managed to lose it to the French in 1204, just six years after it was completed.) Meanwhile, in the Spanish *Reconquista* kingdoms, lavish fortresses such as Monzón and Calatrava sprang up to rival vast Islamic castles in al-Andalus, such as the Alcazaba of Malaga and the Alhambra palace in Granada. And in the Baltic, shortly before work on Caernarfon Castle began, the Teutonic Knights founded Malbork Castle on the banks of the river Nogat, around 50km from the Baltic port of Danzig (Gdansk). Designed to control territory newly seized from the pagan tribes of Prussia, by the end of the Middle Ages Malbork castle (in modern Poland) had become a regional control centre for the Teutonic Knights, covering nearly fifty acres, with room to lodge several thousand knights at any given moment. From the Holy Land to the Atlantic, castle-building had become an integral part of projecting power. At the same time, weapons designers and siege engineers were constantly responding to advances in castle technology, building ever-larger and more flame-proof towers for storming walls, inventing trebuchets capable of hurling rocks the size of modern hatchback cars, and finessing the art of mining below foundations to bring down towers and walls.* In this context, castle-builders like Master James of St George were worth their weight in gold.

MASTER JAMES' PROJECT AT CAERNARFON DID not go up overnight. James was a preternaturally gifted project manager, who was lucky enough to be backed by the full resources of the

---

* As was done by King John's army in 1215 during the siege of Rochester Castle: sappers dug a mine under one of the castle's towers, greased the mine's wooden struts with pig-fat, then set the mine alight. When it collapsed, so did the tower. This is why Rochester Castle today has three sharp corners and one which is rounded, where it was reconstructed in a different style after John's reign was over.

English crown. But he was not a miracle worker, and during the thirty years he spent serving Edward, he usually had at least half a dozen castles under construction at any given moment. To bring a project like Caernarfon from conception to completion could take decades, even without major interruptions. Quarrying, moving, cutting and lifting stone was slow, labour-intensive, dirty, back-breaking toil. It was possible to build walls and other stoneworks for only about eight months a year, since winter frosts prevented lime mortar from setting. And works could easily be derailed at any time by bad weather, lightning, fires, war and other disasters of fate, including attacks by enemy armies. As a rule, peaceful lands did not need giant castles, so tranquil working conditions were not a luxury granted to engineers.*

This was certainly true in north Wales. Unsurprisingly the Welsh did not enjoy the sight of castles such as Caernarfon erupting all over their beloved mountainsides. The scars Edward gouged into the landscape were deep and permanent. To march his armies into Wales from Chester in north-west England, Edward had ordered his engineers to cut broad superhighways through the countryside, and throughout the 1280s and 1290s these teemed not only with knights and infantry, but also with construction traffic serving the castle sites along the route. Even a single castle sucked in vast manpower and natural resources at a fierce rate. For example, in the first ten months of construction at the royal castle of Denbigh, nearly two hundred cartloads of timber had been felled from local woods.[8] At Conwy, two hundred woodcutters and one hundred diggers were hired to work on the foundations alone; when it came to the fabric of the building, four years' worth of iron, steel, nails, tin, stone, lead, glass, brass and labour cost Edward more than £11,000 – a sizeable percentage of his annual royal revenue at a time when he was also funding wars on two fronts.[9] To build six

---

* One of the most vivid examples of this to survive in archaeology is to be found in the ruins of a Templar castle at Jacob's Ford, around a hundred miles north of Jerusalem, where in August 1179 the Ayyubid sultan Saladin sent troops to attack the building site. The remains of workers and their construction tools have all been found left scattered where the men were cut down.

or more fortresses at any given moment required builders by the battalion and building materials by the ton. Timber and stone were ferried to Caernarfon in ships hailing from as far away as Dublin, Calais and Yarmouth; the quarries of Anglesey were raided for all the stone they could provide; expert masons were summoned from Yorkshire to work on the cutting.[10] This was a messy, noisy, disruptive business. The end result of it for the local people was permanent oppression in the shadow of the forts.

By the mid-1290s the Welsh were heartily fed up. In September 1294 they rebelled. During the revolt insurgents tried to put a stop to works at Caernarfon – not so much lying down in front of the bulldozers as setting out to burn the entire building to the ground. The site and half-built town around it was sacked and captured. Newly constructed town walls were pulled down. When the rebellion was crushed, Master James, and his on-site deputy, an expert mason called Master Walter of Hereford, were dismayed to find their progress set back by months, if not years.

Yet the king's dedication to castle-building in general was undimmed. Quite the opposite. Not only did Edward supply Master James and Master Walter with the money, material and men they needed to bring construction back on track, he also gave them yet another enormous project. This was the amphibious castle of Beaumaris, which was planted across the Menai Strait from Caernarfon on the island of Anglesey, and funded even more lavishly.

In 1296, at the height of on-site activity at Beaumaris, Master James reported to the royal Exchequer that he had 'one thousand carpenters, smiths, plasterers and navvies' at work, guarded by 130 soldiers. They laboured long and hard, in weather conditions which – as any visitor to the mountainous region of Snowdonia today will attest – can switch from beautiful to brutal in a few minutes. In total, nearly £15,000 was spent at Beaumaris, yet even so, it remained unfinished at Edward's death in 1307, unfinished at Master James' death in 1309 and unfinished, indeed, in the 1320s.[11] Still, if it was never brought to architectural sign-off, Beaumaris – a more functional, stolid castle than the flight of mythological fantasy at Caernarfon – was still a testament to the ruthless military ambition that burned inside Edward I: his deep need to stamp his power indelibly onto Wales, and to do so by the means of castles built in stone, which would be capable of standing more or less intact for at least five hundred years.

Fortress Europe

NO OTHER ENGLISH MONARCH WOULD EVER devote themselves to castle-building with quite the same vigour as Edward I, who, besides his Welsh projects, also invested heavily in redeveloping the Tower of London and other Plantagenet fortresses at Cambridge, Chester and Corfe. In that sense, the late thirteenth century was a heyday for castle-building, in England, at least. Nevertheless, the monumental stone castle remained a feature of the landscape across the medieval world until the fifteenth century, funded enthusiastically by kings, queens and wealthy aristocrats alike. A brief survey of a few of the greatest castle-building projects of the age will serve to show just how essential the west's most powerful rulers considered them.

In England during the fourteenth century, Edward III refortified England's coastal castles to stand firm against French raids in the Hundred Years War, and spent heavily on erecting satellite forts around the town of Calais, which was seized from the French in 1347. He also invested in major defensive works at Berwick, in the Scottish borderlands. Edward was acutely attuned to the value of good fortifications, and led sieges in person, not least at Calais itself. But Edward's most eye-catching castle-works were not on the front line of battle, but at Windsor, a longstanding royal residence which the king remodelled as a new Camelot and nerve centre of revived English chivalry. This was not a castle in the traditional sense – things would have gone terribly wrong if any fourteenth-century king required a heavy military presence in rural Berkshire. But as a fortified palace, it served an equally important purpose: to tell a story about martial kingship and the romance of royalty. Edward spent £50,000 – a staggering sum – on Windsor, with large new apartment suites, offices and entertaining spaces. Today Windsor Castle still serves as the *de facto* home of English chivalry, particularly when it hosts gatherings of the Order of the Garter in its stunning Gothic chapel of St George (rebuilt in the late fifteenth century by Edward IV and Henry VII), or during its thrice-weekly changing of the guard – a public ceremony which normally attracts hundreds of curious spectators and tourists.

Outside England, castle-building was also heavily in vogue almost everywhere in the west throughout the later Middle Ages. In Hungary, the Mongol invasions of the thirteenth century emphasized the need for castles to defend against marauders from the east; although many older castles were razed by the Mongols, they were rebuilt stronger in the decades after the dreaded Tartars vanished, on the orders of King Béla IV, who demanded a castle on every hilltop in his realm. Further north, an equally far-reaching castle-building programme was undertaken in southern Poland by the fourteenth-century king Casimir III the Great (r. 1333–70) – son of the memorably nicknamed Wladyslaw I the Elbow-high (r. 1320–33). Besides founding Kraków University, reforming Poland's legal code and garnering a reputation as a protector of Jews, whom he offered refuge in Poland during an age of generalized anti-Semitism, Casimir was a prodigious military spender. During his long reign he built or redeveloped around two dozen castles in a chain stretching 100 miles between Kraków and Częstochowa, on the sensitive western border of his realm, which was contested with the neighboring kings of Bohemia. His castles, many of which were perched high on craggy Jurassic-era highland rock formations, are known today as the Eagles' Nests.*

In Germany (where the term Eagles' Nests has closer links with the Second World War than the Middle Ages) castles also

---

* Several of Casimir the Great's Eagles' Nests have today been refurbished as tourist destinations, including Bobolice Castle, which was rebuilt from ruins to reflect its original medieval condition. For an academic verdict on the success of that project (along with other Polish case studies), Żemła, Michał and Siwek, Matylda, 'Between authenticity of walls and authenticity of tourists' experiences: The tale of three Polish castles', *Cogent Arts & Humanities* 1 (2020).

decorated the landscape. The golden age of castle-building here, as elsewhere, was in the twelfth and early thirteenth centuries, when many magnificent fortresses were erected, including Heidelberg, Eltz and Hohenstaufen Castle, perched on a small mountain above Goppingen in the south-western German state of Baden-Württemberg and home to the imperial family of Frederick II Hohenstaufen. The Hohenstaufen were very enthusiastic castle-builders – and needed to be, since their chief dynastic trait was fighting other rulers, particularly popes. However, their most impressive surviving castle lies not in Germany but in southern Italy, where Frederick erected the fortress-cum-hunting lodge Castel del Monte on a hill above Andria, in Apulia. With its eight-sided walls, each joined by an eight-sided tower, Castel del Monte spoke in part to Frederick's political and military aims, but more, perhaps, to his fascination with geometry and mathematics, and his keen interest in Islam. In its footprint, Castel del Monte resembles nothing quite so much as the first level of the Dome of the Rock in Jerusalem,* the city which Frederick returned to Christian control during his crusade of 1228–9. Edward I was not the only thirteenth-century king to import design ideas from the eastern Mediterranean.

Examples of prodigious castle-building could be found everywhere across medieval Europe – with structures and styles varying from region to region and from age to age, according to the tastes of the decade in which they were designed and constructed, and the military or symbolic interests of the ruler or aristocrat who commissioned them. A talented castle-builder like Master James of St George would never go short of work, particularly if he was willing to travel the world and ply his trade in war zones. For those who could stomach the conditions, the medieval west could be a playground. Of course, the good times did not last forever: for by the fifteenth century gunpowder and advances in casting massive cannon meant that no castle could be built that was strong enough to withstand a protracted siege-shelling with

* See chapter 4.

475

live artillery, rather than the mechanical siege engines. Whereas castles built in the thirteenth century were designed to withstand sieges for a year or more, in 1415 it took the English king Henry V just a month to smash the fortified defences of the town of Harfleur to rubble with twelve great guns. With this revolution in battlefield technology, by the sixteenth century, fortress-building was something of an obsolete art, and the golden age of the castle maestro was over. Yet by that stage men like Master James had made their mark. The sight of a great stone castle looming from a German mountaintop or commanding the headland on a stretch of British coastline was now familiar – even comforting. And later rulers would make the most of castles, even if they did not build them in great numbers. During fears of a French invasion of England in the 1540s, Henry VIII considerably strengthened the south coast's string of fortresses. Four hundred years later the largest castle in that region, at Dover, was still a critical part of British military defence strategy: it served as the command centre for the Dunkirk evacuations at the beginning of the Second World War, and was later adapted to include a nuclear bunker in the rock below, for use in the event of a Third World War fought with atomic weapons.

So the castle was in some ways the iconic medieval architectural achievement. It married form and function seamlessly – and often thrillingly. It served practical and political ends. And it was a recurring device in late medieval literature, such as the Arthurian tales and Grail romances. From the fourteenth century onwards the 'Castle of Love' was a commonplace literary metaphor: here the castle might stand for the Virgin Mary, impregnable to the world, touched only by God. Or it could be a more playful symbol in tracts and poems about young love, virtue and vice. Either way, by the end of the Middle Ages the castle had migrated from the physical landscape to the realm of the imagination. Its only rival in the sphere of monumental architecture was the great Gothic cathedral.

Between Heaven and Earth

IN 1239, TWO GENERATIONS BEFORE EDWARD I remodelled northern Wales, the king of France, Louis IX, made a sensational purchase. Of all the kings in his Capetian royal line, Louis was the most ostentatiously pious. Early in his reign he had learned that a major religious relic was on the market. That relic was Christ's Crown of Thorns, which had been offered to creditors in Venice by Baldwin II, the Latin emperor of Constantinople. Baldwin and his Venetian friends had decided they were willing to sell it to the right buyer. Louis was determined the buyer should be him. It was a once-in-a-lifetime opportunity, and he was willing to spend whatever it took. Thus, after some negotiations, he bought the Crown of Thorns for the astonishing sum of 150,000 livres, and had it shipped to France via Venice. The king took delivery of it in the town of Villeneuve l'Archevêque, surrounded by his whole court, standing barefoot and penitential, dressed in only his shirt. He and his brother Robert, similarly attired, then personally transported the crown back to Paris, where it became the centrepiece for a royal relic collection that would later come to include a piece of the True Cross, the tip of the Holy Lance which had pierced Christ's side, and the Holy Sponge from which Jesus had sipped his last mouthful of vinegar before he died.[12] This was as fine a cache of holy treasures as existed anywhere in the west. All Louis lacked was an appropriately grand trophy cabinet in which to display them.

After deliberating a few years Louis decided the best way to showcase his relics was to commission a chapel to house them, built in the latest style, decorated with the finest religious images and stained glass, and endowed with a college of clergy. The result was the Sainte-Chapelle on the Île-de-la-Cité in Paris, a Gothic masterpiece of almost incomparable beauty, which is still one of the greatest architectural marvels in a city that does not lack for them. The building was erected in the middle of the Île's royal palace complex, easily accessible for private worship by the royal family and approved courtiers. Visitors were blessed indeed to set foot inside it. The Sainte-Chapelle followed the very latest Gothic trends: its walls soared, seemingly impossibly high, supported by perilously elongated columns, propped up outside the building by ornately decorated flying buttresses. It was built over two storeys, and in the upper of these, the vaulted ceiling seemed to stretch to the very heavens. The effect from the outside was like a graceful, long-legged stone spider standing on tip-toes; the effect on the inside was little short of sublime. Between every column were high, thin windows, topped with pointed arches and glazed with some of the most dazzling stained glass ever produced. To step inside the Sainte-Chapelle was supposed to feel like floating into heaven – and it still does today. There could not have been a more perfect setting for Louis' expensively acquired relics; nor a better showcase for his vision of himself as a king possessed of all the saintly virtues. Yet if the Sainte-Chapelle was magnificent, it was only one example of the daring and technical genius of the Gothic architects who worked on religious buildings in the thirteenth century. Just as military engineers were pushing castle-building to new levels, so their civilian counterparts were revolutionizing church-building.

WHEREAS CASTLES GAVE PHYSICAL FORM TO the military might of individual medieval lords, cathedrals, churches and chapels stood testament both to the faith of their founders, and the collective piety of the community that lived in and around them. This investment – of both cash and emotion – in great religious buildings went all the way back to the beginning of the Middle Ages.

We have already encountered some of the magnificent structures that sprang from the medieval impulse to build big in the name of God: Constantine the Great's imperial audience hall at Trier, the Basilica di San Vitale in Ravenna, Justinian's Hagia Sophia in Constantinople, great mosques in Medina, Damascus, Jerusalem and Cordoba, Charlemagne's Palatine Chapel at Aachen and the Church of the Holy Sepulchre. Yet if the urge to build vast temples was constant throughout the Middle Ages, its apotheosis in Christian Europe came between twelfth and fourteenth centuries, when some of the most daring, visionary architectural projects in western history were undertaken by builders working in a radical new style that today is known as Gothic. The Gothic movement – named in reference to the barbarians of old, by sneering fifteenth-century Italians, who saw the movement as a hideous perversion of the elegant aesthetic popular in ancient Rome – touched virtually every aspect of the arts, from painting and sculpture to embroidery and metalwork. But nowhere was it more enduring and exciting than in the field of architecture, and specifically in religious building. In western Europe during the first half of the Middle Ages, the dominant style was Romanesque: thick-walled buildings supported with elegant pillars and lit with round-topped windows.[13] Gothic departed radically from this template. Its key motif was the pointed arch, which allowed builders to pull together enormously long and tall buildings, held together by fine stone skeletons, framing almost impossibly thin walls and lit by what could seem like acres of stained glass: colossal yet at the same time dazzlingly light, they were the physical realization of a New Jerusalem, or 'heaven on earth'.[14]

THE FIRST GOTHIC BUILDING PROJECT OF the Middle Ages was the abbey church at St-Denis, on the outskirts of Paris.[15] An abbey had sat there since Carolingian times, and by the early twelfth century, during the reign of Louis VII, it had become the spiritual home of the Frankish kings who claimed to be 'most Christian' (*les rois très chrétiens*) in Europe, if not the world. Unfortunately, the abbey was also in a lamentable condition: small, run-down, and badly in need of an overhaul. Its woeful state brought together even arch-enemies like Bernard of Clairvaux and Peter Abelard: Bernard called St-Denis a 'synagogue of Satan' and Abelard wrote that it was home to 'intolerable obscenities'.[16] To bring the abbey church up to scratch, in the 1130s and 1140s the great statesman-abbot Suger devoted much of his time and energy to renovating it:

making it bigger, grander, and much more beautiful than anywhere else in France.

Central to Suger's vision was the construction of a new, 30m long choir, where, in Suger's words, perpetual Masses might be held 'without the disturbance of crowds'.[17] The choir took three years and three months to build, during which time Suger himself could often be seen rolling up his sleeves on the site, on one occasion personally leading a scouting mission in some woods near Paris to find a load-bearing beam of the size his builders needed.[18] But all the toil bore fruits, for when Suger's choir was complete it was jaw-dropping, with miraculously slender walls and columns casing huge stained-glass windows painted 'by the exquisite hands of many masters from different regions'.[19] The glass depicted scenes from the Old and New Testaments, the lives of the saints and events from the crusades – the second of which was underway at the same time as Suger's works were taking place. But this was not simply decoration. Suger's abbey church was a building that accorded with St Denis' supposed belief that God *was* light, and that through the light of God, the whole world was illuminated to man.[20]

Of course, as with any great church of the Middle Ages, the remodelled Abbey Church at St-Denis was packed with jewelled ornaments, fine sculpture, expensive wax candles, relics including the iron neck-collar that had shackled St Denis himself before his martyrdom, and secular treasures such as a necklace that had belonged to Queen Nanthilda, whose husband King Dagobert was believed to have been the abbey's first benefactor. It also held the *Oriflamme* – the sacred battle-flag representing French kingship. But while these treasures were impressive, it was the architectural form of the new choir that was truly inspirational. Its unprecedented grandeur and unity of vision, massive and exaggerated height, synthesis of ornate detail and elegant space set St-Denis apart from anything that had gone before – which was exactly as Suger had intended. (Not for nothing did that intrepid explorer and ambassador to the Mongols, William of Rubruck, claim that St-Denis was a much finer building than the Khan's palace in Karakorum.) When it was consecrated in 1144, St-Denis set a challenge to every other bishop, architect, engineer and patron of the age: beat that.[21]

Sure enough, they tried. From the 1140s, the Gothic style took off. At first the new movement was characteristic to northern France, where it chiefly influenced rebuilding projects close to nodes of Capetian royal power: the choir of Saint-Germain-des-Prés in Paris, a brand new cathedral in Senlis, and a reconstructed one at Sens, in Burgundy. But by the end of the century, word was out everywhere. Extraordinary new cathedrals were flying up in towns and cities throughout north-west Europe, notably in Cambrai, Arras, Tournai and Rouen. And in Paris, ground was broken on what became perhaps the most famous cathedral in the entire world: Notre-Dame. Reaching more than 100ft (33m) this was the tallest cathedral that had been contemplated to that point, and a marvel of engineering, with ingeniously positioned ranks of flying buttresses allowing the walls to reach four storeys in height.

Building Notre-Dame was a colossal feat of construction: nearly one hundred years separated the moment that Louis VII laid the cornerstone at Easter in 1163 and the completion of the now-iconic circular 'rose' stained-glass windows at either end of the transept. And even then, major works continued to be carried out there until the late fourteenth century.* The expense and effort was prodigious – but so was Notre-Dame's importance as a symbol of Paris and the French kingdom's pre-eminent sophistication and faith. Although the cathedral at Reims was preferred as the coronation site for French monarchs, and St-Denis was their mausoleum, Notre-Dame still exuded cultural and religious power from every grain of its fabric. At a critical moment during the last stages of the Hundred Years War, when the English brought their boy-king Henry VI to be crowned as king of France, they chose Notre-Dame for the occasion. It was every inch fit for this magnificent ceremony.

---

* At the time of writing, the cathedral is once more shrouded in scaffolding, as damage from a serious fire in 2019 is repaired – a process that is scheduled to take even twenty-first century builders at least a decade.

By that time, of course, the Gothic imprint had spread virtually everywhere across Europe. In France it reached its zenith at Beauvais, where the vaulted ceiling of the nave stretched nearly 50m above the earth. This was very slightly higher than a rival cathedral built around the same time in Amiens; the brainchild of a master mason called Robert de Luzarches, Amiens had more internal space than any other building completed in the entire Middle Ages.[22] But Beauvais' superior height was noted and treasured, as the scramble between bishops to commission ever-bigger projects became the ecclesiastical equivalent of an arms-race. (Unfortunately in Beauvais, the quest for height proved hubristic: in 1284 the ceiling vaults collapsed, probably due to engineering errors, and the roof came tumbling in, requiring years of expensive construction to make right.[23]) But if Beauvais was massive, it was hardly pre-eminent. Other fine Gothic cathedrals were built at Chartres, to house relics of the Virgin Mary; at Bourges, where a huge cathedral lavishly decorated with Gothic sculpture was augmented in the fifteenth century with an extraordinary astronomical clock; and as far south as Albi, where a bizarre cathedral, partly modelled on a fortress, was erected after the suppression of the Cathars – its military façade a reminder that while the Church was glorious it was also mighty, and would not tolerate dissent.

So massive, elaborate and difficult were the plans for these vast churches – which dwarfed most other medieval buildings by the same degree to which an elephant might tower over a cow – that works were still underway on some of them well into the sixteenth century. Succeeding generations of masters, labourers and benefactors, who often changed the vision for the finished building as they went along, were bound together across the years by their contribution to what could seem like never-ending projects.

This was by no means a phenomenon limited to France. In Germany, particularly glorious Gothic cathedrals appeared at Cologne and Strasbourg. In the fourteenth century King John of Bohemia and his son, the Holy Roman Emperor Charles VI, undertook an energetic rebuilding of Prague: giving the city a world-class university and a cathedral to match, paid for from a levy on profits from Bohemia's rich silver mines; the cathedral was home to a glorious shrine containing the relics of St Wenceslas,* the tenth-century duke-king who had helped further the cause of Christianity in the realm until he was murdered by his brother, Boleslav.[24] These cathedrals were staunchly French in flavour (reflecting what architectural historians now call the Rayonnant style). Others, however, in cities like Magdeburg, Regensburg and Ulm, did not stick slavishly to French styles, developing instead a German Gothic imprint, characterized by churches and cathedrals with single spires rather than two or more, and very wide roofs covering both the nave and the aisles alongside. Perhaps the most startling twist on the Gothic aesthetic, however, could be seen in buildings such as Pelplin Abbey in Poland, where from 1289 a vast abbey church was built in baked red brick – a necessity given how rare suitable rock-types for large-scale building projects are around the Baltic fringe, but an eye-catching visual departure from the French model nonetheless.

In southern Europe, the picture was more mixed. The Italians were generally lukewarm about the Gothic mania, with the notable exception of the astonishing, wide-fronted, deeply strange beast that was Milan Cathedral, begun during the time of the Visconti dukes in the early fourteenth century but not fully completed until the 1960s, some six hundred years later. In Spain, meanwhile, the Christian ethos that underpinned Gothic form was just one more addition to a rich blend of architectural styles influenced by the strong Islamic and Jewish presence on the peninsula. Some cathedrals – such as those in Barcelona, Burgos and at Palma, on Majorca – might at first glance have been picked up in northern Europe and dropped into Iberia by the angels. But others were profoundly local: Toledo Cathedral, founded in the 1220s, was an idiosyncratic attempt to put Gothic clothing on the city's main mosque; Seville's cathedral, converted from a mosque at the start of the fifteenth century, underwent a similar transformation. These – and others like them in Valencia and Lleida – are weird and

---

* The 'good king' commemorated today in the popular nineteenth-century Christmas carol.

wonderful places, unique products of Spain's variegated history. They also stand testament to the perceived power of Gothic design and decoration to bring a physical structure closer to God.

It would be possible to fill a whole shelf of books with stories about the construction of each of these extraordinary medieval masterpieces. But to understand in detail how much effort went into one, what powerful interests were involved, and why the expense and trouble was worthwhile, we will now return to England, to examine in closer detail the building of the cathedral at Lincoln: a triumph of Gothic construction which produced a building that was, for more than two centuries, the tallest structure anywhere on earth.

Lincoln

LINCOLN CATHEDRAL ORIGINALLY OWED EVERYTHING TO William the Conqueror. After invading England in 1066, the first Norman king undertook a large-scale rearrangement of the country. He built a lot of castles – including the 'White Tower' on the north bank of the river Thames, which became the Tower of London. But he also made significant rearrangements to the fabric and structure of the Church in England. Bishops were integral figures to the new Norman ruling system that William imposed from the top down, and he needed to be sure they were in the right places. Several bishops were therefore ordered to move their headquarters (or 'seats') from the countryside into towns and cities. The mark of William's changes can still be felt all over England today: it is why there is a cathedral at Salisbury and not Old Sarum, at Norwich instead of Thetford, and at Chichester instead of Selsey; and why we have a bishop of Bath and Wells, rather than one or the other. In most cases William's rearrangement of his English bishops and their seats did not involve long-distance removal. But in one case it did. In 1072 Pope Alexander III granted William permission to move the bishop of Dorchester-on-Thames in Oxfordshire 150 miles north-east, to the most distant extreme of his sprawling diocese, in Lincoln.

This was a drastic move, but one that made sense: whereas Dorchester was a pleasant Thames-side town on the edge of the Chiltern Hills, Lincoln was of far greater strategic and political importance. It had been founded by the Romans (as *Lindum Colonia*), occupied for two centuries by the Vikings, and sat at a useful strategic position on the road between London and York, as well as several other river courses and Roman-era thoroughfares. It was close to the east coast, and boasted a very defensible, enormously steep hill (known today, with typical East Midlands unfussiness, as Steep Hill.) And it was also in wild terrain, in need of taming: Norman authority in the region had been strongly resisted in the aftermath of the Conquest by a famous Saxon nobleman known in later outlaw tales as Hereward the Wake.[25]

On Steep Hill William built a castle. Soon after, his bishop Remigius, a Benedictine monk from Fécamp Abbey in Normandy, commissioned a cathedral directly next door. It was largely built in locally quarried limestone, at a time when many other Norman buildings were constructed in stone dug at Caen in Normandy, and imported to England on specially equipped ships.[26] It was completed by 1092, when Remigius died, and then embellished by one of his successors, who installed beautifully carved arches over the doors – inspired by Abbot Suger's works at St-Denis.[27] But this cathedral did not stand untroubled for long. It was burned in a fire of 1124, damaged during the battle of Lincoln in 1141 (when it was used as a makeshift fort) and shaken to its foundations by one of the worst earthquakes in Britain's recorded history in 1185.[28] This was bad luck. Yet in architectural terms it was good timing. In 1186 a new bishop of Lincoln was elected: a French Carthusian monk known in his lifetime as Hugh of Avalon (but in death as St Hugh of Lincoln). Hugh had come to England with a direct interest in building, having been tasked by his Order with constructing a Carthusian charterhouse in Somerset.* His appointment as a bishop meant he could now set his sights much

---

* Building this charterhouse was the financial responsibility of Henry II, a duty he had undertaken as one of his many penances for causing the death of Thomas Becket in 1170.

higher – literally. On the top of Steep Hill Bishop Hugh initiated works to completely transform the cathedral, which, during the following six decades, would rise to a height unseen on earth since the days of the Pharaohs.

The name of the mason (or masons) Hugh hired to oversee his new cathedral is lost, but his team plainly included at least one architect-engineer of the grandest vision, who was familiar with the latest and finest Gothic trends. These included the fine works recently completed on the choir of Canterbury Cathedral, which had been rebuilt under the direction of the great master William of Sens following a devastating fire in 1174; but influences and perhaps craftsmen arrived in Lincoln from further afield too, including Trondheim, across the North Sea in Norway, where a Gothic cathedral had been built in the mid-twelfth century. Now it was not just limestone that was dragged painstakingly up Steep Hill to the building site (probably by teams of oxen hauling carts), but also marble from Peterborough, further away in the diocese, which added a luxurious, sensuous feel to the pillars in an interior that would eventually reach nearly 150m in length. The west front of the original cathedral, through which most visitors would approach, was already intricately decorated with a carved frieze in the Romanesque tradition, depicting events from the Old and New Testaments, ranging from Satan's expulsion from heaven to Christ's Harrowing of Hell.[29] This had survived the ravages of fire, war and earthquake, and now set the tone for a building that would be filled with statues, carvings and reminders to all who entered of both the delights of salvation and the hideous torments of damnation.

A project on the scale of Lincoln's new Gothic cathedral was inevitably more than a lifetime's work, and when Bishop Hugh died in 1200, Lincoln's centre was still a huge construction site, which would have teemed with masons and labourers, carpenters and blacksmiths, the shell of the new cathedral covered with wooden scaffolding and pulley-operated cranes. But by dying, Hugh did his cathedral a great service.

According to a hagiographical account of his life, the bishop had often been seen hauling stone blocks and lime-mortar around the site, assisted by a crippled hod-carrier who was miraculously cured by his willingness to graft in the name of the Lord.[30] (The bishop's normal companion was a tame whooper swan, which he befriended on the day of his consecration and kept as a pet.) In death Hugh was far more than a mere willing pair of hands. In the half-century after his demise his reputation for sanctity, probity and holiness blossomed, until he became the object of a miracle cult. According to Adam of Eynsham, who wrote Hugh's biography in the first decades of the thirteenth century, his sanctity was obvious from the moment a surgeon cut open his fresh corpse to remove the intestines before burial: those who attended this grisly ritual noted with surprise that his bowels were empty of 'water or stool... as clean and immaculate as if someone had already carefully washed and wiped them... the internal organs shone like glass.'[31] And this was only the beginning. During his funeral procession, the candles on his bier would not be blown out, even by strong winds. A mourner with a broken arm was healed by a miraculous dream, while a cutpurse who robbed a woman who had come to pay her respects at Hugh's coffin was struck blind, so that he 'stagger[ed] about aimlessly like a drunkard' until he was captured.[32]

These, and wonders like them, were enough to earn Hugh sainthood in 1220. So Lincoln now became a tourist trap, with thousands of visitors arriving each year to venerate Hugh's shrine (along with a second one that was installed to hold his head). This new footfall necessitated further extension work.[33] But it also paid for it. Thus, at the far east end of the cathedral the 'Angel Choir' was added to house Hugh's remains;* it was so-called for the delightful angel sculptures that decorated it – taking their design cues from Westminster Abbey, which at this time was also

---

* There is another famous Hugh buried in the cathedral, too. In the thirteenth century a cult sprung up around a child known as Little Hugh of Lincoln, whose fate was allegedly to be murdered by Jews in a sacrificial ceremony. The story of the rise and veneration of Little Hugh is a prime example of the pernicious 'blood libel' phenomenon, part of broader fabric of vicious English anti-Semitism in the later Middle Ages which crescendoed in 1290 when Edward I expelled all Jews from the realm.

undergoing massive refurbishments, under the attentive eye of King Henry III.[34]

By the time the Angel Choir was complete in 1280, Lincoln was unquestionably in the first rank of English cathedrals – and this was a very glamorous club in which to sit. In England, Westminster had undergone its elaborate, royal renovations, recentred on the shrine of Edward the Confessor. Canterbury was an imposing seat for the English primate, and contained the world-famous shrine to Thomas Becket. York Minster, seat of the northern archbishop, was undergoing magnificent works of its own. And glorious Gothic building programmes were either underway or complete in every corner of the land: Exeter, Salisbury, Winchester, Gloucester and Wells in the south and west; Ely and Norwich in the east; Durham and Carlisle in the north; Hereford and Worcester in the Welsh borders. Meanwhile, in Wales there had been major works at St David's, Llandaff and St Asaph; Gothic sensibilities had also touched the kingdom of Scotland, where they were notably put into effect at Dunblane and Elgin cathedrals, and at Melrose Abbey.

Out of these various works, a distinct take on Gothic architecture was developing; what are today called the Decorated and Perpendicular styles were hallmarks of English cathedral-building during the later Middle Ages.[35] But it was no accident that there was such creativity and ambition in the British Isles. As we have seen, by the late thirteenth century England in particular was an enormously wealthy kingdom. Its economy was supercharged by the booming wool industry; its churchmen possessed huge tracts of profitable land; its kings commanded a relatively unified state and took a keen interest in monumental building of all sorts, not only in the form of castles. Most of England's Plantagenet monarchs were keenly attuned to the power that they could project through employing world-class master-builders – which is why many English cathedrals have a royal tomb somewhere within.

There was certainly keen royal interest in Lincoln. Part of Bishop Hugh's vision for his remodelled cathedral had been a large tower at the centre of the building, topped with a spire. Unfortunately, during the first decades of the tower's construction, problems arose with its structure, and in 1237 it fell, brought down by its own weight. Repairs were first made in the 1250s under orders from King Henry III, whose interest in architecture was unsurpassed by that of any other king of his dynasty save perhaps Henry VI, who in the fifteenth century founded the majestic Gothic chapels at Eton College and King's College, Cambridge. Then, in the early fourteenth century, Lincoln's tower was enlarged and extended to an even greater height. When it was complete in 1311 its spire, made of wood and finished in lead, was 160m tall. This was some 11m higher than the Great Pyramid of Giza at Cheops in Egypt – which had for almost four thousand years been the tallest man-made structure on earth. Lincoln Cathedral would retain this status until a gale blew the spire down in 1548.*

By the time Lincoln had become a wonder of the world, it had also officially become the repository for royal as well as saintly relics. In the early winter of 1290 Edward I's beloved queen, Eleanor of Castile, died in the village of Harby in Nottinghamshire, just thirty miles away from Lincoln. Eleanor, as we have seen, had been an impeccably dutiful queen, her service to the crown extending to giving birth on the building site of Caernarfon Castle. Edward was distraught by her death and determined to mark with great honour her progress back to London, where she was to be buried. On the first night of this journey, her body was taken to a priory just outside Lincoln's city walls, and her entrails were removed to slow decomposition. On 3 December they were buried in the cathedral, and were later given a fine tomb near St Hugh's shrine.†

Outside in the town was erected the first of a series of twelve 'Eleanor Crosses' – ornately carved stone pillars prominently located in town squares to mark the fact that the queen's remains had rested there. The inspiration for this elaborate and unusual

---

* Even so, nothing taller than Lincoln Cathedral's spire was built anywhere in the world until the Eiffel Tower (300m) in 1887. Today of course, 160m is now considered puny; the tallest building at the time of writing was the Burj Khalifa in Dubai, and this will in due course be superseded by the Jeddah Tower in Saudia Arabia, which when complete is planned to stand at 1,000m.

† The tomb in the Angel Choir today is a Victorian reproduction of the original, which was vandalized beyond repair during the English Civil War in the seventeenth century.

commemoration of Eleanor's procession probably came from France, where twenty years earlier monuments known as *montjoies* were set up along the funeral procession route of Louis IX – he who commissioned the Sainte-Chapelle in Paris to house the Crown of Thorns.[36] The Eleanor Crosses were designed by a team of the best mason-architects working in England at that time: John of Battle, Michael of Canterbury and Alexander of Abingdon. Most are now destroyed or lost, but they were all once Gothic masterpieces in their own right – ordered by a king who understood, as all great medieval rulers did, that a legacy could not be built in blood alone, but had to be certified and made permanent in stone.

Although Edward was, as we have seen, a castle-builder first and a cathedral-builder second, he nevertheless ensured his place in Lincoln Cathedral's extraordinary history. And Lincoln, in turn, earned its own place at the heart of the story of the medieval Gothic adventure. Walking through the ancient doorway in the west front on a quiet afternoon in the twenty-first century, and strolling down the cathedral's vast length to the Angel Choir in the far east, admiring the near-infinite wealth of decorations and sculptures, which stretch so high that many have seldom been glimpsed since the medieval masons who originally carved them descended from the scaffolding some 750 years ago, is one of the most exhilarating experiences you can enjoy – and a testament to the lasting power of this entire age of western architecture.*

Yet before we leave the realm of the medieval builders, there is one last case to consider, from a city that was – and is – only lightly touched by the French-Gothic mania for endless sheets of glass and ceilings that touched the clouds. It is time to pay a visit Florence, which at the turn of the fourteenth century was to be the venue for a great cathedral of its own: suitable for a city so proud

---

* It can, incidentally, help us to understand why Gothic had such a vigorous revival in the nineteenth century, as Victorian architects grasped at a style that seemed to embody all that was magical and grand in western history. The high-point of neo-Gothic, cod-medieval architecture is of course the Palace of Westminster in London, home to the Houses of Parliament, rebuilt by Charles Barry after the fire of 1834 which all but destroyed the medieval structure.

of its own wealth and glory, but hungry for something other than the arches and spires that soared everywhere north of the Alps.

From Spires to Domes

IN THE EARLY 1290S, AROUND THE time that Edward of England was commissioning his last Welsh castles, the Italian artist and sculptor Arnolfo di Cambio was in Rome, working on a tomb. It was located in the old Basilica of St Peter, and its occupant was to be Pope Boniface VIII – *bête noire* of the French king Philip IV, and recipient of the so-called Agnani Slap.* At this time Boniface was still alive, but it was traditional for any self-respecting magnate of Church or state to oversee works on their own tomb, if nothing else to be sure the job was done to their satisfaction. Arnolfo had previously created a fine tomb for a powerful French cardinal, Guillaume de Bray, located in a large church at nearby Orvieto. Before that, he had also served as a court sculptor to Charles of Anjou, brother of Louis IX and king of Naples and Sicily (d. 1285) – producing an uncannily lifelike statue of the king sitting on a throne, wearing a Roman senator's toga. He therefore had a working knowledge of French styles and French attitudes, and a good claim to be the foremost sculptor at work in Italy. Certainly, he was a man fit to build a pope's resting place. Yet Arnolfo had bigger ambitions than statues and tombs. Around 1293 he was invited to fulfil them. The citizens of Florence wanted a new cathedral. They asked Arnolfo to come and build it for them.

Arnolfo had designed one cathedral already, in Orvieto, where he had planned a large Romanesque basilica, on which work had begun around 1290. In Florence, however, the opportunities were much greater. The city had a population of perhaps forty-five thousand people (which made it larger than London), ruled over by an oligarchic government generally dominated by wealthy merchant families. Like many other Italian cities it had been

* See chapter 11.

plagued for most of the thirteenth century by violent civil strife, firstly between a pro-Hohenstaufen imperial faction known as the Ghibellines and a papal faction known as the Guelphs, and subsequently between parties known as the Blacks and Whites.[37] These political tensions often gave rise to brawls, fights, murders, coups, counter-coups, petty revolutions and even all-out war. Yet they did not diminish Florentines' overall sense of civic pride and ability to make money. The streets may not have been safe at night, but they were clean and well laid out, and business in them was booming, as ambitious merchants and bankers harvested huge profits from all across the world.* Florence was already producing or attracting great artists, writers and architects, including the artists Cimabue and his protégé, Giotto, the poet Dante Alighieri and the visionary painter Coppo di Marcovaldo. Florentines also had a particularly acute sense of the political power of buildings: one favourite activity in the aftermath of any bout of political upheaval was for the victorious party to tear down the houses and towers belonging to their disgraced and vanquished rivals. There was plenty for Arnolfo to do.

According to his admiring biographer, the sixteenth-century painter and architect Giorgio Vasari, Arnolfo built or rebuilt half the city of Florence in his time there, including the walls and the famous Palazzo Vecchio, the fortress-like city hall which overlooks the Piazza della Signori. It seems very likely that Vasari was exaggerating. Nevertheless, Arnolfo took on at least three major projects more or less simultaneously. The first was to rebuild the church at the Badia – one of the most prominent Benedictine abbeys in the city (and by tradition, the place where the city's most famous poet, Dante Alighieri, first set eyes on his poetic muse Beatrice). The second was to overhaul the Franciscan church of Santa Croce. The third, and greatest, was to begin work on a replacement for a dilapidated thousand-year-old cathedral dedicated to the city's then-patron St Reparata. And here Arnolfo was given licence to let his imagination run riot.

* See chapter 10.

Had Arnolfo been working in Paris, London or Cologne, his designs for these buildings would surely have followed the French Gothic style. Yet in Italy, architecture was developing along different lines. Arches remained rounded in the Romanesque fashion, rather than pointed. Elaborate systems of flying buttresses and dizzying spires were seldom seen. Walls were walls – thick and strong and structurally sound, rather than frameworks for vast plates of brightly coloured glass. And the gleaming white and yellow limestone so popular north of the Alps was only rarely preferred to sandstone and brick. Although height, size and ornateness of decoration had all become more important in Italian building projects during the thirteenth century there was no pressure whatever on Arnolfo suddenly to bless Florence with its own take on the abbey church of St-Denis.[38] Arnolfo was free to create buildings that would be characteristically Florentine, adopting elements of the Gothic movement, but not slavishly so. His works on the Badia and the Franciscans' church at Santa Croce were elegant but comparatively spare and uncomplicated – although the former is now distinguished by its spired tower, and the latter lavishly decorated with a nineteenth-century neo-Gothic marble façade. (Santa Croce became the burial place for some of Florence's most stellar residents, including Michelangelo, Galileo, Machiavelli and Gioachino Rossini.) His design for the city's new cathedral, however, was ambitious and potentially triumphant.

The cathedral Arnolfo designed directly anticipated the world-renowned building that now occupies the Piazza del Duomo in central Florence: one of the most immediately recognizable places in the world, the centerpiece of Florence's iconic skyline, and a magnet to modern tourists who queue for hours in the baking heat of Tuscan summers to set foot inside for a mere few minutes. To allow for it, workmen tore down a swathe of the city, including the old cathedral of Santa Reparata and another nearby church, and exhumed a graveyard. In the space they cleared, Arnolfo laid the foundations for an oblong nave, 66m in length and 21m wide, with bays on either side. This replicated, almost to the centimetre, his design for the church of Santa Croce, and Arnolfo probably planned his cathedral to mimic Santa Croce's wooden (rather than stone-vaulted) roof. But where the two designs differed was at the eastern end, where Arnolfi envisaged the cathedral rising into a large dome – echoing that marvel of classical engineering which crowned the Pantheon in Rome. The dome would sit on an octagonal base, and around it, three half-octagonal arms would complete the design, while helping to support the anticipated weight of such a complicated structure.[39] It was to be slightly larger than the dome that crowned the Hagia Sophia in Constantinople.[40] This was a majestic plan. The foundation stone was laid in 1296.

As we have already seen, few medieval architects lived to see their cathedrals completed. Arnolfo was no exception. His designs and the start he made on the building work certainly pleased the Florentine authorities – four years into the project Arnolfo was granted freedom from taxation there for the rest of his life and lauded in official city documents as 'a more famous master and greater expert in the building of churches than any other who is known in neighbouring parts.'[41] He was a walking, talking, credit to the city itself. But at some point between 1301 and 1310 he died, and work on his cathedral ground to a halt. A façade at the western end (replaced in the sixteenth century and now largely lost) featured sculptures by Arnolfo, depicting figures ranging from the Virgin Mary to Pope Boniface; around half the nave had probably also been built. But without the cathedral's master the impetus for completing his designs was lost.

There were, to be fair, extenuating political circumstances. In 1311 an aggressive, if short-lived, new German king, Henry VII, marched into Italy to be crowned as Holy Roman Emperor. The Florentines rejected him, and were forced to arm themselves to defend the city against imperial troops. Although Henry died of malaria during his campaign, Florence was subsequently attacked by the pro-imperial ruler of nearby Pisa and Lucca. Strengthening the city walls took precedence over finishing the cathedral. In 1333 Florence also needed a new bridge, after floods swept away the existing *Ponte Vecchio*. True, in the 1330s the genius Giotto built a tall, freestanding, undeniably Gothic cathedral belltower directly alongside Arnolfo's nave. But by mid-century, no more significant work had been done. The cathedral was not quite a white elephant, but it represented unfinished business.

. It took until the late 1360s for Florence's cathedral committee to agree to restart works, under a revised design drawn up by the most respected mason of the day, Neri di Fioravanti, who envisaged enlarging the dome even further than Arnolfo had planned – making it bigger than the Pantheon – and concluding in a small spire. This was a Gothic flourish, but the dome itself smacked of ancient Rome by way of Byzantium and even Arab Jerusalem. It was also, apparently, unbuildable. Neri created a huge scale model of the dome, which was placed in the cathedral nave; every year the building committee members would swear to find a way to realize it.[42] But for decades, no one could see how it was to be done. Not until 1418 – some 122 years after the foundation stone on Arnolfo's original cathedral was laid – did anyone come up with an engineering solution to the conundrum of Florence's *Duomo*. That person was a mathematical genius called Filippo Brunelleschi, who won an open competition for the commission, and was forced to invent entirely new building systems and lifting machines to winch some 4 million bricks into position, during a construction process that took the better part of two decades. It was a gruelling end to a painfully drawn-out project. But when Brunelleschi finished the Dome, the cathedral now known as *Santa Maria del Fiore* was instantly recognized as a marvel of the sort scarcely seen since the death of the classical world a millennium before. Today it is generally recognized as the founding architectural achievement of the Italian Renaissance and the ancestor of the domes that adorned many monumental buildings of the modern age, including St Paul's Cathedral in London, Les Invalides in Paris and the US Capitol in Washington D.C. But for that reason, it belongs to a phase of the Middle Ages that had yet to dawn when Arnolfo di Cambio broke ground in 1296.

That phase – the beginning of the end of the medieval world – began in 1347, when *Santa Maria del Fiore* was a half-built curiosity, born but ungrown and waiting for a genius to bring it to conclusion. The event that turned the world upside-down was a pandemic. It hit western Europe when ships arriving in Italy from the east disembarked not only spices and exotic luxury goods, but a disease worse than any since the age of Justinian. This was the Black Death, which killed around 40 per cent of Europe's population and changed the world forever. The swathe it cut across the west and the reaction of the living to unfathomable death marks the start of the final part of our story.

Part IV

Revolution

13

SURVIVORS

'The past has devoured us, the present is gnawing our entrails...'

GABRIELE DE' MUSSIS,
LAWYER AND PLAGUE CHRONICLER

In the late summer of 1314 a hard rain fell across north-west Europe. It rained and it rained, and it barely stopped throughout the autumn. Rivers rose and fields flooded. Roads and tracks churned up. When the winter passed crops had to be sown in waterlogged fields and it seemed certain the harvest that followed was going to be weak. Then in May 1315 the rains came again, and this time they fell all summer. As the leaden skies unloaded, temperatures remained chilly – and as the year wore on they plummeted. The harvest was indeed a failure, and the next winter was abominably cold. By Easter 1316, people were beginning to starve. An English chronicler recorded the dire conditions among ordinary folk as the cost of grain fluctuated wildly and unpredictably, at times soaring to 400 per cent of its normal level. 'A great famine appeared,' he wrote. 'Such a scarcity has not been seen in our time, nor heard of for a hundred years.'[1]

This was only the beginning. The year 1316 followed the same pattern: chronic rainfall from the spring onwards, a summer that never came, and a freezing winter. In 1317 things were somewhat better, although there was barely enough grain to sow; only in 1318 was there at last a harvest worth the name.[2] Even so, the trouble was not over. Those farm animals which had survived the wet, the cold and the dearth were so weak they fell victim to a lethal, highly contagious, fast-moving disease which whipped around the west. It was probably the virus we now call rinderpest, which gave cows and oxen terrible fevers and diarrhoea, rotted the flesh in their noses and mouths and (more often than not) killed them within two or three weeks. It appeared in Mongolia then spread west, and was soon slashing through herds in central Europe, Germany, France, Denmark, the Netherlands, England, Scotland and Ireland. It killed, on average, 60 per cent of the cattle in any given place.[3] The plague peaked in 1319. But in 1320–1 the return of torrential rain and flooding ruined yet another harvest and grain failed again.

This was a Biblically cruel time, in which the entire agricultural basis for survival was swept away across the west for six years, causing a humanitarian crisis to compare with the worst famines of the twentieth century.[*] In the summer of 1316 alone, 10 per cent of the inhabitants of Ypres in Flanders died. This was not unusual.[4] One chronicler sketched the miserable conditions in England – which quite aside from hunger and murrain was also tormented by runaway inflation, war with Scotland and the hapless governance of King Edward II. 'The usual kinds of edible meat were too scarce, so horse meat became precious and fat dogs were stolen. It was said that men and women in many places secretly ate their own children...'[5] Another annalist agreed: 'Many thousands died in different places... dogs and horses and other unclean things were consumed as food. Alas, land of England! You who out of your abundance once helped other lands, now, poor and needy, are forced to beg!'[6] The latter writer, an eyewitness to what became known as the Great Famine, composed his chronicle in or before the year 1325. Little did he know that the worst lay ahead.

---

[*] Between 3 per cent and 5 per cent of the population of Russia died in the famine of 1921–2; the death rate of the Great Famine of the early fourteenth century was likely two or three times this, although of course absolute numbers were considerably lower, given the smaller population of Europe at the time.

Ice and germs

THE FOURTEENTH CENTURY WAS A TIME of cataclysmic change, particularly for people in the European west. The changes began with the climate. For several hundred years after AD 900 global temperatures had risen: the so-called Medieval Warm Period. But around 1300 they began to drop again – and sharply. This rapid cooling was prompted by a period of intense volcanic activity around the world, during which seismic explosions belched sulfur dioxide and other sunlight-reflecting aerosols into the stratosphere. The climate became so regularly and bitterly cold that watercourses from the Baltic Sea to the River Thames and even the Golden Horn at Constantinople were prone to freezing in winter – phenomena that led to the period between 1300 and 1850 becoming known as the Little Ice Age.[7]

Of course, the onset of the Little Ice Age alone was not the only cause of the Great Famine of 1315–21. Human catastrophes are almost always the result of a delicate interplay between societies and their environments, and at the turn of the fourteenth century, the west was primed for a shock. The European population boom that began around the year AD 1000 had helped spur economic activity, invention and commerce. Yet at the same time it had created deep frailties. Technological improvements in agriculture and food production – heavy ploughs, watermills, windmills and crop rotation systems – allowed farmers to get more from the soil, while the drive to clear forests and drain marshes opened up vast new tracts of land for cultivation. But there were limits – and around 1300 western society had reached them.

There were, put simply, too many people for the technology of the time to handle. The population of England had raced from perhaps 1.5 million at the time of the Norman Conquest to around 6 million on the eve of the Great Famine.* That pattern was broadly mirrored elsewhere, especially in the cities of Europe and the Near East, which quadrupled or more in size from the middle of the

---

* This was a population spike not reached again in England until the eighteenth century.

twelfth century, bringing tens of thousands of people together in conditions that were inevitably cramped and less than sanitary. In the countryside, meanwhile, people were farming ever-smaller plots of land, and cultivating increasingly marginal areas. The result was creeping and eventually chronic overpopulation, which made countries across the west very sensitive to disruptions in their food supply. At the same time, the busy increase in global trade and travel that had begun with the Mongol conquests of the twelfth and thirteenth centuries had quietly opened up the possibility of diseases passing just as freely around the world as silks, slaves and spices. The rinderpest cattle panzootic had shown what was possible for a virulent disease with an abundant and mobile host species. As it would transpire, fourteenth-century humans were every bit as vulnerable as their cows.

THE BLACK DEATH, AS THE PLAGUE pandemic which scythed through Asia, Europe, north Africa and some regions of sub-Saharan Africa from the 1340s is known, began in a similar place to the rinderpest pandemic: with the Mongols.[8] As we have already seen, plague was caused by the bacillus *Yersinia pestis* (or *Y. pestis*), which jumped to humans from steppe rodents such as rats and marmots via flea-bites.[*] Eight hundred years earlier the Justinianic pandemic had ripped around sixth-century Byzantium, killing millions of people. What emerged in the fourteenth century was worse: a new, hyper-infectious mutation of the same illness, which could apparently spread between rats, cats, dogs, birds and people with uncommon ease. Once in a human host it caused similar, ghastly symptoms to the sixth-century pestilence: fever, swellings known as 'buboes' around the groin, armpits and neck, internal bleeding, uncontrollable vomiting and death within a few days.[9] It also developed a pneumonic strain that could be passed from human to human on the breath.

---

[*] See chapter 3.

This hybrid bubonic-pneumonic plague was probably circulating among the Mongols of Central Asia in the early 1330s. It spread outwards through the eastern world during that decade, throughout Transoxania, China and Persia, although it did not seem to make a very serious impact in India.[10] By the mid-1340s it was moving freely among the Mongols of the Golden Horde, and according to traditional plague narratives, it was they who passed it on to westerners during a siege of the Genoese-held port of Caffa on the Black Sea in 1347. An account of the siege, written by an Italian lawyer from Piacenza called Gabriele de' Mussis, described how disease surged through the Mongol army 'as though arrows were raining down from heaven... all medical advice and attention was useless; the Tatars died as soon as the signs of disease appeared on their bodies: swellings in the armpit or groin caused by coagulating humours, followed by putrid fever.'[11] Heavily depleted by sickness, the Mongols abandoned the siege, but not before spreading their germs. In de' Mussis' colourful telling, 'they ordered corpses to be placed in catapults and lobbed into the city in the hope that the intolerable stench would kill everyone inside. What seemed like mountains of dead were thrown into the city, and the Christians could not hide or flee or escape from them, although they dumped as many of the bodies as they could in the sea. And soon the rotting corpses tainted the air and poisoned the water supply... no one knew, or could discover, a means of defence.'[12]

Whether this was strictly true is hard to say. The plague of the 1340s was undoubtedly wickedly infectious, but stench alone is not a disease vector. Be that as it may: soon after the siege of Caffa, plague cases began to appear in Italy at Genoa and Venice, brought there aboard merchant and military boats that may well have travelled from the Black Sea. 'When the sailors [arrived...] it was as if they had brought evil spirits with them,' recalled de' Mussis. 'Every city, every settlement, every place was poisoned by the contagious pestilence, and their inhabitants, both men and women, died suddenly.' In crowded cities, where extended families lived under the same roof in tightly cramped streets, and where rats and other flea-bearing animals abounded, there was no stopping the spread. 'When one person had contracted the illness, he poisoned his whole family,' wrote de' Mussis. 'Mass funerals had to be held and there was not enough room to bury the growing numbers of dead. Priests and doctors, upon whom most of the care of the sick devolved, had their hands full in visiting the sick and, alas, by the time they left they too had been infected and followed the dead immediately to the grave.'[13] Death spread almost unimaginably fast, and as it did so it seemed to shred the whole fabric of the normal world, leaving survivors as bewildered as the dying. It was truly apocalyptic. One eyewitness in Ireland left blank pages at the end of his chronicle, in case by some miracle there were any humans left in the future to carry on his work. 'The past has devoured us, the present is gnawing our entrails, the future threatens yet greater dangers,' wailed de' Mussis.[14] He was not far wrong.

ANYONE WHO HAS LIVED THROUGH A lethal, fast-moving pandemic* will recognize in basic outline the distressing and chaotic situation described here in medieval Italy, as the advance of the sickness turned normal life upside down. The Black Death seemed to have a mind of its own. It moved through populations apparently at will, jumping from city to city and country to country, until it was everywhere. In 1347 it leapt across the Black Sea to Constantinople and Italy, from where it exploded around the Mediterranean. Seafaring merchants bore it to the Holy Land, Cyprus and the Greek islands. Road travellers took it over the Alps to the Holy Roman Empire, including Bohemia.[15] During the spring of 1348 plague was rampant in France; that summer it travelled to England; by 1349 it was spreading northwards towards Scotland and across the sea, east to Scandinavia and west to Ireland. Medieval writers blamed the pestilence variously on God's wrath, the prevalence of vice, the coming of the Antichrist,

---

* The most recent being the global spread of COVID-19, which is at its height as I write these pages.

the impending resurrection of Frederick II Hohenstaufen, the excessive tightness of women's clothes, misalignment of the planets, sodomy, evil vapours, rain, Jewish conspiracy, the tendency of hot and moist people to overindulge in sex and baths, and under-ripe vegetables, which doctors of medicine were sure caused 'windy ulcers'.[16] Desperate people tried prophylactics and remedies ranging from quarantine and laxatives to bloody self-flagellation and plague-themed prayer. But the sad fact was that the plague's spread illustrated nothing so much as the deep interconnection between medieval communities – and their terrible vulnerability to an infection that thrived on human mobility, overcrowding and limited standards of hygiene. *Y. Pestis* had only one biological imperative: to replicate in new hosts. In the absence of microbial biology and vaccine technology, there were no effective medical responses save for total quarantine and patience while the disease ran its course. Once the Black Death was loose, nothing could stop it.

The Black Death's first wave lasted from 1347 until 1351. During that time, in the worst-affected countries, up to 60 per cent of the local population died. This was a staggering mortality rate, which reeling chroniclers understandably exaggerated even further: some suggested that by the end of the pandemic, just one in ten people was left alive. And the Black Death did not just carry off the poor. True, the rich were better able to flee diseased cities for the comparative safety of quarantine in the countryside, a phenomenon the great Italian writer Giovanni Boccaccio memorialized in his *Decameron*, a collection of 100 short stories told by a group of ten affluent young people who escape Florence to dodge infection. But wealth alone could not guarantee immunity, either from the sickness itself or the psychological trauma that came with survival. Edward III of England's beloved daughter Joan was killed by plague in Bordeaux as she travelled to be married in Castile in 1348 – a tragedy that prompted her father to reflect that the death 'seizes young and old alike, sparing no one and reducing rich and poor to the same level'.[17] Joan's prospective father-in-law, Alfonso XI, also died, as did Eleanor, queen consort of the king of Aragon. The Byzantine emperor John VI Cantacuzenus lost his youngest

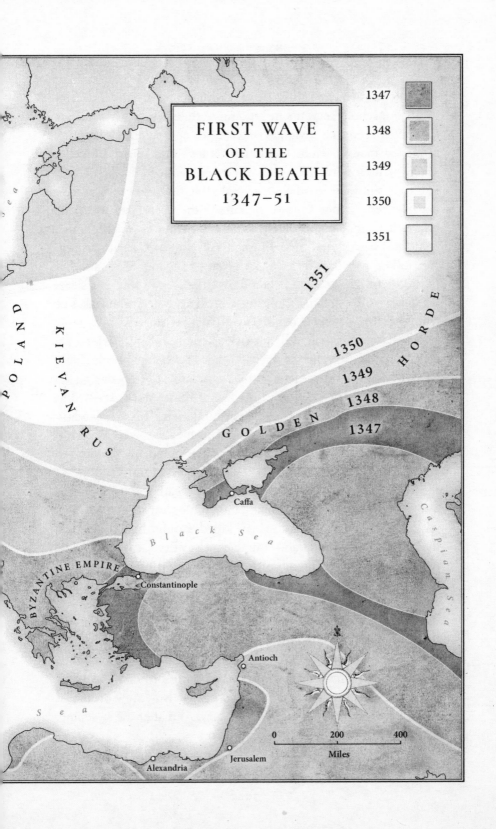

FIRST WAVE
OF THE
BLACK DEATH
1347–51

1347
1348
1349
1350
1351

POLAND

KIEVAN RUS

GOLDEN HORDE

1351
1350
1349
1348
1347

Caffa

Black Sea

Caspian Sea

BYZANTINE EMPIRE

Constantinople

Antioch

Sea

Jerusalem

Alexandria

0   200   400
Miles

son.[18] Pope Clement VI lost three cardinals and around a quarter of his household servants in little more than a year when plague hit the papal court at Avignon. Boccaccio's contemporary Petrarch mourned many friends, including his love and muse, Laura: in letters written while Italy was still in the teeth of the pandemic, Petrarch summed up the survivors' guilt that many must have experienced. In one missive he cursed the year 1348, which he said 'left us lonely and bereft; for it took from us wealth which could not be restored by the Indian, Caspian or Carpathian Sea.' In another, written after he was rocked by the loss of yet another friend, Petrarch wrote as if in a daze: 'The life we lead is a sleep, whatever we do, dreams. Only death breaks the sleep and wakes us from dreaming. I wish I could have woken before this.'[19]

As it was Petrarch did not 'wake' for another quarter of a century, so he was alive to see the Black Death come back. There were major European plague outbreaks in 1361 and 1369, during the 1370s and again in the 1390s. (The last of these attacks seemed to strike particularly hard at boys and young men.) These secondary waves were not as severe as the first, but they caused widespread misery and mortality all the same, and prevented any rebound in population numbers, which remained depressed until the end of the Middle Ages and beyond. So the Black Death was by no means a one-off event, even in simple epidemiological terms. It was a long, drawn-out pandemic which killed around half the people in Europe and comparable numbers elsewhere, cast a shadow over the popular imagination for decades, and brought about a radical reshaping of western demography, political and social structures, attitudes and ideas. Although in one sense a freak, 'Black Swan' catastrophe, the plague also exposed the weaknesses and vulnerabilities of fourteenth-century western society, and either directly or indirectly inspired survivors to seek to change the world they had, by some miracle, clung on to.[20] The Black Death was not just a reaper's scythe: it was also a new broom. It swept hard across the fourteenth century. And after the sweeping, things would never look the same again.

After the Flood

IN SEPTEMBER 1349, ROBERT OF AVESBURY, a clerk who worked for the archbishop of Canterbury at Lambeth Palace, stepped into the streets of London to witness a parade of Flemish flagellants. Around six hundred of these curious characters had recently appeared in the city, and they were now a regular sight. Twice each day they appeared, dressed in simple white, open-backed shifts, wearing caps with red crosses on their heads. 'Each carried a scourge with three tails in his right hand,' wrote Robert. 'Each tail had a knot and through the middle many had fixed sharp nails. They marched in a line, one behind the other, whipping themselves with these scourges on their naked and bloody bodies. Four of them would chant in their own language and another four would chant back like a litany. Three times they would all hurl themselves on the ground... stretching out their hands in the shape of a cross. The singing would continue while, one by one, each would step over the others and give a stroke with his scourge to the man lying under him.'[21]

At this point, organized flagellation had become something of a craze. It began in Italian cities around 1260, in the midst of a fraught period of hunger and destructive warfare between the Guelphs and Ghibellines. The practice subsequently caught on in Germany and north-west Europe. Flagellants sought to atone for their own sins, and those of mankind at large, through organized self-harm.[22] Besides being an interesting reversal of the crusading imperative to hurt other people in the name of Christ, flagellation was also tailor-made for the Black Death, which seemed certain proof that God was angry and needed to be appeased. Of course, as we have already seen, it had no effect whatsoever on the spread of the pandemic. (Today, indeed, we might speculate that large-scale daily gatherings without robust social distancing protocols probably helped transmit plague even faster.) But this did not stop participants from trying. Nor did it dissuade churchmen across the plague-affected lands from organizing less gory, but still abjectly penitential, weekly or bi-weekly parades, in which desperate people called on God to spare them. Edward III spelled out how this worked in a letter to the English bishops in 1349, explaining that 'prayer, fasting and the exercise of virtue' would encourage God to 'repel the plague and illness and confer peace and tranquility and health of body and soul.'[23] Countless other leaders like him urged the same, all to no avail. However, the immediate, religious reflexes that the Black Death set off were only a small part of the human response to the pestilence.

The first economic consequence of the pandemic was to wreak havoc on prices and wages. When Europe's population peaked at the start of the century, there had been abundant workers, many of them bonded to the land in the legally unfree status of serfdom. However, the effect of losing around one in every two people, virtually at a stroke, stood the world on its head and put labour suddenly at a premium. The chronicler Henry Knighton recorded that in 1349 'crops perished in the fields for lack of harvesters'; even where willing workers could be found, the cost to landowners of bringing in their crops rocketed.[24] The sudden population decline also caused a collapse in the price of land rents. In a situation so severe that some villages were wiped out and abandoned forever, land was suddenly dirt cheap, and landlords were scrambling for tenants. Not surprisingly, a double-whammy of soaring wages and plummeting rents sent panic swirling through political societies, whose most powerful members petitioned their rulers to help save them from financial ruin.

In England the government acted quickly. In 1349 and 1351 Edward III's government rushed out legislation (the Ordinance and Statute of Labourers) which made it illegal for workers to claim wages above pre-pandemic rates. These were specified in law: five pence a day for mowing, three pence a day for carpentry or masonry work, two and a half pence a day for threshing wheat, and so on. At the same time it became a legal requirement for every able-bodied person under the age of sixty to work. Begging was outlawed. Workers were not permitted to leave their estates and employers were forbidden to poach them by offering wages in excess of the government's limits. The law was strictly enforced. According to Knighton (who lived in an abbey in Leicestershire and was therefore firmly on the side of the landowner), workers were 'so arrogant and obstinate' that they continued to demand high pay, effectively holding employers to ransom. This resulted in large fines being levied on 'abbots, priors, knights... and others both great and small throughout the kingdom.' At the same time, 'the king caused many labourers to be arrested, and sent them to prison; many escaped and fled to the forests and woods for a time, and those who were captured were severely punished.'[25] The text of the Statute of Labourers made no bones about where the sympathies of legislators lay: the law was aimed, it said, at mitigating 'the malice of servants'.[26]

This attitude – of despising the poor except insofar as they occasionally reminded one of Jesus – was entirely typical in the hierarchical, aristocrat-led societies of the late Middle Ages. Yet in the teeth of a pandemic it was also dangerous. The Black Death's harrying of the western world was more than just a financial inconvenience to be solved by legislation. It brought about an immediate and drastic rearrangement of European demography – which meant power lurched suddenly towards ordinary people. As a consequence, the second half of the fourteenth century saw a sudden rise in violent large-scale popular uprisings against established authorities. They began just as the first wave of the Black Death was beginning to wane, and continued until the end of the 'calamitous' fourteenth century.[27]

POPULAR REBELLIONS HAPPENED THROUGHOUT THE MIDDLE Ages. It would have been strange if they did not. The vast majority of medieval human beings were rural peasants, supplemented after the millennium by significant numbers of urban poor.[28] The lot of these people usually hovered somewhere just above terrible, and there were inevitably moments during the Middle Ages when groups of the dispossessed perceived this to be the fault of their leaders rather than just the way of the world. As a result, from time to time ordinary folk banded together to express their anger and try to effect change.

There were plenty of examples. During the final three centuries of the Roman Empire in the west, southern Gaul and Hispania experienced sporadic popular insurgencies led by rowdy gangs known as the Bagaudae.[29] Constantinople in the fifth century was burned and bloodied by the Nika riots.* Between the tenth and twelfth centuries there were serious urban riots in Italian, French, Flemish and English towns and cities. In the same period countryside risings also occurred from Sicily to Scandinavia. These usually involved disagreements between landlords and their peasant tenants or labourers: either over the right of landlords to impose their authority on traditionally 'free' people, or (in places where lordship was more firmly established) over the type and amount of work that peasants were forced to do as a condition of their existence. But while some of these risings were purely 'popular' – spontaneous orgies of protest, demonstrations of fury and bloodletting enacted solely by the disadvantaged – just as many were what we might now call populist. This is to say they conformed to a model at least as old as Republican Rome (and much in vogue in the early twenty-first century), by which rich, cynical politicians mobilized the poor and attempted to direct their righteous anger against other elites.

Revolts of one or other of these types had occurred in Saxony during the 840s, in Norway in 1030, in Castile in 1111 and in Frisia around the 1230s.[30] Riots swept through the cloth-making towns of Flanders in the 1280s, and flared up again repeatedly thereafter. And some of these had dire consequences. The Norwegian rebels killed their king, Olaf Haraldsson 'the Stout', who was stabbed through the belly with a spear wielded by a rebel called Thórir the Hound.[31] The Frisian rebels, known as the Stedinger, wreaked so much havoc that Pope Gregory IX preached a crusade against them.[32] In Bruges in 1302, a group of townswomen seized a French soldier and sliced him up 'like a tuna fish'.[33] It was always scary, and to many, abhorrent, for in an age before modern notions of democracy or social equality, demonstrations of popular power

---

* See chapter 3.

were something most elites despised. The English poet John Gower captured the sense, common among the well-heeled and urbane, that popular rebellion was a form of natural disaster, to be feared but also to be expected. 'There are,' he wrote, 'three things of such a sort that they produce merciless destruction when they get the upper hand. One is a flood of water, another is a raging fire, and the third is the lesser people, the common multitude; for they will not be stopped, either be reason or discipline.'[34]

Gower was writing in the late 1370s. He had good reason to be alarmed. Around twenty years earlier the northern half of the nearby kingdom of France had been shaken by an outbreak of popular insurrection known as the Jacquerie. At the end of May 1358 a band of irate villagers in Saint-Leu-d'Esserent, about 60km north of Paris on the banks of the river Oise, attacked local nobles, either killing them or running them out of their homes.[35] According to an account written by a churchman from Liège called Jean le Bel, the villagers numbered around one hundred, and were 'without weapons except iron bats and knives.'[36] Nevertheless, they scored an impressive victory over their social betters, and in doing so set off a wave of violence that quickly pulsed outwards through northern France and Normandy.

During the course of the next fortnight, villagers across this region banded together under the leadership of a man called Guillaume Cale and attacked targets standing for wealth, power, privilege and incompetent government. The rebels – men and women who eventually numbered in the tens of thousands – were nicknamed 'les Jacques', referring to the pseudonym 'Jacques Bonhomme' (Jack Goodfellow), which a number of them either adopted or were given by their enemies.[37] To the French chroniclers, the Jacques were 'wicked people… peasants who were dark, short and poorly armed', characterized mainly by their base ignorance and viciousness.[38] And their deeds were, naturally, appalling: burning and demolishing houses, thieving with abandon, raping and murdering.

In truth, it seems that many of the Jacques were fairly restrained, aiming their destruction against those they felt had failed to rule

competently or govern fairly. Nevertheless, the further the news
of the Jacquerie travelled, the more depraved the stories became.
An account written in northern England described the bogeyman
'Jak Bonehomme' as 'a haughty and arrogant man with the heart
of Lucifer' who commanded nearly two hundred thousand rebels,
organized in three battalions, as they marched around the whole
kingdom of France 'taking great booty from the land and sparing
no gentleman or lady. Once they had won over... castles and
towns, they took the lords' wives, beautiful ladies and of great
renown, and slept with them against their will... And in many
places this Jak Bonehomme ripped babies from their mothers'
wombs and with these babies' blood [the rebels] quenched their
thirst and anointed their bodies in contempt of God and the
saints.'[39] Another writer claimed the rebels lit fires and roasted
knights on spits over the flames.

Quite how much of this is true is open to debate. Certainly the
Jacques who rose up in May and June 1358 were angry, numerous
and violent. But they were not the only ones. After exactly two
weeks of disorder, they were crushed by a short, concerted military
campaign led by King Charles II 'the Bad' of Navarre, a singularly
dishonourable and feckless nobleman who was married to the
French king's daughter Joan. Guillaume Cale was tortured and
beheaded. And many of those accused of having taken part were
run to ground, and had their own homes destroyed and their crops
burned. The rebels did not have a monopoly on terror.

What is more, if we are to be scrupulously sympathetic to
circumstances, we might consider the Jacques to have been rather
hard done by. In the aftermath of the Black Death, France was in
a dismal condition. Not only had there been forty years of famine
and plague, but the kingdom was also in the midst of the Hundred
Years War. For a generation large areas of northern France and
Gascony had been subjected to ruinous campaigns by English
armies and hired mercenary companies known as 'routiers'. At the
battle of Poitiers in 1356 the French king, Jean II, had been taken
prisoner; at the time of the Jacquerie he was being held in London.
In Paris, power was fragmented between competing factions, led

by the Dauphin Charles, the king of Navarre, a Parisian merchant called Etienne Marcel and the bishop of Laon. At the moment the Jacquerie erupted, Marcel and the Dauphin were on the brink of war, with their armies stationed outside Paris; there is good reason to believe Marcel encouraged insurrection in the countryside to further his own cause in the capital.

By the standards of any age, this was a hot mess. And in a realm that had suffered the worst pandemic for 800 years, and lost approximately half its population, such incompetence was insufferable. One of the theoretical benefits of the Black Death was that life ought to have been a little easier on survivors, who could look to a future of more land, lower rents, higher wages and brighter things. Instead, everything in France seemed to be getting worse. Modern research has shown the Jacquerie's leaders – Guillaume Cale and his captains – were not dirt-poor serfs, but relatively affluent, educated property-owners, artisans and professionals who expected better than they were getting and who were able to channel and articulate the ire of their communities against a system that seemed to be failing them.[40] That they themselves failed, and the fact that their uprising has latterly become a byword for heedless, bloodthirsty, rustic barbarity does not mean that their grievances were unreasonable or impossible for us to understand today.

Worms of the Earth

JUST AS THE BLACK DEATH OF 1347–51 combined with the draining effects of war to set the context for the Jacquerie in 1358, a generation later a similar pattern emerged elsewhere in Europe. This time it was not only France that was disturbed. During a protracted period of populist fervour, cities and their surrounding areas in Italy, England, Flanders and Normandy were all convulsed with rebellion. These uprisings were not, for the most part, co-ordinated or even directly connected. However, they showed just how brittle public order had become as the fourteenth century drew to a close, and the inhabitants of a world transformed clashed over what it ought to look like.

In the decade after the Jacquerie, there were sporadic stirrings of popular and populist anger across the west. Often the catalyst was disagreement over taxation, which governments across Europe had been trying to extend for several decades, the better to tap the wealth of ordinary people who had traditionally been only lightly touched by it. There was a tax riot in Tournai in 1360, during which prisons were stormed and wealthy merchants' houses vandalized. In the same year a group of artisans and workers in Pisa, whose economy was depressed, plotted a murderous riot in which 'they would kill a large number of the big-shots who controlled the city government wherever and however they could be found, either alone or together.'[41]

Around the same time the so-called Tuchin movement began in southern France, in which disaffected rural workers decided 'to submit no longer to shouldering the yoke of the subsidies [i.e. taxes]'.[42] Dropping off the grid, as we might now put it, they formed sworn brigand companies and 'declared themselves to be the enemies of churchmen, nobles and merchants'. Hostile chroniclers shared horror stories of the Tuchins' crimes: a Scottish envoy called John Patrick was supposedly seized by Tuchins while on his way to Aragon: his captors 'murdered him savagely by crowning him with a trivet of red-hot iron.' Another victim, a priest travelling to Rome, was also tortured to death: 'they cut off the ends of his fingers, peeled the skin from his body with shears, and then burnt him alive.'[43] These and similar stories of Tuchin terror stirred the south of France for twenty years, although of course it may well be that any heinous act in that time was associated to 'Tuchins', and that any group of malfeasants, protestors or criminal ne'er-do-wells seeking quick notoriety might call themselves Tuchins to bolster their reputation.* Whatever the case, the Tuchin movement lasted on and off for more than twenty years. And in doing so it provided a prelude for the most concentrated and widespread

---

* A version of what we now see with international terror brands such as Al-Qaeda and ISIS.

cluster of violent rebellions in the Black Death era, which occurred between 1378 and 1382.

THE 1370S, AS WE HAVE ALREADY seen, saw a serious spike in new plague infections, following on from the first great shock of the 1340s and subsequent waves in the 1360s. The precariousness of the times gave rise to prophecies and popular rumours of strange and wonderful sorts. In Florence, a friar became notorious for predicting that the year 1378 would see 'strange novelties, fears and horrors, such that the worms of the earth will cruelly devour lions, leopards and wolves.' The Antichrist would appear, said the friar, Muslims and Mongols would ally to invade Italy, Germany and Hungary, God would send a flood to rival the one that Noah escaped in the Ark, and wealthy Florentine citizens would ally with common people to 'kill all the tyrants and false traitors'.[44] Neither the monstrous worms, nor the devil nor the flood came, and the friar was thrown into prison by the pope. But on the matter of popular rebellion, he was proved spectacularly right.

In 1378 Florence witnessed the beginning of the Ciompi Revolt, a long struggle in which artisans excluded from the guild system of closed-shop, oligarchic trades unions allied with miserable wool workers to rise up and seize control of the city council. They established a revolutionary government which lasted for nearly three and a half years in various guises, until it was eventually brought down by a counter-revolution led by Florence's old, rich noble families. The Ciompi Revolt very often looked like – and was – a genuine class war; its first leader was an old vegetable-seller who waved a flag known as the banner of justice and uttered little of note except the revolutionary slogan: 'Long live the *Popolo Minuto* [i.e. the little people].' This was not great oratory, but it was symbolic of social divides in Florence, which seemed to be starker than ever before in the 1370s.

According to one anonymous, aristocratic Florentine diarist, in the early stages of the Ciompi Revolt, the rebels 'constructed a gallows in the Piazza della Signoria, which they said was to hang the fat cats', and simultaneously sent out an order that anyone wearing a cloak (a rough way of defining anybody who might be considered a fat cat) 'would be killed without a trial or warning'.[45] The gallows were not used, but the revolution became violent all the same. At one point an unfortunate notary who worked for the city government which was overthrown in 1378 was murdered in the street by a mob. According to the same diarist, 'someone... gave him a big blow with an axe across the head, chopping him in two; then [the crowd] tore him apart at the armpit with his brains spurting out and blood spewing all across the street... they then dragged him along the ground to the foot of the gallows in the Piazza of the Priors, where they hanged him by the feet. Here all the people cut off little pieces of him and stuck them to their lances and axes and carried them around the city, through the streets and into the suburbs.'[46] The revolution did not remain bloody for its long duration, and when the oligarchs returned to power in 1382 they were surprisingly gentle, preferring to restore unity to the city than wreak vengeance on the rebels. Nevertheless, the little people of Florence had shown what was possible when they felt their rights were being trampled, and what severe means they would deploy if their plight was not recognized.

And they were not alone. In France, the last years of Charles V's reign saw severe tax rebellions in cities across the south, including Le Puy, Montpellier and Béziers, where disorder crescendoed in 1379. In 1380, the accession of Charles' twelve-year-old son, Charles VI, sparked renewed protests, this time in the northern towns and cities, where populist-minded burghers (well-off citizens) and nobles joined forces with the mob. The city of Paris and the surrounding countryside were gripped by severe rioting, assaults on public buildings and tax collectors, and attacks on Jews and their property. During the next two years there were further tax riots in the Norman capital of Rouen, in Laon, in Picardy and in towns like Utrecht, in Flanders. Then, in January 1382, Paris rose again, in the so-called rebellion of the hammer men, during which anti-tax rioters ran amok with 'mallets of iron, steel and lead', with which they beat up royal officials and smashed houses.

Caernarfon Castle in north Wales was built for the English king Edward I by the great engineer-architect Master James of St George. It blended state-of-the-art fortification design with hints of the walls of Constantinople, and was intended to claim Welsh national myths for the colonizing English crown.

The reconstructed tomb effigy of Eleanor of Castile, queen of England and wife of Edward I. Eleanor died near Lincoln, so her intestines were removed and interred in the Gothic cathedral there. A royal connection could be invaluable to a medieval cathedral, attracting patronage and tourism to fund its building costs.

Four million bricks were winched into place during the construction of the 'Duomo' on Florence's cathedral of Santa Maria di Fiori in the fifteenth century. The task of building the dome was an architectural puzzle for generations, eventually solved by Filippo Brunelleschi.

The first wave of the Black Death (*below*) killed at least 40 per cent of Europe's population between 1347 and 1351. The terrible mortality led to decades of popular unrest and social upheaval. But it also ushered in an exciting new age of medieval invention and exploration.

Sì non essent registrantes et futuris ministrantes que vident et que audiunt. et illa que eveniunt in diversis

que non viderunt nec sciunt per scripturas edocemur. si nos bene recordemur. que sunt bona ut amemus quid ue malum

In England, waves of plague, a long war with France and punitive taxation sparked the Peasants' Revolt of 1381. During populist riots in London, the archbishop of Canterbury and royal treasurer were murdered, and the government nearly fell.

ivant ce vint le ven
dzedy au matin ce

One of the most famous works of art inspired by the Black Death was *The Decameron*, a collection of tales told by characters who have fled Florence to escape the pestilence. Its author was Giovanni Boccaccio, shown here in a nineteenth-century statue on the exterior of the Uffizi Gallery.

GIOVANNI BOCCACCIO

The Italian poet Petrarch is often cited as the first writer of the Renaissance. The muse for his sonnets was Laura de Noves, pictured here (*left*) in a portrait made after she died during the first European outbreak of the Black Death.

The Arnolfini Portrait (*below left*)by Jan van Eyck pictured a wealthy merchant and his bride. Its playful use of perspective and reflection showed van Eyck at the peak of his powers. He is often said to have invented oil painting.

Salvator Mundi (below) is (at the time of writing) the most expensive painting ever sold at auction. Much of its value lies in the fact that it has been identified as the work of Leonardo da Vinci, the Renaissance polymath whose genius joins the Middle Ages with our own times.

In 1453 the Ottoman sultan Mehmed II besieged Constantinople. This French illustration shows the huge cannon he trained on the ancient city's walls. The fall of the Byzantine capital made trade more difficult in the eastern Mediterranean and encouraged exploration across the Atlantic instead.

Christopher Columbus' journey to the Caribbean in 1492–3 is remembered as a pivotal moment in the history of medieval transatlantic contacts. But he would have gone nowhere without the backing of Isabella of Castile (*right*), one of Spain's 'Catholic Monarchs', who sponsored Columbus after other rulers turned him down.

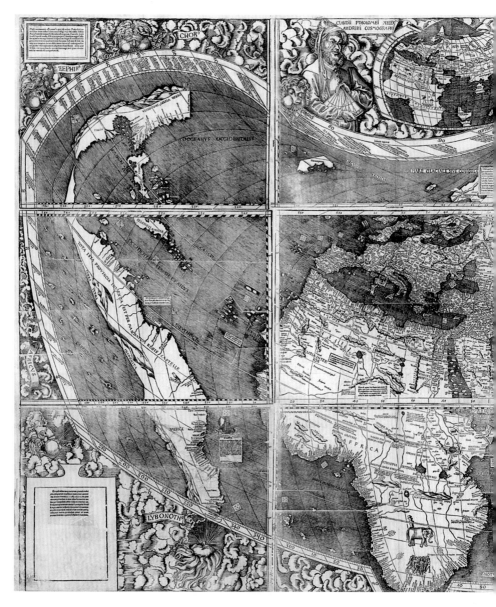

This map (*above*), produced by a German cartographer in 1507, shows a landmass in the western Atlantic, named 'America'. It also shows the Indian Ocean as navigable from the south. Both of these were recent geographical discoveries for late-medieval Europeans.

In 1527 Rome was sacked by an army raised by the future Holy Roman Emperor Charles V. This panorama (*right*) by Peter Brueghel the Elder only hints at the terrible bloodshed unleashed by mutinous imperial troops. The medieval world was well and truly at an end.

Martin Luther was the intellectual architect of what became the Protestant Reformation. His blistering critiques of Catholic doctrine and corruption caused irreparable damage to the medieval Roman Church.

The Gutenberg Bible, produced in 1455, was the first great printed book in western history. The invention of the printing press transformed European politics, culture and religion. It was particularly important in spreading new religious ideas during the Reformation.

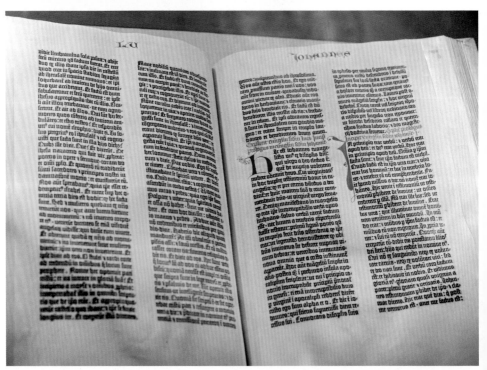

During this feverish period, one contemporary felt the whole realm was teetering on the brink as 'throughout the kingdom of France, the appetite for liberty and the desire to throw off the yoke of the subsidies were burning; a burning rage was brewing.'[47] He was probably right. The Jacquerie of 1358 had been dealt with inside a month. By contrast, some of the rebellions that began in 1378 took several years to dissipate – and as fires were lit far and wide across Europe, it became abundantly clear to governments that in the post-Black Death world, the views and interests of ordinary people would have to be considered, or the consequences could be severe. Nowhere was that lesson made clearer than in England, where a rebellion in the summer of 1381 came perilously close to bringing the royal government to its knees.

Summer of Blood

IN ENGLAND, AS WE HAVE SEEN, King Edward III's government reacted fast to the economic effects of the Black Death, passing labour laws that sought to freeze wages and prevent the pandemic from altering the basic relationship between wealthy landlords and their peasants. To make sure these laws were followed, Edward's ministers set up labour commissions to investigate illegal wage-taking, and punish those who sought to profit from what we would now recognize as the basic market mechanisms of supply and demand. Fines and prison sentences were issued to offenders not only in the immediate wake of the first wave of the pandemic, but for a generation afterwards.

Enforcing the labour laws became something of an official obsession. By the 1370s, as Edward's reign drew to a close, more than two-thirds of the business of royal courts concerned labour violations.[48] And this was not the only way that workers were being targeted. England had a long tradition of serfdom, in which peasants were bound to the land from birth – owing compulsory labour service to their lord, requiring his permission to marry and inherit, and being unfree to leave his estates if they wished. By the middle of the fourteenth century that system was waning, but it was revived by many lords after the Black Death, with many nobles using their own private ('manorial') courts to impose on their peasants old, forgotten obligations to work for free.[49] Villagers had attempted to fight back, hiring lawyers to obtain copies of William the Conqueror's Domesday Book,* hoping the records contained therein would prove they were exempt from exploitation by their own ancient right.[50] But this was futile.

All the while, the standard of English government was drifting. At his peak, Edward III was one of the most brilliant, talented and inspirational kings of the entire Plantagenet dynasty. By the mid-1370s, however, he had ruled for nearly fifty years. He was physically decrepit, losing his mind and surrounded by a corrupt court whose decadence seemed to be typified by his unscrupulous mistress, Alice Perrers. The Hundred Years War, which had brought a succession of magnificent military victories in the 1340s and 1350s, was now costing far more than it brought in. And there was no apparent exit strategy. Tax receipts earmarked for the war seemed to be disappearing into the coffers of courtiers. French pirates were harassing England's southern and eastern ports. In 1376 the 'Good Parliament' severely censured a number of English royal officials. The following year Edward died. His eldest son, a talented warrior and war hero known today as the 'Black Prince', was already dead. That meant that the English crown passed to Edward's grandson, the nine-year-old Richard of Bordeaux. Just as would happen in France in 1380, a major transition to a new reign occurred at a moment of deep social unease and war-weariness, when the new king was a child. Trouble was looming.

The rebellion in England began in the early summer of 1381 in a group of villages around the Thames estuary in Essex and Kent. As was the case elsewhere in Europe, the catalyst was an

---

* This was the comprehensive survey of land, people and rights undertaken at William's command following the Norman Conquest, and completed in 1086. An interesting parallel in modern times is the rumour that circulated in England during the COVID-19 lockdown of autumn 2020: business owners convinced one another that if they posted text of the 1215 Magna Carta on their premises they were exempt from government instructions to suspend trading.

unpopular tax. The government of the boy-king Richard II had been experimenting for several years with new ways of tapping the English people's wealth, and had imposed three successive poll taxes, all of which had been extremely unpopular and were widely evaded. Around Easter a poll-tax collector working near Bicester in Oxfordshire had been set upon and given a sound thrashing. To investigate tax-dodging, as well as these sorts of regrettable incidents, more judicial commissions were sent into the countryside. But this only made things worse. Rumours about the gross misconduct of tax collectors and inspectors began to circulate; it was claimed public officials were lifting up young girls' skirts to see if they were old enough to be assessed for tax. On 30 May, at a judicial session held in the Essex market town of Brentwood, patience with the collectors and their (alleged) methods snapped. Villagers who had gathered in town to attend the sessions told the royal officials they were not for paying their taxes. On what was apparently a pre-arranged signal, the villagers ran the officials out of town. Then they sent messages to their friends on both sides of the Thames to do the same. The message spread like a forest fire, and by the first week of June 1381 the whole of south-east England was in uproar.

As was the case in France during the Jacquerie, the English rising of 1381 was not the preserve of the very poorest in society.* Rather, it was led by what we might call the middling sort – not, for the most part, knights or gentlemen, but village elites who occupied roles of petty responsibility such as constables and parish priests. The rank and file, meanwhile, were typically skilled artisans like carpenters, masons, shoemakers, skinners and weavers.[51] The most famous leaders were Wat Tyler, who may well have served in France in one of the campaigns of the Hundred Years War, and John Ball, a priest originally from Yorkshire, who was well known to the authorities, thanks to a long personal history of preaching egalitarian doctrine, which had earned him incarceration in a Canterbury jail for

---

* The term 'Peasants' Revolt' to describe the English rising of 1381 dates only to the nineteenth century. A more contemporary nickname, which had deliberate undertones of medieval football violence, was 'the hurling time'.

causing a public nuisance. During the rising Tyler operated as a *de facto* captain of the Kent and Essex rebels, while Ball served as their spiritual guide. In early June Tyler, Ball and thousands of likeminded folk marched up the Thames towards London, where they planned to join with disaffected apprentices and workers in a demonstration against the incompetence of Richard II's minority government. They had momentum, confidence and numbers – and no landlord on their route dared stand in their way.

By Wednesday 12 June the Kent and Essex rebels were camped close to London at Blackheath, where a delegation of the capital's aldermen met them, bringing a message from the mayor, William Walworth, not to come any further. The message was not heeded. At Blackheath, Ball preached a famous sermon, whose message was neatly summed up by the couplet 'When Adam delved and Eve span/Who then was the gentleman?'. This rhetorical question revealed the depth of anti-aristocratic feeling that characterized the rebellion, as well as their conviction that Christ was on their side. The rebels regarded the young king Richard with naïve affection, seeing him as the victim of corrupt officials rather than the source of tyranny himself. They claimed to stand for 'King Richard and the true commons', and anyone standing between king and people – either literally or metaphorically – would be considered fair game.

On the morning of Thursday 13 June Tyler and his men moved on from Blackheath to Rotherhithe. There they were visited by their young hero the king and several of his closest counsellors, who had been rowed downriver from the Tower of London on a barge. But the royal party did not dare disembark to parlay with the rebels, who presented an intimidating scene on the riverbank. This reticence frustrated the mob, who proceeded to sack Southwark, London's large suburb on the south bank of the Thames, before turning on London Bridge. It ought to have been impossible to storm the city from the south, since the bridge could be barred to all crossers. Fatefully, however, rebel sympathizers within the city opened the barriers and tens of thousands of rebels poured in. So began two and a half days of semi-organized mayhem which would live long in Londoners' collective memories. Prisons were opened. Legal records were seized and burned in the street. The Savoy Palace, the fine London residence belonging to the king's uncle, John of Gaunt, was stormed and burned to the ground. All hell was let loose.

On Friday 14 June, King Richard invited the rebels to send a delegation to meet him outside the city gates at Mile End. They presented him with demands for a charter that effectively stood the post-Black Death labour laws on their head: serfdom was to be officially abolished, rents limited to four pence per acre, and labour contracts subject to regular negotiation. Richard granted all this. He also told the rebels that if they could bring any traitors to him in person he would see that justice was done. This was a disastrous misstep, and it cost lives. When word of the king's promise was taken back to the city, the protests, which were already rough, turned murderous. Rebels forced their way into the Tower of London and seized the two most senior members of the royal council who were holed up there: Simon Sudbury, the chancellor and archbishop of Canterbury, and Sir Robert Hales, the treasurer. Both were beheaded and their heads put on spikes.

The city was now well and truly out of control, and amid the chaos, further lives were lost. Those slain included various servants of Gaunt (who was himself fortunate to be in northern England at the time of the riots), the keeper of the royal prison in Southwark and, particularly tragically, around 150 Flemish merchants, who were slaughtered for little more than being foreign. The hunt for 'traitors' continued overnight on Friday 14 June and throughout the day on Saturday. Only on Saturday afternoon, when the rebels were drunk, tired and running out of steam, did the city authorities manage to get a grip on the situation. Once more the king offered to meet with the rebels, on a recreation ground outside London's walls known as Smithfield. This time, however, there was a plan.

On the evening of the 15th, the king came face to face with Wat Tyler, who presented an even more radical set of demands than had been issued at Mile End. Now the rebels called for an absolute end to all lordship except the king's and the complete confiscation and redistribution of Church lands. They repeated their demand for an end to serfdom. This was an extraordinary manifesto – far more extreme in its revolutionary vision than even that of the Ciompi rebels in Florence. Understandably, Richard now equivocated, and when Tyler became nervous, Mayor Walworth took over. He tried to arrest the rebel leader, and in the ensuing scuffle, daggers were drawn and Tyler was fatally stabbed. He was dragged off to die at the nearby hospital of St Bartholomew, and Walworth's city militia, which had been waiting in the wings, finally charged in, surrounded the assembled rebels, and sent them packing. London had been saved – but only just.

Nor was England's rising over. Even as London was pacified, disorder was spreading all over the country, from Somerset in the south-west to Beverley in the north-east. Much of it was deliberately co-ordinated. There were major disturbances in East Anglia and the counties immediately north of London. Royal judges and tax collectors were killed, and properties vandalized. In Cambridge, vendettas between townspeople and the university scholars led to brawling and assaults on college buildings. Norwich experienced major rioting, as did York. The disturbances lasted for weeks, and there was an impressive degree of co-ordination among rebels across the country, who shared an egalitarian philosophy and a general interest in having fun, causing trouble and smashing the system. John Ball was only run to ground in mid-July, and by the time he was captured, in the Midlands, he had sent dozens of open letters to his contacts and other rebels around England, urging them in cryptic tones to 'stand together in God's name' and 'chastise well Hob the Robber' and 'be ware or be woe'.[52] Ball admitted to writing these words when he was put on trial at St Albans. Needless to say, he was found guilty of heinous crimes against crown and the country. On 15 July, exactly a month after the London insurrection had ended, Ball was hanged, drawn and quartered.

In the mopping-up operations that followed, another fifteen hundred rebels also died. By the end of the year, the English rising was finally over, and a sense of reactionary vengefulness had taken root at court: the king and his minders wished to make sure that nothing of the sort should ever take place again. According to the chronicler Thomas Walsingham, the fourteen-year-old Richard was particularly bent on revenge. When the men of Essex sent a messenger to the king to enquire politely what had happened to the liberties Richard had promised them at Mile End, the teenager answered him with all the imperious severity of a Mongol khan.

'O you wretched men,' he said.

Detestable on land and sea, you who seek equality with lords are not worthy to live… As you have come here in the guise of envoys, you will not die now but may keep your lives… [But] give this message to your colleagues from the king: Rustics you are, and rustics you are still, you will remain in bondage, not as before but incomparably harsher. For as long as we live and, by God's grace, rule over the realm, we will strive with mind, strength and goods to suppress you so that the rigour of your servitude will be an example to posterity.[53]

Walsingham surely injected Richard's alleged speech with much of his own disdain for rebels who had seriously damaged his home at St Alban's Abbey during the rising in Hertfordshire. Nevertheless, the underlying sense was clear: whatever miseries the lower orders had endured in a century of starvation, plague, perpetual war and climate change, they would be even more cruelly punished if they dared forget their place again. It was neither the first nor the last time in history that revolution would be crushed with overkill. In medieval England, there would not be another popular rising for the better part of seventy years.

'Away traitors, away!'

AS MODERN READERS KNOW, REBELLIONS STILL happen in bursts sometimes: the so-called Arab Spring of 2011, during which populations across Muslim states in north Africa and the Middle East rose up, is one recent example; if we look a little further back we may think of the upheavals of 1848 or the great revolutions of the late eighteenth century, which remade France, America and Haiti. The frenzy of popular and populist rebellion that gripped Europe between 1378 and 1382 deserves to be thought of in this category: as a revolutionary 'moment', in which many people in many places at roughly the same time all sought to change their circumstances by taking to the streets, reacting to different local provocations and crying liberty in different languages, but nevertheless connected to one another thematically and historically.

Of course, the rebels of the late fourteenth century did not change the world as they hoped. Wat Tyler parlayed with Richard II, but he was cut to ribbons for his troubles. The Ciompi took control of Florence for several years, but in the end faded back into obscurity. By the end of the fourteenth century southern France was still plagued by bandits, but people no longer talked of the Tuchin. In the strictest sense, these rebels all failed.

Yet the world *was* changing. Thanks to the Black Death, Europe's population had undergone a long-term adjustment which would last for centuries. As a result, the relationship between landlords and peasants, and city-leaders and workers, could never return to earlier medieval norms. As urban economies continued to develop, cash was confirmed as the key currency of social obligation. In realms like England, serfdom had all but disappeared by the early fifteenth century. Soldiers were almost exclusively mustered on the promise of fixed, salaried contracts, rather than obligation laid on them by liege homage. In the cities, people grumbled about their rulers' tax demands, and still rioted when they felt it was the only way to be heard. But levying taxes on workers as well as rich landlords was no longer outrageous. Moreover, the general sense that the world was teetering on the brink of apocalypse cooled somewhat. Plague, war and famine remained regrettably common features of life. But as the fourteenth century drew to a close, they did not seem to be sent with quite the same ferocity as before. So although revolt and rebellion also remained a feature of medieval society after the fourteenth century, they looked and sounded different. A new age was coming in.

SOME DISORDER AND REBELLION IN THE fifteenth century was born of plain, old-fashioned social tension – a natural feature of towns and cities in almost every age. Universities, which flourished in the century after the Black Death, were a particularly regular source of urban conflict, as students and academics clashed, either with townsfolk or with one another. Student riots had been a feature of city life since at least the year 1200, and they continued to occur until the end of the Middle Ages and well beyond. In France, disorder linked to academics was recorded in Paris in 1404 and Orléans in 1408. In Italy there was an armed stand-off between students in Perugia and the city governor in 1459; in 1467 there were mass brawls between rival gangs of German and Burgundian students at the University of Pavia.[54] In Pavia in 1478 there was an extraordinary one-man rebellion against society, when a student called Bernardino was accused of raping at least two girls, starting a four-man street-fight while arguing over a prostitute, inciting a brawl in a brothel, turning up fully armed to disrupt Carnival celebrations, stealing books, wine, jewellery and even a herd of goats and fighting the city customs officers on several separate nights.[55] (Bernardino's uncle was the duke of Milan, and he perhaps thought that gave him the right.) But student disorder was generally either a matter of internal university politicking or the result of clashes over the privileges due to academics versus those enjoyed by everyone else. Seldom if ever did academics seek to upend any more general established order.

Nor, for the most part, did any other rebels of the later Middle Ages. In 1413 Paris was once again the venue for major public disorder, during the toxic civil war that swirled up during the reign of King Charles VI. For much of his life Charles was tormented by episodes of psychosis which led him to forget his name and who he was, to believe he was made entirely of glass, to run naked about his palaces matted with his own filth and to attack his servants and family. The factions who contested power during the king's maddest episodes were known as the Burgundians and Armagnacs, and both sides sought to involve the citizens of Paris and the common mob in their disputes. In the trouble of 1413, thousands of citizens took up arms, and for much of the spring and summer Paris was on a knife-edge, with popular militias in the streets. A faction of prominent butchers and meat-traders were encouraged by the duke of Burgundy to seize control of the city; the leader of the butchers, known as Simon 'Caboche', put forward an extensive programme of legal reforms to combat government abuses.

For Caboche and his 'Cabochiens', this was success on a level that Wat Tyler or Guillaume Cale could only have dreamt about. Yet the revolt of the Cabochiens was markedly different from those earlier risings. Whereas in the late fourteenth-century rebels sought to overthrow the norms of the post-Black Death world, a generation later rebellion was framed within the existing political structures and discourses of the day. The Cabochiens did not seek to recast the foundations of the French realm, but merely spoke as a powerful voice within its ongoing debates. They were essentially a political movement, rather than a social one, and they were backed strongly by Burgundy himself, one of the most powerful nobles in France – indeed, in Europe. As one chronicler wrote, the butchers were 'spurred on by the duke... who desired to take over the government.'[56] They were political players within a game that might have been violent in character, but was played according to mutually agreed rules.

Much the same was true in England in 1450, when a rebellion broke out in Kent – one of the breeding-grounds of the 1381 rising. Jack Cade's Rebellion, as it was known, was a bloody and frightening burst of violence, during which rebels from the south-east followed a strikingly similar path to Wat Tyler and John Ball's sixty-nine years earlier. Amid acute fears of a French invasion, and with England in the first throes of the protracted series of civil wars that would become known as the Wars of the Roses, ordinary people who were already mustered in militias for coastal defence rose up under the leadership of Cade – a charismatic captain, probably from Suffolk.[57] Protesting against the hapless government around King Henry VI, they marched up the Thames to Blackheath singing a song with the refrain 'away, traitors, away!'.

On arrival at the capital these rebels stormed Southwark, entered the City via London Bridge and set up a kangaroo court outside the Guildhall, where disgraced figures from the royal government were put on trial. The treasurer, Lord Saye and Sele, was beheaded; back in Kent, a military force under the nobleman Sir Humphrey Stafford was ambushed and Sir Humphrey was killed. The king – a timid soul at the best of times – was whisked out of London early in the rising to the relative safety of the Midlands, and it was left to his wife, Queen Margaret, to keep her eye on the battle for London, which was fought between the rebels and the city militia on 5 and 6 July. Cade was eventually captured, beheaded and quartered, but London and southern England remained febrile for the rest of the summer and into the autumn. It was the worst popular insurrection in England during the whole of the fifteenth century, and it rocked the government of the day to its boots.

However, Cade's rebellion, like the rising of the Cabochiens in Paris, was a long way removed from the previous great English rising. Whereas Tyler and Ball had in 1381 imagined a world that could be rebuilt from the ground up, Cade's rebels put forward a political programme that was less idealistic and more practically ambitious. They composed a formal 'bill of articles', complaining of specific abuses by named councilors, and called for detailed reforms to royal policies in Kent and the surrounding counties. They asked that government be taken over by the king's cousin, 'the high and mighty prince, the duke of York', and proposed that the crown reclaim all lands granted out as gifts to nobles and courtiers, for the purpose of balancing the royal books in a time of war.[58] They made no utopian cries for a land in which serfdom was abolished, for the simple reason that serfdom had already all but vanished of its own accord. The complaints of Cade's rebels were a bold, one-sided but educated critique of England's many problems, from a class of people who were now fully engaged in the political process, rather than seeking to ride roughshod over it. They illustrated precisely how far the world had moved on from the agonies of the Black Death era.

SURVIVING THE GREAT FAMINE AND THE Black Death did not turn the whole of the world into rebels. But the popular and populist risings that emerged in the second half of the fourteenth century were certainly early indicators of some of the ways that the catastrophes of that time had shaken medieval society. Hierarchies were challenged vigorously. The ravages of war – either civil or foreign – were not simply accepted as a part of the drudgery of human existence, and when people felt they were being subjected to more misery than they could accept, they rose up and tried to make their voices heard, or else used the chaotic conditions of war as a springboard to launch their campaigns for better conditions. But it did not take long for the most strident phase of post-Black Death insurrection to tail off, and more sophisticated, advanced forms of lower-order rebellion to become the norm.

At the same time, of course, western elites took heed of the potential power of the rebellious lower orders, and tried to direct them to their own ends. In addition to the examples we have already seen, this was particularly evident during the Catalan civil war of 1462–72, when a revolt of bonded labourers known as the *payeses de remensa* was folded into a struggle between King John II of Aragon and Catalan nobles who were trying to limit royal power.[59] Not until the sixteenth century did the west experience another large-scale revolt with the scope and character of those that took place between 1358 and 1382. That was the German Peasants' War of 1524–5, and it was framed not by the traumatic effects of demographic collapse, but by the religious revolution that was breaking across the west in the shape of the Protestant Reformation.*

Protestantism, though, was another matter altogether, and one that we shall turn to shortly, as our journey approaches the end

---

* See chapter 16.

of the Middle Ages. But before we do so, it is time to consider the broader changes that blew through the medieval world in the aftermath of the Black Death. For the last 150 years of the Middle Ages were not simply characterized by political turmoil and popular unrest. They were just as much a time of revolution in the arts, literature, philosophy, poetry, architecture, finance and urban planning. Having survived the onslaught of *Y. Pestis*, the world was suddenly awash with new ideas, discoveries and technologies – some of them revived from the classical era and others invented afresh. What dawned in the fourteenth century and blossomed in the fifteenth was the Renaissance, a time of beauty, genius, invention and inspiration, yet one that had dirt on its belly, and blood beneath its claws. It is on this glorious, dangerous time of rebirth and renewal that we must now cast our eye.

14

RENEWERS

'There was an age that was happier for poets...'

PETRARCH, POET AND HUMANIST

In the week before Christmas 1431, in the great cathedral of Santa Maria del Fiore in Florence, a scholar called Francesco Filelfo gave a lecture about the poetry of Dante. Several hundred high-minded Florentines came to listen. The cathedral in which they gathered was partway through its sensational renovation: at the east end, Brunelleschi's vast *duomo* was coming together, and although it would five years until it was officially finished, this would clearly be a crowning triumph for the city. Filelfo was every inch a fitting character to perform beneath it. He was one of the most exciting thinkers of his day. Educated in Pavia, he had been appointed to teach the arts in Venice at the age of just eighteen. He had then travelled the world, soaking up languages, reading voraciously and immersing himself in politics. He learned Greek in Constantinople, worked as a diplomat at the court of Murad II, sultan of the rising Islamic superpower known as the Ottoman empire[*] and then took postings as an ambassador to Sigismund, king of Hungary and Władisław II, king of Poland. Having married a minor Greek princess called Theodora, he settled back in Italy to pursue a career as a scholar, moving to Florence in the late 1420s. There Filelfo taught rhetoric, translated classical poetry and gave lectures at the recently established university (known as the

---

[*] See chapter 15.

Studio), holding forth on the writers of ancient Greece and Rome.[1] On Sundays and other Christian feast days he declaimed in public about Dante. He could be a magnetic figure. Bright, outspoken, articulate, intellectually vain, personally spiky and obsessed with money, Filelfo was so keen on chasing women that he boasted he must have been born with three testicles. He made enemies easily, particularly among other academics, one of whom called him 'repulsive'.[2] Yet when Filelfo spoke, the city listened.[3]

Dante was a wildly popular subject. The great man had died 110 years earlier, and was regarded in Florence as a literary demi-god. His tomb actually lay in Ravenna, where he had lived after being exiled from his home city in the course of the wars between the Blacks and Whites. Nevertheless, parsing Dante's work – and in particular the *Commedia* (or as it is usually called today, *The Divine Comedy*) – was a favourite pastime of Florentine intellectuals. Not only was the *Commedia* a vivid portrait of hell, purgatory and heaven, written in dancing, interlaced lines of Italian *terza rima*,* rather than staid Latin; it was also packed with gossipy sketches of famous men and women from distant and recent history, who were judged by the poet's pen and sentenced accordingly, either to diabolical torments or the delights of paradise. This gave the *Commedia* – and commentary on it – considerable contemporary relevance and no little potential for causing trouble. Relatives and descendants of many of Dante's subjects were alive and active in Florentine high society, and the poem was germane to their self-image, their worldview and their squabbles. Famous Florentines could be praised, needled or outright slandered through the

---

* Terza rima, which is inextricably connected with Dante, and best suited to Italian, is a scheme in which rhymes alternate and tumble over one another. The pattern is ABA BCB CDC DED (and so on), usually driving towards a final rhyming couplet. Dante is the first major poet known to have worked in terza rima, and it became popular both in the Middle Ages and beyond. Although not perfectly suited to English (which has far fewer rhyming words than Italian), the form was used by Geoffrey Chaucer, the Tudor-era poet Thomas Wyatt, John Milton and any number of nineteenth-century romantics, including George Byron, Percy Shelley and Alfred Tennyson. There is a strong argument to say that in spirit it also informs the work of the twentieth- and twenty-first century's more verbally dextrous rappers – Notorious B.I.G., Jay-Z, Lauryn Hill, Eminem, MF Doom, Kendrick Lamar and so on, although I have yet to find an example of a rapper deploying strict terza rima over the course of an entire track.

medium of Dantean commentary. So when a master of letters –
particularly one with a waspish tongue in his mouth – spoke about
Dante in the city's landmark cathedral, his words mattered.

In December 1431, Filelfo did not just pass textual judgement
on Dante. He also used his platform to throw shade on a faction in
the city led by the fifty-two-year-old banker Cosimo de' Medici.
Since taking over running the Medici bank from his father
eleven years previously, Cosimo had become one of the richest
and most powerful men in Florence. He was heavily involved in
planning and financing wars with nearby city-states, including
Lucca and Milan. He was an instinctive and astute operator, who
specialized in controlling politics from the shadows. But he was
not universally liked, particularly by a conservative, oligarchic
faction led by another super-wealthy Florentine, Rinaldo degli
Albizzi, and one of Filelfo's patrons, Palla Strozzi. In the course of
Filelfo's lecture in the cathedral, the scholar made it clear whose
side he was on. He suggested, half-obliquely, that the Mediceans
were 'ignorant', that they were envious of him and that they
knew nothing about Dante. He accused them of targeting him
for 'hate and persecution', and of being behind attempts earlier in
that academic year to have him permanently removed from his
university teaching posts.[4] This was fighting talk. And it would
come back to haunt Filelfo.

Under Cosimo's leadership the Medici family had begun their
rise not only to hegemony in Florence, but to the rank of a quasi-
royal dynasty, whose sons would eventually include popes and
grand-dukes, and whose daughters would become queens. And
although the peak of their powers lay some way off, in the first
half of the sixteenth century, they were still dangerous people
to cross. A large clan, with interests all over the city, the Medici
sat at the centre of a network of Florentines known as the *amici*
('friends'), whose members ranged from magnates and bankers
to shopkeepers and the ordinary poor.[5] This network could be
mobilized for all sorts of tasks, both noble and underhand. Falling
out with the Medici meant making many enemies, who, if they felt
so inclined, could do a man real harm.

Filelfo tasted the *amici*'s dark power in May 1433. This was nearly eighteen months after he began his verbal attacks on the Medici and their party, and tempers had not cooled. One morning, as Filelfo walked to work at the *Studio*, following the river Arno along the Borgo S. Jacopo, he was accosted by a thug called Filippo, who pulled a sword from his cloak and set about him. Filelfo tried to defend himself with his fists, but he was more of a writer than a fighter. The attack was not fatal (probably by design), but there was a lot of blood. With one 'terrifying thrust' of the blade, Filelfo later wrote, his attacker succeeded 'not only in cutting deep but also in almost amputating my entire right cheek and nose.'[6] Then the goon ran away. After the initial shock and the pain, Filelfo recovered, but he was marked forever with a disfiguring scar. Cosimo was never formally connected with the crime – one of Filelfo's *Studio* colleagues was instead brought to trial by the city authorities and tortured into admitting he had paid Filippo to do the deed. But Filelfo was convinced the Medici patriarch had lain behind it.

In the months following his attack, Filelfo railed against Cosimo and his friends. When political events turned against the Medici in 1433 – Cosimo was accused, with some justification, of having manipulated the conduct of Florence's wars with Lucca to ensure maximum profit for his bank – Filelfo was delighted. He called publicly for formal charges of treason, which could have seen Cosimo put to death. But he failed to convince the city authorities. Cosimo was convicted for offences relating to war profiteering, but merely exiled to Venice, from where he engineered a quick return to power. And when he got back to Florence in 1434, Filelfo found the game was up. Now it was he who was run out of the city. This was not the end of his career by a long chalk: he went on to enjoy distinguished postings under the dukes of Milan and, briefly, Pope Sixtus IV, a depraved and corrupt individual but an enthusiastic patron of the arts. He worked as a professor and court poet and tirelessly composed tracts urging the princes of Europe to revive the spectacle of the mass crusade to deal with the Ottoman Turks. Yet he lived with the physical, reputational and emotional scars he had earned by crossing Cosimo in the 1430s. In 1436 he tried to hire an assassin of his own to kill the Medici boss. But the plot was foiled, and it only served to ensure that, for all the fame and esteemed connections Filelfo made, he was not welcomed back to Florence for nearly fifty years.

Only in 1481 did Cosimo's grandson, Lorenzo 'the Magnificent', invite him back to become professor of Greek at the university. By now, however, Filelfo was eighty-three. His second posting in Dante's city lasted scarcely a heartbeat. He caught dysentery soon after arriving, and was dead within two weeks. He had enjoyed an exciting and varied career, for most of which he had been the greatest Greek scholar in the western Mediterranean. Yet his sharp tongue had cost him his looks and very nearly his life. The way Filelfo saw it, he was an honourable fellow who had stuck to his principles and suffered for it: 'Shame has not allowed me to be a parasite,' he once wrote. 'Nor have I ever learned to flatter, to adulate, or to be a yes-man'.[7] Others saw it differently. 'His wit was nimble,' wrote one contemporary intellectual, drily, 'but he knew not how to keep it in order.'[8]

TODAY FRANCESCO FILELFO IS NOT AMONG the first names that people reach for when they think of the extraordinary intellectual and artistic world that flourished across the west in the late Middle Ages. Rightly or wrongly, his genius and scholarship have not captured the public imagination in the same way as that of some of his contemporaries, particularly the visual artists. The superstars of this age are men like Leonardo da Vinci and Sandro Botticelli, Brunelleschi and Michelangelo, Raphael and Titian, Pico della Mirandola and Machiavelli, Jan van Eyck, Rogier van der Weyden and Albrecht Dürer. Filelfo does not belong in the first rank of these figures, and maybe not even in the second. Yet there is something in his little-known story that sums up the nature of the times.

From the late fourteenth century there flourished, first in Italy and, soon afterwards, beyond the Alps in northern Europe, a cultural movement known as the Renaissance. The Renaissance

– literally, 'rebirth' – was a time in which creative people discovered new (or lost) approaches to literature, the arts and architecture. From these there also sprang novel theories of political philosophy, natural science, medicine and anatomy.

The Renaissance saw revived and intense interest in the glories of ancient Greek and Roman culture, rapid technical advances in painting and sculpture and the dissemination of new ideas about matters such as education and statecraft. Great public art transformed cityscapes. Portraiture gifted politicians with new propaganda tools. The Renaissance rolled and developed across many generations: in the longest historical analysis it was still going in the early seventeenth century. Crucially, right from the start, some of those who lived through the period recognized they were living in a new age. Among the first to state it was Leonardo Bruni, who wrote an epic *History of the Florentine People*, in which he identified the collapse of the western Roman Empire in the fifth century as the end of one great age, and his own times in the early fifteenth century as the culmination of a long road back to civilization.[9] This notion still underpins our sense of the boundaries of the Middle Ages – as the scope of books like this one shows.

The Renaissance was a time when genius and geniuses were unleashed. But patrons mattered as much as auteurs. Art and invention were tightly interwoven with money, power and the ambitions of princes. Clever and creative people flocked to the wealthy to fund their endeavours, while the mighty threw their weight behind artists to help them emphasize their own good taste and the civic sophistication of their home cities. So for every Filelfo there was a Cosimo; each capable of elevating and thwarting the other in roughly equal measure.

For centuries, people have looked back at the Renaissance and seen it as an epochal cultural turn, which marks the boundaries between the Middle Ages and modernity. Today, however, some historians dislike the term, on the grounds that it implies a dearth of invention or any transformations in thought during the centuries that preceded it. Others still have decided to co-opt and dilute the term 'renaissance' by applying it to earlier moments in the Middle Ages; we have already encountered the 'twelfth-century renaissance' on our journey to this point.* So be it. The fact remains that whether we like the term 'Renaissance' or not, it would be a brave or foolish person who denied that the fifteenth century in particular saw a groundswell of cultural and intellectual endeavour, which produced some of the most famous works of art and literature in human history, under the patronage of magnificent, if often rather grubby, customers. So it is to this age that we will now address our thoughts, as we look at the artistic and humanistic explosion of the late Middle Ages, along with the occasionally bloody shenanigans that underpinned it.

The First Humanist

ON GOOD FRIDAY IN 1327, 104 years before Filelfo fell out with Cosimo de' Medici, the young poet and diplomat Francesco Petrarca went to church in the papal city of Avignon. As he later told the story, it was there, on the most solemn day in the whole Christian calendar, that he first clapped eyes on a woman called Laura. She was probably (but not definitely) Laura de Noves, recently married to the nobleman Count Hugh de Sade.

Aged seventeen, Laura de Noves was scarcely out of adolescence, though this was fairly normal for fourteenth-century brides. Six years older, Petrarca, or Petrarch, as he is known today in English, was captivated by her. The attraction was partly physical. A posthumous (and partly imagined) portrait of Laura de Noves kept in the Laurentian Library in Florence shows a pretty woman with a thin, elegant nose, round eyes beneath high-arched brows and a small mouth and chin. But her physical beauty was not everything. Petrarch wrote that when Laura shone 'the rays of her lovely eyes' on him she created 'thoughts of love, action and words'.[10] In a chaste, platonic relationship which began soon after,

---

* See chapter 11.

Laura became his muse. Over the course of his long life and her short one Petrarch would write hundreds of poems about and to her.*

Like Dante, Petrarch wrote most of his best poetry in Italian, rather than Latin. He also perfected the fourteen-line poetic form of the sonnet. Petrarch did not create the sonnet. If it was ever definitively 'invented', then it came from the Sicilian court of Frederick II Hohenstaufen during the early thirteenth century. But he moulded it and mastered it to such an extent that the 'Petrarchan sonnet' is now a staple of Italian poetry, just as the later 'Shakespearean sonnet' is in English.[11]

Petrarch's subject matter in his sonnets (and other early poetry) was more than just romantic love for an unattainable woman. He also used his adoration for Laura as the leaping-off point for an investigation into the mysteries, pleasures and sorrows of human life itself. For nearly one thousand years in the west the standard framework used for discussing these themes had been the contemplation of Christ and his Passion. Now Petrarch stood the traditional model on its head. He was unquestionably a pious Christian – indeed, he was officially a clergyman. Yet he found the sublime in the individual, and not the other way around. He imbued the emotional and interior life of one person with infinite significance and the power to reveal higher truth. Everything still led back to God. But the route was radically different. And Petrarch's approach would come to lie at the core of an overarching aesthetic and moral philosophy known as humanism, which drove the achievements of the Renaissance. Future generations looked on him as the first of the humanists.

In the fourteenth century, it did not take long for Petrarch to make a name for himself. He was a beautiful writer, an enthusiastic correspondent and an irrepressible traveller. When he was a teenager he had rejected his father's advice to settle down and train as a lawyer, knowing already that he wanted to spend his

---

* We might today consider Petrarch a bit of a stalker. The line between flattery and obsession has ever been thin and porous, particularly for poets.

days wandering the world, reading and writing, rather than sitting at his desk in Bologna filing legal briefs. And in the years after he first encountered Laura he indulged this wanderlust. In the 1330s he roamed the cities of France, the German empire, Flanders and the Low Countries, keeping an eye out all the while for scholars to consult and libraries where he could read manuscripts copied from classical sources. He returned regularly to the closest thing he had to a home: a tiny secluded village called Vaucluse, hidden in a valley 30km east of Avignon. But he never fully settled there. The world, with all its natural splendour, its great buildings and its books was a source of irresistible inspiration. In 1337 he visited Rome, and while touring the ruins of the imperial capital became obsessed with stories of the Punic Wars. After this he began writing (in Latin, rather than Italian) a long epic poem called *Africa*, narrating the Second Punic War of 218–201 BC, when Hannibal of Carthage had eventually been bested by Scipio Africanus. *Africa* eventually ran to nine books and nearly seven thousand lines, although Petrarch never considered it finished and would not allow it to be widely circulated while he lived.[12]

By and by his fame grew. So did his circle of powerful friends. In the first half of his career Petrarch worked for Cardinal Giovanni Colonna, a member of the powerful Roman noble dynasty whom Petrarch described in a sonnet as 'Glorious Colonna!'[13] He always moved in high places thereafter. One of his most famous patrons was Robert of Anjou, king of Naples (r. 1309–43), who harboured ambitions to be the pre-eminent ruler in Italy, and understood acutely the value of projecting might by associating with the leading artists and writers of his day. In 1341 Robert made Petrarch a tantalizing offer: come to Rome and be crowned *poet laureate* – an ancient title revived specifically to recognize his brilliance. Petrarch accepted, adding only the flattering condition that King Robert should subject him to a three-day *viva voce* in his palace to make sure he was up to scratch. Robert was tickled pink, and having passed his examination, Petrarch was crowned with a laurel wreath on the Capitoline Hill at Easter 1341. It was a ceremony layered with meaning, the ruins of the Eternal City suggesting both the collapse of an old world and the impending resurrection of the spirit of the ancients.[14] In his coronation oration, Petrarch sang effusive praises to the Romans. Quoting Lucan, he told his audience 'the task of the poet is sacred and great'. He went on:

> There was an age that was happier for poets, an age when they were held in the highest honour, first in Greece and then in Italy, and especially when Caesar Augustus held imperial sway, under whom there flourished excellent poets, Virgil, Varus, Ovid, Horace and many others... But today, as you well know, all this has changed...[15]

Poetry, he argued, had been devalued. Yet poets were able to reveal through their words truths as deep as any of those mined from scripture by theologians – if only their audience would recognize it. As Petrarch put it:

> Poets, under the veil of fictions have set forth truths physical, moral and historical... the difference between a poet on the one hand and a historian or a moral or physical philosopher on the other is the same as the difference between a clouded sky and a clear sky, since in each case the same light exists in the object of vision, but is perceived in different degrees according to the capacity of the observers.[16]

Petrarch's blistering defence of verse, and his wider claim for art as a lens through which to spy the divine, was stirring and challenging in the 1340s. It would take two centuries for his insights to be fully unpacked by writers, artists and thinkers across the west. But his coronation oration eventually came to be seen as a manifesto for the entire Renaissance.[17]

PETRARCH'S LIFE FOLLOWING HIS CORONATION IN Rome could be read, in retrospect, as a model for the new intellectual and cultural world of the Renaissance which burst into life at the end of the Middle Ages. As we have already seen, Petrarch was spared by the Black Death in 1348, but his beloved Laura was not, and nor were many of his friends.* As he grew older, he became lonelier and became more religious. In 1350 he decided to set aside as much worldly pleasure as possible and devote himself to a more reclusive existence of contemplation and study.

Yet like all the greatest medieval minds, Petrarch realized that to immerse himself in Christian thought did not necessarily imply abandonment of the classics. Through his travels and his work he had amassed one of the greatest private book collections in Europe, which included texts that had not been read for many centuries, such as a cache of Cicero's private letters, which he discovered in Verona. Petrarch was also conscientious about organizing his own writing: he arranged his sonnets in a collection known in Italian as the *Canzoniere*; collected letters he had sent over the years to friends such as Boccaccio; and made steady progress on an ambitious lyric poem collection called the *Triumphs (Trionfi)*. This was arranged around six great themes – Love, Chastity, Death, Fame, Time and Eternity – and it charted the mortal and spiritual course of human life all the way through to the afterlife. Thanks to the big ideas in which it dealt, its vivid depictions of suffering, struggle and celebration and the many cameos for famous characters ranging from Old Testament patriarchs to near-contemporary figures like the sultan Saladin, the *Triumphs* was very popular during the later Middle Ages, and much-copied, often in lavishly illustrated manuscripts.

The original text of the *Triumphs* took Petrarch nearly twenty years to complete, and he only finished it in the early 1370s. By that time he was living in Italy, splitting his time between Padua and his nearby country retreat at Arquà. He remained in close contact with the papal court, and although he did not approve of every pontiff who reigned there, he was delighted when the papacy began its return to Rome from its so-called 'Babylonian

---

* See chapter 13.

Captivity' in Avignon in 1367.* Sadly he never lived to see the full Roman restoration, for he died at his desk in Arquà the day before his seventieth birthday, on 19 July 1374; he was reputedly found as if asleep, with his head propped on a Virgil manuscript. Virgil was – and is – usually most closely linked with Dante, who lived a generation earlier than Petrarch. No matter. Together, Dante and Petrarch were the foremost Italian writers of the fourteenth century. They were the equals of their much-admired classical forebears, and the giants on whose shoulders many of the greatest artists and writers of the Renaissance would stand.

LOOKING BACK ON PETRARCH'S LIFE SOME five hundred years after he died, a Swiss scholar called Jacob Burckhardt thought it was possible to pinpoint the exact moment when the Renaissance 'began'. This was Saturday 26 April 1326, when a young Petrarch and his brother Gherardo decided to climb Mount Ventoux, not far from Vaucluse – a peak of nearly two thousand metres, today famous as one of the toughest climbs on the route of the Tour de France. According to Petrarch himself, he had been dreaming of climbing it since childhood, to see what was visible from the top. Neither the fact that it was 'a steep mountain with rocky and almost inaccessible cliffs' nor specific warnings to clear off, given by an old shepherd, could dissuade the brothers. So up they went.[18]

Obviously the climb was horrible. But they pushed through. And in the course of a difficult ascent and descent, Petrarch meditated on the writings of St Augustine. He wrote afterwards that doing so showed him the importance of introspection and physical striving as a source of religious revelation. 'What could be found within, [people] go seeking without,' he wrote. According to Burckhardt, this insight and the idea of climbing the mountain with the simple purpose of experiencing nature for its own sake would never have

---

* The Avignon Papacy had begun in 1309 under Clement V. In 1367 Pope Urban V returned to Rome, but he was forced to leave in 1370. Six years later Gregory XI made the switch back to Rome permanent, although the Church was then wrenched apart by schism, which lasted until 1417. See chapter 16.

occurred to anyone before Petrarch's time – just as both concepts would seem entirely normal to the generations that followed him.[19] This, claimed the historian, is what made Petrarch special.

Today not many people would agree with Burckhardt's assessment about when the Renaissance started. All the same, after Petrarch's death in 1374 there was undeniably a boom in great literature, felt in realms across the west. Boccaccio, who died in 1375, had finished his *Decameron* twenty years earlier. In England the enthusiastic Italophile Geoffrey Chaucer began his *Canterbury Tales* around 1387 and worked on it until his own death in 1400. (Chaucer also translated Petrarch's poetry into English and adapted one of his Latin stories, *Griselda*, as *The Clerk's Tale*.) In France the Venetian-born poet, historian and courtier Christine de Pisan rose to prominence as a star of the French court of the mad Charles VI, where she spun a new and compelling Trojan origin story for the Frankish people, and wrote what was arguably the first ever feminist history, *The Book of the City of Ladies*: a French vernacular compendium of the lives and deeds of great women throughout history. Twenty years after Christine de Pisan completed that book, Leonardo Bruni and Filelfo were at work in Italy. Not long after, probably in the 1440s, Donatello sculpted his famous bronze of David – generally considered the first naturalistic, nude male sculpture of the Middle Ages. Not all of this was Petrarch's doing – either directly or indirectly. But taken together, it was an extraordinary scene.

We shall return to Italy soon. However, before we do, we must look at another vibrant centre of artistic and creative innovation in the early fifteenth century, which lay north of the Alps, in Burgundy. The duchy of Burgundy was the successor state to the vanished kingdom of the same name, which had been folded into the Frankish state in the sixth century AD. Under a family of independent-minded fifteenth-century dukes it reached from the northern banks of Lake Geneva to the North Sea coast of Flanders. Its rulers had not forgotten that they might in other circumstances have been fully fledged monarchs, and they sought to emphasize that in every way possible. They acted as power-brokers in the final chapters of Hundred Years War between England and France. They took the cross and fought as crusaders against the Ottomans. But they were also generous, lavish patrons of arts and artists and in the fifteenth century their ducal court became a hub for creative geniuses from across Europe.

The Good, the Bad and the Lovely

IN NORTH-WEST EUROPE THE WINTER OF 1434–5 was bitingly cold. In England, the Thames froze all the way up to its estuary. Across Scotland ice lay so thick that for weeks on end mill wheels stopped turning, causing mass shortages of flour and bread. And in Arras, in Flanders, where snow fell relentlessly for four months, the townsfolk built elaborate snowmen in the forms of mythical, supernatural, political and historical figures. On one street lay the Seven Sleepers of Ephesus. On another, frosty skeletons cavorted hideously in a *danse macabre*. The allegorical figure of Danger guarded the entrance to the *Petit Marché*. And amid it all stood a snow-woman leading a small force of snowmen-at-arms.[20] She was Joan of Arc (*Jeanne d'Arc*), and she would have been instantly recognizable to any pedestrians who scurried past her along the snowbound streets.

For a brief time during the previous decade Joan – a village girl from Domrémy, in the heart of Burgundian territory in eastern France – was the most famous woman in Europe. In 1425, when she was about thirteen, she had been visited by archangels, who told her to track down the late Charles VI's uncrowned son and heir, known as the Dauphin, and help him drive out of France the English armies that had invaded and conquered much of the northern half of the country.* Amazingly, Joan had followed through with her

---

* It may be helpful to summarize briefly the state of France and the Hundred Years War at this point. As mentioned above (see chapter 13), during the long and troubled reign of Charles VI (r. 1380–1422) France split into two rival camps, known as the Armagnacs and Burgundians. Taking advantage of this political schism, Henry V of England (r. 1413–22) invaded, defeated an Armagnac-French army at the battle of Agincourt (25 October 1415) and proceeded to conquer Normandy and much of the north of the realm. Under the Treaty

mission, and in the late 1420s, now aged around seventeen, she marched alongside the Dauphin's armies as they brought the fight back to the English. Sometimes she dressed in male armour, and although she did not fight, she presented a splendid vision of God's favour, seeming to inspire victory wherever she went. In 1429 she carried a banner alongside French troops as they won the hard-pressed siege of Orléans. The next year she was at the Dauphin's side in Reims Cathedral, dressed in gleaming armour and carrying her banner, when her master was crowned as Charles VII.[21]

In May 1430, however, Joan was captured, at the siege of Compiègne. She was brought to Arras to be imprisoned. Her captor was a nobleman called Jean de Luxembourg, who had been fighting on the English side at Compiègne. He owed his allegiance to England's most important ally, Philip the Good, duke of Burgundy, and through the duke's mediation he sold Joan to the English. One year later, during which time a Church court had convicted her of heresy, Joan was burned at the stake in Rouen. The duke of Burgundy was not in town to watch her die. But he had met with Joan while she was in prison, and although he never revealed what words passed between them, he had shown no compunction about brokering this vulnerable woman's sale to people he must have known would eventually kill her.

Nor, as it turned out, did the duke worry too much about his loyalty to his English allies. Indeed, in the bleak winter of 1434–5, as the late Joan was raised in snow-effigy in Arras, Philip the Good was preparing to abandon the English altogether. Six months after the snows finally melted, in September 1435, Philip agreed the Treaty of Arras with Charles VII. He withdrew all his support for

---

of Troyes (1420) the French recognized Henry and heirs as legitimate successors to Charles VI, effectively securing the final objective of the Hundred Years War, which was to combine the crowns of England and France. This disinherited Charles VI's eldest son the Dauphin, who was on the side of the Armagnacs. None of this would have been possible without Burgundian support for the English. By the early 1430s both Henry V and Charles VI were dead, and Henry's young son, Henry VI, had theoretically succeeded both. France was effectively partitioned in three: the English-controlled northern sector, the Armagnac south and a Burgundian swathe which included Burgundy itself along with Flanders and the Low Countries. An alliance between any two of the active powers was highly disadvantageous to the third.

the English in France, repudiated the claim of the young English king Henry VI to call himself king of France and joined a coalition of powers all vigorously hostile to England, including the kingdoms of Scotland and Castile. It was a stunning blow, from which the English cause would not recover. It led eventually to their final defeat in the Hundred Years War, at the battle of Castillon in 1453. So in the short and even the medium term, the Treaty of Arras was a potent demonstration of the power that the duke of Burgundy could wield on the European stage.

Diplomatic and military historians have spent much time analysing the terms and consequences of the Treaty of Arras. That need not concern us here. What matters is that Philip the Good was a great duke, from a great line of dukes. But his ambition was to be a king. He recognized that in part the job of a great potentate was exercising political cunning and prowess in battle, and ensuring that he was recognized as a genuine force in the perpetual diplomatic games contested between the European realms. Yet he was acutely aware that the perception of power went far beyond occupying ambassadors and armies. It was also a matter of ostentation and courtly spectacle. So it is no coincidence that in the 1430s Philip the Good was positioning himself carefully as more than merely a power-broker. He was also carving out a role as Europe's foremost patron of the arts, who surrounded himself with a coterie of dazzling creative people. Their efforts bore testimony to the regality of this effervescent duke's rule. The greatest of all of these – a painter who was recognized even in his lifetime to have changed the course of western art for good – was Jan van Eyck.

AT THE TIME OF THE TREATY of Arras, van Eyck was in his mid-fifties and one of Philip's close confidants and friends. He was born around 1390, probably in Maaseik (modern Belgium). It seems likely he had an elder brother by the name of Hubert who was also a painter – and art historians have debated at length the precise contribution of Hubert to the van Eyck canon. What is plain is that Jan was the greater of the two by an order of magnitude. As a young man Jan van Eyck travelled around Flanders and the Low Countries practicing his craft, living in Liège and Ghent and working at first on fairly conventional, Gothic-influenced religious scenes showing Christ and the Virgin Mary in various episodes from the gospels. In the early 1420s his patron was a bishop-turned-nobleman called John the Pitiless – so called because when he put down a rebellion in Liège in 1408 he had massacred the rebels to a man. His accomplice in this unpleasant butchery was none other than Philip the Good's father, John the Fearless. But by 1425 John the Fearless and John the Pitiless had both been murdered (the Fearless was bludgeoned to death on a bridge, the Pitiless was assassinated with a poisoned prayer-book). So Philip was pre-eminent in and around Flanders, and van Eyck fell naturally into his orbit. From the spring of that year he was paid 100 *livres parisis* (Parisian pounds) – a handsome wage – to double up as Philip's valet and a sort of painter-at-large, attached to the ducal court but permitted to freelance outside it. The roles suited him perfectly.

The ducal court Jan van Eyck had entered in 1425 was a vibrant, ostentatious, sometimes ribald place. Philip, who was about the same age as van Eyck, was a striking and charismatic figure, described by one chronicler as tall and thin, with veins that bulged all over his body. He shared his family's characteristic aquiline nose, along with a sun-browned face and 'bushy eyebrows which stood out like horns when he was angry'.[22] A portrait by van Eyck's great contemporary Rogier van der Weyden confirms the description. It also backs the chronicler's claim that the duke 'dressed smartly but in rich array'; in van der Weyden's portrait Philip wears a luxurious black gown, the fine jewelled collar of his chivalric Order of the Golden Fleece, and a huge, black turban-like *chaperon* on his head.

Van Eyck must have come quickly to realize that this striking nobleman combined conventional piety with extravagant excess. The duke heard Mass every day, but had papal dispensation to do so between 2 p.m. and 3 p.m. (instead of in the morning) since he liked to feast, drink, dance and party at night, sometimes until dawn, and rose so late that official visitors might be turned away if they showed up while he was still sleeping off the fun.[23] He had impeccable manners, particularly towards women, whom he said were almost invariably the real rulers of their houses and needed to be charmed. But in addition to three wives, he accrued between twenty and thirty-three mistresses, and fathered at least eleven illegitimate children.

The duke also had a remarkably surreal and even slapstick sense of humour. He signed off his private letters with the phrase 'farewell turd'. And he paid one of van Eyck's artist colleagues at court £1,000 to fit out rooms in his castle of Hesdin with practical jokes and booby traps: statues that squirted water at passing courtiers; a boxing-glove contrivance in one doorway 'which buffets anyone who passes through well and truly on the head and shoulders'; further water-jets hidden in the floor to spray up ladies' skirts; and a room that held a speaking wooden hermit, a rain machine in the ceiling to spray fake thunderstorms on visitors and a phoney rain-shelter with a false floor, so that those trying to escape the wet would be dunked into a large sack of feathers.[24]

These contraptions spoke to the duke's zany, slightly cruel streak. But they also sprang from Philip's boundless love of invention and artistry. He spent fortunes on tapestries, elaborately decorated religious vestments, jewelled reliquaries and exquisite illuminated manuscripts.[25] He employed musicians, painters, goldsmiths, writers and other craftsmen on a greater scale than any ruler of his day outside Italy. To inspect his jewellery collection alone was said by its keeper to be a three-day job.[26] And, of course, he hired van Eyck, who blossomed under his patronage, becoming what the sixteenth-century writer Giorgio Vasari called an artistic alchemist; the man who effectively invented oil painting.[27]

Van Eyck did not spend all his time with Duke Philip – he had a contract that did not require him to live at court, but allowed him to work in his own studio, where Philip occasionally dropped in. However, they were together on many important occasions, for van Eyck's work was bound up with Philip's political ambition, and the duke trusted him deeply. From the beginning of his employment van Eyck was used as a diplomat for sensitive embassies: in

1426 he was sent on a mission listed in the duke's records as a 'pilgrimage' – possibly a quiet fact-finding mission to Aragon to sound out King Alfonso V about a marriage alliance and send back portraits of potential brides.[28] He certainly attended a covert mission of this sort to Portugal in 1428: a journey that secured the thirty-year-old Infanta of Portugal, Isabella, as Philip's third wife. At the Portuguese court, Van Eyck probably painted two canvas portraits of the Infanta, which were sent to Burgundy so that the duke could decide whether or not he fancied her. Evidently van Eyck did his job well, for the couple were ultimately married. And his good service earned him not only handsome bonus payments, but Philip's friendship and admiration. By the time of the Treaty of Arras in 1435, Philip had stood as godfather to van Eyck and his wife Margaret's first child, and given the painter a 700 per cent pay-rise – a raise Philip told his vexed accountants was fully justified, since 'we would not find another so much to our liking, nor so excellent in his art and science'.[29] Such was the power of the man with the brush.

And sure enough, by this stage, secure with Philip's backing, van Eyck was reaching the peak of his talent. A likely self-portrait, which hangs in the National Gallery in London, shows a somewhat stern-faced middle-aged man in an elaborate red *chaperon*; it is an absorbingly lifelike feat of oil-painting, electrifying in its use of light and shade to accentuate the drawn skin, the lines on the sitter's face and the glint that dances behind his eyes. But in its day it was revolutionary. Van Eyck came of age at a moment when the flat, idealized or iconic forms of human portraiture that characterized most medieval art had begun to give way to this far more lifelike style of work, alive with depth and rich colour. Just as Petrarch had used poetry to shine a light on the soul, so painters of the fifteenth century were attempting to capture inner truth – the essence of the individual – through portraiture. By the 1430s van Eyck was pushing this trend to new heights with every painting.

Much of van Eyck's gift lay in his acute gaze, his extraordinary command of the brush, his understanding of how to deploy colour, his love for tiny detail and his peerless hand-to-eye co-ordination. But he had also made a technical leap forward. Van Eyck discovered how to dilute oil paint with other essential oils, producing a medium that was exceptionally fluid and subtle, and which allowed the artist to capture in his sitters' faces individual hairs, tiny pimples, broken capillaries and chapped lips. Van Eyck could now render perfectly the fleeting glint of a jewel. He could mimic the way light fell across the folds of clothes. He could capture the craters of the moon. He could freeze a swallow turning on its wing in a distant part of the sky and fix exactly the way that sunlight fell across the gracefully drooping petals of an iris flower. He could recreate the cold horror of daylight reflecting off the curvature of a knight's bloodied plate armour, while capturing at the same time the brutalized thousand-yard-stare in the eyes of its wearer. It was with good reason that van Eyck's contemporary, the Italian humanist writer Bartolomeo Fazio, called him the most prominent painter of his age, and argued that his work deserved to be considered alongside literature as a rarefied art form, and the work of an illustrious sort of man.[30] Van Eyck was, simply, a technical genius. And in the 1430s he had completed two of the greatest paintings of his age.

In 1432 van Eyck finished a twenty-part altarpiece for the cathedral of St Bavo in Ghent (modern Belgium). Known as a 'polyptych' (a multi-panelled, double-sided work), the Ghent Altarpiece may have begun as a collaborative piece with Jan's brother Hubert; but the pedantic historical debate over who did what pales into irrelevance against the majesty of the work as a whole.* At the heart of it sat a panel known as *The Adoration of the Mystic Lamb*, in which angels, bishops, saints, kings, queens, ladies, soldiers, merchants and hermits are gathered around an altar on which the lamb of God stands bleeding from a wound in its breast into a golden chalice. In the upper panels Christ sits enthroned and glorious, surrounded by the Virgin Mary, John the Baptist and angels singing or playing musical instruments. On either 'wing' of

---

* The Ghent Altarpiece has been recently and brilliantly restored, removing the over-painting and varnish of several earlier restorations. It is as close today as it has been for many centuries to the version that van Eyck completed in 1432.

the altarpiece stand Adam and Eve, naked but for their fig-leaves, and, in Eve's case, coyly but inadequately trying to hide what is sometimes cited as the first known medieval depiction of pubic hair. On the back panels of the polyptych – which would be visible when the hinged altarpiece was closed – van Eyck painted scenes of the Annunciation, images of St John the Baptist and St John the Evangelist, and pictures of Joost Vijdt, the mayor of Ghent, and his wife Lysbet, who had ordered the altarpiece in the first place.

Shortly after completing the Ghent Altarpiece, van Eyck worked on another, very different masterpiece: The Arnolfini Portrait. This is a picture of the Italian merchant Giovanni Arnolfini, a cloth-weaver who traded between Lucca and Bruges, and his young wife. The couple stand hand-in-hand in a bedroom illuminated by a single candle, their shoes strewn about the floor and a cheeky little brown lapdog posing between their feet. Beautifully, and somewhat eerily, a mirror on the wall reflects two other people in the room, standing where we presume the artist ought to be. Through the mirror, the room is warped and elongated, telescoping the semblance of depth perspective in the painting, while setting it at odds with the direction of every other significant line in the portrait, which run vertically. Beyond the geometric expertise at play in the image and its exquisite attention to near-microscopic detail, the Arnolfini portrait is a masterpiece of humanist art. The merchant's squint makes it impossible to quite catch his eye, while the burden of time weighing on two partners who seem to be different in age and background is worn plainly on their faces.

BETWEEN THEM, THE GHENT ALTARPIECE AND Arnolfini Portrait confirmed van Eyck as the most accomplished painter of his day. Curiously, neither was commissioned by Philip the Good, the patron who paid van Eyck such a fortune. Yet they were connected to the court all the same. Ghent was a Burgundian-controlled town, and its municipal glory reflected back on the duke. Meanwhile, Arnolfini had helped Philip the Good enhance Burgundy's prestige at the papal court in the 1420s, by supplying him with six fine tapestries to send to Pope Martin V as a gift.[31] It may be that Philip was prepared to retain van Eyck at such huge expense precisely *because* the latter could take his pick of patrons across Europe. For the duke, who amassed fine things at a pace and volume matched by few if any other magnates in the west, being associated with this virtuoso artist – and knowing no one else could claim overall patron status – was enough. Throughout the late 1430s he continued to pay van Eyck his large fee to represent Burgundy, and sent him on more diplomatic embassies where his brush as well as his eyes might be needed. The deal seemed to be that other patrons were welcome to hire van Eyck, and they did so: the lugubrious Burgundian ambassador to England, Baudouin de Lannoy, was one; the wealthy Bruges-based goldsmith Jan de Leeuw another. But they could never have him all to themselves.

Van Eyck died in 1441, while he was working on a painting known as *The Madonna of the Provost van Maelbeke*, commissioned for display in a monastery in Ypres (and today known only in replica). He was buried twice – first in the churchyard and later inside the cathedral church of St Donatian in Bruges, which no longer stands, having been destroyed after the French Revolution. His association with Philip the Good's court had lasted for sixteen years, and although he produced most of his best works for other clients, he would forever be linked with Burgundy. Van Eyck was remembered in courts all across Europe as 'an exquisite master in the art of painting', while other artists – even Italians – would travel hundreds of miles to the Burgundian-controlled towns of Flanders and the Low Countries to study his work, hoping to learn how to recreate his greatest tricks.[32] This was, in the end, why Philip the Good had hired him. He put Burgundy on the map in just as powerful a fashion as any amount of underhand politicking or double-dealing between the English and Armagnacs could do.

Philip outlived his finest artist by two and a half decades, dying at the age of seventy in 1467. By the end of the fifteenth century his descendants had proven unable to transform Burgundy into a kingdom, nor even to maintain it as an independent state: in the 1490s Burgundy was split up and much of its territory rolled into what would become the Habsburg Holy Roman Empire. But the reputation of this fleeting European half-realm for punching far above its weight as a cultural force would endure for centuries afterwards. And Philip's model of accruing magnificence through patronage was now widespread.

'Universal genius'

AROUND 1482 THE THIRTY-YEAR-OLD PAINTER LEONARDO da Vinci wrote a letter to Ludovico Sforza, nicknamed 'Il Moro' (the Moor), who ruled the city-state of Milan. Leonardo was asking Ludovico for a job. He had spent the years before he wrote the letter working in a highly regarded artists' workshop in Florence, run by Andrea del Verrocchio. This had been a wonderful place to train, for Verrocchio was a very fine artist in his own right, who numbered among his clients the richest and most prestigious Florentine families, including the Medici. His studio turned out fine paintings, metalwork, sculpture, ceremonial armour and textiles, and had manufactured the gleaming, hammered-copper ball that crowned Brunelleschi's dome – a feat of artistry and engineering which had required soldering torches made from concave mirrors that concentrated sunlight into a single hot point.[33] While working under Verrocchio, Leonardo had already been given important opportunities to demonstrate his skills: he and his master had collaborated on handsome portraits such as *Tobias and the Angel* (today displayed at the National Gallery in London) and *Madonna and Child* (now in the Berlin *Staatliche Museen*). But as he turned thirty, Leonardo was setting his sights higher. He did not simply desire the chance to be an artist in his own right, or to have his own workshop in Florence. He wanted to be something altogether bigger. In his letter to Ludovico Sforza, he explained what he could do.

'I have designed extremely light and strong bridges, adapted to be easily carried,' wrote Leonardo. 'I know how, during a siege, to take the water out of the trenches... I have methods for destroying

any fortress even if it is founded on solid rock. I have cannons...
that can fling small stones almost resembling a hailstorm.' He
boasted that he could make naval weapons, design mines and
tunnels, and 'make unassailable armed chariots that can penetrate
the ranks of the enemy with their artillery'. He said he could
manufacture guns, catapults, 'and other effective machines not
in common use.' Besides military engineering, he claimed to be
a master of 'architecture and the composition of buildings public
and private, and in guiding water from one place to another...' He
wrote that he would be able to see to completion a famous mooted
Milanese public art project to construct a giant bronze horse in
tribute to Ludovico's late father, Duke Francesco Sforza. And he
mentioned, almost as an afterthought: 'Likewise in painting I can
do everything possible, as well as any other man, whosoever he
may be.'[34]

This letter of Leonardo's, preserved in draft form in his notebooks, shows in cross-section the versatile mind of a medieval man
who has a serious claim to be thought of as the greatest genius in
history. Leonardo set no limits on his interests and there was very
little he could not do. Besides painting several of the most famous
artworks of all time – *Mona Lisa*, *The Last Supper*, *The Virgin of
the Rocks* and *Salvator Mundi** – and drawing the iconic *Vitruvian
Man* – he mastered aspects of anatomy, optics, astronomy, physics
and engineering. The inventions he designed in his notebooks
– among them aircraft and tanks – were often so ambitious that
they were not realized until hundreds of years after his death. His
notes to himself, largely kept in neat, left-handed mirror-writing,
ranged across a vast landscape of intellectual and practical topics.
Leonardo was a polymath, and a fearless thinker. And he knew
it. That was why he wrote to Ludovico Sforza. He reckoned his
abilities, born of an insatiably curious mind and buoyed by great
self-confidence, would be invaluable to a political patron, warrior

---

* *Salvator Mundi* is a relatively recent addition to the list of Leonardo's greatest works; in
part it owes its position on this list to the fact that in 2017 it was sold at auction for slightly
more than $450 million, making it (at the time of writing) the most expensive artwork in
history.

and aesthete such as Il Moro. He was right. After writing the letter Leonardo spent seventeen years working in Milan. And this was only part of a long career, during which Leonardo served many great masters in Italy and France. All were lucky to have him, for he was, as Vasari put it, 'marvellous and celestial'.[35]

LEONARDO WAS BORN IN THE SMALL town of Vinci, about a day's ride from Florence, in 1452. His father was a notary. His mother was a sixteen-year-old peasant girl. They were not married, but at that moment, illegitimacy was no particular disgrace. It simply meant Leonardo was brought up by his grandparents and not given a rigorous Latin education. At the age of twelve he moved from Vinci to Florence with his father, and two years later he was apprenticed to Verrocchio, whose circle may also have included the brilliant painter Sandro Botticelli.[36] Under Verrocchio, students did not just learn to paint and sculpt. They picked up practical geometry and anatomy and studied classical literature, the better to understand the subject matter of the artworks they produced. Leonardo lapped it all up.

By the time he was an adult, in the early 1470s, Florence was an even greater place to be an artist than it had been forty years previously in the days of Cosimo de' Medici and Francesco Filelfo. The effective ruler of the city was now Lorenzo 'the Magnificent' de' Medici, who took over the family business in 1469. Although the Medici bank's finances were creaking – they suffered catastrophic losses though their Bruges branch in the 1470s, when a rogue local manager made massive, unsecured loans to Charles the Bold, duke of Burgundy, the son and successor of Philip the Good – Lorenzo's eagerness to spend his money lavishly made his tenure a golden age of the Renaissance.

A quick census of the artists working and emerging in Florence in the 1470s and 1480s is a roll-call of some of the most brilliant in world history. As well as Verrocchio, Botticelli and Leonardo, the city was home to Domenico Ghirlandaio and the Pollaiuolo brothers. The poet and Greek scholar Angelo Ambrogini (known as Poliziano) was combining his duties as tutor to Lorenzo de' Medici's children with translating Homer's *Iliad* into Latin verse. In 1484 the scholar Giovanni Pico della Mirandola ('a man of almost supernatural genius', said Machiavelli) would arrive to seek Lorenzo's patronage, boasting that he could defend 900 theses on topics ranging from Christian dogma to witchcraft against any and all who dared challenge him.[37] A few years later a thirteen-year-old Michelangelo Buonarroti was apprenticed to the Ghirlandaio workshop; he would grow up to be Leonardo's closest rival as the finest painter of the Italian Renaissance.

The wealth of the Medici family drove much of this creative investment: every year Lorenzo continued the family tradition, established by his grandfather, of ploughing what would today be tens and even hundreds of millions of dollars into cultural endeavours. He did it because he and almost everyone else whose opinion mattered thought it money well spent. For one thing, conspicuous consumption was satisfying in itself – as it remains to billionaires today. For another, Lorenzo was concerned with cultivating his own reputation as a patron of the arts, not least to cover up some of his shadier dealings within the city. And patronage could be useful in diplomacy, too. On occasion Florentine artists were 'loaned out' to other great potentates to cultivate their favour. When he was trying to secure a cardinal's hat for one of his sons, Lorenzo sent the painter Filippino Lippo to Rome to decorate another cardinal's private chapel; it may well be that he encouraged Leonardo to seek favour with the Sforza family in Milan, too.

Yet his patronage was not wholly cynical. Accumulating great art, particularly great art displayed in public settings, was thought to reflect of the inner virtue of the Republic of Florence itself. Machiavelli claimed that Lorenzo spent vast sums on beautiful things in order to 'keep the city abundantly supplied, the people united and the nobility honoured'.[38] To be sure, Lorenzo had personal reasons for doing so – but among them was real civic pride, which in the fifteenth century was inseparable from the business of leadership.

However, while Lorenzo's Florence, the city that produced Leonardo da Vinci, was abundant in beautiful things, it was also violent and dangerous – perhaps even more so than it had been in Cosimo's day. Factional strife in the city could still boil over quickly into spectacular bloodshed – as it did in 1478 in the Pazzi Conspiracy, when assassins of the Pazzi family, backed by Pope Sixtus IV, tried to assassinate Lorenzo and his brother Giuliano in Santa Maria del Fiore cathedral. Public feuding was deeply ingrained in Florentine political culture, and it made its mark on Leonardo: in his notebooks there is a memorable ink sketch of one of the Pazzi conspirators, Bernardo Bandini dei Baroncelli, hanging dead from a noose. (The sketch is accompanied with Leonardo's cheerful notes on the colours of Baroncelli's robes.) To live and work in the vibrant, handsomely funded world of the Renaissance meant accepting its macabre realities and the ubiquity of bloodshed, crime and war. So it was no coincidence that Leonardo positioned himself to Ludovico Sforza as a man who could do more than merely paint like an angel. He knew that to be truly great required a measure of pragmatism – being able to turn one's ingenuity to all manner of ends, including, if necessary, diabolical ones.

Leonardo's seventeen years in Milan were busy and productive. Handsome and charming – 'a man of outstanding beauty and infinite grace', wrote Vasari – he was also gentle-spirited. He adored animals, and would never eat meat. Both inscrutable and gregarious, he made friends easily, though his closest associate was his young assistant Gian Giacomo Caprotti da Oreno, better known simply as Salaì, who was apprenticed to him at the age of ten in 1490. Beautiful, unruly and possessed of a kleptomaniac streak, Salaì combined the roles of Leonardo's muse, helper, protégé, son and (very possibly) lover, staying with him for a quarter of a century. His formative teenage years were spent by Leonardo's side in Milan.

During his time in that city, Leonardo won big commissions, although these were mostly in the civic space, rather than in the realm of military engineering. He consulted on improvement works to Milan's huge and structurally unsound Gothic cathedral. He spent many hours designing theatrical devices for the amusement of Ludovico's courtiers. He painted the two versions of *The Virgin of the Rocks* (which today hang in the Paris Louvre and London's National Gallery). He undertook the gorgeous, intimate, secular portraits known today as *Portrait of a Musician*, *Lady with an Ermine* and *La Belle Ferronnière*. And he devoted more than two years to *The Last Supper* – a mural in the refectory of the convent church of Santa Maria delle Grazie, where curious citizens came to see him sitting all day on his scaffolding, lost to his painting. Meanwhile, in private he studied anatomy, both animal and human. His *Vitruvian Man*, a scientific drawing illustrating the geometric proportions of the human form, also dates to this period in his life. All the while he continued to fill his notebooks with designs for machines, observations on mathematics, studies of natural motion and more besides. It was a wonderfully fruitful period. But it would not last forever.

Of all the bold pitches Leonardo had made Ludovico Sforza in his letter of 1482, the one he came closest to achieving was production of a great bronze horse – the long-talked-about monument to Ludovico's father, Duke Francesco Sforza. In the early months of 1489 he finally got the job, and set up a studio, staffed with half a dozen assistants, where he made plans for the biggest equestrian statue the world had even known – which would stand at three times life size, weigh seventy-five tons, and advertise the might of the Sforza dynasty, who had been in power in Milan only since 1401, and coveted spectacular ways of making up for their lack of pedigree.[39] Leonardo's plans for this gigantic monument were more than audacious: they were visionary. He aimed to cast it in a single piece – a process no one else alive would have conceived or dared to try. By the end of 1493 he had worked through the structural problems of moulding, casting and cooling and was almost ready to begin.

Yet the great horse never materialized. For just at that moment French armies were preparing to invade northern Italy. A fierce, sixty-five-year series of wars for control of the Italian peninsula, waged mainly between France and a newly united kingdom of Spain, was beginning. The Italian city-states would henceforth be in regular military peril. And Ludovico Sforza could not now afford to waste good metal on big horses. He sent the bronze earmarked for Leonardo's statue 250km east to the city of Ferrara, where it was used to manufacture cannon. And that was that. It was a disappointment, although Leonardo was pragmatic enough to know that nothing could be done. 'I know the times,' he wrote.[40] The map of Europe was changing abruptly and dramatically. Artists and artisans had to respond as best they could. Leonardo would never have the luxury of another seventeen-year residency at any court. He would, however, have an even great pick of patrons than before, as war drove up the premium on his artistic and engineering expertise.

In 1499 another French army marched over the Alps to invade northern Italy, deposing Ludovico Sforza (who eventually died in a French dungeon in 1508). Leonardo fled. He headed back to Florence, stopping briefly in Mantua to meet (and sketch) that city's young and single-minded patron of the arts, Isabella d'Este, and in Venice to advise on defensive engineering to guard against possible invasion by the Ottomans. But by 1500 he was home, and working on a new raft of projects.

For a brief spell he was hired by Cesare Borgia: a dangerous, sadistically violent, wanton and extremely cunning military captain and would-be prince, whose father was the debauched and sexually incontinent Pope Alexander VI. Cesare spent the early years of the sixteenth century conquering the smaller cities in the vicinity of Florence, and only resisted taking Florence itself upon receipt of protection money. He hired Leonardo as a military advisor and map-maker, and Leonardo stayed in his service for the better part of a year, even as Borgia besieged, butchered and murdered his way around Italy. There was a cold, pragmatic streak to Leonardo's genius which sat strangely at odds with his gentler, humanistic interests.[41] A patron, it seemed, was a patron. Serving Borgia allowed Leonardo to develop his skills in cartography, bridge-building and fortification design. That was apparently enough for him to overlook any amount of moral squalor.[42]

Perhaps, however, one could only put up with Cesare Borgia for so long. In 1503 Leonardo left his service. He spent the next decade shuttling back and forth between Tuscany and Lombardy – Medici Florence and French-occupied Milan – adapting to the rapid political changes and reversals of fortune that now characterized the wider region. The turbulence and constant upheaval might have shaken a less robust or worldly-wise character. Yet Leonardo seems to have danced constantly forward, the quality of his work remaining in the highest rank despite the difficulties of the times. It was probably in Florence between 1503 and 1506 that he began a portrait of Lisa Gherardini del Giocondo – the *Mona Lisa* – which he would tinker with for the rest of his life.[43] He also worked on a mural (now lost) for the Palazzo Vecchio, which showed a tangle of men and horses in combat at the battle of Anghiari: a clash between Milanese and Florentine-led forces that had taken place in 1440. He and his assistants produced numerous editions of a painting called *Madonna of the Yarnwinder*. In Milan in 1509 he started work on the extraordinary, gender-fluid *Saint John the Baptist*. And he worked on unrealized, grandiose military and civil engineering projects. He planned to divert the river Arno to cause a drought in Pisa, which had rejected Florentine overlordship. He plotted to drain the swamps surrounding the town of Piombino and build an impregnable fortress on the reclaimed land. These came to nothing – but Leonardo never stopped dreaming.

Yet as he dreamed, he aged, and as the sixteenth century dawned, Leonardo found himself an old man. A self-portrait he sketched when he turned sixty in 1512 shows a grizzled, long-nosed, balding figure with a flowing beard and shoulders that are starting to stoop. But he was a grand master, in one of the grandest times. His peers included the spiky, combative, sexually closeted and often downright angry genius Michelangelo, who unveiled his statue *David* in Florence 1504 – yet even Michelangelo had to seek the permission of Leonardo and other Florentine elders to have it approved for display outside the *Palazzo Vecchio*. So his star had not yet waned. And as a result, his patrons now included the most powerful figures in his world. In 1513 one of Lorenzo de' Medici's sons, Giovanni, was elected as Pope Leo X. He decided he could use Leonardo in the papal court, where lavish renovations were underway. In September of that year Leonardo left Florence for Rome, and began the last stage of his life.

LEONARDO'S TIME UNDER THE PATRONAGE OF a Medici pope was not as glorious as perhaps he had hoped. For one thing, he was not part of the most exciting projects at play in the Holy City. Michelangelo had been given the job of decorating the ceiling of the Sistine Chapel, which he completed in 1512. Raphael (Raffaello Sanzio) was painting the papal apartments. These were much younger men, but the plum job of building the new St Peter's Basilica, which was arguably the greatest architectural commission on earth, had gone in 1506 to Leonardo's contemporary Donato Bramante. So although he had fine apartments in the papal palace at the Vatican, he was left more or less to his own devices: studying geometry and reflection; taming a lizard, for which he made a coat from mercury-covered scales; dissecting human bodies and making notes on anatomy. This was all fascinating work, and he was paid a nice salary to do nothing very much. But it was not enough.

In 1516, therefore, Leonardo left Rome and headed out of Italy for the first time in his long life, to serve yet another patron: Francis I, the young and charismatic new king of France. More than forty years younger than Leonardo, Francis was a true child of the Renaissance. Like his contemporary and sparring-partner, Henry VIII of England, Francis was commandingly tall, handsome and possessed of an instinctive love for fine things and the rich fruits of humanism. He came to the throne aged twenty on the first day of 1515, and met Leonardo with the pope at the end of the same year. Tempting Leonardo to France, where he lodged him in the picturesque village of Amboise, was a priceless opportunity to send the world a message about the values of his new French monarchy. It was also a chance for Francis personally to study with the greatest living polymath.

For the next three years Leonardo and Francis enjoyed a mutually pleasant existence in one another's company. Just as he had done in his long years in Milan, Leonardo designed court entertainments. He tinkered with his great paintings, including the *Mona Lisa*. He worked on designs for brand new Renaissance palace and town at Romorantin. He studied mathematics and the movement of water. And he grew gradually, gracefully ancient. After a series of strokes, he died on 2 May 1519. A tradition, begun by Vasari, said that he died with Francis at his bedside – indeed, that he 'expired in the arms of the King'. To Vasari, this was a fitting, noble end for so great a man. Leonardo 'adorned and honoured, in every action, no matter what mean and bare dwelling,' Vasari wrote. 'Florence received a very great gift in the birth of Leonardo, and an incalculable loss in his death.'[44] And it was not just Florence. Every patron who had employed Leonardo, from the murderous Cesare Borgia to the urbane Francis I, had been blessed by his genius; the world was greatly diminished by his passing.

A Golden Age

LEONARDO DA VINCI WAS THE ULTIMATE Renaissance man – so much so that it is often hard for us to conceive of him as the product of the Middle Ages. Yet he was born in the same year as King Richard III of England; he died several decades before the Polish scientist Nicolaus Copernicus proposed that the sun, and not the earth, might sit at the centre of the heavens.* Many of Leonardo's projects – from helicopters to diving bells – were so advanced that they belonged not to his time but to ours. He

---

* Copernicus only published his key text on this topic, *De revolutionibus orbium coelestium*, in 1543, the year of his own death.

is an essentially liminal character – one who belongs to both our worlds, and who has the power to join us emotionally as well as intellectually to the Middle Ages.

In his own time, however, Leonardo was very much *primus inter pares*. Had he never lived – had he been a legitimate child of his father's, sent off to a conventional education and a solid career as a notary – we would still be able to talk of the Renaissance as a landmark, transitional age in western and world history, from which poured forth a torrent of new ideas, methods and styles, across literature, arts and human sciences. Leonardo's peers – from Botticelli and Donatello to Michelangelo and Raphael – would have made sure of that. And of course, it was not only Italians. For although the main wellspring of the Renaissance was in Italy, by the sixteenth century the cultural revolution had begun to touch almost every realm in the west.

In England the humanist writer Thomas More was at work around Henry VIII's court, publishing books including *Utopia*, his satirical work of social commentary and political philosophy. In France, Leonardo's place as the most talented painter at Francis' I's court was taken by Jean Clouet and, later, his son Francois Clouet, whose paintings of French courtly figures such as Francis and his daughter-in-law Catherine de' Medici became as iconic as the English court paintings made in the 1530s by Hans Holbein the Younger. In Poland, the poet Mikołaj Rej began to write in the Polish language and Stanisław Samostrzelnik experimented with new styles of manuscript illumination and fresco, following trends brought east by foreigners such as the Italian Bartolommeo Berrecci and the German painter and stained-glassmaker Hans von Kulmbach.

These creative people – and many others like them – continued to flourish throughout the sixteenth century, and into the early seventeenth. And what remained constant throughout that long period was the close interdependence of patrons and artists, neither of whom could do without one another. Indeed, one of the reasons that the magnificent creativity of the Renaissance lasted so very long after its genesis in the fourteenth century is that the most powerful men and women in Europe were growing ever richer, and gaining access to new sources of gold and precious goods, far beyond the imagination of any generation before them. As a rule, they were always happy to spend their newfound riches on pretty things.

Where, though, did all this wealth come from? The answer lay in the west. In the year that Leonardo died, the German printmaker and artist Albrecht Dürer was bringing many of the techniques and insights of Renaissance drawing and painting to Nuremberg. Dürer was an avid traveller with an insatiable curiosity, and a range and intellect not dissimilar to Leonardo's. He learned much about painting, engraving, anatomy and geometry on his travels to Italy and the Netherlands. He corresponded with other learned and talented figures all over Europe, and like Petrarch long before him he thought hard about the elusive topic of beauty itself. He was as happy making portraits of magnificent monarchs like the Holy Roman Emperor Maximilian I as he was creating pictures of exotic beasts from much further afield. (Dürer's woodcut of a rhinoceros, today in the National Gallery of Art in Washington D.C., is truly sublime.) He took his inspiration from far and wide, and he was usually able to analyse and understand everything he set his eyes on.

Yet when Dürer took a trip with his wife to the Burgundian Low Countries in the late summer of 1520, he saw things he could not easily explain, nor absorb into his work. Travelling through Brussels the couple visited the town hall, where they clapped eyes on a display of gold and silver treasures whose beauty almost defied explanation. These belonged to the Holy Roman Emperor, Charles V, whom Dürer was in the Low Countries to petition for patronage. Dürer noted in his diary what the things he had seen:

...a sun all of gold a whole fathom broad, and a moon all of silver of the same size, also two rooms full of armor... and all manner of wondrous weapons... very strange clothing, bed-covers, and all kinds of wonderful objects of human use, much better worth seeing than prodigies. These things were all so precious that they are valued at 100,000 florins. All the days of my life I have seen nothing that rejoiced my heart so much as these things... and I marvelled at the subtle [ingenuity] of men of foreign lands.[45]

Dürer's rough estimate that the treasure was worth 100,000 florins was in itself almost incredible: his own annual stipend from Charles' predecessor as Holy Roman Emperor was 300 florins – a handsome sum. But his appreciation of the exotic craftsmanship on display was even more important. For in Brussels that year, Dürer was looking at works by artists who had been entirely untouched by the Renaissance. The treasure on display had been brought to Europe from Mexico by Hernán Cortés – an adventurer and *conquistador* who had sailed across the Atlantic and visited the megacity of Tenochtitlán (modern Mexico City). The hoard was a gift from the Aztec ruler Moctezuma II, and it was a mere suggestion of the vast riches that lay in the new lands Cortés and other Europeans had begun to explore in the Americas. So this was the wealth that would fund the next stage of the Renaissance – and much else besides. As the sixteenth century dawned, the world was getting bigger, richer – and bloodier. The map of the globe was expanding. And all the rules were changing.

15

NAVIGATORS

*'It has been a long time since there was a
crusading expedition overseas...'*

SIR JOHN MANDEVILLE,
FOURTEENTH-CENTURY TRAVEL WRITER

The cannon was so massive it took a team of sixty strong oxen and two hundred troops to move it. It had been built by a Hungarian engineer, who was paid handsomely to let his imagination run riot.[1] The gun-barrel was 8m long* and wide enough to fire rocks weighing more than half a ton. Loading it was so laborious that in combat it could only be fired seven times a day. But the slow load-rate was more than rewarded when the monster roared. According to one chronicler who heard it detonate, the blast was loud enough to render bystanders speechless and cause pregnant women to miscarry.[2] City and castle walls in the late Middle Ages had been built to withstand the battering of catapults, mangonels, siege towers and mines. But under an assault from a full-blown field cannon, charged with gunpowder manufactured from 'nitre, sulfur, carbon and herbs', they just disintegrated.[3] This was why, in the spring of 1453, the twenty-one-year-old Ottoman sultan Mehmed II ordered his troops to bring his biggest gun more than two hundred kilometres east, from his headquarters in Adrianople (Edirne) to the outskirts of Constantinople. Mehmed's

---

* This is considerably larger that the combat length of a M777 howitzer, which is the 155mm calibre field artillery piece used today by US, Australian, Canadian and Indian ground troops. The barrel of the M777 is slightly more than 5m long.

army numbered at least eighty thousand people, which, along with his naval fleet, was large enough to keep the Byzantine capital blockaded. But Mehmed needed more than manpower to stand a realistic chance of overrunning the Queen of Cities' famous double walls. Hence the gun: 'a thing most fearsome to see and altogether unbelievable,' wrote the chronicler Michael Kritovoulos of Imbros, who knew and admired Mehmed, and visited Constantinople in the aftermath of the attack.[4]

When Sultan Mehmed laid siege to Constantinople, he had been in sole command of the Ottoman empire for two years.[5] But he had been exercising power and making military decisions from the time he was twelve. He was hardwired to fight. And he was driven by the same impulse that had animated his late father, Murad II, and many sultans before: to expand the boundaries and the glorious reputation of the Ottoman empire across the near east and the Balkans. The bellicose Islamic state had been founded in 1299 by Osman I, a small-time Turkic warlord based in Asia Minor just south of Constantinople. By the mid-fifteenth century Osman's descendants ruled a rising superpower. They controlled much former Byzantine territory in the Balkans, and around half of Asia Minor, where they provided a bulwark between Europe and the Mongols. Taking Constantinople would confirm their claim to be the supreme authority in the eastern Mediterranean, and open up the possibility of further expansion into realms such as Serbia, Hungary and Albania. Regional hegemony lay, tantalizingly, within young Mehmed's grasp.

The artillery bombardment Mehmed aimed at Constantinople from his wonder-cannon and other, smaller bronze pieces was nothing short of terrifying. Kritovoulos did not see the barrage at first hand, but heard later what the firing of the biggest gun was like. 'There was a fearful roar and a shaking of the earth beneath and for a long way off, and a noise such as never was heard before,' he wrote. 'Then, with an astounding thunder and a frightful crashing and a flame that lit up all the surroundings and then left them black... a dry hot blast of air, violently set in motion the stone... And the stone, borne with tremendous force and velocity, hit the wall, which it immediately shook and knocked down, and was itself broken into many fragments and scattered, hurling the pieces everywhere and killing those who happened to be nearby.'[6] Whenever a blast like this took out a section of wall, a turret or a tower, citizens would rush to plug the hole as best they could with rubble. For a while this piecemeal, patch-up strategy prevented Mehmed from sending troops in behind the gun barrage to storm the city. But it was not a long-term solution.

On the night of 28 May 1453, after the siege had lasted forty-seven days, Mehmed's men rushed Constantinople's now very depleted walls. Inside them, a defence force consisting of Greek, Genoese and Venetian troops, under the high command of the Byzantine emperor, forty-nine-year-old Constantine XI Palaiologos, fought bravely, as cannon-blasts erupted, and the dark sky rained arrows, crossbow-bolts and Greek fire.[7] 'There was much shouting on both sides – the mingled sounds of blasphemy, insults, threats, attackers, defenders, shooters, those shot at, killers and dying, of those who in anger and wrath did all sorts of terrible things,' wrote Kritovoulos.[8] But by dawn the defenders had been outgunned, outmanned and overcome. A confused sea-evacuation was underway at the waterfront, while in the streets a savage sack took place. Ottoman soldiers and the sultan's elite bodyguard corps (known as Janissaries) ran rampant.

It was a pitiful, hideous scene. According to Kritovoulos, the Ottomans 'killed so as to frighten all the City, and to terrorize and enslave all by the slaughter.' Churches were plundered and shrines desecrated. Priceless manuscripts were piled and burned in the streets. Women were snatched from their homes and dragged off as slaves. 'Men with swords, their hands bloodstained with murder, breathing out rage, speaking out murder indiscriminate, flushed with all the worst things… like wild and ferocious beasts, leaped into the houses, driving [the Greeks] out mercilessly, dragging, rending, forcing, hauling them disgracefully into the public highways, insulting them and doing every evil thing.'[9]

Maybe fifty thousand Constantinopolitans were taken captive in the days that followed. Thousands more died. Among the fallen was Emperor Constantine, who went down fighting hand-to-hand among his men. His body was never recovered – although several observers thought they had seen his severed head paraded around on a lance in the chaos of the city's fall.[10] Meanwhile, Mehmed II entered Constantinople in splendour, riding a white horse around the streets, admiring the ancient sights and ordering his followers to refrain from damaging them. (Mehmed personally clouted the head of a soldier he found smashing the marble floor of the Hagia Sophia.) He reviewed the captives and chose the prettiest girls and young boys for his own enjoyment. He feasted and got drunk. And he began to make plans to rebuild and regenerate the city, which even before his arrival had been underpopulated and in a state of advanced urban decay.

This was all now Mehmed's prerogative, as victor. For more than eleven hundred years Constantinople had been ruled by Christian emperors – Roman, Byzantine or Latin. Those days were now over. Constantinople was Ottoman. The Roman Empire was dead. As Kritovoulos wrote, 'the great city of Constantine, raised to a great height of glory and dominion and wealth in its own time, overshadowing to an infinite degree all the cities around it, renowned for its glory, wealth, authority, power and greatness, and all its other qualities… thus came to its end.'[11]

Even allowing for poetic hyperbole, this was a defining moment in Constantinople's history – and in the history of the west. After the city's fall, the whole world would be transformed.

THE CONQUEST OF CONSTANTINOPLE IN 1453 shocked Christian Europe in much the same way as Jerusalem's capture by Saladin had done in 1187. This was not surprising. For thousands of Italian merchants and adventurous pilgrims, Constantinople was a vital and glorious gateway to the eastern half of the world. For millions more, Constantinople was an idea. It represented the enduring presence of the Roman Empire on earth and a historical continuity stretching back to time out of mind. For more than a millennium it had been a pillar of the Christian world, which seemed to hold

Turks and the armies of Islam at arm's length. In truth, of course, Byzantium had been too feeble a political entity to do anything of the sort for generations: even before its capture in 1453 the city had been cut off, surrounded by territory already conquered by the Ottomans, its emperors reduced to little more than Ottoman vassals. Nevertheless, like West Berlin after the Second World War, the symbolism of Constantinople's survival was just as important as the reality. If it could fall, where might be next? Rumours went round the west that when Mehmed entered Constantinople for the first time he had thanked Muhammad for granting him victory, and added: 'I pray that he will permit me to live long enough to capture and subjugate Old Rome as I have New Rome.'[12]

This was a frightening thought. The spectre of Islamic armies hammering at the doors of the Vatican has long haunted the nightmares of Christian Europeans. (Not for nothing was it a mainstay of al-Qaeda and ISIS propaganda in the early twenty-first century.) It certainly sent shivers down the spine of fifteenth-century Italians. And as it turned out, their fears seemed to be founded in reality. Mehmed presented an ambiguous figure. On the one hand he allowed Christians, Jews and foreign merchants to continue living more or less unmolested in the city, and he took an interest in Renaissance artists: in 1479–80 he 'borrowed' the talented Venetian painter Gentile Bellini, and had him perform the somewhat un-Islamic task of painting his portrait.[13] Yet on the other, Mehmed changed the name of Constantinople to Istanbul, and turned the Hagia Sophia into a mosque. Although he was capable of enlightened amiability, and was very far from being a religious zealot, he was still a Turk. His followers called him *Fatih* – Conqueror. But Pope Nicholas V called Mehmed a 'son of Satan, perdition and death', and Pope Pius II called him a 'venomous dragon'.[14]

After 1453 Mehmed continued his programme of expansion. He set his sights – and his ships and troops – on conquering lands in eastern Europe, the Black Sea and the Greek islands. In 1454–9 he sent armies into Serbia, eventually annexing it to the Ottoman empire. In the 1460s he seized Bosnia, Albania and the

Peloponnese. From 1463 to 1479 he fought a long and bitter war against the Republic of Venice. As soon as this was settled, in 1480 Mehmed invaded southern Italy, at Otranto, which his men sacked and burned; a small crusade summons was required to reclaim the town the following year. All this was more than enough to convince Europeans that the Turkish threat was not just acute but existential. From the fifteenth century until the seventeenth, the Turk was the bogeyman at the end of Christian Europe's bed.*

Whether or not the Ottomans really deserved that reputation is a moot point, but not one that need detain us here. What really mattered in the late fifteenth century was the effect that the rise of the Ottomans had on broader patterns of global trade, travel and exploration. In that regard, they turned age-old certainties on their head.

For one thing, the Ottoman rise seemed to some to herald the coming of the apocalypse, which according to calculations in Russia was scheduled to arrive before the end of the fifteenth century.[15] For another, it focused minds on other, wider losses in Christendom: specifically the fact that Jerusalem, like Constantinople, also lay in non-Christian hands, and that for generations all too little had been done to pursue its recapture. And for a third, there were now certain practical difficulties in doing business. The great medieval trading states of the Mediterranean were in formidable shape in the mid-fifteenth century. Yet they did not enjoy perfectly harmonious relations with the Ottomans: Venice was at outright war with the Turks for a decade and a half, and lost to them its critical trading-post at Negroponte. Genoa was stripped of its most important Black Sea port, Caffa. Certain specific sectors – such as the lucrative trade in transporting Turkic slaves captured around the Black Sea to Mamluk Egypt – were halted outright.[16] The Ottomans did not suddenly blockade the eastern Mediterranean,

---

* In the medium term, the Ottoman push into Europe was only ended when they were defeated outside the walls of Vienna, Austria, in 1683. Even after this, the Ottoman Empire remained the object of suspicion and some fear until it was finally destroyed by the First World War.

but they made doing business somewhat less attractive than it had been, on both a financial and an ethical basis.

As a result, fifteenth-century European merchant adventurers, in alliance with ambitious new monarchies, particularly in Spain and Portugal, started to consider branching out into other avenues of trade, and devising schemes by which they might source help for the fight-back against the perfidious Turk. Many of them began to look west, across the Atlantic Ocean. It was not very clear what, if anything, lay there. But many explorers and patrons were willing to find out. Their most fervent wish was that navigating the Atlantic might reveal a new passage to the east, which would bypass the Ottoman zone. But as it transpired, they found something very different: the islands and mainland of the Americas, and the abundant, deadly, fragile, wonderful territories of a New World.

Saints, Norsemen and Navigators

PEOPLE HAVE BEEN LIVING IN THE Americas for at least thirteen thousand years, and perhaps more than twice that long.[17] Although archaeologists do not agree on the exact time that humans arrived, most concur that at some moment during the last Ice Age, settlers moved overland out of north-east Asia, picking their way across what was then a land-bridge between Siberia and Alaska, before heading south, either along the Pacific coast or through an ice-free corridor into the American interior. The early peoples of this vast continent survived by gathering plants and hunting animals, making stone tools and spearheads and sheltering in caves. At one site in Chile, modern researchers have found the remains of a large communal wooden tent, protected with animal skins, firepits, tools, the remains of nuts and seeds, and evidence that stone-age people living there grew potatoes, some to eat themselves, and some to trade with other groups more than two hundred kilometres away. (They estimate the cave was inhabited fourteen and a half thousand years ago.)[18] So the first 'Americans' lived much like other Stone Age humans all over the world. However, they did so alone. From the time the great ice sheets melted and the Siberian–Alaskan land bridge was sunk beneath the rising seas, people in the Americas were largely cut off from the rest of the globe. Bounded by the world's two greatest oceans, they developed along a course unaffected by developments elsewhere on earth for more than ten thousand years.

It was once thought that the first medieval voyagers to make contact with the Americas were the southern Europeans of the fifteenth century. Now we know this was not so. Throughout the Middle Ages there were contacts – or claims of contact – from a wide range of other peoples. The sixth-century Irish monk St Brendan sailed extensively around the British Isles, and perhaps as far away as the Faroe Isles.[19] According to his legend, which circulated widely in manuscripts from the tenth century onwards, Brendan put to sea in a wood-framed coracle covered with 'tanned ox-hide stretched over oak bark' and greased with fat. In this, he and a few companions sailed far and wide, enduring hunger and thirst and dodging fire-spewing sea monsters until after many years they discovered an island 'so wide that forty days' wandering still did not bring them to the farther shore.'[20] Some have assumed this meant Brendan sailed all the way across the Atlantic Ocean. In fact, the great island in St Brendan's legend seems to be an allegory for Eden rather than a literal description of the American continent. However, there clearly existed an idea that *something* had to lie west of Ireland, even if no one knew quite what. Some thought there was an island called 'Brazil', where King Arthur was buried. To the brilliant tenth-century Arab geographer al-Mas'udi, the Atlantic Ocean was the 'sea of darkness', which had 'limits neither in its depths nor extent, for its end is unknown.'[21] (Al-Mas'udi reported rumours in Spain that a young sailor from Córdoba called Khoshkhash had once braved this sea and come back 'loaded with rich booty' – but how and where exactly he went was a mystery.)[22] A tradition in Mali said that a fourteenth-century *mansa* (roughly, king or emperor) called Abu Bakr II abdicated his throne to devote his life to crossing the Atlantic, and disappeared, presumed lost at sea. This was all titillating stuff.

But none of it added up to much more than a confection of stories and dreams.

The first medieval people who *are* known to have travelled across the Atlantic* to the Americas were Vikings of the tenth and eleventh centuries.[23] Medieval Scandinavians were some of the most adventurous and outward-bound people on earth,† and they roved as far across the North Atlantic as they did in the rest of the world. By the ninth century, Vikings had settled Iceland. In the 980s an exiled outlaw known as Erik the Red kickstarted the colonization of Greenland.[24] And around the same time, the Norse sagas claimed that several hundred travellers, led either by a married couple called Thorfinn Karlsefni and Gudríd Thorbjarndóttir, or by an explorer called Leif Eriksson, made their way to a place they called Vinland. Here they encountered native peoples they derisively named *skrælingar* (loosely, 'savages'), with whom they bartered and fought, and from whom they abducted children and caught diseases. Historians suspect these *skrælingar* were related to the now-extinct First Nations people known as the Beothuk.[25] But it is not easy to be certain.

What is certain, however, is that around the year AD 1000 there was a small, short-lived Viking settlement in Newfoundland, at a site called L'Anse aux Meadows. The archaeological evidence suggests that for a time about one hundred Norse lived there, felling trees and perhaps using the site as a base for exploring further points on the coast, as far afield as what is now Quebec and even Maine. Almost certainly, L'Anse aux Meadows, or the region more generally, was Vinland. And although the Vikings who stayed there could not possibly have known the extent of the vast continent they had encountered, the fact was that they had set foot on its soil, exchanged goods and arrow-shot with the locals, and sent word of its existence back home. This mattered. They had completed, however briefly and tenuously, a

---

* The Pacific is another matter. There is intriguing archaeological evidence that Polynesian seafarers travelled to the South American continent around the year AD 1000, leaving sweet potatoes and chicken bones there as unwitting mementoes of their visit.
† See chapter 5.

chain of human interaction that linked human societies from the Americas to the Far East.[26]

FIVE HUNDRED AND FIFTY YEARS AFTER Vikings chopped down trees in medieval Vinland, however, meaningful transatlantic exchange had signally failed to develop. The Norse colony at L'Anse aux Meadows, made up of timber buildings and cut-turf houses, was abandoned and burned within a generation of being established. Eventually the Norse also retreated from Greenland. So while the Black Sea, Baltic Sea and Mediterranean all buzzed with commercial shipping, by the late Middle Ages the Atlantic remained a great question-mark on the map of the world. It was a barrier, far more than it was a bridge.

In the fifteenth century, however, things began to change. The process by which the 'far' side of the Atlantic was opened up to regular European traffic was gradual and dilatory. Nevertheless, it happened. And perhaps the most important figure in galvanizing exploration in the Atlantic was a Portuguese prince known to history as Henry the Navigator.

Henry was a younger son of John (*João*) I, king of Portugal, and his English wife, Philippa of Lancaster. He was born in 1394 and grew up at a court that fairly bubbled with political ambition.[27] John I was the first king of a new dynasty called the Aviz, and he wished to raise Portugal to the rank of a major European power.[28] Thus he intervened in the Hundred Years War by signing a perpetual peace treaty with England,* threw open his capital, Lisbon, to Italian banking houses and Flemish merchants, promoting Portugal as a naval stopping-point between the ports of Flanders and England and those of the Mediterranean, and groomed his family to participate in his great project.[29] His children were given first-rate educations, and good marriages: as we have already seen, the

---

* The Anglo-Portuguese alliance sealed with the Treaty of Windsor (1386), which married John I to John of Gaunt's eldest daughter, Philippa, and established concord between the two realms, is often cited as the longest-standing peace deal in history, since England and Portugal have remained at peace ever since.

Infanta Isabella was married to Philip the Good, the wily duke of Burgundy who patronized artists including Jan van Eyck.* Henry and his brothers, meanwhile, were encouraged to help spread Portuguese influence outside the realm, more often than not at the point of a sword.

Territorial expansion was deeply embedded in Portuguese history and identity. The very fact of the kingdom's existence was down to the efforts of generations of crusaders, who fought in the *Reconquista* to carve out their long, thin state along the Atlantic coast of the Iberian peninsula, grinding along year after year, in their wars against the Almoravids, Almohads and *taifa* kings of al-Andalus. This was a long, hard process. Lisbon was only taken from Islamic hands during the Second Crusade in 1147. It took another hundred years to establish the kingdom proper and extend its borders all the way down to the Algarve. But eventually it was done. And by Henry the Navigator's day, there was no more mainland left to conquer. The future lay over the water.

In the summer of 1415, when Henry was twenty-one, he accompanied his father to Ceuta, on the north coast of Morocco, which stood at the mouth of the Strait of Gibraltar: the gateway between the Mediterranean and the Atlantic, once famed as the location of the Pillars of Hercules. Ceuta was ruled by sultan of Morocco, but it held enormous economic allure to the Portuguese, not least because it was a coastal terminus for the camel-caravans that criss-crossed northern Africa, bringing tons of gold every year across the Sahara from mines in the region known as west Sudan.[30] It was also a Muslim-held city, which chimed well with Portugal's history of expansion into land seized from infidels. To take it, King John prepared a huge fleet, packed with tens of thousands of troops and commanded by himself. He had made meticulous plans for the city's capture, so when he launched an assault on the town on 21 August, it fell with minimal fighting, inside a single day. Henry was hurt in the battle, but not seriously. After it was over, the Portuguese converted Ceuta's mosque into a makeshift

---

* See chapter 14.

church and celebrated Mass. Henry was knighted in his armour – 'a splendid thing to see,' wrote one observer – and his father appointed him lieutenant of the city.[31] This gave the young man an interest in Ceuta's survival as a Portuguese possession (a status that was frequently under threat as the indignant Moroccans tried to win it back), and a lifelong fascination with extending Portuguese interests down the long, rich, west African coast.

Although Henry himself was not the hands-on 'navigator' that his historical nickname implies, he was a major patron and cheerleader for sailors who dared venture south to seek land that was only sketchily known. It was no secret that beyond the Sahara lay fabulous natural resources: a well-known world atlas produced on Majorca in 1375 had shown the heartlands of Africa populated by black kings bedecked in gold, and elegant slave-drivers on camel-back, wearing long, luxurious robes. The main problem was access, which relied heavily on Islamic intermediaries. The goal for the Portuguese was to cut out the Saharan camel-trains, and open sea-routes which could bring all the wealth of west Africa directly to the Mediterranean. If they would do that, reasoned Henry, they all stood to make a fortune. (His personal tax on ventures he sponsored was 20 per cent of total profits.) The means were certainly available. Ship technology was improving: the fifteenth century saw the development of the caravel, a light and nimble vessel with triangular sails (lateens) which allowed it to sail over long distances while remaining manoeuvrable around inlets, ports and coastlines. A lateen rig also allowed sailors to beat against the wind, something quite impossible on a square rig.[32] At the same time, improved understanding of Atlantic wind patterns meant navigators knew how to get home from journeys to or beyond the equator: having headed south, one could return north by sailing out into the Atlantic, then circling back in towards Iberia, rather than trying to struggle along the coast. Thanks to these important maritime advances, there was no shortage of volunteers ready to set out into the unknown.

The first expeditions under Henry's auspices departed soon after the battle of Ceuta, and landed, somewhat accidentally, in the Madeiran archipelago, which Henry ordered to be claimed for

Portugal. Not long afterwards, in the late 1420s and early 1430s, the Azores islands were also colonized. In the 1450s a Venetian explorer and slave trader called Alvise Cadamosto laid claim to the Cape Verde islands during an expedition along the Guinea Coast. The explorers who charted these islands saw many things along the way that delighted and astonished them. When Cadamosto passed by Madeira, he marvelled at the fertile, abundant nature of the land, from which many types of useful wood could be harvested, and where sugar cane and grapes* grew easily. 'Many of the inhabitants are rich, like the country itself,' he wrote, 'since the island resembles a garden and everything that grows there is like gold.' The promise of this virgin territory was obvious. 'Because of the perfection of the country for agriculture, [people] have reported seeing ripe grapes in holy week [i.e. at Easter], which is a thing more amazing than anything I have seen,' he wrote.[33]

All the while, Portuguese vessels, many of them under Henry's sponsorship, were also docking on the African mainland, advancing a little further south every sailing season, so that by mid-century the Gulf of Guinea (the coastlines of modern-day Côte d'Ivoire, Ghana, Togo and Benin) was in reach. The business relationships the Portuguese struck with traders in west Africa's coastal cities were often fruitful, although many of them would strike us today as morally abhorrent. One of Africa's longest-standing trades was in human slaves, and the Portuguese had few qualms about joining in. They had dabbled in the market via the Castilian-controlled Canary Islands since the late fourteenth century, but as their contacts in west Africa multiplied, so did their use and desire for African captives, who in some areas could be exchanged for European horses at the rate of between nine and fourteen humans to one animal. From the 1440s the sight of Africans being unloaded as cargo at the Portuguese port of Lagos (on the coast of the Algarve) became a familiar and doleful one. The immorality of the trade troubled at least some observers: in 1444 the chronicler Gomes

---

* Madeira's most famous export today remains fortified wine, produced from grapestocks introduced in the time of Henry the Navigator.

Eanes de Zurara recorded his mixed feelings when he watched caravels in Lagos disembarking 235 African men, women and children, who were cruelly divided up, with families broken and mothers separated from their children, each one taken off for a life of involuntary servitude, hundreds of miles from their homelands.

> What heart, however hard it might be, would not to be pierced with a feeling of pity to see that company? For some hung their heads with their faces bathed in tears, looking at each other. Others stood groaning sadly, looking up to the height of heaven, fixing their eyes upon it and crying loudly, as if asking help of the Father of Nature. Others struck their faces with the palms of their hands, throwing themselves at full length upon the ground. Others made their lamentations in the manner of a song after the custom of their country, and, though we could not understand the words of their language, it seemed to reflect the extent of their sorrow.[34]

Gomes was deeply uneasy about the emotional and physical torture this trade represented. However, the same thoughts did not appear to vex Henry the Navigator, who oversaw the division of the human spoils.

> The Infante was there, mounted upon a powerful horse and accompanied by his retinue, distributing his favours like a man who sought only to gain a small profit from his share; for he made a very speedy distribution of the forty-six souls that constituted his fifth [i.e. his 20 per cent tax on profit], for his chief riches lay in his purpose, and he reflected with great pleasure upon the salvation of those souls that otherwise would have been lost.[35]

To Henry, new lands were for profit. Unbelievers were for baptism. And ends justified means. Henry's mind was steeped in the traditions of crusading and conquest, neither of which were pursuits for the fainthearted. He was the grand master of the

Order of Christ, a reconstituted Portuguese chapter of the Knights Templar, and he involved this order extensively in colonizing Portugal's new territories. He also sent forth his navigators, conquerors and slavers with the backing of Rome. In 1452 and 1456 the Portuguese received papal licence to 'invade, conquer, fight [and] subjugate the Saracens and pagans, and other infidels and other enemies of Christ', to conquer their lands and 'to lead their persons in perpetual servitude'.[36] Conflating the heightened anti-Islamic mood of the mid-fifteenth century with the spirit of adventure and conquest over unbelievers far away from the Holy Lands did not demand a huge leap of imagination. But it gave valuable godly sanction to a military-economic project of the sort that had not been seen since the creation of the crusader states in Palestine and Syria in the twelfth century.

By the time Henry the Navigator died in November 1460 Portuguese explorers had ventured as far along the African coast as Sierra Leone. (Forty years later they had been all the way to the Cape of Good Hope.) They were well placed to be the most powerful trading nation in western Europe, rivalled only by Castile. In the early sixteenth century, the experienced navigator Duarte Pacheco Pereira (nicknamed 'the Portuguese Achilles') laid the credit for this extraordinary programme of expansion squarely with Henry. 'The benefits conferred on [Portugal] by the virtuous Prince Henry are such that its kings and people are greatly indebted to him', wrote Pereira, 'for in the land which he discovered a great part of the Portuguese people now earn their livelihood and the kings [of Portugal] derive great profit from this commerce.'[37] Of those who had – and would – suffer individual and systemic misery for generations thereafter, Pereira said not a word.

Christopher Columbus

ON THE SECOND DAY OF JANUARY 1492 a solemn ceremony took place in southern Spain. At the magnificent palace of the Alhambra, perched amid the hills of Granada, the last Islamic ruler of mainland Spain formally quit his sultanate and his home. Muhammad XII – or 'Boabdil', as he was known to Christians – had begun his rocky reign ten years earlier. But he had found himself squeezed relentlessly by the kingdoms around him. Over the centuries the *Reconquista* wars had whittled away at what little remained of Muslim al-Andalus, and in 1469 Christian Spain had been effectively united in a single super-kingdom, when King Ferdinand II of Aragon married Queen Isabella I of Castile. This had rung the death-knell for the sultanate of Granada, and although it had taken more than twenty years for the end to come, come it had.

Not long after dawn on 2 January, Muhammad, aged a little over thirty, ceremonially surrendered the Alhambra to a Spanish military officer, then rode down to the outskirts of Granada, where he met King Ferdinand and Queen Isabella and gave them the keys to the city. He said to Ferdinand in Arabic: 'God loves you greatly. Sir, these are the keys of this paradise. I and those inside it are yours.' Then gifts were exchanged, and Muhammad's son, who had been a hostage at the Spanish court for nine long years, was released back to his father. Finally Muhammad left. By the end of the year he had settled in Morocco, where he would live out his life in exile.[38] He departed for his new home with tears streaming down his face.

Watching events in Granada that day was a Genoese adventurer called Cristoforo Colombo – or, as he is usually known today, Christopher Columbus.[39] He had been in and around the Iberian peninsula for nearly twenty years, having moved to Lisbon in the 1470s. In that time Columbus had turned himself into a regular Atlantic sea-dog, sailing back and forth to the new Portuguese island outposts in the Azores and Madeira, and venturing further still – far along the Guinea coast and (so he claimed) up into the North Atlantic as far as Iceland.

More than that, however, he had thought long and hard about the shape of the world and the mysteries of its parts unknown. Columbus was an avid reader, and he had studied works by historic travellers ranging from the ancient Greek polymath Ptolemy to the thirteenth-century Venetian adventurer Marco Polo.* He had also pored over a colourful fourteenth-century travelogue – partly derivative of other sources and partly imaginary – supposedly by an English knight called Sir John Mandeville. The author claimed to have written this 'because it has been a long time since there was a crusading expedition overseas, and because many men long to hear about that land [i.e. the former kingdom of Jerusalem] and various countries nearby'. He described regions from Asia Minor to India and recycled hoary old myths such as the tales of Prester John.[40]

Columbus lapped it up. And from his reading, combined with his personal experiences at sea, he came to two broad conclusions. The first was that there was abundant wealth across the Atlantic. If, as Ptolemy argued, the earth was a sphere, then a journey Columbus (incorrectly) reckoned at less than three thousand miles ought to bring a man to the far east, whose dizzying riches Marco Polo and Mandeville had described at length. Columbus' second belief was that by visiting the east he could revive the project of converting a khan or some other great eastern king to Christianity, which he maintained was still the best strategy for combating the 'idolatry' and 'doctrines of perdition' practiced by Muslims around the Mediterranean.[41]

As time went by, Columbus grew, like many a zealot in history, increasingly obsessive about his grand scheme. All he needed was someone to back him. And that was where Ferdinand and Isabella – vanquishers of Muslim sultans, joint governors of the largest realm on the Iberian peninsula, now styling themselves as the 'Catholic Monarchs' – came in. When he brought his scheme to the Spanish court at the end of January 1492, the culmination of many years of largely fruitless nagging and pleading in Spain, Portugal and elsewhere, Isabella finally agreed to support him, granting Columbus the right to call himself Grand Admiral, and claim 10 per cent of the profits of his voyage. For all concerned, it was a gamble. But it paid off.

* See chapter 10.

Between Odysseus' fabled return home to Ithaca from the Trojan Wars and the Apollo 11 mission to the moon in 1969, there has probably been no more famous journey in human history than Columbus' first voyage west, in 1492. The details of it are well known, because Columbus kept a log-book (the original is lost, but its substance is preserved in a digest made by the historian Bartolomé de las Casas). According to this, on 3 August, Columbus set out 'half an hour before sunrise' from Palos, on the southern coast of Spain, taking his three caravels, the *Niña*, *Pinta* and *Santa Maria*, to the Canary Islands. Here locals assured him that his journey would probably be a short one, since every day at sunset 'they saw land to the westward'.[42] If true, this would have implied that the Americas were between three and twenty miles away. Plainly, they were not.

Having made repairs to his ships and awaited a good wind, Columbus struck out west from the Canaries on Saturday 8 September. For the next month he and his crew sailed, keeping a keen eye out for birds, seaweed, crabs, whales and dolphins, all of which Columbus claimed as signs that land was close at hand. But land never seemed to come, and as his crew grew restless, Columbus began to lie to them about how far they had travelled, downplaying the ever more obvious fact that they were hundreds of leagues from anywhere. They spent, in all, thirty-three days at sea. Only on 11 October, with the crew on the brink of mutiny, did a sailor called Rodrigo sight land – a coral island in the Bahamas which they named San Salvador. 'All breathed again and were rejoiced,' wrote Columbus. That night they anchored off-shore, and the next morning Columbus and a small group of his crew went to land in an armed boat, with a banner bearing Ferdinand and Isabella's initials and a crusader-style cross.[43]

They were met on the shore by a very excited and very naked group of men and women, whom Columbus presented with 'red caps and glass beads... also many other trifles'. The delighted islanders swapped these for 'parrots and balls of cotton thread and spears... they very willingly traded everything they had.'[44] It was a happy encounter: 'they became marvellously friendly to us,' wrote Columbus.[45]

The sight of these people filled Columbus with a mixture of emotions. Certainly they were good-looking and young, with light brown skin, 'very straight legs and no bellies, but well-formed bodies'. Yet they seemed almost comically primitive – going about in nothing more than body-paint, paddling long canoes carved from tree-trunks, showing complete unfamiliarity with weapons as basic as swords, and appearing quite naïve about trade. Columbus had come in search of a superior culture, with a court to rival the grand khan's. Instead, *he* was being treated like the alien from a higher species.[46]

One thought, however, occurred to him immediately. Although these islanders were plainly not the trading partners with whom the Catholic Monarchs might found a new world order, 'they should be good servants and very intelligent... and I believe that they would easily be made Christians, for they appeared to me to have no religion.' He decided to take six of them prisoner to bring back to Ferdinand and Isabella, 'so that they can learn to speak'.[47] And he planted the Spanish flag on their island, to signal that he had taken possession of it on behalf of the Catholic Monarchs. Then he set off to find out what else there was to claim.

For the next few weeks Columbus and his crew explored nearby islands. Still hoping he might be somewhere a lot further east than he actually was – on an outlying island of the Japanese archipelago – Columbus was looking for the mainland of 'Cathay'. What he found instead were a number of other small Caribbean islands, and then, in late October and early November, the much larger landmasses of Cuba and Haiti (which he called Hispaniola). His crew was intrigued and cheered by the exotic things that lay everywhere: pearls and gold, herbs and spices, new root vegetables, sweet and juicy fruits, masses of cotton, and 'certain perfumed herbs' which turned out to be tobacco leaves. But they were also appalled at some of the local customs. Columbus' son Ferdinand later wrote that 'the Indians* are accustomed to eating unclean things, such as large, fat spiders and white worms that breed among decayed wood...

---

* This was the generic term for the people of the New World – derived of course from the fact that the first navigators believed they were in the Indies of the east.

They eat some fish almost raw, and immediately on catching them. Before they boil them they tear out their eyes and eat them on the spot. They eat many such things that would not only make any Spanish person vomit, but would poison him if he tried.'[48] This was very much the way of this world: by turns fascinating and grotesque. Columbus said he frequently told his crew it would be impossible to describe to others all the things they had seen when they got back home, for 'my tongue could not convey the whole truth about them, nor my hand write it down.' Meanwhile, the same sense of half-dumbstruck wonder also seemed to grip the people he encountered. On Hispaniola one dignitary indicated to Columbus that his patrons 'must be very great princes, since [they] had sent me fearlessly from so far away in the sky.'[49]

Columbus remained in the new lands until Christmastime. On Christmas Eve he lost one of his ships, the *Santa Maria*, which hit a reef in shallow waters off Hispaniola. Columbus ordered its crew to build a makeshift wooden fort from timbers salvaged from the wreck. He had one of his men demonstrate musket-fire to the Indians, to deter them from attacking the stronghold. He assigned three dozen men to garrison it; they were to be the nucleus of a town he called Christmas Harbour (Puerto de la Navidad), 'the first Christian town and settled country in the western world'.[50] Then on 16 January 1493 he took his two remaining caravels back to sea, heading for Spain to show off everything he had seen and done. Once more it was a long journey, and this time the *Niña* and *Pinta* were separated by storms. But in the first days of March, amid 'a terrible sea and high winds, the whole sky... rent with thunder and lightning', Columbus limped into port at Lisbon. He stopped briefly at the court of the Portuguese king, John II (the great-grandson of John I), regaling the monarch with stories while assuring him that he had not trespassed on Portuguese interests in Africa.* Then he moved on to find his patrons.

---

* Columbus' visit to the Portuguese king hastened the Treaty of Tordesillas, which drew a notional, vertical line of demarcation 370 leagues west of the Cape Verde islands (the Tordesillas Meridian); east of this, all discoveries were deemed to belong to Portugal; west of it, to Castile/Spain.

This time he travelled overland. By mid-April he had tracked down the Spanish court at Barcelona, and when arrived, he was greeted by King Ferdinand in person. They rode through the city side by side, as though Columbus was a prince of the blood. The Catholic Monarchs were thrilled, said Columbus: lit up 'with infinite joy and satisfaction.'[51] After years of struggle, Columbus' belief that something wonderful lay across the Atlantic had been vindicated. Ferdinand's chaplain and court historian, Peter Martyr, was unsure what to make of these discoveries, writing 'one must speak of a new world, so distant is it and devoid of civilization and religion.'[52] But Columbus was sure that all good Christians owed him thanks 'for the great triumph which they will have, by the conversion of so many peoples to our holy faith and for the temporal benefits which will follow, not only for Spain, but all Christendom.'[53] It was the victory he had dreamed about for so long.

ON CLOSE READING OF CHRISTOPHER COLUMBUS' letters and notebooks, he does not present an especially attractive figure. 'The Admiral', as it pleased him to be known, was a braggart and at times an outright liar. He misled his crew about his intentions and the progress of their expedition. He claimed credit for having been the first to spot land in the Bahamas, when he had done no such thing. He took advantage of the good nature of people he met in the new lands; any passing anthropological interest he had in them was second always to his cynical eye for ways in which he and future Spanish expeditions might exploit their resources and labour. And when he came back to Spain he exaggerated his achievements and the potential of his discoveries, claiming Hispaniola was bigger than the entire Iberian peninsula, already replete with beautiful harbours and rich gold mines (it was not); and that Cuba was 'larger than England and Scotland put together.'[54]

Yet despite all this, there is no doubting the scale of his achievement in 1492. Given the comparative standards of medieval technology, contact between the Americas and Europe was only ever going to come from one direction. And although it is certain that if Columbus had not made his voyage, someone else would have done so soon afterwards, the fact remains it was he who had the nerve, the plan and the sheer good fortune to go forth and prosper. History does not have to be made by nice people; in fact our tour of the Middle Ages to this point probably demonstrates that it very rarely is. So whatever Columbus' failings, his flaws, and his prejudices, which are assuredly even more out of step with twenty-first century pieties than they were with those of his own time, he was – and remains – one of the most important figures in the whole of the Middle Ages. And from the moment he returned from the Caribbean it was clear he had opened up a new age in human history.

After reappearing in Spain in 1493, Columbus did not waste much time in planning his next trips west. There would be three in all. In 1493–6 he led a large mission of seventeen ships, arriving in the Caribbean via the Antilles islands, before visiting Puerto Rico and Jamaica. In 1498–1500 he ventured further south, stopping at Trinidad and alighting briefly on the South American mainland at what is now Venezuela. And on his final adventure, in 1502–4, he explored the coastline of Central America (modern Honduras, Nicaragua and Costa Rica). He spent many years at sea, and in foreign lands where the perils of disease, the volatile Caribbean climate and the poisonous politics of settler colonialism were all revealed to him in short order. Over the years he was becalmed, battered by hurricanes, attacked by angry tribes and struck down by sickness. On his third voyage, he was accused of having misused his powers as 'Viceroy Admiral and Governor-General' of the new lands, arrested, imprisoned and shipped back to Spain in chains – an experience that left him bitter until the end of his days. But if Columbus felt he was mistreated, he was not the only one. For as his initial missions of reconnaissance gave rise to many more expeditions to claim and colonize, so began the horrors that would come to be an intrinsic part of European expansion into the New World.

Right from the very beginning, these new lands were wild. The fate of the first garrison Columbus left in Hispaniola in 1493 warned as much. Once the admiral left, his men fell quickly to raiding the local tribes for gold and women, and bickering among themselves. They were soon murdered en masse by a local leader called Caonaobó.[55] When Columbus came back to Hispaniola on his second mission he did not immediately avenge their deaths. But he was no benevolent visitor, either. Despite having specific orders not to maltreat the native people, Columbus did so: demanding tribute from them in gold, kidnapping and enslaving them and building fortresses on their lands. At one point he wrote back to advise the Catholic Monarchs that the best strategy for making an economic success of the new lands would be to impose mass servitude on the local populations, along with forcible conversion to Christianity. Ferdinand and Isabella were less than enthusiastic about such heavy-handed tactics. But in the long run that was neither here nor there. Columbus' brute cynicism was founded in the cold reality of virtually every colonial programme in history. Cruelty and inhumanity were the handmaidens of imperial expansion. There was no reason why the New World should be any different.

The shiploads of would-be settlers and fortune-seekers who came in Columbus' wake to establish outposts on Hispaniola and Cuba were often little different. When 'the Admiral' was arrested during his third expedition, the new Spanish viceroy, a crusading knight called Nicolás de Ovando, took uncompromising measures against the local people known as the Taíno, who were now chafing against the Spanish presence. Ovando had brought hundreds of troops with him to the islands, and set them loose on the unfortunate Taínos. Some were massacred. Their queen, Anacaona, was hanged in public. Many more were taken prisoner, and in dealing with them, Ovando followed old crusader logic: unbelievers captured in war were fair game to be enslaved. They were put to work for the settlers, who by the end of the first decade of the sixteenth century numbered in the thousands. What was more, Ovando also began to import black African slaves to Hispaniola, to work in the gold mines the colonists had dug. The blueprint for colonization was taking shape. And it was a far cry from the mood of excited inquisitiveness that had buzzed around the beach at San Salvador when Columbus first came ashore. Any brief age of innocence in the New World was over before it had begun.

After 1504 Christopher Columbus never went back to the Caribbean. His star had waned after his third expedition, and he generally blamed other people for his downfall, not least King Ferdinand, whom Columbus came to suspect of having been far less a friend to him than Isabella, who died in 1504. Whether this was quite accurate is perhaps not important. Far more significant than Columbus' petty grudges was the now unstoppable momentum of the enterprise that, between them, these three had begun. Columbus died on 20 May 1506, after suffering, wrote his son, from 'gout and other ills and grief at seeing himself so fallen from his high estate.'[56] But as he expired, the Age of Exploration in which he had played a pivotal role was well underway.

By the mid-1520s, Spanish and Portuguese explorers and warriors known as *conquistadores* were swarming not only across the Caribbean, but also around the continental lands we know as Mexico, Guatemala, Florida and coastal Brazil. They brought with them heavy armour, handguns and cannon – the booms from which reliably spread panic among the indigenous people, who had never seen or heard gunpowder before. One of these *conquistadores* was Hernán Cortés, the stiff-necked Spaniard who brought back huge quantities of gold from Mexico after his campaigns of 1519–21, in which his troops crushed and overthrew the Aztec Empire, deposing and probably murdering its last emperor, Moctezuma II. Some of this gold was the treasure that Albrecht Dürer saw displayed in Brussels town hall in 1520; but it was only a fraction of what would eventually be plundered from the New World, where the mainland was found to hold megacities like the Aztec capital Tenochtitlán, which many who saw it judged every bit as glorious as Venice. Deploying superior technology and weapons, and bringing diseases like smallpox, to which the indigenous Americans had little or no resistance, the *conquistadores* swept the ancient realms of the Americas away and established in their place their own transatlantic empires, which they bled in every sense to enhance the glory of their home countries back in Europe. The emergence of these New World empires is one of the great changes which historians today use to discern an end-point to the Middle Ages.

To India, and Beyond

IN THE YEARS BETWEEN THE EARLY fifteenth-century forays down the coast of Africa and the Columbian adventures in the Caribbean, late medieval navigators learned a vast amount about world geography. They identified valuable new sources of raw materials ranging from gold to wood to codfish. What they did not do, however, was to solve the fundamental problem that had stood since Ptolemy's time: whether it was possible to get to the Indies by going west instead of east.

Nothing about the first transatlantic voyages of discovery changed that. Every sailor from Columbus onwards who headed west on a latitude from the Canaries or Cape Verde eventually ran into the islands of the Caribbean, and beyond them the Americas (which were so named in the early sixteenth century for Amerigo Vespucci, a Florentine navigator who charted the coast of Brazil in 1501–2). Heading further north, meanwhile, made little difference. In 1497 John Cabot (Giovanni Caboto), a Venetian sailor in the pay of the first Tudor king of England, Henry VII, set out from Bristol in search of a 'north-west passage' to the far east. He too hit a buffer, encountering lands which were probably Newfoundland (the region of the old Viking settlement at L'Anse aux Meadows) before he turned back. In 1508–9 Cabot's son Sebastian made another attempt, sighting what would later be dubbed Hudson Bay before opting to turn south, scouting the North American coastline as far as the Chesapeake. All of this would transpire to be extremely historically significant, not least when the first North American colonies were established in the later sixteenth century. But none of it brought European powers any closer to a shortcut to the land of the khans.

In 1488, however, a Portuguese captain called Bartholomew Diaz (Bartolomeu Dias) had provided tantalizing evidence that another route might exist. Diaz had been tasked by John II with going further along the African coastline than any European sailor before him, and in the course of a battle with the seas that lasted nearly eighteen months, he succeeded. In February 1488 he rounded the Cape of Good Hope, which he originally dubbed the Cape of Storms, and went as far as Algoa Bay (the inlet east of Port Elizabeth in modern South Africa) before his crew told him frankly that they would slit him ear to ear if he forced them to continue any further. His mission was confirmation that it was possible, if not easy, to sail around Africa; this being so, it followed that a voyage which went on to the north-east would eventually come to India. This was literally world-changing: maps of the world produced after Diaz's journey had to be adjusted to take account of the fact that the Indian Ocean was not, as Ptolemy thought, landlocked by unexplored territory, but could be entered from the south. Armed with this knowledge, and stirred, after 1493, by the achievements of Christopher Columbus in the west Atlantic, the Portuguese were ready to try to push past Diaz's landmark.

The name second only to that of Columbus in the history of late medieval navigation is that of Vasco da Gama. In 1497 da Gama was in his thirties, and a member of the crusading Order of Santiago. He was therefore favoured by King John II, who was the grand master of the Order, and gave da Gama his blessing to explore the Indian Ocean as far as he could. In July the captain departed Lisbon with four ships, 170 men and a licence from the new Portuguese king Manuel I (r. 1495–1521) to do whatever it took to 'make discoveries by sea [in] the service of God and [to] our own advantage'.[57]

He carried out his instructions to the letter. Da Gama sailed south along the African coast as far as Sierra Leone, then courageously, and perhaps a little madly, continued straight ahead, out into the open Atlantic, trusting Diaz's assertion that eventually a westerly breeze would carry his fleet back towards the southern tip of the African continent. He was right, but it took an immense effort of will and survival, and three months at sea without a glimpse of land in any direction. Week after week da Gama and his crew saw nothing except waves, whales and the occasional seabird. No one in recorded history had ever been out at sea for so long. But on Saturday 4 November, at last, land hove into view. Da Gama's crew 'put on our gala clothes, saluted [the captain] by firing our bombards and dressed the ships with flags and standards.'[58] They were on their way.

In late November 1497 the fleet rounded the Cape. By Christmas they were trading with black Africans on the shores they passed, exchanging glass beads, caps and bracelets for fat oxen to roast, and swapping linen cloth for metal. They goggled at birds which brayed like asses and huge sea lions so tough-skinned that they could not be speared. They noted apparently plentiful supplies of minerals like copper, salt, tin and elephant ivory. Only their attempts at evangelizing for Christ seemed to be an outright failure: when the crew stopped to erect a pillar and a holy cross in one African bay, they sailed away to the sight of a dozen tribesmen smashing both to pieces in disgust.[59]

In the new year da Gama and his crew started to experience more difficulties. They were forced to scuttle (i.e. deliberately sink) one of their ships. Many of the men developed scurvy, 'their feet and hands swelling and their gums growing over their teeth so that they could not eat.'[60] In Mozambique, they found a wealthy Muslim population who were contemptuous of their peace-offerings, and they learned that while Prester John was relatively close at hand, he lived deep in the desert, in a place which could only be reached by a long trek on camel-back. When they called at Mombasa (modern Kenya) an apparently friendly welcome soon turned treacherous, as swimmers were sent to sabotage their ships at anchor. Unlike the Caribbean, the Indian Ocean was a sophisticated and highly developed maritime trading zone; although da Gama's cannon proved effective defence when they were occasionally required to let them off, gunpowder was old hat, and the Portuguese enjoyed nothing like the technological advantages that had benefitted Christopher Columbus. Eventually, however, da Gama managed to recruit an experienced local navigator who helped them fix a course away from the African coast, out into open water once more, towards the Arabian Sea.

On 20 May da Gama and his crew reached the coast of southwest India, and anchored in waters just off Calicut (*Kozhikode*, modern Kerala) on the Malabar coast. When the local ruler, known as the Zamorin, sent messengers to ask what they wanted, da Gama was straight and to the point. 'Christians and spices,' he replied. His luck was only partly in. Da Gama found the Zamorin was wholly underwhelmed by his personal status and his suggested terms of trade. He and his crew believed that many of the people of the lands were some sort of Christians. But none of them appeared to be Prester John. The anonymous diary of one of his crew-members recorded that:

> [The men] are of a tawny complexion. Some of them have big beards and long hair, whilst others clip their hair short or shave the head, merely allowing a tuft to remain on the crown as a sign that they are Christians. They also wear moustaches. They pierce the ears and wear much gold in them. They go naked down to the waist, covering their lower extremities with very fine cotton stuffs. But it is only the most respectable who do this, for the others manage as best they are able. The women of this country, as a rule, are ugly and of small stature. They wear many jewels of gold round the neck, numerous bracelets on their arms, and rings set with precious stones on their toes. All these people are well-disposed and apparently of mild temper. At first sight they seem covetous and ignorant.[61]

But 'covetous and ignorant' was a description that could apply just as well to the newcomers, who were roundly outmanoeuvred at virtually every turn in their attempt to strike a trade deal with the merchants and authorities in Calicut, although they remained there from May until the end of August. Nevertheless, while the expedition did not yield instant riches, it proved the larger point for which da Gama had been commissioned. It was possible to reach India without having to negotiate the congested and dangerous Ottoman Mediterranean, or struggling along in Marco Polo's footsteps on an arduous overland journey through Central Asia.

All the same, it was not easy. Da Gama's sea-journey home to Portugal still took nearly a year, during which scurvy, thirst and disease led to the deaths of around half his men, so that he was forced to scuttle a second ship. But when his remaining two vessels finally returned to Portugal in July 1499 they were met with cheers and public celebrations. The king, Manuel I, wrote in triumph to the Catholic Monarchs, Ferdinand and Isabella, announcing that his navigators:

> ...did reach and discover India and other kingdoms and lordships bordering upon it; that they entered and navigated its sea, finding large cities, large edifices and rivers, and great populations, among whom is carried on all the trade in spices and precious stones, which are forwarded in ships... to Mecca, and thence to Cairo, whence they are dispersed throughout the world. Of these [spices, etc.] they have brought a quantity, including cinnamon, cloves, ginger, nutmeg, and pepper... also many fine stones of all sorts, such as rubies and others. And they also came to a country in which there are mines of gold, of which [gold], as of the spices and precious stones, they did not bring as much as they could have done...

The Spanish may have led the way in forays to the New World in the west, but the Portuguese were not far behind them.

AFTER DA GAMA'S FIRST EXPEDITION, THE Portuguese sent a steady stream of missions to India. The second great expedition, much larger than da Gama's, was captained by Pedro Álvares Cabral, who in 1500–1 undertook a massive sea-voyage, first to the coast of Brazil, then east to the Cape of Good Hope and on via Mozambique to Calicut and another point on India's Malabar coast: the kingdom of Cochin. Cabral and his crew came back somewhat battered by storms and running battles fought against Arab merchants in India, who resented the newcomers. But they were laden with spices, which were sold at a huge profit in Europe.

Seeing that the trick was not only a good one, but could be repeated, annual armadas were now sent along a route that became known for hundreds of years afterwards as the *Carreira da India*. Taking advantage of trade winds in the Atlantic and monsoon patterns in the Indian ocean, Portuguese fleets became a regular sight striking out from Lisbon to Cape Verde, south-west to Brazil, back around the southern tip of Africa and thence to India, sometimes through the channel between Mozambique and Madagascar, and at other times around the outside of the latter island. Fleets could number from a handful of ships to more than a dozen, and dedicated departments of the Portuguese royal government oversaw the logistical demands. The state had well and truly thrust itself into sponsoring and underwriting the costs of what became, in effect, a national business. And this mercantile activity was backed increasingly with military force. The Portuguese struck deals to build forts up and down the south-west coast of India and they chastised hostile Indian rulers with broadsides from their cannons. Sea-battles between these European interlopers and merchants native to the Indian Ocean became ever more frequent. But by the end of the first decade of the sixteenth century the Portuguese were appointing permanent governors for their outposts on the Indian mainland, and carving out a settlement centred on Goa.

One hundred and fifty years later, the Portuguese had conquered hundreds of miles of the coastline of India, much of Sri Lanka, swathes of modern Bangladesh and Myanmar, and the tiny peninsula and archipelago of Macau, in southern China. Their ships brought back to Lisbon black pepper, cinnamon, cloves and nutmeg; in the east they traded cotton cloth and gold or silver bullion. In time they would insert themselves as trading intermediaries between the mutually hostile Japanese and Chinese empires, who were on such poor terms that direct trade between them was illegal. On the other side of the world, meanwhile, they had also taken control of Brazil, the stopping point on the first stage of the *Carreira da India*. This was, truly, a world empire, in which Portuguese forts, ports, trading stations, factories and garrisons extended around the known world like a string of pearls. (And it lasted in part right through until modern times: Goa was only ceded back to India in 1961, and Macau in 1999.) The endgame was coming into view.

The Circle Complete

THE VOYAGE THAT SOLVED THE LONG conundrum of sailing west to end up in the east was undertaken by the Portuguese explorer Ferdinand Magellan, who set sail from Seville along the Guadalquivir in August 1519 with the intention of travelling all the way around the world. Magellan – a secretive and extremely pious man who, like Columbus, constantly misled his crew about where they were going and what he hoped to achieve – did not live to see his journey's end.[62] But it was completed all the same, under the captaincy of one of his officers, a Castilian called Juan Sebastián Elcano. The epic, three-year adventure took its intrepid members across the Atlantic, around the southern tip of South America and across the Pacific to the Philippines and Indonesia. After Magellan died, during a battle with natives on the island of Mactan, who would not readily accept the Christian faith he was attempting to foist on them, Elcano saw the mission home across the Indian Ocean, around the Cape of Good Hope and back to Spain. There the patron of the voyage, Charles V, was so thrilled that he granted Elcano a coat of arms bearing the motto 'You first encircled me'.

The journey took a terrible toll on its participants: of nearly three hundred men who set out, fewer than twenty came home. But it was both an exceptional feat of navigation and a symbolic landmark in human progress all the same. The earth, whose shape and nature had been a matter of speculation and mystery since the beginning of recorded history, was now subject to man's full purview. And although many places remained unknown and unexplored by westerners – including the Australasian continent, much of central Africa, the Amazon rainforest, the American interior, Antarctica and the Himalayan peaks – charting these places had become a question that began with the word 'when', not 'if' or 'how'. The line from Magellan and Elcano's circumnavigation to Captain Cook's arrival in Australia, Tenzing Norgay and Edmund Hillary's ascent of Mount Everest and our current age of satellite surveys and Google Earth was long, but it was direct. Before the fifteenth century voyages of European discovery maps of the world were partially completed jigsaws. After them, nowhere above sea level would be off-limits to explorers and navigators.

So the voyages of European discovery were one critical factor in bringing the Middle Ages to a close. Besides the geographical and psychological achievement of Magellan's circumnavigation, they also bore forth a new age of European global empires. Spain and Portugal were the first great maritime powers to start colonizing lands thousands of miles away, but they were followed not long afterwards by the English, French and Dutch, among others. The establishment of these far-flung dominions profoundly changed the nature of global commerce, and it shattered and redrew age-old power structures on every continent in the world. It brought unimaginable wealth and prosperity to some individuals and realms, and foisted hellish misery, slavery and evil on others. The legacy of imperialism is still the subject of fierce and highly emotional debate in the twenty-first century. The full story of the age of European colonial imperialism and its legacy lies way beyond the scope of this book – yet what we cannot deny is that it had its origins in the Middle Ages, when adventurers like Columbus and da Gama set off to seek new ways to travel the world, and came upon wonders which, in the end, were every bit as alluring as those discovered by Marco Polo in the heyday of the Mongol khans.

All of this leaves us with just one more path to explore in our long journey through the medieval world. For in the fifteenth century, just as the nature of the world was changing, so was the shape of the Church. At the same time as new continents and new routes to the east were fundamentally recasting ideas about the medieval earth, a quite different revolution was about to blow apart ideas about the heavens. This was the Protestant Reformation, and it began in Germany during the 1430s, when a goldsmith called Johannes Gutenberg worked out how to print a book.

16

PROTESTANTS

'The Word so greatly weakened the papacy that never a
Prince or Emperor inflicted such damage upon it...'

MARTIN LUTHER

In the autumn of 1455 two goldsmiths went to court in the German city of Mainz. Their dispute, which was heard by the city's ecclesiastical authorities in the dining hall of a Franciscan friary, was about money. The first goldsmith, Johannes Gutenberg, had borrowed 1,600 *guldens* – a small fortune – to invest in equipment, labour and his own time as he built a machine he hoped would change the nature of writing. The second goldsmith, Johann Fust, had loaned the money, hoping the returns on his investment would make him rich. But several years had gone by, and Gutenberg had not turned a profit. Now Fust's patience had run out, and he was seeking restitution by suing his business partner. Either Fust would have his money back, or he would raid Gutenberg's workshop for equipment and goods to the value he was owed. For Fust the case was a matter of pride and propriety. For Gutenberg it was a matter of survival or defeat.

The invention on which Gutenberg had been toiling was a printing press. Throughout the Middle Ages, text had generally been produced by clerks writing longhand with quills and pots of gum-based ink on stretched and treated animal skin known as parchment or vellum. The best clerks were either efficient copyists or gifted artists – and sometimes both. But none were superhuman. They worked page by page, one manuscript at a time.

A long text – a Bible, a book of saints' lives, a tract by Aristotle or Ptolemy – would take a scribe hundreds or even thousands of hours to complete.

Gutenberg saw this as hopelessly laborious, and had spent much of his adult life seeking to revolutionize manuscript-production. He was not the first to conceive of printing: the first printed scroll from China which bears a date (a copy of a Buddhist text called the *Diamond Sutra*) was made with wood-blocks in AD 868, while metal type was in use in Korea from the thirteenth century. But such technology was unknown in the west – until now. Gutenberg's press would allow a small team of printers to set and replicate pages at previously unimaginable volume. Individual letters (known as moveable type) would be cast from metal, then arranged together to form words, sentences and paragraphs. They would then be smeared with oil-based ink and pressed against sheets of vellum or Italian-made paper (another early medieval Chinese invention, only recently imported to the west) as many times as required, printing identical leaves. Although all this was an expensive, difficult process, which required considerable care and attention on the part of a skilled metalworker, it had the potential, Gutenberg thought, to render the old ways of manuscript copying obsolete, and usher in a bold new age of the written word.

The problem was, like all tech entrepreneurs in history, Gutenberg's breadth of ambition and imagination was matched only by his ability to spend other people's money. So when Fust called in his loan, it spelled disaster for Gutenberg's start-up. In November 1455 the court in Mainz found in Fust's favour, and soon after he was allowed to seize Gutenberg's printing presses, his letter-types and his workshop. Even worse, Fust took Gutenberg's commercial stock. For several years Gutenberg had been working on a two-volume printed edition of the Bible: St Jerome's fourth-century Latin Vulgate was to be given a fifteenth-century technological spin. He was all but finished printing it, and had been planning to sell two versions – one printed on paper and a more luxurious, hard-wearing vellum edition. Rumours about the Bible's impending release were whirring around European high society: a papal agent in Germany called Aeneas Silvius Piccolomini* wrote in March 1455 to a Spanish cardinal to tell him that he had seen individual, unbound sheets of it, was very impressed, but expected it to be nigh-on impossible to buy a copy before they all sold out. ('The script is extremely neat and legible, not at all difficult to follow,' wrote Piccolomini. 'Your grace would be able to read it without effort, and indeed without glasses.'[1]) Now Fust, along with one of Gutenberg's apprentices, Peter Schoeffer, took over and saw the project through to completion.

Gutenberg's Bible was duly published by Fust and Schoeffer, and sold before August 1456. It was a large book, designed to be read from a lectern. It had more than twelve hundred pages across its two volumes, laid out in forty-two-line double columns of black, blue and red type, with fine illuminated letters here and there and occasional illustration in the margins.[2] It looked very much like a manuscript. But it was not. Gutenberg's Bible was the first great printed book in the west. It was a landmark in the history of writing and publishing. More than that, however, it was the starting point of a medieval communications revolution. Mechanized printing changed western culture in the fifteenth century as fundamentally and profoundly as the creation of the smartphone changed it at the turn of the twenty-first. It led to sweeping developments in literature and literacy, education and popular politics, cartography, history, advertising, propaganda and bureaucracy.[3] Looking back from the seventeenth century, the philosopher–politician Sir Francis Bacon ranked printing alongside gunpowder and the shipman's compass in having changed 'the appearance and state of the whole world'.[4]

But most important for our purposes, the printing press occupied a central place in the Reformation – the revolution that ripped apart the Roman Church in the sixteenth century. First, printers like Gutenberg provided the tools by which the papacy plunged itself headlong into a crisis of ethics and institutional corruption. Then, printers allowed dissent against the established

* The future Pope Pius II.

order to spread across Europe at breakneck speed. The result was that, in the space of a few short decades, medieval Europe descended into religious and political turmoil, as a new movement – Protestantism – took root, providing the first serious challenge to Catholicism in one thousand years. Charting the beginnings of the Protestant Reformation is our last task before we bring our story of the Middle Ages to an end. It is a journey that will take us from the Mainz workshop of struggling goldworker Johannes Gutenberg to a mutiny in the streets outside the papal palace, and a second, epoch-shifting sack of Rome.

The Indulgences Scandal

THE EARLIEST SURVIVING WESTERN DOCUMENT TO have been printed with a moveable-type press – or at least, the first with an identifiable date on it – is not a Bible or any other sort of book,* but rather a document known as a papal letter of indulgence. It was produced in or near Mainz – perhaps by Gutenberg himself, although this is far from certain – and it was one of many identical such letters that were printed around the same time. The indulgence consists of thirty-one lines of text printed on a sheet of vellum; the only words on it that are not printed are the individualizing details, which have been entered by hand, and tell us that it was issued to a woman called Margarethe Kremer on 22 October 1454.[5]

In the printed text, this indulgence states clearly what it is for. It is addressed from a Cypriot nobleman called Paulinus Chappe, who declares himself a spokesman for the king of Cyprus. That particular monarch was in 1454 being hard-pressed by the Ottoman sultan Mehmed II, who, fresh from the conquest of Constantinople, was taking aim at other Christian-held territories in the eastern Mediterranean. The indulgence explains that since the king of Cyprus is in desperate need of money, Pope Nicholas V has agreed that for three years, anyone who donates to the Church

---

* Technically, books printed before 1500 are known as *incunabula*.

is entitled to go to a confessor and claim complete forgiveness for all their earthly sins. This was, of course, quite a big deal. We do not know what sins Margarethe Kremer had committed which she felt she could not (or did not wish to) atone for by penance or other good deeds. But since 1215 confession had been compulsory once a year for ordinary Latin Christians, who usually made it semi-publicly in ceremonies during Easter. Sin and punishment in the afterlife were real concepts.[6] So the offer of remission was attractive, which was why Margarethe had opened her purse to a papal representative, and bought her indulgence certificate, dated and personalized. As long as she handed it over to a Church confessor by the end of the indulgence's term (in this case, 30 April 30 1455), confessed her sins and truly repented, Margarethe could consider her soul returned to a state of pious blotlessness.[7] Should she be struck by lightning or trampled by a cow or carried off by the plague or murdered by bandits before she had the chance to commit another sin, her passage to heaven would be assured. By buying the indulgence, Margarethe Kremer had paid her fare to paradise.

Indulgences like Margarethe's were commonplace across Europe during the later Middle Ages. The purpose of an indulgence was, at root, simple. It was a cross between a spiritual hall-pass and banknote: a letter issued or underwritten by the pope, which entitled the bearer to claim forgiveness for sins. The advantage to the sinner of buying such a document was straightforward: it reduced the time he or she was doomed to spend suffering the agonies of purgatory. The advantages to the Church in selling it were equally clear: profit, and authority, since cultivating a market in guilt and repentance had obvious implications for social control. Indulgences were issued en masse – a little like modern-day shares, government bonds or lotto tickets – and sold individually for hard cash.

On its own the printed Mainz indulgence issued to Margarethe Kremer might be considered a curiosity: an important artefact in the history of publishing, but little more. Yet its significance goes far beyond its role in the story of the printed word. For the sale of papal indulgences was an issue which in the later fifteenth century came to assume central importance in critiques of the Roman Church as a whole – and one which was used by reformers in northern Europe to pull apart papal authority and public confidence in every aspect of Catholicism. To understand how and why this was so, we need to cast our eye back a little way, and put the development of the papal indulgence into the context of the broader history of the late medieval Church.

THE APOTHEOSIS OF PAPAL POWER IN the Middle Ages came in the early thirteenth century during the reign of Innocent III. For a short time, when Innocent was at the peak of his powers – extending crusading against new enemies both pagan and Christian, excommunicating monarchs who displeased him, and making sweeping reforms to Church law, practice and governance in the Fourth Lateran Council – it seemed possible that the papacy was on course to convert its spiritual authority into political supremacy everywhere from the Holy Land to the Atlantic coast.*

After Innocent, however, no pope found a way to complete the job. Indeed, Innocent's legacy to his successors was an impossibly exaggerated sense of the Church's proper position in directing the great affairs of the west. And as European monarchs deepened and extended their own powers in the thirteenth and fourteenth centuries, more often than not popes found themselves at war with their subjects. During the first half of the thirteenth century they fought with the Hohenstaufen rulers of Germany and Sicily (most notably the emperor Frederick II). That dispute rolled into the long-running Guelph–Ghibelline wars, which plagued Italy's city-states well into the fifteenth century. At the same time, Boniface VIII's violent clash with Philip IV of France during the 1290s and early 1300s culminated not only in Boniface's death but with the wholesale removal of the papacy from Rome to Avignon, where popes sat for sixty-seven years in the orbit of the French crown – a time Petrarch called the papacy's 'Babylonian Captivity'. The

* See chapter 9.

Avignon Papacy lasted from 1309 until 1376, but its end did not make things much better. Only two years later the western Church fell into full-blown schism: a series of Italian popes sat in Rome, while French and Spanish-aligned antipopes ruled from Avignon. In 1410 *another* antipope was set up in Pisa, meaning that for a brief period there were three men who all claimed the papacy. It was a shambles.

The Great Schism was finally resolved at the Council of Constance in 1414–18, which settled the papal tiara on the head of the Italian lawyer Martin V. Yet the residual damage to the reputation of the papacy was lasting and severe. Every man elected to the office still claimed to be the lineal heir of St Peter, and the leader of all the Christian faithful. Popes continued to exercise judgement on matters of world-changing importance – such as the treatment of non-Christian people in the territories of the New World. The blessings of popes and cardinals were still sought for new religious foundations, not least universities and cathedrals. And at the height of the Renaissance popes spent vast sums glorifying Rome, endowing the palatial Vatican headquarters there with some of the most sublime artworks produced in all of human history. Yet if there had ever been a time when popes were beyond criticism or reproach, by the late fifteenth century it was over.

As the authority of popes was by turns eroded, challenged and squandered, critics felt ever freer to voice their disdain for the office and their dissatisfaction with the Roman Church at large. In the 1320s and 1330s the English philosopher and friar William of Ockham saw fit to condemn Pope John XXII as a heretic, and dismissed popes in general as nothing more than men in gaudy hats. 'No one is bound to believe the pope in matters which are of the faith, unless he can demonstrate the reasonableness of what he says by the rule of faith,' Ockham wrote.[8] In the early fourteenth century the Bohemian heretic Jan Hus (who was influenced by the notorious Oxford theologian John Wycliffe*) railed against papal corruption; either Hus or someone in his circle produced

* See chapter 11.

a Latin polemic known as the *Anatomy of the Antichrist*, which explained at painstaking length why the pope was in fact the devil: an 'abomination of desolation', the 'angel of the bottomless pit', a 'he-goat' and a 'wicked and profane prince'.[9] Hus was burned at the stake in 1415 and his supporters were butchered by crusaders. But long before the sixteenth century, when the Reformation is still generally said to have begun, papal supremacy had been downgraded from an assumption to a mere matter of opinion.

When Hus took aim at corruption in Rome, one of his greatest bugbears was the sale of indulgences. The concept of the indulgence was an old one: it originated around the same time as the crusades in the eleventh century, when remission of sins was first granted in exchange for arduous pilgrimage, and subsequently on a large scale to the armies who marched off to fight Christ's enemies.[10] After this, indulgences took on a life of their own, helped significantly by the invention of purgatory – which developed as a Catholic doctrine between 1160 and 1180. During the twelfth and thirteenth centuries indulgences without an obligation to fight Saracens or pagans were sold to willing customers around Europe on an ad hoc basis. And in 1343 Pope Clement VI formalized the system, effectively confirming that indulgences could be bought from approved clerics for cash. Thus was a busy market established, which Hus and many others like him considered a symbol of the intolerable money-grubbing that characterized the Roman Church.

In the 1390s Geoffrey Chaucer satirized indulgences and other clerical swindles in his *Canterbury Tales*, in which the entertainingly venal Pardoner (a common term for an indulgence salesman) prefaces his tale with a pseudo-confession, boasting that he dupes gullible Christian folk into buying fake relics, and berates them so much for their sins that they rush to purchase indulgences from him, making him extremely rich. 'For mine intent,' he says, 'is not but for to win/and nothing for correction of sin'.[11] Chaucer was sending up, with characteristic wry wit, what was by his day a well-worn caricature of the swindling papal huckster. Two decades later Hus – angrier than Chaucer, not nearly as detached and ready to die for his cause – tapped the same theme. He complained that 'one pays for confession, for mass, for the sacrament, for indulgences, for churching a woman,* for a blessing, for burials, for funeral services and prayers. The very last penny which an old woman has hidden in her bundle for fear of thieves or robbery will not be saved. The villainous priest will grab it.'[12] It would be more than a century before gripes like these tipped over from the realms of satire, grumbling, and localized rebellion into full-blown revolution. But the seeds were sown.

GIVEN THE MONEYMAKING POTENTIAL OF INDULGENCES, it should now be obvious why the advent of mechanized printing in the 1450s seemed like a boon to the Church. Tickets to salvation, which had previously to be written out longhand, could now be mass-produced. And they were. In the quarter-century that followed the publication of Gutenberg's Bible, print-shops opened across Europe: in Oxford, London, Paris, Lyon, Milan, Rome, Venice, Prague and Kraków; not long after printers were operating in Portugal, the Spanish kingdoms, Sweden and Istanbul. Print runs for indulgences typically ran from 5,000 to 20,000 copies at a time, and they raised money for both the papal coffers and local projects – usually expensive building works. In 1498 the Barcelona-based printer Johann Luschner printed 18,000 indulgences to benefit the Abbey of Montserrat – along with cheap handbooks describing miracles that had taken place at a battle between the Ottomans and the Knights Hospitaller: an inspiring story designed to motivate customers to contribute to the cause.[13] Around the same time, fundraising for an Austrian monastery at Vorau saw an extraordinary 50,000 indulgences sold within a few months.[14]

So printing was booming – and so was the pardoning trade. Indulgence sellers now had at their fingertips a mass communication medium with which they could make their case, sell their wares

---

* Churching was the ceremony by which a new mother was welcomed back into her Christian congregation following a period of purdah after her delivery.

and line their pockets. What was more, ordinary folk embraced the changing times. Pardoners were not foisting an unwanted product on recalcitrant people. Quite the opposite.[15] Like twenty-first century social media users, medieval men and women rushed to engage with a system that offered them something they actually wanted, even as it turned each one of them into a profit node in a system bigger than they could comprehend. And we might not judge them too harshly for it. In a western world that had been ravaged by the Black Death and tormented by ceaseless petty wars, this new means of offsetting sin and insuring against the tortures of damnation must have seemed both necessary and welcome. It was only gradually, over the course of more than half a century, that the indulgence industry became the target of widespread scholarly complaint, and even longer before it prompted full-blown cultural revolution.

WHAT TIPPED THE INDULGENCE BUSINESS FROM a service into a scandal was, at root, simple greed. In the 1470s Pope Sixtus IV, the notorious and extravagantly nepotistic pontiff whose enemies accused him of all manner of sexual predation, and whispered that he handed out cardinal's hats to boys he fancied, found that his expenses were running away with him. The Italian wars demanded a programme of castle-building in the papal states. The Ottomans continued to threaten Christendom. Closer to home, Sixtus had a grand plan for the glorification of Rome, which included restoring or building dozens of churches, paving and widening the city streets, bridging the Tiber and restoring the papal chapel in the Vatican. (It is after Sixtus that the Sistine Chapel, with the world-famous ceiling eventually painted by Michelangelo, is named.)

One of Sixtus' favoured methods of raising the funds for this work was selling indulgences, and not only for the benefit of the living. Calculating that the market could be grown exponentially if indulgences were available to all souls, wherever they might reside, Sixtus was the first pope to state that indulgences could be bought on behalf of the dead. He slipped this new concept into a papal grant of 1476, which confirmed an existing indulgence for rebuilding the cathedral in the French city of Saintes. Encouraged in his thinking by a theologian and future cardinal called Raymond Peraudi, Sixtus reformulated the Saintes indulgence: it could now be used for 'intercession' – meaning the relatives of souls presumed to be in purgatory could buy it for their late loved ones as well as themselves; the money collected was to be split between Saintes cathedral and a fund for crusading against the Turks.[16] In practice this meant that Sixtus would see a healthy portion of the profits of this indulgence flow into his papal coffers. What happened to the money once it was there was anyone's guess.

Not surprisingly, this dramatic extension of the scope of indulgences raised eyebrows, including those of theologians at the University of Paris.[17] But Sixtus was unmoved. He had bigger things to worry about than disapproving scholars; and the sale of indulgences was too useful a source of papal income to ignore. So the system was enlarged and extended, and indulgences continued to be granted by Rome, printed in their tens of thousands and sold to willing consumers all over the west – particularly in northern Europe, where the appetite for remission of sins and intercession for the dead seemed to grow stronger with every passing year. So Sixtus' papacy passed without any major opposition. Print-shops continued to produce indulgences, and punters continued to snap them up. It was only in the early sixteenth century that disgruntlement about an increasingly corrupt system spilled over into outright attacks on the papacy and the Church. The indulgence that sparked the trouble was launched in a bull known as *Sacrosanctis*. It was issued by Pope Leo X (the second son of Lorenzo 'the Magnificent' de' Medici) with the ultimate aim of financing the wildly expensive reconstruction of St Peter's Basilica in Rome. And it caused a storm. The man whose objections to this scheme kindled the fire that became the Reformation was Martin Luther, a young professor at the University of Wittenberg, who did every bit as much as Gutenberg and Columbus to bring about the death of medieval Europe.

The Ninety-Five Theses

By the end of the fifteenth century printing houses were handling all sorts of material besides Bibles and indulgence slips. Around the year 1500 there were some 27,000 books in print across Europe.[18] And books were only a part of it. Gutenberg himself printed calendars, which detailed religious festivals, or the best times of the month to administer bloodletting and laxatives.[19] Early newspapers were in circulation, publicizing of all manner of wonderful events: in 1492 a German news-sheet told of how a huge meteorite had crashed into the earth near the town of Ensisheim; the following year Latin news-sheets were printed in Paris, Basel and Rome, telling of Columbus' adventures in the 'Indian Sea'.[20] In the same decade the German emperor Maximilian I circulated political announcements throughout his dominions on printed broadsides, and later in his reign he would commission anti-Venetian propaganda pamphlets inciting the people of Venice to rebel against their rulers; these were airdropped over Venetian armies in the field by balloon, much as psy-ops material would be scattered from aircraft during the great wars of the twentieth century.[21]

It is in this context that we must understand the publication of Martin Luther's famous *Ninety-Five Theses*, an expression of outrage at the practice of indulgence-selling which the author published in Wittenberg in the autumn of 1517. The *Theses* were a series of learned propositions pertaining to the state of the western Church, prefaced with an invitation to all who disagreed to come and debate them with Luther.[22] And they were designed for public consideration. Since Luther framed his critique of the Church in the form of an open invitation to an academic debate, it was a matter of protocol that he had them copied and distributed to potentially interested parties. According to later Protestant lore he did this by nailing a copy of them to the door of his local church. This is most likely myth. In fact, the earliest surviving copy of the *Theses* is one Luther mailed to Albert, archbishop of Mainz, on 31 October. But either way, the effect was extraordinary.

Naturally, the easiest way to replicate the *Theses* in the early sixteenth century was to have them printed at Luther's university. However, after their first publication, Luther lost control of the copying and reprinting process. When his *Theses* entered the public domain, they touched a nerve. And they travelled. People heard about them, they wanted to read them and printers reproduced them. Within weeks, as we would now put it, Luther went viral. In the last months of 1517 hundreds of copies of his *Theses* were printed in Germany, some in the original Latin and others in vernacular translation. Within a year Luther's writings were known to intellectuals and booksellers in England, France and Italy.[23] Massive fame was never Luther's ambition or intention, and he suggested later that he was surprised by the furor his *Theses* caused. But of course, the modern history of things going viral tells us that exponential publicity is as often accidental as deliberate. After 1517 the genie was out of the bottle.

Luther once described himself as the son, grandson and great-grandson of peasants, who only had a chance at education because his father left the ancestral village and became a successful copper-smelter in Mansfeld, in the modern German state of Saxony-Anhalt, around a hundred kilometres north-west of Leipzig. Luther was born there in 1483; when he grew up he went to the cathedral school in Magdeburg, and university in Erfurt. In 1505, when he was twenty-two, he had earned his master's degree and taken holy orders as an Augustinian friar.* Three years later he was a theology lecturer in Wittenberg, and there, the year before his thirtieth birthday, he received his doctorate in theology. He specialized in the Psalms and St Paul's letters to the Romans. There was, on the surface of things, nothing much unusual about him.

In the course of Luther's theological enquiries, however, he became increasingly interested in the nature of God's forgiveness,

---

* Or more properly, the Order of Hermits of St Augustine, known in English as the Austin Friars, and not the same as the Augustinian Canons. Luther was a friar, not a canon or a monk (although he is often described as one). The importance of this distinction, given the friars' role in engaging the community through preaching but also through hearing confessions, is discussed by MacCulloch, Diarmaid, 'The World Took Sides', *London Review of Books* 38 (2016), www.lrb.co.uk/the-paper/v38/n16/diarmaid-macculloch/the-world-took-sides.

which he believed was a matter of faith, rather than something which had to be earned by doing things. This may seem now like an arcane and technical distinction. Certainly, it sprang initially from Luther's near-neurotic personal obsession with his own imperfect soul. But as the professor worked through his thoughts he reached conclusions that would have serious political resonance. In a world where the Roman Church built its wealth on the basis that salvation was something to be acquired, either by doing penance or buying one's way closer to salvation, Luther's assertion that the way to heaven was through belief, not deeds, sat very ill. If all one had to do was believe, repent, love one's fellow humans and pray for grace, it was hard to see the point of papal indulgences such as those offered by *Sacrosanctis*, which was promulgated in 1515 and aggressively preached in the German states by a Dominican friar called Johann Tetzel – just as Luther was in the depths of his theological research.

Luther's *Theses* can therefore be seen as the product of his own theological mud-wrestling, given a target in the form of Tetzel's indulgence preaching. As a result, they were both impassioned and politically inflammatory. 'The Pope,' Luther proposed, in the sixth of his *Theses*, 'cannot reduce any guilt.' He went on: 'indulgence preachers falsely claim that one is freed from all punishment and is saved by the indulgences of the pope... [but] the pope cannot reduce the penalties of souls in purgatory.' He took aim at a catchphrase popularly associated with Tetzel, a neat ditty which ran, 'When the coin in the coffer rings, the soul from purgatory springs'. Nonsense, wrote Luther: in fact the indulgence system was a scam in which both sellers and buyers were at fault. 'The one who buys indulgences honestly is as rare as the one who is honestly contrite,' wrote Luther. This was not a completely new critique. As long ago as the twelfth century, the writer Peter of Poitiers had argued that it was outrageous to think that salvation could simply be bought. ('[God] does not consider how much is given, but... from what intention,' Peter wrote.[24]) But Luther was exceptionally frank and personal about it. 'Those who believe that they can be certain of their salvation because they have indulgence letters will be eternally damned, together with their teachers.'[25] Clearly, this was going to be a problem.

One of the reasons Luther's *Ninety-Five Theses* captured imaginations in 1517 was that the pope against whom Luther railed, Leo X, was not just constitutionally spendthrift but genuinely corrupt. Of course, Leo was a Medici – and in Italy this was always an aggravating factor in politics and religion. He also had a very faulty radar for doing the right thing. He was a generous patron of the arts, no doubt, and a cultured intellectual. But he seldom seemed to grasp how badly he compromised both himself and the papal office through his efforts to raise money for his various projects – ranging from rebuilding St Peter's to fighting the Ottomans.

The indulgence preached in Germany was a classic example of Leo's blasé attitude spilling over into naked fiscal turpitude. On a basic level, *Sacrosanctis* represented exploitation: the poor being squeezed to pay for the pleasures of the rich. ('Why does not the pope, whose wealth is today greater than the wealth of the richest Crassus, build this one basilica of St Peter with his own money?' Luther asked, rhetorically, in his *Theses*.)[26] Yet there was more to it. *Sacrosanctis* was in fact the public face of a corporate conspiracy between the leading men of three powerful European families: the Medici (in the form of Pope Leo); Jakob Fugger, head of the Augsburg banking and mining dynasty and a man often said to have been the richest in human history; and Albert, archbishop of Mainz, a member of the politically influential Hohenzollern dynasty and (not coincidentally) the man to whom Luther mailed the first copy of his *Theses*.

The nature of the agreement between these three was broadly thus: Albert, who was already archbishop of Magdeburg, had been permitted by the pope to become archbishop of Mainz at the same time – which made him the most senior churchman in Germany, *and* meant he controlled two of the seven electoral votes which determined the identity of the German emperor. (His brother already controlled a third.) Vast fees were due to Rome as a tax on taking office as an archbishop – but Albert could afford these, thanks to a loan from Fugger, who advanced the money on the basis that he would have the Hohenzollern and their electoral votes in his pocket. Albert, for his part, promised Leo he would do all he could to make sure that German Christians bought as many indulgences as possible, partly because his share of the proceeds could repay his debt to Fugger and partly so that funds would flow rapidly to Leo in Rome for the completion of St Peter's. For the parties involved this was a neat arrangement by which they all got what they wanted – so long as the faithful did their part and kept pumping money into pardons.[27] For onlookers, however – particularly German princes, who worried about the excessive power of the Hohenzollern – it was a highly distasteful deal, which demanded opposition.

This intimate link between high politics and high theology is one reason why Luther's *Theses* became the talk of Europe in 1517 and the years that followed. As he continued to write and preach and explore the wider fields of sin, forgiveness and the nature of God's love, arguments which might in other times have been of interest only to humanist scholars and other academics became highly germane to German electoral politics and the Medici papacy. Moreover, Luther's writings continued to circulate in print. He published more than any other man of his generation – with the possible exception of the brilliant Dutch humanist Desiderius Erasmus. It was as if he could not help himself. The modern edition of his complete works runs to over one hundred volumes, on all manner of subjects, bound together chiefly by the theme of Luther's refusal to dissemble or hide what he believed was the truth about God's love for mankind. Again and again, as Luther's writings riled defenders of the established order, he argued that he was interested only in divinity and grace, and not in the concerns of the world. Yet in time he came to accept that whenever he wrote, his words struck home. 'While I slept or drank Wittenberg beer,' he once wrote, 'the Word so greatly weakened the papacy that never a Prince or Emperor inflicted such damage upon it.'[28]

It took just a year, therefore, for this obscure German doctor to fall squarely into the sights of the Church establishment. In October 1518 Luther was summoned to Augsburg to debate an Italian cardinal, Thomas Cajetan, an expert on Thomas Aquinas, the great thirteenth-century scholar whose writings were considered an intellectual pillar of Church orthodoxy. Although Luther was aware that there were already threats to his liberty and even his life, he went to Augsburg under the protection of Frederick III 'the Wise', elector of Saxony and one of the leading anti-Hohenzollern nobles in Germany. However, after three days of feisty debates with Cajetan, Luther became convinced that if he stayed he risked arrest for heresy. He fled, and went back to his books.

Yet controversy would not now leave him alone, nor he it. In summer 1519 he went to a debate at the University of Leipzig, where he let his tongue run away with him to the extent that he denied papal authority on matters of scripture and argued that the late, loathed Bohemian heretic Jan Hus may have crossed the line occasionally but was by and large a good Christian. Unsurprisingly, the following summer Luther was officially condemned by Pope Leo himself, in a papal bull called *Exsurge Domine* (Arise, O Lord). In response, Luther burned a copy of the bull outside Wittenberg's city gates. And so the battle lines were drawn. In a work written that same year, Luther called the 'Romanists' – Leo, his supporters, and in effect, anyone else who disagreed with him – 'the fellowship of antichrist and the devil', who had 'nothing of Christ but the name'.[29] And all of this was played out in public, via letters and books which were printed and circulated in the universal scholarly language of Latin. Not surprisingly, by the end of 1520 Pope Leo had reached the limit of his patience. On 3 January 1521 he excommunicated Luther, making him a formal enemy of the Church and all its faithful people. It was now incumbent on all who called themselves Christian rulers to stand against the precocious doctor. But if this was intended to silence Luther, it did quite the opposite. Although Leo could not have known it, catastrophe was set in motion.

The Judgement of Kings

IN THE SPRING OF 1521 THE king of England, Henry VIII, put his handsome signature to a book entitled the *Assertio Septem Sacramentorum* ('assertion of the seven sacraments'). Aged twenty-nine, Henry fancied himself as the paragon of Renaissance kingship; he had been given an excellent education and sparred with great humanist writers like Erasmus since his childhood. He was also perpetually eager to find ways to enhance what one courtier called his 'virtue, glory and immortality'.[30] As such Henry took a keen interest in the growing controversy surrounding Luther's writings. Once Luther's books were outlawed by the Church, he had given his approval for mass burnings of them in English cities. Meanwhile, in private, Henry saw an opportunity to burnish his own reputation as a thinker as well as a statesman, by contributing personally to the theological debate. His *Assertio* – a smartly bound, signed edition of which survives in the British royal collection – was a response to Luther's 1520 work *On the Babylonian Captivity of the Church*. In this, the German professor had argued that most of the seven sacraments of the Church (baptism, Eucharist, confirmation, reconciliation, anointing the sick, marriage and holy orders) were pure folly and invention. Only the first two, he pointed out, had any basis in scripture. This was plainly an affront to centuries of Christian tradition. So King Henry – aided by a panel of eminent Oxford and Cambridge university scholars and the great humanist writer Thomas More – picked up his pen, and huffed and puffed his way through a rebuttal.[31] He called Luther an 'infernal wolf' and a 'great member of the Devil'. He said he had dragged up from hell itself 'heresies which ought to lie in eternal darkness'.[32]

In August the king's chief minister, Thomas Wolsey, sent twenty-seven printed copies of the finished *Assertio* to an English clerk at the papal court in Rome. In the covering letter Wolsey asked that one of them be covered in gold cloth and delivered to Pope Leo himself. The clerk was instructed to do this at a moment when the pope was surrounded by as many people as possible, in order that word of the English king's piety and intellect might get around. Once this was done, Wolsey said, the clerk was to petition Leo for a favour. King Henry hankered for an official title which would advertise his Christian magnificence. Ferdinand and Isabella of Spain (Henry's parents-in-law) had been known as 'the Catholic Monarchs'. French rulers, including Henry's contemporary and rival Francis I, styled themselves 'the most Christian kings'. Henry wished to be known as 'the very defender of the Catholic faith of Christ's Church'.[33]

Thanks to Wolsey and his Roman agent, Henry more or less got his way. Pope Leo was shown the *Assertio* that summer. The day after he saw it, he formally granted Henry the right to append his royal style with the Latin words *Fidei Defensor* – Defender of the Faith. (The title has stuck to this day, and is embossed after the monarch's name on British coins.) And Leo's approval made the *Assertio* into a minor bestseller. It went through ten printed editions, and reached a wide European audience, not least when it was translated from Latin into German. Meanwhile, further works by English theologians such as John Fisher, bishop of Rochester and chancellor of Cambridge University, helped to reinforce England's reputation as a bastion of anti-Lutheran orthodoxy, where heretics and reformers were not welcome. By the mid-1520s the English authorities were on ostentatious high alert for Lutheran heresy: German merchants were liable to have their homes raided; sermons against heretics were regularly preached in London; and the government was preparing a plan to resist the arrival of an English-language print edition of the New Testament, being prepared in Cologne by an expatriate scholar called William Tyndale.

In retrospect, of course, there was enormous historical irony in all of this. During the course of his long reign, Henry VIII did not prove to be quite the defender of the Catholic faith he had promised. In the late 1520s he decided he wished to annul his marriage to Queen Catherine of Aragon, with whom he had been unable to father a male heir to the English crown. When Henry could not secure papal approval for an annulment (for reasons that will shortly become apparent), he performed an astonishing religious volte-face. Liberally reinterpreting his role as *Fidei Defensor*, he now took the view that protecting the Christian faith did not in fact require his obedience to the pope, but the opposite. In 1534 he withdrew England from its ancient allegiance to Rome, establishing an independent English Church with himself as supreme head. In the course of all this, Henry discarded Queen Catherine, treating her atrociously, and killed her replacement, Anne Boleyn, three years after marrying her. Wolsey was destroyed and died a broken man. Bishop Fisher and Thomas More were executed for refusing to acknowledge the royal supremacy. And Henry himself, once the scrupulously orthodox scourge of Lutheran heresy, became the poster-boy for anti-papal politics, a turn of events which in the early 1520s would have seemed so implausible as to be hilarious. Although popular religion in England remained obstinately traditional for several generations, Tudor England ended the sixteenth century as the most powerful Protestant nation in Europe, virulently hostile to Catholics until the emancipation campaign of the late eighteenth and early nineteenth centuries. In the grand scheme of English history, the break with Rome was the moment at which contemporaries like the historian and Protestant polemicist John Foxe perceived the Middle Ages ending and a new, modern age beginning.*

However, important though these developments in England undoubtedly were (and, in the age of Brexit, can still seem), the monarch whose stance towards Luther had the most decisive and lasting effect on western history was not Henry, but another of his contemporaries: Charles V, Holy Roman Emperor, king of Spain, Germany, Naples and Sicily, archduke of Austria and ruler of the Burgundian states in the Netherlands. Notwithstanding Henry's pretensions and the ambition of Francis I, Charles was, by some distance, the most powerful European monarch of his time, a foundational figure in the history of realms ranging from the Habsburg empire of central Europe to the kingdom of Mexico.

* See Introduction.

After his death he was remembered (by a friend, admittedly) as 'the greatest man who ever lived'.[34] But long before that, in the 1520s, the positions he adopted towards Luther, Lutheranism and the papacy were of definitive importance in political and religious maelstrom that marked the sunset of the medieval world.

IN LATE JANUARY 1521, JUST A few months before Henry VIII came up with his *Assertio* against Luther, Charles V convened an imperial Diet – a political assembly – in the free city of Worms, a little way south of Frankfurt on the river Rhine. The Diet marked Charles' coronation as German emperor in Aachen the previous autumn: a glorious ceremony in which the young man positioned himself as a new Charlemagne, but one which had also posed numerous awkward questions about the shape and structure of his future government.* Dozens of sensitive issues were up for consideration at the Diet, including matters of German law, concerns about economic policy, and technical queries about the relationship between the empire and the rest of Charles' extensive territories. Afterwards, however, the Diet would be remembered for one thing only: the dramatic scene played out when Luther, dressed in his friar's habit and inflated almost to bursting with his customary righteousness, explained to the new emperor in person why he persisted in dragging the good name of the pope and the Roman Church through the mire.

Luther's hearing at the Diet took place over the course of several days, beginning on the afternoon of 17 April at a special session convened in rooms at Charles' lodging house, which was ordinarily the local bishop's official residence. As in the past, Luther was granted safe conduct to appear at Worms, and his personal safety was guaranteed by his patron, Elector Frederick of Saxony. He had

---

* Born in 1500, Charles had already become ruler of the Burgundian Netherlands as a child in 1506, took command of the conjoined Spanish thrones in 1516, exercising power on behalf of his mother, Joanna 'the Mad' (one of two daughters of the Catholic Monarchs Ferdinand and Isabella; the other was Henry VIII's queen Catherine of Aragon) and ruled Austria after the death of his grandfather Maximilian in 1519.

been promised that if he turned up he would not be arrested and bundled off to Rome to face Pope Leo. Nevertheless, it was clear from the moment he arrived that Charles hoped to induce Luther to recant his most egregious opinions and writings. This was not a recipe for a happy outcome, for as usual Luther could not be silenced by force and would not be silenced by reason.

Over the course of several presentations in Latin and German (which Charles, a native French speaker, struggled to follow) Luther revealed just what a formidable debater and scholar he had become. He rapidly dispelled any hopes that he might crumble when faced with the emperor – or anyone else. And eventually he gave a biting summary of the grounds for his apparently infinite obstinacy. 'As long as my conscience is captive to the word of God,' he said, 'I neither can nor will recant, since it is neither safe nor right to act against conscience. God help me.'[35] Several days later the inevitable verdict was passed. Charles had seen first-hand that Luther was incorrigible, and that he would have to deal with it. The papal bull condemning Luther would have to stand, and the professor and all who followed him would be considered enemies of the empire as well as the Church. 'We shall pursue Martin himself and his adherents with excommunication and use other methods available for their liquidation,' promised Charles.[36] Not for the first time, Luther fled.

Despite Charles' fierce words, however, Luther was safe so long as Frederick of Saxony chose to keep him so. The new emperor fervently wished that Luther would shut up, but he was not about to go to war with his new German subjects over it. So at the start of May Luther was ensconced under Saxon protection in Elector Frederick's fortress of Wartburg, in Eisenach, where he remained for nearly a year, working on books that would deconstruct the basis for monastic vows, forced public confession and even the Mass as it was generally performed in the west. He was also translating the New Testament into German, writing hymns and contemplating ways to force European Jews to convert to Christianity. Although the latter suggested that there were some medieval prejudices so ingrained that even the revolutionary mind of Martin Luther could not overturn them, in almost every other way he was beginning to write the documents on which to build an entirely new Church.

Meanwhile, outside the walls of his castle, Luther's friends and supporters had begun to put his theories into action: celebrating Masses without ordained priests, agitating for free preaching of God's word, vandalizing statues of saints by smashing their heads and hands, and demanding that municipal authorities take action taken against immoral establishments like pubs and brothels. New preachers – some far more radical even than Luther, and many of them out-and-out firebrands – were busy trying to stir up popular enthusiasm for the new religious mindset, with its tight focus on the individual and its rejection of traditional symbols of public authority. The most extreme reformers – led by the Swiss preacher Ulrich Zwingli – had begun to question even sacraments like infant baptism. (For this they became known as Anabaptists.) So from being a shopping basket of theological and heretical positions, Lutheranism was starting to take on the characteristics of a social movement. Yet as it did so, it was developing a highly rancorous character, intolerant of any resistance. Erasmus noted as much when he wrote about Lutheranism in 1524; he complained that among the new thinkers, 'I see some people endowed who are so uncontrollably attached to their own opinion that they cannot bear anything which dissents from it,' and wondered where it would all lead. 'I ask you,' he wrote, 'what sort of sincere judgment can there be when people behave in this way? Who will learn anything fruitful from this sort of discussion – beyond the fact that each leaves the encounter bespattered with the other's filth?'[37] It was not long before these lines appeared prophetic.

'Murderous, thieving hordes'

WHEN LUTHER DECIDED TO LEAVE THE Wartburg fortress and return to Wittenberg, in the spring of 1522, he did so on the basis that the world – or at least, his small corner of it – was ready for wholesale reform. He returned to teaching at the university and continued to write, feverishly at times, composing his new Church and publishing books and pamphlets, trusting in the fact that the authorities' desire to censor the printing press was not at all matched by their ability to control the flow of information.* He enthusiastically encouraged other reform-minded intellectuals in Saxony and as far away as Zurich and Strasbourg to begin dismantling the practices of the Catholic faith and establishing new rites of worship and ecclesiastical groups outside the control of Rome. And he became a keen supporter of clerical marriage – including for himself. In 1525 Luther wed Katharina von Bora, one of several dozen nuns he had helped to escape from a convent near the town of Grimma, smuggled away from their confinement on the back of a herring wagon. This was an important milestone in Luther's personal life, and in his progress as a reformer for whom nothing but the literal word of scripture was sacred. Yet in the same year Luther married, the unintended consequences of his war against old certainties became horribly apparent, when Germany erupted into popular rebellion.

The Peasants' War of 1525 was the amalgamation of a number of separate, disparate protests across southern Germany, which bubbled up slowly during the autumn of 1524, until massive popular rioting swept estates and cities across central Europe throughout the following spring. Like the popular insurrections of the fourteenth century† the first stirrings of rebellion had myriad local causes, but they were brought together by a feeling of generalized, systemic discontent against the wealthy and powerful, and stirred – not surprisingly – by the spirit of the nascent Lutheran Reformation, which was iconoclastic on more than one level. Unlike fourteenth-century rebels, however, the insurgents of 1525 were well served by the printing press, which allowed rebel groups to circulate propaganda and protest literature.[38] Most famously this included the *Twelve Articles* issued in early March on behalf of a group of rebels from villages in Swabia, and written

---

* Not coincidentally, the question of matching governments' desire for censorship with its practical application is a central feature in our present age of communications revolution.
† See chapter 13.

by a Lutheran pamphleteer and preacher called Sebastian Lotzer.[39] This manifesto was a searingly articulate cry for freedom in all its forms, heavily flavoured with calls for religious reform. The rebels called for the rights of villagers to appoint preachers who stuck to the scriptures, for the abandonment of serfdom, and for the return of common land seized by nobles for private use.[40] Copies of the *Twelve Articles* flew from the presses and were widely distributed across Germany, with tens of thousands circulated during the months in which the rebellion was at its peak.

Although rebels like those in Swabia saw themselves as acting well within the pious, scourging spirit of the times, Luther blanched at the means many of them deployed in his name. In Erfurt, in late April, around eleven thousand peasants stormed the city, chalked 'a ploughshare, sickle and hoe crowned with a horseshoe' on the gates of the bishop's palace and ordered that it was 'henceforth to be called the Country Palace', then attempted forcibly to introduce the Lutheran Mass into the city's churches.[41] Meanwhile, in Weinsberg (a little way north of Stuttgart), things were bloodier. According to a local parson, a band of peasants arrived at Weinsberg castle in mid-April, clambered over the walls, kidnapped the wife and children of the local nobleman and governor, Count Ludwig von Helfenstein, plundered his goods and then set off to find the count himself in the nearby town. The townsmen, being Lutherans, let the rebels in. According to the parson, 'Lucifer and all his angels were then let loose; for they raged and stormed no differently than if they were mad and possessed by every devil. First they seized the count, then the nobility and the cavalry, and some were stabbed as they resisted.' One well-to-do townsman tried to seek sanctuary in a church tower. But 'as he called down to the peasants for mercy, offering them money, someone fired a shot up at him and hit him, then climbed up and threw him out of the window.'

After this, the count, his family and servants – more than twenty people in all – were taken to a field outside the town walls and murdered. 'The count offered to give them a barrel of money if they would let him live, but there was no way out but to die,' wrote the parson. 'When the count saw that, he stood stock still until they stabbed him… Thus, all these were driven through with lances… and afterwards dragged out naked and let lie there… After all this, [the peasants] set alight to the castle and burnt it, and then marched off to Würzburg.'[42]

Surely, Luther had not predicted scenes like this when he began his investigations into the scriptural basis for indulgences. Horrified at the crimes being now perpetrated in the name of the reform movement he had begun, he tried increasingly to distance himself from the rebels' actions. His first effort was a pamphlet called *An Admonition to Peace*, which advised the rebels to calm down and negotiate for better conditions. But when that fell on deaf ears he wrote a much less conciliatory tract entitled *Against the Murderous, Thieving Hordes of Peasants*. In this he condemned the peasants for misappropriating the cause of Church reform and using it as a cover to commit horrible sins and crimes, and advocated a strong crackdown by their social betters. Plainly, Luther was shaken by what he had seen. Yet it was all now out of his control.

As the Peasants' War raged, other reformers who had risen to prominence in Luther's wake – notably a radical preacher called Thomas Müntzer – threw themselves into the fight on the side of the rebels. But Luther could not bring himself to join them. Thus he ended up on the side of the nobility, which was not a pretty place to be. In May 1525, after a period of paralysis, the German aristocracy rallied, and crushed the peasants with brute force and extreme vindictiveness.[43] In a series of uncompromising military assaults all over Germany, tens of thousands of peasants were slaughtered; preacher-leaders like Müntzer were captured and tortured to death. On 21 May Luther received a letter from a councilor in his hometown of Mansfeld, relating what punishments had been meted out in the local area.

At Heldrungen they have beheaded five priests. After the greater part of the citizens in Frankenhausen was slain and others taken prisoner, those who remained alive were released at the plea of the women of the town, but on condition that the women should punish the two priests who were still there. Both priests were beaten with cudgels by all the women in the marketplace, it is said, for half an hour after they were dead; it was a sorry deed. Whoever does not take pity on such an act is truly no human being. I fear that it looks as if you are acting as the lords' prophet... There is so much punishment that I fear that Thuringia and the county will only gradually recover... Robbery and murder are the order of the day here...[44]

It was a savage end to a shocking episode – the bloodiest popular uprising in European history before the French Revolution of the late eighteenth century. An imperial Diet of 1526, summoned by Charles V to discuss the official reaction to the rebellion, concluded that 'The common man rather grievously forgot himself,' but recommended lenience so as to prevent further outbreaks of popular rage.[45] This was a rare gracious sentiment. But it was by no means the end of the bloodshed and tumult Luther's protests would bring about.

ALTHOUGH THE GERMAN PEASANTS' WAR WAS a major disturbance to the peace in the heartlands of his empire, Charles V largely delegated the political response to his younger brother, Ferdinand archduke of Austria, who was his *de facto* deputy in central and eastern Europe. This was not for lack of interest, but because Charles was immersed in the events of the Italian Wars. A sporadic struggle between Europe's great powers for supremacy below the Alps had been underway in Italy, on and off, for thirty years. In 1525, as the German peasants were taking up arms, Charles seemed to sniff the possibility of total victory.

The scent emanated from the duchy of Milan. There, on 24 February, an imperial army, led by Charles' experienced commander Charles de Lannoy, attacked a French army besieging the town of Pavia. Lannoy's aim was to drive off the French from Pavia, and ultimately away from the whole duchy. But he did far better than that. In four hours of fighting the imperial army crushed the French, killing many leading French nobles. Even better, the prisoners taken on the battlefield included King Francis I himself. The monarch surrendered gracefully in the field, but he was not treated especially kindly thereafter. Francis was removed from Italy to Madrid, where he was kept for nearly a year. Only in March 1526, when he had ceded to Charles' terms and swathes of territory in a treaty that heavily favoured the empire, was he released. Francis had been forced to transfer to the emperor his claims to Burgundy, Milan and Flanders, and to hand over his two young sons as surety. It was a round humiliation.

It looked like a thunderous triumph for Charles. Yet as things soon transpired, it was not. In the first place, the cost of the long years of fighting which had preceded victory at Pavia was astronomical: on the day that Pavia and Francis were captured, Charles already owed his armies 600,000 ducats – an impossibly massive sum – in back pay.[46] And in the second, King Francis had no intention whatever of keeping to the terms he had agreed.

Almost immediately upon his release, the aggrieved French king made plain his intention to ignore the Treaty of Madrid, which he argued was a disgraceful peace made under duress. For moral and political support he wrote to the papal court. By now Pope Leo was dead. His successor, Adrian VI, had lasted less than two years before he, too, expired. So the new pope was another Medici: Leo's first cousin Giulio, a career churchman of long experience, who had taken the name Clement VII. Clement was almost as wary of Charles V as Francis was. He therefore officially relieved Francis of any undertakings he had given while an imperial prisoner. And there was more. Not only did Clement absolve Francis of his promises, he also committed the papacy to a formal alliance with France, the purpose of which was to drive Charles and his imperial influence out of the whole Italian peninsula. This alliance was called the League of Cognac; its members included France, the papacy, Venice, Milan and Florence. Of course, its very existence was a gross affront to Charles. As he realized the hollowness of his victory, and his obligation to continue fighting a war which was already beyond even his ample means, he became depressed: 'full of dumps and solitary musing', wrote the English ambassador at the imperial court.[47] But there was little time for sulking. Another round of wars in the Italian peninsula was underway.

The Sack of Rome

AT EASTER 1527 A MAD, SEMI-NAKED, ruddy-faced preacher known as Brandano stalked the streets of Rome, prophesying impending damnation. Brandano – who dressed, as Martin Luther had for so long, in the robes of an Augustinian friar – was an expert at gloomy prognostications, and had been in and out of jail in the course of his career, as punishment for disturbing the peace. Now he was at it again: as Clement VII appeared before worshipers at St Peter's on Maundy Thursday, Brandano shimmied up a statue of St Paul, and started screaming at the pope to repent. Calling Clement 'thou bastard of Sodom', he warned the assembled crowds that unless all Romans repented of their monstrous sins, within a fortnight God would send them punishment worthy of the Old Testament.[48] It did not take long for Brandano to be apprehended and thrown once more into a cell. But he had said his piece, and what was more, he would be proven right.

That spring, imperial armies were on the loose in Italy, and marching towards the Holy City. Far from scaring Charles V away from Italy, the formation of the League of Cognac had spurred the emperor to push his chips forward. So too had news from the east, where the Ottomans under their sultan Suleiman the Magnificent had crushed a Hungarian army at the battle of Mohács in 1526 and were now overrunning south-eastern Europe. Subduing his enemies in Italy seemed ever more essential if Charles was to defend Europe from the Turks. Of course, it was still terribly unclear how Charles' troops in Italy were to be paid, or even fed. But his advisors had reasoned that if there was anywhere in Europe where it was possible to live off plunder and the land, it was Italy. What was more, Charles had alighted on a frighteningly opportunistic way to both raise troops and heap pressure on Clement VII. He hinted that he might suspend the penalties against Lutherans that had been imposed at the Diet of Worms six years earlier.[49] And he sent into Italy a huge force of *landsknechte* – fierce German-speaking mercenary units who wielded guns and pike, many of whom were not only hardened storm-troopers, but Lutheran sympathizers. It would be a deadly combination.

The imperial troops in Italy – 20,000 of them in all, split into Spanish, Italian and German factions – were under the command of a general known as Charles, duke of Bourbon: a French traitor who had gone over to the emperor after falling out with Francis I. Unfortunately for all concerned, by the spring of 1527 Bourbon had more or less lost his grip on the army. Unpaid, ill and hungry having spent the winter in the field, mutinous and eager for loot, the troops were now driving Bourbon as much as he was them. Having been in Milan the previous autumn, they flirted with attacking Florence in April, but decided that it would be too hard to take. The real plunder, Bourbon and his troops concluded, was in Rome, where there lay two ways by which they might recoup their pay: either they could force Clement to dig into his pockets, or they could take it as war-spoils. At the end of April they set off from Tuscany in the direction of the Holy City. They marched fast, fording rivers and almost hurtling down Roman roads at a pace of more than twenty miles per day. Less than two weeks later – just as the mad preacher Brandano had predicted – they were at Rome's gates.

It was 5 May when Bourbon and his 20,000 appeared before Rome, and although they had great numbers, the odds looked to be stacked against them, since they had no decent artillery, and half the men were on the brink of starvation. However, desperation was a powerful motivation in itself. They had powered towards the city at such speed that, in the words of the accomplished Florentine historian and Medici associate Luigi Guicciardini, 'those within were not prepared for them either physically or in spirit, and not in any way organized for battle.'[50] Moreover, as the imperial army camped overnight, a fog descended over Rome, reducing visibility to less than six feet – and making it impossible for the city's defenders to fire their own heavy guns.[51] For a few hours the contest would be more or less level.

Around dawn on 6 May Bourbon slung a white cloak over his armour and ordered an assault on the walls of Rome with ladders and sidearms. In his pre-battle speech he offered incentives to the various companies of Spanish, Italian and German troops assembled before him. He spoke of booty and glory, and the 'inestimable wealth of gold and silver' that lay inside the city. With an eye on the Spaniards, he promised that if Rome fell, it would be the start of a world conquest, in which all of Italy and France would follow, after which Charles V would lead his armies against the Ottomans before '[ranging] with you in victory through Asia and Africa... [where] you will have a thousand opportunities to show the whole universe that you have far surpassed the glory and riches of the incomparable armies of Darius, Alexander the Great, or any other ruler known to history.' Then, turning to the Germans, Bourbon decried the godless corruption of Rome's Catholic clergy, who led the citizens 'in lustful and effeminate pastimes... totally committed to amassing silver and gold with fraud, pillage, and cruelty, under the banner of Christian piety...' Taking Rome, he told them, would fulfil the dream of which 'our infallible prophet, Martin Luther, has spoken many times.'[52] There was, it seemed, something for everyone. Bourbon worked his men into a frenzy and let them go.

In the confusion of the thick fog and the early morning, the hungry imperialists took less than three hours to breach Rome's walls. They did so through an old-fashioned combination of scrambling up ladders and pulling at stones with their hands. Yet at the moment that the breakthrough came, disaster struck. Bourbon was in the middle of the action, resting his hand on a scaling-ladder and exhorting the men above him to get to the top of the walls as best they could. Suddenly, through the press of bodies and the mist, a slug fired from a long gun known as an arquebus blasted straight through his head. He was killed on the spot. Around him, on both sides of the Roman defences, a combination of panic and bloodlust set in. Bourbon had been only barely in command of his troops when he was alive. But now he was dead, no one could steer them. Even as the blood seeped from the general's perforated skull, imperial troops who had clambered over Rome's walls and snuck in through vacant cannon-holes were flinging open the gates. The city had been taken by force, and a rampage was assured. More than one thousand years after the cataclysm of AD 410, the barbarians had finally returned.

THE SACK OF ROME IN MAY 1527 lasted for more than a week. Screaming 'Spain! Spain! Kill! Kill!', imperial troops hurtled through into the city and ran wild. They made short work of the few thousand military defenders, including most of the pope's Swiss Guards, who were cut down in front of St Peter's. After that, the city was theirs. Clement himself fled to the Castel Sant'Angelo, the most secure fortress in the city, where he holed up along with several cardinals and a motley band of other citizens who barged in before the portcullis was dropped. He, and those who made it in with him, were the lucky ones. Outside the fortress, anyone who had not managed to slip out of Rome before the gates were re-locked was in deep trouble.

According to Guicciardini, when the imperial army realized 'all the defenders had fled and that they were truly in control of the city, the Spanish troops began to capture houses (along with everyone and everything that was in them) and to take prisoners... The Germans, however, were obeying the articles of war and cutting to pieces anyone they came upon.'[53] It was soon a hellish scene. Women and children were every bit as vulnerable as men, and the clergy were killed along with the laity. Indeed, clerics were expressly targeted. It had been said earlier in the year that the erstwhile commander of the *landsknechte*, Georg von Frundsberg (who left Italy a broken man when the troops began to mutiny in the spring) had gone about with a golden noose on his person, in case he ever had the chance to hang the pope.

Now German mercenaries had a chance to channel that violent mood. Relics including the heads of St Peter, St Paul, St Andrew along with fragments of the True Cross and the Crown of Thorns were 'shamefully trodden underfoot in that fury'.[54] Popes' tombs were ransacked. One group dressed a donkey in priestly vestments and murdered a churchman when he refused to feed the animal the Eucharist.[55] Guicciardini's long and lurid account of the sack made it plain how fiercely anti-clerical the imperialists were – and how easily their attacks on the symbols of papal wealth spilled over into naked inhumanity.

> In the street you saw nothing but thugs and rogues carrying great bundles of the richest vestments and ecclesiastical ornaments and huge sacks full of all kinds of vessels of gold and silver – testifying more to the riches and empty pomp of the Roman curia than to the humble poverty and true devotion of the Christian religion. Great numbers of captives of all sorts were to be seen, groaning and screaming, being swiftly led to makeshift prisons. In the streets there were many corpses. Many nobles lay there cut to pieces, covered with mud and their own blood, and many people only half dead lay miserably on the ground.[56]

Nuns were raped. Priests were killed on their altars. Although there were occasional altercations between the Spanish and Germans about the extent to which churches ought to be despoiled, this was of little use or solace to the clergy themselves, who, if they were not killed outright, could be seen wandering the streets 'in torn and bloody shirts, [with] cuts and bruises all over their bodies from the indiscriminate whippings and beatings they had received. Some had thick and greasy beards. Some had their faces branded; and some were missing teeth; others were without noses or ears...'[57]

All the while, armed companies went house to house, torturing people into revealing the whereabouts of their valuables. Noblemen were forced to empty cesspits with their bare hands to reveal whether they had stashed any booty in the sewage. Some had their noses cut off. Others were force-fed their own genitals. For the invaders, it was all too easy. 'The Romans were surprised, sacked, and slaughtered with incredible ease and enormous profit,' wrote Guicciardini. He was right.

Only slowly did the Romans' torments start to ease. The terrors of the sack lasted for around ten days, and even after this, Rome was still an occupied city. The pope and his circle remained barricaded in the Castel Sant'Angelo for a month, only negotiating their safety on 7 June, at the price of 400,000 ducats. Even then, although most of those who had been cooped up in the fortress were allowed to leave, Clement himself was forced to stay there for his own safety. He was only released in early December – under the cover of darkness, for fear of enraging the rank and file of the occupying army. By this time around eight thousand Romans had been killed by the rampaging imperial troops. And perhaps twice as many again had died from other causes: disease scythed through the Roman population, spread by the invading army and the squalid conditions of a broken city.[58]

This was undoubtedly, the nadir of Clement's papacy. And although he was personally safe, he was forever after under Charles V's thumb. The emperor had been delighted almost beyond measure when the first news of the sack reached his court: one observer said Charles laughed so much that he had hardly been able to eat his supper.[59] The pope was his. Italy might follow. Although there would be many serious challenges throughout the rest of his long reign, this was a defining, generation-shaping achievement. On 22 February 1530 Charles appeared in Bologna and Pope Clement crowned him with the Iron Crown of Lombardy, first seized for the empire so many centuries earlier by Charlemagne. Two days later, on his thirtieth birthday, Charles was officially crowned as Holy Roman Emperor. He paraded around the city with Clement at his side. A wonderful new decade – indeed, a new era – stretched out before him.

THE SACK OF ROME IN 1527 had important consequences, many of which remain with us today. In England it is best known because it derailed King Henry VIII's plans to annul his marriage to Queen Catherine of Aragon. Henry's ministers submitted the request for papal dispensation to divorce while Clement was languishing under effective house arrest in Rome in the autumn of 1527; since Catherine was Charles' aunt, there was no way the request could be granted. As a result, a bull-headed Henry charged down another, far more destructive path: as we have already seen, he withdrew England from the Roman Church, announced his own supremacy in matters of both Church and state and allowed Lutheranism into a realm where previously it had been forbidden. A page was turned in English – and eventually, British and Irish – history and Henry's reign still marks the boundary between the medieval and early modern worlds.

But of course, England was only one part of the story. There were serious consequences all over the west. In Italy, Rome lay half-ruined, its population literally decimated. Any dreams of a united and independent Italy, which had been current in some quarters in the 1530s, now drifted away, not to be revived until the Risorgimento of the nineteenth century. Meanwhile, the peninsula's appeal as a hub for Renaissance artists lay in tatters. It could be argued with long hindsight that the height of the Italian Renaissance passed when Raphael died in 1520 (although Michelangelo was still working in the Sistine Chapel in the 1540s); but the psychological and financial trauma of the sack certainly helped ensure that there was not another late flourish of this wonderful movement. The Spanish, by contrast, were ascendant – and the combination of their swaggering progress through the New World and the Old, along with the formal unification of the Aragonese and Castilian crowns, launched a new golden age on the Iberian peninsula. It was eventually personified by Charles V's son and successor, Philip II, under whose patronage Madrid and the grand palace of El Escorial became the beating heart of European sophistication.

The French, for their part, confounded by events in 1527 and looking for a new partner against the empire, moved towards an alliance with the Ottoman empire. To be sure, that would have astonished generations of medieval French crusaders. Yet it was symbolic of a coming age. The Franco-Ottoman alliance, spawned at the end of the Middle Ages, endured from the mid-sixteenth century until the reign of Napoleon, and it ensured that the Balkans and eastern Europe, up to the borders of Austria, would feel the gravitational pull of Constantinople until the eve of the First World War. Meanwhile, conciliation with the world's leading Islamic power was not the only legacy of the events of 1527 in France. The religious fallout was just as significant. For in the aftermath of Rome's fall, a growing reform movement flourished from the 1530s onwards, spurred by homegrown reformers like John Calvin. By mid-century, groups of Protestants known as Huguenots began to pose serious problems for the French crown, and tensions eventually erupted in the French Wars of Religion, which were fought from the 1560s until the 1590s, cost tens of thousands of lives, and left religious wounds in French society that were still bleeding in the eighteenth century.

Theologically, of course, the sack of Rome had a profound effect on the Catholic Church. Charles V had wished for some time to hold an ecumenical council to decide on a Church-wide strategy for combating Lutheran heresies and the burgeoning Reformation. With the papacy at his command, he eventually had his way. The painfully drawn-out Council of Trent, convened in several sessions between 1545 and 1563, fundamentally restated and redrew the doctrine of the Catholic Church in a form that lasted for 300 years. Much overdue reform was enacted – indulgences were not banned, but their sale was eventually forbidden in 1567. Yet Trent also made it very clear that there could be no reconciliation with the Protestants. So the schism in the western Church which endures to this day was complete – and although neither Luther (who died in 1546) nor Charles (who followed him in 1558) lived to see this confirmed, they and their overlapping bands of supporters had played a fundamental role in ensuring that it was so. It is to their struggles that we must trace the fact that today one-eighth of the world's population – more than 900 million people – are members of a Protestant congregation.[60]

Of course, all this represents only the barest of summaries of the world that was emerging as imperial troops slunk away from the bloodied streets of Rome in 1527. To go any further with it would be to burst the banks of this already voluminous book. But I hope that this, along with the chapters that have gone before, should be sufficient for us to see that by the 1530s, the western world was no longer recognizably medieval. The rise of the printed word, encounters with the New World, the collapse and fracture of the Church militant, the demographic rearrangements caused by waves of the Black Death, the humanistic and artistic revolutions of the Renaissance – all these things and more had recast the shape and feel of the west, in ways that contemporaries explicitly recognized, even as the process was taking place. The Middle Ages did not exactly die on the streets of Rome in 1527 – but afterwards, it was very clear that something had been lost, and was never coming back.

Living in the early twenty-first century, in the midst of our own time of epochal global change, we may recognize a little of this. Our world is also being recast around us, through the combination of a changing global climate, pandemic diseases, technological progress, a revolution in communication and publishing, rapid and uncontrollable mass migration, and a reformation in cultural values centred on the celebration of the individual. Is it possible that we not only can be interested in, but may even sympathize with, the people who lived through the topsy-turvy Middle Ages? Or would that be unhistorical? I shall leave the answer up to you. For it is now late. I have written a lot, and it is time to go. Martin Luther put it well, in the conclusion to a letter he composed in 1530, while hiding from Charles V at a secret location he named only as the Wilderness.

'This is getting too long… more another time,' he wrote. 'Forgive this long letter… Amen.'[61]

NOTES

Introduction

1 The Oxford English Dictionary traces the first use of the word 'medieval' (initially spelled 'mediæval') to 1817.

2 See, for example, Olstein, Diego, '"Proto-globalization" and "Proto-glocalizations" in the Middle Millennium', in Kedar, Benjamin Z. and Wiesner-Hanks, Merry E. *The Cambridge World History V: State Formations* (Cambridge: 2015).

3 Wickham, Chris, *The inheritance of Rome: A history of Europe from 400 to 1000* (London: 2010).

4 Much exciting research on the Middle Ages outside Europe is published in the relatively new *Journal of Medieval Worlds*. For its mission statement, Frankopan, Peter, 'Why we need to think about the global Middle Ages', *Journal of Medieval Worlds* I (2019), pp. 5–10.

Chapter 1

1 Around 40kgs, if wooden chest and treasure are included together. Johns, Catherine, *The Hoxne Late Roman Treasure: Gold Jewellery and Silver Plate* (London: 2010), p. 201.

2 de la Bédoyère, Guy, *Roman Britain: A New History* (revd. edn.) (London: 2013), pp. 226–7. Mattingly, David, *An Imperial Possession: Britain in the Roman Empire* (London: 2006), pp. 294–5. Another historian estimates the price of a slave in today's terms as 'about that of a new car'. Woolf, Greg, *Rome: An Empire's Story* (Oxford: 2012), p. 91.

3 Johns, *The Hoxne Late Roman Treasure*, pp. 168–9.

4 On the soil, ibid., p. 9.

5 Hamilton, Walter (trans.) and Wallace-Hadrill (intro.), *Ammianus Marcellinus / The Later Roman Empire (A.D. 354–378)* (London, 1986) pp. 45–6.

6 The continuity of the concept of Rome as everlasting is summarized usefully by Pratt, Kenneth J., 'Rome as Eternal', *Journal of the History of Ideas* 26 (1965), pp. 25–44.

7 West, David (trans. and ed.), *Virgil / The Aeneid* (revd. edn.) (London: 2003), 1.279, p. 11.

8 De Sélincourt, Aubrey (trans.), *Livy / The Early History of Rome*, (revd. edn.), (London: 2002), p. 122.

9 *Ammianus Marcellinus*, p. 46.

10 Gibbon, Edward, *The History of the Decline and Fall of the Roman Empire: Abridged Edition* (London: 2000), p. 9.

11 The best example of volcanic activity prompting political and social crises around the world is the eruption of the Tambora volcano in Indonesia in April 1815. See Oppenheimer, Clive, 'Climatic, environmental and human consequences of the largest known historic eruption: Tambora volcano (Indonesia) 1815', *Progress in Physical Geography: Earth and Environment* 27 (2003), pp. 230–59.

12 Ibid. pp. 44–9.

13 Graves, Robert (trans.) Rives J. B. (rev. and intro), *Suetonius / The Twelve Caesars* (London, 2007), pp. 15, 3.

14 This description follows Suetonius: ibid. pp. 88–9.

15 Church, Alfred John and Brodribb, William Jackson (trans.), Lane Fox, Robin (intro.), *Tacitus / Annals and Histories* (New York: 2009), pp. 9–10.

16 Graves, *Suetonius / Twelve Caesars*, p. 59.

17 *Aeneid*, VI. 851–54. This translation West, *Virgil / The Aeneid* p. 138.

18 Waterfield, Robin (trans.), *Polybius / The Histories* (Oxford: 2010), pp. 398–399.

19 *Tacitus / Annals and Histories*, p. 648.

20 Ibid. pp. 653–4.

21 Luttwak, Edward N., *The Grand Strategy of the Roman Empire: From the First Century A.D. to the Third* (Baltimore/London: 1976), p. 3.

22 The text of Claudius' speech is preserved on a bronze plaque in the city of Lyon; a detailed account, including senatorial grumbling, is in *Tacitus / Annals and Histories*, pp. 222–4.

23 For a concise discussion of citizenship in the context of identity, Woolf, *Rome: An Empire's Story* pp. 218–229; in the context of social hierarchy, Garnsey, Peter and Saller, Richard, *The Roman Empire: Economy, Society and Culture* 2nd edn. (London/New York: 2014), pp. 131–149.

24 Johnson, Allan Chester, Coleman-Norton, Paul R and Bourne, Frank Card (eds.), *Ancient Roman Statutes: A Translation With Introduction, Commentary, Glossary, and Index* (Austin: 1961), p. 226.

25 Bodel, John, 'Caveat emptor: Towards a Study of Roman Slave Traders', *Journal of Roman Archaeology* 18 (2005), p. 184.

26 On the worldwide context of Roman slavery, Hunt, Peter, 'Slavery' in Benjamin, Craig (ed.), *The Cambridge World History vol. 4: A World with States, Empires and Networks,*

1200BCE–900CE (Cambridge: 2015), pp. 76–100.

27 *Leviticus* 25:44.

28 Hornblower, Simon, Spawforth, Anthony, Eidinow, Esther (eds.) *The Oxford Classical Dictionary* (4th ed) (Oxford: 2012), p. 1375.

29 Trimble, Jennifer, 'The Zoninus Collar and the Archaeology of Roman Slavery', *American Journal of Archaeology* 120 (2016), pp. 447–8.

30 Kenney, E.J. (trans.), *Apuleius / The Golden Ass* (revd. edn.) (London: 2004), p. 153.

31 Jones, Horace Leonard (trans.), *The Geography of Strabo* vol. VI (Cambridge, Mass: 1929), pp. 328–9.

32 This translation Harper, Kyle, *Slavery in the Late Roman World, AD 275–425* (Cambridge: 2011), pp. 35–6.

33 Harper, *Slavery in the Late Roman World*, p. 33.

34 Richardson, John, 'Roman Law in the Provinces' in Johnston, David (ed.), *The Cambridge Companion to Roman Law* (Cambridge: 2015), pp. 52–3.

35 Rudd, Niall (trans.), *Cicero / The Republic, and The Laws* (Oxford: 1998), p. 69.

36 Radice, Betty (trans.), *The Letters of the Younger Pliny* (London: 1969), 10.96, 293–5.

37 Williamson, G.A. (trans.), *Eusebius / The History of the Church* (revd. edn.) (London: 1989), p. 265.

38 MacCulloch, Diarmaid, *A History of Christianity* (London: 2009), p. 196.

39 Hammond, Martin (trans.) *Marcus Aurelius / Meditations* (London: 2014), p. 48.

Chapter 2

1 *Ammianus Marcellinus*, p. 410.

2 Ridley, Ronald T. (trans.), *Zosimus / New History* (Sydney: 2006), p. 79.

3 Bettenson, Henry (trans.), *Saint Augustine / City of God* (London: 2003), pp. 43–4.

4 *Ammianus Marcellinus*, p. 410.

5 For detail on early Hunnic political organization see Kim, Hyun Jin, *The Huns* (London/New York: 2016), pp. 12–36. For a more skeptical view of links between Xiongnu and the fourth-century Huns than is presented here and elsewhere, see Heather, Peter, *The Fall of the Roman Empire: A New History of Rome and the Barbarians* (Oxford: 2006), pp. 148–9.

6 De la Vaissière, Étienne, 'The Steppe World and the Rise of the Huns' in Maas, Michael (ed.), *The Cambridge Companion to The Age of Attila* (Cambridge: 2014), pp. 179–80.

7 De la Vaissière, Étienne, *Sogdian Traders: A History* (Leiden: 2005), pp. 43–4.

8 *Ammianus Marcellinus*, pp. 411–2.

9 Ibid.

10 Cook, Edward R. 'Megadroughts, ENSO, and the Invasion of Late-Roman Europe by the Huns and Avars' in Harris, William V. (ed.), *The Ancient Mediterranean Environment between Science and History* (Leiden: 2013), pp. 89–102. See also Wang, Xiaofeng, Yang, Bao and Ljungqvist, Fredrik Charpentier, 'The Vulnerability of Qilian Juniper to Extreme Drought Events', *Frontiers in Plant Science* 10 (2019) doi: 10.3389/fpls.2019.01191.

11 Letter quoted in Reeve, Benjamin, *Timothy Richard, D.D., China Missionary, Statesman and Reformer* (London: 1912), p. 54.

12 *Zosimus*, p. 79.

13 *Ammianus Marcellinus*, p. 416.

14 Ibid. p. 417.

15 For this argument see Halsall, Guy, *Barbarian Migrations and the Roman West 376–568* (Cambridge: 2007), pp. 172–5.

16 *Ammianus Marcellinus*, p. 418.

17 Ibid. p. 423.

18 Ibid. pp. 424–5.

19 Ibid. p. 433.

20 Ibid. p. 434.

21 Ibid. p. 435.

22 A measured estimate of numbers on both sides can be found in Heather, *The Fall of the Roman Empire*, p. 181.

23 *Ammianus Marcellinus*, p. 435.

24 Ibid. pp. 435–6.

25 Ibid. p. 437.

26 This weather report is via St Ambrose, whose funeral oration for Theodosius attributed the rains and darkness that accompanied the emeror's death as a sign that the universe itself was grieving. See McCauley, Leo. P. et al, *Funeral Orations by Saint Gregory and Saint Ambrose (The Fathers of the Church, Volume 22)* (Washington: 2010), p. 307.

27 Platnauer, Maurice (trans.), *Claudian / Volume II (Book 1)* (New York, 1922), p. 367.

28 Compare, for example the narratives presented in Heather, *The Fall of the Roman Empire*, pp. 203–5 with Kim, *The Huns*, pp. 76–7.

29 *Zosimus*, p. 113.

30 Ibid.

31 Some scholars dispute this date, preferring to place this invasion in 405, which would make it coincidental with Radagaisus' attack on the Italian peninsula. See Kulikowski, Michael, 'Barbarians in Gaul, Usurpers in Britain', *Britannia* 31 (2000), pp. 325–345.

32 Fremantle, W.H. (trans.) *Saint Jerome / Select Letters and Works* (New York: 1893), p. 537.

33 For Orientius, see Halsall, *Barbarian Migrations*, p. 215.

34 *Claudian / Volume II (Book 2)*, p. 173.

35 *Non est ista pax sed pactio servitutis* – recorded by *Zosimus*, p. 114.

36 *Zosimus*, p. 117.

37 *Zosimus*, p. 125.

38 *Livy / The Early History of Rome*, p. 419.

39 Kneale, Matthew, *A History of Rome in Seven Sackings* (London: 2017), p. 24.

40 *Saint Jerome / Select Letters and Works*, p. 577; cf. *Psalms* 79.

41 Winterbottom, Michael (trans.), *Gildas / The Ruin of Britain and other works* (Chichester: 1978), pp. 23–4.

42 *Gildas*, p. 28.

43 *Gildas*, p. 28.

44 *Gildas*, p. 28.

45 *Gildas*, p. 29.

46 Dewing, H.B. (trans.), *Procopius / History of the Wars*, vol. 2 (Cambridge, Mass.: 1916), pp. 30–33.

47 Weiskotten, Herbert T. (trans.), *The Life of Augustine: A Translation of the Sancti Augustini Vita by Possidius, Bishop of Calama* (Merchantville, NJ., 2008), pp. 44–56.

48 For recent scholarship on Vandal north Africa, see the essays collected in Merrills, A. H. (ed.), *Vandals, Romans and Berbers: New Perspectives on Late Antique North Africa* (Abingdon: 2016), esp. pp. 49–58.

49 *Procopius / History of the Wars* vol. 2, pp. 46–9.

50 For a discussion of Quovultdeus' rhetoric and its religious and political context, see Vopřada, David, 'Quodvultdeus' Sermons on the Creed: a Reassessment of his Polemics against the Jews, Pagans, and Arians', *Vox Patrum* 37 (2017), pp. 355–67.

51 See Cameron, Averil et al (eds.), *The Cambridge Ancient History XIV: Late Antiquity, Empire and Successors, A.D. 425–600* (Cambridge: 2000), p. 554.

52 Procopius, *History of the Wars*, vol. 2, pp. 256–57.

53 Mierow, Charles C., *Jordanes / The Origin and deeds of the Goths*. (Princeton University doctoral thesis, 1908), p. 57.

54 Kelly, Christopher, *Attila the Hun: Barbarian Terror and the Fall of the Roman Empire* (London: 2008), p. 189.

55 Kelly, Christopher, 'Neither Conquest nor Settlement: Attila's Empire and its Impact' in Maas, Michael (ed.), *The Age of Attila* (Cambridge: 2015), p. 195.

56 Lenski, Noel, 'Captivity among the Barbarians and its Impact on the Fate of the Roman Empire' in Maas, Michael (ed.), *The Age of Attila* (Cambridge: 2015), p. 234

57 Ibid. p. 237.

58 Cameron, Averil et al (eds.), *The Cambridge Ancient History XIV: Late Antiquity, Empire and Successors, A.D. 425–600* (Cambridge: 2000), p. 15.

59 Brehaut, Earnest (trans.), *Gregory bishop of Tours / History of the Franks*, (New York: 1916), pp. 33–4.

60 Sarti, Laury, *Perceiving War and the Military in Early Christian Gaul (ca. 400–700 A.D.)*, (Leiden: 2013), p. 187.

61 Robinson, James Harvey, *Readings in European History*. Vol 1. (Boston: 1904), p. 51.

62 Given, John (trans.), *The Fragmentary History of Priscus: Attila, the Huns and the Roman Empire, AD 430–476* (Merchantville: 2014), p. 127.

63 Ibid. p. 129.

64 Robinson, George W. (trans.), *Eugippius / The Life of Saint Severinus* (Cambridge, Mass.: 1914), pp. 45–6.

65 Mariev, Sergei (trans.), *Ioannis Antiocheni Fragmenta quae supersunt Omnia* (Berlin: 2008), p. 445.

66 Heather, Peter, *The Goths* (Oxford: 1996), p. 221.

67 Watts, Victor (trans.), *Boethius / The Consolation of Philosophy* (revd. edn.) (London: 1999), pp. 23–24.

Chapter 3

1 Chabot, J-B (trans.), *Chronique de Michel le Syrien, patriarche jacobite d'Antioche, 1166–1199*, vol. 2 (Paris: 1901), pp. 235–8. Also see Witakowski, Witold (trans.), *Pseudo-Dionysius of Tel-Mahre, Chronicle (known also*

as the *Chronicle of Zuqnin) part III*
(Liverpool: 1996), pp. 74–101.

2 *Jeremiah* 9:21.

3 Cf. *Deuteronomy* 8:20.

4 Dewing, H. B. (trans.), *Procopius / History of the Wars, Books I and II* (London: 1914), pp. 455–6.

5 Keller, Marcel, et al., 'Ancient Yersinia pestis genomes from across Western Europe reveal early diversification during the First Pandemic (541–750)', *Proceedings of the National Academy of Sciences* 116 (2019). See also Wiechmann, I and Grupe, G, 'Detection of Yersinia pestis DNA in two early medieval skeletal finds from Aschheim (Upper Bavaria, 6th century A.D.)', *American Journal of Physical Anthropology* 126 (2005), pp. 48–55.

6 Moderchai, Lee and Eisenberg, Merle, 'Rejecting Catastrophe: The Case of the Justinianic Plague', *Past & Present* 244 (2019), pp. 3–50.

7 Procopius, *The Secret History*, p. 36.

8 Cisson, C.H. (trans), *Dante Alighieri, The Divine Comedy* (revd. edn.) (Oxford: 1993), *Paradiso*, 5.130–139.

9 Jeffreys, Elizabeth, Jeffreys, Michael and Scott, Roger, *The Chronicle of John Malalas* (Leiden: 1986), p. 245.

10 Williamson, G. A. and Sarris, Peter (trans.), *Procopius / The Secret History* (revd. edn.) (London: 2007), pp. 33–5.

11 *The Chronicle of John Malalas*, pp. 254–5.

12 *Procopius / The Secret History* pp. 37–9.

13 Moyle, John Baron (trans.), *The Institutes of Justinian* (Oxford: 1906), p. 1.

14 For more on what follows, see Johnston, David (ed.) *The Cambridge Companion to Roman Law* (New York: 2015), pp. 119–48, 356–7 and 374–95.

15 Dewing, H. B. (trans.), *Procopius, On Buildings* (Cambridge, Mass.: 1940), pp. 7–8.

16 Kelley, Donald R., 'What Pleases the Prince: Justinian, Napoleon and the Lawyers', *History of Political Thought* 23 (2002), p. 290.

17 An accessible guide to the context and broad course of this dispute can be found in MacCulloch, *A History of Christianity*, pp. 222–8

18 *The Chronicle of John Malalas*, pp. 253.

19 The chronology of this process is concisely sketched in Constantelos, Demetrios J., 'Paganism and the State in the Age of Justinian', *The Catholic Historical Review* 50 (1964), pp. 372–380.

20 *The Chronicle of John Malalas*, p. 264. For a full discussion of what exactly Malalas meant by this, and the context in which he reported it, see Watts, Edward, 'Justinian, Malalas, and the End of Athenian Philosophical Teaching in A.D. 529', *The Journal of Roman Studies* 94 (2004), pp. 168–182.

21 On the survival of Neoplatonism in Byzantium, see Blumenthal, H. J., '529 and its sequel: What happened to the Academy?', *Byzantion* 48 (1978), pp. 369–385, and Watts, Edward, 'Justinian, Malalas, and the End of Athenian Philosophical Teaching in A.D. 529', *The Journal of Roman Studies* 94 (2004), pp. 168–182.

22 The two most important English-language articles on Justinian, the Hippodrome factions and the Nika riot are Bury, J. B, 'The Nika Riot', *The Journal of Hellenic Studies* 17 (1897), pp. 92–119, and Greatrex, Geoffrey, 'The Nika Riot: A Reappraisal', *The Journal of Hellenic Studies* 117 (1997), pp. 60–86.

23 The dissatisfactions of imperial aristocrats may have played a part in stirring the disorder – some of their alleged complaints are repeated in *Procopius / The Secret History*, pp. 51, 80.

24 *Procopius, History of the Wars, I Books 1–2*, pp. 224–5

25 *The Chronicle of John Malalas*, pp. 277–8.

26 *Procopius, History of the Wars, I Books 1–2*, pp. 230–1.

27 *The Chronicle of John Malalas*, p. 280.

28 *Procopius / On Buildings*, p. 12.

29 Downey, G., 'Byzantine Architects: Their Training and Methods', *Byzantion* 18 (1946–8), p. 114.

30 *Procopius / On Buildings*, p. 13.

31 Swift, Emerson H., 'Byzantine Gold Mosaic', *American Journal of Archaeology* 38 (1934), pp. 81–2.

32 Magdalino, Paul et al, 'Istanbul' in *Grove Art Online* (published online 2003), https://doi.org/10.1093/gao/9781884446054.article.T042556 III.1

33 Cross, Samuel Hazzard and Sherbowitz-Wetzor, Olgerd P. (trans.), *The Russian Primary Chronicle: Laurentian Text* (Cambridge, Mass.: 1953), p. 111.

34 Dewing, H. B. (trans.), *Procopius / History of the Wars, II, Books 3–4* (Cambridge, Mass.: 1916), pp. 88–91.

35 A concise recent narrative is in Merrills, Andy and Miles, Richard, *The Vandals* (Oxford: 2010) pp. 228–33.

36 *Procopius / History of the Wars, II, Books 3–4*, pp. 178–9.

37 *Procopius / History of the Wars, II, Books 3–4*, p. 267.

38 *Procopius / History of the Wars, II, Books 3–4*, pp. 282–3.

39 *Ecclesiastes*, 1:2.

40 *Procopius / History of the Wars, II, Books 3–4*, p. 329.

41 On Ilopango, see Dull, Robert A. et al, 'Radiocarbon and geologic evidence reveal Ilopango volcano as source of the colossal 'mystery' eruption of 539/40 CE', *Quaternary Science Reviews* 222 (2019), accessed online https://doi.org/10.1016/j.quascirev.2019.07.037

42 *Procopius / History of the Wars, II, Books 3–4*, p. 329.

43 This case is made strongly by Harper, *The Fate of Rome*, p. 232.

44 Ibid. pp. 234–5.

45 *Procopius / The Secret History*, pp. 123.

46 Dewing, H.B. (trans.), *Procopius / History of the Wars, V, Books 7.36–8*, (Cambridge, Mass.: 1928), pp. 374–75.

47 *Procopius / On Buildings*, pp. 34–7.

Chapter 4

1 Much of the putative chronology followed below draws on Donner, Fred M., *The Early Islamic Conquests* (Princeton: 1981), pp. 111–55, which discusses the numerous possible reconstructions of events.

2 For this physical description, see Blankinship, Khalid Yahya (trans.), *The History of al-Tabari Vol. XI: The Challenge to the Empires* (New York: 1993), pp. 138, 152.

3 Blankinship, *al-Tabari XI*, pp. 113–4; also see Donner, *Early Islamic Conquests*, pp. 121–2.

4 Kennedy, Hugh, *The Great Arab Conquests* (London: 2007), pp. 79–80 reconciles them; see also Donner, *Early Islamic Conquests*, p. 131.

5 Blankinship, *al-Tabari XI*, p. 160.

6 Wallace-Hadrill, J.M. (trans.), *The Fourth Book of the Chronicle of Fredegar, with its continuations* (Westport: 1960), p. 55.

7 *al-Tabari XI*, pp. 87–8.

8 *The Fourth Book of the Chronicle of Fredegar*, p. 55.

9 Hoyland, Robert G., *In God's Path: The Arab Conquests and the Creation of an Islamic Empire* (Oxford: 2015), p. 45.

10 Holum, Kenneth G., 'Archaeological Evidence for the Fall of Byzantine Caesarea', *Bulletin of the American Schools of Oriental Research* 286 (1992), pp. 73–85.

11 Hoyland, *In God's Path*, p. 45.

12 Bowersock, G. W., *The Crucible of Islam* (Cambridge, Mass., 2017), pp. 48–9.

13 Donner, *Early Islamic Conquests*, pp. 51–2.

14 For this tradition, and a more general 'traditional' history of Mecca and Muhammad, see Lings, Martin, *Muhammad: his life based on the earliest sources* (Cambridge: 1991), p. 3.

15 Bowersock, *Crucible of Islam*, pp. 50–1.

16 Lings, *Muhammad*, p. 26.

17 *Genesis* 16:12. For commentary, see Hilhorst, Anthony, 'Ishmaelites, Hagarenes, Saracens', Goodman, Martin, van Kooten, George H. and van Buiten, JTAGM (eds.), *Abraham, the Nations, and the Hagarites Jewish, Christian, and Islamic Perspectives on Kinship with Abraham* (Leiden: 2010).

18 Hoyland, *In God's Path*, p. 94.

19 Juynboll, Gautier H. A. (trans.), *The History of al-Tabari vol. XIII: The Conquest of Iraq, Southwestern Persia and Egypt* (New York: 1989), p. 7.

20 Ibid. p. 27.

21 Ibid. p. 189.

22 Hoyland, *In God's Path*, pp. 96–7.

23 Fishbein, Michael (trans.), *The History of al-Tabari vol. VIII: The Victory of Islam* (New York: 1997), pp. 35–6.

24 Friedmann, Yohanan (trans.), *The History of al-Tabari vol. XII: The Battle of al-Qadisiyyah and the Conquest of Syria and Palestine* (New York: 1991), pp. 127–8.

25 *The Hadith* (pp. Sahih Bukhari, Vol. 4, Book 52, Hadith 46).

26 *The Hadith* (pp. Sahih Bukhari, Vol. 5, Book 57, Hadith 50).

27 Humphreys, R. Stephen (trans.), *The History of al-Tabari, vol. XV: The Crisis of the Early Caliphate*, (New York: 1990), pp. 252–3.

28 Ibid. pp. 207–11.

29 For a convenient narrative, Hinds, Martin, 'The Murder of the Caliph 'Uthman', *International Journal of Middle East Studies* 3 (1972), pp. 450–469.

30 *al-Tabari XV*, p. 216.

31 Ettinghausen, Richard, Grabar, Oleg, and Jenkins-Madina, Marilyn, *Islamic Art and Architecture 650–1250* (2nd edn.) (New Haven/London: 2001), pp. 15–20.

32 Grabar, Oleg, *The Dome of the Rock* (Cambridge, Mass., 2006), pp. 1–3.

33 Mango, Cyril and Scott, Roger (trans.), *The Chronicle of Theophanes Confessor: Byzantine and Near Eastern History AD 284–813* (Oxford: 1997), pp. 493.

34 Ibid. pp. 493–4. On the names and changing formula of 'Greek Fire', Roland, Alex, 'Secrecy, Technology, and War: Greek Fire and the Defense of Byzantium, 678–1204', *Technology and Culture* 33 (1992), pp. 655–679 and esp. p. 657.

35 Ibid. p. 494.

36 Ibid. p. 548.

37 Ibid. p. 550.

38 *al-Tabari XV*, p. 281–7. See also Kaeigi, Walter, *Muslim Expansion and Byzantine Collapse in North Africa* (Cambridge: 2010), p. 260.

39 Wolf, Kenneth Baxter, *Conquerors and chroniclers of early medieval Spain*, (Liverpool: 1990), p. 132.

40 Ibid., p. 132.

41 Grierson, Philip, 'The Monetary Reforms of 'Abd al-Malik: Their Metrological Basis and Their Financial Repercussions', *Journal of the Economic and Social History of the Orient* 3 (1960), pp. 16–7.

42 On this area see also Bates, Michael L., 'The Coinage of Syria Under the Umayyads, 692–750 A.D.' in Donner, Fred M., *The Articulation of Early Islamic State Structures* (London: 2017).

43 Surah 17:35.

44 Ettinghausen and Jenkins-Madina, *Islamic Art and Architecture, 650–1250*, pp. 24–6.

45 Jones, John Harris (trans.), *Ibn Abd al-Hakam / The History of the Conquest of Spain* (New York: 1969), p. 33.

46 For the legend of St Martin, see Ryan, William Granger (trans.) and Duffy, Eamon (intro), *Jacobus de Voragine, The Golden Legend: Readings on the Saints* (Princeton and Oxford: 2012), pp. 678–686.

47 According to Gregory of Tours, the Merovingian-era basilica – now long vanished – was '160 feet long and 60 wide and 45 high to the vault; it has 32 windows in the part around the altar, 20 in the nave; 41 columns; in the whole building 52 windows, 120 columns; 8 doors, three in the part around the altar and five in the nave.' *Gregory bishop of Tours / History of the Franks*, p. 38.

48 *The Fourth Book of the Chronicle of Fredegar*, pp. 90–1.

49 Stearns Davis, William (ed.), *Readings in Ancient History: Illustrative Extracts from the Sources*, II (Boston: 1913) pp. 362–364.

50 Sherley-Price, Leo (trans.), *Bede / A History of the English Church and People* (revd. ed) (Harmondsworth: 1968), p. 330.

51 Womersley, David (ed.), *Edward Gibbon / The History of the Decline and Fall of the Roman Empire*, vol. III (London: 1996), p. 336.

52 *The Occidental Quarterly* can be quickly found online via a Google search, but I have decided not to give a full reference here to this wretched publication.

Chapter 5

1 Ganz, David (trans.), *Einhard and Notker the Stammerer: Two Lives of Charlemagne* (London: 2008), p. 19.

2 Wallace-Hadrill (ed.), *Chronicle of Fredegar*, p. 102.

3 Ailes, Marianne, 'Charlemagne "Father of Europe": A European Icon in the Making', *Reading Medieval Studies* 38 (2012), p. 59.

4 For a summary of Charlemagne's extraordinary and enduring appeal to would-be European titans, see McKitterick, Rosamond, *Charlemagne: The Formation of a European Identity* (Cambridge: 2008), pp. 1–5.

5 A point I first encountered in MacCulloch, *A History of Christianity*, p. 348.

6 A process which also supposedly provided the origins of the Turks and Macedonians. See Macmaster, Thomas J., 'The Origin of the Origins: Trojans, Turks and the Birth of the Myth of Trojan Origins in the Medieval World', *Atlantide* 2 (2014), pp. 1–12.

7 On the grave-goods see Brulet, Raymond, 'La sépulture du roi Childéric à Tournai et le site funéraire', in Vallet, Françoise and Kazanski, Michel (eds.), *La noblesse romaine et les chefs barbares du IIIe au VIIe siècle* (Paris: 1995), pp. 309–326.

8 Available in modern English translation: Fischer Drew, Katherine (trans.), *The Laws of the Salian Franks* (Philadelphia: 1991).

9 *Einhard and Notker the Stammerer*, p. 19.

10 Ibid.

11 Frankish Royal Annals. This translation: Dutton, Paul Edward, *Carolingian Civilization: A Reader* (2nd edn.) (Ontario: 2009), p. 12.

12 Aurell, Jaume, *Medieval Self-Coronations: The History and Symbolism of a Ritual* (Cambridge: 2020), pp. 128–30.

13 *Chronicle of Fredegar*, p. 104.

14 Davis, Raymond (trans.), *The Lives of the Eighth-Century Popes (Liber Pontificalis)* (Liverpool: 1992), p. 63.

15 Fried, Johannes, *Charlemagne* (Cambridge, Mass., 2016), p. 43. See also McKitterick, Rosamond (ed.),

The New Cambridge Medieval History II c. 700–c.900 (Cambridge: 1995), pp. 96–7.

16 *Chronicle of Fredegar*, p. 106.

17 Ibid. p. 120.

18 *Einhard and Notker the Stammerer*, pp. 34–6.

19 Notker's Deeds of Charlemagne in Ganz (trans.), *Einhard and Notker the Stammerer*, p. 109.

20 Costambys, Marios, Innes, Matthew and MacLean, Simon, *The Carolingian World* (Cambridge: 2011), pp. 67–8.

21 Collins, Roger, *Charlemagne* (Basingstoke: 1998), p. 62.

22 Ganz (trans.), *Einhard and Notker the Stammerer: Two Lives of Charlemagne*, p. 25.

23 Burgess, Glyn (trans.), *The Song of Roland* (London, 1990), p. 85.

24 Ibid. pp. 104–5.

25 Ganz (trans.), *Einhard and Notker the Stammerer: Two Lives of Charlemagne*, p. 36.

26 'Aachen' in *Grove Art Online* https://doi.org/10.1093/gao/9781884446054.article.T000002

27 See Fouracre, Paul, 'Frankish Gaul to 814' in McKitterick (ed.), *The New Cambridge Medieval History*, p. 106.

28 Dutton, *Carolingian Civilization: A Reader* (2nd edn.), pp. 92–5.

29 Ganz (trans.), *Einhard and Notker the Stammerer: Two Lives of Charlemagne*, p. 36.

30 Davis (trans.), *Lives of the Eighth-Century Popes*, pp. 185–6.

31 On this point, Fried, *Charlemagne*, p. 414.

32 Dümmler, Ernst (ed.), *Poetae latini aevi Carolini* I (Berlin: 1881), p. 379.

33 Davis, *Lives of the Eighth-Century Popes*, p. 188.

34 See Dümmler, Ernst, as above. This English translation, Dutton, *Carolingian Civilization: A Reader* (2nd edn.), p. 65.

35 Ganz (trans.), *Einhard and Notker the Stammerer: Two Lives of Charlemagne*, p. 38.

36 Ibid. p. 35 and Fried, *Charlemagne*, p. 425.

37 Ibid.

38 This translation, Dutton, *Carolingian Civilization: A Reader* (2nd edn.), pp. 146–7.

39 These portents were all recorded by Einhard. Ganz (trans.), *Einhard and Notker the Stammerer: Two Lives of Charlemagne*, p. 41.

40 Translation by Dutton, *Carolingian Civilization: A Reader* (2nd edn.), p. 157.

41 More than one historian suggests that it was the shame of not actually being mentioned in the *Ordinatio Imperii* that most goaded Bernard. See McKitterick, Rosamond, *The Frankish Kingdoms Under the Carolingians* (London/New York: 1983), p. 135.

42 The text of the *Ordinatio Imperii* of 817 is conveniently translated in Dutton, *Carolingian Civilization: A Reader* (2nd edn.), pp. 199–203.

43 Translated in ibid. p. 205

44 On the identification of Ragnar as Ragnar Lodbrok, see for example Price, Neil, *The Children of Ash and Elm: A History of the Vikings* (London: 2020), p. 344.

45 Ermentarius of Noirmoutier in Poupardin, René (ed.), *Monuments de l'histoire des Abbeyes de Saint-Philibert* (Paris: 1905), pp. 61–2.

46 Whitelock, Dorothy (ed.), *English Historical Documents I 500–1042* (2nd edn.) (London: 1979), pp. 775–7.

47 Poupardin (ed.), *Monuments de l'histoire des Abbeyes de Saint-Philibert*, pp. 61–2.

48 For a useful summary of, and bibliographical links to, the voluminous scholarship on the location of 'Thule', see McPhail, Cameron, Pytheas of Massalia's Route of Travel', *Phoenix* 68 (2014), pp. 252–4.

49 For an evocative recent description of this, Price, *The Children of Ash and Elm*, pp. 31–63. See also Ferguson, Robert, *The Hammer and the Cross: A New History of the Vikings* (London: 2009), pp. 20–40.

50 A summary and bibliography of the many proposed theses for Viking migration is Barrett, James H., 'What caused the Viking Age?', *Antiquity* 82 (2008), pp. 671–85.

51 Baug, Irene, Skre, Dagfnn, Heldal, Tom and Janse, Øystein J., 'The Beginning of the Viking Age in the West', *Journal of Maritime Archaeology* 14 (2019), pp. 43–80

52 DeVries, Kelly and Smith, Robert Douglas, *Medieval Military Technology* (2nd edn.) (Ontario: 2012), pp. 291–2.

53 Whitelock (ed.), *English Historical Documents I 500–1042* (2nd edn.), pp. 778–9.

54 Price, Neil, *The Children of Ash and Elm: A History of the Vikings*, pp. 438–9.

55 A modern English translation of the edict is Hill, Brian E., *Charles the Bald's 'Edict of Pîtres' (864): A Translation and Commentary* (Unpublished MA Thesis, University of Minnesota: 2013).

56 *Annals of St Vaast*, this translation from Robinson, James Harvey, *Readings in European History* vol 1. (Boston: 1904), p. 164.

57 Christiansen, Eric (trans.), *Dudo of St. Quentin / History of the Normans* (Woodbridge: 1998), p. 22.

58 Price, *Children of Ash and Elm*, p. 350.

59 *Annals of St Vaast*, p. 163.

60 Dass, Nirmal (trans.), *Viking Attacks on Paris: The Bella parisiacae Urbis of Abbo of Saint-Germain-des-Près* (Paris: 2007), pp. 34–5.

61 *Dudo of St. Quentin / History of the Normans*, pp. 28–9.

62 Ibid., p. 46.

63 Ibid., p. 49.

64 Price, *Children of Ash and Elm*, p. 497.

65 Licence, Tom, *Edward the Confessor* (New Haven/London: 2020), p. 48, and see n. 30.

Chapter 6

1 Smith, M. L., *The Early History of the Monastery of Cluny* (Oxford: 1920), p. 10.

2 Ibid., pp. 11–12.

3 Rosè, Isabella, 'Interactions between Monks and the Lay Nobility (from the Carolingian Era through the Eleventh Century)', in Beach, Alison I. and Cochelin, Isabelle (eds.), *The Cambridge History of Medieval Monasticism in the Latin West* I (Cambridge: 2020), esp. pp. 579–83.

4 Smith, *Early History of the Monastery of Cluny*, p. 14 n. 5.

5 *Matthew* 19:21.

6 Voraigne, Jacobus de, *The Golden Legend*, p. 93.

7 Ibid. p. 96.

8 Clark, James G., *The Benedictines in the Middle Ages* (Woodbridge: 2011), pp 8–9.

9 For a summary of the ascetic 'problem' at Chalcedon, see Helvétius, Anne-Marie and Kaplan, Michael, 'Asceticism and its institutions' in Noble, Thomas F. X. and Smith, Julia M. H., *The Cambridge History of Christianity III: Early Medieval Christianities c. 600–c.1100* (Cambridge: 2008), pp. 275–6.

10 Gardner, Edmund G. (ed.) *The Dialogues of Saint Gregory the Great* (Merchantville: 2010), p. 51.

11 Ibid., p. 99.

12 Fry, Timothy (trans.), *The Rule of St Benedict in English* (Collegeville: 2018), p. 15.

13 *The Dialogues of Saint Gregory the Great*, p. 99.

14 This translation, Coulton, C. G. (ed.), *Life in the Middle Ages* IV (Cambridge: 1930), p. 29.

15 Diem, Albrecht and Rousseau, Philip, 'Monastic Rules (Fourth to Ninth Century)', in Beach, Alison

I. and Cochelin, Isabelle (eds.), *The Cambridge History of Medieval Monasticism in the Latin West* I (Cambridge: 2020), pp. 181–2.

16 MacCulloch, *History of Christianity*, p. 354.

17 Cantor, Norman F., 'The Crisis of Western Monasticism, 1050–1130', *The American Historical Review* (1960), p. 48.

18 Sitwell, G. (trans.), *St. Odo of Cluny: being the Life of St. Odo of Cluny / by John of Salerno. And, the Life of St. Gerald of Aurillac by St. Odo* (London: 1958), p. 16.

19 Sherley-Price (trans.), *Bede / A History of the English Church and People*, p. 256

20 Ibid. p. 254.

21 See Morghen, Raffaello, 'Monastic Reform and Cluniac Spirituality', Hunt, Noreen (ed.), *Cluniac Monasticism in the Central Middle Ages* (London: 1971), pp. 18–19.

22 On new conversions, see Raaijmakers, Janneke, 'Missions on the Northern and Eastern Frontiers', Beach, Alison I. and Cochelin, Isabelle (eds.), *The Cambridge History of Medieval Monasticism in the Latin West* I (Cambridge: 2020), pp. 485–501 and Jamroziak, Emilia, 'East-Central European Monasticism: Between East and West?', ibid. II, pp. 882–900.

23 Clark, *The Benedictines in the Middle Ages*, pp. 53–4.

24 Zhou, TianJun, Li, Bo, Man, WenMin, Zhang, LiXia, and Zhang, Jie, 'A comparison of the Medieval Warm Period, Little Ice Age and 20th century warming simulated by the FGOALS climate system model', *Chinese Science Bulletin* 56 (2011), pp. 3028–3041.

25 A thesis fully developed by White, Jr., L., *Medieval Technology & Social Change* (Oxford: 1962), and recently strongly backed by Andersen, Thomas Barnebeck, Jensen, Peter

Sandholt and Skovsgaard, Christian Stejner, 'The heavy plough and the agricultural revolution in medieval Europe', *Discussion Papers of Business and Economics* (University of Southern Denmark, Department of Business and Economics: 2013).

26 One scholar has called this 'vying in good works'. See Moore, R. I. *The First European Revolution, c.970–1215* (Oxford: 2000), p. 75.

27 Smith, *Early History of the Monastery of Cluny*, pp. 143–6, drawing on the near-contemporary Jotsaldus' *Life of Odilo*.

28 For a succinct summary of building works at Cluny during this period, the starting point is Bolton, Brenda M. and Morrison, Kathryn 'Cluniac Order', *Grove Art Online*, https://doi.org/10.1093/gao/9781884446054.article.T018270

29 Fry, Timothy (ed.), *The Rule of St Benedict In English* (Collegeville: 2018), pp. 52–3.

30 On Benedictine music in general see Clark, *The Benedictines in the Middle Ages*, pp. 102–5.

31 Biay, Sébastien, 'Building a Church with Music: The Plainchant Capitals at Cluny, c. 1100', Boynton, S. and Reilly D. J. (eds.), *Resounding Image: Medieval Intersections of Art, Music, and Sound* (Turnhout: 2015), pp. 221–2.

32 Hunt, Noreen, *Cluny under Saint Hugh, 1049–1109* (London: 1967), p. 105.

33 King, Peter, *Western Monasticism: A History of the Monastic Movement in the Latin Church* (Kalamazoo: 1999), p. 128. See also Hunt, *Cluny under Saint Hugh*, pp. 101–3.

34 Shaver-Crandell, Annie and Gerson, Paula, *The Pilgrim's Guide to Santiago de Compostela: A Gazetteer with 580 Illustrations* (London: 1995), pp. 72–3.

35 Mullins, Edwin, *In Search of Cluny: God's Lost Empire* (Oxford: 2006), pp. 72–3.

36 Mabillon, Jean, *Annales Ordinis S. Benedicti Occidentalium Monachorum Patriarchæ vol. IV* (Paris, 1707), p. 562.

37 On the True Cross at Poitiers, see Hahn, Cynthia, 'Collector and saint: Queen Radegund and devotion to the relic of the True Cross', *Word & Image* 22 (2006), pp. 268–274.

38 Werkmeister, O. K., 'Cluny III and the Pilgrimage to Santiago de Compostela', *Gesta* 27 (1988), p. 105.

39 On this dream, Carty, Carolyn M., 'The Role of Gunzo's Dream in the Building of Cluny III', *Gesta* 27 (1988), pp. 113–123.

40 The Vitruvian proportions of Cluny III were first described by Conant, Kenneth J., 'The after-Life of Vitruvius in the Middle Ages', *Journal of the Society of Architectural Historians* 27 (1968), pp. 33–38.

41 Bolton and Morrison, 'Cluniac Order', *Grove Art Online*.

42 Mullins, *In Search of Cluny*, pp. 79–80.

43 Hunt, Noreen, *Cluny under Saint Hugh, 1049–1109* (London: 1967), pp. 145–6.

44 Mullins, *In Search of Cluny*, pp. 197–205.

45 Ibid. p. 221.

46 Canon 12 of the Fourth Lateran Council. The canons are printed and translated in full in Schroeder, H. J., *Disciplinary Decrees of the General Councils: Text, Translation and Commentary* (St. Louis: 1937), pp. 236–296.

47 Greenia, M. Conrad, *Bernard of Clairvaux / In Praise of the New Knighthood* (revd. edn.) (Trappist: 2000), p. 37.

Chapter 7

1 The specks of stardust, known as the Tears of St Lawrence, were caused by the earth passing through the tail of a comet. This insight comes from the essential source in English on the battle of Lechfeld: Bowlus, Charles R., *The Battle of Lechfeld and its Aftermath, August 955* (Aldershot: 2006). Much of what follows on Lechfeld is informed by Bowlus' reconstructed narrative of this complicated and strung-out battle, and on his translations of key contemporary sources, which are collected in his book's appendices.

2 *Widukind's Deeds of the Saxons*, trans. ibid. p. 180.

3 Ibid. pp. 181–2.

4 *Gerhard's Life of Bishop Ulrich of Augsburg*, translated in ibid. p. 176.

5 Ibid.

6 Ibid. p. 181.

7 Archer, Christon I., Ferris, John R., Herwig, Holger H. and Travers, Timothy H. E., *World History of Warfare* (Lincoln: 2002), pp. 136–7.

8 *Xenophon / On Horsemanship* 12.6

9 Hyland, Ann, *The Medieval Warhorse: From Byzantium to the Crusades* (London: 1994), p. 3.

10 Sewter, E. R. A (trans.), Frankopan, Peter (intro.), *Anna Komnene / The Alexiad* (revd. edn.) (London: 2009), p. 378.

11 Keen, Maurice, *Chivalry* (New Haven/London: 1984), p. 23

12 Hyland, *Medieval Warhorse*, p. 11.

13 See, for example, the copy of this wonderful document which is held at the British Library, shelfmark Add MS 11695, f.102 v. It can be viewed online at www.bl.uk/catalogues/illuminatedmanuscripts/record.asp?MSID=8157&CollID=27&NStart=11695

14 The Great Stirrup Controversy is essentially a debate over the thesis of Lynn White Jr., who argued in the 1960s that the arrival of the stirrup in medieval Europe not only changed the way people fought on horseback, but also brought about the rise of feudalism. For a brisk and useful historiographical discussion see

Kaeuper, Richard W., *Medieval Chivalry* (Cambridge: 2016), pp. 65–8.

15 Keen, *Chivalry*, p. 25.

16 Whether 'feudalism' or a 'feudal system' ever formally existed outside historians' minds is one of the greatest and most enduring debates in medieval history, which has been raging in its current form since the 1950s. The architect of the idea of a feudal 'revolution' was Georges Duby – see, for example, Duby, Georges, *The Chivalrous Society* (Berkeley: 1977); an important essay for understanding the demolition of the case is Brown, Elizabeth A. R., 'The Tyranny of a Construct: Feudalism and Historians of Medieval Europe', *The American Historical Review* 79 (1974), pp. 1063–88. For a more recent snapshot of the historiography of feudalism across Europe, see also the essays in Bagge, Sverre, Gelting, Michael H., and Lindkvist, Thomas (eds.), *Feudalism: New Landscapes of Debate* (Turnhout: 2011). For a local study focusing on north-west Europe, see West, Charles, *Reframing the Feudal Revolution: Political and Social Transformation between the Marne and the Moselle, c.800–c.1100* (Cambridge: 2013).

17 Christon et al, *World History of Warfare*, p. 146.

18 On Hungary, see Bak, Janos M., 'Feudalism in Hungary?', in Bagge, Gelting and Lindkvist (eds.), *Feudalism: New Landscapes of Debate*, pp. 209–12.

19 *Historia Roderici* translated in Barton, Simon and Fletcher, Richard, *The World of El Cid: Chronicles of the Spanish Reconquest* (Manchester: 2000), p. 99.

20 Ibid. p. 100.

21 Kaeuper, *Medieval Chivalry*, p. 69.

22 Ibid. p. 101.

23 Ibid.

24 Ibid. p. 109.

25 Ibid. pp. 111–2.

26 Ibid. p. 113.

27 Ibid. p. 117.

28 Ibid. p. 133.

29 Ibid. p. 136.

30 Ibid. p. 137.

31 Fletcher, Richard, *The Quest for El Cid* (Oxford: 1989), p. 172.

32 Barton and Fletcher, *World of El Cid*, p. 138.

33 *El Canto de mio Cid* lines 1722–26, translation via https://miocid.wlu.edu/

34 Fletcher, *The Quest for El Cid*, p. 174.

35 The Spanish–Arab poet Ibn Bassam, translated in ibid. p. 185.

36 Livesey, Edwina, 'Shock Dating Result: A Result of the Norman Invasion?', *Sussex Past & Present* 133 (2014), p. 6.

37 *Song of Roland*, p. 154

38 Ibid. ch. 245.

39 At the time of writing the most recent screen treatment of the Arthurian legends are Guy Ritchie's *King Arthur: Legend of the Sword* (2017) and Frank Miller and Tom Wheeler's Netflix series *Cursed* (2020).

40 Kibler, William W., *Chrétien de Troyes / Arthurian Romances* (revd. edn.) (London: 2001), pp. 382–3. This passage also inspires the first pages of Barber, Richard, *The Knight and Chivalry* (revd. edn.) (Woodbridge: 1995), p. 3.

41 E.g. Asbridge, Thomas, *The Greatest Knight: The Remarkable Life of William Marshal, the Power Behind Five English Thrones* (London: 2015), which is the current standard biography.

42 Holden, A. J. (ed.), Gregory, S. (trans.) and Crouch, D., *History of William Marshal* I (London: 2002), pp. 30–1.

43 Ibid. pp. 38–9.

44 Ibid.

45 Ibid. pp. 52–3.

46 Ibid. pp. 60–1.

47 Crouch, David, *Tournament* (London: 2005), p. 8.

48 Translated in Strickland, Matthew, *Henry the Young King* (New Haven/ London: 2016), p. 240.

49 *History of William Marshal* I, pp. 186–7.

50 Kibler (trans.), *Chrétien de Troyes / Arthurian Romances*, pp. 264–5.

51 Holden et al (eds.), *History of William Marshal* I, pp. 268–9, 276–277.

52 Ibid. pp. 448–9.

53 Holden et al (eds.), *History of William Marshal* II, pp. 60–3.

54 This translation Gillingham, J., 'The Anonymous of Béthune, King John and Magna Carta' in Loengard, J. S. (ed.), *Magna Carta and the England of King John* (Woodbridge: 2010), pp. 37–8.

55 Holden et al (eds.), *History of William Marshal* II, pp. 406–7.

56 Morris, Marc, *A Great and Terrible King: Edward I* (London: 2008), p. 164.

57 Ibid.

58 A vast subject, introduced well in the English context by Harriss, Gerald, *Shaping the Nation: England 1360–1461* (Oxford: 2005), pp. 136–86.

59 As advertised and surveyed exhaustively in Sainty, Guy Stair, Heydel-Mankoo, Rafal, *World Orders of Knighthood and Merit* (2 vols) (Wilmington: 2006).

60 Jones, Dan, 'Meet the Americans Following in the Footsteps of the Knights Templar', *Smithsonian* (July 2018), archived online at www.smithsonianmag.com/history/meet-americans-following-footsteps-knights-templar-180969344/.

Chapter 8

1 For a narrative of the battle of Manzikert, Haldon, John, *The Byzantine Wars* (Stroud: 2008), pp. 168–81.

2 For an outline of this topic, see Jones, Dan, *Crusaders: An Epic History of the Wars for the Holy Lands* (London: 2019), pp. 30–41. For a more detailed treatment, Morris, Colin, *The Papal Monarchy: The Western Church, 1050–1250* (Oxford: 1989).

3 See Cowdrey, H. E. J., 'The Peace and the Truce of God in the Eleventh Century', *Past & Present* 46 (1970), pp. 42–67.

4 The best account of the motivations for the First Crusade as a response to pleas from Byzantium is Frankopan, Peter, *The First Crusade: The Call From the East* (London: 2012).

5 This translation, Robinson, I. S., *Eleventh Century Germany: The Swabian Chronicles* (Manchester: 2008), p. 324.

6 Cowdrey, H. E. J. (trans.), *The Register of Pope Gregory: 1073–1085: An English Translation* (Oxford: 2002), pp. 50–1.

7 Ryan, Frances Rita and Fink, Harold S. (eds.), *Fulcher of Chartres: A History of the Expedition to Jerusalem, 1095–1127* (Knoxville: 1969), pp. 65–6.

8 Sweetenham, Carole (trans.), *Robert the Monk's History of the First Crusade: Historia Iherosolimitana* (Abingdon: 2016), p. 81.

9 See Chazan, Robert, *In the Year 1096: The First Crusade and The Jews* (Philadelphia: 1996).

10 Edgington, Susan (trans.), *Albert of Aachen / Historia Ierosolimitana: History of the Journey to Jerusalem* (Oxford: 2007), pp. 52–3.

11 *Anna Komnene / The Alexiad*, pp. 274–5.

12 Ibid., pp. 383–4

13 Edgington (trans.), *Albert of Aachen / Historia Ierosolimitana*, p. 145.

14 Hill, Rosalind (ed.), *Gesta Francorum et Aliorum Hierosoliminatorum: The Deeds of the Franks and the Other Pilgrims to Jerusalem*, (Oxford: 1962), pp. 19–20.

15 Edgington (trans.), *Albert of Aachen / Historia Ierosolimitana*, pp. 284–5.

16 Hill, John Hugh and Hill, Laurita L. (trans.), *Raymond d'Aguilers / Historia Francorum Qui Ceperunt*

Iherusalem (Philadelphia: 1968), p. 127.

17 Richards, D. S. (trans.), *The Chronicle of Ibn al-Athir for the Crusading Period from al-Kamil fi'l Ta'rikh* I (Farnham: 2006), p. 22.

18 The journey is narrated in entertaining fashion in the Norse sagas. See Hollander, Lee M. (trans.), *Snorri Sturluson / Heimskringla: History of the Kings of Norway* (Austin: 1964), pp. 688–701.

19 Wilkinson, John, Hill, Joyce and Ryan, W. F., *Jerusalem Pilgrimage 1099–1185*, (London: 1988), p. 100.

20 Ibid. p. 171.

21 Riley-Smith, Jonathan, *The First Crusaders, 1095–1131* (Cambridge: 1997), pp. 169–188.

22 Jacoby, David, *Medieval Trade in the Eastern Mediterranean and Beyond* (Abingdon: 2018), pp. 109–116.

23 Galili, Ehud, Rosen, Baruch, Arenson, Sarah, Nir-El, Yoram, Jacoby, David, 'A cargo of lead ingots from a shipwreck off Ashkelon, Israel 11th–13th centuries AD', *International Journal of Nautical Archaeology* 48 (2019), pp. 453–465.

24 Ryan and Fink (eds.), *Fulcher of Chartres: A History of the Expedition to Jerusalem*, p. 150.

25 Eugene's crusading bull *Quantum Praedecessores* (1145), translated in Riley-Smith, Jonathan and Louise (eds.), *The Crusades: Idea and Reality, 1095–1274* (London: 1981), pp. 57–9.

26 Berry, Virginia Gingerick, *Odo of Deuil / De Profectione Ludovici VII in Orientam* (New York: 1948), pp. 8–9.

27 Bédier, J. and Aubry, P. (eds.), *Les Chansons de Croisade avec Leurs Melodies* (Paris: 1909), pp. 8–10.

28 The best introductory survey to the Second Crusade is Phillips, Jonathan, *The Second Crusade: Extending the Frontiers of Christianity* (New Haven: 2008).

29 Babcock, Emily Atwater and Krey, A. C. (trans.), *A History of Deeds Done Beyond the Sea: By William Archbishop of Tyre* II, (New York: 1943), p. 180

30 The best introduction to this topic is Christiansen, Eric, *The Northern Crusades* (2nd edn.) (London: 1997).

31 The most recent biography is Phillips, Jonathan, *The Life and Legend of the Sultan Saladin* (London: 2019).

32 Broadhurst, Roland (trans.), *The Travels of Ibn Jubayr* (London: 1952), p. 311.

33 Barber, Malcolm and Bate, Keith, *Letters from the East: Crusaders, Pilgrims and Settlers in the 12th–13th Centuries* (Farnham: 2010), p. 76.

34 Lewis, Robert E. (ed.), *De miseria condicionis humane / Lotario dei Segni (Pope Innocent III)* (Athens, GA: 1978).

35 McGrath, Alister E., *The Christian Theology Reader*, p. 498.

36 Bird, Jessalyn, Peters, Edward and Powell, James M., *Crusade and Christendom: Annotated Documents in Translation from Innocent III to the Fall of Acre, 1187–1291* (Philadelphia: 2013), p. 32

37 The essential texts on the Fourth Crusade are Phillips, Jonathan, *The Fourth Crusade and the Sack of Constantinople* (London: 2011) and Angold, Michael, *The Fourth Crusade: Event and Context* (Abingdon: 2014).

38 Andrea, Alfred J. (trans.), *The Capture of Constantinople: The 'Hystoria Constantinoplitana' of Gunther of Pairis* (Philadelphia: 1997), p. 79.

39 Magoulias, Harry J. (trans.), *O City of Byzantium, Annals of Niketas Choniates* (Detroit: 1984), p. 316

40 Riley-Smith, *The Crusades: Idea and Reality*, p. 156.

41 Ibid. pp. 78–9.

42 Ibid. p. 81.

43 See Barber, Malcolm, *The Trial of the Templars* 2nd edition (Cambridge: 2006); Jones, Dan, *The Templars: The*

Rise and Fall of God's Holy Warriors
(London: 2017).

Chapter 9

1 Peters, Edward (ed.), *Christian
Society and the Crusades 1198–1229.
Sources in Translation including
The Capture of Damietta by Oliver
of Paderborn*, (Philadelphia: 1971),
p. 113.

2 The text of Jacques de Vitry's details
letter on 'King David' is known as the
Relatio de Davide, and can be read (in
French) in Huygens, R. B. C. (trans.),
*Lettres de Jacques de Vitry, Edition
Critique* (Leiden: 1960), pp. 141–50.

3 The famous forged letter from Prester
John to the Byzantine Emperor
Manuel I Komnenos is translated in
Barber, Malcolm and Bate, Keith,
*Letters from the East: Crusaders,
Pilgrims and Settlers in the 12th–13th
Centuries* (Farnham: 2013), pp. 62–8.

4 On the relationship between Prester
John and 'King David', see Hamilton,
Bernard, 'Continental Drift: Prester
John's Progress through the Indies'
in Rubies, Joan-Pau, *Medieval
Ethnographies: European Perceptions
of the World Beyond* (Abingdon:
2016).

5 Smith, Richard, 'Trade and
commerce across Afro-Eurasia', in
Kedar, Benjamin Z. and Weisner-
Hanks, Merry E., *The Cambridge
World History Vol. 5: Expanding
Webs of Exchange and Conflict, 500
C.E.–1500 C.E.* (Cambridge: 2013),
p. 246.

6 de Rachewiltz, Igor (trans.), *The
Secret History of the Mongols: A
Mongolian Epic Chronicle of the
Thirteenth Century* I (Leiden: 2006),
p. 1.

7 Ibid. p. 13.

8 Pederson, Neil, Hessl, Amy E.,
Baatarbileg, Nachin, Anchukaitis,
Kevin J. and Di Cosmo, Nicola,
'Pluvials, droughts, the Mongol
Empire, and modern Mongolia',
*Proceedings of the National Academy
of Sciences* (25 March, 2014).

9 Biran, Michael, 'The Mongol Empire
and inter-civilizational exchange', in
Kedar, Benjamin Z. and Weisner-
Hanks, Merry E., *The Cambridge
World History Vol. 5: Expanding
Webs of Exchange and Conflict, 500
C.E.–1500 C.E.* (Cambridge: 2013),
p. 538.

10 Ibid. p. 546.

11 de Rachewiltz (trans.), *The Secret
History of the Mongols*, p. 133.

12 Ibid. p. 116.

13 Ibid. p. 179.

14 Boyle, J.A. (trans.), *Genghis Khan:
the history of the world conqueror /
by 'Ala-ad-Din 'Ata-Malik Juvaini*
(Manchester: 1997), p. 107.

15 McLynn, Frank, *Genghis Khan: The
Man Who Conquered the World*
(London: 2015), p. 299.

16 Translation: Ibid. p. 327.

17 Michell, Robert and Forbes, Nevill
(trans.), *The Chronicle of Novgorod
1016–1471* (London: 1914), p. 64.

18 Ibid. p. 66.

19 Richard, D. S., *The Chronicle of Ibn
al-Athir for the Crusading Period from
al-Kamil fi'l Ta'rikh* III, (Farnham:
2006), p. 215.

20 For a colourful discussion of the
various possible causes of Genghis'
death, see McLynn, Frank, *Genghis
Khan*, pp. 378–9.

21 Colbert, Benjamin (ed.), *The Travels
of Marco Polo* (Ware: 1997), p. 65.

22 Michael, Maurice (trans.), *The Annals
of Jan Długosz: Annales Seu Cronicae
Incliti Regni Poloniae* (Chichester:
1997), p. 180.

23 A detailed account of the crusade
against the Mongols is Jackson, Peter,
'The Crusade against the Mongols',
Journal of Ecclesiastical History 42
(1991), pp. 1–18.

24 Ibid. p. 15 n. 72

25 Martin, Janet, *Medieval Russia,
980–1584* (2nd edn.) (Cambridge:
2007), p. 155.

26 Zenokovsky, Serge, *Medieval Russia's Epics, Chronicles and Tales* (New York: 1974), p. 202. See also Martin, *Medieval Russia*, p. 151.

27 For the narrative of Giovanni's journey, Hildinger, Erik (trans.), *Giovanni da Pian del Carpine, Archbishop of Antivari, d. 1252 / The story of the Mongos who we call the Tartars* (Boston: 1996), pp. 88–113. This quote, p. 91.

28 Ibid. p. 93.

29 Ibid. p. 95.

30 Ibid., p. 34.

31 Ibid., p. 39.

32 Ibid. p. 48.

33 Ibid. p. 99.

34 Ibid. p. 107.

35 For a full discussion of the missions sent east, many of them by Pope Innocent IV, see De Rachewiltz, Igor, *Papal Envoys to the Great Khans* (London: 1971).

36 Jackson, Peter (ed.), *The Mission of Friar William of Rubruck* (Abingdon: 2016), p. 291.

37 Ibid. p. 303.

38 Ibid. p. 316.

39 For a discussion of the various proposed causes of Möngke's death and their original sources, Pow, Stephen, 'Fortresses That Shatter Empires: A look at Möngke Khan's failed campaign against the Song Dynasty, 1258–9', in Jaritz, Gerhard, Lyublyanovics, Kyra, Rasson, Judith A., and Reed, Zsuzsanna (eds.), *Annual of Medieval Studies at CEU* 23 (2017), pp. 96–107.

40 Barber and Bate, *Letters from the East*, pp. 157–9.

41 Martin, *Medieval Russia*, p. 156.

42 Gibb, H. A. R. (trans.), *Ibn Battuta: Travels in Asia and Africa 1325–1354* (London: 1929), p. 166.

43 Jackson, Peter, *The Mongols and the West, 1221–1410* (Abingdon: 2005), p. 236.

44 Ibid. p. 237.

45 Jamaluddin, Syed, 'Samarqand as the First City in the World under Temür', *Proceedings of the Indian History Congress* 56 (1995), pp. 858–60.

46 Biran, 'The Mongol Empire and inter-civilizational exchange', pp. 553–4.

47 Weatherford, Jack, *Genghis Khan and the Quest for God* (New York: 2016).

Chapter 10

1 Latham, Ronald (trans.), *Marco Polo / The Travels* (London: 1958), p. 33.

2 Ibid. p. 112.

3 Ibid. p. 113.

4 Ibid. p. 41.

5 Ibid. p. 74.

6 Ibid. p. 76.

7 Ibid. p. 79.

8 Ibid. p. 88.

9 Ibid. p. 90.

10 Ibid. p. 194

11 Ibid. p. 256.

12 Ibid. p. 261.

13 Ibid. p. 287.

14 Ibid. pp. 299–303.

15 Ibid. pp. 213–31.

16 Ibid. p. 61.

17 Ibid. p. 149.

18 Ibid. p. 155.

19 Blegen, Nick, 'The earliest long-distance obsidian transport: Evidence from the ~200 ka Middle Stone Age Sibilo School Road Site, Baringo, Kenya', *Journal of Human Evolution* 103 (2017), pp. 1–19.

20 Barjamovic, Gojko, Chaney, Thomas, Cosar, Kerem and Hortaçsu, Ali, 'Trade, Merchants and the Lost Cities of the Bronze Age', *The Quarterly Journal of Economics* 134 (2019), pp. 1455–1503.

21 Holland, Tom (trans.), *Herodotus / The Histories* (London: 2013), p. 318.

22 Lopez, Robert S., *The Commercial Revolution of the Middle Ages, 950–1350* (Cambridge: 1976), p. 8.

23 McCormick, Michael, *Origins of the European Economy: Communications and Commerce, A.D. 300–900* (Cambridge: 2001), pp. 729–34.

24 Hunt, Edwin S. and Murray, James, *A History of Business in Medieval Europe, 1200–1550* (Cambridge: 1999), pp. 20–3.

25 Hunt and Murray *History of Business in Medieval Europe*, p. 26.

26 Lopez, *Commercial Revolution*, pp. 60–1.

27 On other regional fairs, particularly after 1350, see Epstein, S. R., 'Regional Fairs, Institutional Innovation, and Economic Growth in Late Medieval Europe', *The Economic History Review* 47 (1994), pp. 459–82.

28 Blockmans, Wim, 'Transactions at the Fairs of Champagne and Flanders, 1249–1291', *Fiere e mercati nella integrazione delle economie europee secc. XIII-XVIII – Atti delle Settimane di Studi* 32, pp. 993–1000.

29 Boyle, J. A. (trans.), *The History of the World-Conqueror / 'Ala-ad-Din 'Ata Malik Juvaini* (revd. edn.) (Manchester: 1997), p. 272.

30 Lloyd, T. H., *The English Wool Trade in the Middle Ages* (Cambridge: 1977), pp. 1–3.

31 The Bardi banker Francesco Balducci Pegolotti's advice to Florentine merchants doing business with the Chinese formed part of his merchants' handbook *La Practica della Mercatura*. See Evans, Allan (ed.), *Francesco Balducci Pegolotti / La Practica della Mercatura* (Cambridge, Mass.: 1936). See also Lopez, *Commercial Revolution*, pp. 109–11 and Hunt, Edwin S., *The Medieval Super-Companies: A Study of the Peruzzi Company of Florence* (Cambridge: 1994), pp. 128–9.

32 Hunt, Edwin S., 'A New Look at the Dealings of the Bardi and Peruzzi with Edward III', *The Journal of Economic History* 50 (1990), pp. 151–4.

33 The Ordinances of 1311, translated in Rothwell, Harry (ed.), *English Historical Documents III: 1189–1327* (new edn.) (London: 1996), p. 533.

34 Evans, Allen (ed.), *Francesco Balducci Pegolotti / La Practica della Mercatura* (Cambridge, Mass: 1936), pp. 255–69.

35 Hunt, 'A New Look at the Dealings of the Bardi and Peruzzi with Edward III', pp. 149–50.

36 Power, Eileen, *The Wool Trade In Medieval English History* (Oxford: 1941), p. 43.

37 See Fryde, E. B., 'The Deposits of Hugh Despenser the Younger with Italian Bankers', *The Economic History Review* 3 (1951), pp. 344–362.

38 Ibid. Of course, the danger to the historian is that in seeing an abundance of new records he or she assumes a revolution in practice; but even taking that into consideration, it is clear that commerce was booming in the later Middle Ages.

39 Lloyd, *The English Wool Trade in the Middle Ages*, pp. 144–50.

40 Ormrod, Mark, *Edward III* (New Haven: 2011), p. 230.

41 Hunt, *Medieval Super-Companies*, pp. 212–6.

42 Hunt, 'A New Look at the Dealings of the Bardi and Peruzzi with Edward III', is most sceptical about Villani's estimate of Edward's indebtedness and historians' acceptance of it.

43 Puga, Diego and Trefler, Daniel, 'International Trade and Institutional Change: Medieval Venice's Response to Globalization', *The Quarterly Journal of Economics* 129 (2014), pp. 753–821.

44 Axworthy, Roger L., 'Pulteney [Neale], Sir John (d. 1349)', *Oxford Dictionary of National Biography*.

45 Turner, Marion, *Chaucer: A European Life* (Princeton: 2019), pp. 22–8.

46 Ibid. pp. 145–7.

47 Barron, Caroline M., 'Richard Whittington: The Man Behind the Myth', in Hollaender, A. E. J. and Kellaway, William, *Studies in London History* (London: 1969), p. 198.

48 Saul, Nigel, *Richard II* (New Haven: 1997), pp. 448–9.

49 Barron, 'Richard Whittington: The Man Behind the Myth', p. 200.

50 See Sumption, Jonathan, *Cursed Kings: The Hundred Years War IV* (London: 2015), p. 208

51 Barron, 'Richard Whittington: The Man Behind the Myth', pp. 206, 237.

52 Sutton, Anne F., 'Whittington, Richard [Dick]', *Oxford Dictionary of National Biography* (2004).

53 Sumption, *Cursed Kings*, pp. 419–21.

54 Barron, 'Richard Whittington: The Man Behind the Myth', p. 237.

55 Curry, Anne, *Agincourt* (Oxford: 2015), pp. 189–90.

Chapter 11

1 Bouquet, Martin (ed.), *Receuil des historiens des Gaules et de la France* 21 (Paris: 1855), p. 649. See also Crawford, Paul F., 'The University of Paris and the Trial of the Templars' in Mallia-Milanes (ed.), *The Military Orders, Volume 3: History and Heritage* (London: 2008), p. 115.

2 Ibid. pp. 244–5.

3 According to Clement V, Philip had buttonholed him about the Templars at the papal coronation in Lyon in 1305. See Barber, Malcolm and Bate, Keith (ed. and trans.), *The Templars* (Manchester: 2002), p. 243.

4 Barber, Malcom, *The Trial of the Templars* (2nd edn.) (Cambridge: 2006), p. 80.

5 In a bull known as *Pastoralis Praeeminentiae*, issued in November 1307. For a more detailed narrative of events in the downfall of the Templars see Barber, *The Trial of the Templars* or Jones, *The Templars*.

6 Cheney, C. R., 'The Downfall of the Templars and a Letter in their Defence' in Whitehead, F., Divernes, A. H, and Sutcliffe, F. E., *Medieval Miscellany Presented to Eugène Vinaver* (Manchester: 1965), pp. 65–79.

7 These translations in Barber and Bate, *The Templars*, pp. 258–60.

8 Barber and Bate, *The Templars*, p. 262.

9 Crawford, 'The University of Paris and the Trial of the Templars', p. 120

10 This translation Barney, Stephen A., Lewis, W. J., Beach, J. A, Berghof, Oliver (eds.), *The Etymologies of Isidore of Seville* (Cambridge: 2006), p. 7

11 On hedgehogs, see Eddy, Nicole and Wellesley, Mary, 'Isidore of Seville's Etymologies: Who's Your Daddy?', *British Library Medieval Manuscripts Blog* (2016), https://blogs.bl.uk/ digitisedmanuscripts/2016/04/ isidore-of-seville.html

12 Falk, Seb, *The Light Ages: A Medieval Journey of Discovery* (London: 2020), p. 83.

13 Barney et al (eds.), *The Etymologies of Isidore of Seville*, p. 16.

14 Ibid. p. 7.

15 Wright, F.A. (trans.) *Jerome / Select Letters* (Cambridge, Mass.: 1933), pp. 344–47.

16 Haskins, Charles Homer, *The Renaissance of the Twelfth Century* (Cambridge, Mass: 1927), p. 34.

17 On Bec, ibid. p. 38.

18 For an introductory overview to this topic, Spade, Paul Vincent, 'Medieval Philosophy', in Edward N. Zalta (ed.), *The Stanford Encyclopedia of Philosophy* (Summer 2018 Edition), and for more detail, Klibancky, Raymond, *The continuity of the Platonic tradition during the middle ages, outlines of a Corpus platonicum medii aevi* (London: 1939).

19 One retrospective diagnosis is cerebral palsy. For the contemporary description of Hermann's ailment see Robinson, I. S., *Eleventh Century Germany: The Swabian Chronicles* (Manchester: 2008), p. 108.

20 Ibid.

21 Ibid. p. 110. See also Falk, *The Light Ages*, pp. 49–50.

22 See Burnett, Charles, 'Morley, Daniel of' in *Oxford Dictionary of National Biography*.

23 After Haskins, *The Renaissance of the Twelfth Century*.

24 Ibid. pp. 129–31.

25 Smith, Terence, 'The English Medieval Windmill', *History Today* 28 (1978).

26 See Nardi, Paolo, 'Relations with Authority', De Ridder-Symoens, H. (ed.), *A History of the University in Europe* I (Cambridge: 1992), pp. 77–9.

27 Turner, Denys, *Thomas Aquinas: A Portrait* (New Haven: 2013), p. 12.

28 The sequence of events portrayed here and below relies on the biographical summary in Stump, Eleonore, *Aquinas* (London: 2003), pp. 3–12.

29 Parts of this enormous work can be consulted in the easily available McDermott, Timothy, *Aquinas / Selected Philosophical Writings* (Oxford: 2008).

30 Aston, T. H., 'Oxford's Medieval Alumni', *Past & Present* 74 (1977), p. 6.

31 This translation by Markowski, M., retrieved via https://sourcebooks. fordham.edu/source/eleanor.asp

32 De Mowbray, Malcolm, '1277 and All That – Students and Disputations', *Traditio* 57 (2002), pp. 217–238.

33 De Ridder-Symoens, *A History of the University in Europe* I (Cambridge: 1992), pp. 100–1.

34 Many of the implications of Arundel's Constitutions are explored in Ghosh, K. and Gillespie, V. (eds.), *After Arundel: Religious Writing in Fifteenth-Century England* (Turnhout: 2011). My thanks to Dr David Starkey – a modern-day condemned heretic – for prompting me to think of Arundel in this context.

Chapter 12

1 *Calendar of Various Chancery Rolls: Supplementary Close Rolls, Welsh Rolls, Scutage Rolls, A.D. 1277–1326* (London: 1912), p. 281.

2 The details of the execution were recorded by the Oxfordshire chronicler Thomas Wykes. See Luard, H. R., *Annales Monastici* vol. 4 (London: 1869), p. 294.

3 For a biography of Master James see Taylor, A. J., 'Master James of St. George', *The English Historical Review* 65 (1950), pp. 433–57.

4 For this and an excellent account of Caernarfon's construction, Colvin, H. M. (ed.), *The History of the King's Works I: The Middle Ages* (London: 1963), pp. 369–95.

5 Gantz, Jeffrey (trans.), *The Mabinogion* (London: 1973), pp. 119–20.

6 For a plan of the castle, Colvin (ed.), *History of the King's Works* I, p. 376.

7 Barratt, Nick, 'The English Revenue of Richard I', *The English Historical Review* 116 (2001), p. 637.

8 Colvin, *History of the King's Works* I, p. 333.

9 Ibid. p. 344.

10 Ibid. pp. 371–4.

11 Ibid. pp. 395–408.

12 Bradbury, J. M. *The Capetians: Kings of France 987–1328* (London: 2007), p. 205.

13 For an introduction to this topic, see Stalley, Roger, *Early Medieval Architecture* (Oxford: 1999).

14 Bony, Jean, *French Gothic Architecture of the 12th and 13th Centuries* (Berkeley: 1983), p. 61. Special thanks also to Dr Emma Wells for her guidance on this huge topic, and for sharing with me advance excerpts from her forthcoming book: Wells, Emma, *Heaven on Earth* (London: 2022).

15 See for example Clark, William W., 'Early Gothic', *Oxford Art Online*, https://doi.org/10.1093/gao/9781884446054.article.T024729

16 Panofsky, Erwin and Panofsky-Soergel, Gerda (eds.), *Abbot Suger on the Abbey Church of St.-Denis and its*

Art Treasures (2nd. ed.) (Princeton: 1979), p. 6.

17 Ibid. pp. 48–9.

18 Erlande-Brandenburg, Alain, *The Cathedral Builders of the Middle Ages* (London: 1995), pp. 141–2.

19 Panofsky and Panofsky-Soergel, *Abbot Suger on the Abbey Church of St.-Denis*, pp. 72–3.

20 Scott, Robert A., *The Gothic Enterprise: A Guide to Understanding the Medieval Cathedral* (Berkeley: 2003), p. 132.

21 Wilson, Christopher, *The Gothic Cathedral: The Architecture of the Great Church, 1130–1530* (London: 2000), p. 44.

22 Erlande-Brandenburg, *Cathedral Builders of the Middle Ages*, p. 47.

23 For speculation as to the exact cause of Beauvais' vaults' failure, Wolfe, Maury I. and Mark, Robert, 'The Collapse of the Vaults of Beauvais Cathedral in 1284', *Speculum* 51 (1976), pp. 462–76.

24 Wilson, *The Gothic Cathedral*, p. 224.

25 Foyle, Jonathan, *Lincoln Cathedral: The Biography of a Great Building* (London: 2015), p. 19.

26 Erlande-Brandenburg, *Cathedral Builders of the Middle Ages*, p. 105–7.

27 Foyle, *Lincoln Cathedral*, pp. 34–5.

28 Although England does not sit on any major seismic fault-lines, it has a relatively busy history of earthquakes. See Musson, R. M. W., 'A History of British seismology', *Bulletin of Earthquake Engineering* 11 (2013), pp. 715–861, which makes passing mention of the 1185 quake. See also Musson, R. M. W., 'The Seismicity of the British Isles to 1600', *British Geological Survey Open Report* (2008), p. 23.

29 On the old west front, Taylor, David, 'The Early West Front of Lincoln Cathedral', *Archaeological Journal* 167 (2010), pp. 134–64.

30 Garton, Charles (trans.), *The Metrical Life of St Hugh* (Lincoln: 1986) p. 53.

31 Douie. Decima L. and Farmer, David Hugh, *Magna Vita Sancti Hugonis / The Life of St Hugh of Lincoln* II (Oxford: 1985), p. 219.

32 Ibid. p. 231.

33 On which, see Harrison, Stuart, 'The Original Plan of the East End of St Hugh's Choir at Lincoln Cathedral Reconsidered in the Light of New Evidence', *Journal of the British Archaeological Association* 169 (2016), pp. 1–38.

34 Wilson, *The Gothic Cathedral*, p. 184.

35 Ibid. pp. 191–223.

36 Ibid. p. 192.

37 For a summary of these overlapping conflicts, see Hibbert, Christopher, *Florence: The Biography of a City* (London: 1993), pp. 18–34.

38 For arguments as to why Italy rejected the Gothic movement so prevalent elsewhere, see Wilson, *The Gothic Cathedral*, pp. 258–9.

39 The most detailed analysis of Arnolfo's design, along with an argument for him as the definitive architect of Florence's great cathedral, is Toker, Franklin, 'Arnolfo's S. Maria del Fiore: A Working Hypothesis', *Journal of the Society of Architectural Historians* 42 (1983), pp 101–20.

40 King, Ross, *Brunelleschi's Dome: The Story of the Great Cathedral in Florence* (London: 2000), p. 6.

41 See Poeschke, Joachim, 'Arnolfo di Cambio' in *Grove Art Online* https://doi.org/10.1093/gao/9781884446054.article.T004203

42 King, *Brunelleschi's Dome*, p. 10.

Chapter 13

1 Childs, Wendy R. (trans.), *Vita Edwardi Secundi* (Oxford: 2005), pp. 120–1. On price fluctuations, see Slavin, Philip, 'Market failure during the Great Famine in England and Wales (1315–1317), *Past & Present* 222 (2014), pp. 14–8.

2 The standard work on the Great Famine is Jordan, William C., *The*

Great Famine: Northern Europe in the Early Fourteenth Century (Princeton: 1996). Also see Kershaw, Ian, 'The Great Famine and Agrarian Crisis in England 1315–1322', *Past & Present* 59 (1973), pp. 3–50 and, more recently, Campbell, Bruce M. S., 'Nature as historical protagonist: environment and society in pre-industrial England', *The Economic History Review* 63 (2010), pp. 281–314.

3 Slavin, Philip, 'The Great Bovine Pestilence and its economic and environmental consequences in England and Wales, 1318–50', *The Economic History Review* 65 (2012), pp. 1240–2.

4 Kershaw, 'The Great Famine', p. 11.

5 Johannes de Trokelowe, in Riley, H. T. (ed.), *Chronica Monasterii S. Albani* III (London, 1865), pp. 92–95. Cannibalism was also reported in Ireland. Kershaw, 'The Great Famine', p. 10 fn. 41.

6 Childs (trans.), *Vita Edwardi Secundi*, p. 120–3.

7 See, for example, Miller, Gifford H. (et al.), 'Abrupt onset of the Little Ice Age triggered by volcanism and sustained by sea-ice/ocean feedbacks', *Geophysical Research Letters* 39 (2012), https://doi.org/10.1029/2011GL050168; Zhou, TianJun (et al.), 'A comparison of the Medieval Warm Period, Little Ice Age and 20th century warming simulated by the FGOALS climate system model', *Chinese Science Bulletin* 56 (2011), pp. 3028–41.

8 Recent research has argued strongly for the existence of Black Death south of the Sahara in the Middle Ages. See Green, Monica H., 'Putting Africa on the Black Death map: Narratives from genetics and history', *Afriques* 9 (2018), https://doi.org/10.4000/afriques.2125

9 See for example the description of symptoms and transmission via animals and birds in Bartsocas,

Christos S., 'Two Fourteenth Century Greek Descriptions of the "Black Death"', *Journal of the History of Medicine and Allied Sciences* 21 (1966), p. 395.

10 Horrox, Rosemary (trans. and ed.), *The Black Death* (Manchester: 1994), p. 9. For India's apparent lack of infection, see Sussman, George D., 'Was the Black Death in India and China?', *Bulletin of the History of Medicine* 85 (2011), pp. 332–41.

11 This translation Horrox, *The Black Death*, p. 17.

12 Ibid.

13 Ibid. p. 19.

14 Ibid.

15 The notion that Bohemia was miraculously passed over by the Black Death was popular for a long time but has recently been disproven. See Mengel, David C., 'A Plague on Bohemia? Mapping the Black Death', *Past & Present* 211 (2011), pp. 3–34.

16 Horrox, *The Black Death*, pp. 111–184, *passim*.

17 Ibid. p. 250.

18 Bartsocas, 'Two Fourteenth Century Greek Descriptions', p. 395.

19 Ibid. pp. 248–9.

20 I refer to a 'Black Swan' event broadly as defined in Taleb, Nassim Nicholas, *The Black Swan: The Impact of the Highly Improbable* (London: 2008).

21 Thompson, Edward Maunde (ed.), *Adae Murimuth Continuatio Chronicarum / Robertus De Avesbury De Gestis Mirabilibus Regis Edwardi Tertii* (London: 1889), pp. 407–8.

22 Cohn, Norman, *The pursuit of the millennium: revolutionary millenarians and mystical anarchists of the Middle Ages* (London: 1970), p. 125.

23 Horrox, *The Black Death*, p. 118.

24 Lumby, J. R. (ed.), *Chronicon Henrici Knighton vel Cnitthon, Monachi Leycestrensis* II (London: 1895), p. 58.

25 Ibid.

26 For an English extract and summary of the Statue of Labourers see Myers, A. R. (ed.), *English Historical Documents IV, 1327–1485* (London: 1969), pp. 993–4.

27 As labelled by Tuchman, Barbara, *A Distant Mirror: The Calamitous Fourteenth Century* (New York: 1978).

28 Wickham, Chris, 'Looking Forward: Peasant revolts in Europe, 600–1200' in Firnhaber-Baker, Justine and Schoenaers, Dirk, *The Routledge History Handbook of Medieval Revolt* (Abingdon: 2017), p. 156.

29 Wickham, Chris, *Framing the Early Middle Ages*, pp. 530–2.

30 Wickham, 'Looking Forward', pp. 158–62.

31 Hollander, Lee M. (trans.), *Snorri Sturluson / Heimskringla: History of the Kings of Norway* (Austin: 1964), p. 515.

32 See Cassidy-Welch, Megan, 'The Stedinger Crusade: War, Remembrance, and Absence in Thirteenth-Century Germany', *Viator* 44 (2013), pp. 159–74.

33 Cohn Jr., Samuel, 'Women in Revolt in Medieval and Early Modern Europe' in Firnhaber-Baker and Schoenaers, *The Routledge History Handbook of Medieval Revolt*, p. 209.

34 Wilson, William Burton (trans.), *John Gower / Mirour de l'Omme (The Mirror of Mankind)* (Woodbridge: 1992), pp. 347–8.

35 A short, classic summary of this rebellion is Cazelles, Raymond, 'The Jacquerie' in Hilton, R. H. and Aston, T. H., *The English Rising of 1381* (Cambridge: 1984), pp. 74–83. The new standard work in English, is Firnhaber-Baker, Justine, *The Jacquerie of 1358: A French Peasants' Revolt* (Oxford: 2021).

36 This translation, Cohn Jr., Samuel K. *Popular Protest in Late Medieval Europe* (Manchester: 2004), pp. 150–1.

37 On the labelling of the Jacques, Firnhaber-Baker, Justine, 'The Eponymous Jacquerie: Making revolt mean some things' in Firnhaber-Baker and Schoenaers, *The Routledge History Handbook of Medieval Revolt*, pp. 55–75.

38 Jean Froissart, translation by Cohn Jr., *Popular Protest in Late Medieval Europe*, pp. 155–8.

39 *Anonimalle Chronicle* translated in ibid. pp. 171–3.

40 Firnhaber-Baker, Justine 'The Social Constituency of the Jacquerie Revolt of 1358', *Speculum* 95 (2020), pp. 697–701.

41 Cohn Jr., *Popular Protest in Late Medieval Europe*, p. 121.

42 Ibid. p. 99.

43 Ibid. p. 100.

44 Ibid. p. 235.

45 Ibid. p. 217.

46 Ibid. p. 219.

47 Ibid. p. 269.

48 See Putnam, B. H., *The enforcement of the statutes of labourers during the first decade after the Black Death, 1349–59* (New York: 1908).

49 See Jones, Dan, *Summer of Blood: The Peasants' Revolt of 1381* (London: 2009), pp. 15–16.

50 Faith, Rosamond, 'The "Great Rumour" of 1377 and Peasant Ideology' in Hilton and Aston, *The English Rising of 1381*, pp. 47–8.

51 Prescott, Andrew, '"Great and Horrible Rumour": Shaping the English revolt of 1381', in Firnhaber-Baker and Schoenaers, *The Routledge History Handbook of Medieval Revolt*, p. 78.

52 Ball's letters are conveniently collected in Dobson, R. B., *The Peasants' Revolt of 1381* (2nd edn.) (London: 1983), pp. 380–3.

53 This translation, ibid. p. 311.

54 Cohn Jr., *Popular Protest in Late Medieval Europe*, pp. 341–6; Davies, Jonathan, 'Violence and Italian universities during the Renaissance', *Renaissance Studies* 27 (2013), pp. 504–16.

55 Davies, 'Violence and Italian universities during the Renaissance', p. 504.

56 Cohn Jr., *Popular Protest in Late Medieval Europe*, p. 345

57 For a short summary in context of the Wars of the Roses, see Jones, Dan, *The Hollow Crown: The Wars of the Roses and the Rise of the Tudors* (London: 2014), pp. 111–9.

58 Cade's demands are printed in Dobson, *The Peasants' Revolt*, pp. 338–42

59 O'Callaghan, Joseph F., *A History of Medieval Spain* (Ithaca: 1975), pp. 614–5.

Chapter 14

1 For a brief history of the Studio, Grendler, Paul F., 'The University of Florence and Pisa in the High Renaissance', *Renaissance and Reformation* 6 (1982), pp. 157–65.

2 On Filelfo's character, see Robin, Diana, 'A Reassessment of the Character of Francesco Filelfo (1398–1481)', *Renaissance Quarterly* 36 (1983), pp. 202–24.

3 There were proposals, indeed, to erect a special chair in the cathedral on which Filelfo could sit to read aloud from Dante. See Parker, Deborah, *Commentary and Ideology: Dante in the Renaissance* (Durham: 1993), p. 53.

4 Gilson, Simon, *Dante and Renaissance Florence* (Cambridge: 2005), p. 99.

5 Hollingsworth, Mary, *The Medici* (London: 2017), pp. 80–1.

6 This translation Robin, Diana, *Filelfo in Milan* (Princeton: 2014), pp. 19–20.

7 Ibid. p. 45.

8 George, William and Waters, Emily, *Vespasiano da Bisticci / The Vespasiano Memoirs* (London: 1926), p. 409.

9 Hankins, James (trans.), *Leonardo Bruni / History of the Florentine People Volume I: Books I-IV*

(Cambridge, Mass.: 2001), xvii-xviii, pp. 86–9.

10 Sonnet 9 – 'Quando 'l pianeta che distingue l'ore'. Kline, A.S. (trans.), *Petrarch / The Complete Canzoniere*, (Poetry in Translation, 2001), p. 26.

11 Of course, in his own sonnets Shakespeare was in part reacting against Petrarchian convention. Thanks to Dr Oliver Morgan for briefing me on Petrarch and Renaissance poetry.

12 Mustard, Wilfrid P., 'Petrarch's Africa', *The American Journal of Philology* 42 (1921), p. 97.

13 Sonnet 10. —'Gloriosa columna in cui s'appoggia'. *Petrarch / The Complete Canzoniere*, p. 27.

14 Regn, Gerhard and Huss, Bernhard, 'Petrarch's Rome: The History of the Africa and the Renaissance Project', *MLN* 124 (2009), pp. 86–7.

15 Translated by Wilkins, Ernest H., 'Petrarch's Coronation Oration', *Transactions and Proceedings of the Modern Language Association of America* 68 (1953), pp. 1243–4.

16 Ibid. p. 1246.

17 Ibid. p. 1241.

18 Bernardo, Aldo (trans.), *Francesco Petrarch / Letters on Familiar Matters (Rerum Familiarium Libri) Volume 1: Books I-VIII* (New York: 1975), p. 168.

19 Middlemore, S. (trans.), *Burckhardt, Jacob / The Civilization of the Renaissance in Italy* (London: 1990), pp. 194–7.

20 Vaughan, Richard, *Philip the Good: The Apogee of Burgundy* (new edn.) (Woodbridge: 2002), p. 67, drawing on Besnier, G., 'Quelques notes sur Arras et Jeanne d'Arc', *Revue du Nord* 40 (1958), pp. 193–4.

21 The best modern biography of Joan is Castor, Helen, *Joan of Arc: A History* (London: 2014). For the Dauphin's coronation, see pp. 126–7.

22 George Chastellain, translated in Vaughan, *Philip the Good*, p. 127.

23 Ibid. p. 128

24 Ibid. p. 138. Van Eyck may have contributed to these joke-rooms; he certainly had a hand in refurbishments at Hesdin. See Martens, Maximiliaan et al (eds.), *Van Eyck*, (London: 2020), p. 74.

25 Martens, Maximiliaan et al (eds.), *Van Eyck* (London: 2020), p. 22.

26 Vaughan, *Philip the Good*, p. 151.

27 De Vere, Gaston (trans.), *Giorgio Vasari / Lives of the Most Excellent Painters, Sculptors and Architects* I (London: 1996), p. 425.

28 Martens et al (eds.), *Van Eyck* (London: 2020), p. 70.

29 Ibid. p. 74.

30 Ibid. p. 141.

31 Vaughan, *Philip the Good*, p. 151.

32 Martens, Maximiliaan et al (eds.), *Van Eyck* (London: 2020), p. 22.

33 Kemp, Martin, *Leonardo by Leonardo* (New York: 2019), p. 10.

34 Richter, Irma A. (ed.), *Leonardo da Vinci / Notebooks* (Oxford: 2008), pp. 275–7.

35 De Vere (trans.) *Giorgio Vasari / Lives of the Most Excellent Painters*, p. 625.

36 Isaacson, Walter, *Leonardo da Vinci: The Biography* (London: 2017), p. 34.

37 *Machiavelli / The History of Florence* Book 8, ch 7.

38 Ibid.

39 Isaacson, *Leonardo*, pp. 160–2.

40 Ibid. p. 169.

41 On the general relationship between Leonardo and Cesare, see Strathern, Paul, *The Artist, the Philosopher and the Warrior: Leonardo, Machiavelli and Borgia: A fateful collusion* (London: 2009).

42 See Richter, *Leonardo da Vinci / Notebooks*, pp. 318–24.

43 Marani, Pietro C., *Leonardo da Vinci: The Complete Paintings* (new edn.) (New York: 2019), p. 179.

44 De Vere (trans.), *Giorgio Vasari / Lives of the Most Excellent Painters*, p. 639.

45 This translation, Hess, Peter, 'Marvellous Encounters: Albrecht Dürer and Early Sixteenth-Century German Perceptions of Aztec Culture', *Daphnis* 33 (2004), p. 163 n. 5.

Chapter 15

1 Magoulias, Harry J. (trans.), *Decline and Fall of Byzantium to the Ottoman Turks* (Detroit: 1975), pp. 200, 207.

2 Ibid. p. 201.

3 Gunpowder recipes had been circulating in the Mediterranean world since the mid-thirteenth century, probably having been brought west during the Mongol conquests. For this particular description of its recipe, see Riggs, Charles T. (trans.), *Mehmed the Conqueror / by Kritovoulos* (Princeton: 1954), p. 46.

4 Riggs, *Mehmed the Conqueror / by Kritovoulos*, p. 43. Also see Harris, Jonathan, *Constantinople: Capital of Byzantium* (2nd edn.) (London: 2017), p. 192.

5 The classic biography of Medmed in English translation is Babinger, Franz, *Mehmed the Conqueror and his time* (Princeton: 1978).

6 Riggs, *Mehmed the Conqueror / by Kritovoulos*, p. 45.

7 For a vivid narration of the night hours of the siege, Crowley, Roger, *Constantinople: The Last Great Siege, 1453* (London: 2005), pp. 203–16.

8 Riggs, *Mehmed the Conqueror / by Kritovoulos*, p. 69

9 Ibid. pp. 72–3.

10 Crowley, *Constantinople*, p. 230.

11 Riggs, *Mehmed the Conqueror / by Kritovoulos*, p. 69

12 Schwoebel, Robert, *The Shadow of the Crescent: The Renaissance Image of the Turk, 1453–1517* (New York: 1967), p. 11 See also Crowley, *Constantinople*, p. 241.

13 For a discussion of the diplomatic and cultural significance of the Bellini portrait, Gatward Cevizli, Antonia, 'Bellini, bronze and

bombards: Sultan Mehmed II's requests reconsidered', *Renaissance Studies* 28 (2014), pp. 748–65.

14 Freely, John, *The Grand Turk: Sultan Mehmet II – Conqueror of Constantinople, Master of an Empire and Lord of Two Seas* (London: 2010), pp. 12–13.

15 Frankopan, *The Silk Roads* (London: 2015), p. 199.

16 Balard, Michel, 'European and Mediterranean trade networks', Kedar and Weisner-Hanks, *Cambridge World History V*, p. 283

17 For a summary of the state of research, Gruhn, Ruth, 'Evidence grows for early peopling of the Americas', *Nature* 584 (August 2020), pp. 47–8.

18 Ugent, Donald, Dillehay, Tom and Ramirez, Carlos, 'Potato remains from a late Pleistocene settlement in southcentral Chile', *Economic Botany* 41 (1987), pp. 17–27.

19 For an entertaining if idiosyncratic study of St Brendan see Ashe, Geoffrey, *Land to the West: St Brendan's Voyage to America* (London: 1962).

20 Webb, J. F. (trans.), *The Age of Bede* (revd. edn.) (London: 1998), pp. 236, 266.

21 Sprenger, Aloys (trans.), *El-Masudi's Historical Encyclopaedia Entitled 'Meadows of Gold and Mines of Gems'* I (London: 1841), pp. 282–3

22 Ibid.

23 For a summary of the current work on Polynesian–American contact in the Middle Ages, see Jones, Terry L. et al (eds.), *Polynesians in America: Pre-Columbian Contacts with the New World* (Lanham: 2011).

24 An excellent recent account of Viking explorations in Iceland, Greenland and North America can be found in Price, *Children of Ash and Elm*, pp. 474–94.

25 Ibid. p. 491.

26 On the idea of a 'globalized' world around AD 1000, see Hansen, Valerie, *The Year 1000: When Explorers Connected the World – and Globalization Began* (London: 2020).

27 The standard English-language biography of Henry the Navigator is Russell, P. E., *Henry the Navigator: A Life* (New Haven/London: 2000).

28 For a brief summary of the circumstances of John I's accession, Disney, A. R., *A History of Portugal and the Portuguese Empire I* (Cambridge: 2009), pp. 122–8.

29 Cervantes, Fernando, *Conquistadores: A New History* (London: 2020), p. 6.

30 Up to thirty tons of gold was brought to the Mediterranean markets each year from African mines. See Kea, Ray A. 'Africa in World History, 1400–1800', Bentley, Jerry H., Subrahmanyam, Sanjay and Weisner-Hanks, Merry E. *The Cambridge World History VI: The Construction of a Global World 1400–1800 C.E. / Part I: Foundations* (Cambridge: 2015), p. 246.

31 Gomes Eanes de Zurara, translated in Newitt, Malyn, *The Portuguese in West Africa, 1415–1670: A Documentary History* (Cambridge: 2010), p. 27

32 On sail technology in the fifteenth century, Parry, J. H., *The Age of Reconnaissance: Discovery, Exploration and Settlement, 1450–1650* (London: 1963), pp. 53–68, 88.

33 Alvise da Cadamosto, translated in Newitt, *The Portuguese in West Africa*, pp. 55–7

34 Gomes Eanes de Zurara translated in ibid. p. 150

35 Ibid. p. 151.

36 This translation, Adiele, Pius Onyemechi, *The Popes, the Catholic Church and the Transatlantic Enslavement of Black Africans 1418–1839* (Hildesheim: 2017), pp. 312–3.

37 From Pereira's *Esmeraldo de Situ
    Orbis*, translated in Newitt, *The
    Portuguese in West Africa*, p. 44.
38 For this episode, including reported
    speech, Drayton, Elizabeth, *The
    Moor's Last Stand: How Seven
    Centuries of Muslim Rule in Spain
    Came to an End*, (London: 2017),
    pp. 113–27.
39 Cohen, J. M. (trans.), *Christopher
    Columbus / The Four Voyages*
    (London: 1969), p. 37.
40 Bale, Anthony (ed.), *John Mandeville
    / Book of Marvels and Travels*
    (Oxford: 2012).
41 Ibid. p. 37.
42 Cohen (trans.), *Christopher
    Columbus / The Four Voyages*, p. 40.
43 Ibid. p 53.
44 Ibid.
45 Ibid. p. 55.
46 Bergreen, Laurence, *Columbus: The
    Four Voyages 1492–1504* (New York:
    2011), p. 14.
47 Cohen (trans.) *Christopher Columbus
    / The Four Voyages*, p. 56.
48 Ibid. p. 81.
49 Ibid. p. 89.
50 Ibid. p. 96.
51 Ibid. p. 114
52 This translation Parry, *The Age of
    Reconnaissance*, p. 154.
53 Cohen (trans.), *Christopher
    Columbus / The Four Voyages*, p. 123.
54 Ibid. pp. 117–9.
55 Cervantes, *Conquistadores* (London:
    2020), p. 31.
56 Cohen (trans.), *Christopher
    Columbus / The Four Voyages*, p. 319.
57 Ravenstein, E. G. (trans.), *A Journal
    of the First Voyage of Vasco da Gama,
    1497–1499* (London: 1898), p. 113.
58 Ibid. p. 5.
59 Ibid. p. 13.
60 Ibid. p. 21.
61 Ibid. pp. 49–50.
62 On Magellan, Bergreen, Laurence,
    *Over the Edge of the World: Magellan's
    Terrifying Circumnavigation of the
    Globe* (New York: 2003).

Chapter 16

1 This translation, Davies, Martin,
   'Juan de Carvajal and Early Printing:
   The 42-line Bible and the Sweynheym
   and Pannartz Aquinas', *The Library* 17
   (1996), p. 196.
2 Readers can inspect digital pages of
   the paper and vellum editions via the
   British Library website. See www.
   bl.uk/treasures/gutenberg/ . It is also
   available in a handsome two-volume
   facsimile edition: Füssel, Stephan
   (ed.), *The Gutenberg Bible of 1454:
   With a commentary on the life and
   work of Johannes Gutenberg, the
   printing of the Bible, the distinctive
   features of the Göttingen copy, the
   'Göttingen Model Book' and the
   'Helmasperger Notarial Instrument'*
   (Köln: 2018).
3 Eisenstein, Elizabeth L., 'Some
   Conjectures about the Impact of
   Printing on Western Society and
   Thought: A Preliminary Report', *The
   Journal of Modern History* 40 (1968),
   pp. 1–56.
4 Bacon, Francis, 'Novum Organum',
   in Montagu, Basil (trans.), *The Works
   of Francis Bacon, Lord Chancellor
   of England: A New Edition* vol. 14
   (London: 1831), p. 89.
5 Ing, Janet, 'The Mainz Indulgences
   of 1454/5: A review of recent
   scholarship', *The British Library
   Journal* 9 (1983), p. 19.
6 There were, however, interesting
   regional variations in the popular
   enthusiasm for purgatory and
   penitential deeds. See MacCulloch,
   Diarmaid, *Reformation: Europe's
   House Divided 1490–1700* (London:
   2003), pp. 10–16.
7 Eisermann, Falk, 'The Indulgence
   as a Media Event: Developments in
   Communication through Broadsides
   in the Fifteenth Century' in Swanson,
   R.N. (ed.), *Promissory Notes on the
   Treasury of Merits Indulgences in
   Late Medieval Europe* (Leiden: 2006),
   pp. 312–3.

8 On Ockham, and for this translation, MacCulloch, *A History of Christianity*, p. 559.

9 Buck, Lawrence P. '"Anatomia Antichristi": Form and Content of the Papal Antichrist', *The Sixteenth Century Journal* 42 (2011), pp. 349–68.

10 For a concise history, Shaffern, Robert W., 'The Medieval Theology of Indulgences' in Swanson (ed.), *Promissory Notes*, pp. 11–36.

11 *Geoffrey Chaucer / The Canterbury Tales* (London: 1996), p. 315.

12 Macek, Josef, *The Hussite Movement in Bohemia* (Prague: 1958), p. 16

13 Eisenstein, Elizabeth, *The Printing Press as an Agent of Change: Communications and Cultural Transformations in Early-Modern Europe* (Cambridge: 1979), p. 375.

14 Eisermann, 'The Indulgence as a Media Event', p. 327 n. 50.

15 MacCulloch, *Reformation*, p. 15; Duffy, Eamon, *The Stripping of the Altars: Traditional Religion in England 1400–1580* (New Haven: 1992), p. 288.

16 The text is printed in Jenks, Stuart (ed.), *Documents on the Papal Plenary Indulgences 1300–1517 Preached in the Regnum Teutonicum* (Leiden: 2018), pp. 224–66.

17 Croiset Van Uchelen, Ton and Dijstelberge, Paul, 'Propaganda for the Indulgence of Saintes' in Blouw, Paul Valkema et al, *Dutch Typography in the Sixteenth Century: The Collected Works of Paul Valkema Blouw* (Leiden: 2013), p. 25.

18 Collinson, Patrick, *The Reformation* (London: 2003), pp. 34–5.

19 Füssel, Stephan, *Gutenberg and the impact of printing* (Aldershot: 2003), p. 149.

20 Ibid. pp. 151–2.

21 Ibid. pp. 155–6.

22 For an English text of the Ninety-Five Theses, Russell, William R. (trans.), *Martin Luther / The Ninety-Five Theses and Other Writings* (New York: 2017), pp. 3–13.

23 Smith, Preserved, 'Luther and Henry VIII', *The English Historical Review* 25 (1910), p. 656.

24 Translated in Shaffern, 'Medieval Theology of Indulgences', p. 15.

25 Russell (trans.), *Martin Luther / The Ninety-Five Theses* pp. 4–6.

26 Ibid. p. 12.

27 MacCulloch, *Reformation*, p. 121.

28 See Collinson, Patrick, *The Reformation* (London: 2003), p. 27.

29 Wace, Henry and Buccheim (trans.) C.H., *Luther's Primary Works: Together with his Shorter and Larger Catechisms*, (London: 1846), p. 175.

30 St. Clare Byrne, Muriel (ed.) *The Letters of King Henry VIII* (New York: 1968), p. 11.

31 On the vexed question of the *Assertio*'s real authorship, see Rex, Richard, 'The English Campaign against Luther in the 1520s: The Alexander Prize Essay', *Transactions of the Royal Historical Society* 39 (1989), pp. 85–106.

32 O'Donovan, Louis (ed.), *Assertio Septem Sacramentorum or Defence of the Seven Sacraments by Henry VIII, king of England* (New York: 1908), pp. 188–9.

33 Brewer, J. S., (ed.) *Letters and Papers, Foreign and Domestic, Henry VIII, Volume 3, 1519–1523* (London: 1867), No. 1510, p. 622.

34 Luis Quijada, translated in Parker, Geoffrey, *Emperor: A New Life of Charles V* (New Haven: 2019), xvii.

35 Forell, George W., Lehmann, Helmut T. (eds.), *Luther's Works* vol. 32, (Philadephia: 1958), pp. 112–3.

36 This translation, Hendrix, Scott H., *Martin Luther: Visionary Reformer* (New Haven: 2015), p. 105.

37 Rupp, E. Gordon and Watson, Philip S. (trans.), *Luther and Erasmus: Free Will and Salvation* (London: 1969), p. 37.

38 Graus, František 'From Resistance to Revolt: The Late Medieval Peasant Wars in the Context of Social Crisis'

in Bak, Janos (ed.), *The German Peasant War of 1525* (Abingdon: 2013), p. 7.

39 Cohn, Henry J., 'The Peasants of Swabia, 1525' in ibid., p. 10. See also Sreenivasan, Govind P., 'The Social Origins of the Peasants' War of 1525 in Upper Swabia', *Past & Present* 171 (2001), pp. 30–65.

40 An English translation is provided in ibid. pp. 13–18.

41 Official account of the disorder in Erfurt, this translation, Scott, Tom, and Scribner, Bob (trans.), *The German Peasants' War: A History in Documents* (Amherst: 1991), pp. 185–8.

42 Translated in ibid. pp. 157–8.

43 On aristocratic reaction to the rebellion, Sea, Thomas F., 'The German Princes' Responses to the Peasants' Revolt of 1525', *Central European History* 40 (2007), pp. 219–40.

44 Translated in ibid. p. 291.

45 Ibid. p. 318.

46 Hook, Judith, *The Sack of Rome 1527* (2nd edn.) (Basingstoke: 2004), p. 46.

47 See Parker, *Emperor*, p. 162.

48 Hook, *Sack of Rome*, p. 156.

49 Parker, *Emperor*, p. 168.

50 McGregor, James H. (trans.), *Luigi Guicciardini / The Sack of Rome* (New York: 1993), p. 78.

51 Kneale, *Rome: A History in Seven Sackings*, p. 194.

52 McGregor, *Luigi Guicciardini*, pp. 81–2. See also Hook, *Sack of Rome*, p. 161.

53 McGregor, *Luigi Guicciardini*, p. 97.

54 McGregor, *Luigi Guicciardini*, p. 98

55 Kneale, *Rome: A History in Seven Sackings*, p. 201

56 McGregor, *Luigi Guicciardini*, p. 98

57 Ibid. p. 114

58 Sherer, Idan, 'A bloody carnival? Charles V's soldiers and the sack of Rome in 1527', *Renaissance Studies* 34 (2019), p. 785. See also Hook, *Sack of Rome*, p. 177.

59 Parker, *Emperor*, p. 172.

60 On the broader legacy of Protestantism to political systems and values, Ryrie, Alec, *Protestants: The Faith that Made the Modern World* (New York: 2017), pp. 1–12.

61 Russell (trans.), *Martin Luther / The Ninety-Five Theses* p. 121.

BIBLIOGRAPHY OF WORKS
CITED IN THE TEXT

Primary Sources

—, *Calendar of Various Chancery Rolls: Supplementary Close Rolls, Welsh Rolls, Scutage Rolls, A.D. 1277–1326*, London: HM Stationery Office, 1912.

—, *Cronica di Giovanni Villani: A Miglior Lezione Ridotta* V, Florence: Per Il Magheri, 1823.

—, *Geoffrey Chaucer / The Canterbury Tales*, London: Penguin Popular Classics, 1996.

Andrea, Alfred J. (trans.), *The Capture of Constantinople: The Hystoria Constantinoplitana of Gunther of Pairis*, Philadelphia: University of Pennsylvania Press, 1997.

anon., *The Ecclesiastical History of Socrates… Translated from the Greek, with some account of the author, and notes selected from Valesius.*, London: Henry G. Bohn, 1853

Babcock, Emily Atwater and Krey, A. C. (trans.), *A History of Deeds Done Beyond the Sea: By William Archbishop of Tyre* (2 vols.), New York: Columbia University Press, 1943.

Bale, Anthony (ed.), *John Mandeville / Book of Marvels and Travels*, Oxford: Oxford University Press, 2012.

Barber, Malcolm and Bate, Keith (ed. and trans.), *The Templars: Selected Sources*, Manchester: Manchester University Press, 2002.

Barber, Malcolm and Bate, Keith (eds.), *Letters from the East: Crusaders,*

Pilgrims and Settlers in the 12th–13th Centuries, Farnham: Ashgate, 2013.

Barney, Stephen A., Lewis, W. J., Beach, J. A, Berghof, Oliver (eds.), *The Etymologies of Isidore of Seville*, Cambridge: Cambridge University Press, 2006.

Barton, Simon and Fletcher, Richard, *The World of El Cid: Chronicles of the Spanish Reconquest*, Manchester: Manchester University Press, 2000.

Bédier, J. and Aubry, P. (eds.), *Les Chansons de Croisade avec Leurs Melodies*, Paris: Champion, 1909.

Bernardo, Aldo (trans.), *Francesco Petrarch / Letters on Familiar Matters (Rerum Familiarium Libri): Vol. 1: Books I–VIII*, New York: Italica Press, 1975.

Berry, Virginia Gingerick, *Odo of Deuil / De Profectione Ludovici VII in Orientam*, New York: W. W. Norton, 1948.

Bettenson, Henry (trans.), *Saint Augustine / City of God*, London: Penguin Classics, 2003.

Bird, Jessalyn, Peters, Edward and Powell, James M. (eds.), *Crusade and Christendom: Annotated Documents in Translation from Innocent III to the Fall of Acre, 1187–1291*, Philadelphia: University of Pennsylvania Press, 2013.

Blankinship, Khalid Yahya (trans.), *The History of al-Tabari Vol. XI: The*

Challenge to the Empires, New York: State University of New York Press, 1993.

Bouquet, Martin (ed.), *Receuil des historiens des Gaules et de la France 21*, Paris: V. Palmé, 1855.

Boyle, J.A. (trans.), *Genghis Khan: The History of the World-Conqueror / 'Ala-ad-Din 'Ata Malik Juvaini* (revd. edn.), Manchester: Manchester University Press, 1997.

Brewer, J. S., (ed.), *Letters and Papers, Foreign and Domestic, Henry VIII, Volume 3, 1519–1523*, London: HM Stationery Office, 1867.

Brehaut, Earnest (trans.), *Gregory bishop of Tours / History of the Franks*, New York: Columbia University Press, 1916.

Burgess, Glyn (trans.), *The Song of Roland*, London, Penguin Classics, 1990.

Chabot, J-B (trans.) *Chronique de Michel le Syrien, patriarche jacobite d'Antioche, 1166-1199*, Vol. 2, Paris: E. Leroux, 1901.

Christiansen, Eric (trans.), *Dudo of St. Quentin / History of the Normans*, Woodbridge: The Boydell Press, 1998.

Church, Alfred John and Brodribb, William Jackson (trans.), Lane Fox, Robin (intro.), *Tacitus / Annals and Histories*, New York: Alfred A. Knopf, 2009

Cohen, J. M. (trans.), *Christopher Columbus / The Four Voyages*, London: Penguin Classics, 1969.

Cohn Jr, Samuel K. (trans.), *Popular Protest in Late Medieval Europe*, Manchester: Manchester University Press, 2004.

Colbert, Benjamin (ed.), *The Travels of Marco Polo*, Ware: Wordsworth Editions, 1997.

Cowdrey, H. E. J. (trans.), *The Register of Pope Gregory: 1073–1085: An English Translation*, ,Oxford: Oxford University Press, 2002.

Cross, Samuel Hazzard and Sherbowitz-Wetzor, Olgerd P. (trans.), *The Russian Primary Chronicle: Laurentian Text*, Cambridge, Mass.: The Medieval Academy of America, 1953.

Dass, Nirmal (trans.), *Viking Attacks on Paris: The Bella parisiacae urbis of Abbo of Saint-Germain-des-Prés*, Paris: Peeters, 2007.

Davis, Raymond (trans.), *The Lives of the Eighth-Century Popes (Liber Pontificalis)*, Liverpool: Liverpool University Press, 1992.

de Rachewiltz, Igor (trans.), *The Secret History of the Mongols: A Mongolian Epic Chronicle of the Thirteenth Century* (2 vols.), Leiden: Brill, 2006.

de Sélincourt, Aubrey (ed.) *Livy / The Early History of Rome*, (revd. edn.), London: Penguin Books, 2002.

de Vere, Gaston du C. (trans.), *Giorgio Vasari / Lives of the Painters, Sculptors and Architects*, 2 vols, London: Everyman's Library, 1996.

Dewing, H. B. (trans.), *Procopius / History of the Wars, I, Books 1–2*, Cambridge, Mass.: Harvard University Press, 1914.

Dewing, H. B. (trans.), *Procopius / History of the Wars, II, Books 3–4*, Cambridge, Mass.: Harvard University Press, 1916.

Dewing, H. B. (trans.), *Procopius / On Buildings*, Cambridge, Mass.: Harvard University Press, 1940.

Dobson, R. B. (ed.), *The Peasants' Revolt of 1381* (2nd edn.), London: The Macmillan Press Ltd., 1983.

Douie, Decima L. and Farmer, David Hugh, *Magna Vita Sancti Hugonis / The Life of St Hugh of Lincoln* (2 vols.), Oxford: Clarendon Press, 1985.

Dümmler, Ernst (ed.), *Poetae latini aevi Carolini* I, Berlin: Apud Weidmannos 1881.

Edgington, Susan (trans.), *Albert of Aachen / Historia Ierosolominitana: History of the Journey to Jerusalem*, Oxford: Clarendon Press, 2007.

Evans, Allan (ed.), *Francesco Balducci Pegolotti / La Practica della Mercatura*,

Cambridge, Mass.: The Medieval Academy of America, 1936.

Fischer Drew, Katherine (trans.), *The Laws of the Salian Franks*, Philadelphia: University of Pennsylvania Press, 1991.

Fishbein, Michael, *The History of al-Tabari, Vol. VIII: The Victory of Islam*, New York: State University of New York Press, 1997.

Forell, George W. and Lehmann, Helmut T. (eds.), *Luther's Works* vol. 32, Philadelphia: Muhlenberg Press, 1958.

Friedmann, Yohanan, *The History of al-Tabari, Vol. XII: The Battle of al-Qadisiyyah and the Conquest of Syria and Palestine*, New York: State University of New York Press, 1991.

Fremantle, W.H. (trans.) *Saint Jerome / Select Letters and Works*, New York: Christian Literature Company, 1893.

Fry, Timothy (trans.), *The Rule of St. Benedict In English*, Collegeville: Liturgical Press, 2018.

Füssel, Stephan (ed.), *The Gutenberg Bible of 1454: With a commentary on the life and work of Johannes Gutenberg, the printing of the Bible, the distinctive features of the Göttingen copy, the Göttingen Model Book and the 'Helmasperger Notarial Instrument'*, Köln: Taschen, 2018.

Gardner, Edmund G. (ed.), *The Dialogues of Saint Gregory the Great*, Merchantville: Evolution Publishing, 2010.

Gantz, Jeffrey (trans.), *The Mabinogion*, London: Penguin Classics, 1973.

Ganz, David (trans.), *Einhard and Notker the Stammerer: Two Lives of Charlemagne*, London: Penguin Classics, 2008.

Garton, Charles (trans.), *The Metrical Life of St Hugh of Lincoln*, Lincoln: Honywood Press, 1986.

George, William and Waters, Emily (trans.), *Vespasiano da Bisticci / The Vespasiano Memoirs: Lives of Illustrious Men of the XVth Century*,

London: George Routledge & Sons, 1926.

Gibb, H.A.R. (trans.), *Ibn Battuta / Travels in Asia and Africa 1325-1354*, London: Routledge & Kegan Paul Ltd, 1929.

Given, John (trans.), *The Fragmentary History of Priscus: Attila, the Huns and the Roman Empire, AD 430–476*, Merchantville: Evolution Publishing, 2014.

Graves, Robert (trans.) and Rives J. B. (rev. and intro), *Suetonius / The Twelve Caesars*, London: Penguin Books, 2007.

Greenia, M. Conrad (trans.), *Bernard of Clairvaux / In Praise of the New Knighthood* (revd. edn.), Trappist: Cistercian Publications, 2000.

Hamilton, Walter (trans.) and Wallace-Hadrill (intro.), *Ammianus Marcellinus / The Later Roman Empire (A.D. 354–378)*, London: Penguin Books, 1986.

Hammond, Martin (trans.), *Marcus Aurelius / Meditations*, London: Penguin Classics, 2014.

Hankins, James (trans.), *Leonardo Bruni / History of the Florentine People Volume I: Books I–IV*, Cambridge, Mass.: Harvard University Press, 2001.

Hildinger, Erik (trans.), *Giovanni da Pian del Carpine, Archbishop of Antivari, d. 1252 / The story of the Mongols who we call the Tartars*, Boston: Branden Publishing Company, 1996.

Hill, John Hugh and Hill, Laurita L. (trans.), *Raymond d'Aguilers / Historia Francorum Qui Ceperunt Iherusalem*, Philadelphia: American Philosophical Society, 1968.

Hill, Rosalind (ed.), *Gesta Francorum et Aliorum Hierosoliminatorum: The Deeds of the Franks and the Other Pilgrims to Jerusalem*, Oxford: Clarendon Press, 1962.

Holden, A. J. (ed), Gregory, S. (trans.) and Crouch D., *History of William*

Marshal (3 vols.), London: Anglo-Norman Text Society, 2002–06.

Holland, Tom (trans.), *Herodotus / The Histories*, London: Penguin, 2013.

Hollander, Lee M. (trans.), *Snorri Sturluson / Heimskringla: History of the Kings of Norway*, Austin: University of Texas Press, 1964.

Horrox, Rosemary (trans. and ed.), *The Black Death*, Manchester: Manchester University Press, 1994.

Humphreys, R. Stephen (trans.), *The History of al-Tabari, Vol. XV: The Crisis of the Early Caliphate*, New York: State University of New York Press, 1990.

Huygens, R. B. C. (trans.), *Lettres de Jacques de Vitry*, Edition Critique, Leiden: Brill, 1960.

Jackson, Peter (ed.), *The Mission of Friar William of Rubruck*, London: Hakluyt Society, 1990.

Jeffreys, Elizabeth, Jeffreys, Michael and Scott, Roger (eds.), *The Chronicle of John Malalas*, Leiden: Brill, 1986.

Jenks, Stuart (ed.), *Documents on the Papal Plenary Indulgences 1300–1517 Preached in the Regnum Teutonicum*, Leiden: Brill, 2018.

Johnson, Allan Chester, Coleman-Norton, Paul R and Bourne, Frank Card (eds.), *Ancient Roman Statutes: A Translation With Introduction, Commentary, Glossary, and Index*, Austin: University of Texas Press, 1961.

Jones, Horace Leonard (trans.), *The Geography of Strabo, vol VI*, Cambridge, Massachusetts: Harvard University Press, 1929.

Jones, John Harris (trans.), *Ibn Abd al-Hakam / The History of the Conquest of Spain*, New York: Burt Franklin, 1969.

Juynboll, Gautier H. A. (trans.), *The History of al-Tabari vol. XIII: The Conquest of Iraq, Southwestern Persia and Egypt*, New York: State University of New York Press, 1989.

Kenney, E.J. (trans.), *Apuleius / The Golden Ass* (revd. ed.), London: Penguin Books, 2004.

Kibler, William W. (ed.), *Chrétien de Troyes / Arthurian Romances* (revd. edn.), London: Penguin Classics, 2001.

Kline, A.S. (trans.), *Petrarch / The Complete Canzoniere*, Poetry in Translation, 2001.

Latham, Ronald (trans.), *Marco Polo / The Travels*, London: Penguin Books, 1958.

Lewis, Robert E. (ed.), *Lotario dei Segni (Pope Innocent III) / De Miseria Condicionis Humane*, Athens, GA: University of Georgia Press, 1978.

Luard, H. R. (ed.), *Annales Monastici* vol. 4, London: Longmans, Green, Reader and Dyer, 1869.

Lumby, J. R. (ed.), *Chronicon Henrici Knighton vel Cnitthon, Monachi Leycestrensis* II, London: Rolls Series, 1895.

Mabillon, Jean (ed.), *Annales ordinis S. Benedicti occidentalium monachorum patriarchæ*, vol. 4., Paris, 1707.

Magoulias, Harry J. (trans.), *O City of Byzantium, Annals of Niketas Choniates*, Detroit: Wayne State University Press, 1984.

Magoulias, Harry J. (trans.), *Decline and Fall of Byzantium to the Ottoman Turks*, Detroit: Wayne State University Press, 1975.

Mango, Cyril and Scott, Roger (trans.), *The Chronicle of Theophanes Confessor: Byzantine and Near Eastern History AD 284–813*, Oxford: Clarendon Press, 1997.

Mariev, Sergei (trans.), *Ioannis Antiocheni Fragmenta quae supersunt Omnia*, Berlin: W. de Gruyter, 2008.

McCauley, Leo. P. et al, *Funeral Orations by Saint Gregory and Saint Ambrose (The Fathers of the Church, Volume 22)*, Washington: The Catholic University of America Press, 2010.

McDermott, Timothy (ed.), *Aquinas / Selected Philosophical Writings*, Oxford: Oxford University Press, 2008.

McGregor, James H. (trans.), *Luigi*

Guicciardini / *The Sack of Rome*, New York: Ithaca Press, 1993.

Michael, Maurice (trans.), *The Annals of Jan Długosz: Annales Seu Cronicae Incliti Regni Poloniae*, Chichester: IM Publications, 1997.

Michell, Robert and Forbes, Nevill (trans.), *The Chronicle of Novgorod 1016–1471*, London: Camden Society Third Series, 1914.

Middlemore, S. (trans.), *Burckhardt, Jacob / The Civilization of the Renaissance in Italy*, London: Penguin Classics, 1990.

Montagu, Basil (trans.), *The Works of Francis Bacon, Lord Chancellor of England: A New Edition* vol. 14, London: William Pickering, 1831.

Moyle, John Baron (trans.), *The Institutes of Justinian*, (Oxford: Clarendon Press, 1906).

Myers, A. R. (ed.), *English Historical Documents IV, 1327–1485*, London: Eyre & Spottiswoode, 1969.

Newitt, Malyn (ed.), *The Portuguese in West Africa, 1415–1670: A Documentary History*, Cambridge: Cambridge University Press, 2010.

O'Donovan, Louis (ed.), *Assertio Septem Sacramentorum or Defence of the Seven Sacraments by Henry VIII, king of England*, New York: Benziger Brothers, 1908.

Panofsky, Erwin and Panofsky-Soergel, Gerda (eds.), *Abbot Suger on the Abbey Church of St.-Denis and its Art Treasures* (2nd. ed.), Princeton: Princeton University Press, 1979.

Peters, Edward (ed.), *Christian Society and the Crusades 1198-1229. Sources in Translation including 'The Capture of Damietta' by Oliver of Paderborn*, Philadelphia, University of Pennsylvania Press, 1971.

Platnauer, Maurice (trans.), *Claudian* (2 vols), New York: G. P. Putnam's Sons, 1922.

Poupardin, René (ed.), *Monuments de l'histoire des Abbeyes de Saint-Philibert*, Paris: Alphones Picard et Fils, 1905.

Radice, Betty (trans.), *The Letters of the Younger Pliny*, London: Penguin Books, 1969.

Ravenstein, E. G. (trans.), *A Journal of the First Voyage of Vasco da Gama, 1497–1499*, London: Hakluyt Society, 1898.

Richards, D.S. (trans.), *The Chronicle of Ibn al-Athir for the Crusading Period from al-Kamil fi'l Ta'rikh* (3 vols.), Farnham: Ashgate, 2006.

Richter, Irma A. and Wells, Thereza (eds.), *Leonardo da Vinci / Notebooks*, Oxford: Oxford University Press, 2008.

Ridley, Ronald T. (trans.), *Zosimus / New History*, Leiden: Brill, 1982.

Riggs, Charles T. (trans.), *Mehmed the Conqueror / by Kritovoulos*, Princeton: Princeton University Press, 1954.

Riley-Smith, Jonathan and Louise (eds.), *The Crusades: Idea and Reality, 1095–1274*, London: Edward Arnold, 1981.

Riley, H. T. (ed.), *Chronica Monasterii S. Albani III*, London: Rolls Series, 1866.

Riley, Henry Thomas (ed.), *The Comedies of Plautus* vol. 1, London: Henry G. Bohn, 1912.

Robinson, George W. (trans.), *Eugippius / The Life of Saint Severinus*, Cambridge, Mass: Harvard University Press, 1914.

Robinson, I. S. (trans.), *Eleventh Century Germany: The Swabian Chronicles*, Manchester: Manchester University Press, 2008.

Robinson, I. S. (trans.), *Eleventh Century Germany: The Swabian Chronicles*, Manchester: Manchester University Press, 2008.

Robinson, James Harvey (ed.), *Readings in European History* vol. 1, Boston: Ginn & Company, 1904.

Rothwell, Harry (ed.), *English Historical Documents III: 1189–1327* (new edn.), London: Routledge, 1996.

Rudd, Niall (trans.), *Cicero / The Republic and The Laws*, Oxford: Oxford University Press, 1998.

Rupp, E. Gordon and Watson, Philip S. (trans.), *Luther and Erasmus: Free Will and Salvation*, London: John Knox Press, 1969.

Ryan, Frances Rita and Fink, Harold S. (eds.), *Fulcher of Chartres: A History of the Expedition to Jerusalem, 1095–1127*, Knoxville: University of Tennessee, 1969.

St. Clare Byrne, Muriel (ed.), *The Letters of King Henry VIII*, New York: Funk & Wagnalls, 1968.

Schroeder, H. J. (trans.), *Disciplinary Decrees of the General Councils: Text, Translation and Commentary*, St Louis: B. Herder, 1937.

Scott, Tom, and Scribner, Bob (trans.), *The German Peasants' War: A History in Documents*, Amherst: Humanity Books, 1991.

Sewter, E. R. A (trans.) and Frankopan, Peter (intro.), *Anna Komnene / The Alexiad* (revd. edn.), London: Penguin Classics, 2009.

Sherley-Price, Leo (trans.), *Bede / A History of the English Church and People* (revd. edn.), Harmondsworth: Penguin Classics, 1968.

Sitwell, G. (trans.), *St. Odo of Cluny: being the Life of St. Odo of Cluny / by John of Salerno. And, the Life of St. Gerald of Aurillac by St. Odo*, London: Sheed & Ward, 1958.

Sprenger, Aloys (trans.), *El-Masudi's Historical Encyclopaedia Entitled Meadows of Gold and Mines of Gems* vol. I, London: Oriental Translation Fund of Great Britain and Ireland, 1841.

Sweetenham, Carole (trans.), *Robert the Monk's History of the First Crusade: Historia Iherosolimitana*, Abingdon: Routledge, 2016.

Thompson, Edward Maunde, (ed.), *Adae Murimuth Continuatio Chronicarum / Robertus De Avesbury De Gestis Mirabilibus Regis Edwardi Tertii*, London: Rolls Series, 1889.

Wace, Henry and Buccheim, C.H. (trans.), *Luther's Primary Works: Together with his Shorter and Larger Catechisms*, London: Hodder & Stoughton: 1846.

Wallace-Hadrill, J.M. (trans.), *The Fourth Book of the Chronicle of Fredegar, with its continuations*, Westport: Greenwood Press, 1960.

Waterfield, Robin (trans.), *Polybius / The Histories*, Oxford: Oxford University Press, 2010.

Watts, Victor (trans.), *Boethius / The Consolation of Philosophy* (revd. ed.), London: Penguin Books, 1999.

Webb, J. F. (trans.), *The Age of Bede* (revd. edn.), London: Penguin Classics, 1998.

Weiskotten, Herbert T. (trans.), *The Life of Augustine: A Translation of the Sancti Augustini Vita by Possidius, Bishop of Calama*, Merchantville, NJ.: Evolution Publishing, 2008.

West, David (trans. and ed.), *Virgil / The Aeneid* (revd. edn.), London: Penguin Books, 2003.

Whitelock, Dorothy (ed.), *English Historical Documents I 500–1042* (2nd edn.), London: Routledge, 1979.

Wilkinson, John, Hill, Joyce and Ryan, W. F., *Jerusalem Pilgrimage 1099–1185*, London: The Hakluyt Society, 1988.

William R. (trans.), *Martin Luther / The Ninety-Five Theses and Other Writings*, New York: Penguin Classics, 2017.

Williamson, G.A. (trans.), *Eusebius / The History of the Church* (revd. edn.), London: Penguin Books, 1989.

Williamson, G. A. and Sarris, Peter (trans.), *Procopius / The Secret History* (revd. edn.), London: Penguin, 2007.

Wilson, William Burton (trans.), *John Gower / Mirour de l'Omme (The Mirror of Mankind)*, Woodbridge: Boydell & Brewer, 1992.

Winterbottom, Michael (trans.), *Gildas / The Ruin of Britain and other works*, Chichester: Phillimore, 1978.

Witakowski, Witold (trans.), *Pseudo-Dionysius of Tel-Mahre, Chronicle (known also as the Chronicle of

Zuqnin) part III, Liverpool: Liverpool University Press, 1996.

Wolf, Kenneth Baxter (trans.), *Conquerors and chroniclers of early medieval Spain*, Liverpool: Liverpool University Press, 1990.

Womersley, David (ed.), *Edward Gibbon / The History of the Decline and Fall of*

the Roman Empire, vol. III, London: Penguin Classics, 1996.

Wright, F.A. (trans.), *Jerome / Select Letters*, Cambridge: Harvard University Press, 1933.

Zenokovsky, Serge (ed.), *Medieval Russia's Epics, Chronicles and Tales*, New York: E. P. Dutton, 1974.

Secondary Sources

Abu-Lughod, Janet L., *Before European Hegemony: The World System A.D. 1250–1350*, New York: Oxford University Press, 1991.

Adiele, Pius Onyemechi, *The Popes, the Catholic Church and the Transatlantic Enslavement of Black Africans 1418–1839*, Hildesheim: Georg Olms Verlag, 2017.

Angold, Michael, *The Fourth Crusade: Event and Context*, Abingdon: Routledge, 2014.

Asbridge, Thomas, *The Greatest Knight: The Remarkable Life of William Marshal, the Power Behind Five English Thrones*, London: Simon & Schuster, 2015.

Ashe, Geoffrey, *Land to the West: St Brendan's Voyage to America*, London: Collins, 1962.

Aurell, Jaume, *Medieval Self-Coronations: The History and Symbolism of a Ritual*, Cambridge: Cambridge University Press, 2020.

Babinger, Franz, *Mehmed the Conqueror and His Time*, Princeton: Princeton University Press, 1978.

Bagge, Sverre, Gelting, Michael H., and Lindkvist, Thomas (eds.), *Feudalism: New Landscapes of Debate*, Turnhout: Brepols, 2011.

Bak, Janos (ed.), *The German Peasant War of 1525*, Abingdon: Routledge, 2013.

Barber, Malcolm, *The New Knighthood: A History of the Order of the Temple*,

Cambridge: Cambridge University Press, 1994.

Barber, Richard, *The Knight and Chivalry* (revd. edn.), Woodbridge: Boydell Press, 1995.

Beach, Alison I. and Cochelin, Isabelle (eds.), *The Cambridge History of Medieval Monasticism in the Latin West* (2 vols.), Cambridge: Cambridge University Press, 2020.

Beard, Mary, *SPQR: A History of Ancient Rome*, London: Profile Books, 2015.

Benjamin, Craig (ed.), *The Cambridge World History vol. 4: A World with States, Empires and Networks, 1200 BCE–900 CE*, Cambridge: Cambridge University Press, 2015.

Bentley, Jerry H., Subrahmanyam, Sanjay and Weisner-Hanks, Merry E., *The Cambridge World History VI: The Construction of a Global World 1400–1800 C.E. / Part I: Foundations*, Cambridge: Cambridge University Press, 2015.

Bergreen, Laurence, *Columbus: The Four Voyages 1492–1504*, New York: Viking, 2011.

Bergreen, Laurence, *Over the Edge of the World: Magellan's Terrifying Circumnavigation of the Globe*, New York: William Morrow, 2003.

Blouw, Paul Valkema et al, *Dutch Typography in the Sixteenth Century: The Collected Works of Paul Valkema Blouw*, Leiden: Brill, 2013.

Bony, Jean, *French Gothic Architecture of*

the 12th and 13th Centuries, Berkeley: University of California Press, 1983.

Bowersock, G. W., The Crucible of Islam, Cambridge, Mass., Harvard University Press, 2017.

Bowlus, Charles R., The Battle of Lechfeld and its Aftermath, August 955, Aldershot: Ashgate, 2006.

Boynton, S. and Reilly D. J. (eds.), Resounding Image: Medieval Intersections of Art, Music, and Sound, Turnhout: Brepols, 2015.

Bumke, Joachim, The Concept of Knighthood in the Middle Ages, New York: AMS Press, 1982.

Cameron, Averil et al (eds.), The Cambridge Ancient History XIV: Late Antiquity, Empire and Successors, A.D. 42--600, Cambridge: Cambridge University Press, 2000.

Castor, Helen, Joan of Arc: A History, London: Faber & Faber, 2014.

Chazan, Robert, In the Year 1096: The First Crusade and The Jews, Philadelphia: Jewish Publication Society, 1996.

Christiansen, Eric, The Northern Crusades (2nd edn.), London: Penguin, 1997.

Clark, James G., The Benedictines in the Middle Ages, Woodbridge: Boydell Press, 2011.

Cohn, Norman, The Pursuit of the Millennium: Revolutionary Millenarians and Mystical Anarchists of the Middle Ages, London: Temple Smith 1970.

Collins, Roger, Charlemagne, Basingstoke: Palgrave Macmillan, 1998.

Collinson, Patrick, The Reformation, London: Weidenfeld and Nicholson, 2003.

Colvin, H. M. (ed.), The History of the King's Works I: The Middle Ages, London: HM Stationery Office, 1963.

Crouch, David, Tournament, London: Hambledon & London, 2005.

Crowley, Roger, Constantinople: The Last Great Siege, 1453, London: Faber & Faber, 2005.

Curry, Anne, Agincourt, Oxford: Oxford University Press, 2015.

de la Bédoyère, Guy, Roman Britain: A New History (revd. edn.), London: Thames & Hudson, 2013.

De la Vassière, Étienne, Sogdian Traders: A History, Leiden: Brill, 2005.

De Rachewiltz, Igor, Papal Envoys to the Great Khans, London: Faber & Faber, 1971.

De Ridder-Symoens, H., A History of the University in Europe I, Cambridge: Cambridge University Press, 1992.

DeVries, Kelly and Smith, Robert Douglas, Medieval Military Technology (2nd edn.), Ontario: University of Toronto Press, 2012.

Disney, A. R., A History of Portugal and the Portuguese Empire vol. I, Cambridge: Cambridge University Press, 2009.

Donner, Fred M., The Articulation of Early Islamic State Structures, London: Routledge, 2017.

Drayton, Elizabeth, The Moor's Last Stand: How Seven Centuries of Muslim Rule in Spain Came to an End, London: Profile Books, 2017.

Eisenstein, Elizabeth, The Printing Press as an Agent of Change: Communications and Cultural Transformations in Early-Modern Europe, Cambridge: Cambridge University Press, 1979.

Erlande-Brandenburg, Alain, The Cathedral Builders of the Middle Ages, London: Thames & Hudson, 1995.

Ettinghausen, Richard, Grabar, Oleg, and Jenkins-Madina, Marilyn, Islamic Art and Architecture 650–1250 (2nd edn.), New Haven/London: Yale University Press, 2001.

Falk, Seb, The Light Ages: A Medieval Journey of Discovery, London: Allen Lane, 2020.

Ferguson, Robert, The Hammer and the

Cross: A New History of the Vikings, London: Allen Lane, 2009.

Firnhaber-Baker, Justine, The Jacquerie of 1358: A French Peasants' Revolt, Oxford: Oxford University Press, 2021.

Firnhaber-Baker, Justine and Schoenaers, Dirk, The Routledge History Handbook of Medieval Revolt, Abingdon: Routledge, 2017.

Fletcher, Richard, The Quest for El Cid, Oxford: Oxford University Press, 1989.

Foyle, Jonathan, Lincoln Cathedral: The Biography of a Great Building, London: Scala, 2015.

Frankopan, Peter, The First Crusade: The Call From the East, London: Vintage, 2012.

Frankopan, Peter, The Silk Roads: A New History of the World, London: Bloomsbury, 2015.

Freely, John, The Grand Turk: Sultan Mehmet II – Conqueror of Constantinople, Master of an Empire and Lord of Two Seas, London: I. B. Taurus, 2010.

Fried, Johannes, Charlemagne, Cambridge, Mass.: Harvard University Press, 2016.

Füssel, Stephan, Gutenberg and the Impact of Printing, Aldershot: Ashgate, 2003.

Garnsey, Peter and Saller, Richard (eds.), The Roman Empire: Economy, Society and Culture (2nd edn.), London/New York: Bloomsbury Academic, 2014.

Ghosh, K. and Gillespie, V. (eds.), After Arundel: Religious Writing in Fifteenth-Century England, Turnhout: Brepols, 2011.

Gibbon, Edward, The History of the Decline and Fall of the Roman Empire: Abridged Edition, London: Penguin Classics, 2000.

Gilson, Simon, Dante and Renaissance Florence, Cambridge: Cambridge University Press, 2005.

Goodman, Martin, van Kooten, George H. and van Buiten, JTAGM (eds.), Abraham, the Nations, and the Hagarites: Jewish, Christian, and Islamic Perspectives on Kinship with Abraham, Leiden: Brill, 2010.

Grabar, Oleg, The Dome of the Rock, Cambridge, Mass.: Belknap Press, 2006.

Haldon, John, The Byzantine Wars, Stroud: The History Press, 2008.

Halsall, Guy, Barbarian Migrations and the Roman West 376–568, Cambridge: Cambridge University Press, 2007.

Hansen, Valerie, The Year 1000: When Explorers Connected the World – and Globalization Began, London: Viking, 2020.

Harper, Kyle, The Fate of Rome: Climate, Disease, & the End of an Empire, Princeton/Oxford: Princeton University Press, 2017.

Harper, Kyle, Slavery in the Late Roman World, AD 275–425, Cambridge: Cambridge University Press, 2011.

Harris, Jonathan, Constantinople: Capital of Byzantium (2nd edn.), London: Bloomsbury, 2017.

Harris, William V. (ed.), The Ancient Mediterranean Environment Between Science and History, Leiden: Brill, 2013.

Harriss, Gerald, Shaping the Nation: England 1360–1461, Oxford: Oxford Univeristy Press, 2005.

Haskins, Charles Homer, The Renaissance of the Twelfth Century, Cambridge, Mass: Harvard University Press, 1927.

Heather, Peter, The Fall of the Roman Empire: A New History of Rome and the Barbarians, Oxford: Oxford University Press, 2006.

Heather, Peter, The Goths, Oxford: Blackwell Publishing, 1996.

Hendrix, Scott H., Martin Luther: Visionary Reformer, New Haven: Yale University Press, 2015.

Hibbert, Christopher, Florence: The Biography of a City, London: Penguin, 1993.

Hollaender A. E. J. and Kellaway, William, Studies in London History, London: Hodder & Staunton, 1969.

Hollingsworth, Mary, *The Medici*, London: Head of Zeus, 2017.

Holton, R. H. and Aston, T. H., *The English Rising of 1381*, Cambridge: Cambridge University Press, 1984.

Hook, Judith, *The Sack of Rome 1527* (2nd edn.), Basingstoke: Palgrave Macmillan, 2004.

Hornblower, Simon, Spawforth, Anthony and Eidinow, Esther (eds.), *The Oxford Classical Dictionary* (4th edn.), Oxford: Oxford University Press, 2012.

Hoyland, Robert G., *In God's Path: The Arab Conquests and the Creation of an Islamic Empire*, Oxford: Oxford University Press, 2015.

Hunt, Edwin S., *The Medieval Super-Companies: A Study of the Peruzzi Company of Florence*, Cambridge: Cambridge University Press, 1994.

Hunt, Edwin S. and Murray, James M., *A History of Business in Medieval Europe, 1200–1550*, Cambridge: Cambridge University Press, 1999.

Hunt, Noreen, *Cluny Under Saint Hugh, 1049–1109*, London: Edward Arnold, 1967.

Hunt, Noreen (ed.), *Cluniac Monasticism in the Central Middle Ages*, London: Macmillan, 1971.

Hyland, Ann, *The Medieval Warhorse: From Byzantium to the Crusades*, London: Grange Books, 1994.

Isaacson, Walter, *Leonardo da Vinci: The Biography*, London: Simon & Schuster, 2017.

Jackson, Peter, *The Mongols and The West, 1221–1410*, Abingdon: Routledge, 2005.

Jacoby, David, *Medieval Trade in the Eastern Mediterranean and Beyond*, Abingdon: Routledge, 2018.

Johns, Catherine, *The Hoxne Late Roman Treasure: Gold Jewellery and Silver Plate*, London: The British Museum Press, 2010.

Johnston, David (ed.), *The Cambridge Companion to Roman Law*, New York: Cambridge University Press, 2015.

Jones, Dan, *Crusaders: An Epic History of the Wars for the Holy Lands*, London: Head of Zeus, 2019.

Jones, Dan, *The Templars: The Rise and Fall of God's Holy Warriors*, London, Head of Zeus: 2017.

Jones, Dan, *Summer of Blood: The Peasants' Revolt of 1381*, London: William Collins, 2009.

Jones, Dan, *The Hollow Crown: The Wars of the Roses and the Rise of the Tudors*, London: Faber & Faber, 2014.

Jones, Terry L. et al (eds.), *Polynesians in America: Pre-Columbian Contacts with the New World*, Lanham: AltaMira Press, 2011.

Jordan, William C., *The Great Famine: Northern Europe in the Early Fourteenth Century*, Princeton: Princeton Universtiy Press, 1996.

Kaeigi, Walter, *Muslim Expansion and Byzantine Collapse in North Africa*, Cambridge: Cambridge University Press, 2010.

Kaeuper, Richard W., *Medieval Chivalry*, Cambridge: Cambridge University Press, 2016.

Kedar, Benjamin Z. and Weisner-Hanks, Merry E. (eds.), *The Cambridge World History Vol. 5: Expanding Webs of Exchange and Conflict, 500 C.E.–1500 C. E.*, Cambridge: Cambridge University Press, 2013.

Keen, Maurice, *Chivalry*, New Haven/London: Yale University Press, 1984.

Kelly, Christopher, *Attila the Hun: Barbarian Terror and the Fall of the Roman Empire*, London: The Bodley Head, 2008.

Kemp, Martin, *Leonardo by Leonardo*, New York: Callaway, 2019.

Kennedy, Hugh, *The Great Arab Conquests*, London: Weidenfeld & Nicolson, 2007.

Kim, Hyun Jin, *The Huns*, London/New York: Routledge, 2016.

King, Peter, *Western Monasticism: A History of the Monastic Movement* in the Latin Church, Kalamazoo: Cistercian Publications, 1999.

King, Ross, Brunelleschi's Dome: The Story of the Great Cathedral in Florence, London: Penguin Books, 2000.

Klibancky, Raymond, The continuity of the Platonic tradition during the middle ages, outlines of a Corpus platonicum medii aevi, London: Warburg Institute, 1939.

Licence, Tom, Edward the Confessor, New Haven/London: Yale University Press, 2020.

Lings, Martin, Muhammad: His Life Based on the Earliest Sources, Cambridge: The Islamic Texts Society, 1991.

Lloyd, T. H., The English Wool Trade in the Middle Ages, Cambridge: Cambridge University Press, 1977.

Loengard, J. S. (ed.), Magna Carta and the England of King John, Woodbridge: Boydell & Brewer, 2010.

Lopez, Robert S., The Commercial Revolution of the Middle Ages, 950–1350, Cambridge: Cambridge University Press, 1976.

Luttwak, Edward N., The Grand Strategy of the Roman Empire: From the First Century A.D. to the Third, Baltimore/London: The Johns Hopkins University Press, 1976.

Maas, Michael (ed.), The Cambridge Companion to The Age of Attila, Cambridge: Cambridge University Press, 2015.

Maas, Michael (ed.), The Cambridge Companion to the Age of Justinian, Cambridge: Cambridge University Press, 2005.

MacCulloch, Diarmaid, A History of Christianity, London: Allen Lane, 2009.

MacCulloch, Diarmaid, Reformation: Europe's House Divided 1490–1700, London: Allen Lane, 2003.

Macek, Josef, The Hussite Movement in Bohemia, Prague: Orbis, 1958.

MacGregor, Neil, A History of the World In 100 Objects, London: Allen Lane, 2010.

Mallia-Milanes (ed.), The Military Orders, Volume 3: History and Heritage, London: Routledge, 2008.

Marani, Pietro C., Leonardo da Vinci: The Complete Paintings (new edn.), New York: Abrams, 2019.

Martens, Maximiliaan et al (eds.), Van Eyck, London: Thames & Hudson, 2020.

Martin, Janet, Medieval Russia, 980–1584 (2nd edn.), Cambridge: Cambridge University Press, 2007.

Mattingly, David, An Imperial Possession: Britain in the Roman Empire, London: Allen Lane, 2006.

McCormick, Michael, Origins of the European Economy: Communications and Commerce, A.D. 300–900, Cambridge: Cambridge University Press, 2001.

McKitterick, Rosamond, Charlemagne: The Formation of a European Identity, Cambridge: Cambridge University Press, 2008.

McKitterick, Rosamond, The Frankish Kingdoms under the Carolingians, London/New York: Longman, 1983.

McKitterick, Rosamond (ed.), The New Cambridge Medieval History II c.700 – c.900, Cambridge: Cambridge University Press, 1995.

McLynn, Frank, Genghis Khan: The Man Who Conquered the World, London: Bodley Head, 2015.

Merrills A. H. (ed.), Vandals, Romans and Berbers: New Perspectives on Late Antique North Africa, Abingdon: Routledge, 2016.

Merrills, Andy and Miles, Richard, The Vandals, Oxford: Blackwell Publishing, 2010.

Moore, R. I., The First European Revolution, c.970–1215, Oxford: Blackwell Publishing, 2000.

Morris, Colin, The Papal Monarchy: The

Western Church, 1050–1250, Oxford: Clarendon Press, 1989.

Morris, Marc, A Great and Terrible King: Edward I, London: Hutchison, 2008.

Mullins, Edwin, In Search of Cluny: God's Lost Empire, Oxford: Signal Books, 2006.

Nicholson, Helen, The Knights Hospitaller, Woodbridge: The Boydell Press, 2001.

Noble, Thomas F. X. and Smith, Julia M. H., The Cambridge History of Christianity III: Early Medieval Christianities c.600–c.1100, Cambridge: Cambridge University Press, 2008.

Norman, Diana (ed.), Siena, Florence and Padua: Art, Society and Religion 1280–1400 Volume II: Case Studies, New Haven: Yale University Press, 1995.

O'Callaghan, Joseph F., A History of Medieval Spain, Ithaca: Cornell University Press, 1975.

Orme, Nicholas, Medieval Schools: Roman Britain to Renaissance England, New Haven: Yale University Press, 2006.

Ormrod, Mark, Edward III, New Haven: Yale University Press, 2011.

Parker, Deborah, Commentary and Ideology: Dante in the Renaissance, Durham/London: Duke University Press, 1993.

Parker, Geoffrey, Emperor: A New Life of Charles V, New Haven: Yale University Press, 2019.

Parry, J. H., The Age of Reconnaissance: Discovery, Exploration and Settlement, 1450–1650, London: Weidenfeld and Nicholson, 1963.

Phillips, Jonathan, The Second Crusade: Extending the Frontiers of Christianity, New Haven: Yale University Press, 2008.

Phillips, Jonathan, The Life and Legend of the Sultan Saladin, London: Bodley Head, 2019.

Phillips, Jonathan, The Fourth Crusade and the Sack of Constantinople, London: Jonathan Cape, 2011.

Pope-Hennessy, John, Italian Gothic Sculpture, London: Phaidon Press, 1955.

Power, E., The Wool Trade in Medieval English History, Oxford, 1941.

Price, Neil, The Children of Ash and Elm: A History of the Vikings, London: Allen Lane, 2020.

Putnam, B. H., The Enforcement of the Statutes of Labourers During the First Decade After the Black Death, 1349–59, New York: Columbia University Press, 1908.

Reeve, Benjamin, Timothy Richard, D.D., China Missionary, Statesman and Reformer, London: S. W. Partridge & Co., 1912.

Riley-Smith, Jonathan, The First Crusaders, 1095–1131, Cambridge: Cambridge University Press, 1997.

Robin, Diana, Filelfo in Milan, Princeton: Princeton University Press, 2014.

Rubies, Joan-Pau, Medieval Ethnographies: European Perceptions of the World Beyond, Abingdon: Routledge, 2016.

Russell, P. E., Henry the Navigator: A Life, New Haven/London: Yale University Press, 2000.

Ryrie, Alec, Protestants: The Faith that Made the Modern World, New York: Viking, 2017.

Sainty, Guy Stair and Heydel-Mankoo, Rafal (eds.), World Orders of Knighthood and Merit (2 vols.), Wilmington: Burke's Peerage & Gentry, 2006.

Sarti, Laury, Perceiving War and the Military in Early Christian Gaul (ca. 400–700 A.D.), Leiden: Brill, 2013.

Schwoebel, Robert, The Shadow of the Crescent: The Renaissance Image of the Turk, 1453–1517, New York: St Martin's Press, 1967.

Scott, Robert A., The Gothic Enterprise: A Guide to Understanding the Medieval

Cathedral, Berkeley: University of California Press, 2003.

Shaver-Crandell, Annie and Gerson, Paula, *The Pilgrim's Guide to Santiago de Compostela: A Gazetteer with 580 Illustrations*, London: Harvey Miller, 1995.

Smith, M. L., *The Early History of the Monastery of Cluny*, Oxford: Oxford University Press, 1920.

Stahl, Alan M., *Zecca: The Mint of Venice in the Middle Ages*, Baltimore: Johns Hopkins University Press, 2000.

Stalley, Roger, *Early Medieval Architecture*, Oxford: Oxford University Press, 1999.

Strathern, Paul, *The Artist, the Philosopher and the Warrior: Leonardo, Machiavelli and Borgia: A Fateful Collusion*, London: Jonathan Cape, 2009.

Strickland, Matthew, *Henry the Young King*, New Haven/London: Yale University Press, 2016.

Stump, Eleonore, *Aquinas*, London: Routledge, 2003.

Sumption, Jonathan, *Cursed Kings: The Hundred Years War* IV, London: Faber & Faber, 2015.

Swanson, R.N. (ed.), *Promissory Notes on the Treasury of Merits Indulgences in Late Medieval Europe*, Leiden: Brill, 2006.

Taleb, Nassim Nicholas, *The Black Swan: The Impact of the Highly Improbable*, London: Penguin, 2008.

Taylor, Arnold, *Studies in Castles and Castle-Building*, London: The Hambledon Press, 1985.

Tuchman, Barbara, *A Distant Mirror: The Calamitous Fourteenth Century*, New York: Albert A. Knopf, 1978.

Turner, Denys, *Thomas Aquinas: A Portrait*, New Haven: Yale University Press, 2013.

Turner, Marion, *Chaucer: A European Life*, Princeton: Princeton University Press, 2019.

Vallet, Françoise and Kazanski, Michel (eds.), *La noblesse romaine et les chefs barbares du IIIe au VIIe siècle*, Paris: AFAM and Museé des Antiquiteés Nationales, 1995.

Vaughan, Richard, *Philip the Good: The Apogee of Burgundy* (new edn.), Woodbridge: Boydell Press, 2002.

Weatherford, Jack, *Genghis Khan and the Quest for God*, New York: Viking, 2016.

West, Charles, *Reframing the Feudal Revolution: Political and Social Transformation between the Marne and the Moselle, c.800–c.1100*, Cambridge: Cambridge University Press, 2013.

Wheatley, Abigail, *The Idea of the Castle in Medieval England*, Woodbridge: York Medieval Press, 2004.

White, Jr., Lynn, *Medieval Technology & Social Change*, Oxford: Oxford University Press, 1962.

Whitehead, F., Divernes, A. H., and Sutcliffe, F. E. (eds.), *Medieval Miscellany Presented to Eugène Vinaver*, Manchester: Manchester University Press, 1965.

Wickham, Chris, *The Inheritance of Rome: A History of Europe from 400 to 1000*, London: Penguin Books, 2010.

Woolf, Greg, *Rome: An Empire's Story*, Oxford: Oxford University Press, 2012.

Journal Articles and Theses

Ailes, Marianne, 'Charlemagne "Father of Europe": A European Icon in the Making', *Reading Medieval Studies* 38 (2012).

Andersen, Thomas Barnebeck, Jensen, Peter Sandholt and Skovsgaard, Christian Stejner, 'The heavy plough and the agricultural revolution in medieval Europe', *Discussion Papers of Business and Economics* (University of Southern Denmark, Department of Business and Economics: 2013).

Aston T. H., 'Oxford's Medieval Alumni', *Past & Present* 74 (1977).

Barjamovic, Gojko, Chaney, Thomas, Cosar, Kerem and Hortaçsu, Ali, 'Trade, Merchants and the Lost Cities of the Bronze Age', *The Quarterly Journal of Economics* 134 (2019).

Barratt, Nick,' The English Revenue of Richard I', *The English Historical Review* 116 (2001).

Barrett, James A., 'What caused the Viking Age?', *Antiquity* 82 (2008).

Bartsocas, Christos S., 'Two Fourteenth Century Greek Descriptions of the Black Death', *Journal of the History of Medicine and Allied Sciences* 21 (1966).

Baug, Irene, Skre, Dagfnn, Heldal, Tom and Janse, Øystein J., ,'The Beginning of the Viking Age in the West', *Journal of Maritime Archaeology* 14 (2019) .

Besnier, G., 'Quelques notes sur Arras et Jeanne d'Arc', *Revue du Nord* 40 (1958).

Blegen, Nick, 'The earliest long-distance obsidian transport: Evidence from the ~200 ka Middle Stone Age Sibilo School Road Site, Baringo, Kenya', *Journal of Human Evolution* 103 (2017).

Blockmans, Wim, 'Transactions at the Fairs of Champagne and Flanders, 1249–1291', *Fiere e mercati nella integrazione delle economie europee secc. XIII–XVIII – Atti delle Settimane di Studi* 32 (2001).

Blumenthal, H. J., '529 and its sequel: What happened to the Academy?', *Byzantion* 48 (1978).

Bodel, John, 'Caveat emptor: Towards a Study of Roman Slave Traders', *Journal of Roman Archaeology* 18 (2005).

Brown, Elizabeth A. R., 'The Tyranny of a Construct: Feudalism and Historians of Medieval Europe', *The American Historical Review* 79 (1974).

Buck, Lawrence P., 'Anatomia Antichristi: Form and Content of the Papal Antichrist', *The Sixteenth Century Journal* 42 (2011).

Bury, J. B, 'The Nika Riot', *The Journal of Hellenic Studies* 17 (1897).

Campbell, Bruce M. S., 'Nature as historical protagonist: environment and society in pre-industrial England', *The Economic History Review* 63 (2010).

Cantor, Norman F., 'The Crisis of Western Monasticism, 1050–1130', *The American Historical Review* (1960).

Carty, Carolyn M., 'The Role of Gunzo's Dream in the Building of Cluny III', *Gesta* 27 (1988).

Cassidy-Welch, Megan, 'The Stedinger Crusade: War, Remembrance, and Absence in Thirteenth-Century Germany', *Viator* 44 (2013).

Conant, Kenneth J., 'The After-Life of Vitruvius in the Middle Ages', *Journal of the Society of Architectural Historians* 27 (1968).

Constantelos, Demetrios J., 'Paganism and the State in the Age of Justinian', *The Catholic Historical Review* 50 (1964).

Davies, Jonathan, 'Violence and Italian universities during the Renaissance', *Renaissance Studies* 27 (2013).

Davies, Martin, 'Juan de Carvajal and Early Printing: The 42-line Bible and the Sweynheym and Pannartz Aquinas', *The Library* 17 (1996).

De Mowbray, Malcolm, '1277 And All That – Students and Disputations', *Traditio* 57, (2002).

Dull, Robert A. et al, 'Radiocarbon and geologic evidence reveal Ilopango volcano as source of the colossal "mystery" eruption of 539/40 CE', *Quaternary Science Reviews* 222 (2019).

Eisenstein, Elizabeth L., 'Some Conjectures about the Impact of Printing on Western Society and Thought: A Preliminary Report', *The Journal of Modern History* 40 (1968).

Epstein, S. R., 'Regional Fairs, Institutional Innovation, and Economic Growth in Late Medieval Europe', *Economic History Review*, 47 (1994).

Firnhaber-Baker, Justine, 'The Social Constituency of the Jacquerie Revolt of 1358', *Speculum* 95 (2020).

Frankopan, Peter, 'Why we need to think about the global Middle Ages', *Journal of Medieval Worlds* 1 (2019).

Fryde, E. B., 'The Deposits of Hugh Despenser the Younger with Italian Bankers', *The Economic History Review* 3 (1953).

Galili, Ehud, Rosen, Baruch, Arenson, Sarah, Nir-El, Yoram, Jacoby, David, 'A cargo of lead ingots from a shipwreck off Ashkelon, Israel 11th–13th centuries AD, *International Journal of Nautical Archaeology* 48 (2019).

Gatward Cevizli, Antonia, 'Bellini, bronze and bombards: Sultan Mehmed II's requests reconsidered', *Renaissance Studies* 28 (2014).

Greatrex, Geoffrey, 'The Nika Riot: A Reappraisal', *The Journal of Hellenic Studies* 117 (1997).

Green, Monica H., 'Putting Africa on the Black Death map: Narratives from genetics and history', *Afriques* 9 (2018).

Green, William A., 'Periodization in European and World History', *Journal of World History* 3 (1992).

Grendler, Paul F., 'The University of Florence and Pisa in the High Renaissance', *Renaissance and Reformation* 6 (1982).

Gruhn, Ruth, 'Evidence grows for early peopling of the Americas', *Nature* 584 (August 2020).

Hahn, Cynthia, 'Collector and saint: Queen Radegund and devotion to the relic of the True Cross', *Word & Image* 22 (2006).

Harrison, Stuart, 'The Original Plan of the East End of St Hugh's Choir at Lincoln Cathedral Reconsidered in the Light of New Evidence', *Journal of the British Archaeological Association* 169 (2016).

Hill, Brian E., 'Charles the Bald's "Edict of Pîtres" (864): A Translation and Commentary', Unpublished MA Thesis, University of Minnesota (2013).

Hinds, Martin, 'The Murder of the Caliph 'Uthman', *International Journal of Middle East Studies* 3 (1972).

Holum, Kenneth G. , 'Archaeological Evidence for the Fall of Byzantine Caesarea', *Bulletin of the American Schools of Oriental Research* 286 (1992).

Hunt, Edwin S., 'A New Look at the Dealings of the Bardi and Peruzzi with Edward III', *The Journal of Economic History* 50 (1990).

Ing, Janet, 'The Mainz Indulgences of 1454/5: A review of recent scholarship', *The British Library Journal* 9 (1983).

Innes, Matthew, 'Land, Freedom and the Making of the Medieval West', *Transactions of the Royal Historical Society* 16 (2006).

Jackson, Peter, 'The Crusade against the Mongols', *Journal of Ecclesiastical History* 42 (1991).

Jamaluddin, Syed, 'Samarqand as the First City in the World under Timur', *Proceedings of the Indian History Congress* 56 (1995).

Jones, Dan, 'Meet the Americans Following in the Footsteps of the Knights Templar', *Smithsonian* (July 2018)

Kershaw, Ian, 'The Great Famine and

Agrarian Crisis in England 1315–1322', *Past & Present* 59 (1973).

Kılınç, Gülşah Merve et al, 'Human population dynamics and Yersinia pestis in ancient northeast Asia', *Science Advances* 7 (2021).

Kulikowski, Michael, 'Barbarians in Gaul, Usurpers in Britain', *Britannia* 31 (2000).

Livesey, Edwina, 'Shock Dating Result: A Result of the Norman Invasion?', *Sussex Past & Present* 133 (2014).

MacCulloch, Diarmaid, 'The World Took Sides', *London Review of Books* 38 (2016).

Macmaster, Thomas J., 'The Origin of the Origins: Trojans, Turks and the Birth of the Myth of Trojan Origins in the Medieval World', *Atlantide* 2 (2014).

McPhail, Cameron, 'Pytheas of Massalia's Route of Travel', *Phoenix* 68 (2014).

Mengel, David C., 'A Plague on Bohemia? Mapping the Black Death', *Past & Present* 211 (2011).

Moderchai, Lee and Eisenberg, Merle, 'Rejecting Catastrophe: The Case of the Justinianic Plague', *Past & Present* 244 (2019).

Moore, John C., 'Innocent III's De Miseria Humanae Conditionis: A Speculum Curiae?', *The Catholic Historical Review* 67 (1981).

Musson, R. M. W., 'A History of British seismology', *Bulletin of Earthquake Engineering* 11 (2013).

Musson, R. M. W., 'The Seismicity of the British Isles to 1600', *British Geological Survey Open Report* (2008).

Mustard, Wilfrid P., 'Petrarch's Africa', *The American Journal of Philology* 42 (1921).

Oppenheimer, Clive, 'Climatic, environmental and human consequences of the largest known historic eruption: Tambora volcano (Indonesia) 1815', *Progress in Physical Geography: Earth and Environment* 27 (2003).

Pederson, Neil, Hessl, Amy E., Baatarbileg, Nachin, Anchukaitis, Kevin J. and Di Cosmo Nicola, 'Pluvials, droughts, the Mongol Empire, and modern Mongolia', *Proceedings of the National Academy of Sciences* (25 March 2014).

Pow, Stephen, 'Fortresses that Shatter Empires: A Look at Möngke Khan's Failed Campaign Against the Song Dynasty, 1258–9', *Annual of Medieval Studies at CEU* 23 (2017).

Pratt, Kenneth J., 'Rome as Eternal', *Journal of the History of Ideas* 26 (1965).

Puga, Diego and Trefler, Daniel, 'International Trade and Institutional Change: Medieval Venice's Response to Globalization', *The Quarterly Journal of Economics* 129 (2014).

Regn, Gerhard and Huss, Bernhard, 'Petrarch's Rome: The History of the Africa and the Renaissance Project', *MLN* 124 (2009).

Rex, Richard, 'The English Campaign against Luther in the 1520s: The Alexander Prize Essay', *Transactions of the Royal Historical Society* 39 (1989).

Robin, Diana, 'A Reassessment of the Character of Francesco Filelfo (1398–1481)', *Renaissance Quarterly* 36 (1983).

Roland, Alex, 'Secrecy, Technology, and War: Greek Fire and the Defense of Byzantium, 678–1204', *Technology and Culture* 33 (1992).

Sea, Thomas F., 'The German Princes' Responses to the Peasants' Revolt of 1525', *Central European History* 40 (2007).

Sherer, Idan, 'A bloody carnival? Charles V's soldiers and the sack of Rome in 1527', *Renaissance Studies* 34 (2019).

Slavin, Philip, 'The Great Bovine Pestilence and its economic and environmental consequences in England and Wales, 1318–50', *The Economic History Review* 65 (2012).

Slavin, Philip, 'Market failure during the Great Famine in England and Wales (1315–1317)', *Past & Present* 222 (2014).

Smith, Preserved, 'Luther and Henry VIII', *The English Historical Review* 25 (1910).

Smith, Terence, 'The English Medieval Windmill', *History Today* 28 (1978).

Sreenivasan, Govind P., 'The Social Origins of the Peasants' War of 1525 in Upper Swabia', *Past & Present* 171 (2001).

Sussman, George D., 'Was the Black Death in India and China?', *Bulletin of the History of Medicine* 85 (2011).

Swift, Emerson H., 'Byzantine Gold Mosaic', *American Journal of Archaeology* 38 (1934).

Taylor, A. J., 'Master James of St. George', *The English Historical Review* 65 (1950).

Taylor, David, 'The Early West Front of Lincoln Cathedral', *Archaeological Journal* 167 (2010).

Toker, Franklin, 'Arnolfo's S. Maria del Fiore: A Working Hypothesis', *Journal of the Society of Architectural Historians* 42 (1983).

Trimble, Jennifer, 'The Zoninus Collar and the Archaeology of Roman Slavery', *American Journal of Archaeology* 120 (2016).

Ugent, Donald, Dillehay, Tom and Ramirez, Carlos, 'Potato remains from a late Pleistocene settlement in southcentral Chile', *Economic Botany* 41 (1987).

Underwood, Norman, 'When the Goths Were in Egypt: A Gothic Bible Fragment and Barbarian Settlement in Sixth-Century Egypt', *Viator* 45 (2014).

Vopřada, David, 'Quodvultdeus' Sermons on the Creed: a Reassessment of his Polemics against the Jews, Pagans, and Arians', *Vox Patrum* 37 (2017).

Wang, Xiaofeng, Yang, Bao and Ljungqvist, Fredrik Charpentier, 'The Vulnerability of Qilian Juniper to Extreme Drought Events', *Frontiers in Plant Science* 10 (2019).

Watts, Edward, 'Justinian, Malalas, and the End of Athenian Philosophical Teaching in A.D. 529', *The Journal of Roman Studies* 94 (2004).

Werkmeister, O. K., 'Cluny III and the Pilgrimage to Santiago de Compostela', *Gesta* 27 (1988).

Wilkins, Ernest H., 'Petrarch's Coronation Oration', *Transactions and Proceedings of the Modern Language Association of America* 68 (1953).

Wolfe, Maury I. and Mark, Robert, 'The Collapse of the Vaults of Beauvais Cathedral in 1284', *Speculum* 51 (1976).

Wood, Jamie, 'Defending Byzantine Spain: frontiers and diplomacy', *Early Medieval Europe* 18 (2010).

Żemła, Michał and Siwek, Matylda, 'Between authenticity of walls and authenticity of tourists' experiences: The tale of three Polish castles', *Cogent Arts & Humanities* 1 (2020).

Zhou, TianJun, Li, Bo, Man, WenMin, Zhang, LiXia, and Zhang, Jie, 'A comparison of the Medieval Warm Period, Little Ice Age and 20th century warming simulated by the FGOALS climate system model', *Chinese Science Bulletin* 56 (2011).

PICTURE CREDITS

1. Universal Images Group/Getty
2. Dan Jones
3. Fine Art Images / Bridgeman Images
4. Dan Jones
5. Pictorial Press Ltd/Alamy
6. JLImages/Alamy
7. Digital Commons @ Winthrop University
8. Realy Easy Star/Toni Spagone/Alamy
9. Dan Jones
10. The Picture Art Collection/Alamy
11. Germanisches National Museum/Bridgeman Images
12. Leemage/Getty
13. Science History Images/Alamy
14. ventdusud/Shutterstock
15. Hemis/Alamy
16. Album/Alamy
17. Granger Historical Picture Archive/Alamy
18. Dan Jones
19. World History Archive/Alamy
20. Photo 12/Alamy
21. Anonymousz/Shutterstock
22. ART Collection/Alamy
23. World History Archive/Alamy
24. robertharding/Alamy
25. Dan Jones
26. Historic Collection/Alamy
27. Dan Jones
28. Pere Sanz/Shutterstock
29. Dan Jones
30. Umberto Shtanzman/Shutterstock
31. Album/Alamy
32. Granger Historical Picture Archive/Alamy
33. Classic Image/Alamy
34. Iberfoto/Bridgeman Images
35. FineArt/Alamy
36. VCG Wilson/Corbis/Getty
37. Leemage/Corbis/Getty
38. Fine Art Images/Heritage Images/Getty
39. World History Archive/Alamy
40. incamerastock/Alamy
41. Jim West/Alamy
42. Granger Historical Picture Archive/Alamy

INDEX